Sep. 1995

To
  Robert Kent

My best personal regards
Good luck in your career.

D1201229

Practical
Homicide
Investigation
Tactics, Procedures,
and Forensic Techniques

Second Edition

CRC SERIES IN
PRACTICAL ASPECTS OF CRIMINAL AND FORENSIC INVESTIGATIONS

VERNON J. GEBERTH, BBA, MPS, FBINA *Series Editor*

Practical Homicide Investigation: Tactics, Procedures, and Forensic Techniques, Second Edition
Vernon J. Geberth

The Counter-Terrorism Handbook: Tactics, Procedures, and Techniques
Frank Bolz, Jr., Kenneth J. Dudonis, and David P. Schulz

Forensic Pathology
Dominick J. Di Maio and Vincent J. M. Di Maio

Interpretation of Bloodstain Evidence at Crime Scenes
William G. Eckert and Stuart H. James

Tire Imprint Evidence
Peter McDonald

Practical Drug Enforcement: Procedures and Administration
Michael D. Lyman

Practical Aspects of Rape Investigation: A Multidisciplinary Approach
Robert R. Hazelwood and Ann Wolbert Burgess

The Sexual Exploitation of Children: A Practical Guide to Assessment, Investigation, and Intervention
Seth L. Goldstein

Gunshot Wounds: Practical Aspects of Firearms, Ballistics, and Forensic Techniques
Vincent J. M. Di Maio

Friction Ridge Skin: Comparison and Identification of Fingerprints
James F. Cowger

Footwear Impression Evidence
William J. Bodziak

Practical Aspects of Kinesic Interview and Interrogation Techniques
Stan Walters

Practical Fire and Arson Investigation
John J. O'Connor

A Practical Methodology of Forensic Photography
David R. Redsicker

Practical Gambling Investigation Techniques
Kevin B. Kinnee

Practical Aspects of Interview and Interrogation
David E. Zulawski and Douglas E. Wicklander

Practical Investigation Techniques
Kevin B. Kinnee

Practical Homicide Investigation

Tactics, Procedures,
and Forensic Techniques

Second Edition

VERNON J. GEBERTH, BBA, MPS, FBINA
Lieutenant Commander (Retired)
New York City Police Department

CRC Press
Boca Raton   Ann Arbor   London   Tokyo

Library of Congress Cataloging-in-Publication Data

Geberth, Vernon J.
  Practical homicide investigation : tactics, procedures, and
forensic techniques / Vernon J. Geberth. — 2nd ed.
      p.   cm. — (CRC series in practical aspects of criminal and forensic
investigations)
  Originally published: New York : Elsevier, ©1990, in series:
Elsevier series in practical aspects of criminal and forensic investigations.
  Includes bibliographical references and index.
  ISBN 0-8493-9507-0
  1. Homicide investigation—United States. I. Title. II. Series.
[HV8079.H6G4 1993]
363.2′59523—dc20   92-37535
                                                              CIP

  This book contains information obtained from authentic and highly regarded sources. Reprinted material is quoted with permission, and sources are
indicated. A wide variety of references are listed. Reasonable efforts have been
made to publish reliable data and information, but the author and the publisher
cannot assume responsibility for the validity of all materials or for the consequences of their use.
  Neither this book nor any part may be reproduced or transmitted in any
form or by any means, electronic or mechanical, including photocopying,
microfilming, and recording, or by any information storage or retrieval system,
without prior permission in writing from the publisher.
  CRC Press, Inc.'s consent does not extend to copying for general distribu-
tion, for promotion, for creating new works, or for resale. Specific permission
must be obtained in writing from CRC Press for such copying.
  Direct all inquiries to CRC Press, Inc., 2000 Corporate Blvd., N.W., Boca
Raton, Florida 33431.

© 1993 by CRC Press, Inc.

No claim to original U.S. Government works
International Standard Book Number 0-8493-9507-0
Library of Congress Card Number 92-37535
Printed in the United States of America   8 9 0
Printed on acid-free paper

This book is dedicated to
the men and women entrusted with the profound duty
and responsibility of investigating sudden and violent death.

In memory of those *innocent* victims of homicide
and their surviving families, who must find the
strength to go on without their loved ones.

May justice prevail

The Lord God said...

𝕿𝖍𝖔𝖚 𝕾𝖍𝖆𝖑𝖙 𝕹𝖔𝖙 𝕶𝖎𝖑𝖑

THE FIFTH COMMANDMENT   Book of Exodus, 20 of THE HOLY BIBLE

THE OATH OF
PRACTICAL HOMICIDE INVESTIGATION

HOMICIDE INVESTIGATION IS A PROFOUND DUTY. AS AN OFFICER ENTRUSTED WITH SUCH A DUTY, IT IS INCUMBENT UPON YOU TO DEVELOP AN UNDERSTANDING OF THE DYNAMICS AND PRINCIPLES OF PROFESSIONAL HOMICIDE INVESTIGATION.

PRACTICAL HOMICIDE INVESTIGATION SUGGESTS THAT "THINGS BE DONE RIGHT THE FIRST TIME", AND "KNOWLEDGE IS POWER". KNOWLEDGE WHICH HAS BEEN ENHANCED WITH EXPERIENCE, FLEXIBILITY AND COMMON SENSE.

PRACTITIONERS MUST BE PREPARED TO USE TACTICS, PROCEDURES, AND FORENSIC TECHNIQUES IN THEIR PURSUIT OF THE TRUTH: AND THEN FOLLOW THE COURSE OF EVENTS AND THE FACTS AS THEY ARE DEVELOPED TO THEIR ULTIMATE CONCLUSION.

DEATH INVESTIGATION CONSTITUTES A HEAVY RESPONSIBILITY, AND AS SUCH, LET NO PERSON DETER YOU FROM THE TRUTH AND YOUR OWN PERSONAL COMMITMENT TO SEE THAT JUSTICE IS DONE. NOT ONLY FOR THE DECEASED, BUT FOR THE SURVIVING FAMILY AS WELL.
    AND REMEMBER; "YOU'RE WORKING FOR GOD."

Lt. Cmdr. (Ret.) VERNON J. GEBERTH
NEW YORK CITY POLICE DEPARTMENT
COMMANDING OFFICER
BRONX HOMICIDE TASK FORCE

© Vernon J. Geberth, 1988

Contents

12   The Investigation of Sex-Related Homicides   295

13   Collection of Evidence   333

Editor's Note

This textbook is part of a series entitled, "Practical Aspects of Criminal and Forensic Investigations."

This series was created by Vernon J. Geberth a retired New York City Police Department Lieutenant Commander, who is an author, educator, and consultant on homicide and forensic investigations.

The series has been designed to provide contemporary, comprehensive, and pragmatic information to the practitioner involved in criminal and forensic investigations by authors, who are nationally recognized experts in their respective fields.

Foreword

"Investigating a homicide is both an art and a science, a blend of the practical and the scientific. Without that realization, and that *blend* which includes a coordinated effort by a team of specialists, the chance of a successful case solution is greatly diminished."

— P.R.B.

Vernon Geberth, a former New York city police homicide commander and a friend of mine for many years, is not only an experienced and knowledgeable violent crimes investigator, he is a very talented writer and lecturer on the subject. The first edition of this book, *Practical Homicide Investigation: Tactics, Procedures, and Forensic Techniques,* has been acclaimed as the bible of homicide, and his articles on the investigation of violent crime have been read by police officers throughout the country.

This revised edition should be considered as a primary text for the criminal justice student and the police academy trainee. The book should be on the reading list for uniformed officers who are invariably first to arrive on scene, and all newly assigned detectives. Experienced homicide investigators will find the book to be a valuable resource and a reminder that regardless of how many crime scenes we process, we never stop learning. I am also quite sure that members of the court and bar will have occasion to use the book as a reference and to judge the quality and integrity of procedures and techniques used by the police in a major case investigation.

The text is exceptionally well organized. Chapters 1 through 8 chronologically define all aspects of the initial investigation on scene. Chapters 9 through 18 focus on special procedures and techniques that must always be considered in a major crime investigation. The new sections on suicide, autoerotic fatalities, and sex related homicides are highly informative and will alert even the most experienced investigator of the mind-set pitfalls that can occur in the investigation of equivocal deaths.

Good crime scene photos are the next best to being on scene. Many photographs used in this edition are presented for the first time. Perhaps not for the faint hearted, each photo presents one or more lessons in the importance of "detail observation" while processing a crime scene. Comments made in the chapter on management and supervision of a criminal investigation are long overdue. Vernon identifies traditional problems and suggests solutions. Information to consider in establishing written policy and procedures is included.

Vernon's experience with DNA cases fully qualifies him to present information related to this particular process of identification from the viewpoint of the police homicide investigator. His case study examples of genetic fingerprint comparison and his "Preservation Sample and Minimum Amounts" checklist should be read by every officer involved in the investigation of violent crime.

This book leaves no question that now, more than ever, a homicide investigation must be based on a mix of the practical and the scientific. The new material and descriptive photos in this text combined with the procedures and techniques outlined in Vernon's first book will place this edition in the category of a police text classic, an authoritative standard on the subject.

Pierce R. Brooks
Captain, L.A.P.D. (Ret.)

Preface

This second edition of *Practical Homicide Investigation: Tactics, Procedures and Forensic Techniques* provides practical and conventional information to all detectives responsible for conducting intelligent investigations into violent and sudden death.

This revised text is based on my twenty-five years of law enforcement experience. Formerly a New York City detective, detective supervisor, homicide commander, and now a nationwide consultant, I have integrated this knowledge with my associations with experts in the sphere of forensic science and criminal investigation. I include personal interviews from other homicide authorities, and present an extensive search of forensic literature offering as many actual case histories as possible. *My intention is to provide a comprehensive and practical resource text that will serve as an investigation guide.*

The Uniform Crime Reports (UCR) indicate that crime rates and violence have continued to increase over the past decade. The proliferation of drugs and drug violence has resulted in an unprecedented increase in drug-related murders, placing an additional strain on the resources and capabilities of law enforcement.

Today's criminals are new and more violent types of offenders who literally operate with impunity within our criminal justice system. They are killers without morals or conscience. In fact, I liken them to "thinking" predators who kill for the thrill, fun, convenience, or the purposeful intent of preventing their own identification.

Today's criminals are sophisticated and aware of the limitations of law enforcement. Many of these offenders are "graduates" of the penal system, and have been duly schooled by "jailhouse" lawyers as to just what the police can and cannot do. While our cities grow and become more impersonal, more and more people refrain from "getting involved." Add to these factors some of the restrictive court decisions that prevent authorities from effectively prosecuting offenders, and one can readily understand the frustrations of the homicide investigator.

As we prepare to enter the twenty-first century with advanced forensic and technological changes within the law enforcement community, we should be cognizant of an important prerequisite. In my professional opinion, "The investigation of homicide and the initial actions by the police at the homicide crime scene will and/or may eventually determine whether or not the crime is ever solved or the guilty person brought to justice."

Computerized law enforcement data-based systems, which include N.C.I.C., VI-CAP, R.I.S.S., and other intelligence networks, have provided state-of-the-art electronic technology to the criminal investigator.

LETN and other satellite and cable networks provide the law enforcement community with the contemporary issues and strategies for effective crime fighting techniques.

The scientific community has developed forensic techniques that put criminal investigation on the cutting edge of science. DNA technology promises to be the future of forensic law enforcement operations.

It should be noted, however, that these advanced technologies will never replace the homicide detective.

The basic criminal investigative techniques stressed throughout this text are essential for effective inquiry into sudden and violent death.

The homicide detective, in order to be successful, must have an eye for details and the ability to recognize and evaluate evidence. He or she must have an above-average intelligence in order to absorb the many details that arise. And, most importantly, he or she must be able to effectively interview and interrogate the many different persons with whom he or she will come into contact. In my opinion, the ingredients of an effective homicide investigation are *flexibility* and *common sense*.

The investigation of murder necessitates a certain tenacity and perseverance that transcends the ordinary investigative pursuit. Homicides are solved because the detective cares. The homicide detective becomes the advocate for the victim and the surviving family. That explains how a case three, five, or fifteen years old is eventually solved.

Homicide investigation is an aggressive business. Not everyone is qualified for the mission-oriented commitment of death investigation. *Your* homicide case is *yours* forever. It may stay with you throughout your career and sometimes your life. I know this because I have been there.

You must be prepared to use tactics and strategies for any given situation. Skilled interrogation is paramount to the successful investigation of murder. "Good-guy and bad-guy" scenarios never grow old. Any number of tactics might be employed in seeking the truth, and the limit is only set by your imagination, initiative, and the boundaries of the law. A homicide investigator is street-smart and book-wise. The knowledge that he or she develops must then be further enhanced with experience, flexibility, and common sense.

One thing is certain, homicide is a tricky and devious business. It has been my experience that when you add murder to human nature, people's behaviors become a series of contradictory maneuvers involving all the ramifications of the human mind.

Many factors complicate effective investigation, such as interpersonal conflicts, politics or the classic scenario of bureaucracy, hypocrisy, and utter incompetence of certain persons in public agencies. Whether it be the apathy and indifference of society or the ridiculous over-concern over the defendant's rights by the courts, the homicide detective must be able to overcome these obstacles and concentrate on what results he or she can obtain from the scene, and pursue the case with dedication and perseverance.

The text begins with a comprehensive discussion of the homicide crime scene, and evolves chronologically from the initial notification to police that a homicide has occurred, to how the police should react to this notification, and to what procedural steps are necessary in order to conduct an intelligent homicide investigation. The early chapters act as an instructional guide to the patrol officer, including *A Patrol Officer's Checklist*. The text then proceeds into the details of criminal investigation at the scene. I have added a new *Investigator's Homicide Checklist* that helps officers review their own actions at the scene and refreshes their respective memories.

The book then delves into the more technical aspects of homicide investigation, augmented by additional pictures and illustrations with pertinent case histories, which graphically portray exactly what to look for and what to do at the crime scene.

I have revised the suicide and autoerotic death sections of the first edition and have given additional wound structure and injury photographs to aid the practitioner in properly assessing the mode of death. An entirely new section on DNA technology, with appropriate case histories, has been added to give the reader an understanding of this exciting new forensic tool.

Additional chapters dealing with sex-related homicide investigation and investigative assessment through criminal profiling have been added to the text, to enable the investigator to recognize the different classifications of sex-related death and enable the detective to make an early assessment of possible suspects based on the psychodynamics of the event.

The chapter on management has been restructured to provide guidance to police administrators on the make-up and mission of the investigative unit that handles the homicide investigation. There is a *Supervisor's Homicide Checklist* to help field supervisors to properly coordinate and direct activities at the crime scene.

I also include a complete *Police Related Shooting Checklist* that provides the police manager with recommendations on effective documentation of crucial information later used in departmental review. The procedure defined in this checklist is absolutely essential in the event of any subsequent civil action against the agency.

An expanded *Glossary* has been added to aid the reader with the many medical, anatomical, scientific, psychological, and technical terms used in the text.

This revised edition stresses the basics, indicates the practicalities of certain investigative techniques, and provides the reader with patterns upon which to build a solid foundation for a prosecutable case. There is deliberate repetition throughout the text: I have strategically placed these cues throughout because certain investigative principles can never be stressed enough.

In real life, you get only one shot at the homicide crime scene and a limited opportunity to question the suspect. Therefore, I recommend that the reader follow the *investigative checklists and basic principles* in this text. Remember, things are not always as they appear to be; and do it right the first time, you only get one chance.

                                                                                          Vernon J. Geberth

Acknowledgments

I wish to personally acknowledge and thank the many people and agencies who have contributed to the second edition of *Practical Homicide Investigation: Tactics, Procedures, and Forensic Techniques.* Their professional expertise, suggestions, photos, case histories, and reviews encouraged me to successfully complete this second edition, which has been considerably expanded beyond my original textbook. I have listed these persons in alphabetical order and sincerely apologize to anyone I may have inadvertantly ommitted. Richard Agnoletto, Technician, Bronx District Attorney's Office, Video Unit; Karen Beauchamp, Investigator, Arapahoe County Sheriff's Department, Littleton, Colorado; Mary Ellen Beekman, Agent, Federal Bureau of Investigation, New York Office; Lisa Bennett, DNA Forensic Scientist–Lifecodes Corporation, Valhalla, N.Y.; Bergen County Prosecutor's Office, Bergen County, New Jersey; John Besesi, Professional Photographer; Anthony Besesi, Professional Photographer; Lieutenant Ray Biondi, Homicide Bureau, Sheriff's Department Sacramento County California; Robert Bisbee, Retired Detective, N.Y.P.D.; Det. Sgt. Robert Bittle (Ret.), Judicial Investigator, 12th Prosecutorial District State of North Carolina; Det. Sgt. Gary M. Borman, Squad Commander–Detective Bureau, New York City Police Department; Robert M. Boyd (deceased), Retired Commander Homicide Squad, Metropolitan Police Department, Washington, D.C.; Det. Lieutenant Michael P. Bramble, Squad Commander, N.Y.P.D., Detective Bureau; William Brinkhous, Investigator, Office of the Chief Medical Examiner, Chapel Hill, North Carolina; Charles S. Brofman, Attorney, Former Bureau Chief and Prosecutor, District Attorney's Office; Captain Pierce Brooks, (Ret.), Los Angeles, California Police Dept. and National Homicide Consultant; Bureau of Alcohol, Tobacco, and Firearms–U.S. Treasury; Bruce Cameron, Editorial Director *Law & Order Magazine*, Wilmette, Illinois; Homer Campbell, Odontologist Secretary, American Board of Forensic Odontology; Thomas C. Childrey, Assistant Supervisor, North Carolina State Bureau of Investigation; Det. Victor Cipullo, Bronx District Attorney's Office, New York City Police Department; City of New York Police Department's Detective Bureau; Shelia Coleman, Marketing Assistant, Elsevier Science Publishing Company, Inc.; Det. Richard Collins, (Ret.) New York City Police Department; Criminal Investigations Division (C.I.D.), U.S. Army; Det. Sgt. Kevin Cronin, Suffolk County Homicide, Suffolk County, New York; Det. John T. Croston, (Ret.) Bronx Homicide Task Force, New York City Police Department; Det. Sgt. Victor Cruz, Homicide–Bronx Detective Area, Squad Commander 42 PDU; Det. Clint Daniels (Ret.), Morgue Division–New York City Police Department; Delaware State Police Homicide Unit; Captain Edward Denning, Bergen County Prosecutor's Office; Detectives of the Former 7th Homicide Zone, South Bronx Squad, New York City Police Department's Detective Division; Det. Jose A. Diaz, Bronx Homicide Task Force–N.Y.P.D.; Orly DiLullo, Chief of Police, Liberty Police Department, Youngstown, Ohio; Dominick J. DiMaio, M.D., Pathologist, Former Chief Medical Examiner City of New York; Jim Dooley, Investigator Fairfax County Police Department, Fairfax, Virginia; Major John Dotson, Wichita Police Department, Former Homicide Commander, Wichita, Kansas; Lieutenant Paul Dotson, Wichita Police Department–Homicide Bureau, Wichita, Kansas; John E. Douglas, Supervisory Special Agent, NCAVC, FBI Academy, Quantico, Virginia; Edwin T. Dreher, Retired Deputy Chief, Office of the Chief of Detectives, New York City Police Department; Drug Enforcement Administration–Quantico, Virginia; Joseph Dubinski, M.D., New York City Medical Examiner's Office–Tour Doctor; William G. Eckert, M.D., Medical Examiner, Wichita, Kansas, Milton Helpern International Center for the Forensic Sciences; Harvey Eisner, Technician, Bronx District Attorney's Office, Video Unit; Captain Alan Ellingsworth, Commander Homicide Unit, Delaware State Police, Dover, Delaware; Terry M. Fail, Postal Inspector, United States Postal Inspections Service–California; Federal Aviation Administration–Washington, D.C.; Federal Bureau of Investigation; Florida Department of Law Enforcement–F.D.L.E.; Det. Thomas Fitzgerald, New York City Police Department, 47 Precinct Detective Squad; Robert W. Fox, Chief of Police, Sevierville Police Department, Sevierville, Tennessee; Det. William F. Franks, Stony Point, N.Y. Police Department; Det. Kevin Freely, (Ret.) Bronx Detective Area–N.Y.P.D.; Colonel Michael D. Gambrill, Baltimore County Police Department, former Homicide Commander; Betty Pat Gatliff, Forensic Sculpture;

Beth Gilmer-Jones, Investigator, Geary County Sheriff's Department, Kansas; Arthur D. Goldman, D.D.S., Forensic Odontologist, Vice-President American Academy of Forensic Sciences; Colonel Thomas P. Gorden, Chief–Department of Public Safety, New Castle County, Delaware; Billy G. Green, Training Supervisor North Carolina State Bureau of Investigation, Raliegh, North Carolina; Sgt. Frank Griffen, Homicide Investigator, Connecticut State Police; Lieutenant Colonel James J. Hackett, Chief of Detectives, St. Louis, Missouri Police Department; George O. Haggerty, Captain of Detectives, New Castle County Department of Public Safety, New Castle County, Delaware; William Hagmaier, Supervisory Special Agent, Behavioral Science Unit, NCAVC, FBI Academy, Quantico, Virginia; Det. Robert M. Harris, First Grade Detective–Bronx Homicide, New York City Police Department; Robert R. Hazelwood, Supervisory Special Agent, Behavioral Science Unit, NCAVC, FBI Academy, Quantico, Virginia; Robert J. Hazen, Supervising Fingerprint Specialist, FBI Academy, Quantico Virginia; Det. James Hedrick, New Castle County Police Department, New Castle county, Delaware; Det. Frank Henry, New York City Police Department, Detective Division; Special Agent Dayle L. Hinman, Criminal Assessment and Profiling Program–Florida Department of Law Enforcement; Det. Joseph Horgas, Arlington County Police Department, Arlington, Virginia; Millard Hyland, Chief Medical Examiner, County of Westchester, N.Y., Former Deputy Chief Medical Examiner, New York City; Sgt. Harvey Jackson, Homicide Investigator, Salt Lake City, Utah Police Department; Det. Sgt. Ken Jako, Kalamazoo County Sheriff's Department, Criminal Division; Thomas N. Jordan, Investigator, Bureau of Police Services, State College, Pennsylvania; Kansas Law Enforcement Training Center–K.L.E.T.C.; Nick T. Kaylor, Postal Inspector, United States Postal Inspections Service–California; John J. Kelly, Prosecutor, Chief State's Attorney, State of Connecticut; Det. Lt. Raymond F. Krolak, Commander–Investigative Division, Colonie Police Department, Colonie, New York; Bruce LaBrie, Laboratory Specialist, Kalamazoo Police Department, Michigan; Det. Lt. Andrew J. Leffew, Region 10 Detective Unit, Manistee, Michigan; Lowell J. Levine, D.D.S., Forensic Odontologist, President American Academy of Forensic Sciences; Lifecodes Corporation DNA Laboratory, Valhalla, New York; Det. Robert Lloyd, Former Detroit Police Department Crime Scene Detective, Crime Scene Specialist, Thornton Police Department, Thorton, Colorado; Christopher Longueira, Chief Video Technician Bronx District Attorney's Office, Video Unit; Det. 1st Grade Andrew Lugo, Bronx Homicide, City of New York Police Department's Detective Division, Formerly assigned to 7th Homicide Zone; Leslie I. Lukash, M.D., Forensic Pathologist, Chief Medical Examiner, Nassau County, New York; Frank MacAloon, Editor Emeritus, *Law &*

Order Magazine; Maryland State Police, St. Mary's and Prince Georges County Trooper Investigators; John Marzulli, Investigative Reporter, New York Daily News, New York City; Thomas McCarren, Homicide Detective, Retired–New York City Police Department Detective Bureau; Det. Earl McKee, University of Utah Police Department; Lorah McNally, Forensic Scientist, Forensic Laboratory Supervisor Lifecodes Corporation; Murray S. Miron, Ph.D., Syracuse University; Thomas J. Mullane, Homicide Detective First Grade–Bronx Homicide, N.Y.P.D.; Christopher D. Munger, Special Agent, Training Coordinator, New York Office of the FBI; Deputy Chief Bill Murray, Albany, N.Y. P.D.; New Mexico State Police–Investigations Division; New York City Housing Police Department–Detective Division; New York City Police Department–Officers and Members; New York State Police Bureau of Criminal Investigation; Lt. John Nolan, Commanding Officer, Homicide, Nassau County Police Department; North Carolina State Bureau of Investigation; Lt. Thomas Nye, Director, NELEOA, Warwick, Rhode Island Police Dept.; New Jersey Prosecutor's Office, Ocean County; John P. O'Malley, Homicide Detective Bronx Homicide Task Force, N.Y.P.D.; Karlis Osis, Ph.D., Director, American Society of Psychical Research; Pennsylvania State Police–Trooper Investigators; Sam Pennica, Investigator, North Carolina State Bureau of Investigation, Raliegh, North Carolina; James C. Peppard, Homicide Det. (Ret.), Apprehension Unit–Bronx Homicide Task Force, N.Y.P.D.; Det. Raymond Pierce, Criminal Profiling Unit, New York City Police Department; Lt. Raymond Pietranico, New York City Housing Police, C.O. Training Division; Vincent Pizzo, Deputy Chief, New York City Housing Police Chief of Detectives; John W. Plansker, Inspector Detective Commander DAOS–Manhatten, Former Homicide Zone Commander; The Polaroid Corporation; James C. Power, Inspector, Commanding Officer, Manhatten North Detectives, New York City Police Dept., Former Commander of Manhatten Homicide; Sean Powers, Technician Bronx District Attorney's Office, Video Unit; Mary Ann Pulchinski, Homicide Detective, New York City Police Department; John A. Reeder, Chief of Police, Logan Township, Altoona, Pennsylvania; Martin Reiser, Ed. D. Hypnotist, Director of Behavioral Science Services, Los Angeles Police Department, Los Angeles, California; Noreen Renier, Psychic, Consultant to the FBI; Robert K. Ressler, Supervisory Special Agent, Behavioral Science Unit, NCAVC, FBI Academy, Quantico, Virginia; Jack D. Reyes, Homicide Detective New Castle County Department of Public Safety, New Castle County, Delaware; Yong Myun Rho, M.D., Pathologist, Deputy Chief Medical Examiner City of New York; Cpt. Peter Robbins, Commanding Officer, Detective Division, Greenwich, Connecticut Police Dept.; Det. 1st Grade Arnold Roussine, Crime Scene Unit, City of New York Police Department;

Michael P. Scallin, Inspector, Criminal Investigation Division, Newport, Rhode Island Police Dept.; Det. Sgt. (Ret.) James Scaringe, Crime Scene Unit, City of New York Police Department; Monique Scofield, Psychic–Consultant; George Scroope, Homicide Detective, Retired Homicide Detective 7th Homicide Zone, New York City Police Department; Stephen G. Scurti, Chief of Police, Stony Point, N.Y. Police Department; Joseph Scurto, Technician, Bronx District Attorney's Office Video Unit; Det. Sgt. James Sharkey, New Castle County Department of Public Safety, New Castle County, Delaware; Robert Shaler, Ph.D., Director of Serology–City of New York Medical Examiner's Office, Former Director of Forensic Science, Lifecodes Corporation, Valhalla, N.Y., National expert on DNA technology; Harry L. Shapiro, Ph.D. Forensic Anthropologist, American Museum of Natural History; Det. Sgt. (Ret.) Robert J. Sklenarik, Squad Commander, New York City Police Department's Detective Division; Mjr (Ret.) Richard T. Spooner, U.S. Marine Corps, Quantico, Virginia; Louis N. Sorkin, Forensic Entomologist, American Museum of Natural History; Suffolk County, N.Y. Police Department's Homicide Squad; Suffolk County, N.Y. Prosecutor's Office–Homicide Bureau; Lt. Col. James K. Sullivan, Prince William County Police, Manassas, Virginia; James V. Taylor, Ph.D., Forensic Anthropologist, Lehman College, Bronx, N.Y. Department of Anthropology; Patty A. Tedesco, Composite Artist, City of Aurora Police Department, Aurora, Colorado; Raymond M. Theis, Homicide Detective, Bronx Homicide Task Force, New York City Police Department; Virginia E. Thomas, Author, Technicourse, Inc.; Laren Thorsen, Coordinator Public Security Training, Northwestern Michigan College; John T. Tierney, Homicide Detective, Apprehension Unit–Bronx Homicide Task Force, N.Y.P.D.; John M. Tracy, Homicide Detective (Ret.) Detective 1st Grade, Bronx Homicide Task Force–N.Y.P.D.; Pamela Tully, Special Agent North Carolina State Bureau of Investigation; United States Coast Guard Intelligence Division; United States Park Police–Washington, D.C.; United States Postal Inspections Service; Det. Sgt. Frank Viggiano, New York City Police Department, Squad Commander, 47 Pct. Det. Squad; Robert L. Waters, Homicide Detective, Bronx Homicide Task Force, New York City Police Department; Dennis Watkins, Chief Prosecutor, Trumbull County Prosecutor's Office, Trumbull County, Ohio; Mark W. Weaver, Federal Aviation Administration; Lawrence Welch, Esq., F.B.I. (Ret.), Director Kansas Law Enforcement Training Council (K.L.E.T.C.), University of Kansas; John Wisniewski, Inspector, U.S. Postal Inspections Service, Washington, D.C., Headquarters Division; Wichita, Kansas Police Department–Investigative Division; Jay B. Wright, Ph.D., Executive Director, New York Fair, Trial/Free Press Conference, Syracuse University, New York.

A special word of thanks is extended to: Pierce Brooks, an internationally recognized authority on the subject of homicide investigation, who graciously provided the foreword; George Novotny, former Senior Consulting Editor at Elsevier Science Publishing Company, Inc., who assisted in negotiations and encouraged me to revise this text; David Dionne, former Marketing Director and present Acquisitions Editor, who so effectively designed the marketing program of this text and the other texts within my series; Phil Schafer, Editorial Manager, who was the desk editor on the first edition of this book. It should be noted that Phil took a personal interest in the production of this Second Edition and made significant editorial and design contributions. I would also like to acknowledge the team efforts of Bruce Robinson as Desk Editor and Jose Garcia as Senior Designer for the text.

To my wife and family, I wish to extend a very special acknowledgment: to my children, Vernon, Robert, Christopher, and Laura Marie, and, of course, my wife Laura who assisted me with her support and encouragement in this endeavor.

The Homicide Crime Scene

1

The homicide crime scene is, without a doubt, the most important crime scene a police officer or investigator will be called upon to respond to. Because of the nature of the crime (death by violence or unnatural causes), the answer to "What has occurred?" can only be determined after a careful and intelligent examination of the crime scene and after the professional and medical evaluation of the various bits and pieces of evidence gathered by the criminal investigator. These bits and pieces may be in the form of trace evidence found at the scene, statements taken from suspects, direct eyewitness accounts, or autopsy results.

Homicide investigation is a highly professional and specialized undertaking, which requires years of practical experience coupled with a process of continual education and training. However, homicide investigation is not the exclusive purview of the investigator, nor are all homicides solved because detectives are "smarter" than patrol officers. In fact, successful homicide investigation often depends on the initial actions taken by patrol officers responding to any given scene. Technically speaking, all police officers have a responsibility to actively and skillfully contribute to the crime solving process.

Whether it be the operator, who initially takes the call and obtains a crucial piece of information, or the officer in a patrol car, who responds to a "homicide run" and detains a key witness or suspect, the fact is that practical homicide investigation is based on the cooperation of patrol officers and detectives working together toward the common goal of solving the homicide.

The three basic principles involved in the initiation of an effective homicide investigation are as follows.

1. Rapid response to the homicide crime scene by patrol officers. This is imperative in order to protect evidentiary materials before they are destroyed, altered, or lost.
2. Anything and everything should be considered as evidence. Whether this evidence is physical or testimonial, it must be preserved, noted, and brought to the attention of the investigators. The *only* evidence collected at this point of the investigation is eyewitness accounts or spontaneous statements of a suspect at the scene.
3. After the scene is secured, immediate and appropriate notification must be made to the homicide investigators.

The importance of preserving the homicide crime scene and conducting an intelligent examination at the scene cannot be overemphasized. If a murder case ends in failure or an officer is embarrassed in court, the primary reason may very well be an inadequate examination of the homicide scene or a failure to implement good basic crime scene procedures as outlined in this text.

The Crime Scene

The investigation of homicide usually starts at the point where the body is originally found. This location is referred to as the *primary crime scene.*

It should be noted, however, that there may be two or more crime scenes in addition to the location where the body is found. These additional crime scenes may include:

where the body was moved from,

where the actual assault leading to death took place,

where any physical or trace evidence connected with the crime is discovered (this may include parts of the body),

a vehicle used to transport the body to where it is eventually found.

Still other areas related to the primary crime scene include the point of forced entry, the route of escape, the suspect (clothing, hands, and body), and the suspect's residence.

It is important that responding police officers be aware of this multiple-crime scene possibility. Therefore, during the initial receipt of information by the police concerning a possible homicide, the officer

Multiple Crime Scene. Location of the assault leading to death. This is the crime scene as well as the location where the body was found.

should attempt to ascertain the exact location of the situation requiring police investigation and possible additional locations that may need coverage.

At the Crime Scene

Any item *can* and *may* constitute physical evidence; therefore, it is imperative that nothing be touched or moved at the scene before the arrival of the investigators. If the need arises that something at the scene be immediately secured or removed before it is destroyed or lost, the officer handling the evidence must document its location,

Crime Scenes. Locations through which the body was dragged and where it was found. Each is considered a part of the total crime scene (A-E).

(continued)

appearance, condition, and any other feature that might affect the investigation. The officer must be sure to inform the homicide detective of the item's original position so that it does not lose its evidentiary value.

The crime scene, especially in homicide cases, is proof that a crime has been committed. It often contains many or all of the elements of the *corpus delecti*, and provides an abundance of physical evidence that may connect a suspect or suspects to the crime.

Remember, once an item of evidence has been moved or altered it is impossible to restore it to its original position or condition.

Therefore, with malice aforethought, I once again stress the importance of protecting and preserving the crime scene.

The Homicide Investigation Starts at the Crime Scene

The reason why the homicide investigation starts at the crime scene is twofold: 1) The police are usually called to this location by the person who discovers the body, a witness to the crime, or, in some

Newly Damaged Areas. The crime scene may involve many different locations in addition to where the body was found. Here you can see the presence of broken glass, bloodstains, and other objects indicating violence. This area should be safeguarded and preserved for the crime scene process.

instances, the victim. 2) In homicide cases, the location where the body is discovered yields an abundance of physical evidence and serves as a base of inquiry.

From an investigative point of view, the body and its surroundings (including associative evidence and other factors unique to any specific crime) provide the professional homicide detective with significant information on which to base an investigation. For example, an intelligent examination of the scene may reveal the identity of the victim, the approximate time of death, and important evidence and/ or clues to the circumstances of the death.

There is a principle in homicide investigation that refers to a theoretical exchange between two objects that have been in contact with one another. This theory of *transfer* or *exchange* is based on the following facts.

1. The perpetrator will take away traces of the victim and the scene.
2. The victim will retain traces of the perpetrator and may leave traces of himself on the perpetrator.
3. The perpetrator will leave behind traces of himself at the scene.

It is important to repeat that anything and everything may eventually become evidence. The list of items that may constitute physical and/or testimonial evidence is as extensive as the number, type, and causes of homicide itself. Whether it be the *res gestae* utterances of the suspect murderer at the scene or an important piece of trace evidence, the fact remains that the homicide crime scene is the logical and proper point to start the murder investigation.

Determining the Dimensions of the Homicide Crime Scene

The cardinal rule in homicide cases is to *protect* and *preserve* the crime scene. However, before a crime scene can be protected it must be identified as such. In order for the officer to make an intelligent evaluation of the crime scene, he must have an idea of what constitutes physical evidence and where the boundaries of the scene should be established in order to protect the evidence.

Some examples of physical evidence which may be found at the crime scene are listed below. Although the list does not include all types of evidence, these are the three types most frequently found at the homicide crime scene.

The patrol officer, who has the duty of responding to the scene as quickly as possible, begins the investigation by securing the immediate area. Upon confirming that the victim is dead, an assessment is then made by this officer to determine boundaries.

Objects	Body materials	Impressions
Weapons	Blood	Fingerprints
Tools	Semen	Tire tracks
Firearms	Hair	Footprints
Displaced furniture	Tissue	Palm prints
Notes, letters, or papers	Spittle	Tool marks
Bullets	Urine	Bullet holes
Vehicles	Feces	Newly damaged areas
Cigarette/cigar butts	Vomit	Dents and breaks

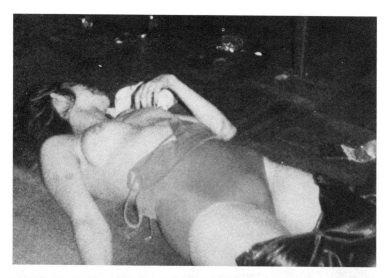

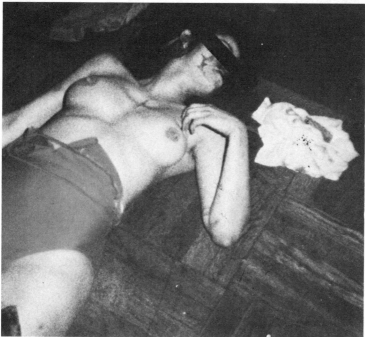

Crime Scene—Basic Death Investigation. Observe the partially clad body of a female. It is important to note that in the early stages of a death investigation you cannot be sure of anything. This apparent case of a sex slaying is actually a natural death due to a ruptured aneurysm. The deceased had been in bed with her boyfriend when she suddenly passed out. He tried to dress her and had placed her on the floor to attempt resuscitation.

Fire Scene. Observe a victim who has died in a fire. Apparently, the victim was lying in his bed when he was overcome. Notice the deep charring and splitting of the skin. Although this is a typical fire death scene, the cause of death should not be assumed until the pathologist has made a careful examination of the deceased. In fact, this was a typical fire death case. Many times arson is used to cover-up a homicide; therefore, the immediate concern of the investigator at such cases should be the scene examination.

Crime Scene. The victim was stabbed and beaten. There is evidence of a struggle: the apartment is in disarray with various broken objects strewn about the room, and blood has been splattered around the room. (*Courtesy* Det. Morris Hill Warren, Ohio Police Department.)

Technically speaking, the homicide crime scene begins at the point where the suspect changed intent into action. It continues through the escape route and includes any location where physical or trace evidence may be located.

Practically speaking, at this stage of the investigation it is next to impossible to know the exact boundaries of the scene. The best course of action for the officer is as follows.

1. Clear the largest area possible. The scene can always be narrowed later.
2. Make a quick and objective evaluation of the scene based on:
   a. location of the body,
   b. presence of any physical evidence,
   c. eyewitness statements,
   d. presence of natural boundaries (a room, a house, a hallway, an enclosed park, etc.).
3. Keep in mind the possibility of a multiple series of crime scenes.

If the crime scene is indoors, the job of making this determination and securing the area is relatively easy to accomplish. If the scene is outdoors, the determination will have to be based on the type of location, pedestrian and vehicular traffic, crowds, paths of entry and exit, weather conditions, and many other factors peculiar to that specific location.

In any event, the first officer should not examine the contents of the scene. He should, however, stabilize the scene by isolating the body and immediate area, including any visible evidence, from all other persons.

Protecting the Crime Scene

The homicide crime scene must be protected from entry by unnecessary or unauthorized persons so that physical evidence will not be altered, moved, destroyed, lost, or contaminated. Other police officers, including supervisory personnel, who do not have a specific or valid reason for being at the crime scene, should be regarded as *unauthorized persons.*

Probably no other aspect of homicide investigation is more open to error than the preservation and protection of the crime scene. The first official acts taken at the scene will either help to bring the investigation to a successful conclusion or will negatively affect both the entire investigation and eventual prosecution of the case.

Therefore, it is incumbent upon the first officer arriving at the scene to perform this first and necessary aspect of the investigation: *Safeguard the location as quickly and as effectively as possible.* (See Chapter 2, "First Officer's Duties on Arrival at the Scene.")

The first police official to arrive at the crime scene is usually the patrol officer, the agency's primary crime-fighting tool, who is expected to respond immediately to any incident where there is a report of a crime or an opportunity to apprehend a criminal. The patrol officer is also the department's representative, responsible for conducting the preliminary investigation, which begins when the officer arrives at the scene.

In homicide cases, the responding officer's duties in the preliminary investigation may simply be to arrive at the scene, observe enough to know that assistance from investigators is required, and protect the scene so that evidence is not destroyed or changed.

Scene protection may be as simple as closing a door to the room where the body is discovered, or as complex as roping off an area of several blocks. There is no definite method or rule for establishing the boundaries of all crime scenes at first glance. As information becomes available at the scene, various other locations may also have to be secured in order to retrieve important physical and trace evi-

Crime Scene Cards. These cards can be used to indicate that a particular area is restricted to authorized personnel only.

dence. Many times I have been at the scene of a homicide in one location and (as a result of information developed from witnesses or evidence located at the primary scene) had to immediately secure a second and third location, a vehicle, and even a building's fire escape and alleyway, used as an escape route by the perpetrator.

Obviously, the best places for obtaining physical evidence are nearest to where the critical act occurred, such as in the immediate vicinity of the victim. However, other areas related to this primary crime scene should not be overlooked. For example,

the point of forced entry,

the route of escape,

the suspect himself (i.e., clothing, hands, body, etc.),

the location of the weapon or other physical evidence,

a vehicle, which was used in the crime,

the suspect's residence,

the location where the assault leading to death took place,

the location whence the body was moved.

The list of locations that may need protection from contamination are as extensive as the crime is complex.

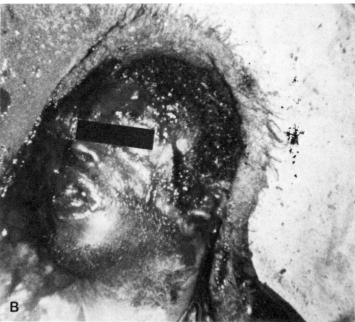

Blunt Force Injuries. Here you can see the degree of injury caused by blunt force. In this case the victim was repeatedly struck with a heavy metal crow bar while he slept. **A.** Note the blood splattering on the surrounding area. **B.** Note the head and immediate area and the extreme lacerations and large amount of blood.

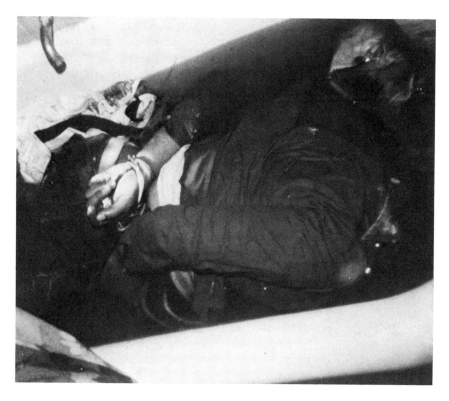

Homicide: Asphyxia by Drowning. Although rare, drowning can be employed as a means of homicide. Observe the body of a victim immersed in the water of a bathtub. The deceased's hands have been bound and the body lies face down in the water. (The water has been discolored by the victim's blood.) This slaying took place after a "crew" decided to rip-off the victim. (A crew is best defined as a loosely knit association of street kids, whose sole occupation is criminal behavior.) The victim had been set up by a couple of street girls, who promised the victim sex. They kept him busy while the male members of the crew broke into the victim's apartment. The victim was then tortured by the crew members who, after ransacking the apartment, eventually drowned him.

The scene should be secured by the use of *ropes, barricades, autos, additional officers,* and even *volunteers from the crowd* if necessary. The use of *crime scene cards* and reflective ribbon can be effective scene indicators. However, the presence of a uniformed officer is essential in order to reinforce scene protection during this phase of the investigation.

Once all injured persons and the deceased have been attended to and all emergency conditions cleared up (such as extinguishing fires, removing hostages in barricade situations, clearing any crowds, taking the suspect into custody, etc.), the officers who have secured the scene should review their actions and make adjustments to provide for the safeguarding of any additional evidence that may have been overlooked during those first critical moments.

The police officer or criminal investigator endeavoring to *protect* and *preserve* the homicide crime scene will find that he or she faces a number of obstacles. It is impossible to list all the conceivable events that may occur at any given scene. However, there are five basic factors or "scene contaminators" that seem to crop up at almost every crime scene. These factors can either by themselves or in combination with other events create problems and do irreparable damage to the scene.

Weather. This factor, especially if the scene is outdoors, can create serious problems in that much of the physical evidence—for example, the body, blood, other body fluids, and residues—is subject to change and/or erasure by rain, snow, wind, direct sunlight, and extreme temperature.

Relatives and friends of the victim. They may be so sickened by the sight of the scene that they begin to cleanup and put things back where they "belong." They are also capable of destroying and secreting any notes or evidence of suicide in order to "protect" the family name.

Suspects or associates. They may attempt to destroy or remove incriminating evidence. It is important to note that if a suspect is taken into custody a short distance away from the scene, he should NOT be returned to the actual crime scene. He may contaminate the scene either by adding something to it, or more importantly, negate the value of any trace evidence originally imparted by him or to him from the scene.

Curious onlookers, souvenir collectors, ordinary thieves. This group encompasses those at the scene either out of curiosity or a desire to steal or to take something as a souvenir. They can introduce confusing fingerprints, alter the condition of the scene, add to crowd-control problems, and in many instances steal pieces of evidence. (During my homicide assignment in the South Bronx, we often used to joke of how a murder weapon could never be heard to hit the ground in the Bronx, because so many would-be felons were on hand to catch it.)

Other members of police agencies and high-ranking officials. They usually are not assigned to the case, but come along to "help." In my

Homicide Crime Scene—Gunshot Victim. This victim was gunned down by robbers and died instantly at the scene. Notice the profuse bleeding from the head wound.

opinion this is the biggest problem encountered in protection of the crime scene.

1. They usually contaminate or destroy valuable trace evidence, either because they don't know what they are doing or because they get in the way.
2. Police officers are naturally curious. However, this curiousity can prove very disadvantageous at the homicide crime scene. Sometimes, for no other reason than "to get a better look at the body," inquisitive officers will unnecessarily walk into the secured area to render their "unofficial diagnoses of death." From my point of view there is no reason for ten or fifteen additional *police* medical opinions. Many times items of trace evidence, thought to be valuable physical evidence, turn out to be something left by police officers who were present at the scene and were smoking, running water, etc.

Basic Death Investigation—Outdoor Scene. Investigators must be cautious each time they are presented with a death investigation. No one can be sure at the start if the deceased is the victim of a homicide or the death is due to other causes. In some instances, preliminary examination of the body and scene will indicate conclusive evidence of murder. However, in a case like the one shown, all you know for sure is that you have a dead body in the woods.

Outdoor Scene—Natural Death. This case turned out to be a natural death due to exposure. The deceased, an outpatient from a mental institution, had apparently been drinking in the woods and fell asleep. The elements eventually took effect. She expired. An empty whiskey bottle was found underneath the body, and there was no evidence of assault. This death was determined to be of natural causes after autopsy. However, the scene examination is vitally important to the pathologist so that the findings can be compared with evidence found at the scene.

Basic Death Investigation—Crime Scene. Here you can see the body of a male, pants apparently pulled down to knees and bruises on the face and arms. The body is in a position which suggests that it was "dumped" at the location. Ironically, this is not a homicide, in fact, the deceased is actually the "bad-guy" in the scenario. Investigation revealed that the deceased, who was accompanied by another, was a rip-off artist; they "worked" the local lover's lane, which was under a major suspension bridge. Their particular M.O. was as follows. After couples parked their cars, these two characters would suddenly appear on each side of the car and, at gunpoint, order the occupants out and rob them. The night before the body was found, these two characters had robbed at least two couples. On their last rip-off they selected a foursome. Not satisfied with just robbing them, they decided to bully the two males. However, the two would-be victims wrested the guns from the "bad-guys" and gave chase in the darkened park. The deceased and his partner made it to the bridge and began running against traffic to the other side. About midway, the decedent decided to jump to what he believed was a walkway. Instead of a walkway, he found air and fell about 200 feet down to where the body was discovered. The two couples who were robbed, unaware of this event, reported the robbery attempt to the police and submitted the guns they had taken. Later on, police questioned the dead man's partner, who showed up at a local hospital with a bullet wound he had received during the abortive robbery, and all the pieces began to fall together.

---

3. The mere presence of additional police officers just standing around or leaning against a doorway may grind valuable trace evidence into the ground or carpet, or may smear a print.

4. Last but certainly not least in the "hit parade" of scene contaminators is the high-ranking police official. It is important to note that *rank does not preclude scene contamination.* Even though some of these misguided officials think they are able to "walk on water," the fact is that they are just as capable of messing up the scene as the lowest ranking police officer who unintentionally walks on through. Many times, especially if the case is sensational or noteworthy, high-ranking officials such as the mayor, the chief of police, fire chiefs, judges, and even the chief prosecutor may appear on the scene. They are usually there to "assist" in operations, but their "assistance" and overall contribution to scene preservation is usually less than helpful. If you are lucky, you may be able to divert them to an area outside the crime scene or to the command post. Or you may gain their cooperation by asking them, in the interests of protecting the scene, that they keep everyone out. In any event, tact will definitely be required in these situations.

Outdoor Scene. Here you see the body of a female who has been "dumped" in the woods. A preliminary examination of the victim indicated that she had been shot in the head and body.

The primary objective in this phase of the investigation is to preserve the body and immediate surrounding area exactly as they were when the body was discovered.

Remember, although the protection of the crime scene is the responsibility of the first officer, all officers responding to and arriving at the scene have an equal responsibility in this duty.

Realistically speaking, various units and additional personnel respond to homicide crime scenes. The toughest job confronting the *first officers* is the effective safeguarding of the crime scene from these additional police officers, emergency services people, and other officials. Obviously, certain personnel must enter the crime scene in connection with their official duties. The first officers, who are safeguarding the crime scene, should identify and document the presence of these officials by maintaing a *Crime-Scene Sign-In* procedure to assure crime-scene integrity and prevent unauthorized personnel from engaging in what I refer to as "crime-scene sightseeing." During my 23 years of active police service, I have come to realize that, "If anything can go wrong, it will go wrong at the crime scene."

This is especially true at incidents that receive an inordinate amount of media attention. It seems as if every official and his/her brother and/or sister feel the need to "show their presence" at the scene.

My solution to this oftentimes impossible situation is quite simple. I suggest that the officers establish *two* crime scenes.

1. The *first* or *primary crime scene* is the location where the actual event occurred, or the area where you expect to recover physical evidence. *This is the real crime scene.*
2. The *second* or *secure area crime scene* is an area set aside from the general public. This allows for all those special dignitaries and high-ranking guests who arrive an opportunity to violate at least one police line in order to establish their importance. It will also serve to keep them within an area where they will be "out-of-the-way" of actual crime-scene operations and preclude any further contamination by official presence.

First Officer's Duties: General

2

This chapter will concentrate on the following events, which initiate a homicide investigation.

1. The actions that should be taken by police officers and police personnel who first receive a report of a possible homicide.
2. The actions that should be taken by a police officer when a witness or passerby reports a possible homicide in person.
3. The actions that should be taken by first officers on arrival at the homicide crime scene.
4. The preliminary investigation that should be initiated by the first officer.

Notification of a Possible Homicide: The Official Notification to the Police

The first notification to the police department of an actual or suspected homicide, or an incident that may develop into one, is usually received by telephone. This first call may simply be a request for assistance for an injured person, a call stating that there were "shots fired," or a report of a screaming man or woman. This first call to the police does not always provide sufficient data to enable the officer to assess the true nature and extent of the incident. Under circumstances where the information received suggests the possibility of a homicide, the person receiving the information should do the following.

1. Obtain and record the following information.
   a. The exact time the call was received.

  b. The exact location(s) of occurrence.

  c. Whether the perpetrator(s), suspicious person(s), or vehicle(s) are still at the scene. Try to get any descriptive information and direction of flight for the immediate transmission of alarms and/or notification to other patrol units.

  d. Where the person calling the police is located, and whether that person will remain. If not, where he or she can be contacted.

  e. The *name, address,* and *phone number* of the person reporting the incident.

2. Request the caller's assistance.

  a. Where practical, if the person making the report seems of suitable age and discretion (calm, etc.), request his or her assistance in safeguarding the location of occurrence. This request should be put into specific terms; for example,

   1. that no one be admitted other than law enforcement personnel or medical people,

   2. that nothing be disturbed.

3. When dispatching officers and units to the scene.

  a. The dispatcher should be aware of the multitude of first officer duties that may be required and should dispatch sufficient personnel and equipment to handle the situation based on the data obtained from the first notification.

  b. Make appropriate notifications to supervisors and to the homicide/detective unit.

4. Switchboard operators and communications personnel receiving emergency calls to police.

  a. Switchboard operators and other police personnel should be aware that in many cases the person making the call to the police is actually the perpetrator, who may not identify himself or herself as such. Should the caller indicate that he or she has just killed someone, the necessary information should be obtained in an ordinary and *detached* manner, the radio cars dispatched, and the operator should attempt to keep the caller on the line in the expectation that the call will still be in progress when the dispatched officers arrive. These officers can then verify that call with the switchboard operator, thereby preparing the basis for a later courtroom presentation.

  b. Even if the operator cannot keep the caller on the line until the arrival of the responding police, the operator should be alert to any identifying characteristics of the caller for later voice identification.

  The first officer or person receiving notification should, as soon as possible, reduce to writing the word-for-word content of the call or conversation.

Remember, the individual who first reported the incident may later become a suspect and the exact words he or she used become critical to the case.

Most departments today, especially in major cities, record all incoming calls as a matter of official procedure. In departments that either cannot afford this type of operation or do not wish to record all calls, there is still the option to invest in an inexpensive tape recorder with a telephone "pick-up." This equipment can then be activated manually by the switchboard operator to record any calls of importance, with specific instructions to record incoming calls relating to homicide or any other serious crime.

Recording of the initial call, especially if the call is made by the perpetrator, can be of invaluable importance later on in the investigation. I recall one case in particular where the common-law husband of the deceased called the police and reported that he had found his wife wandering around the neighborhood in a dazed and beaten condition. This call, which was received through our central 911 system, was automatically taped before the "job" was given to the unit concerned. The patrol unit was given the assignment, responded to the address, and found the woman DOA. They interviewed the complainant, who had mistakenly changed his original story. The complainant did not realize his original call to the police had been recorded. The officers, realizing the discrepancy, notified the homicide division and went along with the husband's story. Upon our arrival, we examined the body, listened to the husband's account of what had happened, and interviewed the first officers, who clued us in to the discrepancies they had observed. It was soon obvious that the common-law husband of the deceased was our suspect. His original call to "central" about finding his wife wandering around in a dazed and beaten condition was apparently forgotten as he became thoroughly enmeshed in a much more involved "fairy tale." He was now claiming that his wife had been a victim of rape and burglary, because he had found her in a nude and beaten condition when he arrived home. He was promptly advised of his constitutional rights, and we allowed him to give a full statement relative to the supposed rape and burglary. He steadfastly denied that he had beaten his wife and continued to embellish his story in an attempt to explain the inconsistencies that we inquired about. However, when I requested the Communications Division to rerun the original taped call, there was our suspect telling a completely different story on tape. Needless to say, upon being confronted with this verbal piece of evidence, and hearing from his own mouth his original "fairy tale," he changed his mind and gave us a complete confession. His story was that she had returned to the apartment after being out with her friends drinking. He had been home

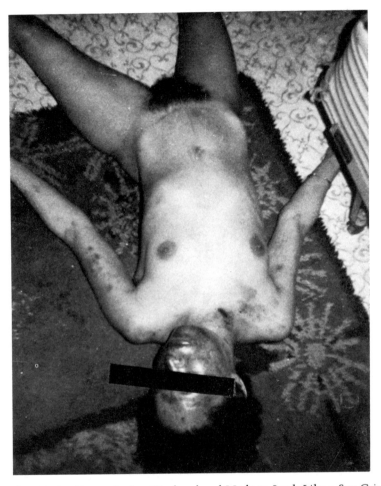

911 Job—Victim Beaten by her Husband and Made to Look Like a Sex Crime. A vicious assault, rape, and burglary *or* a cover-up for murder? This woman was brutally beaten to death by her common-law husband, who then tried to cover up his deed by stripping the clothes off the body and placing it in this position to indicate a rape.

drinking and brooding about her "running around." When she returned, they had an argument, and he proceeded to beat her. And in his drunken rage, he killed her. He couldn't get rid of the body, because there were still people on the front stoop of his building and in the streets. So he undressed her, attempted to cleanup some of the blood (he didn't do a very good job), waited for a while, and then called the police to say that he had found her outside. While he was waiting for the police he came up with the rape and burglary idea.

It is, therefore, very important that the first officer responding to the homicide crime scene *note the time of the call* and/or any initial information, especially if informed of the crime by a passerby or witness. The initial *time* and the officer's *observations* are crucial to the investigation of homicide. Even while responding to the scene and departing from the patrol vehicle, the officer should remain observant and alert to any unusual activity or actions by persons at the scene.

First Notification of Homicide Received in Person by Patrol Officer

If the first notification is received in person by an officer on patrol, he should immediately note the time and the exact information. The person reporting it should be requested to accompany the officer, and this person should be returned to the vicinity of the crime scene and detained for the investigators.

It is important to note that valuable information is often irrevocably lost because the person who reported the homicide to the police officer is allowed to wander off in the confusion at the scene or is not detained for the homicide detective.

If for some reason the officer cannot detain this person, he should at least obtain sufficient identification and other personal information so that the follow-up investigator can interview this important witness at a later date.

Remember, when returning this reporting person to the possible homicide location, never allow him or her to enter the actual crime scene itself. You may contaminate this scene either by adding something to it, or by negating the value of trace evidence which will be found later on and may point to the possible perpetrator.

There is always the possibility that the person reporting the crime is actually the killer. I remember one incident where my partner and I were on investigative patrol in Harlem in an unmarked detective auto. I should point out that these unmarked autos are about as nondescript as a fire engine to the knowing eyes of a criminal. In any event, we had just entered West 117th Street off Lenox Avenue when we observed a male running out of an alley. At about the same time, this male spotted us. He came running up to us and excitedly stated, "There's a man getting killed in the alley." At first impulse, we were about to go charging into the alley; however, being street-wise and suspicious of this sudden show of good citizenship, we grabbed him by the arm and brought him along with us into the alley. There had been a homicide all right. Apparently, our "good citizen" had killed a fellow addict over a bag of "junk." Two addicts who were making a futile attempt to revive the deceased quickly identified our "guest" as the killer. He still had the bloody knife in his pocket and there was blood on his shirt and pants. Maybe if we had not been in a high-crime area, or suspicious of our "good citizen's" intentions, we might have gone charging into the alley, only to discover that we had allowed the perpetrator to walk away. It wouldn't be the first time a suspect had pulled this off. Keep in mind that the next person who comes running up to you yelling murder may be the killer.

Remember, do not go running off without detaining this reporting witness or at least obtaining sufficient identity for follow-up investigators.

First Officer's Duties on Arrival at the Scene

In almost all instances, the first officer to arrive at any homicide crime scene is the uniformed patrol officer. Rarely is the patrol officer a witness to the actual homicide. He usually arrives a short time after in response to a radio transmission or emergency call made by some citizen who has either witnessed the crime or has stumbled upon the homicide scene.

There is no doubt in my mind that the initial actions taken by the first officer may determine whether or not there will be a successful homicide investigation.

On arrival at the homicide crime scene, the situation confronting the first officer can fall anywhere between these two extremes:

1. He might be met by one individual, calm and composed, who directs him to a body which manifests obvious, conclusive signs of death, in a location which is easily secured, and/or safeguarded; or
2. The scene might be filled with people milling about, shouting and/or weeping, the perpetrator may still be at the scene or just escaping, the victim may still be alive and in need of immediate medical assistance, and the scene itself may be a public or quasi-public place which is difficult to safeguard.

Whatever the situation at the scene, the first officer has three primary duties.

1. Determining whether the victim is alive or dead and the necessary actions to be taken.
2. Apprehending of the perpetrator, if still present, or giving the appropriate notifications if he is escaping or has escaped.
3. Safeguarding the scene and detaining witnesses or suspects.

Protection of Life

Each case, of course, will require a different pattern of responses, but the major principle which should guide the first officer is the *protection of life*. The protection of life includes not only that of the victim, where there is a possibility of saving him; but also others on the scene including the suspect and the officer himself. Situations such as barricaded felons exchanging fire with responding police units as a victim lies in the line of fire, possible hostages, and the ever-increasing instances of terrorist acts, obviously will require additional police responses, including requests for specialized units.

However, under ordinary circumstances, wherever there is any doubt as to death, the officer should presume that there is life and proceed accordingly. First officers should, therefore, be aware of the signs of death.

Breath Stoppage. The cessation of breathing is best determined by observation of the abdomen just below the point where the lowest rib meets the breast bone (see arrow).

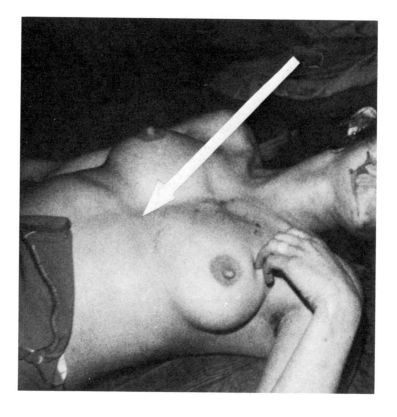

Breath stoppage. This is best determined by observation of the upper part of the abdomen, just below the point where the lowest rib meets the breastbone. Any *up* and *down* motion here, however slight, is indicative of breath and life. Where there is no motion, breathing may have either stopped or be too shallow to be observed. However, death must not be presumed from the cessation of breathing alone.

Cessation of pulse. In most cases the heart continues to beat after the cessation of breathing for a short period of time, anywhere from a few seconds to a few minutes. Pulse can be detected by placing the tips of the fingers on the undersurface of the radial bone (at the base of the thumb) and firmly pressing inward. The absence of *pulse*, coupled with the cessation of breathing, generates a high probability of death.

Eye reflexes. During life, the pupils of the eyes are round and equal in size, and the eyeball is extremely sensitive. At death, the muscles which control the pupils relax, causing them to lose their symmetrical appearance. They may differ in size. The eyelids become flabby in death, and if they are opened by someone, they will remain open.

Pulse. A pulse can be detected by placing the tips of one's fingers on the undersurface of the radial bone. In addition, the pulse can also be detected by placing one's fingertips on the temple or flat portion of the side of the victim's forehead.

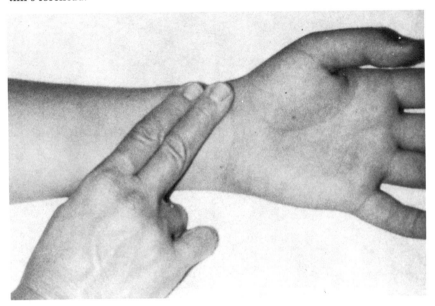

Finally, whereas in life touching the eyeball will cause some reactive movement of the eyeball or eyelid, no such reaction occurs in death. The absence of eye reflexes, coupled with the cessation of pulse and breath, is a conclusive sign of death.

Of course, there are other conclusive signs of death which are somewhat obvious and require little or no examination, such as *rigor mortis*, *lividity*, and *putrefaction*. These will be discussed in greater detail in Chapter 9.

It should be noted, however, that the officer is not expected to perform the functions of a physician. If there is the slightest doubt whether or not the victim is dead, it should be resolved in favor of the presumption of life.

Safeguarding the Scene and Detaining Witnesses or Suspects

The first officer at the scene of a homicide is immediately confronted with a multitude of problems which he must quickly analyze so as to take the necessary steps. Quickness, however, does not imply haste. The first officer's actions must be deliberate and controlled. When the assignment information, communicated to him by radio, passerby, or telephone suggests an incident which is or may become a homicide, the officer, as he approaches the given location, must become *scene conscious*. He must be alert to important details which are transient in nature and which may be subject to chemical change. Changes may occur by dissipation, or simply by being moved by persons on or arriving at the scene. These may include, but are not limited to:

1. The condition of doors and windows, whether closed or ajar, locked or unlocked. Whether shades are drawn or open, the position of shutters or blinds, etc.
2. Odors, such as perfume, after-shave lotion, gas, marijuana, cigar or cigarette smoke, gunpowder, chemicals, putrefaction, etc.
3. Evidence which may be obliterated or damaged on the approach to the central scene, such as tire marks on the roadway, stains such as blood or other body fluids, fibers, shell casings either on the floor or in high grass or soil. In addition there may be discarded cigarettes or cigars, matchsticks, a weapon, fingerprints, and even personal property of the perpetrator left behind in his haste to get away.
4. Whether lights and light switches are *on* or *off*. Condition of electrical appliances—on or off, warm or cold.
5. Original position of furniture or articles which may have been moved in order to get to the victim to render first aid, to make a

determination of death, etc. (If ambulance personnel arrived before patrol units, patrol officer should get their identification and determine what, if anything, was moved or touched.)

In most instances the first officer will face an emergency condition at the homicide crime scene. However, he must maintain a professional image which will enable him to perform effectively during this preliminary response stage. The first officer should direct his attention to isolating the body and immediate surroundings from all other persons. This procedure alone will usually call for a great deal of tact in dealing with members of the family who may be present, sympathetic neighbors, and the curious, whether strangers or other police officers who have responded.

In this phase of preservation of the scene and removal of unauthorized persons, the first officer in his diligence to remove unnecessary persons should be careful not to chase off possible witnesses or others who have important information. Do not overlook the possibility that one of the people you might chase off could be the perpetrator. I remember spending an entire nightwatch tour trying to locate a suspect, who had literally been chased from the area by uniform officers while they were attempting to secure a homicide crime scene, which occurred at a street location. The suspect, who was intoxicated and generally abusive, claimed to be a friend of the victim and had been pushing his way to the front of the crowd to get a better look and "see if the man was really dead." He had been admonished several times to remain behind police lines; however, he wasn't complying. One of the officers, probably out of sheer frustration, grabbed him by his coat collar and the back of his belt and literally tossed him out onto the street. The officer followed this up with an appropriate description of what he would do to the suspect if the suspect returned. Needless to say, the suspect took the officer's friendly advice and "got into the wind"; he disappeared. When the investigators arrived, they began questioning persons in the area and soon learned that the suspect and the deceased had been seen together earlier in the evening drinking and quarreling over a debt the deceased refused to pay. A witness to the murder was located as were various pieces of evidence that linked the suspect to the crime. Only one problem remained, the suspect couldn't be found because the officers had scared him away.

The first officer may even have to guard against his own overzealousness or desire to impress superiors by being the first to discover some piece of evidence, and inadvertently destroy its value by picking it up. He may also have to overcome sheer curiosity, or walking onto the scene "just to get a better look."

In addition, it is important to keep in mind that all personal habits of the officers at the scene must be carefully controlled. These include, but are not limited to, cigarette or cigar smoking, use of the toilet in the crime scene, discarding any foreign substance at the scene, using the telephone, etc.

Remember, at this stage of the investigation, the only evidence that should be collected by the patrol officer is eyewitness or testimonial in nature such as res gestae or spontaneous utterances of a suspect.

The First Officer Initiates the Homicide Investigation

The first officer who is confronted by the homicide crime scene has a very involved responsibility. Although the formal investigation will be conducted by detectives or the criminal investigator, it is the *first officer* who has the responsibility of initiating the investigation. I have provided ten practical rules of procedure which may be used as a guide in initiating a professional homicide investigation.

1. Arrest the perpetrator if you can determine by direct inquiry or observation that he or she is the suspect. (As a general rule, do not question him or her at this stage.)
2. Detain all persons present at the scene.
3. Attempt to assess and determine the entire area of the *crime scene* including paths of entry and exit and any areas that may include evidence.
4. Isolate the area and *protect the scene.* Seek assistance if necessary. Notifications must be made to superiors, investigators, and specialized units. (Use crime scene cards.)
5. Refrain from entering the scene and/or disturbing, touching, or using any item found therein. *Never use the crime scene as a command post or the telephone as a communications center.* In communicating with the station house or headquarters, the first officer should *not,* unless absolutely necessary, use a telephone instrument at the scene. This necessity *should* be determined by common sense and priorities. The first officers should instead establish a temporary command post outside the central crime scene, preferably where there are at least two phones available, one for incoming and one for outgoing calls. In the early stages of the investigation, there is a definite need for rapid communication between the various centers of investigation.
6. Identify and, if possible, retain for questioning the person who first notified the police.
7. Separate the witnesses so as to obtain independent statements.
8. Exclude all unauthorized persons from entering the crime scene until the arrival of the investigators. This, of course, includes police officers not directly involved in the crime scene investiga-

Chalk Lines Around Body at Crime Scene. You are *not* to draw lines around the body at a crime scene unless the body is to be removed. This photo shows evidence that the crime scene had been visited by a "Chalk Fairy." "Chalk Fairy" is a term used to describe mysterious police officers who feel the need to draw lines around the body and then disappear when investigators attempt to find out who contaminated the scene.

tion. The detective supervisor and the investigator assigned are, of course, allowed entry into the scene for evaluation purposes. Other unavoidable exceptions may include the medical examiner, or a doctor or clergyman. In any event, establish a pathway in and out so as to avoid unnecessary disturbance.

9. Keep a *chronological log* containing the name, shield number, command, and title of any police official who enters; the name, serial number, and hospital of any medical personnel, ambulance driver, or technician; and the names and addresses of any civilians entering the crime scene.

10. Take notes.

Although this list may seem very simplistic and basic, I can assure you from experience that in the confusion that permeates the homicide crime scene, it is inevitable that such a fundamental principle as not touching or using the phone is invariably forgotten as the need

Telephone in Crime Scene. In this close-up photo of a telephone in a typical homicide crime scene, it is obvious that the phone has been handled by someone who has been bleeding. (This may include the perpetrator as well as the victim.) It is imperative that this valuable evidence is not touched or disturbed before a forensic examination is made. Telephone instruments often contain latent prints. The first officer should be aware of the existence of "trace evidence" on telephone instruments and not use the telephone to communicate with the police station or other police units until it has been processed for evidence. Although this particular telephone obviously contains trace evidence, it should be noted that any object at the scene may contain latent prints or other evidence and should be treated accordingly.

Remember, never use the crime scene as a Command Post or the telephone as a communications center.

---

for communications overwhelms good technique. Many times I have responded to a homicide in an apartment, only to find that the telephone was now being used as a communications line and one of the rooms as an office or command post. Needless to say, valuable trace evidence is irrevocably lost because of this careless procedure.

Dealing with Emergencies at the Scene

It should be noted that rules and procedures are only a guide to assist the first officer in performing his or her functions at the homicide crime scene. The true test, however, in any given crisis is *common sense.* Often he or she does not have the luxury of "clinical textbook conditions" to direct his or her performance. Practically speaking, it is usually the street-wise officer who manages to come up with the appropriate solution in an emergency that occurs in an otherwise routine job, because he or she possesses flexibility and common sense— the two ingredients necessary in an emergency.

Sometimes the first officer is faced with hysterical or violent persons, who may include the perpetrator and/or his hostile family and friends, or the family and friends of the deceased either bent on revenge or so overcome with grief that they become irrational. In addition, especially within inner-city enclaves, hostility may result from a general distrust of the police, or any number of factors ranging from misunderstanding of the police function to the real or imagined grievances of the citizens involved, neither of which is amenable to correction by the first officers responding to the crime scene.

In situations like these, the first officer would be foolhardy *not* to pick up any weapons connected with the crime scene, in order to preclude their use by those present against either the officer or another person. Protection of life would in that case take precedence over the general rule of not picking up or disturbing any evidence at the scene. However, the officer should continue to remain scene conscious, disturbing only that which is necessary and being careful to note the location, position, and condition of each item before it is moved or changed.

I remember one crime scene in a South Bronx social club that resembled *The Shoot-out at the O.K. Corral.* There were two bodies lying on the floor, a number of guns strewn about, and a large angry group of combatants who had been temporarily "neutralized" by the responding police. The first officers had instinctively retrieved the guns to prevent further bloodshed. Common sense would dictate removing the weapons before you have an increased body count or you lose the evidence to the local gun collectors.

In extreme cases, it may even be necessary to move the body and abandon the scene. However, *this is a last resort,* only undertaken when police officials at the scene either cannot maintain police lines or are forced by conditions that indicate there will be a further loss of life to innocent bystanders or injury to police officers at the scene.

Such a situation could occur when a militant or radical group has just lost its leader through an assassination, or any incident which may trigger a large-scale civil disturbance. In these cases, if the officers have access to the body, they should, consistent with their own safety, attempt to remove the body from the crowd. While doing so, they should attempt to note the original position, any new blood flow, any rigor or lividity if present, and any other information which may assist in the investigation by the pathologist and detectives later on.

In such situations, there will usually be a number of news media representatives, including still and movie photographers. Police officials at the scene should enlist the assistance of these cameramen and photographers in getting as many photos as possible, with an accent on the persons present at the scene. In addition, there is usually ample time to arrange for police photographers to be present to take intelligence films. If conditions allow, it may even be possible to have these police photographers take the necessary crime scene shots before you move the body, taking special note of the crowd. These photos and newsfilms can later be reviewed for evidence and information.

I recall one such episode which occurred in New York City during a "Unity Day" rally in the early seventies. A major member of organized crime, who had arranged for a rally against alleged "police and FBI harassment," was about to address a large assemblage when suddenly he was shot. Although there were uniformed police officers only a few feet away, they were completely helpless in the chaos that followed. In addition to this attempted "hit," there were literally dozens of guns drawn by both the personal bodyguards of the victim and by members of the opposite faction. The bewildered police officers also drew their guns, but couldn't tell the "good guys" from the "bad guys"; they withheld their fire. However, there were several shots fired. A supposed suspect was killed, no one knew by whom, there were guns strewn all over the place, and there were several ongoing struggles within the crowd. The police were at a complete disadvantage in maintaining any type of original crime scene. However, a later review of the film coverage taken by the major networks and the intelligence photos taken by police and FBI photographers were invaluable in re-creating the original scene and identifying possible perpetrators as well as suspected members of organized crime who were present during the shooting.

Conclusion

In conclusion, the police officer who is responding to or confronted by the homicide crime scene should prepare to take *five basic steps* upon arrival. If he executes them carefully, he will have initiated a proper professional investigation.

The homicide crime scene is not an everyday occurrence for most officers. Usual police activities are either emergencies, requiring automatic reaction, or routine handling of called-for-services. The officer who confronts the homicide crime scene, however, finds himself somewhere between these two extremes. He must therefore force himself to adapt to the situation. I offer the acronym ADAPT as a basic, five-step approach.

A   Arrest the perpetrator, if possible.

D   Detain and identify witnesses and/or suspects for follow-up investigators.

A   Assess the crime scene.

P   Protect the crime scene.

T   Take notes.

First Officer's Duties: Specific

Chapter 2 concerned the general responsibilities of the first officer who confronts the homicide crime scene. This chapter will treat related situations that call for a *specific* response on the part of the first officer. These specific duties concern the following:

The suspect in custody,

Transporting the suspect,

Examination of the suspect for evidence,

The dying declaration,

The victim removed to the hospital,

The victim pronounced dead at the hospital,

The officer's duties at the hospital,

The victim confirmed dead at the scene,

Handling witnesses at the scene,

Additional officers at the scene,

Handling news media personnel at the scene,

The documentation of events by the first officer.

In addition, I have included, in this chapter, a patrol officer's checklist, which the officer at the scene can use to refresh his memory about what vital information must be obtained and duties accomplished in the initial investigation of homicide. Some of the information in this chapter may seem repetitive. It is meant to be. Based on my experience, some elements of investigatory procedure need to be reinforced by repetition.

The Suspect in Custody

If the first officer takes a suspect into custody based on the officer's observations, information, or probable cause developed at the scene, he should *not* as a general rule interrogate him. The interrogation should be conducted by the investigator later on.

Suspect in Custody—Deceased Confirmed Dead at Scene. The deceased, a sixteen-year old female, was accidentally shot by her boyfriend while he was practicing his quick-draw with a shotgun, which he wore in a sling under his arm. The boyfriend, a suspect in some local armed robberies (with a shotgun), had been showing-off when the gun discharged. Hearing the blast and screams, neighbors called the police. Three patrol units arrived within minutes of the "shots fired" call. They disarmed the boyfriend at gunpoint, detained the group involved, and notified the detectives. In such situations, the perpetrator is obvious. The patrol officers should take the suspect into immediate custody, based on their observations at the scene. It is better, however, if the suspect is questioned later-on by the investigators and not interrogated by the patrol officers. If the suspect is talkative and wants to make a statement to the patrol officers, then by all means the statement should be taken. Make sure, however, that the suspect has been properly advised of his or her Miranda rights.

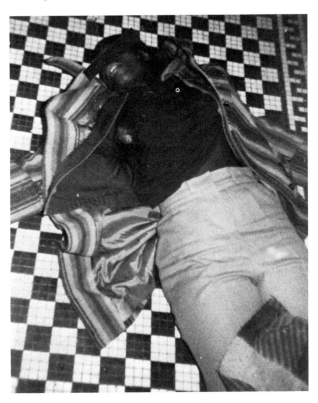

```
┌─────────────────────────────────────────────────────────────┐
│                                                             │
│                    MIRANDA WARNING                          │
│   1.  You have the right to remain silent.                  │
│   2.  Anything you say can and will be used against you in a court of law. │
│   3.  You have the right to talk to a lawyer and have him present with │
│       you while you are being questioned.                   │
│   4.  If you cannot afford to hire a lawyer, one will be appointed to │
│       represent you before any questioning, if you wish one. │
│                                                             │
│                        WAIVER                               │
│   After the warning and in order to secure a waiver, the following ques- │
│   tions should be asked and an affirmative reply secured to each question. │
│   1.  Do you understand each of these rights I have explained to you? │
│   2.  Having these rights in mind, do you wish to talk to us now? │
│                                                             │
└─────────────────────────────────────────────────────────────┘
```

Miranda Warnings Card.

Practically speaking, however, there are certain types of homicide cases that readily indicate the culpability of the suspect. In addition, there are instances when the suspect is quite talkative and insists on confessing or telling "his side of the story" to the officer. Under these circumstances, the officer should immediately advise the suspect of his constitutional rights under the Miranda ruling, make sure the suspect understands these rights, obtain an intelligent waiver from the suspect, and then allow him or her to make a statement.

I recommend that the officer advise the suspect of his rights using an official form, or a "Miranda Warnings" card, issued by most departments to their officers. This will insure that the rights have been given in a proper manner, and the card can later be presented in court upon the challenge of the defense attorney that his client wasn't properly advised by the officer.

Under the Miranda ruling the suspect must be told the following.

1. You have the right to remain silent and refuse to answer any questions. Do you understand?
2. Anything you say can and may be used against you in a court of law. Do you understand?
3. You have the right to consult an attorney before speaking and to have an attorney present during any questioning. Do you understand?
4. If you cannot afford an attorney, one will be provided for you without cost. Do you understand?
5. Now that I have advised you of your rights, are you willing to answer questions without an attorney present?

If the defendant understands his rights and answers in the affirmative to each of the above questions, an intelligent waiver has been obtained. It should be noted that there are specific rules for non-English speaking suspects and juveniles.

Transporting the Suspect

Sometimes a patrol officer will be requested to transport a suspect to the station house while investigators remain at the scene. If the suspect is to be transported to the police station by patrol officers, these officers should be instructed *not* to interrogate him or her. If the suspect insists on volunteering information, or talking about the case, the officers should listen, remember, and later make notes of any statements made. It is important to note that an interrogation by officers who are not familiar with the facts of the homicide investigation may do more harm than good, and perhaps completely damage the case.

From a practical point of view, it is usually better if the suspect is interrogated by the investigator who is assigned to the case. The homicide investigators are in the best position to question the suspect based on their firsthand knowledge of the investigation, which includes examination of the crime scene, interviews with the first officers, and questioning of witnesses or any others who may have information relative to the case. Obviously, the investigator will be able to determine whether or not the suspect's statements are consistent with the facts of the homicide investigation.

Examination of the Suspect for Evidence

The examination of the suspect for evidence should be performed by the investigator or homicide detective assigned to the case, or another investigator familiar with the investigation. However, in the event that the patrol officer has effected the arrest, or has taken the suspect into custody, he should be aware that there may be physical or trace evidence on the suspect, his clothing, and/or his shoes. My advice is that the officer examine the suspect for any evidence, and preserve the clothes and shoes which can be vouchered as evidence in connection with the investigation. (See Chapter 8.)

The Dying Declaration

If the victim is still alive, the officer must be alert to the possibility of obtaining a *dying declaration*. This can be performed while waiting for the ambulance or en route to the hospital. Officers should be knowledgeable in the requirements of a valid dying declaration. I would recommend that the department issue a checklist or card to patrol officers which will assist them in obtaining a legally admissible statement, which may later prove invaluable in firmly establishing whether or not a crime has occurred and investigating the circumstances surrounding that crime. However, it may be used in a criminal trial only for the death of the declarant. (See Chapter 5, "Obtaining a Dying Declaration.")

The statement can be either oral or written. In any event, the officer should reduce the statement to writing and have the declarant either sign it or make his mark. It is recommended that there be a witness present. However, neither the absence of a witness nor the inability of the declarant to write this statement affects its admissibility.

The Victim Removed to the Hospital

Upon arrival of the ambulance, the officer should guide the intern and/or ambulance attendants to and through the central crime scene via a preselected route, so that there is no destruction or unnecessary damage to any physical or trace evidence. Whatever they touch or move must be observed by the officers on the scene and reported to the investigators when they arrive. An officer should ride in the rear of the ambulance with the victim and remain with him at the hospital, making sure not to interfere in any way with required medical treatment. If the prognosis is that the victim is likely to die, the officer's presence is necessary should the victim make some statement or recall some important fact not previously disclosed.

The officer at the hospital should attempt to have the victim's clothing removed intact. If cutting is necessary, however, it should not be done through any holes, cuts, or tears caused by bullets, knives, or other weapons and instruments. To facilitate this procedure, it is recommended that hospital emergency room personnel be contacted in advance to secure their future cooperation when and if such a situation arises. I would suggest that the investigative supervisor contact the hospital administrator and discuss matters of mutual concern. This liaison between homicide commanders and representatives of the hospital can be advantageous to both parties in getting the job done.

The Victim Pronounced DOA at the Hospital

If the victim is pronounced DOA (dead on arrival) or dies at the hospital, the officer should obtain the necessary information consisting of name of attending physician, cause of death, time of death, and any other factors which may pertain to the investigation. The officer

Victim Still Alive. Here you see a homicide crime scene where the body has been removed. The victim was still alive when the police arrived. He was rushed to the hospital in a patrol unit, while other officers secured the scene for the investigators. The chalk outline indicates the position of the body when police arrived. This is good procedure. However, if the victim is obviously dead and the body is not going to be removed *do not* draw any chalk lines around the deceased. In this case, first officers at the scene detained witnesses to the slaying. The officers in the patrol unit, which rushed the victim to the hospital, were able to learn the nick-name of the assailant from the victim before he died. When the victim was pronounced dead at the hospital, the officers notified the patrol units at the scene and the homicide squad was dispatched. As a result of the professional and thorough handling of this incident by the patrol units, the detectives were able to effect an arrest within 24 hours.

should then immediately communicate with the detective or detective supervisor at the scene, relay this information, and then be guided by any further instructions he may receive.

The Officer's Duties at the Hospital

At the first opportunity, the officer at the hospital should communicate with the investigators at the crime scene in order to keep them advised of any developments at the hospital. In turn, the officer will receive such information as is necessary in order to be able to talk intelligently to the victim should he or she regain consciousness, or should the opportunity arise to obtain a dying declaration.

The Victim Confirmed DOA at the Scene

If the first officer arriving at the scene finds a body showing conclusive signs of death, the body should not be disturbed. Sometimes, inexperienced officers feel a need to "do something," particularly in the presence of family or friends of the deceased. They may feel compelled to cut down a body which has been suspended in a hanging, or otherwise disturb it, even when there are such obvious signs of death as rigor, lividity, and incipient putrefaction. In some instances, officers feel that they should immediately search the decedent so as to quickly identify him or her, or obtain "all the information" for the desk officer when they call in their report. Once again, I emphatically state that the body should not be searched or disturbed until all other investigative processes have been completed and the medical examiner has completed his on-the-scene examination.

I would strongly suggest, based on past experience, that the search and inventory of the deceased be conducted in the presence of a supervising officer, and if possible a member of the family or other civilian, in order to minimize a later charge of theft from the body, which unfortunately arises from time to time in dead-body cases. If the officer does cut down a hanging body because there are no conclusive signs of death, he must be careful first to observe the position of the knot when the body is suspended, and then to leave the knot intact.

Handling Witnesses at the Scene

All witnesses present at the scene upon the officer's arrival must be detained for the investigators. The officer should also be alert to the possibility that one of the witnesses who "discovered" the body may in fact be the perpetrator. If the suspect is taken into custody at the scene, he should ordinarily be detained for the investigators or removed as soon as additional assistance arrives to protect the scene. Keep in mind scene contamination.

Keep witnesses and/or suspects separate from one another, or where circumstances make this situation impossible, at least attempt to prevent discussion of the incident either in the hearing of or between these persons. At the same time, officers should be alert to any declarations which may be admissible under the *res gestae* rule. As soon as the circumstances and number of officers present permit, the witnesses should be moved outside the crime scene area, or at the very least away from the central crime scene. Witnesses should not ordinarily be moved to the station house until the investigators arrive, to permit them to obtain the details basic to the investigation and crime scene search.

The first officer should report all conversations with the witnesses to the investigators when they arrive, and, at the first opportunity, make careful written notes of such conversations.

At times, the person who discovers the body, the witnesses, or perhaps members of the immediate family may be so distraught that some well-meaning person or physician may suggest that they be given a sedative. Officers present should attempt to delay this medication until the arrival of the investigators. Persons who are sedated are often unable to be spoken to for several hours or even until the next day. This could become particularly critical when the sedated individual emerges as a possible suspect or perpetrator of the crime. As always, this situation will require tact and discretion.

Additional Officers at the Scene

As other officers arrive, care must be taken that they conduct themselves in an appropriate manner. Too often, officers who have not seen each other for a while meet at crime scenes and drift into irrelevant conversation during the lulls that occur while waiting for the investigators, the crime scene technicians, the morgue wagon, and so on. At times this banter produces snickers or outright laughter which can be heard by members of the family or friends of the victim. The image of the officers, the department, and police in general may thus be downgraded or even ruined in the eyes of that family, the neighborhood, or even the entire community. This is one of the reasons that I recommend that officers, especially additional reinforcements, arriving at homicides, be directed to report to the command post, which should be away from the central crime scene area. There they can await assignments and be supervised without their conversations being overheard.

Handling News Media Personnel at the Scene

If newspaper or television people arrive on the scene, they should *not* be permitted access and *no* information should be given to them at this time. In addition, if there are any witnesses or suspects being detained, it is imperative that they be kept away from the media. The first officers can best accomplish this task by firmly insisting that *no unauthorized persons* are allowed to interview or ask questions of anyone present in the interests of justice.

First officers should tactfully explain that all information about the case will come from the chief investigator or the detective supervisor in charge at the scene. It can be explained that it would be unfair to make some information available, piecemeal, to some members of the press, which would not be equally available to all others, and that such information will be made uniformly available as soon as possible. This approach must be taken by all members of the department, whether at the scene, the hospital, the morgue, the station house, or still on patrol.

Such an *interests of justice* or *cooperation* appeal will usually be sufficient to handle preliminary inquiries by the press. Most press personalities and news reporters who have dealt with the police before can appreciate the emergency nature of this phase of the investigation and know that any information must come from a ranking official or detective supervisor. However, the first officers may encounter an overzealous or pushy character who insists that the police have no right interfering with the freedom of the press. In these instances, merely exercise good police procedure and courteously remove him or her from the crime scene, just as you would remove any other unauthorized or unnecessary person. (See Chapter 14, "The News Media in Homicide Investigations.")

The Documentation of Events by the First Officer

The first officer (and indeed all officers taking part in the investigation) must be *time-conscious*. He must, as soon as circumstances permit, record the time he was dispatched, the time he arrived on the scene, the time he requested assistance, and so on. Time may become an important factor in terms of the suspect's alibi. Accurate recording of time also makes for a more precise investigation and contributes to a more professional report. In addition, accuracy as to time will create a more favorable impression in court.

The first officer, as well as other officers who arrive on the scene prior to investigators, should realize that they will have to enumerate all their activities at the scene to the investigators when they arrive. The officers should be mindful that they too may be subpoenaed to court later on and their notes subject to review.

The investigators must be informed of *everything* that was touched, moved, or altered in any way, either by the officers or by others who were at the scene when the officers arrived. Officers must not smoke, flush toilets, run tap water, use the bathroom facilities, or anything else at or near the crime scene *unless absolutely necessary*.

As soon as the first officers have performed their immediate duties, they should take advantage of any lulls or waiting time to record times, details, conversations they have had, names and addresses of witnesses or persons known to have been on the scene, and any other information pertinent to the investigation.

When the investigators arrive, the officers should immediately fill them in, out of the hearing of the family, witnesses, suspects, and any others present, on all that has transpired up to that point. The investigators will now assume responsibility, at whatever point that they cut into the investigation, for the conduct of the investigation from that point on.

The Changing Sequence of Command

All officers should be aware of the changing sequence of command at homicide crime scenes. The first officer on the scene is in command until a uniformed officer of higher rank, or an investigator arrives on the scene. The ranking uniformed man will be in charge until the arrival of his superiors or an investigator. As soon as the investigator arrives, he will assume command from that point forward. He in turn will be superseded by an investigator of superior rank. Department regulations should provide for such shifts of command in these situations so as to avoid conflict and maintain a professional investigation.

Patrol Officer's Checklist

As a practical matter the first officer's responsibilities in the preliminary investigation of homicide are divided into three specific duties:

1. Preserve life,
2. Arrest the suspect,
3. Protect the scene.

The officer should record all homicide information in his memo book or notebook as soon as possible, preferably as it is obtained. This book should be retained for later court purposes and shown to the investigator when he arrives at the scene. All dead-body calls should be handled as homicides in this preliminary stage.

I have provided the following checklist of first-officer duties in order to assist the officer at the scene in refreshing his memory as to what vital information he should secure.

INITIAL CALL/RECEIPT OF INFORMATION

☐ Record exact time and type of call patrol unit received. (In systems using modern computerized and recorded radio transmissions, unit can check with Communications.)

☐ If first notification is received in person: detain this person for investigators. If unable to detain for some reason, obtain sufficient identification and information for follow-up investigator.

ARRIVAL AT THE HOMICIDE CRIME SCENE

☐ Record the exact time of your arrival and/or notify Communications that you are on the scene.

☐ Enter the immediate crime scene area to view victim. (Only one officer should enter scene. Use only one path of entry and exit.

☐ Determine if victim is alive or dead.

☐ Arrest the perpetrator if present.

☐ If there is a possibility of life, summon ambulance and apply appropriate first-aid procedures.

☐ If circumstances indicate the victim is near death or dying, attempt to obtain a dying declaration.

☐ If ambulance crew is present before your arrival, determine if the crew or anyone else moved the body or any items within the crime scene. If there were any items moved record the following:

    ☐ What alterations were made.

    ☐ When the alterations were made.

    ☐ Purpose of the movement.

    ☐ Person who made the alteration.

☐ Record the names, serial numbers, and hospital of ambulance crew present at the scene.

☐ If the victim is dead, record the official time of pronouncement by ambulance attendant.

☐ *If suspect has just fled the scene, initiate a wanted alarm.*

☐ Record any alterations to the crime scene that were made as a matter of investigative necessity. For example,

    ☐ Lights turned on or off.

    ☐ Door opened, closed, locked, or unlocked.

    ☐ Body moved or cut down.

    ☐ Windows opened, closed, locked, or unlocked.

    ☐ Furniture moved; anything touched.

    ☐ Gas turned off, appliances turned off, motor of vehicle on or off.

PROTECTION OF THE CRIME SCENE

- ☐ Attempt to assess the entire crime scene, including paths of entry and exit, and any areas that may include evidence. *(Remember the possibility of a multiple crime scene.)*

- ☐ Establish a perimeter, secure and protect the scene by isolation and physical barriers such as ropes, cones, and other equipment as necessary.

- ☐ Record names, addresses, dates of birth, and telephone numbers, etc. of all persons present at the crime scene.

- ☐ Remove all persons from the immediate area. *(Be careful not to chase off witnesses or the perpetrator, who may still be present.)*

- ☐ If victim is removed from scene by ambulance, an officer should accompany victim to hospital riding in rear with victim (for possible dying declaration).

- ☐ An officer should remain at scene in order to provide for its security.

- ☐ If the victim's clothes are removed at hospital, an officer should maintain control (victim's clothes are evidence).

- ☐ Request additional units as needed to protect the scene.

- ☐ If it is necessary that a clergyman or doctor enter the scene, have an officer accompany him through the designated path of entry and caution this person about contamination and/or alteration.

NOTIFICATIONS

- ☐ Make notifications by telephone if possible (police radios are often monitored by the press).

- ☐ *Never*, unless absolutely necessary, use a telephone inside the crime scene. Such necessity would involve a life-or-death situation, the need for immediate transmission of alarms, etc.

- ☐ Notify the investigators or homicide division.

- ☐ Record time of notification and who was notified.

- ☐ Establish a temporary headquarters out of central crime scene (preferably a location with two phones, one for incoming, one for outgoing).

- ☐ Broadcast any alarms for suspects or descriptions of perpetrators from command post to guarantee uniformity and possibility of verification.

☐ Notify Communications of the telephone numbers of the command post to facilitate communications between the various units.

PRELIMINARY INVESTIGATION

☐ Initiate and maintain a chronological log recording the names, shield numbers and commands of any police officers entering the crime scene. In addition record the names, addresses, etc. of any civilians who may have to enter as well as names, titles, and serial numbers of any ambulance personnel. This log should reflect the entry and exit of any person who enters the crime scene.

☐ Isolate and separate witnesses or suspects. Do *not* permit any conversations relative to the crime. Hold witnesses and suspects for the investigators.

☐ Establish a path of entry and exit based on observation of scene.

☐ For any civilian at the scene, record identifying information and their knowledge of the crime.

☐ Do not touch, move, or alter anything in the scene. If you do, record it.

☐ Do *not* smoke in the crime scene.

☐ Do not flush toilets or run tap water in sinks or bathtubs. If it has been done, record it.

☐ Refer all newspaper and media inquiries to the investigators.

☐ Stand by for investigators and assist them as required.

☐ Advise and inform investigators of all that has transpired since arrival of first officer.

SUSPECT IN CUSTODY

☐ Determine if the suspect is armed (search for weapons). If weapon is recovered, record description and location. Maintain custody pending arrival of investigators who will instruct as to vouchering and disposition.

☐ Handcuff suspect and isolate him/her from any witnesses and/or associates. (Use rear handcuff method.)

☐ If suspect is arrested outside crime scene, *do not return him/her to scene.*

☐ If suspect is arrested inside crime scene, *remove him/her immediately. (Remember scene contamination.)*

☐ Note and preserve any evidence found on suspect, advise investigators.

☐ Do *not* permit suspect to wash hands or use toilet (you may lose evidence).

☐ Do not permit any conversation between suspect and any other parties.

☐ Do not initiate any interrogation (wait for the investigators). However, in certain types of homicides the first officer will take statements. *Make sure, however, that suspect has been warned of his rights* before taking any statement. As a general rule, no interrogation.

☐ Carefully record all spontaneous statements (*Res gestae* rule).

☐ Observe and record behavior of suspect (e.g., nervous, erratic, emotional, unemotional, drunk, under influence of drugs, any unusual behavior, etc.).

SUICIDE AND ACCIDENTAL DEATHS

☐ If death appears to be suicidal or accidental, handle as homicide, pending arrival of investigators.

    ☐ Secure immediate scene, detain witnesses.

    ☐ Preserve all evidence, e.g., notes, weapons, pills, vials, drugs, etc. in their original position.

    ☐ Notify investigators.

    ☐ If vehicles are involved, do not allow removal until photos have been taken by crime-scene technicians.

    ☐ If suicide is by hanging and death is evident, *do not cut body down.*

    ☐ If body is cut down because death is not evident, *make cut above the knot.*

    ☐ If relatives are present, get any background information which may assist investigators.

The Preliminary Investigation at the Scene: The Detectives

4

The purpose of this chapter is to provide the homicide investigator/ detective with flexible guidelines to follow in the preliminary investigation of death. The principles set forth in this section are intended to help the detective and chief investigator at the homicide crime scene to systematically check and review all the facts applicable to the investigation.

This chapter will cover the sequence of events starting with the initial notification to the detectives that a homicide has occurred, and then proceed chronologically through the investigative duties and direction of activities at the scene, including direction of uniformed personnel, interview of first officers, handling curious onlookers and witnesses at the scene, interview of ambulance personnel, the canvass, and the preliminary medical examination. Subsequent chapters will address the specific investigative methods employed at the scene. However, this preliminary phase of homicide investigation is the most critical and deserves special attention because this phase sets the tone for the entire investigation.

Initial Receipt of Information

Homicide investigation is probably the most exacting task confronting the criminal investigator. It begins with the initial notification that a homicide has occurred.

Investigators are rarely the first officers at the scene of a homicide. The body is usually discovered by friends, relatives, or citizens who in turn notify the police or call for an ambulance. The notification to detectives or investigators is usually made through department channels.

The response of the homicide investigator and detective supervisor must be methodical. In order not to overlook the obvious, the most basic details should be recorded. I personally recommend that the investigator start a separate steno pad or notebook for use in each homicide investigation.

The first entry should be the receipt of information that a homicide has occurred, including:

date and time of notification,

method of transmission, e.g., telephone, radio, or in person,

name, rank, shield number, and other data indentifying the person who is reporting the information to detectives,

complete details of the information and event.

Many times, either from a false sense of urgency and/or a desire to take immediate action, investigators will get caught up in the excitement or confusion that often permeates the homicide crime scene. Subsequently, they may lose the "cool, calm, and detached" projection necessary to assume control and initiate the investigation. A good thing to keep in mind is the fact that the deceased isn't going anywhere; and, more important, that the patrol officers are already at the scene taking preliminary action.

Prior to leaving for the scene, the investigator should instruct the person notifying him or her that patrol officers at the scene should:

preserve the crime scene,

hold all witnesses and/or suspects,

avoid using telephones located within the crime scene,

initiate a *personnel log* accounting for all activities at the scene, including identification of all persons who have had access to the scene,

record the license numbers and vehicle information of all autos in the area of the crime scene (if applicable).

Arrival at the Scene

When the investigator arrives at the scene, he should note the following:

time of arrival,

the exact address of the scene,

persons present (officers, ambulance or medical people, relatives, friends, etc.),

the condition and position of the body (personally verify death; see Chapter 2 "First Officer's Duties on Arrival at the Scene"),

information concerning death,

weather conditions,

outside lighting conditions in nighttime situations,

points of observation (locations where persons such as the local busybody could have observed what happened).

In addition the investigator should stop and observe the area as a whole, noting everything possible before entering the actual crime scene for the detailed examination. Only the investigator and detective supervisor should enter the homicide crime scene, of course, with the exception of the first officers, and even then only to confirm death and observe scene conditions.

Homicide investigators must be certain to record the time and place of events and any measurable evidence. It only takes a few moments of the investigator's time to record this information, which may prove vital to the investigation. Basically, there are three reasons for this emphasis on preliminary note-taking.

1. The question of *time* is frequently the first subject covered in a cross-examination. If the investigator cannot be sure of the time of events, he may lose credibility on the rest of the testimony.
2. The subject of *time* may very well be the basis of an alibi.
3. Note-taking forces the investigator to slow down. It thereby sets a calmer tone for subsequent events at the scene, and also causes the investigator to pay attention to details in order to record them in the notebook.

A procedure I have found effective is to photograph the crime scene upon arrival. This can be done either with a Polaroid camera, available at the homicide office and maintained for crime scene use, or with an Instamatic camera, which can be carried in your pocket for ready use at any time. I find the Instamatic with built-in flash device good because of its convenience and simplicity. A photo taken at this point is a priceless record of how the crime scene appeared when the first detectives arrived.

The Crime Scene Unit or police photographer will take any number of photographs of the homicide crime scene, which will be submitted into evidence for the prosecution. However, those first pictures taken before the arrival of additional personnel and supervisors usually prove to be quite valuable.

Properly Prepared Crime Scene: Victim Dead. This photo was taken immediately on arrival of the investigators at the scene; you can see that uniformed officers have cordoned-off the area to preserve the scene. The emergency medical people have covered the body with a sheet after pronouncing the victim dead. It is a good procedure to obtain pictures of the people in the crowd. Often, witnesses to the event including possible suspects will be watching the police activities at the scene. If their pictures have been taken, you may be able to identify or locate these persons later on in the investigation.

Describing the Scene

A complete description of the dead body and the surrounding area, covering the following items, should be entered in the notebook of the investigator upon arrival. (Although some of the points I have listed may seem quite obvious, I can assure you from my own experience that the obvious is sometimes overlooked, especially during this initial phase, as you attempt to "cover all the bases.")

1. Sex, appearance, age, build, color of hair of the deceased and a description of the deceased's clothing.
2. Evidence of injury and apparent cause of death.
3. Are the bloodstains wet or dry?
4. What is the condition of the body (lividity, rigor, etc.)?

5. Describe the color of the blood (bright red or brown).
6. Note any tears in clothing and evidence of gunshot or stab wounds.
7. Careful examination of the hands. Are there any wounds or a weapon?
8. Note whether or not there is any jewelry (rings, watches, gold chains, etc.). If there is no jewelry, make a negative notation. The defense has been known to resort to dirty tactics during trials. If they can make you appear like a thief to discredit your testimony, *they'll do it.*
9. Describe the immediate surroundings. (See Chapter 7.)
   a. Position of body in relation to articles in the room.
   b. Note doors, windows, furniture, etc.
10. If a weapon is nearby, take detailed notes. Do not handle.
11. Look for bullet holes or fired shells. Note: do not collect at this stage of the investigation. (See Chapter 8.)
12. In poison and drug-overdose cases, note presence of drugs, bottles, or glasses.

Implementing Crime Scene Procedures

The first thing the investigator should do after confirming death is to take charge of the crime scene. In the absence of the detective supervisor, the homicide detective is responsible for the professional investigation, of which the preliminary investigation at the crime scene is the most important and sensitive aspect. Therefore, extreme care must be exercised to preserve and protect the scene, because even the smallest detail can suddenly assume vital importance in the case. Failure to implement proper crime scene techniques may irreparably damage the investigation. I have found that the best course of action is to treat each dead-body call like a criminal homicide until the facts prove differently.

If the crime scene is outdoors, a wide area surrounding the body should be cordoned off for later systematic examination. The patrol officers should be directed to isolate the body and secure the immediate surroundings from all persons.

If the crime scene is indoors, the job of securing the location is relatively easy to accomplish. It may be as simple as closing the door. The biggest problem is removing unauthorized persons from the scene. The investigation should begin with the walkway and front entrance to the structure. These areas and the location where the body lies should be considered part of the scene and appropriately secured.

The homicide detective should determine what areas are to be included or excluded from the crime scene and decide whether or not the homicide involves multiple scenes. (See Chapters 1 and 2.)

I remember responding to a particularly vicious incident in which the victim, a young newspaper delivery girl, was repeatedly stabbed and assaulted during a sex attack on a roof landing. Upon arrival, I was informed by the patrol supervisor that the crime had taken place on the roof landing and that an officer had been assigned to safeguard the scene. I conducted a preliminary survey of the scene and surrounding area and discovered at least five additional locations involved in this original crime scene. These included the roof, an adjoining roof landing, an elevator, and two interior staircases, none of which had been secured and all of which contained various bits of trace evidence. Additional personnel were requested and these areas were cordoned off for the later crime scene search and process.

Direction of Uniformed Personnel at the Scene

The detective supervisor and homicide detective assigned to the case are in complete command at the scene of the homicide. They have the authority to exclude everyone—including other police officers, the news media, and any other unauthorized persons—except the medical examiner or coroner. Often, follow-up investigations of crime scenes have disclosed that valuable evidence was destroyed by the mere presence of police personnel.

Actions such as standing or walking in the scene or leaning against doorways or walls may alter or destroy valuable trace evidence such as latent prints, blood, hair, or skin specimens. If the crime scene can be adequately controlled, the chances of contamination will be minimized. The homicide people should explain these facts to the patrol supervisor and uniformed officers and request their cooperation in keeping *all* unauthorized and unnecessary personnel away from the crime scene.

Sometimes, high-ranking police personnel may inadvertently destroy valuable evidence. Although rank does not preclude scene contamination, I wouldn't advise an officer to tell some high-ranking officer that he has just "screwed up" the crime scene. Instead, the homicide supervisor should be apprised, who then might be able to gain some cooperation from the ranking official by requesting assistance in preserving the scene and keeping everyone out. Tact will be required in this type of situation.

Sometimes a patrol officer will have taken evidence into custody before the arrival of the investigators. There are many situations where officers will be forced to retrieve evidence or secure firearms either because of safety or the possibility of destruction. They should be directed to properly safeguard this evidence, as they now are involved in the "chain of custody," and to make proper notations in their official reports so that this evidence can later be submitted into evidence. (See Chapter 13.) Likewise, if an officer effects an arrest at the scene based on his personal observations, the officer should be placed under the supervision of the homicide investigator by the detective supervisor. This procedure will assure that the officer is properly guided during the subsequent homicide investigation. In some instances, it may be necessary to "detail" a patrol officer to the Homicide Division during the investigation.

Uniformed personnel at the scene should remain at their posts until relieved by the investigator, although they may be used to transport witnesses or suspects for the investigators at the scene. (See Chapter 3.)

The Teamwork Approach

The detective supervisor and homicide investigator are faced with a crime of the utmost gravity, one which is fraught with a complexity of possible motives and methods and a variety of physical evidence. Therefore, *teamwork* is required for a successful homicide investigation, and it is the detective supervisor and homicide investigators who must set the tone for this teamwork approach as they coordinate the different people involved in the responsibility of the inquiry into death, for example:

the patrol service or uniform division,

the detective division and other homicide detectives,

the medical examiner or coroner,

the crime scene technicians or fingerprint experts,

the District Attorney,

medical and ambulance personnel,

other agencies such as the FBI if the homicide involves a federal employee.

Directing the Investigation at the Scene

Homicide investigators should attempt to obtain all pertinent information from the first officer—out of the hearing of any witnesses, the press, or the public—before taking charge of the investigation. As mentioned earlier, the detective should confirm the fact of death for himself. The investigator must also see that the duties of the first officer have been accomplished.

Duties of the Detective Supervisor on Arrival at the Scene

The detective supervisor or chief investigator, upon arrival, will assume the responsibility for conducting the homicide investigation and will replace the initial investigator as the ranking officer in charge of the case.

It is extremely important that the detective supervisor and the homicide investigator not permit themselves to fall into a fixed routine. Previous experience is invaluable but can become a hindrance when allowance is not made for new possibilities.

Remember, each homicide case is distinct and unique and may require a fresh approach or perspective. Keep an open mind.

Practically speaking, no one at this stage of the investigation has all the answers, nor can anyone know for sure exactly what direction the case will take. However, the investigators should be guided by certain basic procedures at the scene.

1. Ascertain that there is an investigator at the scene, and that the crime scene is amply protected. Confer with the investigator and be brought up to date on the status of the investigation. Solicit any opinions or theories and objectively evaluate these with your independent observations. Determine any investigative needs and make assignments as necessary.
2. Confer with the ranking uniformed officer at the scene, and interview the first officer so that proper instructions can be given to responding investigators.
3. Priority should be given to the removal of the suspect and/or witnesses to the police station. Each witness should be transported separately. However, before they are transported, the witnesses should be briefly interviewed by the investigators at the scene so that they may have the advantage of the witnesses' observations to guide their investigation at the scene. Written statements can be obtained later on at the police station and the information transmitted back to the detective supervisor at the scene.
4. Use an assignment sheet to indicate assignments as given. This sheet should contain the identification of officers assigned, the location of the assignment, the duties assigned, and the time the assignment was given. Later on it can be used as a control device to assure that official reports are obtained from the investigators assigned. In addition to fixing responsibility for certain investigative duties, the assignment sheet will eliminate duplication of effort as additional assignments are made and put on the sheet.
5. If a suitable communications center or command post has not

been established by the patrol officers, the investigator or supervisor should take immediate steps to arrange for one. The station house, Communications Division, and the detective command should be apprised of the telephone numbers of the command post to facilitate rapid communication to and from the scene.

6. Designate an officer to keep a running timetable of events, including arrivals and departures at the scene. When the scene is released, the timetable should be turned over to the detective supervisor.

7. If the victim has been removed to the hospital, insure that proper action is being taken at the hospital regarding any dying declarations, clothing, evidence, etc. (See Chapter 3.) It is advisable to have a detective contact the hospital and confer with the patrol officer and/or doctor. It may even be necessary to assign a detective to assist the officer in these procedures.

8. If the suspect has fled the scene, the investigator and detective supervisor must ascertain exactly what alarms have been transmitted, if any, and the exact information contained therein. Upon verification and the development of any new information, these alarms should be retransmitted.

9. Provide for the dissemination of information to all units involved in the homicide investigation. Ideally, all investigators should be aware of all aspects of the case. It is up to the detective supervisor to coordinate and disseminate this information to the "troops." Properly informed officers can better perform their own assigned functions and contribute more intelligently to the overall effort. This is especially true for those officers assigned to conduct canvasses. (See Chapter 4, "The Canvass.") Uniformed officers assisting at the scene must also be made to feel that they are part of the team.

10. On occasion, too many officers respond to the homicide crime scene. The detective supervisor should not hesitate to direct these officers to return to their original assignments if they are not needed.

Preliminary Interview of the First Officer

The detective must ascertain that the scene is *intact*—that nothing has been added or removed since the arrival of the responding police. To determine this he goes directly to the first officer. A preliminary interview with the first officer can provide an up-to-date appraisal of the crime scene as well as an assessment of what has transpired since the discovery of the body.

The homicide investigators should obtain a detailed account of what the officer or officers have seen and done. Usually, the officers will offer an opinion as to cause, manner, and circumstances of death. Investigators should receive these opinions objectively and graciously. However, they should not allow themselves to be influenced prior to making their own observations. Often the first officers' opinions provide a valuable lead in the investigation. In keeping with the teamwork principle, give credit where credit is due. If a patrol officer's performance at the scene is outstanding or proves instrumental in solving the investigation, I personally recommend that an official report be forwarded to the officer's commander. This report should be initiated by the detective supervisor at the scene and sent through channels so that this officer will receive proper recognition.

Remember, in order to effect a successful homicide investigation, everyone involved must work together—homicide investigation is a team effort and not a one man show.

When interviewing first officers, emphasis should be placed on their activities in the immediate area of the crime scene—for example, how they gained entry into the scene, the position of the body on arrival, things they may have touched or moved, condition of the doors and windows, odors, whether the lights were on or off, etc. (See Chapters 2 and 3.) It may prove valuable to have first officers document their activities and observations on official reports. In addition, I recommend that the investigator assigned to interview the first officers prepare an official report for review by the patrol officer to assure that it is correct, and then have the officer sign the investigator's report which will become part of the homicide investigation.

I have found that it is a good idea to keep the first officers at the scene to answer any questions about the appearance of certain objects when they arrived. In addition, they can report any observations of persons who were in the area when they arrived or who expressed some interest in the activities of the police. I recall one case in which the police had been called to the scene by the fire department after firemen discovered a body on fire in a basement of a South Bronx tenement. Two patrol officers in the vicinity responded immediately and arrived as firemen were still extinguishing the fire. The fire officer in charge advised the two police officers that an individual at the scene had been quite helpful and had directed firemen through the unlit basement to the source of the fire. These two police officers, taking note of the fact that inhabitants of the area were often less than civic-minded, detained this "good citizen" pending arrival of myself and other detectives from the 7th Homicide Zone. They advised us of his actions and detained him as a witness. Needless to say, it wasn't long before we were able to reconstruct what had occurred. Our "witness" had been staying with the deceased in a rear room of the basement. They were both from Jamaica and belonged to the Rastafarians sect (a Jamaican subculture that often deals in marijuana and other illegal activities) and apparently had a falling-out over business resulting in a shooting that left the deceased with a bullet in his head. Why our good citizen just didn't take off, I'll never know, but he stayed with the cadaver all night. The next day he bought kerosene at the corner hardware store, dragged the body to the front of the basement, poured the liquid over it, and lit it up. However, he didn't expect the initial burst of flame and smoke. His immediate problem was keeping the flames down. The people on the first floor, spotting the smoke emanating from the basement, called the fire department. A fire company returning to its station, and still in the area from a previous alarm, responded and arrived in less than a minute. The suspect, finding himself trapped between the body and the firemen, decided to play the part of a good citizen. The two street-wise police officers, however, didn't buy his act, and he was detained. After gathering some trace evidence and interrogating our "witness," an arrest was made and our good citizen charged with murder.

The interesting thing to note in this particular case is the actions of the first officers. They took the initiative and detained this person based on their initial observations and "gut feeling." As a result, homicide detectives were provided with a suspect and were able to successfully conclude the investigation.

Interview of Ambulance Personnel

Frequently an ambulance crew represents the first official agency to arrive at the scene of a homicide. Sometimes these ambulance attendants can render invaluable assistance to the investigator. Since their obligation is to view the body and give medical assistance if the victim is still alive, one or more members of the crew have probably been on the scene and close to the body. Often the perpetrator will still be on the scene and may even engage the ambulance crew in conversation or make an admission. In addition, the deceased may utter a name or description of the assailant. Furthermore, many people who were present when the assault took place will not leave when the ambulance arrives, but instead will stand around to "watch the show." When the police units begin to arrive, these persons suddenly make themselves scarce.

It is up to the homicide investigators to find out exactly what took place before the arrival of police. The investigators must interview each member of the ambulance crew who was present at the scene.

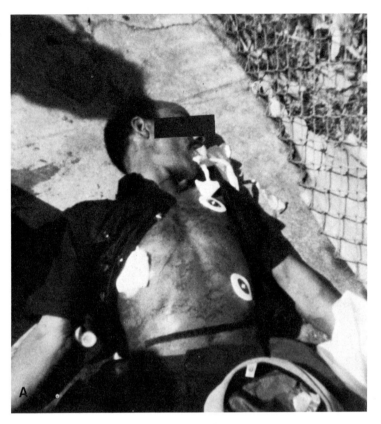

Properly Prepared Crime Scene: Victim Alive. Observe how a crime scene can change prior to the arrival of the investigators. In this case the deceased was still alive when the uniform officers and emergency medical technicians arrived. The body was obviously moved, and the scene changed while first aid measures were given to save the man's life. It is important to obtain the

Ambulance crew members are not trained criminal investigators and may inadvertently have altered the crime scene in some small but highly significant way. Obtain their names, serial numbers, unit numbers, hospital affiliation, and times of arrival and pronouncement of death. Every detail of their actions should be known, for example, how they gained entry if the scene is indoors, the path of entry if outdoors, things they may have touched or moved in order to get to the body, movement of the body, what areas they were present in, and their observations. They should answer such questions as: Who was present? Did the deceased say anything? Were they smoking? If so, did they discard their cigarettes and where did they discard them? etc.

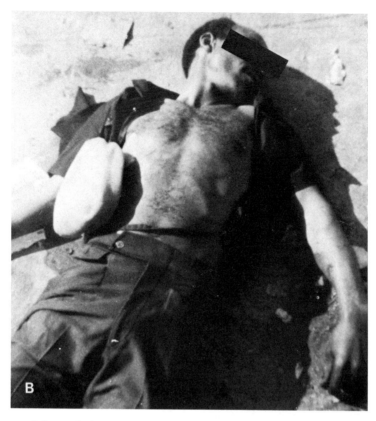

identity of the ambulance personnel and to note their initial observations and recollections of events at the scene when they first arrived. **A.** The man has just been pronounced dead after emergency treatment. **B.** Emergency medical equipment has been removed from the victim.

Handling Curious Onlookers

Using courtesy and a calm professionalism in dealing with civilian crowds can be to your advantage. You may be able, for example, to gain the crowd's cooperation in maintaining police lines pending arrival of additional personnel, or to persuade an onlooker to come forward with some valuable information. This is especially important in areas known for their distrust of and hostility to the police. In some areas, especially in inner cities, the mood of the crowd may turn ugly depending on how the police maintain lines and direct the crowds.

Do not engage in any verbal rhetoric with the "village idiot." You may rest assured that in every crowd there is the drunk, the clown, the self-elected spokesman of silliness, the troublemaker, the junkie, or the fool. Your refusal to get involved with such a character may very well be the key to getting the crowd on your side, and through nothing more than plain old-fashioned peer pressure this person will be neutralized. Furthermore, when the crowd begins to empathize with your function, additional information may be provided by witnesses who were at first reluctant to come forward.

As an investigator you can usually assume a different role than that of the uniformed patrol officer. Persons who have been directed by patrol officers to stand back will instinctively resent the authority, yet may still have a desire to give information to the police. My advice is to take advantage of this and actively solicit their cooperation. People will usually tell a homicide detective things they wouldn't tell another officer.

Furthermore, when dealing with curious onlookers in a crowd, you never know who has information and who will come forward with it. I recommend that you get some of your people, who do not look like detectives, into the crowd. I remember an incident in the South Bronx that the 7th Homicide Zone had responded to. It was a street scene, and the deceased was lying on the sidewalk surrounded by a large crowd of onlookers, most of whom were conversing in Spanish. One of the homicide detectives, who was Puerto Rican, began to mingle with the crowd and ask questions in Spanish. A man he was speaking with suddenly turned to another person in the crowd and said in Spanish, "Hey, look over there, that guy has some nerve. First he kills the "dude," and then he comes back with all these cops standing around just to look at the body." Needless to say, the detective in the crowd alerted his counterparts but remained in the group to watch and listen. When the other detectives suddenly broke into the crowd and grabbed the suspect, the persons who had been discussing the incident were overheard to say: "Wow, those detectives are really smart. How did they know he killed that man?"

The detective who had infiltrated the crowd not only identified the suspect but came up with two additional witnesses who were brought into headquarters for formal statements.

Handling Witnesses at the Scene

Although the homicide crime scene offers an abundance of informational and evidentiary material, the identity of the perpetrator will usually be uncovered through the intelligent interviewing of witnesses.

The homicide detective should determine the identity of all witnesses who have been at the scene. Valid identification, including names, date of birth, residence and business addresses (with zip codes and telephone numbers) should be obtained in the event that later contact is necessary. It is imperative that the witnesses be separated, and each one should be interviewed individually as soon as possible after the event. The best procedure is to assign homicide detectives to take an informal statement immediately upon arrival while the case officer (the investigator assigned to the case) goes over the crime scene and establishes some basic information about the crime. This procedure assures that a candid statement is obtained before any deterioration of memory takes place either because of a time lapse or a desire "not to get involved."

Usually, a person who tells a detective one story won't suddenly change it later on when a formal statement is taken. These initial interview results should immediately be made known to the homicide supervisor and the case officer to assure sensible direction of activities at the scene. The location for the subsequent formal interview of witnesses should be an office or other place where there is privacy and the necessary recording equipment available. I recommend that witnesses be transported to the station house for formal statements immediately after the initial information has been obtained at the scene. If patrol officers provide the transportation, they should be reminded to keep parties separated both en route and at the police station.

The formal statement should be taken and each witness evaluated by the homicide detectives assigned to the investigation. Needless to say, the homicide supervisor and the investigator who originally took the preliminary statement should confer in this evaluation. This phase becomes crucial when dealing with persons who do not speak English and require an interpreter. The interviewing officer should make sure that the interpreter is phrasing the question properly so that there is no misunderstanding of the meaning of the question, and that the exact response—and not the interpreter's assumption of what the interviewee meant—is recorded. If possible, have an officer who speaks the language conduct the interview with the case officer. Together they can formulate the questions and evaluate the responses.

Obviously, the eyewitness to the fatal act is the most valuable. However, other witnesses may have important information which places the suspect at the homicide crime scene or supplies the motive for the crime, or they may be able to provide personal information about the suspect.

Remember, it is important to keep the witnesses separated from one another.

Witnesses who have conferred with each other may change their stories, not from a desire to mislead the police, but from a very basic factor in human behavior. One or more persons in a group may force their dominant personality on the group, and the other witnesses will compromise their stories so as not to disagree or offend the stronger personalities, or to seem "stupid" by having seen something no one else saw.

In other instances, however—especially when dealing with criminals or persons sympathetic to criminal enterprise—there may be a conscious effort to mislead and thwart police inquiry into the crime.

The detective should realize these possibilities when questioning prospective witnesses and must be thorough and patient. He must get the witnesses to relax and talk about themselves. He should encourage them to tell the story in their own words. Of course, when dealing with the criminal sympathizer or "bad-guy" type, questioning will have to be more along the lines of authority, and you will look for any weaknesses or fears you can perceive. Usually these types are not too anxious to have the police probing into their life style and may be willing to cooperate either for a price or just to "get the cops off their back." Sometimes you may be lucky enough to have something on them, such as a lesser crime, which can be traded off for information on the homicide. In reality, as I look back on my career, especially in some of the areas where we conducted homicide investigations, *many* of our witnesses were brought in in handcuffs. Often the only good thing you could say about the deceased was that he was *dead;* today's deceased was usually yesterday's perpetrator.

Dealing with these criminal types is always frustrating and dangerous. You never know for sure which side of the fence they are on, nor can you be sure of their motivation, or when they will turn on you. Your best defense, of course, is the proper documentation of their activities. Make sure that you confer with your supervisors or commanders. In certain instances, the Office of the District Attorney must be consulted, especially if part of the "deal" concerns court consideration or lack of prosecution in return for testimony against a suspect in the homicide.

Effective interviewing is an art that requires constant improvement. It is a very time-consuming procedure, but often invaluable for the discovery of information. In this interviewing phase, team effort is especially important. There is an enormous work load generated in a very short time at a homicide crime scene. This work load is further compounded by the element of time. There just isn't enough time for one or two homicide investigators to perform all the necessary duties and conduct careful interviews. The detective supervisor should assign enough investigators to conduct these preliminary interviews and be kept up to date with the results. This information should be made available to the other investigators involved so that they can proceed intelligently with their duties.

The Canvass

A *canvass* is a door-to-door inquiry or brief interview with persons on the street by which detectives attempt to gain information about a specific incident. It is an important investigative tool and a vital part of the preliminary investigation at the homicide crime scene.

The detective supervisor should assign investigators to conduct a preliminary canvass of the surrounding area including the approach and escape routes from the crime scene, while the case officer performs his functions at the scene. As the detectives conduct the canvass, their primary purpose should not be to conduct in-depth interviews, but to locate possible witnesses or persons who may have information about the crime. Canvassers should obtain the name and address of each person spoken to, whether the person provides information or not. Where no one is at home or there are additional residents who should be interviewed, this should be noted so that the parties can be reached during a recanvass. Likewise, locations that are negative should be recorded for the follow-up investigation. Because of the vast amount of information generated in a short period of time at the homicide crime scene, I recommend that everyone involved in the investigation possess a notebook. Each apartment, place, or person canvassed should be recorded in the investigator's notes for later official reports or a recanvass, as the case may warrant.

At times it may be necessary to recanvass or extend the canvass to include additional areas. The thoroughness of the procedure is the determining factor of success. On the recanvass, a witness who was reluctant to talk the first time or someone who was inadvertently missed will be located. Also consider the physical location of the crime scene in relation to the area canvassed; that is, don't miss the back of the building. I remember one case where an extensive canvass was conducted in a number of buildings that faced the front of a location where a vicious burglary homicide had taken place. The canvass proved negative until someone realized that no one had canvassed the buildings which faced the rear. These buildings were on another street around the corner from the murder site. This particular canvass resulted in locating a witness who had observed two males climbing up a fire escape toward the victim's apartment. This witness was able to make a positive identification of the suspects in the case. The ironic part of the story is that the witness had not made any connection between this event and the murder and would never have

<u>WITNESSES</u>

Name _____   Address _____

M ____ F ____ Race _____ D.O.B. _____ Age _____ Tele. # _____

Height _____ Weight _____ Build _____ Complexion _____

Welfare # _____ Social Security # _____

Drivers License # _____ Auto Driven and Reg. # _____

Wife or Husbands Name _____ Address _____

Welfare # _____ Social Security # _____ Tele. # _____

D.O.B. _____ Age _____ Social Status _____

Girlfriend or Boyfriends Name _____ Tele. # _____

Last Known Address ____ _____ D.O.B. _____ Age _____

Welfare # _____ Social Security # _____

Number of Children _____ Names and Ages _____

School Attending _____

Address _____

Mother's Maiden Name (or Family Name)_____

Address _____ Tele. # _____

Business Address _____ Tele. # _____

Photo

Area Frequents _____ Place of Birth _____

Miscellaneous Information _____

Witness Knows Perpetrator Personally? _____ (Yes/No)   How? _____

Did Witness I.D. Perpetrator _____ (Yes/No)   How? _____

Case # _____ Officer Assigned _____ Homicide # _____

Date of Interview _____ Interviewing Officer _____

Witness Form. This form that can be employed to assure that investigators obtain as much information as possible for later contact. In certain cases it may be advisable to obtain a Polaroid photograph of your witness.

CANVASS QUESTIONNAIRE

(Identify Yourself and Purpose of Canvass)

Name: (last)   (first)   (middle)   Date of Birth:

Address: Phone:

Employment (company name—type of work):   Address: Phone:

Other Residents of This Address: (names and ages)

Did you know of the offense?   ☐ Yes   ☐ No

How did you first learn of it?   (when?)

Did you know the victim?   ☐ Yes   ☐ No

What was your relationship with the victim?   (if knew, date, time, and location last seen or talked to)

Were you on the crime scene at anytime?   (explain)

What knowledge do you have of the crime?

Typed statement taken from this witness?   ☐ Yes   ☐ No

Reporting officer   (name)   (unit)   (date)   (time)

Canvass Questionaire.

CANVASS QUESTIONNAIRE

Street, Avenue, Road, etc. _____

Number (or name if no number) _____

If Apartment or Office Building (name) _____

Occupants (full name and age)

                                                               Questionnaire
Completed

1. _____   Yes – No

2. _____   Yes – No

3. _____   Yes – No

4. _____   Yes – No

5. _____   Yes – No

6. _____   Yes – No

Officer Recording _____

Time _____ Date _____

Canvass Questionaire.

come forward if not located and interviewed by the investigators on the subsequent canvass.

Also consider whether an immediate canvass is necessary. The type of crime or the hour of day or night may determine this. For instance, in an organized crime hit in an area frequented by persons friendly to criminal enterprise, it will probably be necessary to come back at a later time and talk to people out of the hearing or observation of criminal sympathizers and neighbors. A common mistake is to attempt a canvass in the middle of the night. You'll make a lot more enemies than friends if you start ringing doorbells at 3:00 A.M. Wait until a reasonable hour and then do the canvass.

Many homicides have been solved because a good canvass per-

The Canvass. When doing a canvass it is imperative that the investigators consider the buildings and locations which overlook the rear of the crime scene as well as the front of the location. In this particular case, the canvass of apartments which overlooked the rear of the subject building and the building's fire escapes provided police with the description and eventually the identity of the murderer.

formed by a determined group of canvassers uncovered some vital information, including a motive, or even an eyewitness. These canvassers were detectives who didn't just go through the motions, but took the time to effectively elicit information from the people canvassed. It is extremely important to keep in mind when instituting a canvass not to assign officers arbitrarily just because you are supposed to do a canvass. Usually at the homicide crime scene there will be numerous personnel—sometimes more than can be effectively utilized. A common error committed by some supervisors is to indiscriminately assign these people to do a canvass, a practice that can do more harm than good. This is not to say that the supervisor shouldn't "shotgun" a number of investigators into an initial canvass, but the personnel selected should be either good at this investigative technique or have an interest in the particular investigation. The extra personnel can then be used for some of the other jobs that become necessary during the course of events at the scene.

The assigned detective or member of the team conducting the homicide investigation should conduct formal interviews with anyone located by the canvassers. Likewise, the detective supervisor should be kept up to date with any information uncovered by the canvassers. In this way both the supervisor and the team will be aware of all developments in the case and be better able to put this information into proper perspective.

The correctly done canvass is an invaluable investigative technique that can provide:

an actual eyewitness to the crime,

information about the circumstances of the crime,

an approximate time of occurrence and/or estimate of time of death,

information about the deceased—identity, habits, friends, etc.,

a motive for the crime.

The Preliminary Medical Examination at the Scene

In homicide cases a medical examiner or coroner is responsible for performing an investigation to determine the cause, manner, and mode of death. (See Chapter 14.) The medical examiner's or coroner's office is responsible for conducting an autopsy later on. Ideally, the investigation at the scene should be carried out by the same pathologist who will later perform the autopsy. However, in jurisdictions that lack a medical examiner system or have a large number of homicides this is not always possible. In most cases, the medical examiner or coroner must rely on the information provided by the medical examiner or medical investigator at the scene, and from the detectives investigating the homicide.

Since the physical aspects of the scene and the cadaver can never be replaced in quite the same manner after a body has been moved, the body, under ordinary circumstances, should not be moved before an examination by the medical examiner or coroner.

The preliminary medical examination should not, however, be undertaken until the crime scene has been photographed and sketched in its original condition. (See Chapters 6 and 7.) If the medical examiner arrives before the crime scene technicians or police photographer, he or she should be requested to delay the examination until after the scene documentation has been accomplished.

The medical examiner should be brought up to date on all aspects of the case as soon as he or she arrives. This includes any determinations or observations made by the investigators at the scene or in the course of the preliminary investigation.

Remember, the teamwork aspect can never be overemphasized, especially in this preliminary medical examination at the scene.

The scene investigation by the medical examiner or coroner includes identification of the deceased, examination of the body, evaluation of the circumstances of death, and removal of evidence from the body. Therefore, it is important that these medical experts obtain as much information as possible about the facts surrounding death so that later autopsy findings can be properly evaluated. For example, an ambulance may have responded and the attendants attempted resuscitation. This information could become important in evaluating rib fractures, facial trauma, or other internal injuries that could have been caused during the resuscitation attempts.

The medical investigation at the scene may indicate the following:

1. The apparent cause of death, by correlating the injuries with the manner in which they occurred. In homicide deaths which are the result of stabbing or shooting, the determination of cause of death may be made at the scene. In some suspicious deaths, the medical examiner may observe *petechial hemorrhages* in the lining of the eyes and eyelids, alerting the police to asphyxial death.
2. Whether injuries are antemortem or postmortem.
3. Whether the deceased, after the initial injury, fell or struck other objects at the scene, thereby causing further injury.
4. Whether the body came to rest upon an object which, due to pressure, produced a postmortem injury (*artefact*) which could be erroneously interpreted as contributory or responsible for death.
5. The approximate time of death (indicated by such signs as loss of body heat, rigor mortis, lividity, etc.).

The best advice I can give to homicide detectives at the scene is to take the medical examiner or coroner into your confidence, tell him about your theories, and ask questions. If you don't understand some obscure terminology, get clarification (in other words, ask the medical examiner to translate it into English or layman's terms). These medical practitioners can give advice concerning medical aspects of the case and later provide information derived from the postmortem examination and the results of any toxicological analysis. The detective supervisor and homicide investigator should seek their advice. Such conferences and exchanges of information often result in a modification of an investigator's approach to a case or a particular aspect of it.

Historically, medical examiners and coroners have enjoyed a good working relationship with homicide investigators, based on expertise and professional cooperation, which tends to complement the investigation. I have been at many homicide crime scenes where the medical examiner has been more than helpful to the investigator by answering the many questions that arise during this preliminary inquiry.

Doctors who specialize in forensic medicine usually have an ardent interest in homicide cases. Often they can be helpful in reconstructing the scene and formulating the sequence of events. Since their inquiry is directed toward the circumstances that led to death, the manner in which death occurred, and whether or not the condition of the body is consistent with the cause of death, what they determine is essential to the investigation. Each professional is aware of the other's duty and capability, and by working together and exchanging information that they can usually arrive at a final determination of what actually occurred.

Specific Investigative
Duties at the Scene

5

The purpose of this chapter is to provide practical information and guidelines for the homicide investigator to follow when confronted with additional responsibilities and specific duties at the scene. A section on handling buried-body cases has been included which may prove useful as a general guide for the investigation of this unique type of scene. The following subjects will be dealt with in this chapter:

The suspect in custody,

Interrogation of the suspect at the scene,

Examination of a suspect for evidence,

Evaluation of the suspect's demeanor and mental capacity,

Obtaining a dying declaration,

Handling buried-body cases.

The chapter concludes with an investigative checklist which can be used by the homicide investigator and detective supervisor to systematically check and review his or her actions at the scene.

The Suspect in Custody

When the suspect has been taken into custody by patrol officers, the immediate responsibility of the detectives or homicide investigators should be the following.

1. Insure that the suspect has been removed from, or is not allowed to enter, the primary crime scene. The isolation of the suspect is

necessary in order to prevent scene contamination or destruction of evidence.

2. Interview the arresting officer(s), out of the hearing of the suspect, in order to determine the scope of their initial investigation, the location of any physical evidence, and the probable cause for the arrest of the suspect including any statements made by the suspect or witnesses.

3. Instruct these officers, upon completion of this preliminary interview, to document in writing their observations and activities at the scene, including any overhears or statements made by the suspect, as well as any information provided by witnesses or informants.

4. Ascertain whether or not the suspect has been given his or her Miranda warnings by the patrol officers, to assure the admissibility of any culpable statements made to these officers.

Interview and Interrogation of the Suspect in Custody

The investigators, upon their arrival, take charge of the investigation and are responsible for the interrogation of the suspect. Prior to any interview or interrogation, the detective must again advise the suspect of the Constitutional Rights as specified under the Miranda ruling. The detective should make note of this Miranda warning to the suspect in his or her notebook, indicating the time, date, location, and presence of any witnesses including counsel.

It may be advantageous to conduct a preliminary interrogation of the suspect while he or she is still at the scene. This questioning is usually directed toward the recovery of any weapons or other evidence and is used to gauge the scope of the search. The actual formal interrogation, however, should take place later at the police station, where conditions are more favorable. Furthermore, the investigator will have been able by then to complete the preliminary investigation and will have the advantage of information and observations from the scene.

In some instances, the suspect may insist on confessing or telling his or her story immediately. If the suspect is quite talkative or wishes to make a statement to investigators at the scene, do not delay the interview.

Practically speaking, any statement from a suspect is crucial to the investigation. Although the initial statement may be self-serving, a little less than truthful, or even a complete falsehood, this declaration by the suspect is a valuable piece of evidence which may later be presented in court. If the investigator delays or postpones taking an official statement until he or she gathers "all the facts," the suspect may change his or her mind about making a statement, or request an attorney, and this valuable evidence will be lost forever.

Under circumstances where the suspect wishes to make a statement, the investigator should

- immediately advise the suspect of his or her Constitutional rights under the Miranda ruling, utilizing a "rights card" or Miranda form;

- make sure that the suspect understands his or her rights by requesting a response;

- obtain an intelligent waiver of these rights from the suspect (preferably a signature of the suspect on the Miranda form);

- allow the suspect to make a complete statement;

- *take notes,* reduce the statement to writing, and have the suspect sign it.

The importance of documentation, especially in custodial interrogation situations, cannot be overemphasized. This is the reason why I strongly recommend that the Miranda warnings be given from a rights card and that the particular card utilized be preserved as evidence. In addition, persons who are given Miranda warnings should be requested to put their signatures on a Miranda form in order to assure the admissibility of any statements in court.

A favorite trick of defense counsel is to distort any custodial interrogation by innuendo, suggesting that there was some impropriety on the part of the police in obtaining statements from a defendant. If the investigator has taken proper notes of the procedures utilized in obtaining any statements, along with notes of the responses of the suspect to these warnings, he or she will have eliminated a possible source of embarrassment in future court proceedings.

When dealing with minors, the Miranda warnings must be given to the parent(s) as well as the underage suspect. Both the parent(s) and the minor must intelligently waive their rights before an interrogation can proceed.

Examination of a Suspect for Evidence

The examination of the suspect for evidence should be performed by the investigator assigned to the case or an experienced detective assigned to the investigation. The ability to recognize and recover trace evidence from a suspect or his or her clothing is a prerequisite to successful search of suspects. During this preliminary phase of the homicide investigation, especially when the suspect is still at the scene, it is not practical to conduct an extensive examination for trace evidence. However, officers should be aware of the possible evidentiary value of the clothing and shoes worn by the suspect as well as any bruises, cuts, or injuries on the hands, face, or other parts of the suspect's body. When the suspect is brought to the police station, a more thorough examination can be undertaken. (See Chapter 8, "Physical Examination of a Suspect in Custody.")

When the suspect is transported to the police station by patrol officers for further examination, the officers transporting the suspect should be advised to preserve the suspect's clothing and shoes for evidence of trace materials and cautioned not to allow the suspect to wash his or her hands or to engage in any activity that may alter or destroy any trace evidence. These instructions should be communicated to all personnel who will be responsible for the custody of the suspect prior to an extensive examination and search by the investigators. I remember reading about a police matron who had been assigned to guard a female murder suspect. The matron allowed the suspect to wash the victim's blood off her blouse while she was in police custody. During the trial the matron was asked by the prosecutor why she had allowed the suspect to wash off the blood. The matron claimed she wasn't advised by the detectives to preserve the clothing of the suspect and that the detectives "hadn't told her anything." Needless to say, her ignorance of the forensic value of the victim's blood on the blouse was compounded by the failure of the investigators to properly instruct and advise her.

Evaluation of the Suspect's Demeanor and Mental Capacity

When a suspect has been taken into custody, the investigator should make an evaluation of the suspect's demeanor and mental capacity based on observations from the time of his or her arrest to the subsequent arraignment. This observation and documentation is necessary to prepare against a possible diminished-capacity defense, which is usually based on the contention that the defendant, at the time the offense was committed, was not able to determine right or wrong because of his or her mental state. Or the defendant may attempt to claim insanity based on mental incapacity. The defense of diminished capacity is a popular one because the police often fail to take proper precautions during the initial investigation. The following are some important observations that should be recorded in the investigator's notebook.

1. Does the suspect speak rationally or irrationally?
2. Does he or she answer in a straightforward or evasive manner?

3. Is the response to questioning intelligent or confused?
4. Does the suspect have control over his or her actions?
5. What is the suspect's emotional condition?
6. Is there any evidence of intoxication, or does the suspect appear to be under the influence of any drugs?
7. Does the suspect give any reasons for his or her actions?

When investigators interview witnesses, they should attempt to obtain as much information as possible regarding the actions of the suspect prior to the crime, during the crime, and immediately after the crime. Any indications of the suspect's demeanor and mental capacity should be recorded. The witnesses should be asked the following questions.

1. What was the suspect's appearance at the time of the crime?
2. How did the suspect act?
3. Could the witness determine the suspect's demeanor or mental state?
4. Did the suspect act rationally or irrationally?
5. Was the act a cold-blooded or unemotional thing?
6. Did the suspect scream or yell?
7. How did the suspect commit the act?
8. Was the suspect under the influence of alcohol or drugs?
9. Did the suspect say or do anything during or after the crime?
10. Did the suspect attempt to flee or cover up the crime?

Often investigators neglect to obtain witnesses' opinions of the suspect during the initial inquiry because they have been trained to gather only "facts." However, independent observations of and opinions about a person's behavior can be vitally important in establishing the existence or nonexistence of diminished capacity in court. From an investigative point of view, these witnesses' observations and opinions should be documented by the detective in preparation for the later prosecution.

Obtaining a Dying Declaration

If the victim is still alive when investigators arrive at the scene, they should attempt to obtain a statement. Likewise, if a victim has been removed to the hospital, detectives should immediately be dispatched so that they may interview him or her. In cases where the victim is seriously injured and death will undoubtedly occur, investigators must be alert to the possibility of obtaining a dying declaration. This can be obtained while waiting for the ambulance, en route to the hospital, or while the victim is in the hospital. As long as investigators do not interfere with life-sustaining measures, nor hinder medical personnel by their presence, there should be no problems.

The dying declaration may prove invaluable in firmly establishing whether or not a crime has occurred, and, more importantly, who was responsible. In order to obtain a legally admissible declaration, however, certain conditions must exist. They are as follows.

1. The victim must believe that he or she is going to die.
2. The victim must have no hope of recovery.
3. The declaration or statement must refer to
   a. The manner and circumstances which brought about the victim's condition and ultimate death.
   b. The identity of the person responsible.
4. The declarant must die.
5. The declarant must have been otherwise competent and rational.

The dying declaration can be used in a criminal trial only for the death of the declarant. If the victim survives, he or she must testify later on in court.

Questions to be Asked in a Dying Declaration

There are no set guidelines for the exact sequence of questions one should ask when attempting to obtain a dying declaration. Basically, you will want to establish through your questions that the witness is competent, lucid, and does believe that he or she is about to die. Here are some questions that the investigator may find helpful.

1. What is your name?
2. Where do you live?
3. Do you now believe that you are about to die?
4. Have you any hope of recovery?
5. Are you willing to make a true statement of how and why you were injured?

Documentation of the Dying Declaration

The statement can either be oral or, if feasible, written by the declarant. Ideally, the investigator will have a cassette recorder available during this event. In any case, the officer should reduce the statement to writing and have the declarant either sign it or make his or her mark. It is recommended that there be a civilian witness present; however, the fact that there was no witness available or that the declarant was unable to write or sign the statement does not effect the admissibility of the declaration in court.

Handling Buried-Body Cases[1]

Conducting crime scene searches involving the discovery and excavation of buried bodies requires special techniques and planning. Certain procedures, which must be followed in order to locate and recover pieces of physical evidence, involve the need for assistance and cooperation between law enforcement and forensic science. The necessary equipment should be available, as should the forensic experts in case their services are needed. An example of some of the experts who can assist the investigator in this procedure are the medical examiner or forensic pathologist, the forensic archeologist, the forensic odontologist, the forensic entomologist, and the botanist. I recommend that the homicide investigator contact these experts prior to their actual need at the scene of a buried-body case. I have found that these experts are usually happy to cooperate as long as they are acting as part of a team. If provided with an undisturbed crime scene, they can contribute to the overall success of an investigation.

The Discovery of the Buried Body

Buried-body cases usually come to the attention of the police as a result of an accidental find, or, more rarely, from information provided by an informant or in the course of a confession. Accidental finds may be made by a passerby, a hunter, or a construction worker involved in some type of excavation, who then notifies the police. The police respond to the site to verify the discovery and then notify the investigators. As with any crime scene, the basic principles of scene protection and isolation should immediately be instituted. (See Chapter 2, "First Officer's Duties on Arrival at the Scene.")

The investigators should not allow themselves to be rushed into an immediate excavation of the remains. Instead, if the body has not already been removed from the burial site, they should request the services of an archeologist when they notify crime scene technicians and the medical examiner.

From an investigative point of view, there is generally no need to immediately excavate the body at this stage of the investigation. I

---

[1]The information on handling buried-body cases is based on an article written by Robert M. Boyd, former Commander, Homicide Squad, Metropolitan Police Department, Washington, D.C. This article appeared in the *FBI Law Enforcement Bulletin*, February 1979.

recommend the following procedures (all of which will be discussed fully in Chapters 6, 7, and 8).

1. Photographs should be taken of the entire area including the site and any item of evidentiary value (tire tracks, weapons, tools, articles of clothing, etc.).
2. Photographs should be taken in black-and-white and color; photographs of any items located in the scene should be taken with and without markers.
3. The area should be mapped out and a crime scene sketch prepared.
4. The path used by the person discovering the body should be marked off and this route should be followed by all investigators and personnel at the scene.
5. A systematic search of the surrounding area should be instituted using metal detectors and any other aids that might be applicable. If any evidence is discovered, it should be photographed separately and included on the crime scene sketch.
6. If daylight hours are limited, postpone the search and excavation until morning.
7. If the weather poses a problem, wait for proper conditions. The area of the grave can usually be protected by the erection of a tent over the site.

The Excavation

The term *site* refers to the entire area of excavation or disturbance and includes not only the grave, but the immediate area contiguous to the grave. The excavation should be conducted under the direction of a forensic archeologist and should begin with the clearing of the ground around the actual burial site. This is done to locate the dimensions of the hole. At this point measurements should be taken and the site rephotographed. In addition, two sketches should be drawn to show both plan and elevation views of the grave.

When a grave is dug, excavated soil is placed on the surface. As a result, the surface vegetation is usually compressed or broken off. When the grave is refilled, some of this surface vegetation is probably placed in the hole. Furthermore, if the body has been buried for some time, roots of trees or bushes may grow through the remains. This is where the botanist comes into play. The botanist can provide you with estimations of how long the vegetation has been damaged or the length of time necessary for the root structures in the remains to have reached their present stage of development. If any dead insects, insect larvae, or maggots are located at the site, they should be collected for examination by a forensic entomologist. (See Chapter 9.)

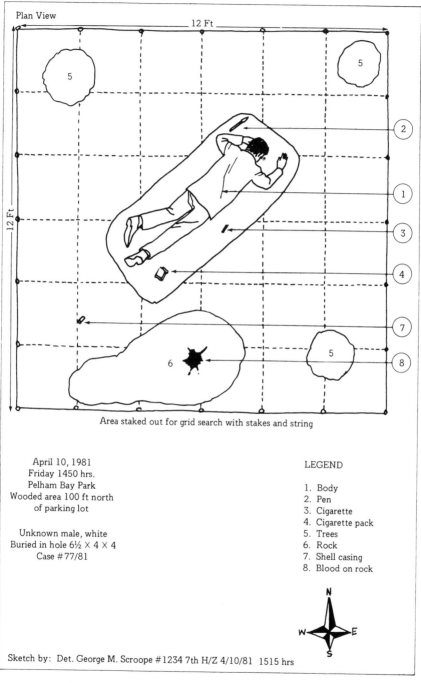

Plan View

Area staked out for grid search with stakes and string

April 10, 1981
Friday 1450 hrs.
Pelham Bay Park
Wooded area 100 ft north
of parking lot

Unknown male, white
Buried in hole 6½ × 4 × 4
Case #77/81

LEGEND

1. Body
2. Pen
3. Cigarette
4. Cigarette pack
5. Trees
6. Rock
7. Shell casing
8. Blood on rock

Sketch by: Det. George M. Scroope #1234 7th H/Z 4/10/81 1515 hrs

Excavation of Buried Body, Plan View Sketch.

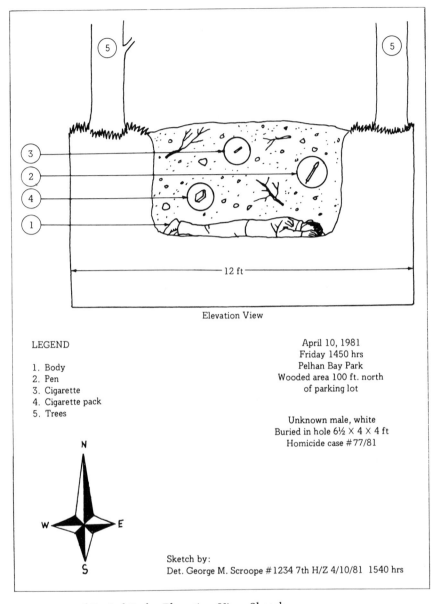

Elevation View

LEGEND

1. Body
2. Pen
3. Cigarette
4. Cigarette pack
5. Trees

April 10, 1981
Friday 1450 hrs
Pelhan Bay Park
Wooded area 100 ft. north
of parking lot

Unknown male, white
Buried in hole 6½ × 4 × 4 ft
Homicide case #77/81

Sketch by:
Det. George M. Scroope #1234 7th H/Z 4/10/81 1540 hrs

Excavation of Buried Body, Elevation View Sketch.

This is the reason why the excavation must proceed at an orderly and systematic pace. The soil should be removed in somewhat even layers, about four to six inches deep, and sifted through screens. As items are located and recovered, they should be photographed and plotted on the elevation and plan view drawings to indicate their actual locations. In addition, samples of the soil should be taken as each item is recovered.

The Body

When the body is uncovered, it should immediately be photographed in the condition of discovery before any disturbance. If the medical examiner is there, and the body has soft tissue present, there should be a preliminary scene examination by the pathologist. The body should then be placed on a clean sheet to preserve any additional evidence which may not be readily observable at the scene. The body and sheet should then be removed to a morgue for further examination and autopsy.

After the body has been removed, the grave should again be photographed, and the area which was under the body carefully searched and excavated several more inches. The use of a metal detector at this stage may prove valuable, especially if bullets were fired into the body as it lay in the grave.

The identification of the remains, especially in cases where the body is badly decomposed, will call for the expertise of the forensic anthropologist and the forensic odontologist working along with the medical examiner or coroner. The various methods and techniques are presented in Chapter 10.

Search for a Buried Body

In cases where an informant or confession reveals the existence of a buried body, the immediate problem facing the investigator is locating the site. Unless the exact location is given, the information may be so vague that it involves an area of several acres. Good planning will be necessary to locate and isolate the scene. Practically speaking, the more that is known about the circumstances of the crime, the better your chances are of locating the site. For example, where was the victim killed? If the victim was killed elsewhere, the location of the site may be close to a road or path. If the killing took place at the site, then the victim may have been forced to walk some distance. The element of time will have a bearing on the condition of any vegetation or the grave itself. The grave may have sunk or there may still be surplus dirt on the mound.

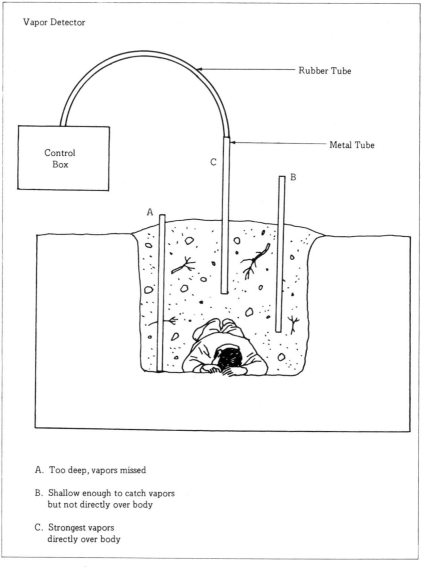

Vapor Detector.

A. Too deep, vapors missed

B. Shallow enough to catch vapors but not directly over body

C. Strongest vapors directly over body

The following methods may be used to locate the burial site:

1. Search by aircraft. Prior to a foot search, this method can be used to cover a wide area and locate visually a sign of soil or vegetation disturbance. In addition, the use of thermal infrared photography, which can detect the heat of a decomposing body, can sometimes be utilized depending on the length of time the body has been bur-

ied. Aerial photographs should be taken of the suspected area both before, and, if the search is successful, after.

2. Search by foot. Mechanical aids are a must in this type of search. (See Chapter 8, "Methods of Crime Scene Search.")

3. Probing. This is the most practical method of ground search. It is done with a steel rod which is about four to five feet long with a "tee" handle on one end and a sharp point at the other. The probe is inserted into the suspected area. If the ground is soft it is left in place, all probing is halted, and a vapor detector is brought into play. The probing should follow a systematic pattern so as not to miss any locations.

4. The vapor detector. This instrument can detect the presence of body gases formed as a result of decomposition. It can be used to locate a cadaver prior to any excavation. Its value is quite evident when several suspected areas must be checked. It can also be used under concrete (roadways, patios, floors) after a small hole is bored through the concrete.

The Investigative Checklist

The homicide detective faces a monumental task at the crime scene. There are a multitude of duties to perform, and each event needs to be documented according to a routine procedure. This routine procedure is necessary so that valuable information or observations are not overlooked. Although each homicide is distinctive and unique, there are certain basic steps to be pursued at all crime scenes. This Investigative Checklist is designed to be utilized by detectives involved in the investigation of sudden and violent death. Although extensive, it is not all-inclusive. The investigator is advised to simply utilize this Checklist as a guide to refresh the memory.

Remember, the fundamental rule in homicide investigation is the documentation of events in the investigator's notebook.

DOCUMENTATION OF THE INITIAL REPORT

INITIAL RECEIPT OF INFORMATION

☐ Date and time of initial report.

☐ Method of transmission—report received by.

☐ Reporting party—officer, dispatcher, etc.

☐ Complete details.

ARRIVAL AT THE HOMICIDE: DEATH SCENE

☐ Record exact time of arrival.

☐ Record the exact address of the crime scene.

☐ Record the outside weather/temperature conditions.

☐ Record outside lighting conditions.

☐ Interview the *first officer* and other police personnel at the scene to determine the sequence of events since their arrival.

    ☐ Crime discovered by—Date and time of initial call. Complete details of initial police report.

    ☐ Determine the scope of the patrol officer's initial investigation at the scene.

        ☐ Protection of the crime scene.

        ☐ Notifications, alarms, teletypes.

        ☐ Preliminary investigative results.

☐ Record persons present at the scene.

    ☐ Police officers and law enforcement personnel.

    ☐ Ambulance and/or emergency personnel.

    ☐ Family and/or relatives and friends of victim.

    ☐ Witnesses, including persons detained by patrol officer.

        ☐ Keep witnesses separated.

        ☐ Provide for witness security and availability.

PRELIMINARY INSPECTION OF THE BODY AT THE CRIME SCENE

☐ Victim pedigree—name and address if known (includes the following: Sex, race, and age).

☐ Location of the victim: description of body and scene.

    ☐ Have the patrol officer personally escort you through the scene to the body using same path used by responding police.

☐ Personally determine and verify death.

☐ Note condition of the body.

☐ Ascertain whether or not there are any suspects in custody (see "The Suspect in Custody" procedure).

☐ Are there any additional victims?

    ☐ Is this a multiple murder? (If yes, establish separate case numbers and provide for additional documentation.)

☐ Officially assign investigator to case.

☐ If identity of victim(s) is known, get a background check.

IMPLEMENT CRIME SCENE CONTROL PROCEDURES

☐ Determine the scope of the general crime scene—assessment.

☐ Take preliminary photographs with Instamatic or Polaroid camera to "freeze" the crime scene and provide for review by additional investigators as they arrive at the scene (Polaroid photos are preferred for immediate viewing).

☐ Stabilize the scene by identifying and establishing perimeters.

    ☐ If crime scene was not established by patrol officers, secure and protect the scene by isolation (ropes, barriers, etc.).

    ☐ Establish outside and inside perimeters (only authorized personnel allowed within respective perimeters).

    ☐ Remember, the two crime scene theory: The *general area* for police and other official personnel at the scene, and the *forensic area* where the body as well as any other evidence may be located.

☐ Assign patrol officers as needed to effectively safeguard scene.

☐ Update and expand crime scene protection as necessary. Is this a multiple scene? Are there additional areas to protect?

☐ Establish a single path of entry and exit to the crime scene.

☐ Implement procedures to safeguard all evidence found at scene.

INITIATE A CRIME SCENE LOG

☐ Assign an officer to obtain the names of all police and emergency personnel who responded to the original call.

☐ Assign an officer to record the names of all personnel and civilians involved in the investigation at the crime scene.

☐ Allow no entry to the crime scene except to authorized personnel involved in the official investigation.

☐ Record arrival/departure times of all officials (this includes medical examiner or coroner, state's attorney, crime scene technicians, etc.).

☐ This crime scene log should be delivered to detectives upon release of the crime scene.

ESTABLISH A POLICY FOR CRIME SCENE INTEGRITY

☐ Do not touch, move, or alter anything at the scene until full documentation has been completed (*observe, describe, record*).

☐ *Record any alterations to the crime scene that were made as a matter of investigative necessity or emergency police response.*

☐ Lights turned on or off?

☐ Doors opened, closed, locked, or unlocked?

☐ Body moved, or body cut down?

☐ Windows opened, closed, locked, or unlocked?

☐ Names of all parties who moved the body prior to and during police presence at the scene.

☐ Any furniture moved or anything touched?

☐ Gas turned on or off? Appliances turned on or off?

☐ If vehicle involved, is engine off or on? Is the motor cold, cool, warm, or hot?

☐ *Do not use any telephone(s)* located inside the crime scene.

☐ Coordinate activities at the scene and direct investigators by *fixing* responsibility for the performance of certain duties.

☐ Implement procedures to protect the evidence from damage by weather or exposure, and the presence of police personnel.

☐ *Do not allow smoking* by anyone in the crime scene.

☐ *Do not turn water on or off. Do not flush toilets. Do not use any facility in the scene.*

☐ Record condition of lights, lamps, and electric appliances, such as TVs, radios, clocks, etc.

ESTABLISH A COMMAND POST OR TEMPORARY HEADQUARTERS

☐ Select a location out of the central crime scene, preferably a location with two phones (cellular phones): one for outgoing and one for incoming telephone calls.

☐ Notify communications and/or the station house of the telephone numbers of the *command post* to facilitate communications between the various units concerned.

☐ Make notifications as necessary from this location.

    ☐ Crime scene technicians.

    ☐ Medical examiner/coroner or representatives.

    ☐ Additional investigators or police personnel.

    ☐ Prosecutor/district attorney/solicitor's office.

AMBULANCE PERSONNEL

☐ If ambulance personnel were present before investigator's arrival, determine if the crew or anyone else moved the body or any other items within the crime scene. If yes, record the following:

- [ ] When were the alterations made?
- [ ] Purpose of the movement.
- [ ] Persons who made the alterations.
- [ ] The time of death as pronounced by the ambulance or paramedic crew.

INITIATE A CANVASS

- [ ] Initiate a *canvass* of the immediate area by assigning sufficient personnel to locate any witnesses or persons who may have information about the homicide or death.
- [ ] Assign a supervisor or coordinator to organize the canvass.
  - [ ] Utilize *canvass control sheets.*
- [ ] Assure that canvassers are provided with *all* information from the investigation and scene so that they may properly solicit information from prospective witnesses. (*This includes photos of the deceased taken in life, if available.*)
- [ ] Have investigators *check vehicles* and *record registration* numbers of autos in the immediate area.
- [ ] Require official reports from *canvassers* indicating:
  - [ ] Negative locations (locations with no results).
  - [ ] Locations that have been canvassed, indicating number of persons residing therein.
  - [ ] Positive locations for possible follow-up and reinterview.
  - [ ] Information relating to the event being canvassed.
  - [ ] Utilize the *canvass questionnaire forms.*

WEAPONS

- [ ] If a weapon is discovered, *do the following:*
  - [ ] *Firearms*—do not attempt to unload.
  - [ ] Record where the weapon is located.
  - [ ] Safeguard the weapon for forensic examination.
  - [ ] Have the weapon photographed before further examination.
  - [ ] If the weapon is a firearm, consider an examination of the suspect's hands for residue analysis.
  - [ ] Determine if the weapon is from the premises.
  - [ ] Determine if there is any *blood* or any *other trace evidence* on the weapon.

THE SUSPECT IN CUSTODY

☐ If the suspect is arrested and present at the scene, make sure that he or she is *immediately removed* from the crime scene and not returned to the scene unless the clothing of the suspect is secured. This procedure is necessary to *prevent crime scene contamination.*

☐ Safeguard all evidence found on the suspect, including *blood, weapons, debris, soil, proceeds of crime,* etc.

☐ Ensure that the suspect *does not wash his or her hands,* nor engage in any conduct which may alter or destroy evidence.

☐ Record any spontaneous statements made by the suspect(s).

☐ Do not permit any conversation between the suspect and any parties present.

SUSPECT IN CUSTODY: INTERROGATION AT THE SCENE

If the suspect is in custody at the scene, and circumstances indicate that immediate interrogation of the subject would be beneficial to the investigation, the following steps should be taken.

☐ *Advise* the suspect of his or her rights under the Miranda ruling prior to any custodial interrogation. (This should be done from a Miranda Rights card.)

☐ Determine if the suspect fully understands his or her rights.

☐ *Obtain an intelligent waiver* of these rights from the suspect prior to any questioning.

☐ *Document* this procedure in the investigative notebook.

☐ Allow the suspect to make a full statement.

☐ Reduce this statement to writing and have the suspect sign it.

☐ Keep the suspect *isolated* at all times from other suspects, witnesses, prisoners, and any personnel not connected with the investigation.

☐ Advise any officers transporting the suspect not to engage the suspect in any conversation or questioning. However, if during transport the suspect makes any statement, the officers should document this information.

☐ If the suspect is brought to the police station, he or she should be placed in a separate holding cell.

☐ Alibi statements should be documented and recorded in the investigator's notebook.

☐ Any self-serving statements should also be recorded and documented, in the event the suspect later changes his or her story.

CRIME SCENE PROCESSING

☐ The crime scene search should not be undertaken until all photographs, sketches, measurements, dusting for prints, and written documentation have been completed (*except for emergency situations*).

CRIME SCENE PHOTOGRAPHS

The following photographs should be taken.

☐ Photos of the entire location where the homicide took place.

☐ Photos of contiguous areas and sites.

☐ Photographs of the crowd or any bystanders (*surreptitiously*).

☐ Photos of suspect(s) and/or witnesses, if applicable.

    ☐ Photos of suspect's clothing and shoes.

    ☐ Photos of any injuries (body, face, hands, etc.).

☐ *Do not add any chalk marks* or markers prior to taking the original crime scene photographs. Markers can be added later on for close-up shots.

☐ Take photos from the *general to the specific*.

DOCUMENTATION OF CRIME SCENE PHOTOGRAPHS

☐ Date and time photos are taken.

☐ Exact location of photographs.

☐ Description of item photographed.

☐ Compass direction (north, south, east, or west).

☐ Focus distance.

☐ Type of film and camera utilized.

☐ Lights and weather conditions.

☐ Number of exposures.

☐ Identification of photographers.

☐ Eliminate extraneous objects, including any police equipment.

☐ Show the relationship of the scene to its surroundings.

    ☐ Outdoor scenes—fixed objects as they relate to the scene from eye level.

    ☐ Indoor scenes—objects in the room such as doors, windows etc., to "fix" the body to the crime scene.

RECOMMENDED CRIME SCENE PHOTOGRAPHS

☐ Front entrance of building.

☐ Entrance to the room or apartment where the deceased is found.

- [ ] Two (2) full-body views.
- [ ] A general view of the body and crime scene.
- [ ] A close-up shot of the body.
- [ ] Photos of any visible wounds.
- [ ] If the body has been removed, photos should be taken of the body's original location.
- [ ] Photos of possible entrance or escape routes used.
- [ ] Areas where any force was used for entry or exit.
- [ ] Area and close-up views of any physical evidence such as *bloodstains, weapons, shell casings, hairs, fibers,* etc.
- [ ] Fingerprints (plastic, bloodstained, and latents)—as well as any "lifts"—should be photographed before removal.
- [ ] *After body has been moved,* additional photos should be taken.
    - [ ] Areas beneath the body.
    - [ ] Any additional evidence found beneath the body.

THE CRIME SCENE SKETCH

- [ ] Make a simple line drawing of the crime scene, either in the investigative notebook or on a separate sheet of paper.
- [ ] The following information should be included.
    - [ ] Measurements and distance.
    - [ ] A title block consisting of:
        - [ ] Name and title of sketcher.
        - [ ] Date and time the sketch was made.
        - [ ] Classification of crime.
        - [ ] Identification of victim(s).
        - [ ] Agency's case number(s).
        - [ ] Names of any persons assisting in taking measurements.
        - [ ] Precise address of the location sketched and compass *North.*
    - [ ] A *legend,* to identify any object or articles in scene.
    - [ ] A *scale,* to depict measurements used.

THE CRIME SCENE SEARCH

- [ ] Establish the perimeters of the crime scene and document this location by crime scene photographs and sketches, including written documentation.
- [ ] Reconstruct aspects of the crime in formulating the search.

☐ Ascertain the legal basis for the search prior to any seizure of evidence.

☐ Visibly locate any physical evidence and determine which evidence should be gathered before any destruction or any alteration takes place.

☐ Establish the method of search based on your investigative theory, size of the area to be searched, and any other factors that arise while conducting this phase of the inquiry.

☐ Areas that should be processed:

  ☐ The point of entry.

  ☐ The escape route.

  ☐ The suspect and his or her clothing, including injuries.

  ☐ The location where any physical evidence or weapons may be located.

  ☐ A vehicle used in the crime.

  ☐ The suspect's residence.

  ☐ The location where the actual assault leading to death took place.

  ☐ Location from which the body was moved.

DUST FOR FINGERPRINTS

The following areas should be processed for "latent prints."

☐ Areas of entry and exit.

☐ Weapons or objects which were apparently handled.

☐ Door handles.

☐ Telephone instruments.

☐ Windows.

☐ Glasses.

☐ Light switches.

☐ Newly damaged areas.

☐ Objects that may have caused death.

☐ Objects missing from their original location.

Note that some areas to be processed may require the use of chemical reagents such as luminol, ninhydrin, cynoacrylate, etc., in order to obtain latent print evidence. Consider these options before dusting.

DESCRIPTION OF THE DECEASED

A complete description of the body should be documented in the investigator's notes, including the following information.

- ☐ The position of the body.
- ☐ Sex.
- ☐ Race.
- ☐ Appearance.
- ☐ Age.
- ☐ Build.
- ☐ Color of hair.
- ☐ Description of clothing.
- ☐ Presence or absence of any jewelry.
- ☐ Evidence of any injuries (bruises, bite marks, wounds, etc.).
- ☐ Condition of the body.
  - ☐ Livor mortis.
  - ☐ Rigor mortis.
  - ☐ Decomposition (describe in detail).
  - ☐ Blood wet or dry.
  - ☐ Insect activity.
  - ☐ Putrefaction.
- ☐ Is the condition of the body consistent with known facts?
- ☐ Note and record the condition of the victim's hands for signs of evidence (defense marks, hairs, fibers, etc.).
- ☐ Note and record any creases and folds on victim's clothing.
- ☐ What is the condition of the victim's pockets?
- ☐ Examine the *immediate area surrounding the body* for evidence.
- ☐ Record the direction and size of any bloodstains.
- ☐ Check the clothing and shoes for any *trace evidence.*

PRELIMINARY MEDICAL EXAMINATION AT THE SCENE

- ☐ Record the time of arrival of the coroner/medical examiner.
- ☐ Obtain a preliminary estimate on the time of death.
- ☐ Document the apparent cause of death after conferring with the medical examiner/coroner.
- ☐ Are injuries consistent with the suspected weapon involved?
- ☐ *Release of the body:*
  - ☐ Use a new or laundered sheet to wrap body before removal.
  - ☐ Bag the hands of the victim with paper bags (*not plastic*) to preserve any trace evidence under fingernails.

VICTIM: HOSPITAL INFORMATION

If victim was removed to hospital, dispatch investigators, if available, or patrol unit to obtain the following information.

- ☐ Name, address, and phone number of the hospital.
- ☐ Attending doctor (name, address, and phone).
  - ☐ Name of officer interviewing doctor.
  - ☐ Doctor's diagnosis.
  - ☐ If pronounced dead, get time and date.
  - ☐ If admitted at hospital, get time and date.
- ☐ *Was the victim interviewed? Yes or no?*
  - ☐ Name of officer conducting interview.
  - ☐ *Dying declaration?*
    - ☐ Obtain witnesses, preferably doctor or nurse.
- ☐ Obtain names, addresses, phone numbers of all emergency room and hospital personnel involved in treatment.
- ☐ Obtain names, addresses, phone numbers of all ambulance or paramedic personnel involved in emergency and transport.
- ☐ Names, addresses, phone numbers of anyone who accompanied victim to hospital.
- ☐ *Evidence obtained and/or impounded at hospital.*
  - ☐ Establish chain of custody—identity of person at hospital who impounded any evidence.
  - ☐ Obtain any clothing worn by the deceased for forensic examination.
- ☐ *Obtain names of all police personnel at hospital.*

EVIDENCE PROCESS AND CONTROL PROCEDURES

- ☐ Ensure that all evidence is properly marked and packaged.
- ☐ Establish a *chain of custody.*
- ☐ Designate a *searching officer to take charge of all evidence.*
- ☐ Record the name and unit designation of all persons participating in the homicide crime scene search.
- ☐ Photograph all evidence in its original position (*in situ*).
- ☐ Record the position and location of *all* evidence on the *crime scene sketch* and the *investigative notebook.*
- ☐ Record the name of any officer or person discovering any physical evidence and the location where it was recovered.

- ☐ Measure the location of any evidence found from two (2) separate fixed points of reference.
- ☐ *Weapons*
    - ☐ Are there any shell casings present?
    - ☐ Any bullet holes or spent rounds?
    - ☐ Determine how many shots were fired.
    - ☐ Position of bullets in revolver (*record by diagram*).
    - ☐ Safety on or off?
    - ☐ Is firearm loaded or unloaded? *Bullet in chamber?*
- ☐ Are the wounds consistent with the suspected weapon?
- ☐ Is there any trace evidence on the weapon?

RELEASE OF THE HOMICIDE CRIME SCENE

Critical decision: Authorities should hold onto the crime scene as long as possible in the event that further process, investigation, or review becomes necessary as additional information becomes available.

- ☐ *Do not release* the scene prior to the completion of the canvass and any interviews of witnesses or interrogation of suspect(s).
- ☐ Have the deceased's mailbox searched and note the date of any mail found therein.
- ☐ Note the telephone numbers of any phones at the scene.
- ☐ If the scene is to be abandoned temporarily during certain investigatory procedures, provide for the continued crime scene protection during the absence of investigators. *The assignment of patrol officers to assist detectives at the crime scene is highly recommended.*
- ☐ Before leaving the crime scene, look over the entire area from *the perspective of the defense counsel* to make sure you have "*covered all the bases.*"
- ☐ Gather all materials used in the crime scene processing, such as film packs, Polaroid negatives, flash bulbs, notes, tape, evidence containers, etc.
    - ☐ Cause these materials to be removed from the scene for destruction and disposal at another location.
    - ☐ Utilize large plastic garbage bags at the crime scene for disposal of materials generated during the search.

It is important to note that the extent of the crime scene search can be ascertained by the examination of these types of materials if they are left behind at the crime scene by the authorities.

SUICIDE: INVESTIGATIVE CONSIDERATIONS

☐ *Evaluation of the wounds:*
  ☐ Could the deceased have caused the injuries and death?
  ☐ Was the person physically able to accomplish the act?
  ☐ Are the wounds within reach of the deceased?
  ☐ Are the wounds grouped together?
  ☐ Is there more than *one (1) cause of death?*
  ☐ Describe the *nature* and *position* of the injuries.
  ☐ Are there any hesitation marks?

☐ *Psychological state of the victim:*
  ☐ Obtain a background of the victim from family and friends.
    ☐ This includes medical as well as social information.
  ☐ Were there any *warning signs* indicated by the victim? (See listing of these under "Psychological Autopsy.")
  ☐ Were there any recent deaths in the family?
  ☐ Is there any indication of a recent upset or stress?
  ☐ Did the victim leave any notes?
    ☐ Request a sample of the victim's handwriting for a comparison analysis with any note found at scene.
    ☐ Request a sample of the victim's handwriting for an analysis in case a note is later discovered.
  ☐ Did the deceased have any close personal relationships, any close friends, etc.?
    ☐ *Interview these persons as soon as possible.*

☐ *Any prior mental disease or defect:*
  ☐ Has the deceased been under any professional treatment?
  ☐ Had the deceased ever attempted suicide in the past?
  ☐ Has anyone in the family ever committed suicide?
  ☐ Was the deceased a heavy drinker?
  ☐ Was the deceased on any medication?
  ☐ Was there a history of drug abuse?

☐ *Recognized warning signs and extreme danger signs in suicides.*
  ☐ *Warning signs:*
    ☐ A change in sleeping habits (sleeping more than usual or staying up much later), followed by sadness.
    ☐ A change in eating habits—weight loss or lack of appetite.

- ☐ A lack of interest in sex—a loss of the sex drive.
- ☐ A sudden drop in grades or school attendance—young people.
- ☐ A loss of work interest—adults.
- ☐ Loss of interest in favorite activities, hobbies, or sports.
- ☐ Loss of interest in friends, family, etc.—*isolation.*
- ☐ A preoccupation with *death,* or an unusual interest in art or music dealing with death (*teenagers'* "heavy Metal," rock, etc.; *adults'* preoccupation with death and afterlife).
- ☐ Loss of interest in personal hygiene and appearance.
- ☐ Involvement with drugs, including an abuse of alcohol.
- ☐ *Extreme danger signs:*
  - ☐ Suddenly becoming cheerful or calm after a depression. A sudden *euphoria* or burst of activity. This could mean that the person has resolved the inner conflict by deciding to take his or her own life. *The decision has been made.*
  - ☐ Giving away prized possessions.
  - ☐ Speaking of life in the *past tense,* For example, saying, "I've loved you," or "You've been a good mother."

AUTOEROTIC FATALITIES (ACCIDENTAL ASPHYXIA):
INVESTIGATIVE CONSIDERATIONS

Deaths which result during solo sex-related activities.

- ☐ Is the victim nude or sexually exposed?
- ☐ If the victim is a male, is he dressed in feminine attire?
- ☐ Is there evidence of masturbatory activity?
- ☐ Are sexually stimulating paraphernalia present (vibrators, dildos, other sexual fantasy aids or pornography, etc.)?
- ☐ Is bondage present (ropes, chains, blindfolds, gags, etc.)?
- ☐ Are the restraints interconnected?
- ☐ Is there protective padding between the ligature and neck?
- ☐ Is there evidence of infibulation?
- ☐ Is there evidence of fantasy (erotic literature, diaries, fantasy drawings, etc.) or fetishism?
- ☐ Are there any mirrors or other reflective devices present?
- ☐ Is the suspension point within the reach of the victim?
- ☐ Is there evidence of prior such activities (abrasions or rope burns on the suspension point, photographs, etc.)?

☐ Is there a positioned camera?

☐ Does the victim possess literature dealing with bondage, escapology, or knots?

☐ Is there any indication of suicidal intent?

FATAL FIRES: INVESTIGATIVE CONSIDERATIONS

☐ Was the fire *intentional* or *accidental?*

☐ Was the victim *alive* or *dead* before the fire?

    ☐ *Many times arson is used to conceal a homicide, disguise a crime scene, or destroy evidence.*

☐ *The fire incident:*

    ☐ Identify the fire officer in charge of firematic operations.

        ☐ Obtain the name, rank, assignment, and unit responsibility of all fire personnel involved in the operation.

        ☐ Obtain copy of chief's report describing the firematic operations taken to extinguish the fire. This includes:

            ☐ Determination of *origin/cause—suspicious* or other.

            ☐ Was the fire incendiary? What accelerant was used?

☐ *Suspicious designation—general determination factors:*

    ☐ Rate of burning not consistent with type of combustibles present in the location at the time of fire.

    ☐ A person died as a result of the fire.

    ☐ *Questionable* or *multiple points of origin* of the fire.

    ☐ Firefighter(s) noticed odor of gasoline or other accelerant.

    ☐ Cause not readily determined.

☐ *Maintenance of the fire crime scene:*

    ☐ Determine the condition of the scene based upon firematic operations (body moved, debris removed, building collapse, etc.).

☐ *Investigation at the scene:*

    ☐ Interview survivors as soon as possible.

    ☐ Interview people with an interest in the fire, who may still be present, at the scene while firefighters are working.

    ☐ Interview firefighters who have first-hand knowledge of the conditions within the building.

    ☐ Obtain information on all injured, evacuated, and relocated persons for interview.

☐ Interview any ambulance, paramedic, or other emergency crews, including *Red Cross personnel* who assisted with operations.

☐ *Initiate an investigative canvass* (see "Initiate a Canvass").

☐ Assign a fire investigator or arson expert to begin an *origin/cause* investigation at the scene to make an official determination of the fire incident.

☐ *Record the crime scene—conduct the crime scene examination.*

☐ Examination of the body.

　☐ Investigative considerations in arson cases:

　　☐ Identity of the victim.

　　☐ Was victim dead or alive?

　　☐ Is victim face-up or face-down? (Usually, when people collapse, they fall face forward.)

　　☐ Does the body evince a *pugilistic attitude* (a boxing pose or fetal position caused by the effect of heat upon the muscles)?

　　☐ Post mortem lividity (should be pink to cherry-red due to the inhalation of carbon monoxide if the person was alive and breathing during fire).

　　☐ Blistering. (Blisters surrounded by pink ring can be considered as having occurred before death. *However, the medical examiner makes final call.*)

☐ *Determination of arson:*

　☐ The determination of arson must be based upon expert opinion. This opinion is established after a careful review of the facts as well as the ability of the expert to "read the fire," which provides the investigator with the necessary legal basis for an arson determination and subsequent prosecution.

Selected Reading

Deickman, Edward A. *Practical Homicide Investigation.* Springfield, Illinois: Charles C. Thomas, 1961.

Harris, Raymond I. *Outline of Death Investigation.* Springfield, Illinois: Charles C. Thomas, 1962.

Hendrix, Robert C. *Investigation of Sudden and Violent Death.* Springfield, Illinois: Charles C. Thomas, 1972.

Hughes, Daniel J. *Homicide Investigative Techniques.* Springfield, Illinois: Charles C. Thomas, 1974.

International Association of Chiefs of Police. *Criminal Investigations.* 2nd ed. Gaithersburg, Maryland, 1970.

O'Hara, Charles E. *Fundamentals of Criminal Investigation,* 5th ed. Springfield, Illinois: Charles C. Thomas, 1980.

Snyder, LeMoyne. *Homicide Investigation,* 3rd ed. Springfield, Illinois: Charles C. Thomas, 1977.

Soderman, H. and O'Connell, J. J. *Modern Criminal Investigation,* 5th ed. New York: Funk & Wagnalls, 1962.

Spitz, Werner U. and Fisher, Russell S. *Medicolegal Investigation of Death.* Springfield, Illinois: Charles C. Thomas, 1973.

Svensson, Arne; Wendel, Otto; and Fisher, Barry A. J. *Techniques of Crime Scene Investigation,* 3rd ed. New York: Elsevier North Holland, Inc., 1981.

Westen, Paul B. and Wells, Kenneth M. *Criminal Investigation—Basic Perspectives,* 2nd ed. Englewood Cliffs, New Jersey: Prentice-Hall, Inc., 1974.

The Crime Scene Photographs

6

Crime scene photographs are permanent and comprehensive pieces of evidence which may be presented in a court of law to prove or disprove a fact in question. During the preliminary stage of homicide investigation it is impossible to determine all of the things which may become relevant or important later on. Therefore, it is imperative that photos be taken of the entire area and location where the crime took place, including any sites contiguous with the original crime.

Remember, you only get one shot at the homicide crime scene, so obtain as much information and documentation as possible.

The Value of Crime Scene Photographs

The old adage, "One picture is worth a thousand words," is certainly appropriate when considering the value of crime scene photography. Although an investigator can verbally describe the homicide crime scene, photographs are able to present the same facts in a more accurate and easily understood manner. In addition, photography enables the investigator to stop the clock at any given instant and obtain a durable record which remains long after other more fragile evidence has dissipated. From an investigative point of view, crime scene photographs are practical and valuable tools which can:

1. Pictorially re-create the original crime scene.
2. Refresh the investigator's memory and recall significant details which may have been overlooked or forgotten.

3. Review particular aspects of the case.
4. Provide a new slant on the case.
5. Refresh the memory of witnesses.
6. Illustrate details of a scene and the relationship of objects to the crime.
7. Provide proof of injury or wound.
8. Make comparisons.
9. Brief newly assigned investigators.
10. Convey the crime scene and circumstances of the crime to a jury and serve as a *visible* piece of evidence.

Crime Scene Photography and the Investigator

The investigator should have a basic understanding of photography and be able to operate some of the more simple photographic equipment available today. An easy-to-use camera should be provided for use by the investigators at the homicide crime scene. Such cameras as the Instamatic and many of the Polaroid models are simple to operate and ideal for obtaining a record of the crime scene before any changes occur.

The type of camera that is recommended for crime scene photography is one which provides a large negative. A camera such as the 4 × 5 or the 120 model is preferred because the larger negatives provide better clarity and resolution upon enlargement. The 35mm camera, because of its versatility and relative simplicity, is an excellent substitute for the large-negative types if they are not available. Investigators can be trained to operate the 35mm camera in a short time.

Although investigators may be able to operate the 35mm camera or the Instamatics and Polaroids, they should enlist the assistance of a professional with sophisticated equipment for the proper documentation of the homicide crime scene. Most departments maintain police photographers or specialized personnel to photograph crime scenes. In the absense of police personnel, civilian professionals can be employed. However, they should be advised of the legal requirements involved. The primary duty of the investigator will be to maintain the homicide crime scene in a condition that assures the integrity of the photos.

Admissibility of Photographic Evidence

The homicide investigator should have an understanding of the techniques and legal requirements necessary to insure that the crime scene photos will be admissible in court. The basic premise involved in crime scene photography is that the photographs are a true representation of the homicide crime scene as it was at the time the incident was reported. Therefore, before a detailed examination of the crime scene is undertaken, and before any items are moved or even touched, the crime scene must be photographed.

The photographer should show the relationship of one object to another by moving from the general to the specific. Several photos of

The Chalk Fairy. Here you see the deceased lying in the position in which he was found. This crime scene photo may possibly be "inadmissible." While the first officers were securing the scene, a "chalk fairy" suddenly had the irresistable impulse to draw chalk lines around the body.

Remember, do not draw any chalk lines nor place markers in the crime scene until an original photograph can be obtained depicting the scene as it was when the police first arrive.

the general view should be taken at eye level in a clockwise direction or from each point of the compass (north, south, east, and west). The photographer should start at the outside perimeter of the scene and work toward the central scene. In addition, the photos of the body should indicate its position in relation to some landmark or permanent point of reference. The entire roll of film should be exposed in each investigation. Never leave partially exposed film in the camera for another investigation, or the evidentiary value of the crime scene photographs may be jeopardized.

Do not add any chalk marks or markers to the scene before a long shot and close-up detail shot are obtained. Defense counsel can argue that the crime scene photographs are not an accurate representation of the scene as it was upon discovery of the crime because the police have added markers or chalk lines. If chalk lines or markers are needed to pinpoint the location of a small item, such as bloodstains, hair, or similar articles, photos should first be taken without the markers and then additional photos taken with the markers.

The number of photos taken is usually determined by the case. There is no limit on the number that can be taken. Practically speaking, it is always better to overshoot a scene than to miss some vital shots.

As each photo is taken, an accurate record should be made in the investigator's notebook. In addition, an entry should be made on an official photo log. Some agencies maintain logs or preprinted forms for use at crime scenes in order to assure the proper documentation of crime scene photographs. In any event, the following information should be recorded.

 1. the date and time,
 2. the exact location,
 3. a brief description of the detail being photographed,
 4. the compass direction (north, south, east, or west),
 5. the focus distance,
 6. the type of film and camera utilized,
 7. any special equipment utilized,
 8. light and weather conditions,
 9. the number of exposures,
10. the identity of the photographer.

The photographer should keep possession of the exposed film for delivery to the laboratory for processing. After these photos are developed, the above information should be entered either on the back of each photo or on an appropriate form indicating each photo by number.

The comprehensive log is necessary to assure the admissibility of the crime scene photos in court. The log includes the ten points mentioned above, as well as the chain of custody from exposure to final disposition and storage of the film and negatives.

In addition, the police laboratory should keep an evidence log containing the following information.

1. the identity of the individual delivering the film for process (name, rank, serial number, etc.),
2. date and time the film was received for processing,
3. results of development,
4. number of prints requested,
5. location of original negatives,
6. identity of the person receiving developed prints and/or negatives if there is no central storage.

In the event that a commercial laboratory is used to process the film, the management should be requested to cooperate in adhering to the rules of evidence handling. This should include limiting the number of personnel handling the evidence film, as well as guaranteeing the security of the film and negatives. Needless to say, the commercial firm utilized to process any evidentiary material should be a reputable establishment.

Photographing the Homicide Crime Scene

Recording the homicide crime scene is a major facet of the investigation. It is extremely important that this be accomplished before anything is touched or moved at the scene. Also, it is important while photographing the scene to eliminate persons or items—including officers and police equipment—that do not belong in the scene.

As mentioned earlier in the chapter, the photographer should attempt to show the relationships of objects to each other by shooting from the general to the specific, should take several photos of the general view, and should start at the perimeter and work toward the body. This is followed by close-up shots of the body and any significant pieces of physical or trace evidence. Important items of evidence, such as weapons, should be photographed as they appear at the scene.

Remember, no chalk marks or markers before you get a long shot and a close-up shot of the body and any other evidence.

Outdoor Locations

Outdoor locations should be photographed showing the central scene and the surrounding area in order to show the relationship of the scene to its surroundings and give the viewer a point of reference.

These photos should be taken at eye level to show exactly how the scene appeared to the investigators or witnesses. If the homicide takes place in a large area, or the surrounding street locations become significant, aerial photos are often helpful in providing a better perspective.

Indoor Locations

Indoor locations are more restricted than outdoor ones; however, the same principles apply. The photographer takes several overall shots in order to relate the scene to its surroundings. He then photographs the body, showing its position and relationship to objects in the room. Indoor locations may include several rooms in a house, an entire apartment or an individual room, the interior of a closet, an office, a hallway, a fire escape, a cellar, etc. The extent of the indoor photos depends on the facts of the case. The position of any windows and doors should be photographed, and exterior photos should be taken of locations—backyards, entranceways, neighboring residences, etc.—that show the premises from the outside.

The Body

Photos of the body should include a general and close-up view and at least two full-body shots, one from each side. The photos must be taken *in situ* before the body is moved and should show any significant aspects of the crime as well as the body's position in the scene. Any defense wounds on the body should be photographed at the scene and later on at autopsy.

It is recommended that additional identification photos of the deceased be taken at the morgue, prior to autopsy and after the body has been cleaned of any blood or grime. Sometimes the facial features will be so distorted that it is impossible to get an identification photo. In these cases, pictures should be taken of any scars or other markings, including tattoos, for later identification purposes. Photographs should also be taken of any wounds or injuries that caused death or are significant to the investigation. These photos should be taken before and after the body has been cleaned in order to show the specific extent of injury and the character of each wound in exact detail. Photographs of any wounds should include a standard or metric ruler along with an I.D. label indicating case numbers and other pertinent information. In homicide cases where the victim has received wounds from bite marks, it is recommended that the photographs be taken with a 1 × 1 *fingerprint* camera such as the one produced by Polaroid. These fingerprint cameras will provide the necessary detail needed for comparison and examination of the wound later on. Remember to use

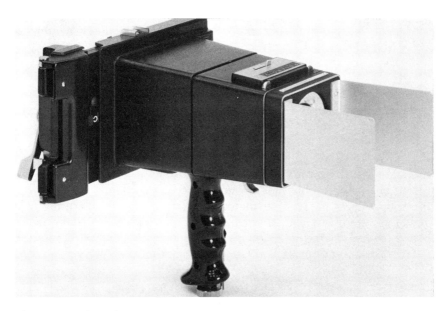

The CU-5 Polaroid Camera.

CU-5 Polaroid Camera—Bite Mark. The effect of using a CU-5 Polaroid camera to record bite-mark evidence. Notice the rule of measure to show actual size and area of the bitemark. In this case the victim, who was not killed, had received a bitemark on her left breast during a struggle with her assailant. The investigators, with the victim's cooperation and permission, photographed the injury. An odontologist can make valuable determinations based on this type of evidence.

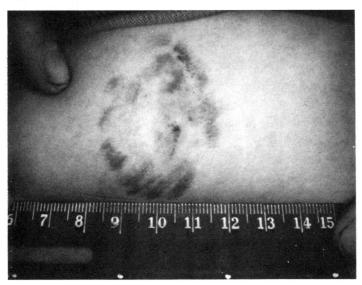

a ruler or scale to obtain an accurate measurement. (See Chapter 15, "Bite-Mark Identification.")

Suspects

It is important to note that crime scene photographs are not limited to places, objects, or dead bodies. Many times a suspect's appearance will indicate that he or she has been in some sort of altercation. Suspects may have blood on their hands or body, and there may be blood on their clothes. They may have scratches or cuts on their hands, or there may be some superficial wounds on their face or body. In addition, there may be some visible material on the suspect that links him or her to the crime scene. Crime scene photographs must be taken before this valuable and important evidence is lost. However, in order to assure admissible crime scene photos, the suspect must be

Hands of the Suspect. Both hands of this suspect, who has been charged with homicide, show evidence of a violent struggle, as indicated by the arrows, and are actually part of the crime scene. These photos should be taken in black and white and color, with a marker.

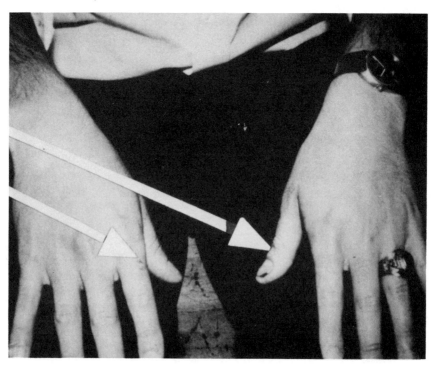

in custody, be under arrest, or agree to *pose* after having been advised of his constitutional rights.

Type of Film

I recommend that crime scene photographs be taken in color and black-and-white. Often an issue of color may arise that cannot be resolved by black-and-white photos. I recall an investigation involving a homicide in a rooming house where the suspect had allegedly brought a blue sweatshirt into the room of the deceased. He had changed the shirt because blood from the victim was splattered all over it. The suspect then threw the shirt on a pile of rags after wiping up some of the blood and left the shirt behind. Later on a witness was located who had observed the suspect wearing a blue sweatshirt before the crime was committed. The witness attempted to locate the sweatshirt in the black-and-white crime scene photos but failed to make an identification. Had we been using color film as well as black-and-white, we would have been able to point out the sweatshirt as a piece of evidence.

Photos taken in color give a much more realistic portrayal of the crime scene, which graphically depicts the events to the viewer. However, in certain instances, defense counsel has effectively precluded the submission of color prints into evidence because color was "too inflammatory." There are other occasions where details shot in color are not clear enough for comparison purposes, e.g., latent fingerprint evidence. In any event, if the crime scene photographs are taken in both black-and-white and color, the investigator can choose between the two.

Recommended Crime Scene Photographs

There is no limit on the number or types of photos one may decide to take at any given crime scene. However, there are certain photographs which should be taken in all homicide investigations. I recommend that the following crime scene photographs be obtained as a matter of routine.

1. The front entrance or walkway to the building or dwelling where the homicide took place; or the external perimeter of an outdoor crime scene wherein the body lies.
2. The entrance to the apartment or room where the deceased is discovered.
3. Two full-body views (one from each side). If the body has been removed, the original location where the body was discovered should be photographed.

Evidence *In Situ.* This knife was left behind by the killers after it had been used to torture and slay the victim, who was also shot as well as stabbed. The knife had been thrust deep into the deceased's chest, to where the blood-mark appears on the blade.

4. Two photographs relating the body location to its general surroundings, from opposite and/or diagonal sides.
5. Possible entrance and/or escape routes of the perpetrator or perpetrators to and from the crime scene.
6. Areas where force was used for entry or exit.
7. Area and close-up view of evidence *in situ.* In addition to the body, this would include bloodstains, weapons, shell casings, hairs, fibers, or any other physical or trace evidence.
8. If a large outdoor area is involved, take aerial photographs to relate scene to surroundings.
9. Photographs of suspect, if in custody, with attention to any new wounds or injuries or presence of physical or trace evidence.
10. Photographs of witnesses either surreptitiously or as a matter of record, depending on the circumstances of the case.

On completion of these preliminary crime scene photographs, the homicide supervisor should make it a standard practice to keep the photographer at the scene in the event the crime scene search uncovers additional items or details which should be photographed. Many times, after a body has been moved, additional evidence is discovered underneath, such as shell casings, spent rounds, a weapon, etc. These items should be photographed *in situ* before collection, with a refer-

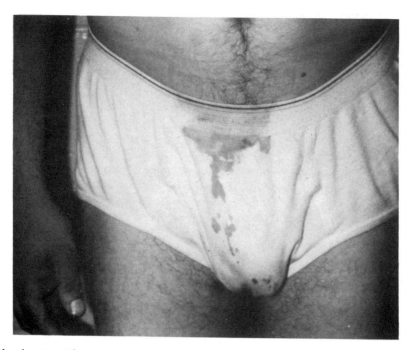

Bloodstains. The suspect's underwear reveals bloodstains and other evidence from a rape-homicide. The suspect, who raped and killed a homeless woman staying in an abandoned building, was apprehended shortly after the crime. This photograph should also be accompanied by a "stand-up" photo identifying the suspect by face as well as additional photos of the individual evidence.

ence in the investigator's notebook as to the original location and the discovery.

Practical Application of Crime Scene Photography

In addition to the general application of crime scene photography to the overall investigative process, there are instances when the camera can perform what the investigator cannot. For instance, in street homicides, especially in cities, there is always the possibility that the suspect or a witness to the fatal act may still be in the crowd of onlookers. I personally recommend that pictures be taken of these people either surreptitiously while photographing the scene, or directly before anyone in the crowd realizes that their presence is being documented. In addition, if you have videotape capability, tape the crowd and their reactions. It usually proves to be quite interesting, and may help you to locate persons later on for questioning.

I remember two incidents where crime scene photos helped us to

Aerial Shot. It is a good procedure to obtain aerial views of the murder scene in certain cases.

break a case. On one occasion, while on investigative patrol, we heard a radio broadcast of a possible homicide and a request for detectives to respond. Since we were close by, we arrived as the crowd was still being directed behind hastily erected barriers. As the detective who was with me approached the scene, I stood back and began to take pictures of the surrounding crowd with my Instamatic camera. Later on we discovered that there was a witness to the shooting in the crowd. This witness never would have come forward had we not "captured" his presence on film.

In another case, we were at the scene of a street homicide when we received information that one of the perpetrators was in the crowd. We could not verify this information, nor make an arrest, because the source had made himself scarce and we did not have enough probable cause to make an arrest. I instructed the crime scene photographer to surreptitiously photograph the crowd while taking the crime scene photos. Later on when we showed these blown-up crowd shots to our witness, he positively identified the suspect as one of the participants.

Videotaping

The use of videotape is becoming increasingly popular and has been employed with excellent results in the investigation of homicide. The technical expertise involved is certainly within the ability of the homicide investigator or crime scene technician and should be considered a viable adjunct to other methods employed in the recording of crime scenes.

Advantages of Videotaping

Videotaping has the following advantages:

1. It provides a more realistic and graphic portrayal of the homicide crime scene.
2. It tends to capture the atmosphere of the scene, especially when the homicide detective is narrating the events as they are being depicted on film.
3. It can be used to record suspects' statements. This is especially beneficial if suspects later on change their story or deny having made a confession to police. It should be noted that defendants must be given their Miranda rights on the video prior to videotaping their statements. In addition, a clock which is visible in the background should be employed to record the total time of interview.
4. It can be utilized to record a dying declaration. Often a victim under treatment in a hospital may be diagnosed as critically injured and likely to die. If the victim is coherent, the investigator should attempt to elicit a dying declaration. The use of videotape enhances and permanently documents this legal procedure.

5. It can be used to record a line-up. This recording can be utilized to depict to the jury the exact position of the defendant and can be shown to additional witnesses in an attempt to identify suspects.

Videotaping Procedure

The best results in videotaping are obtained when the investigators employ a team method. One investigator should act as the technician while the other describes or narrates the events as they are being filmed. However, personnel at the scene should be cautioned to remain quiet during this taping, as such conversation may prove distracting or embarrassing. I recall a case that was being videotaped that involved a brutal sex act and murder. The suspect was found lying on top of the deceased female by an employee of the building. The suspect had been sodomizing the dead woman when he was "interrupted." The condition of the victim and the act that had been perpetrated were so heinous that officers at the scene were quite descriptive in their opinions of what should be done to the "perp" (perpetrator). The suspect eventually pleaded guilty and the videotape was never presented. Needless to say, however, if the tape had ever been played in court, the defense counsel would have had a field day depicting the police as crude and vindictive, not to mention unprofessional.

The videotaping should begin at the perimeter of the scene or outside the location and progress toward the central scene and the body. Long shots as well as close-ups should be taken in a slow and systematic manner. This is accomplished by first "panning" the entire area and then focusing or "zooming" in on the central scene and corpse. In order to document the location or position of the body, the technician should photograph any landmarks or permanent structures as points of reference to give a perspective on the position of the body.

When videotaping small items of evidence, a scale should be included to show the actual size of the item being filmed. The same principle used in crime scene photographs applies to videotaping. In order for the videotape to be admitted into evidence the scene must be "intact" and not have been changed. The scene should first be filmed without any markers or scales and then filmed with the necessary visual aids. In addition, the videotape must be in original condition without any erasures or editing in order to be admissible as evidence.

When videotaping suspect statements it is important to record the suspect's demeanor during the interview. Frequently a suspect will involuntarily demonstrate some sort of body language that will indicate nervousness or uneasiness at certain questions. This tape can later be played back for evaluation and analysis by the investigator. A review of the tape and the suspect's reactions may form the basis for a different approach or a concentration on certain points of the interrogation.

It should be noted that there is a difference of opinion on whether or not suspects' statements should be videotaped. Certain experts feel that the implementation of such a system may create additional problems in the prosecution if *all* statements are not taped, by providing the defense counsel with ammunition to challenge those statements. For example, if a confession or statement is not videotaped, for any number of legitimate reasons, does this mean the agency was attempting to hide something? Because of this, the decision to videotape statements must be given careful consideration.

Conclusion

In conclusion, the application of photography to the documentation of the homicide crime scene is certainly within the capability of the average investigator. Photography is an important element of professional law enforcement that provides an objective, comprehensive, and impartial re-creation of the crime scene as it was upon discovery. It is up to the investigators to provide this vital ingredient, either by taking the photos themselves or by preserving the scene until the arrival of police photographers.

Selected Reading

O'Hara, Charles E. *Fundamentals of Criminal Investigation*, 5th ed. Springfield, Illinois: Charles C. Thomas, 1980.

Scott, James D. *Investigative Methods.* Reston, Virginia: Reston Publishing Company, Inc., 1978.

Ward, Richard H. *Introduction to Criminal Investigation.* Reading, Massachusetts: Addison-Wesley Publishing Co., 1975.

The Crime Scene Sketch 7

The *crime scene sketch* is a simple line drawing that indicates the position of the body in relation to *fixed* and *significant* objects in the scene. It supplements both the written reports and the crime scene photographs. Photographs, because of camera perspective and distortion, do not always depict the exact location in which objects are situated or the relation of one object to another. The crime scene sketch is an excellent visual aid which allows for the removal of unnecessary details and the inclusion of significant material. Practically speaking, the homicide crime scene sketch can become one of the most useful tools of the homicide investigator.

The Sketch

A drawing of the crime scene is the simplest and most effective way to present measurements and to identify those items that the investigator deems significant, including the location of the victim's body, the location of any physical or trace evidence, the position of the weapon, and objects which may be significant to the overall scene. In addition, the drawing permits the deletion of irrelevant or distracting items which appear in photographs. In addition to creating a diagram which is specific and selective, the crime scene sketch can be used to:

1. Refresh the memory of the investigator.
2. Refresh the memory of the witness(es).
3. Refresh the memory of the cooperative suspect to assist in detailing his or her actions at the scene.
4. Develop a clearer understanding of what happened and determine

the relative likelihood of various possibilities. For instance, persons may be requested to trace their particular movements on copies of the original sketch.

5. Explain to a jury or witness the specifics of a case that may otherwise be too complex or confusing. The value of the crime scene sketch is that its clarity and simplicity motivate understanding.

The crime scene sketch should show the position of doors, windows, staircases, as well as other objects of significance, including blood, weapons, stains, and any other trace evidence identified.

The *rough sketch* should be prepared by the investigator at the scene. He may either use graph paper, which is excellent because it provides lines, or draw the sketch in his notebook. The most important element of the rough sketch is careful attention to measurements and distance. The ability of the investigator to draw is a definite asset; however, the rough homicide crime scene sketch need not be a Rembrandt production.

The rough sketch should contain a *legend*. The legend will explain any numbers or symbols used, and give identification numbers assigned to the case, the identity of the sketcher and person taking the measurements, and a reference to compass direction North.

Many municipalities have a city engineer or graphic arts section with personnel who may, under the direction of the homicide investigator, prepare a professional *smooth* or *finished crime scene sketch*.

In some cases, an existing map or blueprint may be utilized to graphically portray the crime scene. I remember directing investigations involving homicides or shootings on New York City Housing Authority property. The Housing Authority, because it is a city agency, maintained blueprints of all properties under its jurisdiction. While at the scene, we obtained the blueprint of the particular project involved and used the blueprint as our crime scene sketch. Since a blueprint or map will already bear the scales and landmarks of the area, all the investigator need do is add the significant objects in the instant case to the finished blueprint, being careful to measure distances and follow the scale provided in the finished plan.

It should be noted that the original sketch is evidence and, as such, must never be altered, changed, or otherwise tampered with after the investigator has completed his drawing at the scene. In addition, the investigator must assure that this original sketch is properly safeguarded even after a smooth or finished sketch is prepared by an expert draftsman. The original crime scene sketch *must not* be mutilated or destroyed. Often, especially in cases where the smooth or finished sketch is prepared for court presentation, the defense counsel will attempt to prevent its introduction or to diminish its value by

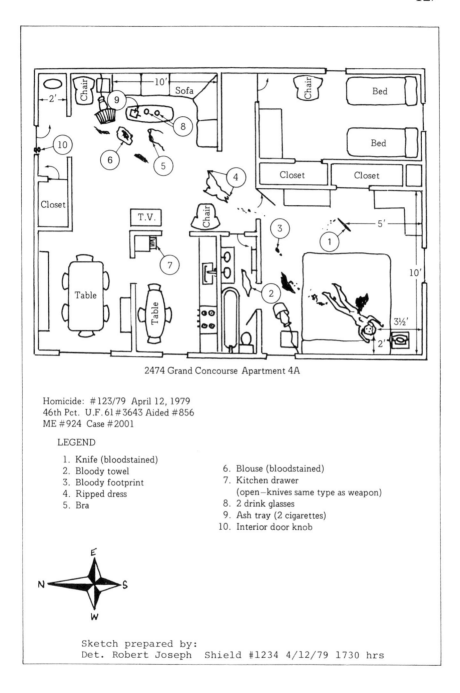

2474 Grand Concourse Apartment 4A

Homicide: #123/79 April 12, 1979
46th Pct. U.F. 61 #3643 Aided #856
ME #924 Case #2001

LEGEND

1. Knife (bloodstained)
2. Bloody towel
3. Bloody footprint
4. Ripped dress
5. Bra
6. Blouse (bloodstained)
7. Kitchen drawer
   (open—knives same type as weapon)
8. 2 drink glasses
9. Ash tray (2 cigarettes)
10. Interior door knob

Sketch prepared by:
Det. Robert Joseph Shield #1234 4/12/79 1730 hrs

Finished Crime Scene Sketch. Includes case numbers, date and times, the identity of the drawer, and a legend.

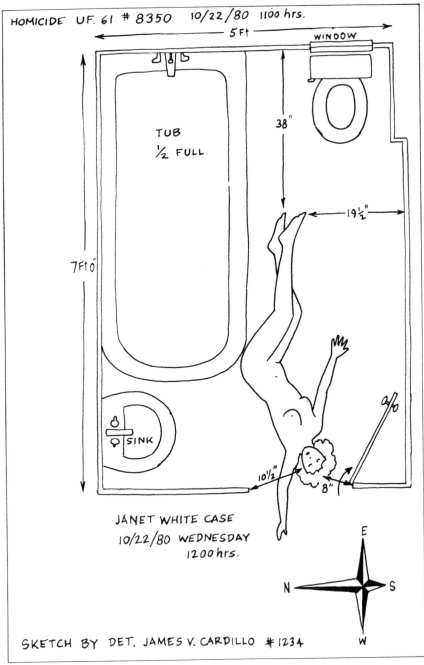

HOMICIDE U.F. 61 # 8350   10/22/80   1100 hrs.

5 Ft

WINDOW

TUB ½ FULL

38"

19½"

7 Ft 0"

SINK

10½"

8"

JANET WHITE CASE
10/22/80 WEDNESDAY
1200 hrs.

E
N — S
W

SKETCH BY DET. JAMES V. CARDILLO # 1234

Rough Sketch. This sketch was made in the investigator's notebook, while at the scene. It is nothing more than a simple line drawing, which indicates the position of objects and gives measurements.

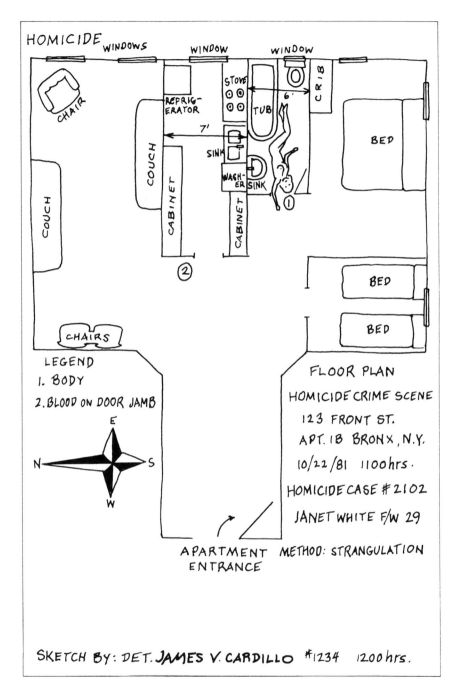

Rough Sketch. The floor plan of the entire apartment of the preceding sketch.
Any number of sketches can be prepared in any case.

demanding to examine the original rough sketch. Defense counsel will then compare the rough sketch to the finished product and attempt to discover some inconsistencies or discrepancies.

Preparing the Crime Scene Sketch

Obviously, a determination must be made regarding what is to be sketched. If you are dealing with a single room, a line drawing or projection-type sketch may be employed. If the crime scene involves two or more rooms, you should utilize a simple line drawing which follows a floor-pattern technique.

In order to assist the investigator in preparing the crime scene sketch I have provided some practical examples and guidelines.

1. Necessary items:
    a. Notebook, paper $(8^{1}/_{2}'' \times 11'')$ or graph paper with $^{1}/_{2}''$ squares, which can be used to scale feet. (Remember to leave an ample margin for the legend.)
    b. Soft lead pencil with eraser.
    c. Straight edge or ruler.
    d. Steel tape (preferably 100′ length).
2. Measurements:
    a. All measurements must be taken from *fixed* points, for example, doors, windows, walls, chimney, stairs, etc.
    b. Measurements should be exact, and should be taken with a steel tape or ruler.
    c. One investigator should sketch while another officer takes the measurements.
    d. In drawing the sketch, the investigator can estimate the relative distances or positions of items, since this rough sketch is not a scale drawing and art work and technical detail do not have to be perfect. However, there should be an accurate measurement taken and recorded in the sketch.
    e. If distances are measured by pacing off, this should be indicated by the number of paces. (This procedure is *not* recommended, but may be used in the absence of proper measuring devices.
3. Methods of obtaining measurements:
    a. *Straightline.* Two measurements are made, one from each side of the object, to a fixed point in the diagram. This method is usually employed to mark positions of furniture or evidence along a wall.
    b. *Rectangular coordinates or perpendicular distance method.* Two measurements are taken at right angles of an item to the nearest two permanent objects, usually the walls. This is the

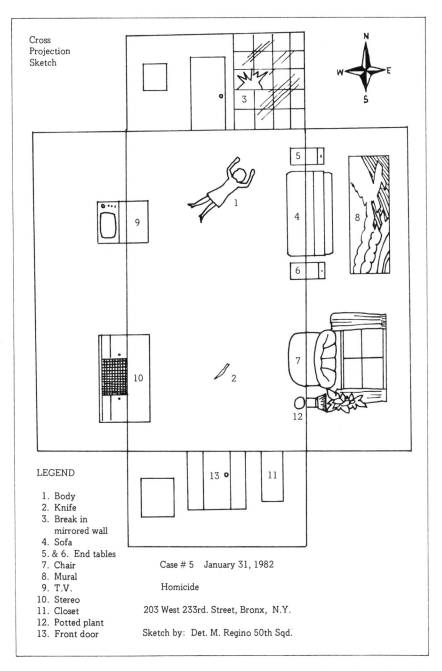

Cross
Projection
Sketch

N
W E
S

LEGEND

1. Body
2. Knife
3. Break in
   mirrored wall
4. Sofa
5. & 6. End tables
7. Chair
8. Mural
9. T.V.
10. Stereo
11. Closet
12. Potted plant
13. Front door

Case # 5   January 31, 1982

Homicide

203 West 233rd. Street, Bronx, N.Y.

Sketch by: Det. M. Regino 50th Sqd.

Cross-Projection Sketch. All objects are drawn as if seen from above, but the walls are folded down and the items are drawn as if the room was a cardboard box with its sides flattened.

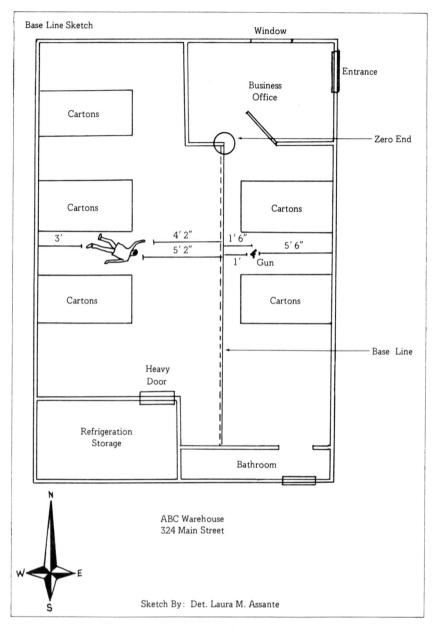

Base Line Sketch

Window

Entrance

Business
Office

Cartons

Zero End

Cartons

Cartons

3'

4' 2"

1' 6"

5' 2"

5' 6"

1'

Gun

Cartons

Cartons

Base Line

Heavy
Door

Refrigeration
Storage

Bathroom

N
W — E
S

ABC Warehouse
324 Main Street

Sketch By: Det. Laura M. Assante

Base Line Sketch. The base line method of sketching can be used when there is a scene without a convenient straight line or boundaries such as a warehouse or large outdoor area. In this sketch the cartons are movable and the inside area large. By drawing a base line through the scene you create a point of reference. Each end of the baseline should be identified and there should be a starting point or zero end.

most practical method for marking the location of the body and other evidence. There are more accurate methods; however, I find this to be the simplest and most useful at the scene.

c. *Polar coordinates or triangulation.* By utilizing a compass and a protractor the investigator locates two fixed points and transfers this information to the sketch. Measurements are then taken from these two fixed points to the object, forming a triangle. Where the two points intersect is the exact location of the object.

d. *Base line.* This method is used for a scene that does not have convenient straight perimeter boundaries, e.g., a large wooded area or the interior of an expansive warehouse. A straight line is drawn through the scene, and each end is located and measured. A starting point is designated and the line is then used as a point of reference for all other measurements. The line can follow a seam or some other naturally existing line.

e. *Two fixed points.* This is a simple method whereby the investigator takes *two* straight-line measurements to *two* fixed points within the scene. There is no need for a right angle, but the two points used should not be close together.

4. The title block:
   a. The professional and legally correct crime scene sketch must contain the following official documentation and information:
      1. The name and title of the investigator who drew the sketch.
      2. The date and time that the sketch was made.
      3. The classification of the crime (homicide, assault, etc.).
      4. The identification of the victim.
      5. The agency's case number.
      6. The names of any persons assisting in taking measurements.
      7. The precise address of the location sketched.
      8. Reference points used during the sketching, including compass direction North, with appropriate indications.
      9. The legend. The purpose of the legend is to identify every article or object by either number or letter and explain the significance of these characters on the crime scene sketch. The legend also includes the scale used and a reference to any notes taken and measurements recorded in connection with the investigation.
      10. Any other pertinent information which is practical to the investigation at the scene (for example: the season, the ground condition—muddy, dry; traffic or lack of traffic; slope of the ground; site—abandoned building, public place,

134

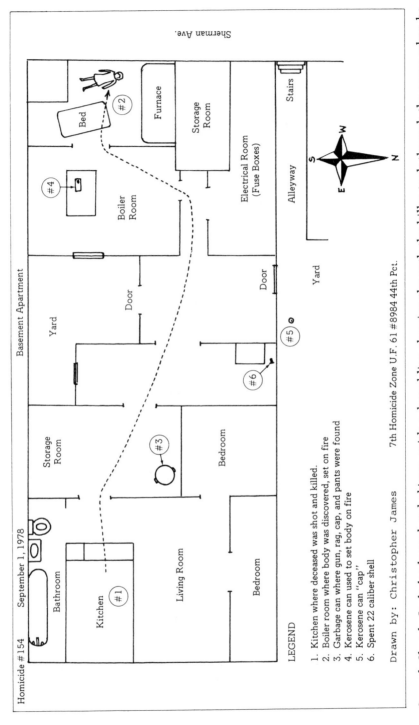

Smooth Sketch. Includes legend and objects, with a dotted line showing the path the killer took through the scene when he disposed of the body.

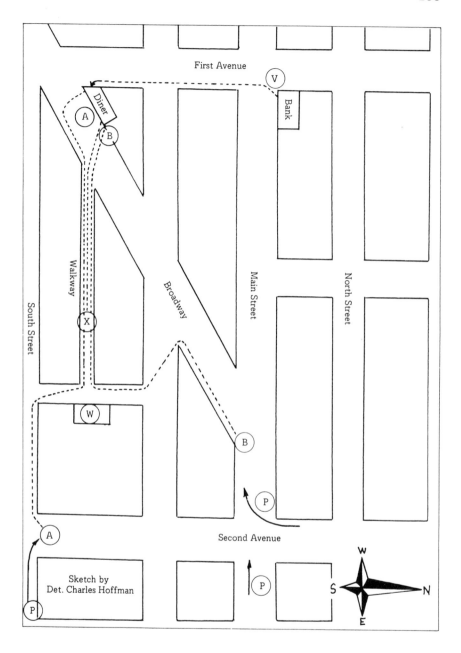

Street Location Sketch. This type of sketch is useful when dealing with several locations and pinpointing the movement of various persons. Symbols and letters can be used to show the movements of the persons involved. For example, V is the victim, A and B are the perpetrators, P represents the police, and W is the civilian witness. X is the crime scene.

transportation facility; the position of the camera in any crime scene photographs; etc.).

It is important to note that any number of crime scene sketches may be employed during the investigation at the scene, especially in multiple-crime scene situations. Therefore, it is imperative that any sketch used be properly documented in the investigator's notebook along with descriptions and other pertinent information.

Selected Reading

O'Hara, Charles E. *Fundamentals of Criminal Investigation*, 5th ed., Springfield, Illinois: Charles C. Thomas, 1980.

Scott, James D. *Investigative Methods*. Reston, Virginia: Reston Publishing Company, Inc., 1978.

Ward, Richard H. *Introduction to Criminal Investigation*. Reading, Mass.: Addison-Wesley Publishing Co., 1975.

The Homicide
Crime Scene Search

8

The search of the homicide crime scene is the most important phase of the investigation conducted at the scene. Decisions of the courts restricting admissibility of testimonial evidence have significantly increased the value of physical evidence in homicide investigations. Therefore, law enforcement personnel involved in the crime scene search must arrange for the proper and effective collection of evidence at the scene.

Physical evidence, which has been referred to as the "unimpeachable witness," cannot be clouded by a faulty memory, prejudice, poor eyesight, or a desire "not to get involved." However, in order for physical evidence to be admissible, it must have been legally obtained. A United States Supreme Court decision of June, 1978 *(Mincey* v. *Arizona)* has severely restricted the right of the police to search certain homicide crime scenes without a search warrant. For example, a warrant is required when the suspect and the deceased both share a possessory right to the premises to be searched. Homicides involving common-law relationships, husbands and wives, or family disputes, will ordinarily necessitate that the detective secure a warrant before the premises can be searched.

Practically speaking, if there is any possibility that evidence you are about to seize for use in a homicide prosecution requires a search warrant, get the warrant. You'll save yourself a lot of headaches later on.

Physical evidence refers to any tangible article, small or large, which tends to prove or disprove a point in question. It may be used to reconstruct the crime, identify the participants, or confirm or discredit an alibi.

Homicide crime scenes usually contain an abundance of physical or trace evidence. Therefore, the detective supervisor should organize the crime scene search so as to collect as much physical evidence as possible. In addition, the search must be based on constitutionally legal grounds, and the evidence collected must be properly documented and handled so that it may be presented in court later on.

Methods of Crime Scene Search

The method selected for search of the crime scene is usually determined by the size, location, and complexity of the scene. There are many criminal-investigation textbooks which describe various types of crime scene search. However, there are actually only five basic methods which are universally accepted. These are: 1) the *strip* method, 2) the *spiral* method, 3) the *wheel* method, 4) the *grid* method, and 5) the *zone* method. Practically speaking, it doesn't really matter which method you select, as long as the search is both systematic and complete.

Formulating the Search

The search for evidence begins with the isolation and protection of the scene. The searcher must ascertain that the scene is intact and then proceed to reconstruct the events that have transpired since his arrival.

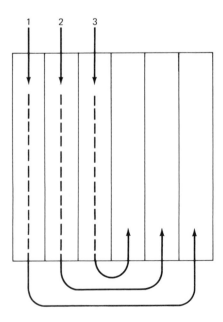

Strip Method. This method can be used effectively if the area to be covered is large and open. It is relatively quick and simple to implement and may even be performed by a single investigator in a limited area such as a room.

Spiral Method. This method sometimes called the circle method is effective in a small area. However, as the
circle widens, evidence can be overlooked. The searcher begins either at
the center or the perimeter and moves
in a circular path.

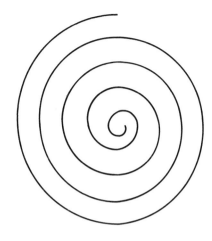

Wheel Method. The searchers gather
at the center of the scene and move
out in spokelike directions. The obvious drawbacks in this method are
the possibility of ruining evidence
when gathering at the center and the
ever-increasing distance between
searchers as the investigators move
outward.

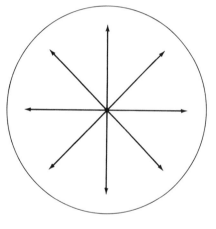

Grid Method. This is the best procedure to cover a large area. The
searchers move parallel to one another and cover the same area twice.
There are a number of variations of
this method. The grid method is considered the most thorough system for
covering large areas with a number of
searchers.

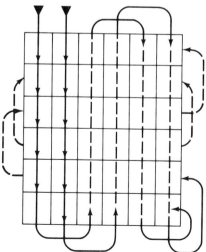

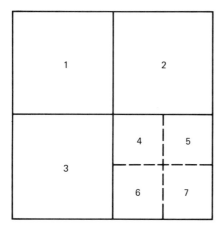

Zone Method. The area is to be searched is divided into squares or sectors. An officer is assigned to each zone or set of squares if the zones are further divided. This method is effective for indoor locations.

Obviously, the best places for obtaining physical evidence are nearest to where the critical act occurred, such as in the immediate vicinity of the homicide victim. However, other areas related to the primary crime scene must not be overlooked; for example,

the point of forced entry,

the route of escape,

the suspect (clothing, hands, body, hair, etc.),

the location where the weapon is or may be located,

a vehicle that was used in the crime,

the suspect's residence,

the location where the assault leading to death took place,

the location where the body was moved from.

Before entering the crime scene, the detective supervisor and the homicide investigator must determine its boundaries, decide how to approach it, and determine if there is any fragile evidence present that requires immediate attention. The crime scene should then be photographed and sketched. (See Chapters 6 and 7.)

The scope of the search is usually determined by a theory or hypothesis agreed on by the investigators, based on their initial observations of the scene. The theory emerges from a set of simple assumptions of *how* and *why* the homicide occurred and the sequence of events that followed. This theory is utilized to guide the investigator in discovering physical evidence. However, remember that *anything* and *everything* may be evidence and become significant later on. Therefore, every item at the scene must be handled as evidence until determined otherwise.

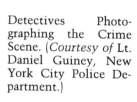

Detectives Photographing the Crime Scene. (*Courtesy of* Lt. Daniel Guiney, New York City Police Department.)

The investigators must keep in mind that their theory is provisional. If new evidence emerges that suggests a different sequence of events, they must be willing to reassess and modify their theory as the new facts dictate. I have been at many different homicide scenes over the years and have seen initial theories change over and over again. The key to success in this phase of the investigation is *flexibility.* Practically speaking, use your common sense in this process. Don't get bogged down in theory and hypothetical speculation. Many times the answer you are looking for is right in front of your nose. The problem is that with all the events going on at the scene, it is sometimes easy to miss a simple observation. Your instincts should not be discounted. They can bring you back to reality or direct you to a situation that would otherwise have slipped by.

Crimes of violence such as homicide usually involve some sort of struggle—a break, use of weapons, use of physical force—or other contact between the perpetrator and the deceased. Therefore, there is a good possibility that trace evidence will be found and recovered. Remember the basic theory of transfer and exchange. (See Chapter 1, "The Homicide Investigation, at the Crime Scene.")

Detectives Measuring the Position of the Body. (*Courtesy of* Lt. Daniel Guiney, New York City Police Department.)

In formulating the search plan there may be some critical areas that you will want to cover immediately, or there may be some question as to what is or is not evidence. Don't be influenced by the original report, the police call, or any initial statements. Note this initial information and then make your own determination based on the total information available. Ask yourself the following questions.

1. Is the death caused by:
   a. Homicide?
   b. Suicide?
   c. Accident?
   d. Natural causes?
2. Do the facts, the scene, the statements, and physical evidence support this explanation?
3. If the death is homicide,
   a. What was the means or agency of death?
   b. Is the homicide excusable or justifiable?

c. Does it appear that any effort was made to purposely mislead the police? For example:
   1. A simulated burglary.
   2. Arson.
   3. Murder made to look like suicide.
   4. Suicide made to look like murder. (Insurance case?)
d. Is there more than one possible cause of death?
e. Are the witness statements consistent with the facts?
f. Is the time element consistent with the condition of the scene?
   1. Are the bloodstains wet or dry?
   2. What is the condition of the body (rigor, lividity, etc.)? (See Chapter 9.)
g. Is there a weapon involved?
   1. Was there more than one weapon used? What does this suggest?
   2. Are the wounds consistent with the weapon suspected?
   3. Is the weapon from the premises?
   4. If the weapon was a firearm,
      a) Are there any shell casings present?
      b) Are there any bullet holes or spent rounds present on the ground, the walls, the ceiling?
   5. Is there a weapon under the body?
   6. Was the deceased armed?

During this, self-cross-examination, do not make any final evaluation, since you are merely forming a theory to assist you in planning the search. However, you should estimate as closely as possible the time and place of the homicide. In addition, you should have a general idea of how much evidence you plan to collect. During this stage you will be depending on hard work, common sense, and keeping an open mind.

The Homicide Kit

If the search is to be successful, certain equipment and logistical support must be available to the homicide investigators. Many departments maintain a forensic or crime scene unit that responds to major crimes with sophisticated equipment necessary to conduct an extensive crime scene search.

I recommend that homicide units maintain a portable homicide kit with the equipment necessary to provide for the collection and documentation of evidence from the scene. A practical kit can be assembled at nominal cost and will usually prove to be invaluable to the investigator at the scene. Although any number of items may be included, a good homicide kit should contain the following.

crime scene cards

plain paper

graph paper ($8^{1}/_{2}'' \times 11''$)

pencils and marking pens

straight-edge ruler

steno pads

clipboard

measuring tape (100' steel)

eraser

box of envelopes

adhesive tape

Scotch tape

surgical gloves

cotton gloves

rope (100')

swivel mirror with 12" handle

magnifying glass

magnet extension rod

saline solution

cotton cloth

safety pins

1 box of cotton swabs (Q-tips)

tongue depressors (50)

specimen bottles (6 bottles, 3-4 oz. size)

forceps tweezers

tape steel (12')

evidence tags

paper towels

antiputrefaction masks

pill boxes

1 scissors (8")

street directory

school compass

paper bags

plastic bags with zip lock

tape recorder with microphone

flashlight (2-cell or 9-volt)

cassette recorder with extra batteries

blank tape cassettes

simple camera (Polaroid or Instamatic)

extra film

telephone pick-up

AC/DC hook-up

thermometer

spotlight (12-volt, 50' extension)

light socket extension cord

electric extension cord

screwdriver (multiple-head)

pliers

hammer with nails

box of chalk

lumber crayons

ball of twine

razor blades

knife (multipurpose)

vise grips

wire cutters

crowbar or pry bar (2')

collapsible shovel

saw (keyhole type)

putty knife

coveralls

fingerprint kit

The Search

The most practical search method is to begin at the point where the body is first discovered and work in an outward direction until the entire room or location has been covered.

Remember, do not smoke or dispose of any cigars, cigarettes, matches, gum wrappers, or any other item that may be confused with evidence at the scene.

Once the search method has been determined, it is up to the detective supervisor to coordinate the efforts of the investigators in order to provide for location of physical or trace evidence, systematized search techniques, a chain of custody, and the recording of evidence.

The search should begin with an examination for latent fingerprints—before any item is touched or moved, the crime scene technician should "dust" for prints. The supervisor should direct this phase by indicating what areas he wants examined. If possible, an attempt is made to determine points of entry and exit for latent impressions. In addition, any weapons or objects that were apparently handled by the suspect, as well as all door handles, telephones, windows, glasses, light switches, etc., should be dusted. Special attention should be given to objects which may have caused death, newly damaged areas, or items apparently missing from their original location. It is important to note that a good latent print will place the suspect at the scene.

Remember, it's your case. You only get one shot at the crime scene, so make sure you do it right.

Direct the fingerprint people. If you do not direct that certain areas be dusted, they may not be. Tell the crime scene people or technicians what you want, and then make sure that you get it. All visible details should be observed and described before dusting anything, in the event that something might have to be moved. Note the location of any stains, weapons, etc.

During the initial search, each possible item of evidence should be measured from a fixed location (see Chapter 7, "Preparing the Crime Scene Sketch"). The measurements along with a complete description should be entered in the investigator's notebook. This information should also be recorded on the crime scene sketch.

Any latent prints located during this preliminary dusting should first be photographed and then "lifted." The photo should be taken with an identifying label in order to document the lift, in case the lift

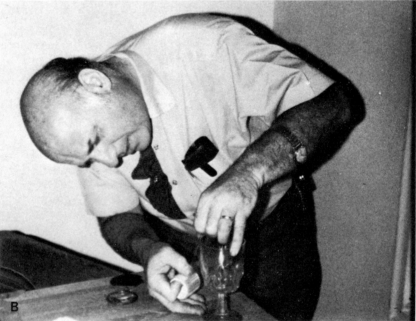

Dusting. **A.** A crime scene detective is evaluating a latent print, which has been brought-up after "dusting." **B.** The detective is preparing to lift the latent print using lifting tape.

fails. The photo can then still be used for identification and comparison.

Examination of the Body at the Scene

The actual examination of the body should not begin until all photographs and sketches are completed. In addition, a complete description of the body as well as any clothing must be obtained, including:

sex,

race,

appearance,

age,

build,

color of hair,

evidence of injury and apparent cause of death,

condition of the body (rigor mortis, lividity, etc.),

color of blood (wet or dry?),

position of body relative to objects of significance at the location.

The investigator should then concentrate on recording a complete description of the clothing as follows:

position of clothes,

condition of clothes (buttoned, unbuttoned, twisted sideways or pulled down, inside out, zippered or unzippered),

damage to clothes (rips, tears, cuts, holes, etc.),

stains: blood, saliva, vomit, semen, phlegm, urine, or feces. Where are they? What are they? Is there any direction of flow?

After a complete description of the clothing and any significant position, condition, damage, or stains have been noted, the investigator begins a careful examination of the body starting with the head and working down to the legs. This description will necessitate moving the body to look for any wounds or evidence of further injuries that are not visible in the original position.

1. The head:
   a. Are the eyes open or closed?
   b. Is the mouth open or closed?
   c. What is the position of the head in relation to the body?
   d. What is the color of the skin (lividity, etc.)?
   e. Is there any blood present? (Describe.)
   f. Are there any visible wounds? (Describe.)

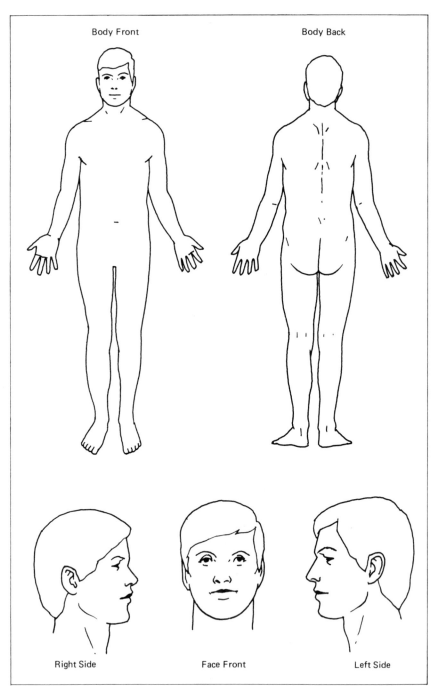

Body Front
Body Back

Right Side
Face Front
Left Side

Wound Chart. This can be used by the investigator to record observations of injuries to the deceased.

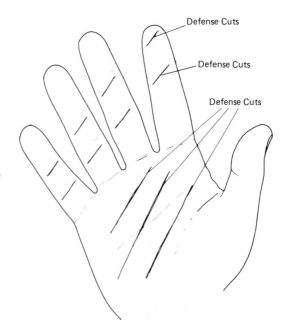

Defense Cuts

Defense Cuts

Defense Cuts

Sketch of Defense Wounds on Hand.

Right-Hand—Palm Up

    g. Is there any foreign material on the head (soil, mud, etc.)?
    h. What is the condition of the deceased's hair (neat or messy)?
    i. Any phlegm, saliva, or vomit present?
2. The trunk:
    a. The position of the trunk (twisted or bent over, on side or back, etc.).
    b. Any injuries. (Describe.)
    c. Presence of any stains (blood, semen, vomit, etc.).
    d. Presence of any hairs or fibers.
    e. Presence of any foreign substances on the trunk (soil, mud, grease, tar, paint, etc.).
3. Arms and legs:
    a. Position of each arm and leg.
    b. Presence of any injuries.
    c. Presence of any stains.
    d. Any foreign matter on the legs or arms?
    e. Are there any defense wounds on the hands, arms, legs, or feet?

Remember, note the presence or absence of any jewelry—rings, watches, etc.—on the body, including any mark on the body indicating that such objects have been worn.

Preserving Trace Evidence. Following examination at the scene, the hands have been bagged to preserve any trace evidence, which may be found under the finger-nails. It is recommended that the investigator use pa-per bags.

In most cases, it is good to bag the hands of the deceased with paper bags. This will preserve any trace evidence which may be found under the fingernails later on during autopsy. A paper bag is used because plastic tends to accelerate putrefaction, especially if there is any blood on the hands. In addition, plastic does not allow the skin to "breathe" and may even change the chemical composition of certain trace evidence.

The area under the body must be carefully examined, bearing in mind that extensive bleeding may create pooling which conceals bullets, cartridge casings, or other small items of evidence. If the body has been lying on soft earth, bullets may be embedded in the soil. If any such items are found, they should be photographed in the position in which found before being collected and marked.

Remember, appropriate notation should be made on the crime scene sketch and in the investigator's notebook.

While this procedure is particularly important in cases of apparent death from gunshot wounds, it should be followed as a matter of routine in all cases.

Release of the Body

The body should not be moved until completion of the preliminary investigation at the scene. The medical examiner or coroner, if responding, should have the opportunity to view the body in its original position. This can be very helpful to these officials in carrying out their responsibilities. After the homicide investigator and medical examiners have completed their work at the scene and details noted, the question arises as to when the body can and should be released.

This decision is critical. Because the consequences of the decision are irrevocable, removal should only be undertaken after due consideration of several factors.

1. Before the body is removed, it should be wrapped in a clean sheet to preserve any evidence or residue for later analysis.
2. If the medical examiner is not going to conduct an immediate autopsy and the body will be lying in the morgue until the following day, there should be no rush to remove the body, particularly in cases of apparent homicide where there are no witnesses and no named perpetrator or arrests. If the body is not in a public place, the location can easily be secured. The reason for this procedure is that information may come to light during the canvass or while talking to witnesses at the station house that may require some additional photos or other police procedure with respect to the body. If the body has been removed hastily, this opportunity will be lost.
3. If an immediate autopsy is to be conducted by the medical examiner, then the removal should be directed only after conferring with the investigators doing the canvass and the interviewing teams at the station house, to determine if there is any new information which may require additional things to be done with the body.
4. If the body is in a public place and the medical examiner has completed his scene examination, and the crime scene work has been accomplished, the detective supervisor can release the body, usually after checking with his detectives at the station house and with the officers doing the canvass.
5. If the body is in a public place and the medical examiner is not responding, the chief investigator will authorize the removal after the crime scene work has been completed.
6. As previously discussed under conditions of violent crowds or pub-

lic disorders, etc., the body may have to be removed immediately. (See Chapter 1, "Dealing with Emergencies at the Scene.")

The Scene

A technique which I have found useful is to have someone who is thoroughly familiar with the scene go over it with you, bit by bit, first visually and then physically, being careful not to touch any items. This person can identify the usual positions of objects in the scene. You can then get a complete inventory on the spot. Instruct them to take their time, and ask if they recognize any inconsistencies or "foreign" material present. Have them point out the usual position of drapes, curtains, blinds, pictures, statues, ashtrays, etc. Obtain a detailed report. You may even want them to examine the scene along with an investigator so that they may point out new stains, signs of disorder, or any factor inconsistent with the life style of the deceased.

The ideal situation in any crime scene search is to have one officer designated the "searching officer," whose responsibility is to search and take the evidence into custody. Other homicide detectives can assist by taking notes of locations where objects are found and even participating in follow-up searches. However, these officers assisting the searching officer should *not* handle any evidence. Instead, they can alert the searching officer, who will take any significant evidence into custody. This procedure limits the chain of custody and makes the recording of evidence more uniform and professional.

Since items tend to fall to the ground, especially in a violent struggle or confrontation, the floor is the best place to begin the search after examining the body. As the search progresses, the investigators may move from the floor or ground to waist height, and from waist height to ceiling. The areas to be searched depend on the type of homicide. If the homicide is the result of a robbery or burglary, you will want to check the entire apartment or house for locations where the intruder "searched" for valuables. If the homicide was the result of a shooting, you will want to check the walls and ceiling for any bullet holes or spent rounds; any carpeting or rugs should also be rolled back or lifted up for examination.

If the murderer "cleaned up" after the crime, you must examine such additional locations as sinks and sink traps or garbage areas. If there are narcotics involved, you might have to locate a "stash" or secret hiding place. The murderer may have fixed something to eat, or may have taken something from a refrigerator. Did the killer turn the light off or on? Does the scene give an appearance of being ransacked? Was the door unlocked or locked? Are the windows open or closed? Where is the point of entry? These are all questions you should ask yourself.

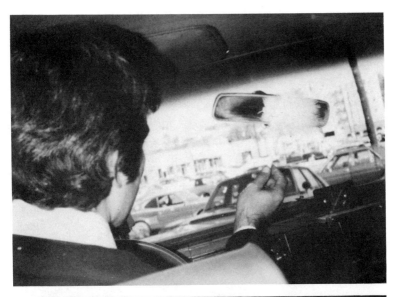

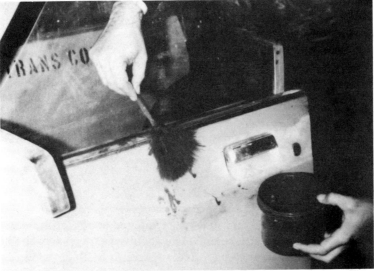

Dusting for Latent Prints. A robbery-homicide of a cab driver has taken place. The stolen taxicab was abandoned a short distance from the scene of the shooting. The mortally wounded driver was pulled from the driver's seat and left lying in the street. The taxicab, which was safeguarded and secured by patrol officers, was towed to an indoor police facility. It is imperative that nothing inside the cab be touched or moved until "dusted." These photos show a detective dusting the critical areas for latent print evidence. Evidence was recovered from the door and rearview mirror, which the perpetrator had adjusted as he drove from the scene.

Remember the theory of exchange and transfer.

Locations where any physical or trace evidence may be found depend on the individual crime and the actions of the suspect or suspects at the scene, and will vary from scene to scene. However, certain areas and objects should always be given attention:

under rugs or carpets	elevator shaft
under chair cushions	tops of cabinets or furniture
doorjambs	chimney
light fixtures	refrigerators
behind drapes or curtains	statues
garbage pails or bags	behind pictures or clocks
wastebaskets	sewers
hampers or soiled clothes	drainpipes
ashtrays	ventilation ducts
ceilings	behind desks set against walls
suspended ceilings	closets
walls	backs and bottoms of drawers
under chairs	inside ovens
under beds	inside cabinets
mirrors	kitchen or bathroom towels
telephones	sinks, toilets, or tubs
signs of a party	counter tops
glasses	windows
stairs	any newly damaged area
passages	garments
back yards	mailboxes
behind boxes or cartons	

The ability to recognize and discover evidence at the crime scene is a prerequisite of successful search. The acquired expertise of the homicide investigator and the detective supervisor will probably determine what trace evidence is found.

It is in this search phase that one can see the need for close cooperation between the investigators and the forensic scientist. It is imperative that the officers performing the search have a working knowledge of handling physical evidence. (See Chapter 12.) Most major departments maintain a forensic or crime scene unit with trained personnel to assist in the search of major crime scenes. These officers have the expertise and equipment necessary to work under the detective supervisor for the proper retrieval of physical evidence.

Information sources such as papers, personal effects, address books, etc., and any other property which may aid in the investigation should be taken by the homicide detectives for later perusal and disposition. The patrol or uniformed division should be responsible for the administrative search and safekeeping of any valuables or property of the deceased. These items can be vouchered and safeguarded at headquarters for later disposition to the property clerk, medical examiner, coroner, or family of the deceased.

Any photos of the deceased taken in life should be collected to use in the canvass to clearly identify the victim to persons interviewed, as well as personal acquaintances or associates of the victim. If photos are not available at the scene, they should be obtained from the victim's family, friends, or employer, or from yearbooks or a driver's license. Photos should have a good likeness of the deceased just prior to death so as not to confuse the person they are shown to.

Examining the Outdoor Scene

The general techniques of crime scene search apply to all homicide crime scenes; however, the outdoor scene poses additional problems for the investigator. For example,

1. The scene usually does not have easily defined borders.
2. The "floor" of the scene is usually rough and irregular and may be composed of hills, valleys, bodies of water, swamps, sand, or other natural contours.
3. The investigation is vulnerable to weather conditions. Rain or snow may have washed much trace evidence away, or the threat of a storm may force immediate procedures to collect evidence in a manner that precludes efficient collection of all evidence.
4. The investigator does not have the luxury of electricity, running water, telephones, or other common conveniences found indoors.
5. Daylight is limited, be prepared to return to the scene the following day.

The investigator's actions at outdoor scenes are usually determined by the weather and the time of day. I have provided some practical procedures to follow. However, they are presented only as a guide. Each individual case will dictate how an investigator will retrieve evidence.

1. Rope off the largest area possible and secure the scene.
2. Establish a path of entry and exit, usually the original path taken by the person who discovered the body. It should be examined for any possible trace evidence and then staked off or marked. All per-

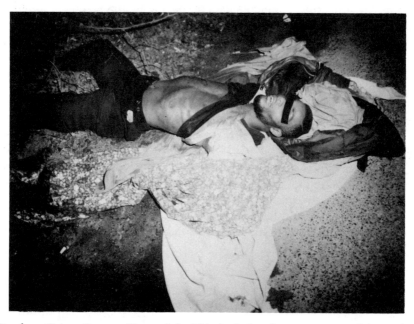

Outdoor Crime Scene—Dump Job. This body has been transported from the place of occurrence to an outdoor dump site. Apparent is that the killers used bed clothing, probably from the scene to carry the body.

sons approaching the area should be cautioned to use this route and not deviate from the established path.

3. The body and immediate surrounding area should be systematically examined before any weather or lighting conditions change. One of the recommended methods of crime scene search should be used. Get additional people to the scene to implement this procedure.

4. If the weather is obviously contributing to or about to destroy trace evidence, collect the evidence as soon as possible even though some additional evidence may be missed, lost, or destroyed.

Remember, some evidence is better than no evidence.

Examples of Evidence Found Outdoors

1. Pollen, vegetation, soil, or seeds may be found on the suspect or the victim. The investigator should collect any foreign matter found on either the suspect or the body for later comparison. However, each individual item must be separately packaged and labeled in order to assure proper examination and admissibility in court later on.

Tire Marks. Here you see the tire impression of the murderer's automobile. The killer had used the auto to transport the victim's body to the place of discovery. Investigators at the scene discovered this tire mark during the crime scene search. This evidence should be preserved through photography and casting.

2. *Foot and tire impressions* may appear on the soil. In addition to gathering samples for laboratory analysis, these impressions must be sketched, photographed, and properly casted for later comparison purposes. When gathering this type of evidence several control samples should be secured for later analysis.
3. *Trees, shrubbery,* and, *fencing* should be examined for any trace evidence that may have been transferred during sudden contact. Fibers, hair, threads, and other material may be affixed to these objects and should be collected and preserved for later comparison with either the victim or the suspect.
4. *Bloodstains, seminal fluid, saliva or phlegm, brain matter, hair, feces,* or *any other biological evidence* are not only subject to rapid change and destruction, but are almost impossible to locate in heavily vegetated terrain. Likewise, these pieces of trace evidence are subject to insect activity and are likely to be washed away if it rains on the scene.
5. *Bullets* and *casings* may be located if the investigator closely ex-

amines any foliage or newly broken parts of shrubbery. In some instances the bullet may have lodged in a tree, causing telltale damage to the bark, or there may be pieces of twigs or branches that are lying on the ground in the line of trajectory. The area immediately surrounding the body should be examined for any shell casings and bullets embedded in the ground under the body.

6. *Oil or gasoline traces.* When vehicles are driven through tall grass or weeds there is a transfer of this material from the underside of the vehicle to the vegetation. This residue should be collected for later comparison.

7. *Crankcase traces.* If a vehicle has been driven through an area of heavy foilage or rocky terrain, there will be traces of this material on the crankcase that can be compared.

8. *Any foreign material at the scene.* Many times, a suspect unwittingly will leave traces of himself at the scene that may be gathered and compared later on, e.g., cigarettes or cigars, toothpicks, etc. In addition, there may be some sort of struggle resulting in a lost item of clothing such as a button or piece of jewelry that can link the suspect to the scene.

9. *Foreign material found on the body.* Sometimes the body may reveal traces of evidence that come from a distinctive location. For instance, the body and clothing may indicate that the deceased was a mechanic or cement worker, or there may be traces of sawdust or coal dust on the corpse.

In the event that the body has to be moved before an extensive examination is conducted at the scene, I recommend that it be wrapped in a clean sheet so that any trace evidence remaining on the clothing will be preserved for later inspection.

Examining an Outdoor Scene at Night

Under ordinary circumstances, the examination of the outdoor crime scene should not be undertaken at night. However, there are certain procedures that should be immediately performed: 1) the area should be effectively secured and safeguarded; 2) the body should be photographed; and, 3) the body should be safeguarded against any additional damage due to exposure to the elements. In addition, any changes that occur since discovery should be noted in the investigator's notebook.

The reason for postponing the search until daylight is that it is utterly impossible to detect minute traces of evidence under nighttime conditions. If some larger pieces of evidence are discovered that are not subject to dissolution, they should be covered or secured pending daylight, since their significance can be better realized in connection

Outdoor Crime Scene at Night and in the Daytime. These two photos show the same scene. **A.** Taken at night. **B.** Taken during the daytime. It is obvious that the investigator has a much better chance of locating evidence under daytime conditions.

Outdoor Scene. A detective points out a piece of evidence in an outdoor scene. The evidence is the metal handle of a portable radio, which was taken from the deceased and tossed into a fire by his killers. This homicide took place at night, and a complete search would have been impossible. Instead, preliminary photos were taken of the body before removal and a later search was postponed until daylight. The homicide took place in a wooded section of a public park and is typical of an outdoor crime scene where a search is usually hampered by lighting conditions or weather. In cases like these you are better off if you delay the search until daylight.

with the overall scene. However, if you are faced with a sudden change in the weather, delaying the search until daylight may prove disastrous to the investigation. Obviously, there can be no set procedure to cover all possibilities, so—as in all other aspects of homicide investigation—be flexible and use your common sense.

Physical Examination of a Suspect in Custody

The suspect and his or her clothing should be considered part of the homicide crime scene search. If the suspect is in custody at the scene, he or she should be immediately removed. If the suspect is apprehended a short distance away, he or she should not be allowed to return to the central crime scene. Instead, the suspect should be isolated for a preliminary examination for evidence.

Remember, if a suspect is allowed access to the crime scene, you will negate the value of any evidence found on the suspect which came from the scene, or destroy the value of any evidence imparted by the suspect to the scene.

The examination of the suspect for evidence should be performed by the investigator assigned to the case or by an experienced detective assigned to the crime scene search. The examination must be conducted in a manner that precludes any possible destruction or loss of evidence. In addition, the search for evidence on the person of a suspect requires that the investigator be able to recognize certain materials and marks as related to the actual crime. This ability to recognize and recover trace evidence is a prerequisite to successful search of suspects.

The suspect's clothing and shoes should be closely examined for any trace material from the scene or evidence of the crime. These items should be seized and vouchered as evidence. If the suspect has any visible injuries or marks that might link him or her to the crime, such as bruises, bite marks, scratches, cuts, or injuries on the hands, face, or other parts of the body, photographs should be taken in black-and-white, and color, using a scale or marker.

Many homicides involve a struggle where both participants receive injuries. Color photographs of these injuries, both to the suspect and deceased, are valuable pieces of evidence which can be presented in court.

It is important to note that once a person is under arrest, he or she has no reasonable expectation of privacy. Suspects under arrest can be subjected to a thorough examination and body search. Under certain conditions, if the case warrants, the investigator should have the suspect undress over a clean sheet or large paper to prevent the loss or destruction of any physical evidence on the clothing, and examine the suspect for any injury. Of course, female suspects subjected to body searches should be processed by female officers, and male suspects processed by male officers, in order to avoid any criticism or objection later on.

If patrol officers have been assigned to transport a suspect to the police station, or are assisting in the examination of the suspect for evidence, they should be cautioned to use extreme care and to preserve the suspect's clothing and shoes for examination for trace evidence. Furthermore, they should be instructed not to allow the sus-

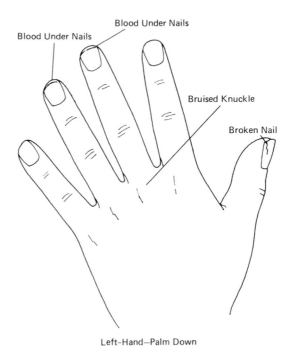

Left-Hand—Palm Down

New Injuries. The suspect's hands indicate new injuries, which he had received during the struggle with the deceased. A simple sketch can be prepared by the investigator either by tracing his own hand or the suspect's hand and then drawing in the locations of injury. This is usually done in connection with a photograph of the suspect's hands.

pect to wash his or her hands nor engage in any activity that may alter or destroy any evidence. I have seen instances where suspects have "cleaned" themselves with urine and spittle to remove blood from their hands or bodies.

When evidence is located on the suspect, the same procedures utilized in other crime scene searches must be applied.

1. Photographs of the evidence *in situ*, and close-ups of the evidence.
2. The evidence should be described and documented in the investigator's notebook.
3. A sketch should be prepared of the area where evidence is found and the location noted on the sketch. This procedure is quite simple. If the evidence is found on the hands, for example, merely trace your own hand (right or left, depending on which hand of the suspect evidence is found) and indicate on the sketch where this evidence is located. The same procedure, without tracing, can be employed for the face and other parts of the body. Use a simple

line drawing of the body part concerned, with appropriate notations.
4. The material should be collected in a manner that preserves its value.

Residue Testing

If the homicide involves a shooting, and the suspect is apprehended within a short time or is in custody at the scene, the investigator may want to consider subjecting the suspect to residue testing. The Trace Metal Detection Test (TMDT) is an examination which determines whether or not a person has been in contact with metal. However, its practicality is questionable, since the touching of any metal may give positive results or may show no results whatsoever.

A more specific type of examination for determining if a person fired a gun is the test for barium and antimony, employing neutron activation analysis. The discharge of a firearm *may* contaminate the shooter's hand with significantly larger amounts of the elements antimony and barium than normally found on an individual who has not fired a weapon. (The contamination results from a "blow-back" of primer residues from the cartridge.)

According to the FBI's *Handbook of Forensic Science*, these residues can be removed for analysis by swabbing the back of the index finger, thumb, and connecting web area of the hand with a moistened cotton swab containing a 5 percent nitric acid solution. It is recommended that two separate swabs be used and that both hands be treated. The swabs should then be placed in separate sealable containers. In addition, a control sample of two moistened swabs not used on the subject should be submitted along with the other swabs to the FBI laboratory for comparison purposes.

In order for the examiner to properly interpret this data from the swabs submitted for analysis, the FBI requests that the following information be provided:

1. A brief resume of the case.
2. The time and date of the shooting.
3. The time and date the hands were swabbed.
4. Location of shooting, i.e., indoors, outdoors.
5. Treatment afforded the suspect, i.e., if wounded, were the hands washed or contaminated in any way during medical treatment?
6. Activity of the subject from arrest until specimens were obtained, i.e., washing of hands, fingerprinting, etc.
7. Description of the firearm used: caliber, type, manufacturer.
8. Brand of ammunition used.

9. Subject right- or left-handed.
10. Subject's occupation.

Practically speaking, this test may have no forensic value at all to your investigation. Although antimony and barium are components customarily found in most primer mixtures, they are also commonly found in nature and may have come from some other source. The problem from an investigative point of view is that most testings are inconclusive in that the examiner cannot positively state that the quantity found is sufficient for determining that a gun was definitely fired by the suspect.

You may want to administer this test, however, in order to preclude any attempt by defense counsel to make an issue of why his or her client was not given this examination. Nevertheless, even if you do subject the suspect to this type of examination and the results are positive, defense counsel could bring in another forensic expert who could dispute the results and challenge your findings based on a different interpretation.

The decision to test or not to test must be determined by the facts of the particular investigation. The investigator should always be aware that residue testing, because of its ambiguous results, can be a two-edged sword that could possibly damage the later prosecution.

Release of the Scene

The decision to release the scene should be carefully considered. Obviously, the problem with releasing the scene prematurely is that soon thereafter information may come forth which would have required different photos or search for and collection of other items. The scene should never be released before the initial canvass is completed, all the known witnesses interviewed, and the suspect in custody questioned fully. In some cases, it may be necessary to secure the scene and post a guard pending interview of witnesses who cannot be immediately located, or in other instances to hold the scene until completion of the autopsy. This may not always be practical, but it is a recommended procedure in case additional examinations or searches are necessary as a result of information obtained during autopsy. Of course, if the autopsy is being conducted while the investigators are still at the scene, any such additional information can be immediately communicated to the chief investigator at the scene. Autopsy findings should always be made available to the homicide investigators as soon as possible to help them in their investigation and in questioning witnesses.

Before releasing the scene, the chief investigator should remember that any good defense attorney will visit the crime scene at his first opportunity. From this inspection he will be able to guage the nature, character, and extent of the investigation at the scene. He will be alert to things which may have been overlooked; to areas which have been dusted and not dusted; to the shape, pattern, and location of blood and other stains; to flash bulbs, film packs, and other debris which the investigators may have carelessly left at the scene. During police activities at the scene the chief investigator should see that all waste materials from the lab work and photography are deposited in one container in a location which will not interfere with other activities, and that this container is removed before the scene is released.

The detective supervisor or chief investigator would do well to check over the whole crime scene from the point of view of the defense attorney before releasing it. Before abandoning the scene and securing it against re-entry, make sure that you have all your equipment and notes, including any portable radios (which seem to have a way of disappearing at crime scenes). It would be embarrassing if you had to break into the recently secured crime scene to retrieve something that was left behind.

Conclusion

The homicide detective and detective supervisor have the responsibility of locating physical and trace evidence and assuring that this evidence is gathered in proper fashion for delivery to the police laboratory. It is up to them to interpret and evaluate the lab results with all the other information developed during the investigation. Hopefully, the total results obtained from the homicide investigation will do what the deceased cannot do, point the finger at the murderer.

Practically speaking, all murders are distinctively different and unique. However, there is one solid base on which to build the case—the determinations you have made from your study of the crime scene and how you apply that knowledge. Keeping in mind the theory of transfer and exchange, you can be sure the minute a killer "does his thing," whether it's a carefully premeditated crime or a spur-of-the-moment impulse, he must go places, handle objects, and move things. The murderer will do this without thinking, either on purpose or by accident. This is the rationale behind a good crime scene search.

Remember, you only have one shot, so do it right the first time.

Selected Reading

Hughes, D.J. *Homicide Investigative Techniques.* Springfield, Illinois: Charles C. Thomas, 1974.

Kirk, Paul L. *Crime Investigation.* New York: John Wiley and Sons, 1974.

O'Hara, Charles E. *Fundamentals of Criminal Investigation,* 5th ed. Springfield, Illinois: Charles C. Thomas, 1980.

Scott, James D. *Investigative Methods.* Reston, Virginia: Reston Publishing Company, Inc., 1978.

Svensson, Arne, Wendel, Otto, and Fisher, Barry A. J. *Techniques of Crime Scene Investigation,* 3rd ed. New York; Elsevier North Holland, Inc., 1981.

Ward, Richard H. *Introduction to Criminal Investigations.* Reading, Massachusetts: Addison-Wesley Publishing Co., 1975.

Estimating Time of Death

9

If the circumstances surrounding death indicate the possibility of homicide, then both the body and immediate surrounding area become crucial in estimating *time of death.* Time is one of the most important factors of consideration in a murder case. It may very well convict a murderer, break an alibi, or eliminate a suspect. Estimating the time of death, especially in cases where there are no witnesses, is critical to the investigation. A good homicide man is going to want to know the time of death in order to establish a foundation for further inquiry.

Time may focus attention on various suspects. For example, the deceased may have had an appointment with someone at a specific time. Or, in cases of "exclusive opportunity" (where only certain persons are present during a specific time, e.g., husband and wife during the evening) if one of those persons is found in nightclothes the following afternoon dead from a beating, and the estimation of time of death places the incident in the range of 3 to 6 A.M., the spouse is sure to be the suspect.

A definite time of death (given by witnesses who noted time) can corroborate or disprove a suspect's alibi.

In civil matters, time may be the factor that determines whether or not an insurance policy was in effect or was void. Most insurance companies include "suicide clauses" in their policies whereby they are released from contract to pay if the insured commits suicide within a specific time, usually within one year after becoming insured. Furthermore, in probating a will, it can be crucial to learn whether the husband or wife died first, since the estate usually goes to the one who expired last.

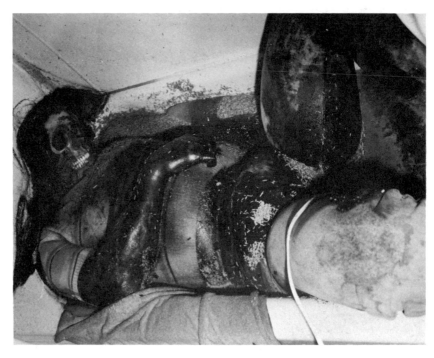

Putrefaction and Insect Activity. These photographs depict the body of a man in a bathtub, fully clothed and lying in the water. The cause of death was electrocution. A hair dryer was found in the tub. This event occurred indoors during the summer time. The body is in an advanced state of decomposition due to the extensive maggot activity.

Throughout the years, forensic scientists and pathologists have searched for a definitive method of determining time of death, yet at present there is no single reliable method. Moreover, it is impossible to fix the exact time of death; hence, we refer to an estimated time. Based on an appreciation of a large number of variables, an experienced pathologist can arrive at a reasonable estimation of time of death; usually placing it within a range of hours. The process is subject to error, especially if some crucial piece of information is omitted. It should be noted, however, that this estimation certainly represents more than just an educated guess. It is a scientifically derived opinion based on a totality of specific factors distinctive to each particular case compared with ordinary time factors attributed to the pathological changes that occur in a human body.

Although the homicide investigator is not expected to have the knowledge of a forensic pathologist, he would certainly do well to have some basic understanding of the postmortem changes that occur

in the human body and the effect of time and atmosphere on the cadaver, on blood pools, and on stains, so that he can make intelligent observations at the scene.

I have found that it is good procedure to take notes of the appearance of the deceased and any blood at the scene so that you can relate to the medical examiner exactly what you observed. The investigator should also interview the first officer for his observations of the scene along with the exact time of his arrival. These observations will be helpful in the analysis of approximate time of death when coupled with the results of the medical examination and autopsy. Generally speaking, the sooner after death a body is found, the more accurate and precise the estimation of time of death. A "fresh" body gives a better time-frame than one which is in advanced putrefaction. However, it is utterly impossible to fix the exact hour and minute that life ceased unless you were there at the moment of death.

The Process of Dying

To understand what takes place in the body after death, one must first have some basic knowledge of the processes that occur in the living body. During life, the systems of the human body have the capacity to maintain themselves by providing oxygen to all the body tissues. In addition, the system provides for the removal of waste products that result from body functions. This is accomplished by the circulation of blood through the arteries and veins. The heart keeps the supply of oxygen continually flowing by its pumping action. As the blood deposits oxygen to the tissues, it picks up the waste products and returns to the lungs where a new supply of oxygen is obtained. During this process, the body is able to defend itself from bacteria and germs within the body. Upon death, however, these bacteria grow at will and begin to release enzymes which dissolve the internal body components. The changes that occur in the dead body are recognized ·as *postmortem decomposition.*

The body begins to decompose from the time of death, in a manner dependent on any number of variables such as temperature, time, location of the body (outdoors, indoors, in soil, in water, in the desert, etc.), humidity, air currents, physical condition, clothing, etc. Externally, insects and animal life may attack the remains so as to further

Putrefaction and Insect Activity. Identification was made through forensic odontology.

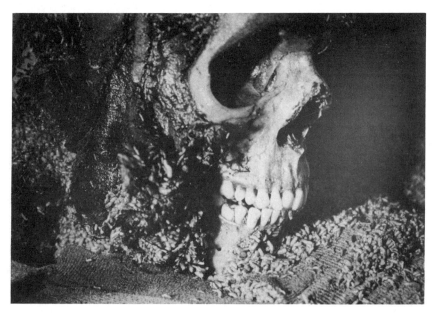

disfigure the body. These changes in the human body result from the same process one observes in an unrefrigerated piece of meat when it rots.

Dying is a process, and estimating the time of death depends on those factors that occur during that process. Death can be said to occur in stages, and a "smart" medical examiner will want to see the scene before he attempts to make any determination about the time of death.

Body Changes After Death

Color. Upon death the heart ceases to function. As a result, the blood and its life-giving properties cease to circulate through the body. As the blood settles into the dependent capillaries of the lower portions of the body, it gives the upper surfaces of the skin a waxy or translucent look. The lips and nails lose their normal pinkish or life-like color.

The blood, which has ceased to circulate, changes from a bright red to a deep purplish color as it loses oxygen. This is apparent even in persons with darker skin. This is the beginning of *lividity*, the pro-

Postmortem Changes in the Body. Notice the lack of postmortem changes over pressure areas. (*Courtesy of* Dr. Dominick J. DiMaio, Former Chief Medical Examiner, City of New York.)

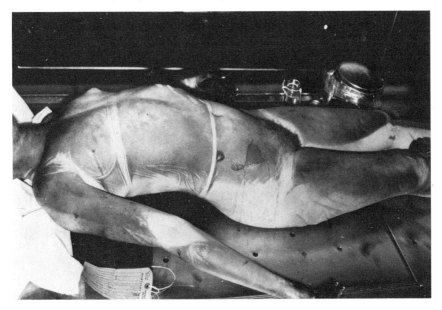

cess whereby the blood settles into dependent capillaries and eventually "fixes" in certain areas of the body.

Eyes. The eyes, which are the most sensitive area of the human body, do not react to light, touch, or pressure in death. The cornea or clear part of the eye becomes slightly milky or cloudy within eight to ten hours after death. In fact, to the experienced observer, the eyes alone will indicate that death has occurred.

Loss of body heat. During life the body maintains an approximate temperature of 98.6 degrees Fahrenheit. After death, the body gives off heat until it becomes the same temperature as the surrounding medium. The rate of cooling can be an important measurement in the estimation of time of death. Body temperature can be taken by rectum with a thermometer to obtain an accurate reading. The environmental temperature should be taken at the same time if the body temperature is to have any meaning. Never take the temperature by inserting a thermometer into a wound; the body, when the wound was received, was probably standing or sitting, not lying face down or in a supine position. If a thermometer or probe is carelessly inserted into the wound, it will probably cause additional damage to the organs or tissues beneath the wound entrance or destroy or distort the *wound track.* In addition, in gunshot cases it may destroy or obscure the ballistics value of a spent round lodged within the *wound track.* From a practical viewpoint, there are "just too damn many" variables that affect the rate of cooling, such as size and amount of fat on the body, clothing, the position of the body (bent upon itself or lying flat on surface), age of the victim, drafts, environmental humidity, etc.— that it is almost impossible to calculate them all. I recommend to investigators who want to get a rough idea of just how long the body has been dead that they place the palm of their hands on a protected surface of the body, such as under the arms. *If the body is warm, death occurred a few hours ago; if the body is cold and clammy, death occurred anywhere between eighteen and twenty-four hours ago.*

Rigor mortis. The process of *rigor mortis* is the result of a stiffening or contraction of the body muscles related to chemical changes occurring within the muscles after death. As a general rule, rigor mortis begins two to four hours after death. Contrary to popular belief, rigor mortis starts at the same time throughout the entire body; however, it is first observed in the jaws and neck. It then seems to progress in a head-to-foot direction and is complete in eight to twelve hours after death. At this stage, the jaws, neck, torso, and upper and

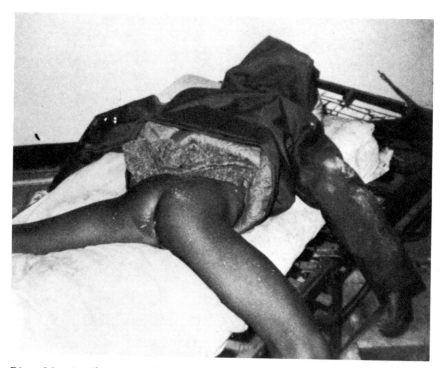

Rigor Mortis. This young boy was found literally "frozen" in the position of assault. He had been brutally sodomized and stabbed to death. Rigor mortis has resulted in "fixing" the body in the position in which it was lying at the time of death.

lower extremities are literally "stiff as a board" and, in this marked state of stiffening, resist any change in position. Rigor "fixes" the body in the position assumed at death. I had one particular case where the body of a young boy who had been brutally murdered and sodomized became literally "frozen" in the position of assault. A body seated in a chair at death will remain in that position, with arms and legs fixed in the position of a seated individual, even after removal.

This complete rigor begins to disappear about eighteen to thirty-six hours after death, and in the average body is completely gone within forty-eight to sixty hours.

A word of caution: this factor is the poorest of the gauges used in estimating time of death because of the many variables involved. The various theories on rigor mortis are loaded with contradiction and misinterpretation. For example, obese people do not always develop rigor, skinny people develop it fast; heat speeds up the process of rigor, while cold retains it; a fight or body shock usually accelerates it;

174

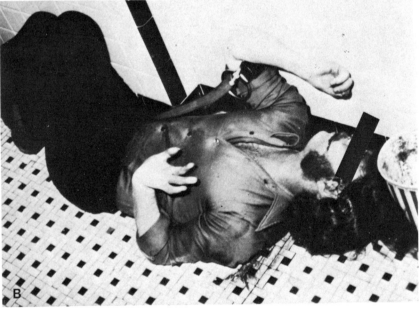

Rigor Mortis and Lividity. The effects of rigor mortis and lividity on the body.
A. The body in the position it was found. **B.** The body after it has been turned
over. Notice the rigidity and discoloration. The victim was an apparent overdose case. Any evidence of drugs or drug paraphernalia at the scene must
be sent with the body to the pathologist for subsequent evaluation.

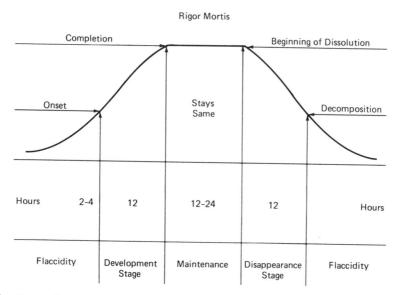

The General Time Elements Involved in Rigor Mortis.

no two bodies even under similar circumstances develop it at the same time, etc.

Practically speaking, if the underarms are warm to the touch and the body is without rigor, death probably occurred less than three hours earlier.

Cadaveric spasm. Under certain conditions the stiffening of the hands or arms may take place immediately at the time of death. This is known as *cadaveric spasm* and is often confused with rigor mortis. It is not uncommon for persons who had a firearm or a knife in their hand at the time of death to clutch it tightly in their hands after death. Also, suicides have been known to have the weapon clutched tightly in their hands after death. It is important from the investigator's point of view to note such clutching of weapons, since you can be sure that the person held this weapon at the time of his or her death. It is impossible to "duplicate" this spasm. For example, a person attempting to place the weapon in the deceased's hand after death cannot get the same type of tight grasp. Cadaveric spasm remains until putrefaction.

Postmortem lividity. Also known as *livor mortis,* this is caused by the pooling and settling of blood within the blood vessels from the effect of gravity. It appears as a purple discoloration of the skin. Dur-

Cadaveric Spasm. The deceased's hand tightly clutches the weapon in cadaveric spasm, which is instantaneous rigor mortis.

Rigor Mortis. Note the rigid body as the officers remove the victim from the water. The cause of death was drowning through traumatic asphyxia. The body is completely "fixed" as a result of the rigor mortis, which is the stiffening of the body's muscles after death. The deceased's arms and legs are as hard as wooden boards.

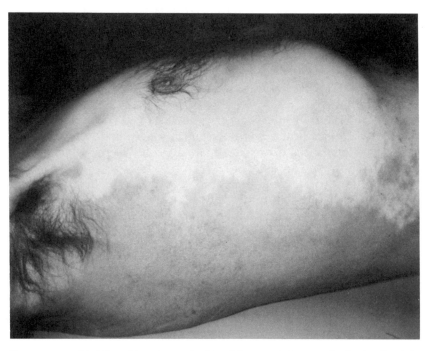

Postmortem Lividity. Note how the blood has settled towards the back of the decedent's body suggesting that the body has lain upon its back after death.

ing life, the pumping action of the heart maintains a constant flow of blood through the numerous vessels of the body. Upon death, this pumping action ceases, and the blood pools within the dependent portions of the body. The location of livor mortis is determined by the position of the body after death. If the body is lying face down, livor will develop on the front of the body rather than on the back. The observation of lividity is important for two reasons: 1) it gives the investigator a general idea how long the body has been dead; 2) it tells you definitely whether or not the body was moved after death. For example, if lividity is observed on the back of the body found lying face down, you can be sure that the body had originally been on its back. Lividity begins about thirty minutes after death and becomes "fixed" in eight to ten hours. *Fixed* means that the livor has settled in one position for more than eight hours and can no longer be significantly shifted by changing the position of the body. However, parts of the body that remain in direct contact with an object, such as the floor, a piece of pipe or wood, or even the weapon, will remain white, as the pressure will not allow the blood to settle into the dependent capillaries.

If when lividity first develops, the investigator presses his finger firmly against the discolored skin, the pressure will cause "blanching." When pressure is released, the discoloration returns. After four or five hours the discoloration becomes clotted and pressure will not cause blanching.

The investigator should know that the discoloration will not be the same for all types of death. For instance, a person whose death was caused by inhalation of carbon monoxide will have a livor mortis which is cherry-red in color. If a person lost a great deal of blood, there will be little or no discoloration; or in cases where death was caused due to heart failure or asphyxia, there will be a deep purple color. These observations should be recorded and the coloration of the lividity evaluated with the later toxicological examination performed at autopsy.

Suppose you have a body that is cool to the touch, rigor has set in in the neck and jaws, and when you press against the lividity it does not blanch. Under ordinary conditions, you can assume that the body has been dead about six to eight hours. Notice I said *ordinary* conditions, and watch the word *assume.*

Remember, you are dealing with tricky circumstances, and even the experienced pathologist will have to weigh all the facts before he attempts an estimate.

Gastrointestinal tract contents. Although commonly referred to as stomach contents, this also includes digested and undigested matter within the entire body. The presence of food particles in the stomach and upper small intestine provides still another source of information to the pathologist regarding time of death. From an investigator's point of view, the presence of food on the table may offer some assistance if the victim maintained a routine eating time. When and what the deceased ate for his last meal is important information for the pathologist who will do the autopsy.

Various ingested food materials remain within the stomach for variable periods of time, depending on the nature and size of the meal. It has been determined through extensive research that under ordinary circumstances the stomach empties its contents four to six hours after a meal. If the stomach, at autopsy, is found to be filled with food, and digestion of the contents not extensive, it is reasonable to assume that death followed shortly after the meal. If the stomach is entirely empty, death probably took place at least four to six hours after the last meal. If the small intestine is also empty, the probability is that death took place at least twelve or more hours after the last meal. In certain cases the medical examiner will be able to determine the type of food which still remains in the stomach, if matched with the last known meal. This can help establish a time period.

Of course this determination will be made by the medical examiner conducting the autopsy. I have been present at many autopsies where the stomach contents were examined and it was quite discernible what foodstuffs were ingested by the deceased prior to his death. In certain cases it is good procedure to obtain a control sample of the food products found at the crime scene, which were apparently eaten by the deceased, for comparison with the stomach contents, especially in cases which involve the possibility of murder by poison or suicide by ingesting toxins or deadly drugs.

Putrefaction. As soon as death occurs, the bacteria or micro-organisms within the intestinal tract escape from the bowel into the other

Putrefaction: Outdoors. Because the weather was cold at the scene, the putrefaction is not as advanced as it would be in warmer weather. However, the body is bloated and the tissues show signs of deterioration.

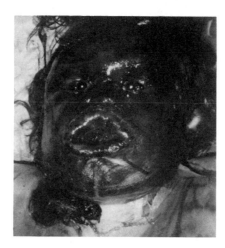

Putrefaction Indoors. (**A**) Note the bloated face of the deceased. This victim's body was found indoors during the summertime. He had been dead for only sixty hours when discovered.

Postmortem Birth. (**B**) Note the dead fetus between the legs of the deceased. The woman, who was 7 months pregnant, died from a heart attack. As the body began to decompose, the putrefactive gases and bloating caused the fetus to descend and the baby was expelled from the mother's womb. (*Courtesy of* Dr. Dominick J. DiMaio, Former Chief Medical Examiner, City of New York.)

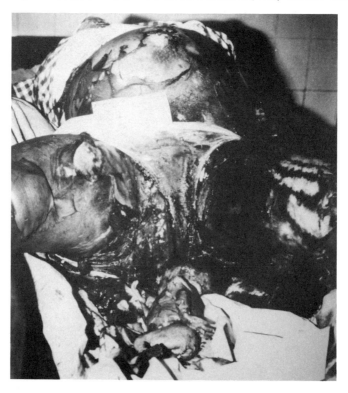

tissues of the body. As they grow, they begin to produce gases and other properties that distort and discolor the tissues of the body. As a result, the body begins to swell. The rate of decomposition depends on the temperature, ground conditions, amount of clothing, size of the body, etc. For example, a body in a warm climate will not only encourage insect attack from the outside, but will also increase the interior bacteria development and subsequent tissue attack from within. As the tissues inside are destroyed and enzymes released, the gases formed emit a foul and sickening smell.

This particular method of determining time of death is very inaccurate because of the variables involved. The putrefactive changes disfigure the facial features making visual identification by relatives impossible. Postmortem changes may also alter the appearance of and may camouflage antimortem injuries. When bloating and darkening occurs, it may be difficult to determine the race and color of the deceased.

Since putrefaction, just like rigor mortis, is subject to a great variation, the estimate will have to be based on other sources derived from both the autopsy and the scene. It has been established that even in deaths occurring as a result of the same cause, with identical environmental conditions, one body showed an advanced state of putrefac-

Marbling. Produced by hemolysis of blood vessels with reaction of hemoglobin and hydrogen sulfide and development of red, purple, or greenish black discoloration along the vessels.

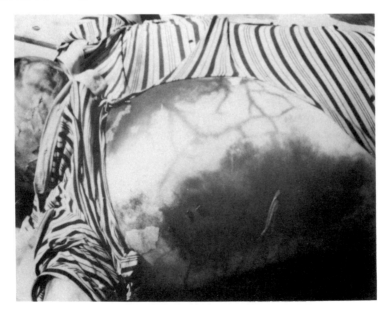

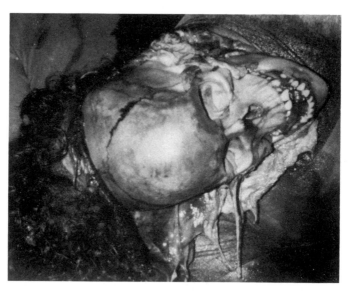

Postmortem Animal Feeding. Bodies are also subject to animal feeding both indoors and outdoors. This woman's face was eaten by the family dog, which increased putrefactive changes to the internal components of the body. You can also observe skin slippage on the woman's scalp, as her hair separates from the skull.

tion while the other showed little change. The general signs of putrefaction are:

1. Greenish discoloration of abdomen and genitals.
2. Veins in skin blue or purplish due to pigment of decomposing blood. (This is referred to as *marbling*.)
3. After the body fluid dries, a yellow parchmentlike membrane forms.
4. After several days:
   a. Abdomen swells, body bloats (from gas).
   b. Fluid emits from mouth and nose (the source being the lungs and stomach).
   c. Rectum may empty.
   d. Skin blisters, resembling peeling sunburn.

Adipocere. This is a greasy, soaplike substance which develops on the surface of a body that has been lying in a moist area such as a swamp or in damp soil. It is due to chemical changes that occur in the body fats—hydrogenation of body fats into fatty acids. It develops mostly in warm weather and usually forms in a few weeks. The material is rancid smelling and floats in water. Adipocere usually covers

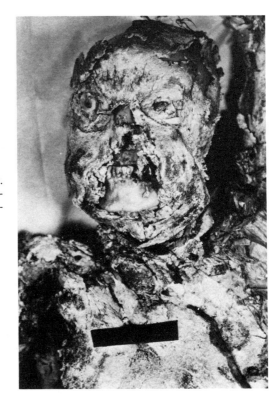

Adipocere. (*Courtesy of* Dr. Leslie I. Lukash, Chief Medical Examiner Nassau County, New York.)

the face and buttocks, but any part of the body can be affected. Where present, the internal organs are usually in good shape, having been dehydrated and mummified in the process.

Mummification. The conditions that produce mummification are the exact opposite of those which cause adipocere. If death occurs in a hot dry place with an adequate and constant circulation of dry air, and body fluids are rapidly absorbed, the body tissues become hard and dry instead of decomposing. The mummification process delays putrefaction, and as a result the form of the body may be preserved for years.

External Agents of Change

Insects

Various insects may eat the flesh of, or lay eggs on, the body of the deceased. Observation of insect larvae can aid in the estimation of time of death. This is an example of the assistance that an *entomol-*

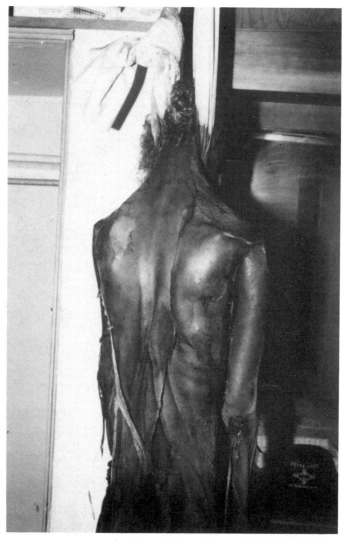

Mummification. In this photo we see the effects of mummification upon a body of a man who hung himself. The mummification was due to the hot and dry climate and circulation of dry air where this death took place. (*Courtesy of* Det. Jerry Fariss Las Cruces, New Mexico Police Department, Criminal Investigations Division.)

ogist—insect expert—can lend to the investigator. Many insects develop from eggs and then progress through growth stages before emerging as adult insects. The time element involved in this developmental stage is rather constant for any given species. For instance, the adult female housefly deposits eggs upon the remains, usually on the eyes, mouth, nostrils, and wounds. These eggs become maggots which then feed off the body. The usual time span for hatching of the maggot is twenty-four hours.

Development time varies among the various species of flies. Temperature and humidity play very important roles in this developmental stage, as do other factors. The larvae may even go into a period of suspended animation if conditions do not warrant further development.

The bluebottle or blowfly is the most common type found on remains discovered outdoors. The investigator at the scene and the medical examiner at the autopsy should collect some specimens for examination by an entomologist. The entomologist can identify the specific insect and provide an estimated time frame based on the stage of growth or development of the larvae. In addition, the experienced entomologist can possibly identify the stage of the life cycle and ultimately the season of the year in which death occurred.

In order to assist the entomologist in making an accurate determination, the following procedure for collection and preservation of specimens is recommended:

1. Collect some maggots from the remains and place them in a KAAD solution. (This is a mixture of kerosene and alcohol along with certain other ingredients for preservation). If this solution is not available, place the sample in hot water first, then in a bottle containing alcohol, and then seal it. The hot water bath will prevent the alcohol from shriveling the sample and maintain the specimen in a condition for examination.
2. Collect some live maggots as a control sample and place them in a separate container.
3. Collect any pupae (hard shell-like casings or cocoons) from around the site, under the body, and from the corpse. Keep the samples separated. The presence of pupae usually provides a minimum time span of approximately two weeks. However, there may be several cycles involved, and the determination should be left up to the entomologist.

Note that the type of maggots found on the body may be significant. For example, the presence of larvae from a housefly found on a body outdoors will indicate that the body had previously lain indoors.

In addition to flies and maggots, a body is also subject to insect attack from different types of beetles and ants and even worms that bore their way into the body. The recommended procedure for collecting all insect samples is to place them in alcohol for preservation.

The forensic entomologist has knowledge of many of the habits of insects and other invertebrates most likely encountered on the corpse and/or in the immediate surroundings of the scene. Seemingly insignificant data to the untrained eye such as insects not found on the body, habitat information, and climatological conditions can be observed by the entomologist. This knowledge enables him to form certain determinations and opinions of how long the body has been at the scene.

In keeping with the team concept of homicide investigation, I recommend that an entomologist, if available, be brought to the scene to assist the investigators. The entomologist's expertise will ensure that proper entomological techniques are employed and the collection of specimens conducted as it should be.

Plants

Bodies found lying on the ground are usually in areas that are abundant with plant life. A competent *botanist* can estimate the age of vegetation found under the body in relation to the vegetation found in the immediate surrounding area. Samples of the sod and vegetation found under the body, as well as a control sample from the immediate area, should be collected for examination.

Remember, keep the two samples in separate containers to prevent any contamination.

The botanist can then examine these samples and may be able to determine how long the body has lain in a particular location. Although this information will not provide an estimate of time of death, it can contribute a relevant time factor to the investigation.

Animals

Bodies are also subject to animal feeding, both indoors and outdoors. Animals feed off the remains of a dead human body just as they feed off any other piece of meat.

Household pets as well as rats and other rodents often attack the body in indoor locations. I investigated one scene in which the deceased's dogs had actually begun to devour the body. Outside locations increase the chances of this occurrence, since many wildlife creatures are carnivorous. Bodies that have been mutilated by domestic and wildlife creatures or insect activity may give an appearance of gross injury, which is not necessarily associated with an antemortem attack. In addition, certain portions of the body may have been carried away or are missing from the cadaver due to animal activity. Practically speaking, investigators must be careful not to jump to any false conclusions based on their initial observations at scenes of this type.

Bodies in Water

Similarly, marine life, especially crabs, are known to nibble on "floaters" or bodies in the water. In addition, movements of the currents and/or contact with marine propellers will further add to disfigurement. These types of postmortem injuries require the knowledge and interpretation of the forensic pathologist, so as not to mistake the injury for one that occurred in life.

From an investigative point of view, the body exposed to the air for one week is equivalent to a body submerged in water for a two-week

Bloated Body of a "Floater." This female body had been in water for approximately one week. Notice the effects of submersion and postmortem changes in the tissue.

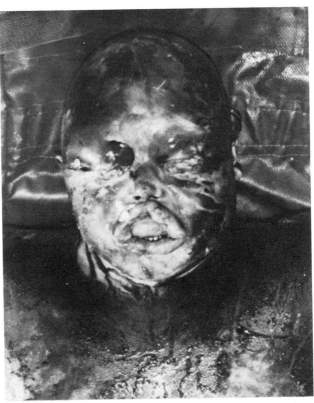

period. The following are some general time spans associated with bodies in water:

hands swollen after several days,

outer layer of skin separated from the body within five to six days, skin of the hand and fingernails separated from the body in eight to ten days,

seaweed vegetation on body within eight to ten days,

floating—in warm water eight to ten days, in cold water two to three weeks.

Information Derived from the Scene

Even though certain pathological changes in the body after death are subject to measurement, the variables involved require additional supportive information before an estimate of time of death can be made. Data obtained by the investigator relative to events associated with the deceased is of utmost importance. This is where the work of the homicide detective really comes into play.

The date and time the deceased was last seen alive gives the detective a starting point to begin the task of narrowing the time of death. The status of the deceased's home or apartment lends additional information—e.g., are there any current newspapers, milk deliveries, mail in the mailbox, dishes in the sink, food on the table, etc.? Are the electric lights on or off? If the lights are burned out, is the light switch in an *on* or *off* position? Are the shades drawn or open?

The detective will want to reconstruct the deceased's last known movements. These would include who spoke to him or her last and where the deceased was prior to being found (at home, at work, with a friend, etc.). The failure of the deceased to perform a daily routine, such as picking up the newspaper, reporting for work, jogging, calling friends or family, or any other personal habit which was routine in his or her life, will also help narrow the time frame.

Another factor to be considered is the weather. For example, if the deceased is found outdoors covered with snow, and the ground beneath is dry, it is important to know what time the snow started in the area. It would be safe to assume that the body was on the ground before the snow fell.

In cases where there has been a struggle and the deceased has a broken watch, or there is a clock in the room that has been damaged, causing it to stop, the time of death can be pinpointed if the investigator can ascertain if the timepiece was in working order prior to death, and if it kept correct time.

Remember, the presence of prepared food on the table may offer assistance in determining time of death if the investigator can ascertain that the victim maintained a routine eating time.

Information derived from the scene as well as knowledge of any personal habits of the deceased will play an important part in the final estimate of time of death.

Conclusion

The estimate of time of death is complex. Before you lock yourself into a specific time frame, it is imperative that all the information available be examined by competent experts. If the time of death tends to fix responsibility for the death, or becomes the factor that points the finger at a particular suspect, then the estimate must be based on positive facts and interpreted by the experienced pathologist.

The physical manifestations of death discussed in this chapter, as well as the autopsy findings, the deceased's personal habits, the medical opinion regarding *survival interval* (the period between the infliction of injury and death), and the statements of witnesses must be taken into consideration in the final analysis.

Therefore, complete cooperation between the experienced homicide investigator and the medical examiner/coroner is essential if there is to be an intelligent estimate of time of death.

Selected Reading

Deickman, Edward A. *Practical Homicide Investigation.* Springfield, Illinois: Charles C. Thomas, 1961.

Harris, Raymond I. *Outline of Death Investigation.* Springfield, Illinois: Charles C. Thomas, 1962.

Hughes, Daniel. *Homicide Investigative Techniques.* Springfield, Illinois: Charles C. Thomas, 1974.

Snyder, LeMoyne. *Homicide Investigation,* 3rd ed. Springfield, Illinois: Charles C. Thomas, 1977.

Spitz, Werner, and Fisher, Russel. *Medicolegal Investigation of Death.* Springfield, Illinois: Charles C. Thomas, 1973.

Svensson, Arne, Wendel, Otto, and Fisher, Barry A. J. *Techniques of Crime Scene Investigation,* 3rd ed. New York: Elsevier North Holland, Inc., 1981.

The Identity of the Deceased

10

The purpose of this chapter is to provide practical information on identifying deceased persons and to assist the homicide investigator in the difficult and often frustrating task of identifying badly decomposed bodies or skeletal remains.

Most deceased persons are readily recognizable to relatives and friends and can be officially identified for law enforcement purposes. Decomposition and dismemberment pose problems, since ordinary means of identification such as photographs and fingerprints are not effective. The criminal investigator should be aware of the contributions forensic experts, such as forensic anthropologists and odontologists, can lend to the process of identification of human remains.

I recommend that the homicide investigator establish personal contact with these forensic people and include them in the investigative team.

Remember, joint contribution to a team effort is not only professional, but effective as well.

The Identification

The identification of the victim is critical because in order to prove a charge of homicide, it must be established that a named or described person is in fact dead. (This verification of death is usually made by a physician; however, in many jurisdictions an ambulance technician's pronouncement of death is sufficient.) Furthermore, from an investigative point of view, identification provides a starting point and direction for the inquiry.

Practically speaking, most homicide victims are killed by someone they knew. Therefore, the identity of the deceased may provide you with motive and establish a clue to the identity of the killer. In addition, even in "stranger-homicides," the identity of the victim will furnish information about his or her movements, which may establish time of occurrence and other information about the crime. Knowing the identity allows the investigator to find out:

the family, spouse, and relatives of the deceased,

the friends, lovers, and neighbors of the deceased,

the residence of the deceased (which will provide additional information about the deceased),

his or her business associates,

whether or not the deceased was involved in criminal enterprise,

where the deceased socialized and locations frequented,

habits and routines of the deceased,

the character of the deceased,

personal information and life style of the deceased, enemies of the deceased (If you know the enemies of the deceased, you can consider one of them—a business competitor, a spouse, a lover, etc.—as a suspect).

Identification at the Scene

Personal Identification

In many cases there are relatives or acquaintances present who will make an identification to the police at the scene. Usually this identification will be sufficient for investigative purposes, pending official identification by some member of the family to the medical examiner or coroner. The investigator, however, should still pursue established practices of identification. The body should be photographed, a complete description of the body and clothing should be obtained, information relative to medical and dental data should be gathered, and a request for blood-typing at autopsy should be made. In addition, all dead bodies, especially in homicide cases, must be fingerprinted.

I recall a case which took place in another jurisdiction, north of New York City. A suspect was shot and killed during a narcotics rip-off by the would-be victims. The police who had responded to the shooting arrested the would-be victims and a female accomplice of the dead man, and seized a gun as well as other evidence. The woman gave the police a fictitious name for the deceased. Although fingerprints were taken during the autopsy, they were mistakenly put in the dead file under the fictitious name. No record check was ever made. However, a separate investigation by New York City police was undertaken because the gun used in the aborted stickup was the same caliber as one used in three New York City homicides during similar rip-offs. An additional set of prints was taken by the City detectives for comparison with latents obtained during the homicide investigations, and a record check was conducted at New York City Bureau of Criminal Identification. The gun was also subjected to ballistics tests in New York City and was positively identified as the same weapon used in the three homicides. The record checks revealed that the dead suspect was not the person named by his accomplice, but was in fact a wanted escapee who had already been identified as a murder suspect along with his female partner. The female accomplice had purposely misled police in an attempt to avoid identification. Her ruse would have worked, had it not been for the second fingerprint record check. Although she gained temporary freedom, she was rearrested in New York and subsequently indicted for murder on the three outstanding homicide cases. The original prints should never have been simply filed before a record check.

Obviously, an oversight such as this can result in a wrong identification, and identity should be positively established before the body is released and the case closed.

Clothing and Possessions

The clothes and possessions—such as driver's license, social security card, and I.D. card—of the deceased are the best sources of tentative identification at the scene. The pockets of the deceased should be searched for any other material documents or photos. This information and a Polaroid picture of the deceased, if the body is in good condition, can be utilized by investigators to attempt to locate family or friends and verify identity. The clothing should be preserved for future identification.

Identification by Photographs

If the body is in good condition, a color photograph should be taken of the face. A full facial shot and a profile as well as detailed pictures of any tattoos, scars, and the ears (which are distinctive) should be obtained. If the body is found indoors and there are photos of the deceased therein, they should be retrieved and duplicated with a 1 × 1 fingerprint camera and distributed to the investigators doing the canvass.

Remember, the body should be photographed before autopsy with and without clothes.

This should be done even in cases where the body is in decomposition. In addition, x-rays should be taken of unidentified bodies since there may be medical records available which can be used to make an identification. I recall a case where the headless and handless bodies of two young women were found in a midtown motel. The murderer had poured a flammable liquid over the bodies and set them on fire in an attempt to prevent identification. Extensive medical and pathological efforts were employed to established identity. The autopsy revealed a three-inch surgical scar on the abdomen of one of the victims. This scar eventually provided police with the identity of the victim, a twenty-two-year-old prostitute. The killer was eventually caught after he committed a series of similar mutilation-sex killings in the metropolitan area. However, the key to his involvement in the New York City killings was the identity of the torso. A search warrant was obtained for the suspect's residence, and items belonging to the twenty-two-year-old victim were found in his home.

Description of the Body

A complete description of the body should be obtained, with emphasis on any deformities, markings, abnormalities, and distinctive traits. The ears make a good identifying feature, because even in the event of decomposition and other changes they remain the same. The following information should be obtained if possible.

1. Name (if papers or documents indicate name—tentative only)
2. Sex
3. Age (date of birth if available or estimated age)
4. Race, color, and nationality
5. Length or height
6. Build (be careful in cases of decomposition)
7. Shape of face (square, round)
8. Neck (thin, large, adam's apple, etc.)
9. Hair (color, length, type—curly or kinky, wavy or straight)
10. Beard or moustaches
11. Forehead (high, protruding, receding hair line, etc.)
12. Eyebrows, eyes, lashes (bushy, thin, fake, etc.)
13. Ears (cauliflower, large, small, deformed, etc.)
14. Nose (small, large, base of nose)
15. Chin, jaw (protruding, receding, square, round, etc.)
16. Mouth, teeth (condition of teeth, missing, spaces, size of lips, etc.)

17. Lips (thin or thick)—note decomposition
18. Hands (small, large, rough or smooth, etc.)
19. Fingers (long or short, marks of any rings, jewelry, etc.)
20. Feet (big, small, shoes, etc.).

Clothing

Clothing should be examined for identification marks. The use of laundry marks and dry-cleaning tags by commercial cleaners can be traced to specific locations. In addition, there are manufacturers' marks and, in some instances, serial numbers for valuable items.

Jewelry and Watches

Most items of jewelry are quite distinctive and may contain inscriptions or jewelers' marks. In addition, there are wear patterns that are distinctive to certain items, and the rare "special piece" that can be identified as belonging to a certain individual.

The more expensive watches can be traced to their source of retail sale, and, if the watch was worked on by a watchmaker or jeweler, the item will usually have some marking which will identify the particular craftsman.

In the absence of fingerprint and/or positive identification, the investigator should attempt to obtain as much information as possible from the clothing, jewelry, body, and material found in the pockets, as well as photographs, with a view toward publication of this information in local papers and on radio and television. Many identifications have been obtained with appeals to the public for information.

I remember one case in which the body of a young woman was found dead in the wooded area of a park. The women had apparently been shot, "execution style." The body was stripped of all identification except jewelry. One of the pieces of jewelry was quite distinctive. It consisted of a caricature of a devil's head with two diamond eyes and ruby mouth. This item and five or six other pieces of jewelry were carefully described, as was the body and clothing of the deceased. The description was given to the press, with a request for anyone with information to please call the police. Twenty-four hours later we received a call, based on the description of the devil ring. A positive identification was obtained and the case continued.

Fingerprints

The fingerprints of the deceased matched with fingerprint records on file provide positive identification. If the victim does not have fingerprints on file, the comparison and match of the deceased's prints with latent prints taken from the dead person's home or place of employment is sufficient to prove identity. In the absence of identification by immediate family, fingerprint records represent conclusive evidence of identity.

The circumstances of death and the condition of the body usually determine whether or not good fingerprints can be obtained. The methods utilized to obtain prints from dead bodies range from the simple to the complex.

Obtaining Fingerprints from Dead Bodies

A standard fingerprint card, preferably a thin one, can be cut into two strips, one strip for each set of five. The fingers are inked either with a roller or pad. Each inked finger is then placed on the strip in the corresponding box. The strip is held in a curved holder or spoon. The finger is pressed against the strip and an impression is obtained.

If there is rigidity in the fingers, the joints can be bent back and forth several times until they are sufficiently flexible. You may have to take several prints before you get a good impression. Select the best impression and paste this on the respective section of the fingerprint card.

Remember, be careful not to mix up the prints.

In cases where the skin is dried out or shriveled up, as in mummification, the fingers are amputated and immersed in a softening solution or water for several days until the skin softens. Each finger is placed in a separate bottle and each bottle is numbered 1 through 5 for each hand. It is imperative that these fingers not be mixed up. This procedure should not be undertaken without the permission of the medical examiner, who usually will do the cutting. The examination will be performed by a technician or laboratory.

If the fingers have been immersed in water or the body is that of a "floater," a fingerprint technician or expert is the best person to attempt to obtain prints. There are various procedures employed, depending on the condition of the body. If the fingers are shriveled or wrinkled, but the skin is still intact, a print can be obtained by filling out the finger, injecting water under the skin until the finger's normal contour has been restored. The best instrument for this procedure is a hypodermic syringe with a fine needle so as not to break the skin. It is recommended that a string be tied around the finger directly above the hole after injecting the water to prevent the fluid from leaking out. Also, the point should not be too close to the skin since the pressure may break the skin.

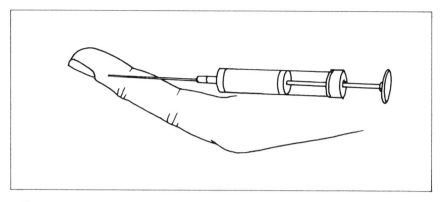

Filling Out a Finger. Injection of water into a finger, which has become shriveled or wrinkled, so that the fingerprints can be obtained. It is recommended that the fluid be injected to restore the finger's normal contour and that a string be tied above the needle hole to prevent the water from leaking out.

Skin Separating from the Hand. This "floater" was removed from one of New York City's rivers. In some instances, the entire outer layer of skin from the hand can be removed intact.

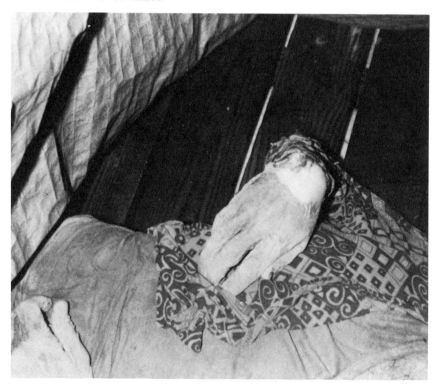

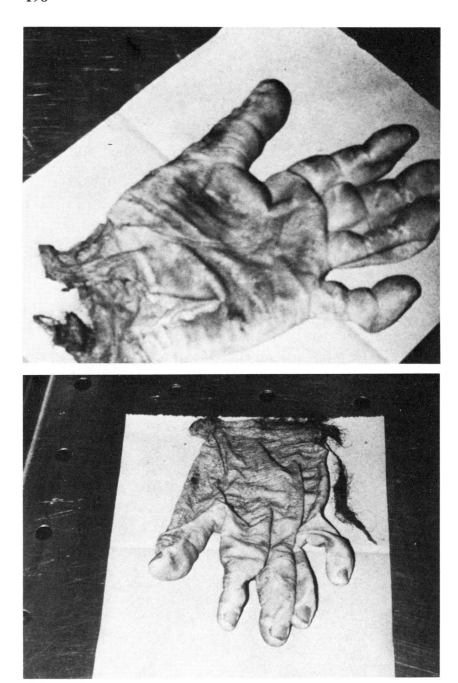

Skin Removed from the Hand. Here the entire epidermis of the hand has been removed intact from the body of a "floater." A fingerprint technician will be able to effectively obtain prints from this fragile tissue.

Sometimes the skin will be so loose that it will come off the hand like a glove and can be cut away from the fingers. Each tip should be placed in a separate test tube, so as not to mix up the prints. The tubes can then be sealed with water and sent to the FBI Laboratory for examination.

In certain cases, the technician can remove the skin and place it over his own finger (wearing a thin surgical glove), and "roll" the skin as if it was his or her own finger. Another method used to obtain prints is by brushing black fingerprint powder on the fingers and removing the impression by "lifting" the print with transparent fingerprint tape. The tape is then placed on the fingerprint card in the respective box.

Remember, once again, be careful not to mix up the fingers or prints and place the proper lift in the right box.

Advanced decomposition will necessitate special lab techniques, the use of photography with side lighting to emphasize ridge patterns, and more sophisticated procedures that are beyond the capability of the ordinary investigator.

Fingerprint impressions and finger stalls can be sent to the FBI Laboratory for identification by mailing as follows:

Director
Federal Bureau of Investigation
10th and Pennsylvania Avenue, N.W.
Washington, D. C. 20537

Attention: Identification Division, Latent Print Section.

The Teeth

Dentition provides an excellent means of identification, especially when antemortem records and x-rays of the deceased are available for comparison. Forensic odontology—the scientific application of dentistry to legal matters—has become a viable asset to the law enforcement community. According to Dr. Levine,[1] a small but growing nucleus of dentists in this country today have been trained to respond to the needs of law enforcement officers, the legal profession, and forensic pathologists.

Forensic odontologists work on problems involving identification,

---

[1]Dr. Lowell J. Levine is President of the American Academy of Forensic Sciences and Consultant to the New York City and Nassau County Medical Examiner's Office.

bite marks, and dental and oral injuries. In addition, they are invaluable in the identification of bodies in mass disasters, where the only semblance of human remains may be a jaw fragment, shattered teeth, or broken dentures.

As a result of modern dental procedures involving restoration such as tooth capping and root canal work, dentists have made extensive use of x-rays and molds, both of which are accurate records of oral anatomy. Fillings and caps are highly individual, and jawbone construction provides information based on certain anatomical landmarks that never change in an individual.

Practically speaking, in cases where the remains have been badly mutilated or burned, are in advanced putrefaction, or have been submerged in water for a long period of time, etc., the possibility of obtaining any fingerprints of value is quite remote. This is where the forensic odontologist can be of assistance. Using powerful cameras, x-rays, and medical records, he or she can, through examination of the dentition and jawbones of the deceased, provide the investigator with information about the deceased, including age, general facial characteristics, race, socioeconomic group, occupation or habits, positive identification, and bite-mark identification.

Age

The eruption of teeth in the human body is a relatively predictable process during the early years of growth. The forensic odontologist can provide a rather accurate estimate of age of persons under fourteen. The first teeth, referred to as baby teeth or deciduous teeth, make their appearance from seven months to two years. The loss of these baby teeth and the eruption of the first permanent molars begins at approximately five years of age and continues into the early teens. After age fourteen, the forensic odontologist relies on the wear patterns. As a general rule, the older a person becomes, the more his or her teeth show evidence of wear, dental repair, and gum recession. The forensic odontologist, using microscopic and radiological (x-ray) examination of dentition, can estimate the age of an adult within five years' accuracy. Estimates of age for the prepubertal child can be calculated within six months by examining the stage of development of the permanent tooth buds.

General Facial Characteristics

By comparing certain aspects of the configuration of teeth and jaws, a forensic odontologist can roughly determine the shape of the face. According to certain experts there are three basic shape formations,

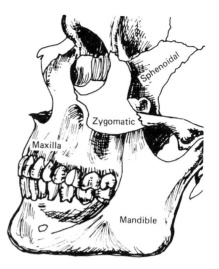

Normal Anatomic Position
of the Teeth and Jaws.

square, tapering, and ovoid. These computations, however, are not infallible and are subject to different interpretations.

An important factor used in arriving at facial contour is the positions, the lower front teeth fit inside the upper front teeth and are in direct contact with the upper teeth. The exceptions to this rule can help in identifying facial features. The following are possible conditions:

1. Normal anatomical position.
2. Overbite: In this case, the lower teeth fail to meet the upper front teeth because of a protruding upper jaw. This results in an over-prominence of the upper jaw, accompanied by an underprominence of the lower jaw, resulting in a receding chin. This is commonly referred to as the "Andy Gump" look.
3. Prognathic: In this case, the lower teeth protrude beyond the upper teeth. The lower jaw and chin are excessively prominent. This is referred to as the "Fearless Fosdick" look.

It should be noted that there are now operations whereby these abnormalities can be corrected, resulting in drastic changes in profile. These procedures are known as orthognathic surgery.

Race

The forensic odontologist can sometimes determine the race of the deceased by examination of the jawbones and teeth. There are certain anthropological traits within races which make such a determination possible. However, with mixed races it is extremely difficult. From a practical point of view, the investigator would obtain a more definite determination from the physical anthropologist, who may even have to utilize a computer.

Socioeconomic Group

The socioeconomic group and relative economic status of a person may be estimated by the quality of dental treatment he or she obtained in life. The forensic odontologist bases his determination on the general oral hygiene of the deceased and the manner and type of dental restoration. For instance, missing teeth which have not been replaced, unfilled cavities, and a generally poor dentition would indicate a low economic status. On the contrary, gold inlays, root canal work, and prostheses such as well-made bridgework and dentures indicate that the individual was able to afford good dental treatment. Expensive dental work is readily observable to the odontologist during examination.

Occupation or Habits

In some instances, habits of the deceased which have caused dental change will be noted during a forensic examination. For example, the holding of nails between the teeth, which is a habit of carpenters, or the playing of certain musical instruments, like the trumpet, causes a distinctive type of wear which may provide a clue as to occupation. Furthermore, habits such as holding a pipe between the teeth or long-time cigar smoking will be evidenced by both wear patterns and heavy tar accumulation.

Positive Identification

Practically speaking, this is the most valuable information which can be learned from an examination of the teeth. Forensic odontology is probably the most effective means available to the investigator for arriving at a positive identification in cases where fingerprints are unobtainable or there are no matchable fingerprints of the deceased on file.

It should be noted that no two sets of teeth are exactly alike. A full complement of teeth is thirty-two. Each tooth has five surfaces, with various fissures and grooves. The arrangement of the teeth within the jaw is different for each person. In addition, there are individual differences in the arch of the palate and the mode of occlusion (bite).

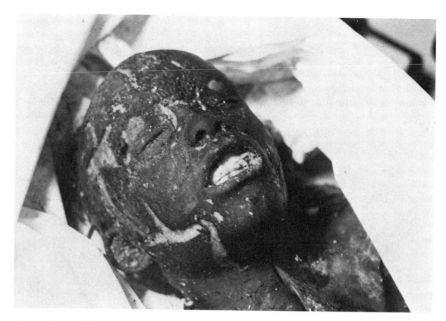

Arson-Homicide Victim. A 6-year old boy was burned beyond recognition. Positive identification was obtained from teeth. (*Courtesy of* Dr. Arthur D. Goldman, Forensic Odontologist.)

X-rays of Victim's Teeth. **A.** X-rays are postmortem. **B.** X-rays are antemortem. Identification was based on the shapes of crowns and root form. (*Courtesy of* Dr. Goldman, Forensic Odontologist.)

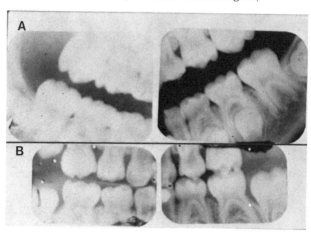

Add to these individual physiological differences the many types of dental operations, such as caps, fillings, root canal work, crowns, dentures, prostheses, and other surgical procedures, and one realizes that the teeth are quite distinctive. In fact, there are literally thousands of identifying characteristics of teeth.

Modern equipment utilized by dentists today, specifically the high-speed, air-driven handpiece, has allowed dentists to undertake many more sophisticated dental treatments and operations. These advanced procedures have created the need for comprehensive dental examinations, involving x-rays and molds of teeth, both of which are highly accurate and individualized. In addition, all dentures have manufacturers' brands that may be traced to a specific dental laboratory in a specific area. In some instances, the dentist will personalize the appliance by engraving the patient's name or social security number on the denture. When attempting to identify an edentulous (toothless) person, the forensic odontologist will take an impression of the palate and upper arch, since the palate's anatomical form and characteristics are distinct. In addition, even an old denture may prove useful in identification procedures. If the investigator can locate this denture, it can be examined by the odontologist. Many people are like "pack rats" and save even the most useless articles; so too do wearers of dentures. Often an investigator who needs to locate an old denture for identification purposes will be surprised to find two or three such appliances.

Military service and private and governmental insurance programs have made dental services available to most of our population. Since comprehensive dental examinations are mandatory prior to treat-

Engraved Denture. This Denture has been engraved by the dentist. The denture, along with antemortem records, led to the identification of the victim who had been kidnapped and slain. (*Courtesy of* Dr. Goldman, Forensic Odontologist.)

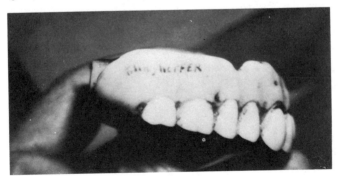

ment, a wealth of dental information on our citizens is now in the hands of the dental profession, insurance companies, and government agencies.

If the investigator can locate the dental records of the deceased, the forensic odontologist can make an absolute and positive identification. It is for this reason that experts in the field of odontology recommend the data banking of dental information by computer. This knowledge would certainly aid in the identification of unknown homicide victims and greatly assist in the tremendous job of identifying bodies in mass disasters.

Bite-Mark Identification

This particular phase of forensic odontology will be discussed in more detail in another section (see Chapter 15, "Bite-Mark Identification"). However, as a practical matter, the investigator who is at the scene of a homicide where teeth either have been used as a weapon, or the body indicates that the murderer may have assaulted the victim by inflicting bite marks, must view these wounds as evidence. Bite marks are specific to the person who has inflicted them. In addition, saliva washings should be obtained for later serological comparison. It is important to note, however, that these washings must take place before the lapse of too much time.

I recommend that the investigator, using a 1 × 1 fingerprint camera, or a 35mm camera with color film, obtain photos of these marks. Side lighting is sometimes useful to accent the marks. In addition, a scale should be included in the photo to assist the experts in their later examination and comparison of the bite marks and evaluation of any impressions obtained from possible suspects.

Inquiries Relative to Forensic Odontology

There is a national organization of forensic odontologists where investigators may request information or obtain the location of an odontologist within his or her specific geographic area. The address is:

The American Board of Forensic Odontology, Inc.
Administrative Office: The Forensic Sciences Foundation
11400 Rockville Pike
Rockville, Maryland 20852

In addition, I have corresponded with Dr. H.R. Campbell, DDS, who is Secretary of the American Board of Forensic Odontology. He processes many requests for listings of current certified diplomats to various law enforcement agencies. He can be reached at the following address:

6800-C Montgomery NE
Albuquerque, N.M. 87109

The Bones

The examination of skeletal remains by a physical anthropologist can provide certain basic classifications which may assist police in determining the identity of the deceased. Depending upon the completeness and condition of these skeletal remains, the forensic examination can supply the age of the deceased at the time of death, as well as his or her sex, race, height, and other individual characteristics such as, right- or left-handedness, overweight or underweight, well or poorly developed musculature, and, prior bone injuries. The exami-

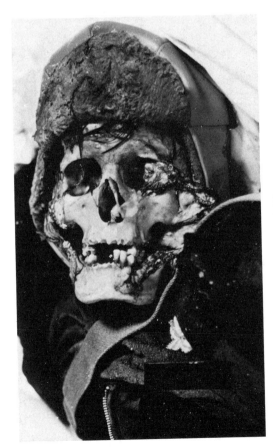

Skeletal Remains of a Body Found Outdoors. (*Courtesy of* Dr. Leslie I. Lukash, Chief Medical Examiner, Nassau County, New York.)

nation can also determine the cause of death in certain cases, and ascertain whether the bones are human or animal.

Estimates of age, sex, race, and stature do not provide positive identification of an individual. However, they become an integral part of the identification process when compared with unique characteristics and matchable records of the deceased made in life. An example of such records, which would yield positive identification, are medical records (operations, births, amputations, etc.), dental records, and antemortem x-rays.

The investigator, armed with the information provided by the anthropologist's examination of skeletal remains, now has a general description of the deceased which can be compared with missing persons reports, registered ownership records if there is property involved, and official records.

Age

A trained radiologist and physical anthropologist can provide an estimate of age, based on skeletal remains, which ranges from somewhat unpredictable to considerably accurate depending on the age of the deceased. After age thirty the reliability of the formulas used by scientists to gauge age decreases, and tooth structure gives a better estimate of age than do the gross bones after that age.

Anthropologists use formulas based on the *epiphyses* of bones (the stage of uniting of bones, a condition which varies with age) to make their determinations.

Basically, science has determined that the bones develop from small areas known as *ossification centers*. These ossification centers produce calcium and other minerals which are deposited to form bone. Many of the ossification centers start their production during the early months of fetal life, while others do not completely finish producing bone until the early twenties. Anthropologists have worked out a series of formulas to estimate age based on the appearance of these different ossification centers. X-ray examination can with considerable accuracy determine age up to twenty-five years.

Another determining factor in estimating age is the skull. The skull is composed of several curved bones joined together along irregular lines called *sutures*. As an individual approaches the early twenties, these sutures begin to fill up with bone and close. This process continues with age and follows a distinct pattern. Anthropological studies of these patterns resulted in the establishment of a formula whereby scientists could determine the age of an individual by examination of the skull. Suture closing, however, is not as reliable as first predicted. Instead, scientists have developed a new scheme,

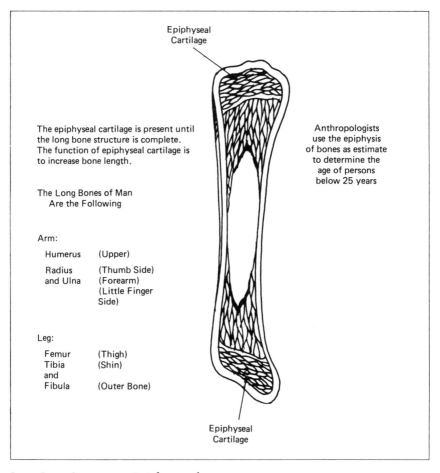

Epiphyseal
Cartilage

The epiphyseal cartilage is present until
the long bone structure is complete.
The function of epiphyseal cartilage is
to increase bone length.

Anthropologists
use the epiphysis
of bones as estimate
to determine the
age of persons
below 25 years

The Long Bones of Man
Are the Following

Arm:

Humerus (Upper)

Radius (Thumb Side)
and Ulna (Forearm)
(Little Finger
Side)

Leg:

Femur (Thigh)
Tibia (Shin)
and
Fibula (Outer Bone)

Epiphyseal
Cartilage

Long Bone Structure—Epiphysis of Bone

which yields both an estimate of age and an error of estimate. Most estimates of age for remains of persons between thirty and eighty years of age are given in seven-to-ten-year brackets.

The pelvic bone can also be used to determine age. There are various changes in the structure of the bone which occur within approximately five-year intervals.

In addition, there are studies that indicate that calcification begins in the cartilages of the larynx and ribs at about fifty-five years of age, and that males in the age bracket of thirty-five to forty show a presence of arthritic lipping in certain joints, especially in the vertebral column. At present, research is being conducted on calculating age based on spectrographic evaluation of bone particles, a procedure still under evaluation.

Although the criminal investigator need not comprehend the technical aspects of these anthropological computations, he would do well to be aware of their value in the identification process.

Sex

If an anthropologist has the whole skeleton to examine, sex can be determined with 90 percent accuracy. Male skeletons are larger than female skeletons, and the bone surfaces of the male are rougher than those of the female. The pelvic bone, however, is the most accurate indicator of sex. Since the female pelvis is designed for childbearing, its difference is readily observable to the trained eye of the anthropologist. Scars of parturition on the pelvic bone not only help to determine sex, but can also provide evidence that the deceased has borne one or more children.

In addition, anthropologists now have a variety of metrical techniques, such as the *ischium-pubis index*, to assist them in determining sex.

Male and Female Pelvis. The pelvis bone is the most accurate indicator of sex. If you look closely at the two drawings below, you may observe the different structure between male and female pelvis. Of course, to the trained eye of the anthropologist the differences are readably discernible.

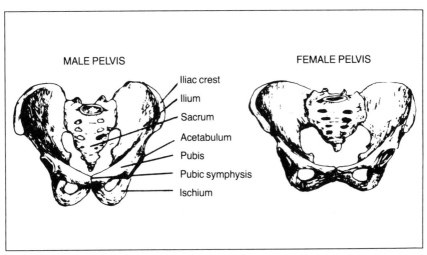

MALE PELVIS   FEMALE PELVIS

Iliac crest

Ilium

Sacrum

Acetabulum

Pubis

Pubic symphysis

Ischium

Race

Through the application of sophisticated statistical procedures to skull dimensions, anthropologists can now determine the race of the skeletal remains. Because of the number of mixed racial heritages in this country, the variables are considerable and a computer is often used to sort out all the information. Determining the race of an individual utilizing the skull is almost without error. However, without the skull the possibility for error drastically increases.

Height and Other Individual Characteristics

In determining height, several different formulas have been devised based on the measurement of the long bones. The most accurate method is based on the measurement of the long bones compared with a simple table. While there is some slight variation in different races, the height can in general, be determined within an inch of accuracy.

The anthropologist can determine whether the person was overweight or emaciated, and, by examining the muscle attachments to the bone, whether the remains are from a muscularly well developed person. In addition, the skeleton reveals whether or not the person was right- or left-handed, since the bones of the dominant arm are slightly longer. Certain characteristics of the *scapula* (shoulder blade) and *clavicle* (collarbone) also help to determine handedness.

The bones will readily indicate whether or not there has been past trauma such as a fracture. If the antemortem x-rays can be obtained, this information will provide positive identification of the deceased.

Determination of Cause of Death

In some instances, the bones will readily reveal the cause of death. For instance, the skull is most likely to yield important evidence of direct violence in gunshot cases or direct blunt force injuries. The penetration of a bullet through the skull will be easily recognizable from its telltale pattern. Likewise, evidence of injuries to the skull or other bones by a hammer, crowbar, or other weapon will be evident upon examination. In addition, if a person died as a result of one of the metallic poisons, the poison can still be extracted from the bones years later.

Determination of Whether the Bones
Are Human or Animal

The first two questions in identifying unknown skeletal remains are: 1) Are they human? and 2) Is more than one person or animal represented? A complete human skull is readily identifiable as human. However, the investigator may be confronted with pieces of broken jaw, bone fragments, teeth, or other parts of a skeleton. Practically speaking, law enforcement personnel should consider all pieces of skeleton human until experts determine otherwise. For example, parts of bear paws are misidentified more often as human than any other animal. In addition, many animal skeletons lacking the telltale skull have been thought to be those of a small child. I remember one incident in the South Bronx that confused the hell out of the police. A body of an apparently nude, decapitated male was found lying in the gutter. The body weighed about 300 pounds. The case was reported as a "possible homicide." Although this was not a skeleton, I bring this case to your attention because upon medical examination at the scene it was discovered to be the body of a full-grown skinned gorilla!

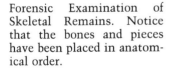

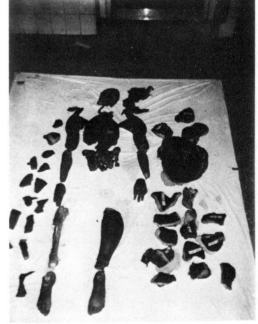

Forensic Examination of Skeletal Remains. Notice that the bones and pieces have been placed in anatomical order.

Often bones or remains can fool people. Therefore, it is imperative that the investigator suspect each case to be human until proven otherwise.

Examination of the Bones

The examination of the bones should be performed by the forensic experts, particularly the physical anthropologist, the radiologist, and the forensic odontologist. Although this phase is beyond the skill of the criminal investigator, it is the investigator who will set the stage for the successful evaluation of this evidence by following certain preliminary procedures. These include photographing and sketching the remains before moving them, consulting with the medical examiner and anthropologist for any instructions, and, if there is more than one skeleton, keeping the parts separate and assigning them in consecutive numbers.

Facial Reconstruction

Facial reconstruction from the skull is a method sometimes used in forensic anthropology to identify skeletal remains. In fact, according to Dr. Harry L. Shapiro, Curator Emeritus of the Anthropology Department of The American Museum of Natural History, facial reconstruction is a procedure that has been used for years by anthropologists to recreate general physiological features of an individual based on information derived from skeletal remains. Although, the physical anthropologist can arrive at an osteo-biography of an individual based on the examination of the bones, Doctor Shapiro is quick to caution the investigator that determination of individuality based on these findings is subject to error. As he points out in his own reconstruction of a skull called "The Peking Man," the reconstruction is an approximation of what a general or nonspecific Peking Man looked like. Doctor Shapiro contends that arriving at an individual or specific face based on examination of the skull and bones leaves too much margin of error because the soft-tissue features—such as shape of eyelids, mouth width, lip thickness, lower part of the nose, and ears—are not necessarily indicated by the skull's shape. However, there is a relatively new process of facial reconstruction which combines both the science of anthropology and artistic judgment based on anatomical knowledge and experience. It is called forensic sculpture.

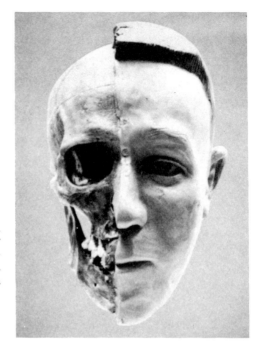

Facial Reconstruction. This restoration technique is employed in forensic anthropology to recreate an identity from a human skull. This particular restoration was created by Ms Betty Pat. Gatliff, Forensic Sculptor and her associate, Dr. Clyde C. Snow, Ph.D. Physical Anthropologist. (*Reprinted with permission from* Ms Betty Pat. Gatliff Skullpture, Inc., 1026 Leslie Lane Norman, Oklahoma 73069 and Mr Mark Weaver, Public Affairs Officer AAC-5, Federal Aviation Administration, P.O. Box 25082 Oklahoma City, Oklahoma 73125.)

Forensic Sculpture

Forensic sculpture—the creation of an identity out of skeletal remains—is a specialty that combines both art and science. Practically speaking, it should be employed only after all other means of identification have proven fruitless.

In fact, Ms. Betty Gatliff, a forensic sculptor, and her associate Dr. Clyde C. Snow, a physical anthropologist, both of whom pioneered work on facial reconstruction, are more than candid in their evaluation and recommendations of their method.[2] They advise that facial reconstruction be employed only as a last-ditch effort by law enforcement authorities. However, by the same token, they report a 70 percent success rate on the reconstructions they have created.

The forensic sculptor and the physical anthropologist collaborate to construct the facial features of the unknown skeletal remains on the basis of the underlying cranial architecture. First, the anthropologist examines the skull to determine sex, race, and approximate age. This information is important because the depths of the soft tissue of the

---

[2]These practitioners can be reached through Skullpture, Inc., 1026 Leslie Lane, Norman, Oklahoma 73069.

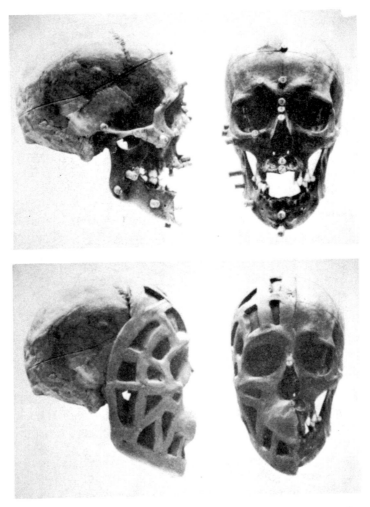

Facial Reconstruction. (*Reprinted with permission from* Ms Betty Pat. Gatliff Skullpture, Inc., 1026 Leslie Lane Norman, Oklahoma 73069 and Mr Mark Weaver, Public Affairs Officer AAC-5, Federal Aviation Administration, P.O. Box 25082 Oklahoma City, Oklahoma 73125.)

face are different in males and females and in the three major racial groups; Mongoloid, Caucasoid, and Negroid. The anthropologist looks for evidence of individual anatomical peculiarities, diseases, or injuries that could influence a person's facial features during life. Depending on the completeness of the skeleton, the anthropologist will be able to determine whether the deceased was fat or thin and if the

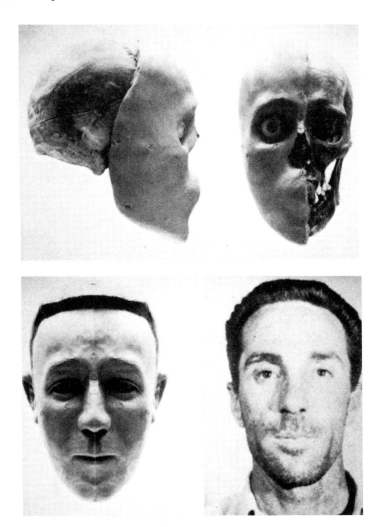

person was muscular. In addition, both the anthropologist and the sculptor will want to see any clothing or other items which may provide clues as to hair color and style.

Armed with the anthropological information, the sculptor begins the reconstruction by placing small blocks or cylinders which correspond to the average thickness of the soft tissue over certain bony

81-10 HUMAN SKELETON FROM STONE COUNTY, MISSISSIPPI
(Mississippi State Crime Laboratory Case #80-2800)

BACKGROUND

This skeleton was discovered by two hunters in a wooded area near Wiggins, Mississippi, on October 5, 1980. The hands and feet were bound with heavy baling twine. Moderate quantities of dried soft tissues were adherent to the bone. A considerable amount of medium-dark brown, shoulder length hair was recovered. In a dark-green plastic bag found with the remains was a page from the March 3, 1980, issue of the Las Vegas (Nevada) *Mirror.*

TIME OF DEATH

Based upon the degree of soft tissue preservation, the season of discovery and local climatic factors, death is estimated at about *2-6 months* prior to discovery.

AGE AT DEATH

Based on symphyseal morphology, cranial suture closure and other age-related skeletal features, the age at death is estimated at *40 ± 6 years* (34-46 years). The lack of vertebral osteophytosis makes the lower part of this range (34-40 years) somewhat more likely than the upper part.

SEX

Cranial and sexual morphology is *female.* Discriminant function analysis of the cranium and postcranial skeleton also yield diagnoses of female.

RACE

Cranial morphology is *Caucasoid.* Discriminant function analysis of cranial measurements confirms this diagnosis. Hair is also Caucasoid in color and form.

STATURE

Using the Trotter-Gleser formula for white females, stature estimated from the combined lengths of the femur and tibia is *64 ± 3 inches.*

PHYSIQUE

Muscle attachments areas are well developed, especially in the upper extremities. These findings suggest a rather *muscular, compact physique* characteristic of a woman who was physically active through either occupation or athletics.

Facial Reconstruction: Description Used. (*Reprinted with permission from* Dr. Clyde C. Snow, Clinical Anthropologist.)

HANDEDNESS
Scapular beveling and length differences in upper extremity bones suggest that this individual was *right-handed.*

PARITY
A very small, poorly developed preauricular sulcus is present on the right innominate; on the left innominate, the sulcus is absent. These borderline findings suggest that this individual was either nulliparous or, possibly, may have given birth to a child many years previously.

OLD DISEASES, INJURIES, ANOMALIES
1. Healed nasal fracture with nasal bridge deviation to the right.
2. Healed fracture of lateral end of right clavicle.
3. Slight porotic hyperostosis suggests at least one episode of chronic iron deficiency anemia.

TRAUMA
There is evidence of postmortem damage to the ribs and some smaller bones of the hands and feet by small carnivoral scavengers. The only evidence of possible circum-mortem trauma is a linear fracture of the right 7th rib.

CAUSE OF DEATH
Aside from the rib fracture suggestive of *possible* blunt force trauma, there is no evidence of the cause of death.

MANNER OF DEATH
Probable Homicide

SUMMARY
This skeleton is that of a white female who was around 40 ± 6 years of age at the time of her death from unknown causes. Location of the body and binding of the hands and feet indicate homicide as manner of death. The victim was about 5' 4'' ± 3'' in height and was somewhat more muscular than the average female. She was right-handed and had suffered a fractured nose and broken right collar bone some years prior to her death. Death is estimated to have occurred about 2–6 months prior to the discovery of her skeleton.

date

Clyde Collins Snow, Ph.D.
Forensic Anthropology Consultant

218

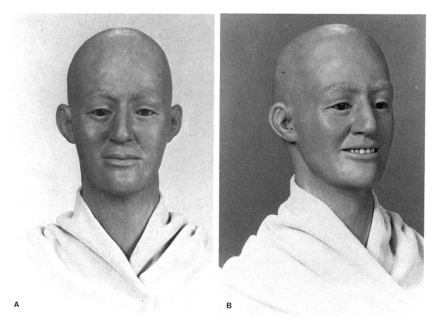

A   B

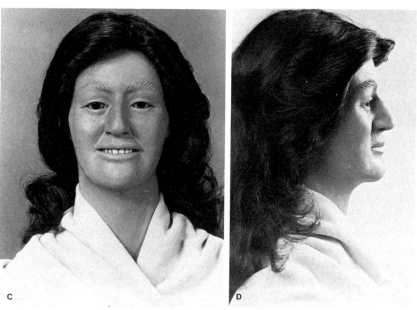

C   D

Composite of Unidentified Deceased Homicide Victim of the preceding Figure Created by Facial Reconstruction by Dr. Snow and Ms Gatliff. (*Courtesy of* Trooper T.P. Naylor Mississippi Highway Patrol.)

landmarks. These blocks are then glued to the skull. Using the tissue-depth blocks as contour guides, the face is built up in clay as shown in steps A through D. Soft-tissue features which have no necessary correlation with the underlying bone present unique problems. According to Ms. Gatliff, determining the contour and shape of these soft-tissue locations challenges the anatomical knowledge, artistic judgment, and the experience of the artist.

When the facial reconstruction is completed, the sculptor selects a wig based on the color, length, and style of the hair found with the remains. If no hair is found, the sculptor bases the selection on other factors inferred from the bones, clothes, and artifacts found with the body.

The completed facial reconstruction is then photographed and the photos given to the law enforcement agency that requested the service. The agency usually, through the cooperation of the media, distributes these photos and circulates the information so as to reach as many persons as possible, with a request to call the police with any information. Any information as to identity will enable authorities to obtain dental records, antemortem x-rays, and other evidence necessary to provide positive identification.

Although this particular method is relatively new and based on a limited number of cases, both Dr. Snow and Ms. Gatliff are optimistic about improved techniques and research in the field, resulting in additional data on soft-tissue depths.

Practically speaking, the homicide investigator must ask himself the following question: "Will facial reconstruction enable me to identify my homicide victim?" If the answer is yes, this method certainly deserves serious consideration, especially after all else has failed.

Conclusion

The identification of the deceased is obviously critical to the overall success of the homicide investigation. The same principle that applies to estimating time of death, however, applies to determining the identity of the deceased: the "fresher" the body, the better the chances.

The normal methods of identification, such as informational sources found at the scene, photographs, and fingerprints can be performed by the investigator. The more technical aspects of identification involving radiological examination, forensic odontology, and physical anthropology require the assistance of scientists and experts from various fields. The homicide investigator does not have to possess the expertise of these scientists, but he or she should have a working knowledge of their availability and potential for determining the identity of the deceased.

I have had the pleasure of working with two distinguished forensic odontologists, Dr. Lowell J. Levine, President of the American Academy of Forensic Sciences and consultant to the New York City and Nassau County Medical Examiner's Office; and Dr. Arthur D. Goldman, DDS, Vice President of the American Academy of Forensic Sciences and consultant to the Rockland County Medical Examiner's Office in New York State.

Dr. Levine and Dr. Goldman contributed their expertise to this chapter by reviewing the section on "Teeth" and providing me with personal opinions and practical information, which I have included herein.

Dr. Harry L. Shapiro, Curator Emeritus of the Anthropology Department of the American Museum of Natural History in New York City, is a renowned educator and scholar whose work in the field of forensic anthropology is widely known. He very graciously provided me with his personal experiences and practical information relative to the section on bones. Dr. James Taylor, Lehman College, Bronx, New York, is a forensic anthropologist. He personally reviewed the material on bones and contributed his experience with criminal investigations. Dr. Taylor is director of the Metropolitan Forensic Anthropology Team located at Lehman College, C.U.N.Y. The team is composed of a forensic anthropologist, a forensic odontologist, a criminalist, and an archeologist.

In addition, I interviewed Ms. Betty Gatliff, a forensic sculptor, whose expertise in facial reconstruction has gained her recognition in the field of forensic science. Her technique, based on anthropological interpretations and an "artist's eye," is used to create an identity or face from a human skull. This field is relatively new to law enforcement; however, there has been some remarkable success with this method, and further research is being undertaken to improve the technique.

Selected Reading

Angel, J. Lawrence. "Bones Can Fool People." *F.B.I. Law Enforcement Bulletin*, January 1974.

Gatliff, Betty Pat and Snow, Clyde C. "From Skull to Visage," *The Journal of Biocommunication* (1979).

Krogman, W.M. *The Human Skeleton in Forensic Medicine*. Springfield, Illinois: Charles C. Thomas, 1962.

Levine, Lowell J. "Forensic Odontology Today—A New Forensic Science." *F.B.I Law Enforcement Bulletin*, August 1972.

Levine, Lowell J. et al. "The Use of Dental Characteristics in The Identification of Human Remains," *Oral Surgery, Oral Medicine, Oral Pathology* 35 (1973): 275–281.

O'Hara, Charles E. *Fundamentals of Criminal Investigation*, 5th ed. Springfield, Illinois: Charles C. Thomas, 1980.

Shapiro, Harry L. "Forensic Anthropology." *Annals of New York Academy of Sciences.* Curator Emeritus American Museum of Natural History, New York, N.Y. Personal Interviews.

Snyder, LeMoyne. *Homicide Investigation,* 3rd. ed. Springfield, Illinois: Charles C. Thomas, 1977.

Stewart, T.D. *Essential of Forensic Anthropology.* Springfield, Illinois: Charles C. Thomas, 1979.

———. "Identification by Skeletal Structures." In *Gradwohl's Legal Medicine,* edited by F.E. Camps. 2nd ed. Baltimore: The Williams and Wilkens Company, 1968, pp. 123–154.

———. "What the Bones Tell—Today." *F.B.I. Law Enforcement Bulletin,* February 1972.

Stewart, T.D., ed. "Personal Identification in Mass Disasters." Washington, D.C.: Smithsonian Institution, 1970.

Svensson, Arne, Wendel, Otte; and Fisher, Barry A.J. *Techniques of Crime Scene Investigation,* 3rd ed. New York: Elsevier North Holland, Inc., 1981.

Modes of Death

From an investigative point of view, it is imperative that the detective have a practical understanding of the manner, means, and mode of several kinds of death. (See Chapter 14, "Purpose of the Autopsy.") During the course of basic death investigations, the investigator will be confronted by various situations and types of death. Since this chapter cannot conceivably cover all of the possibilities involved, it will address the more common methods of death:

Gunshot and firearm wounds, Asphyxia deaths,

Cutting wounds, Autoerotic deaths,

Stabbing wounds, Suicides,

Blunt force injuries, Arson and fire deaths.

Poisons,

In order to provide only the basic knowledge necessary to conduct an intelligent investigation, I have purposely avoided a technical and in-depth discussion of the pathology of wounds, injuries, and forms of death.

Gunshot Wounds

Gunshot wounds may resemble stab wounds in external appearance. However, there are certain physical characteristics of gunshot wounds that will assist the investigator in differentiating stab wounds from wounds caused by firearms. In addition, certain wounds will provide the investigator with a clue to the circumstances under which they occurred.

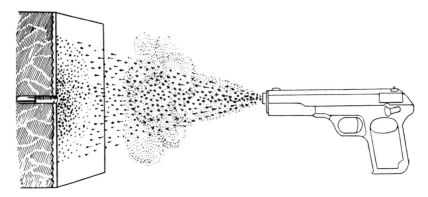

Close Shot—Greater Distance. Unburned powder grains but no smoke deposits in the zone of blackening. (*Reprinted from* A. Svensson, O. Wendel, and B. A. J. Fisher, *Techniques of Crime Scene Investigation*, 3rd ed., New York: Elsevier North Holland, Inc., 1981.)

In order to appreciate the nature of gunshot wounds one must first understand what takes place as a bullet is fired from a weapon and what happens to the body as this projectile or bullet strikes it.

Basically, when a firearm is discharged, four things occur:

1. Fire or flame is emitted from the barrel.
2. Smoke then follows this flame.
3. The bullet emerges from the barrel.
4. Additional smoke and grains of both burned and unburned gunpowder follow the bullet out of the barrel.

As this material exits the barrel, it spreads out like a funnel. As the distance from the barrel increases, the density of the pattern decreases, i.e., the flame doesn't go very far, the smoke goes a little further, the powder grains travel different distances depending upon individual factors, and the bullet travels the greatest distance of all.

Depending on the material present on the body or clothing, and the degree of density, it *may* be possible to determine the distance involved. To make this determination, it is necessary to conduct test firings with similar ammunition.

The Projectile Striking the Body

There are two basic types of wounds.

1. *The entrance wound:*
   a. Generally smaller than an exit wound.

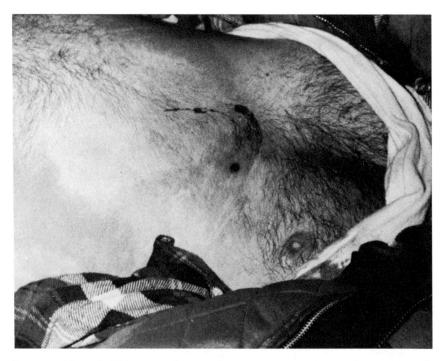

Entrance Wound. This was taken at the crime scene. Notice the neat round hole with smudging around the wound.

   b. Typically round, neat hole with an abrasion collar, and a gray or black ring around the edges.

   c. Comparatively small amounts of blood.

2. *The exit wound:*

   a. Generally larger than an entrance wound.

   b. Ragged and torn in appearance, shreads of tissue extruding.

   c. Generally a greater escape of blood than entrance wounds and possible profuse bleeding.

The Nature and Extent of Gunshot Wounds

There are a number of factors that will effect the characteristics of the wound and change its appearance. For example,

The distance	Passage through clothing
Ricocheting	The type of weapon
Type of ammunition used	The part of the body affected
Passage through body	

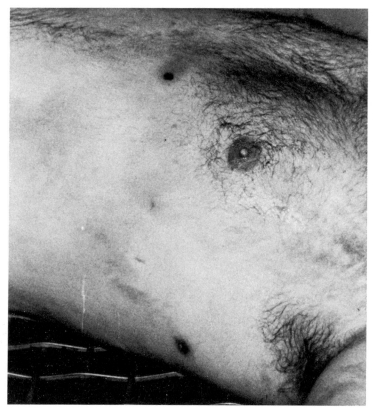

Bullet Wounds. Observe the chest area of this male victim, who has been
shot twice. Notice the smudging and powder collar around the wound.

The homicide investigator should have a working knowledge of the
pathology of wounds and the effect of a firearms discharge on the
human body. Human skin is very elastic and resistant. When a projectile or bullet strikes the skin, it causes an indentation. As the bullet perforates the skin and bores through, it causes a circular perforation and an *abrasion collar*, which is caused by the damage to the
skin as a result of the friction between the bullet and the stretched,
indented skin. In addition to this perforation and abrasion collar,
there will be a blackening effect around the wound's edges caused by
the discharge of lubricants, smoke particles, and grime from the barrel of the weapon onto the bullet. The skin actually wipes this residue off the bullet as the bullet enters the tissue.

The skin which has been stretched by the bullet then returns to its

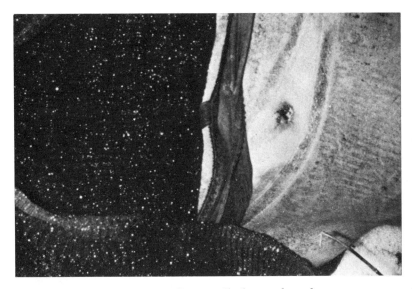

Exit Wound. This type of wound is usually larger than the entrance wound. It is jagged and torn in appearance.

Diagram of a Bullet Penetrating the Skin. The skin is pressed inward, stretched, and perforated in the stretched condition, after which it returns to its original position. The entry opening is smaller than the diameter of the bullet. Immediately around the opening is the contusion ring, since the bullet rubs against this part of the skin and scrapes off the external layer of epithelial cells. (*Reprinted from* A. Svensson, O. Wendel, and B. A. J. Fisher, *Techniques of Crime Scene Investigation*, 3rd ed., New York: Elsevier North Holland, Inc., 1981.)

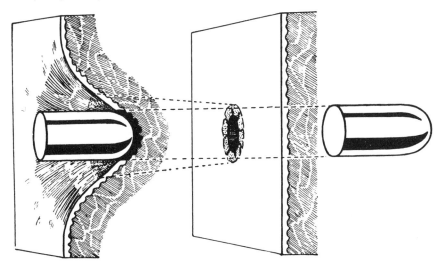

normal or former position. This will make the wound appear smaller than the projectile which has passed through it. The resistance of the skin is evidenced by the fact that many times a bullet will go clear through the body only to be stopped by the skin on the opposite side.

A bullet usually travels in a straight line as it passes through the soft tissue of the body. However, if the bullet hits bones, its direction is unpredictable and will be determined by the velocity of the bullet, the size and shape of the bone, and the angle at which it strikes the bone. In some instances the bone may be shattered, creating additional projectiles of bone fragments which cause even further tissue destruction. The exit wound will be both large and ragged as this impacted tissue and bullet push their way through.

As mentioned above, a bullet hitting a bone may deflect. Often a bullet fired into the chest cavity or skull will be deflected because of angle, and instead of entering straight into the body may travel under the skin, sometimes encircling the entire chest or head of the victim.

Smudging or Smoke

a. Smoke and soot deposited around the wound.
b. Dirty and grimy appearance.
c. Is easily wiped off the skin.
d. Indicates that the gun was held close to the victim, but was not in actual contact.
e. Clothes should be held for examination.

Searing

A yellow singeing effect due to the discharge of flame from the muzzle.

Tattooing or Stippling

a. Pinpoint hemorrhages due to the discharge of burned powder.
b. Unburned powder or pieces of metal of the bullet from the blast are driven into the skin.
c. Unlike "smudging," cannot be wiped off the skin.

Reentry

If the bullet has already passed through another part of the body and reenters, an irregular wound will result which may appear as an exit perforation.

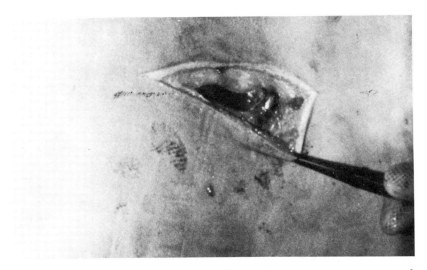

Recovery of a Bullet during an Autopsy. Observe the pathologist, recovering the bullet that has come to rest subcutaneously in the victim's back. The bullet entered the chest area, traveled through the ribs, heart, and lungs; it was stopped by the skin on the opposite side.

Tattooing or Stippling. The bullet entrance wound is surrounded by pinpoint hemorrhages due to the discharge of burned powder and fragments, which have been driven into the skin. This is a result of a "close shot". (Courtesy of William K. Brinkhous, Investigator, North Carolina Office of the Chief Medical Examiner, Chapel Hill, North Carolina.)

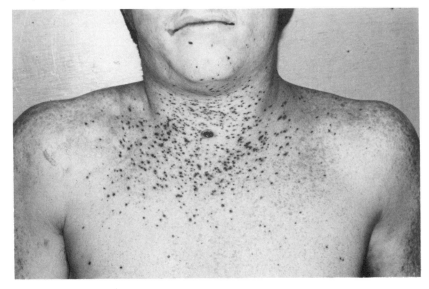

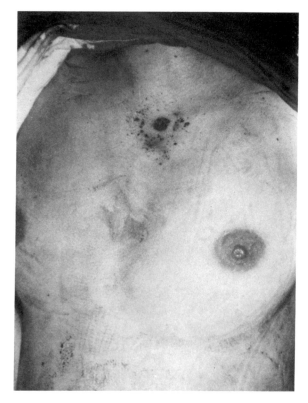

Tattooing and Near Contact Wound. A near-contact type wound with a clustered tattooing around the entrance wound (results from the gun's muzzle
pressed directly to the victim's chest. The wound is a perforating type with the
bullet exiting the victim's back. The muzzle blast caused the tattooing.

Ricocheting

Similarly, if a bullet has struck another object before entering the body,
the entry wound will be irregular.

Shotgun Wounds

The shotgun, specifically the 12-gauge, is the most common weapon
confronting law enforcement, and it is the most deadly.

a. Massive tissue destruction.
b. Wadding will usually be embedded in the wound if the shotgun is
   fired within ten feet of the victim.
c. Wadding can provide the investigator with 1) the type of shot,
   2) the gauge of the gun, and 3) possible evidence to identify the gun
   used.

Effect of High Velocity Ammunition. This woman was hit in the face at close range with a bullet from a 30.06 rifle.

Contact Wounds

a. Muzzle of the gun is held directly against the skin at discharge.
b. Shape is result of penetration of bullet and escape of flame and expanding gases.
c. The perforation will be larger than the diameter of the bullet.
d. Wound is dirty looking.
e. Skin edges are ragged and torn.
f. Charring of skin tissue due to tremendous heat from muzzle blast.
g. Particularly large and marked tissue destruction when the contact wound is in the head or over bones. There will be a characteristic cross-shaped or star-shaped wound, sometimes referred to as stellate. Due to the force of the explosion and the gases against the skull there is an expansion under the scalp, producing a ragged and torn wound that is much larger than an exit wound.

It should be noted that the contact wound is the exception to the general configuration of entrance and exit wounds.

In some instances, the muzzle of the gun may be in contact with the skin and the underlying organs allow for the expansion of gases. The result will be a *muzzle stamp* or *brand* whereby the muzzle of the

gun causes an abrasion on the body outlining the muzzle of the barrel and front sight. In this situation the wound will not be ragged but clean and round, because the charring and destruction takes place under the skin. This is the exception in contact wounds.

Bullet Track

The *bullet track* is the path of the bullet or projectile as it passes through the body. In certain instances the on-scene examination may readily indicate the direction of fire if the classic entrance/exit wounds are present. The bullet track is usually straight but may be bent, changed, or erratic, depending on any number of factors. The most common cause for change of track is when the bullet or projectile has hit or been deflected by bone. However, keep in mind that outer

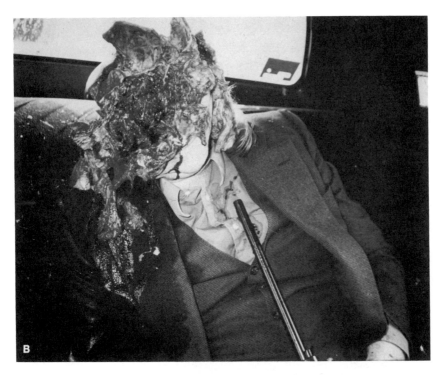

Suicide by Rifle. (**A**) This suicide victim's locale, the interior of a vehicle, shows the effect of the blast. Note the brain matter on the interior roof as well as the back seat of the car. (**B**) We see a close-up of the same victim and the extensive damage inflicted by the blast. The victim committed suicide by placing the barrel of a .308 rifle into his mouth and by pulling the trigger. (Courtesy of Det. Lt. Raymond Krolak, Commander, Investigative Division, Colonie, New York Police Department.)

garments may deflect the path of the bullet, or the wounded person may have fallen and been hit again. Other factors that may affect bullet tracks are:

a. The velocity of the bullet (high or low), which will determine the direction of track.
b. The type of bullet (lead or copper jacket), which will determine how far the projectile traveled.
c. The ricochet factor—increasing size and number of projectiles— which can give a wrong impression as to size and number of wounds.

Remember to note your observations, but be prepared to reevaluate your thinking in light of additional information.

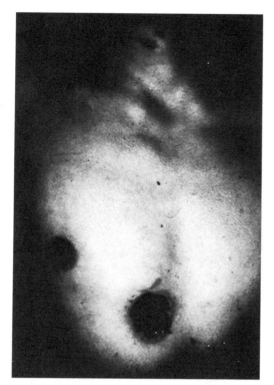

Shotgun Entrance Wound to Chest.

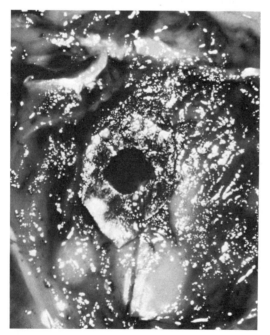

Internal View of the Preceding Wound to Chest Area.

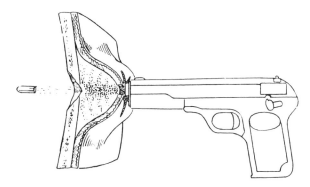

Contact Shot. The weapon is pressed against the head or the body; consequently, gasses from the explosion expand between the skin and the bone producing a bursting effect and a ragged entrance wound. (*Reprinted from* A. Svensson, O. Wendel, and B. A. J. Fisher, *Techniques of Crime Scene Investigation,* 3rd ed., New York: Elsevier North Holland, Inc., 1981.)

The bullet track is important in ascertaining the direction of fire. However, this determination must be made by the forensic pathologist, who can properly evaluate entrance and exit wounds through both microscopic and physiological methods conducted during the autopsy.

Contact Wound to the Side of the Head.

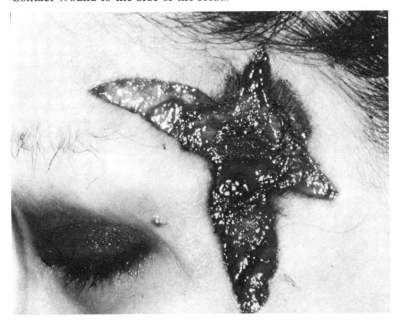

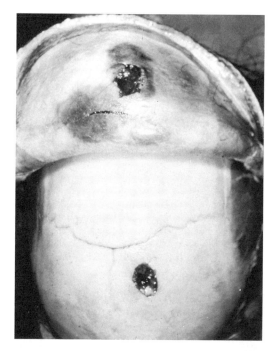

Internal View of a Contact Wound to the Skull after the Scalp has been Pulled Back to Expose the Cranium.

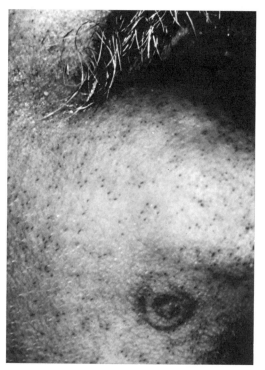

Muzzle Stamp from a Contact Wound to the Area that Involves Soft Tissue. Notice the imprint of the gun barrel.

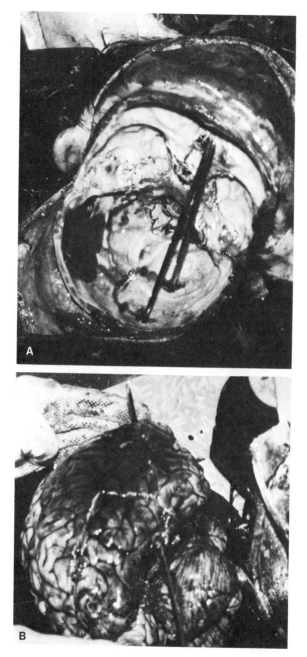

Bullet Track. Observe the skull cavity. **A.** Two separate probes inserted into the entrance wounds of the projectile. **B.** The direction of the bullet through the brain. Both (A) and (B) indicate the bullet track of the projectile. The pathologist will be able to make a determination of the direction and travel based on this procedure.

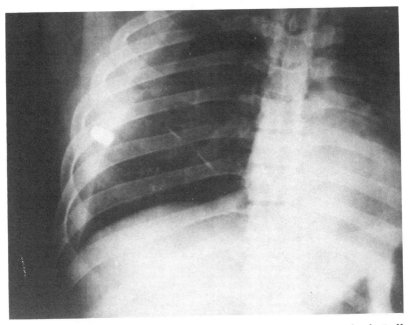

Locating a Lodged Bullet. This x-ray shows the bullet lodged in the chest cavity of the male victim.

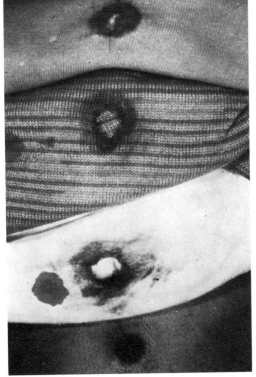

Tracing the Bullet Track through the Victim's Clothing into the Skin. Notice the smudging; this was a close shot to the victim.

Cutting Wounds

An incision or cut-type wound is caused by a sharp instrument or weapon and is generally longer than it is deep. The cut or incised wound is deepest where the weapon was first applied to the skin. If the cutting is done parallel to the lines of cleavage, the edges of the wound will remain together. If the cutting is across the lines of cleavage the wound will be gaping or open.

The incised wound usually involves the skin and underlyng tissue, but may be deep enough to slice bones or organs. It is difficult to determine whether or not cutting wounds are antemortem or postmortem. Therefore, only the pathologist should attempt to make this determination.

Characteristics of cutting wounds are:

Clean and sharp edges,

Minimum bruising,

Longer than deep,

No bridging of skin,

Bleeds freely.

It should be noted that it is extremely difficult to make any determination of the type of instrument or weapon used.

Lines of Cleavage. **A.** Body. **B.** Head.

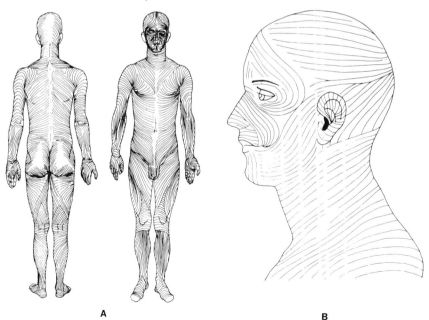

A   B

240

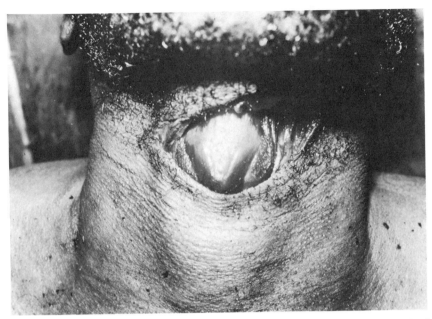

Incised Wound: Neck (*Courtesy of* Dr. Dominick J. DiMaio, Former Chief Medical Examiner, City of New York.)

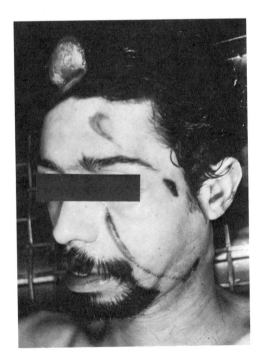

Incised Wound: Face and Head. (*Courtesy of* Dr. Dominick J. DiMaio, Former Chief Medical Examiner, City of New York.)

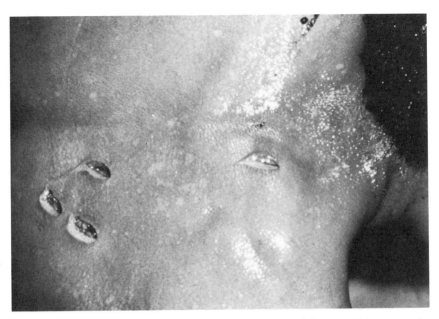

Stabbing Wounds. The victim's back shows a series of deep stabbing wounds, received during a street fight.

Stabbing Wounds

Stabbing wounds are piercing wounds which may extend through the tissue and bone into the vital organs. They are caused by relatively sharp pointed instruments such as knives, screwdrivers, ice picks, daggers, scissors, or pieces of glass.

Stab wounds vary according to the type of weapon employed and how it was used in the attack, (thrust, pulled out, twisted, etc.) The principle involving lines of cleavage is also applicable to stab wounds. The shape of the stab wound *may* indicate what type of weapon or blade was used. However, like a bullet wound, the stab wound will be smaller than the blade which caused it due to the elasticity of the skin. The type of wound is, therefore, determined by estimates of minimum and maximum size. Sometimes the knife hilt may bruise the skin and leave an identifiable mark.

Characteristics of stabbing wounds are:

Deeper than wide,

Possible damage to vital organs beneath skin and bone,

Internal bleeding with little or no external blood,

May indicate type of weapon used.

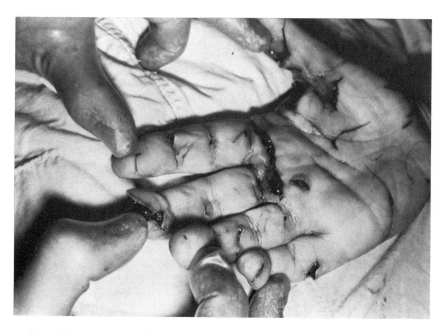

Defense Wounds to the Hand. (*Courtesy of* Dr. Dominick J. DiMaio, Former Chief Medical Examiner, City of New York.)

The pathologist will examine the wound track and can determine the position of the deceased when he or she was stabbed. In addition, if the victim fought with the assailant there will be evidence of *defense wounds* on the hands and arms and between the fingers. Many times, the victim will have grabbed the knife only to have it pulled away by the assailant. This will leave a deep gash in the palm or on the undersurface of the fingers.

The type of weapon, the direction of injury, and the position of the victim are all factors which can be ascertained by a careful examination of the stab wound. The clothing of the victim should always be obtained for later inspection to determine the position of the deceased during the attack and to correlate injuries to the body with tears or rips in the clothing.

Blunt Force Injuries

Blunt force injuries are evident by outward signs such as lacerations and bruising. However, lack of external injuries does not mean that blunt force was not applied. In many instances, internal damage to organs occurs without any external sign of violence.

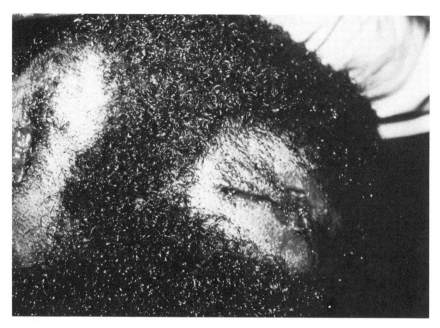

Laceration of Scalp from a Blunt Force Instrument. (*Courtesy of* Dr. Dominick J. DiMaio, Former Chief Medical Examiner, City of New York.)

Lacerations

A laceration is a tear in the tissue which may be external (on the skin) or internal (such as a torn spleen). The torn edges of the skin will be ragged and bruised, and bridges of connective tissue may be stretched across the gap.

Chopping Wounds

These wounds are caused by a heavy object which has an edge, e.g., an axe. A wound produced by an axe will not only cut into the skin, but will also cause contusions and structural damage to the body parts beneath. There will be a deep gaping wound, with contusions and structural damage.

Blunt force injuries are usually directed at the head of the victim. The evidence of injury to the head is evident in the lacerations of the scalp or the blackening of the eyes. However, a severe injury to the head need not be accompanied by evidence of laceration or eye trauma. A person may receive a blow to the head and appear to be all right, only to die later as a result of an internal hemorrhage.

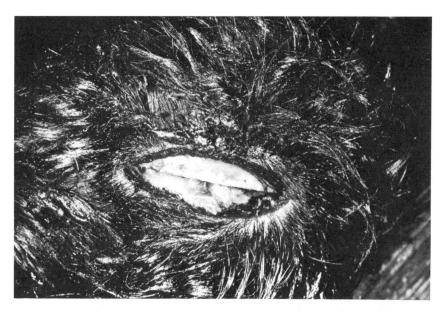

Depressed Skull with Multiple Contusions—Chopping-Type Wound. The weapon here was an ax. (*Courtesy of* Dr. Dominick J. DiMaio, Former Chief Medical Examiner, City of New York.)

Blunt Force Injury. Multiple face and skull injuries. (*Courtesy of* Dr. Dominick J. DiMaio, Former Chief Medical Examiner, City of New York.)

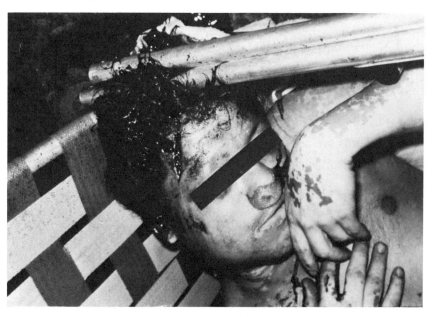

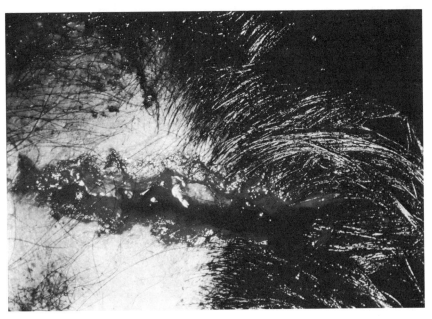

Pattern Injury. A blunt force injury to the head. Notice how the pattern of the weapon matches that of the wound. (*Courtesy of* Dr. Dominick J. DiMaio, Former Chief Medical Examiner, City of New York.)

The Internal Effect of a Blunt Force Injury to the Skull. (*Courtesy of* Dr. Dominick J. DiMaio, Former Chief Medical Examiner, City of New York.)

Injuries to the brain in the back of the head are more likely to be fatal than injuries to the brain in the front part of the skull. This information must be well known in the underworld, since in many execution-type murders the victim is found face down and shot through the back of the head.

Blunt force injuries to abdominopelvic cavity, which contains many organs, can cause severe internal bleeding and death. The most common injury within this area is a torn spleen. However, damage to the liver, intestines, and bladder is relatively easy to cause when blunt force is directed to the body.

Bone injuries also result from the use of blunt force. In a fractured skull, the direction of the cracks or fractures may make it possible to determine the direction of force.

Poisons

Practically speaking, murder by poisoning is extremely rare. Investigators are usually confronted with cases in which the victim has committed suicide by taking an overdose of pills or ingesting something dangerous in order to cause death. Other cases of poisoning are

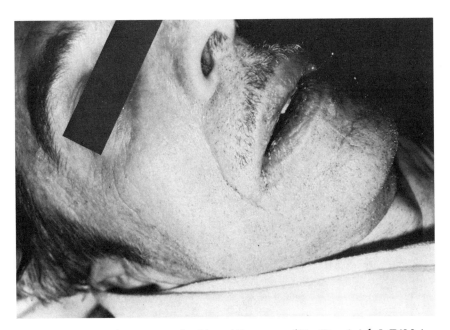

Overdose—Seconal Stains on the Lips. (*Courtesy of* Dr. Dominick J. DiMaio, Former Chief Medical Examiner, City of New York.)

usually accidental and involve narcotic overdoses or the inadvertent taking of the wrong medication.

The examination at the scene and the intelligent questioning of witnesses, members of the family, and others is of paramount importance in determining whether the mode of death was a homicide, suicide, or accident.

Many times, the initial investigation at the scene will reveal the presence of a suspected material or fluid. This material should be retrieved by the detective for later toxicological analysis. Any glasses, cups, or other containers which the deceased may have been drinking from, as well as a sample of the fluid or material believed to have been ingested by the deceased, must also be obtained. Any liquid evidence should be placed in a sterile container, sealed, and delivered to the medical examiner/coroner. Any residue or solid material should be placed in a clean paper bag for similar disposition.

In certain cases, it will be obvious to the police that the death was due to the introduction of some poisonous substance. Drug overdoses are the most common. Any drug paraphernalia or residue found at the scene, including hypodermic needles or syringes, should be collected and forwarded to the pathologist. It is important to secure any needles in order to prevent injury or infection by cutting oneself. A cork placed on the end of the needle will be sufficient to prevent the needle point from scratching or cutting anyone during transportation.

In some instances, a corrosion or burning around the mouth may be present. This usually indicates the consumption of some sort of caustic substance. If a person is desperate, as are most suicides, he or she may ingest a corrosive chemical such as lye or one of the common household cleaners. However, any number of chemicals or substances can be introduced into the human body to cause death. The investigator must be alert to the presence of any material found near the body.

The most important fact to keep in mind is that the scene examination and investigation into the events leading to the death must be thorough and complete. The medicolegal autopsy will determine the type and quantity of the poisonous substance involved. However, determination of the mode of death will be based on the police investigation at the scene.

Deaths by Asphyxia

Death by asphyxia can occur through any number of circumstances. The most common, however, are:

Strangulation (manual or ligature),

Hanging,

Drowning,

Inhalation of poison gases,

Suffocation.

In fact, any death in which air is cut off from the victim is considered to be asphyxial in nature. This would also include those which have been classified as *sexual asphyxia* and *autoerotic deaths*, which are discussed later in this chapter.

Strangulation

Direct strangulation involves the choking of a person, either manually (by the hands) or mechanically (using a ligature). However, strangulation can also occur through such means as Judo moves, use of forearms or legs, as in yoking, and use of instruments employed in combat to restrict air flow or to render an assailant unconscious by cutting off the supply of oxygen to the body.

In ligature-type homicides, any number of instruments can be employed, such as ropes, wires, pieces or clothing, etc. Any type of ma-

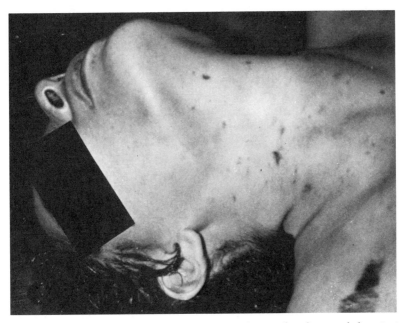

Asphyxiation: Strangulation. Observe the marks on the throat of the victim, which were caused by the fingernails of the assailant as he choked her.

Hanging Case. Clothesline ligature used. Notice the marks of ligature on the neck of the victim. (*Courtesy of* Dr. Dominick J. DiMaio, Former Chief Medical Examiner, City of New York.)

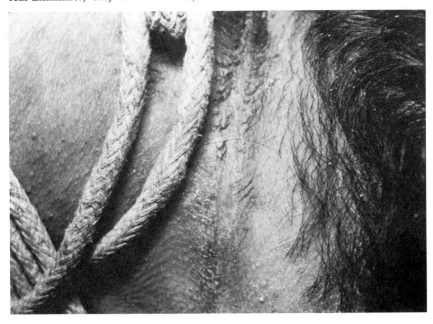

terial or action which causes a person to stop breathing is considered to be asphyxial.

A cord, wire, or similar instrument will leave an obvious groove on the victim's throat which resembles the mark on a hanging victim. The pathologist can often tell the investigator whether or not the marks left on the throat by the assailant's fingernails during the attack took place from the rear or the front of the victim.

Strangulation homicides will cause damage to the interior structures of the neck, throat, and larynx, which will be evident to the forensic pathologist who performs the autopsy.

The investigator can make certain observations at the scene which may enable him or her to determine the manner of death. For example:

1. The presence of new abrasions, bruises, or fingernail marks on the throat of the victim may indicate a strangulation.
2. The presence of *petechial hemorrhages* (minute blood clots which appear as small red dots) in the *conjunctivae* (the mucous membrane lining the inner surface of the eyelids) are presumptive evidence of strangulation.
3. Evidence of trauma to the tongue. Many times persons who are asphyxiated will bite their tongue.

I remember one case I responded to that had been initially reported to the police as a suicide. When I arrived at the scene, I observed the nude body of a young woman lying on the floor next to the tub in the bathroom. The tub was half full of water, and the body was still wet, as though it had been submerged. The husband, who was distraught and crying, stated to the police that he had found his wife submerged in the tub upon returning to the apartment. He had pulled the body from the tub and had attempted mouth-to-mouth resuscitation. He also added that his wife had been despondent and had probably committed suicide by taking an overdose of pills and drowning herself in the tub. Officers at the scene had recovered a prescription bottle next to the victim. The general condition of the scene and the statements of the husband seemed to indicate the possibility of suicide.

I examined the body and noticed a slight bruising in the neck area. The husband explained that upon finding his wife submerged in the tub he had attempted to resuscitate her and had held her by the throat to force air into her lungs. However, when I opened the eyelids of the deceased and examined the conjunctivae, I observed the presence of petechial hemorrhages, and was immediately convinced that the death was, in fact, homicidal and not suicidal, as the husband claimed.

Later on, we learned that the husband had been fighting with his wife and he strangled and killed her. In order to cover up his crime,

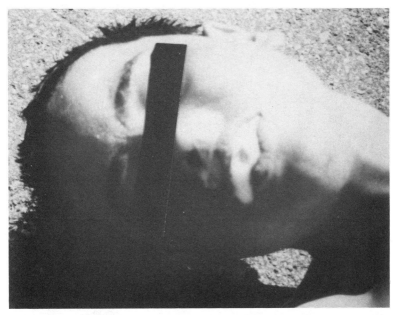

Asphyxia Due to Drowning. The white frothy fluid in the mouth and nostrils of the deceased, hemorrhagic edema fluid, is common in drowning victims.

he filled the tub with water, removed his wife's clothing, and placed her in the tub. He held her under the water to simulate the drowning and then removed her body and placed in on the floor next to the tub. In fact, he had even placed the half-empty bottle of pills next to her body to show to the responding police.

It should be noted that the autopsy would have readily revealed that the death was due to manual strangulation. However, the observation of petechial hemorrhages at the scene gave the investigators a head start on their murder investigation. They made further inquiries of the facts and circumstances at the scene and gathered additional evidence. When the suspect was eventually confronted with this evidence, he made a full confession to the police.

Hanging

Incidents of hanging are usually suicidal or accidental, as in autoerotic deaths. However, the investigator must be alert to incidents in which a hanging may have been purposely staged in order to cover up another crime, thereby making a homicide appear to be suicide.

Hanging deaths must be thoroughly investigated by both the detec-

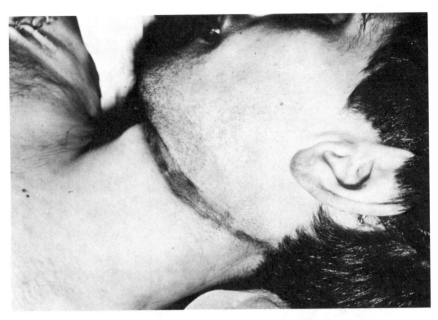

Suicide by Hanging. Notice the groove mark on the neck. (*Courtesy of* Dr. Dominick J. DiMaio, Former Chief Medical Examiner, City of New York.)

tive and the medical examiner/coroner. Practically speaking, the homicide investigator should be aware of certain characteristics of hanging deaths:

1. A body need not be completely suspended in order to suffer asphyxia. If a suicide has fastened a rope, noose, or other type of material around the neck and attached the other end to a doorknob, towel rack, or other hook-type object, and then allowed his or her throat to be contracted; asphyxia will take place, whether or not other portions of the body are in contact with the floor. A majority of the body weight supported by the ligature will effect the required result.
2. If the material used is small or ropelike, there will be a deep groove across the neck, usually high up.
3. Minute areas of bleeding due to the rupture of small blood vessels in the skin will cause small black-and-blue marks to appear within the area of the groove line. This type of rupture indicates that the person was alive when the hanging took place.
4. Persons who have died as a result of asphyxia may expel urine or feces.
5. Postmortem lividity will be pronounced in the head, above the ligature, and in the arms and lower legs due to gravity.

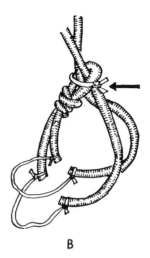

A   B

Removing a Noose from the Neck of a Body. The knots should not be disturbed or loosened. **A.** A fixed noose should be cut off and the ends immediately bound together. **B.** With a running noose, the position of the knot on
the standing part is fixed, after which the noose is cut off. If the noose consists of a number of parts, they should be cut and the ends bound
together. (*Reprinted from* A. Svensson, O. Wendel, and B. A. J. Fisher, *Techniques of Crime Scene Investigation*, 3rd ed., New York: Elsevier North Holland, Inc., 1981.)

It should be noted that if the body is obviously dead, and there is
no need for immediate lifesaving methods to be employed, nothing
should be touched, handled, or otherwise disturbed until the body
and scene have been photographed. If the material around the neck
must be removed, the knot or tie should not be touched. Instead, the
material should be cut in an area which does not disturb the knot.
When the noose is cut, the ends should be tied together with string
to show the original position.

Actually, this procedure is usually performed by the pathologist
who performs the autopsy. There is no need to remove the noose
from the dead person at the scene unless there is the possibility that
the victim is still alive.

Drowning

This type of asphyxia is the direct result of liquid entering the breathing passages, preventing air from going to the lungs. Practically speaking, a person need not be submerged to drown. As long as the mouth
and nose are submerged in any type of liquid, drowning will occur.

I remember one case in which a *crew* (violent urban youth gang)

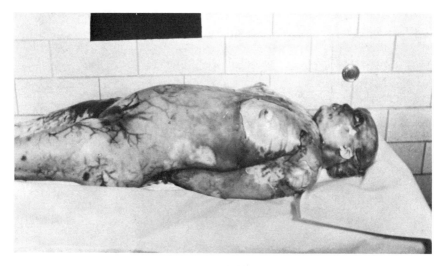

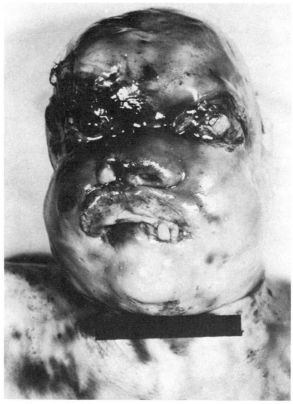

"Floaters." **A.** Bloated body of a floater, which shows the effect of submersion and drowning asphyxia. **B.** Close-up of the same floater's face. (*Courtesy of* Dr. Leslie I. Lukash, Chief Medical Examiner, Nassau County, New York.)

had forced their way into the victim's apartment. They proceeded to torture the man and then tied his hands and feet together. He was then carried to the bathroom, where one of the youths had filled the tub. The victim was placed facedown into the half-filled tub. They held his face under the water until he stopped squirming. The cause of death was drowning.

The most indicative characteristic of drowning is the white foam which forms as a result of the mucus in the body mixing with water. The presence of this white lathery foam in the mouth and windpipe prevents air from entering and contributes to the asphyxia. Bodies which have been in the water for long periods of time are subject to additional damage or injury which is unrelated to the actual drowning. (See Chapter 9, "External Agents of Change.") Most bodies will sink upon drowning only to rise later when the gases from putrefaction begin to inflate the body, causing it to rise to the surface. The amount of time before this occurs depends upon water temperature, the condition of the body (fat or thin), and other variables such as currents. The victim of a drowning will often be found grasping objects such as mud, grass, or other material found in the water.

Inhalation of Poison Gases

The most common type of asphyxia results from the breathing in of certain chemicals, such as carbon monoxide. These deaths are best determined after toxicological testings are made of the blood. At the scene, examinations sometimes will indicate the possibility of carbon monoxide poisoning if the lividity is cherry red. However, this is only a rough gauge, and before attributing the death to carbon monoxide, the investigator should await the results of the autopsy.

Suffocation

Suffocation or smothering occurs when the passage of air through the mouth and nose is blocked. The mechanisms necessary to accomplish this suffocation vary. If the smothering is homicidal, hands may be placed over the mouth and nose, or a pillow forcibly compressed over the face, or a plastic bag, gag, or other obstruction forced into the mouth. When the suffocation is done with the hands, there may be evidence of scratches on the face.

I remember reading about one particularly brutal suffocation in which two teenage boys forced pebbles down the throat of a youngster to prevent him from telling his parents that they had stolen his bike.

Other types of death which are not homicidal but are attributed to suffocation are those which occur in accidents such as industrial

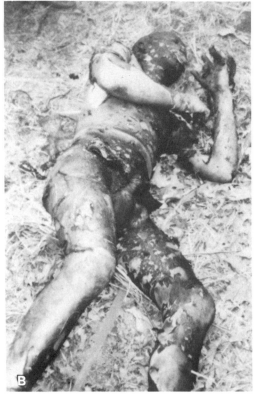

Burned Body. (**A**) The classic pugilistic attitude is assumed by a body as a result of the coagulation of the muscles due to heat. The deceased doused himself with gasoline and ran until he collapsed. The gasoline burned the clothing off the body. (**B**) Note the severe burning and positions of the arms on the body after it has been turned over. Self-immolation is extremely rare.

cave-ins, or where a person has dirt, sand, or other powdery material blocking the mouth, nose, and airway.

Arson and Deaths by Fire

It should be noted that acts of arson to commit homicide and to cover up homicides have become very common. Therefore, homicide investigators should have some basic knowledge of arson-type fires and be familiar with the effects of fire on the human body, in order to properly interpret events at the scene.

Practically speaking, the average investigator lacks the expertise to thoroughly investigate crimes of arson. However, most arson-related homicides are very amateurish, and it will be obvious to the investigator that there is something wrong. The presence of flammable liquids, several points of origin of the fire, and intensity of the blaze are examples of clues which may indicate arson. Meaningful interpretations of these clues, however, must be left to the experts, since, arson investigation is highly technical and complex. Therefore, death inves-

Scalding Burns. This woman was scalded to death in her shower. A defective water heater had heated the water to a temperature of approximately 200° F.

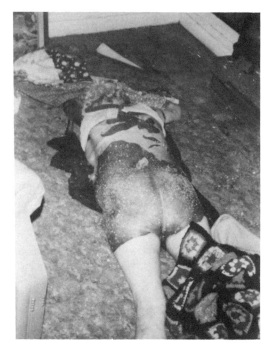

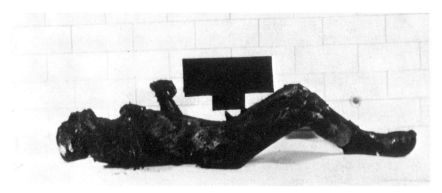

Pugilistic Attitude. This position is assumed by bodies in fire. (*Courtesy of* Dr. Leslie I. Lukash, Chief Medical Examiner, Nassau County, New York.)

tigations in which arson is the cause of the death, or has been employed by the killer to cover up the crime, require that the homicide detective team up with the arson investigator.

The discovery of a body or bodies in a burned-out building or vehicle presents additional investigative problems. The mode of death could be natural, suicidal, accidental, or homicidal. The body may be too badly burned even to recognize whether it is male or female, or there may be evidence or gross injury and dismemberment. The investigators will have to rely on the pathologist to interpret these injuries and make determinations of the cause of death at the autopsy.

Deaths caused by fire generally result from the inhalation of noxious gases and fumes created by the fire. The victim is usually dead prior to any burning or charring of the flesh. The pathologist will be able to determine the critical question of whether or not the victim was alive at the time of the fire. In addition, the pathologist will be able to make certain determinations regarding cause of death. The examination at autopsy will reveal the wounds or injuries which actually caused the death despite the tissue damage done by the fire. Most incidents of arson are perpetrated to destroy evidence or conceal the crime by destroying the body. However, the body does not burn as easily as most people believe. Instead, the body resists the destructive forces of the fire with amazing durability, allowing the pathologist to make determinations from the remains. If the body was alive at the time of the fire, it will evidence 1) smoke stains around the nostrils, in the nose, and air passages, 2) carbon monoxide in the blood, and 3) blistering and marginal reddening of the skin. Burned bodies usually assume a distorted position referred to as the *pugilistic* attitude or position, caused by the contraction of muscles due to the heat of the fire, and not as some persons believe because the victim was alive at the time of the fire. All bodies will react in this manner. The skin will crack, giving the impression of wounds, and bones may break, or the heat will cause the cranium to crack or shatter. All these factors will be properly interpreted by the pathologist.

Suicide Investigation

The rationale behind suicide, the intentional taking of one's own life, can be as simple or as complex as life itself. The person who commits suicide may see his or her actions as some sort of solution to a severe physical or psychological dilemma. Oftentimes, a police investigator will find a note indicating that the victim had suffered psychological torment, or was severely depressed. The note might even suggest that he or she believed that suicide was the last resort. Many of the suicide notes I have seen over the years indicate the acute depression of persons who have taken their lives.

Although depression may be the primary motive for the suicide, other factors frequently play a part. Alcohol, drugs, stress, frustration, fear, anger, hostility, and guilt may lay the groundwork for suicide. Others may actually take their own life in order to punish the survivors, i.e., their family, co-workers, or even society in general for some conceived wrongdoing.

I recall reading a *Daily News* story and seeing on television a particularly bizarre case in which the victim had planned his death for approximately seven months. He had promised reporters that his story would be "The Story of the Decade" (*Daily News*, January 24, 1987, p. 6).

The victim was a state official, who had been found guilty of bribery earlier in the year. On the day of his death, he called for a news conference ostensibly to resign from public office. As he read his statement, he urged the reporters and camera crews to keep their lenses on him. He then pulled a .357 magnum handgun from a manila envelope and placed it into his mouth, pointing the barrel of the gun up toward his brain. He fired and effectively blew his brains out for the viewing audience.

Depression does not discriminate. It effects the young and old alike. Teenage suicides have been described as epidemic in proportion to their representation within society. According to a 1987 study conducted by The Centers for Disease Control in Atlanta, Georgia, more than 5,000 people between the ages of 15 and 24 take their own lives each year. This problem is invisible until it strikes one's own neighborhood. Periodically, the nation's newspapers and television networks may cover this phenomenon by reporting a series of events including "Teenage Suicide Pacts." Ironically, the media attention often results in further teenage suicides. The course of action would be to seek out professional assistance and create programs within the school system to deal with this problem.

The Investigation

Investigatively speaking, all death investigations should be handled as homicide cases until the facts prove differently. The resolution of the mode of death as suicide is based on a series of factors that eliminate homicide, accident, and natural causes of death.

It has been my experience that suicide cases repeatedly cause more problems for the investigator than homicide investigations. There is the possibility that suicide notes may have been taken or destroyed. In addition, the weapon and/or other evidence may have been removed prior to the arrival of the police. Also it is not surprising to encounter misdirected grief and/or anger. The surviving family grieves the loss of a loved one and is faced with the psychological uncertainty of whether or not they could have prevented the act.

I remember one case in which an 84-year-old woman was found with a gunshot wound to her head. The police had been notified of the death by a daughter of the deceased. Unbeknownst to the police, the deceased had been suffering from terminal cancer and had been very depressed. Her daughter, who had unsuccessfully attempted to call the mother at home, went to the mother's house. She opened the door with a key and discovered her mother's body. She saw a .32 caliber handgun, which she immediately recognized as an old family heirloom. The daughter removed the gun from the premises, along with some personal papers and a codicil she found in her mother's dresser drawers. She went home, got rid of the gun, and then called the police to report that she hadn't been able to get through to her mother. She requested the police to respond to her mother's apartment and she would meet them there.

Needless to say, when we arrived, we were looking at a burglary/homicide case and not a possible suicide. Later that week, we were called by the family's priest, who advised us of what had taken place. The case was properly reclassified as a suicide.

Many times the surviving family cannot or will not accept the fact that a relative has committed suicide. They have been known to accuse the police of a cover-up, or to petition state and federal agencies to review the local investigation with the belief that they can change the outcome.

One of the most bizarre cases of suicide I ever investigated involved the suicide death of an attractive 27-year-old woman. She was discovered in her sister's fiancé's apartment with a cut throat and three stab wounds to the chest. She had been hiding at the apartment from a boyfriend, who at first was our primary suspect. However, upon a complete and thorough death investigation, it was soon discovered that the circumstances of her death, as well as the evidence obtained by investigators during the crime scene search, indicated this death to be suicide. The cutting to the throat was superficial with a stigma of

Decomposed Body. Notice the bloating and peeling of skin. (*Courtesy of* Dr. Dominick J. DiMaio, Former Chief Medical Examiner, City of New York.)

Sexual Mutilation—Evisceration. This female victim of lust murder has been eviscerated. The killer then engaged in anthropophagy. (*Courtesy of* Lt. Ray Biondi, Commanding Officer Homicide Bureau, Sacramento, California Sheriff's Department.)

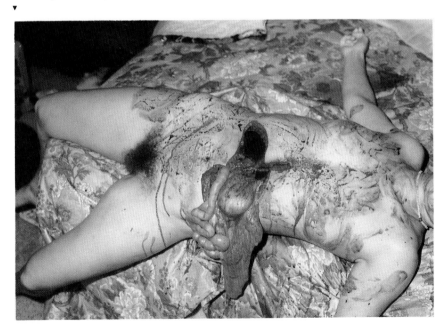

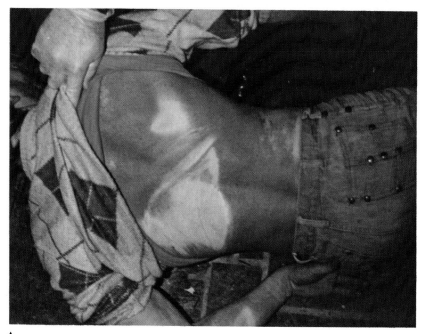

Lividity. Notice the white pressure areas or "blanching" on the victim's back.

Putrefaction. Note the bloating and decompositional blisters as well as the greenish discoloration around the area of the abdomen. This is a classic example of *autolysis,* the breakdown of cells and organs from the aseptic chemical process caused by intracellular enzymes.

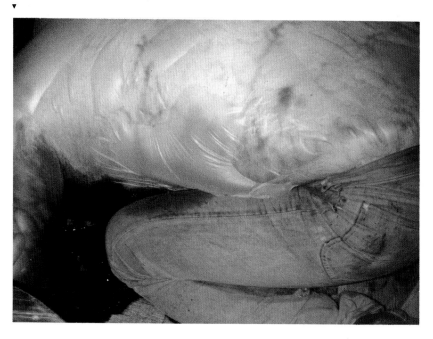

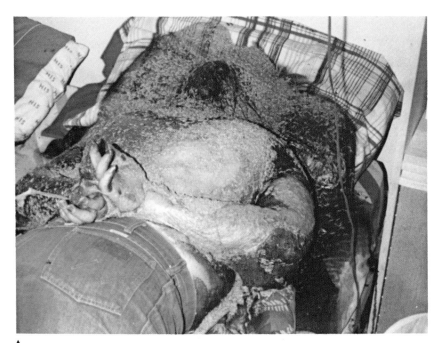

Insect Infestation.

Close-up of a
Floater's Face.

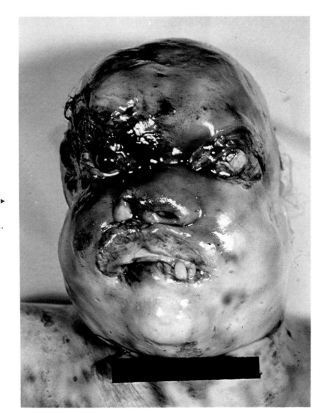

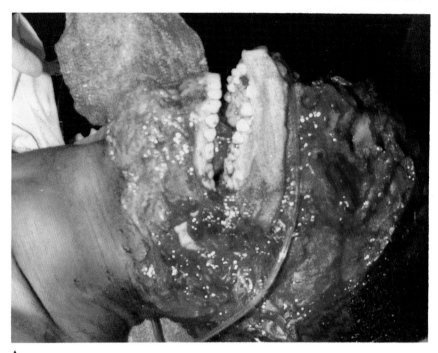

Self-Mutilation. This young man, under the influence of "angel dust," peeled his face from his skull with pieces of a mirror and fed the flesh to his pet dogs. He survived due to the large amount of drugs anesthetizing his system.

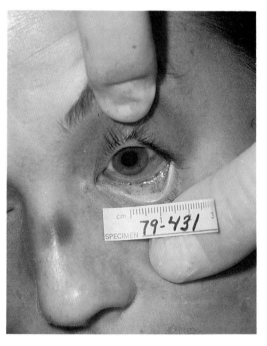

Petechial Hemorrhage. Minute blood clots appear as small red dots in the conjunctivae (the mucous membrane lining the inner eyelid)—presumptive evidence of strangulation. (*Courtesy of* William K. Brinkhous, Investigator, North Carolina Office of the Chief Medical Examiner, Chapel Hill, North Carolina.)

hesitation. The stabbing to the chest was self-inflicted. The weapon came from the scene. The premises were locked from inside. Her palm prints were found on the blade of the kitchen knife. A note found at the scene, although not a classic suicide note, did indicate the victim's depression. A handwriting analysis revealed that the deceased had written the note. A background check of the deceased indicated drug and alcohol abuse. Interviews of family and friends were conducted. Additional evidence was discovered that indicated the deceased had first tried to kill herself with a rifle found in the apartment. There were no signs of a struggle, nor signs of forced entry into the locked apartment. The medical examiner, who responded to the scene, confirmed that the death was suicide.

However, the following day an associate medical examiner, who lacked the expertise of the medical examiner at the scene and the homicide detectives involved in the case, reclassified the case as a homicide. Her rationale was that she had never seen a body with three stab wounds to the chest and a cut throat. She made this determination without consulting the "tour" doctor, who had been at the scene. She disregarded his official notes, refused to discuss the case with me or the detectives, and adamantly insisted that this case was a homicide. As a result of her incompetance and the family's insistence, this case was subject to review by the State Attorney General's Office, the New York City Department of Investigation, and the NYPD Internal Affairs Division.

I would later have the pleasure of conferring with her superiors and having the case properly reclassified as suicide. However, the damage was done; to this day the family of that girl is convinced that their daughter was killed by the boyfriend. It was easier for them to believe that their child was killed than to accept the fact that she killed herself.

The investigator should be aware of three basic considerations to establish if a death is suicidal in nature.

1. The presence of the weapon or means of death at the scene.
2. Injuries or wounds that are obviously self-inflicted, or could have been inflicted by the deceased.
3. The existence of a motive or intent on the part of the victim to take his or her own life.

It should be noted that the final determination of suicide is made by the medical examiner/coroner after all the facts are evaluated. However, the investigation at the scene and an inquiry into the background of the deceased may indicate the presence of life-threatening behavior or activities that suggest suicidal intent. Of course, the medical examiner/coroner is supposed to avail him or herself of the input of the investigators, who were present at the scene and conducted the death investigation.

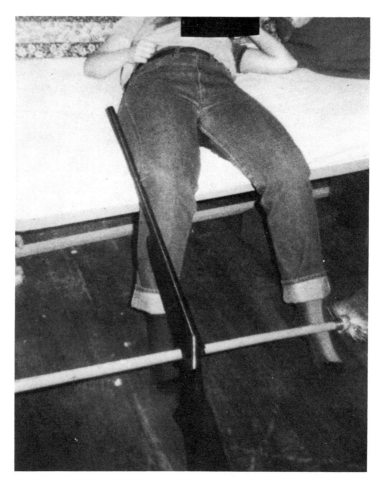

Suicide. Observe the broom handle, which has been placed through the trigger guard. The deceased had apparently placed her feet against the broom handle to put pressure on the trigger, causing the firearm to discharge into her chest.

Suicide. Same case as the preceding figure. A. The deceased is lying on her back, the bullet wound is evident in her chest area. B. With her blouse pulled up, notice the entrance wound directly into the chest cavity. The deceased had used birdshot. If the shot had been of a higher caliber, the wound would have been larger and might have exited from the opposite side.

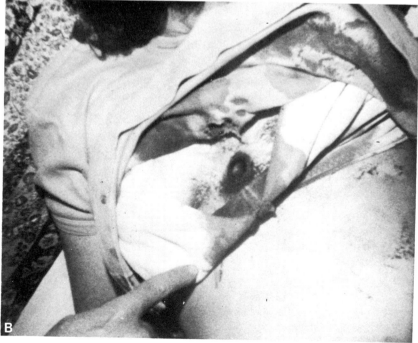

The Weapon

The weapon or means of death should be present in cases of suicide. However, the absence of a weapon does not necessarily indicate that death was due to a homicide. The weapon could have been stolen or otherwise disposed of prior to the arrival of the authorities (as seen in the case of the heirloom handgun). Furthermore, family members have been known to conceal weapons and/or suicide notes in order to collect on an insurance policy. There have been many cases recorded in which the suicide victim has arranged to make his or her death appear to be a homicide for a number of reasons.

If the weapon is observed in the hands of the deceased, the investigator should examine the hand to see if the weapon is clutched tightly, due to *cadaveric spasm* (instantaneous rigor mortis) (see Chapter 9, Body Changes After Death). It is not uncommon for persons who had a firearm or knife in their hand at the time of death to clutch it tightly *after* death, and many victims of suicide have been found tightly grasping their weapon. It is important to note such clutching of weapons, as you can be sure that the person held this weapon at the time of his or her death. A person attempting to place a weapon in the deceased's hand after death would *not* be able to recreate the same grasp.

Suicide which Appears to be Homicide. Notice the extreme violence to the body. (*Courtesy of* Dr. Leslie I. Lukash, Chief Medical Examiner, Nassau County, New York.)

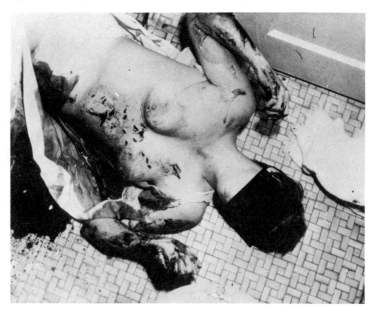

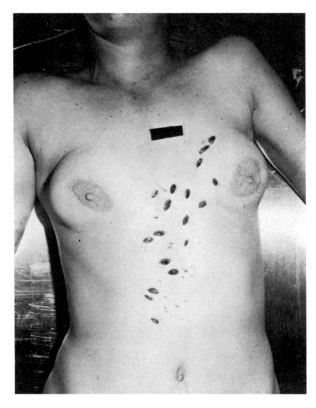

Victim at the Morgue. Observe the victim of the preceding figure after she was cleaned at the morgue. Notice the number of wounds. (*Courtesy of* Dr. Leslie I. Lukash, Chief Medical Examiner, Nassau County, New York.)

Weapon Used by the Victim of the Preceding Figure. (*Courtesy of* Dr. Leslie I. Lukash, Chief Medical Examiner, Nassau County, New York.)

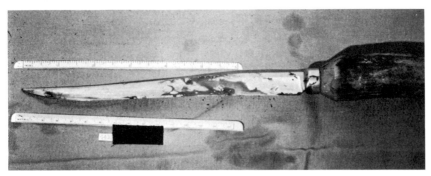

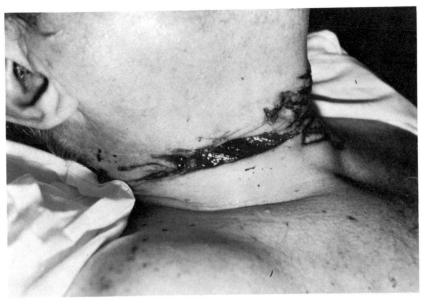

Hesitation Marks. Notice the marks on the throat of the victim. (*Courtesy of* Dr. Domminick J. DiMaio, Former Chief Medical Examiner, City of New York.)

The weapon need not be in the hand of the deceased in order for the death to be a suicide. It is important to note the survival time factor, time between injury and death, which may have enabled the deceased to perform any number of activities, including disposal of the weapon or leaving the original location where he or she first attempted suicide.

Wounds

Injuries and wounds in suicides may be very similar to those observed in homicides. However, certain observations that the wounds found on the body are consistent with homicide or suicide should be made. For example, a person found dead from multiple stab wounds of the back would certainly *not* be considered a victim of suicide. Likewise, in suicide cases, there appear to be preferences and avoidances for certain parts of the body.

If the victim used a knife to commit suicide, the wounds will usually be on the throat or wrists. If the injury is a stab wound, it will generally be through the heart. The investigator should closely examine any slashing-type wounds for evidence of *hesitation marks*, which appear as parallel slashes alongside the mortal wound and are indicative of suicide. The investigator should not jump to any conclusions based on hesitation marks, as an assailant, who is knowledgeable about these factors, might leave similar markings to cover up a homicide.

If the victim uses a gun, their target will likely be their head, followed by the heart. Head shots are usually found in the temple, the forehead, or directly into the mouth. The wounds will be close-range as opposed to long-range. There should be evidence of powder burns and/or smudging. In some instances, there may even be evidence of hesitation gunshot wounds or evidence of other shots fired prior to the fatal shot. The investigator should examine the hands of the deceased for evidence of any blood or tissue splattering.

It is important to remember that wounds are never too painful to a person determined to take his or her own life. Deranged persons may inflict several extensive wounds on themselves before they collapse and die. I reviewed one case in which the deceased had attempted to hang himself with an electrical cord, but the cord broke under his weight. He then cut open his stomach with an eight-inch knife and systematically removed his intestines, which he cut into pieces using a pair of tinsnips. Investigators at the scene recovered an eight-inch knife, a pair of tinsnips, scissors, and towels containing blood and intestines.

Just as investigators should not presume homicide based merely on the extent of injury, they should not be fooled by the method. Although suicide by fire is extremely rare, gasoline is readily available and can be a convenient weapon. Ironically, I have found more women resorting to death by fire than men. I presume that the reason for this situation is that men are perhaps more likely to obtain firearms.

Motives and Intent

The manner of death may be important in determining suicidal intent. For example, people who hang themselves or jump to their deaths from fatal heights have certainly indicated an intention to take their lives. Similarly, deaths that involve a combination of methods (poisoning, shooting, slashing, inhaling gas, etc.) show an extreme desire to die.

There are numerous motives to consider in suicide cases. I have found from my own personal experience, however, that some people's motives never surface; the motive died with the deceased. Some of the more common motivations are as follows:

Depression,	Marital or family crisis,
Drugs,	Severe emotional trauma,
Alcohol,	Psychological problems,
Stress,	Physical deterioration,
Frustration,	Loss of a loved one,
Fear,	The death of a child,

Anger,	Financial situations,
Hostility,	Teenage problems,
Guilt,	Loss of employment,
Terminal illness,	Despair,
Illness in the family,	General inability to cope with life.

I remember a case in which the body of the deceased was found at the base of a high drop. There was evidence of some cutting on the wrists and it was apparent that he had jumped or fallen from the ledge approximately 70 feet above. An examination of the body, however, indicated that his wallet was missing. A further examination of the area on the ledge failed to locate the wallet or any type of blade that could have been used to cut the wrists. The deceased had been at work the previous day and seemed to have been fine. Friends and family of the deceased had not noticed any suicidal tendencies. The case was definitely shaping up into a real mystery. Later in the day, we received a call from a neighboring jurisdiction. The police had recovered the wallet belonging to the deceased in a motel room. The room was very bloody and it appeared that there had been an assault in the premises. Further examination, however, disclosed a suicide note, an empty bottle of pills, and a bloody razor blade. Apparently, the deceased had gone to the motel room to take his own life. He had cut both wrists, consumed the contents of the prescription bottle, and bled all over the place. When death did not occur, he left the motel, got into his car, and drove approximately ten miles back to New York City. He then selected a relatively high building in the area and jumped to his death. The suicide note, which was recovered by police, indicated that the deceased was extremely upset with his life and had planned to kill himself at the motel.

Suicide Notes

The presence of a suicide note certainly suggests suicide. However, the investigator should conduct a further inquiry to ascertain whether or not the note is genuine. Was it written by the deceased? Was it written voluntarily? The investigator should collect the note in a manner that will preserve any latent fingerprints. Known writings of the deceased should be collected for comparison.

Excerpts are provided below of a few suicide notes from cases I have investigated over the years in order to add some insight into the "thinking" of a person who has chosen suicide as the final solution to a real or imagined problem.

The psychology of suicide becomes an integral part of the professional investigation, and often the note provides the detective with a basis of inquiry into the background of the victim for a later psychological autopsy.

> Dear Mom and Dad, I guess the past ten years escapades have finally paid off—with my Life . . . I'm sorry I'm letting alot of people down, who had faith in me, but I no longer had any faith in myself . . .

This case involved a young man, who had a serious alcohol problem. The actual note was two pages, and contained his telephone number and home address. The note was found in his vehicle, which had been parked on the George Washington Bridge in New York City. The note also contained a drawing that indicated he had jumped into the waters of the Hudson River. His body was found approximately five days later.

> To my family, I just got a little tired. It's not your fault, but I want you to know I love you very much . . . Love always Dad.

This case involved the suicide of a police officer. I knew this man for some 15 years and would never have suspected that he would ever take his own life. I remember interviewing his wife, who told me, "This was not the (Jack) you or I knew. He changed. There was a drastic change during the week. I think it was the medication he was taking." Jack, not his real name, had been prescribed drugs for an infection. The prescription had put him into a deep depression.

> Last will and testament, Everything goes to (Jim) with the exception of the things that belong to (John) I love you all.

This case involved a young woman, who had moved to New York City from the midwest and had become depressed with her life. Although she had a good job as a nurse in a hyperbaric center, her real goal was to be in fashions. She decided to kill herself in front of her place of work. She probably decided that no one would miss her and she didn't want to die alone, so she took her pet dog with her. She hooked-up a vacuum cleaner hose, which she taped to the exhaust pipe of her car, and ran the hose into her vehicle. She was found by her fellow employees the next morning.

> Now, (Eva) doesn't have to say Oh she a pain now I'm dead. Now everybody is happy. I hope I wasn't a problem to nobody but if I was now I am not . . . I hope I didn't cause so much trouble. Tell everybody I say goodbye. Have a Happy thanksgiving . . .

This was an extremely sad case involving a 12-year-old girl, who took her life rather than risk being sexually abused any further by her father. The young girl, who was staying with relatives, believed that her father, who had recently been released from prison, might take her back to live with him. Investigation indicated that she had been abused since she was five years old. She shot herself with an unlicensed .38 caliber handgun after swallowing a number of pills.

> Brother and sister, we didn't have anything else in this world. Please put our bodies in the same coffin . . . We love you all . . . Don't be sad about us. Everything is in God's hands . . .

This was a classic "Lover's suicide pact." The two bodies were found in a motel; both of them had been shot through the head. The male was found with the gun by his hand. They were both lying in bed. The note was found on a lamp table next to a Chinese symbol, which meant eternity.

Background Information

It is important to note that the deceased may have indicated an intent to commit suicide through activities and statements prior to death. Any diaries, unmailed letters, or similar writings should be examined for information that may explain the death. Many suicide deaths are preceded by verbal threats of self-destruction and other indications of despondence. In some instances these threats are made to people whom the deceased respects or highly regards. In other instances sudden change in behavior is shown by subtle actions, such as increasing life insurance, giving away prized possessions, disregarding doctor's advice, or abuse of alcohol or drugs.

Psychological Autopsy

The *psychological autopsy* is a collaborative procedure involving law enforcement and mental health experts who attempt to determine the state of mind of a person prior to the fatal act. By examining the victim's life-style and interviewing the victim's friends and relatives, they determine whether the death was accidental or involved suicide.

Warning Signs

A change in sleeping habits—sleeping more than usual or staying up much later—followed by sadness.

A change in eating habits—weight loss or lack of appetite.

A lack of interest in sex—loss of sex drive.

A sudden drop in grades or school attendance—young people; loss of work interest—adults.

Loss of interest in favorite activities, hobbies, or sports.

Loss of interest in friends, family, etc.—isolation.

A preoccupation with death, or an unusual interest in art or music dealing with death—teenagers; preoccupation with death and the afterlife—adults.

Loss of interest in personal hygiene and appearance.

Involvement with drugs, including abuse of alcohol.

Extreme Danger Signs

Suddenly becoming cheerful or calm after a depression—a sudden euphoria or burst of activity. This could mean that the person has resolved the inner conflict by deciding to take his or her life. The decision is made.

Giving away prized possessions.

Speaking of life in the past tense—e.g., saying, "I've loved you," or "You've been a good mother."

Investigation Considerations

EVALUATION OF THE WOUNDS

1. Could the deceased have caused the injuries and death?
2. Was the person physically able to accomplish the act?
3. Are the wounds within reach of the deceased?
4. Are the wounds grouped together?
5. Is there more than *one* cause of death?
6. Describe the *nature* and *position* of the injuries.
7. Are there any hesitation marks?

PSYCHOLOGICAL STATE OF THE VICTIM

1. Obtain a background of the victim from family and friends. This background should include medical as well as social information.
2. Were there any *warning signs* indicated by the victim?
3. Were there any recent deaths in the family?
4. Is there any indication of a recent upset of stress?
5. Did the victim leave any notes? Request a sample of the victim's handwriting for analysis in case a note is later discovered.
6. Any close personal relationships, close friends, etc.? Interview as soon as possible.

ANY PRIOR MENTAL DISEASE OR DEFECT

1. Has the deceased been under any professional treatment?
2. Had the deceased ever attempted suicide in the past?
3. Has anyone in the family ever committed suicide?

272

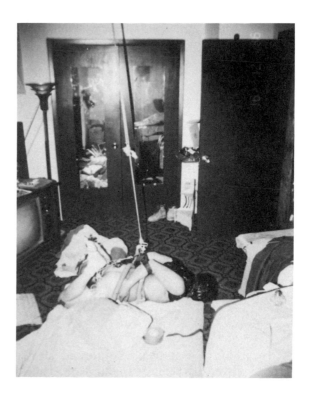

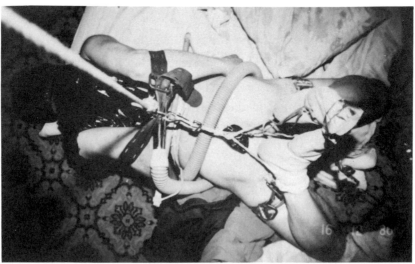

Autoerotic Death Involving Bondage Fantasy. A 35-year-old male expired during an autoerotic act. His fantasy involved bondage. He has a black garbage bag
over his head. His body is bound in several areas, with his feet tied together. His

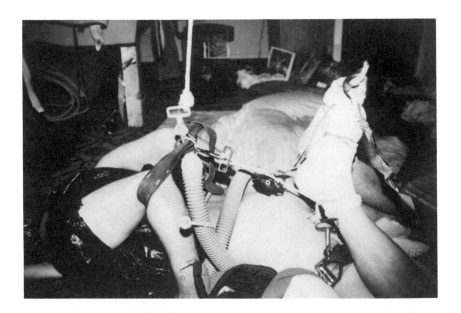

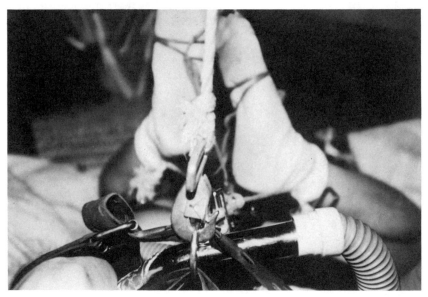

arms are bound behind his back with belts, which are attached to a metal hook. All of the bindings are interconnected and join a metal clasp that is attached to a rope with a loop knot, which is connected to a hook in the ceiling. As bizarre as this appears, the deceased was able to tie himself up in this fashion and reportedly had done this a number of times without injury. (Courtesy of Sgt. David Vanderploeg, Village of Glenview Police Department, Glenview, Illinois.)

4. Was the deceased a heavy drinker?
5. Was the deceased on any medication?
6. Was there a history of drug abuse?
7. Was there a history of physical or psychological abuse to the deceased?

Sexual Asphyxia: The Phenomenon of Autoerotic Fatalities

Autoerotic deaths, or deaths attributed to solo sex-related activities, are not common. Nonetheless, as cases have been recorded by police and medical examiner/coroners in various jurisdictions, the homicide detective should be aware of them. The cause of death may be asphyxia, but the mode of death, based on first observation, may be classified as either suicide or homicide, when in fact it is actually an accident that occurred during a dangerous autoerotic act.

Most of the literature on the subject of autoeroticism analyzes the involvement of teenage boys and older men, who through certain ritualistic activities obtain some sort of sexual gratification. The bodies usually have been discovered nude, attired in female clothing, or in normal attire. It should be noted, however, that there are documented cases of female participants. The investigator confronted with a female

Autoerotic Death: Female. Notice the material around the ligature to prevent any marking of the neck. (*Courtesy of* Special Agent Robert R. Hazelwood, Behavioral Science Unit, FBI Academy, Quantico, Virginia.)

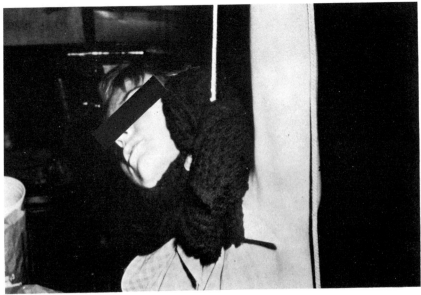

victim found under these circumstances is cautioned to assess carefully all of the information available before jumping to any conclusions. In some cases there is evidence of infibulation and other autosadistic acts. Contraptions or ligatures with padding, to prevent visible marks of this activity, are often used to cause the hypoxia, which is oxygen deprivation.

Doctor H. L. P. Resnick, an author and researcher in this field states that, "A disruption of the arterial blood supply resulting in a diminished oxygenation of the brain . . . will heighten sensations through diminished ego controls that will be subjectively perceived as giddiness, light-headedness, and exhilaration. This reinforces masturbatory sensations."[1]

A combination of ritualistic behavior, oxygen deprivation, danger, and fantasy appears to bring about sexual gratification for these people. According to Robert R. Hazelwood, Supervisory Special Agent, "Death during such activity may result from: 1) a failure with the physiological mechanism; 2) a failure in the self-rescue device; 3) a failure on the part of the victim's judgment and ability to control a self-endangering fantasy scenario."[2]

This author cites the results of some 150 cases, which were the basis for an in-depth study and subsequent textbook, *Autoerotic Fatalities* (D. C. Heath and Company, 1983)[3] by Supervisory Special Agent Robert R. Hazelwood, Dr. Park Elliot Dietz, M.D., M. P. H., Professor of Law, Behavioral Medicine and Psychiatry at the University of Virginia, and Ann Wolbert Burgess, R.N., D.N.Sc., Associate Director of Nursing Research, Department of Health and Hospitals, Boston, Massachusetts. In my opinion, their text is the most thorough and comprehensive study to date on the subject of autoerotic fatalities.

According to their text, approximately 500 to 1000 people die from autoerotic asphyxiation each year in the United States. Many times this type of case has either been misclassified or gone unrecognized due to lack of knowledge, misinformation, or misguided efforts on the part of the surviving family to "cover-up" what is perceived to be an embarrassing situation.

I have personally investigated and assessed over 100 of these investigations. Oftentimes, during a class presentation on the subject of autoerotic deaths, one of the participants will remark how his department had a case like the ones being presented and that the death had been classified as either a suicide or homicide.

I became involved in one case after reading a *New York Daily News* article that described the suicidal death of a 17-year-old. Based upon my professional experience in the investigation of this type of death, I immediately recognized the possibility of an accidental autoerotic fatality. The following day I called the Detective Commander of the local jurisdiction with whom I had grown up and I felt would be open to my speculations. He filled me in on the details of his investigation, which further assured me that this alleged suicide was in fact a tragic accident. In this incident, the crime scene had been changed. The brother of the deceased had discovered the body, removed the ligature from his brother's neck, and re-dressed him out of embarrassment. I learned that the detective supervisor had never heard of autoerotic fatalities. After I provided him with the necessary information, the case was properly reclassified. More importantly, the surviving family was made aware of the actual circumstances of their son's death. The family, who had been blaming themselves, could not understand why their son would commit suicide. We enlisted the services of a family priest to assist in explaining what had happened to their son. Although at first they were astonished and embarrassed (a typical response in this type of case), they were greatly relieved to learn that their son had not taken his own life due to some unknown personal or family problem, but had died accidentally. In fact, this family actually wanted to go public to warn other parents of this phenomenon. I counseled them against going public, but advised them they could work anonymously to accomplish the same objective without exposing their family to any further trauma.

Periodically, one will read a story in the local newspaper that focuses on one or more deaths believed to be teenage suicides. I remember one particular story in my area that made reference to a "Teenage Suicide Epidemic." The series of stories that followed these initial events was directed toward warning the public about this devastating public health problem. There was a call for a renewed effort in bringing suicide prevention programs into the schools as public health officials sought a solution for what was percieved to be the contagious effect of suicide among teenagers. Parents, teachers, and public health officials were mobilized in an effort to identify a motive for these unexplained deaths. Ironically, it was discovered that half of the reported suicides were actually autoerotic fatalities. However, the focus of attention on this issue, although initially misinterpreted, was instrumental in identifying other potential problems and issues of concern regarding suicide.

Some syndicated publications have reported on the phenomena of autoerotic fatality quite accurately. Stories with headlines such as, "Answers Sought in Unusual Deaths" or "Six Deaths in Past Year Stir Warning," and "Medical Examiner Concerned about Bizarre Fatal Accidents," actually provide a genuine insight into these types of deaths. Of course, there is always the possibility that publicity about this phenomenon may actually increase incidents. I believe, however, that persons predisposed to this type of behavior will neither be encouraged nor discouraged by the presentation of information on sexual asphyxia. Instead, I believe that certain details need to be made public for the purposes of alerting people to the dangers of this potentially lethal practice. As a result, I agreed to an interview with the Associated Press entitled, "Autoerotic Deaths—Shocking Practice Often Mistaken for Teen Suicide."[4] Parents, who have the responsibility of raising their children, as well as educators and others responsible for the public welfare of society have a right to information and need to be educated about this phenomena. I have investigated and consulted on a number of autoerotic deaths involving teenage boys. Teenagers, who are going through a period of sexual experimentation, are extremely vulnerable to peer suggestions. Teenagers have traditionally developed their own life-styles, which involve different pleasures, amusements, and pastimes than those of their parents. They have their own slang, music, expressions, dancing, TV programs, movies, etc. Often parents are not even aware of their children's socialization into the teen culture. They are certainly not privy to their children's secret conversations, social groups, and/or risk-taking ventures, which explains their total shock, horror, and disbelief when advised of this phenomenon.

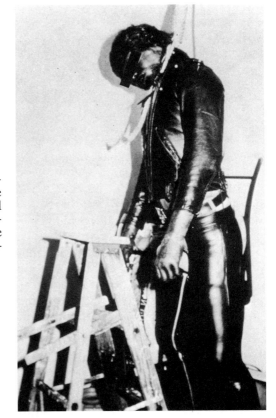

Autoerotic Death: Asphyxiation/Hanging. Notice the bondage. (*Courtesy of* Special Agent Robert R. Hazelwood, Behavioral Science Unit, FBI Academy, Quantico, Virginia.)

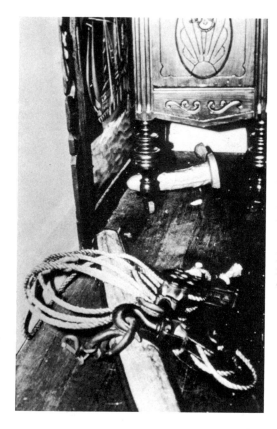

Materials Used in Autoerotic Activities. Evidence of materials used in the bondage and autoerotic activities found in the apartment of the victim in the preceding figure. (*Courtesy of* Special Agent Robert R. Hazelwood, Behavioral Science Unit, FBI Academy, Quantico, Virginia.)

I supervised one investigation where a 16-year-old boy's mother showed him an article about autoerotic deaths in a newspaper so that he would be aware of the dangers. He offhandedly remarked to his mother, "Those kids are stupid. They don't know what they're doing." His mother missed the significance of the remark. Her son was engaged in such activities himself and was found dead two weeks later, the victim of an autoerotic fatality.

In most of the cases in which I was involved, the teenage victim was made aware of the practice through "word-of-mouth." There have been cases, especially those involving adult practitioners, where the victim had learned of this activity through pornographic magazines, X-rated movies, underground publications, the media, and even novels.

Preliminary Investigation at the Scene

Every autoerotic fatality is unique because the circumstances surrounding this activity are based upon the person's fantasy and perception of what is considered sexually stimulating. The death scene will vary according to the victim's age, resources, and/or sexual interests. However, there are some common denominators to suggest that the death may be accidental.

There are five criteria for determining death during dangerous autoerotic practices:

1. Evidence of a physiological mechanism for obtaining or enhancing sexual arousal that provides a self-rescue mechanism or allows the victim to voluntarily discontinue its effect.
2. Evidence of solo sexual activity.
3. Evidence of sexual fantasy aids.
4. Evidence of prior dangerous autoerotic practice.
5. No apparent suicidal intent.[5]

The most common method practiced during this type of activity is neck compression or hanging, with some sort of padding between the neck and the ligature to prevent any markings left by the tightening noose or rope. However, more elaborate and exotic methods such as chest compression, airway obstruction, and oxygen exclusion with gas or chemical replacement have been found.

Asphyxial Deaths—The Pathology of Autoerotic Death

Asphyxiation is the end stage of significant interference with the exchange of oxygen and carbon dioxide. According to Drs. Dominick J. DiMaio and Vincent J. DiMaio, both nationally renowned forensic pathologists, "Asphyxial deaths are caused by the failure of the cells to receive and/or utilize oxygen. This deprivation of oxygen may be partial (*hypoxia*) or total (*anoxia*)."[6]

Asphyxial deaths can be grouped into three categories: suffocation, strangulation, and chemical asphyxia. The most common form of asphyxial death in autoerotic fatalities is strangulation, which is characterized by the closure of the blood vessels and air passages of the neck from hanging or ligature. The suspension of the body may be complete or incomplete. In sexual asphyxia cases, the body is usually in touch with the ground. There may be elaborate bindings of the body and hands of the victim. However, an analysis of these bindings will reveal that the victim was capable of binding him or herself.

Suffocation is the second most frequently occurring form of autoerotic death, which may result from covering the mouth and nose with a plastic bag or mask, or in what is described as proximal or positional asphyxia, such as in chest compression.

Chemical asphyxia takes place when oxygen is excluded by inhaling noxious gases. The most common chemical asphyxial deaths involving autoerotic activities are with nitrous oxide.

The practitioners of this activity often are aware of the possibility of death and may even have taken precautions against a fatal act, but die as a result of a miscalculation. It would appear that the victim, who may be intent upon achieving an orgasm, misjudges the existent hypoxia already present and the time required to reach orgasm by masturbation. The victim loses consciousness and succumbs to the fatal cerebral anoxia.

I had the opportunity to review a case in which the victim had set up a video camera to record his autoerotic fantasy. The victim, who was married with children, had selected an isolated area in the family home to create some sort of execution scenario for his fantasy. He had placed a large sheet over the funishings in the room to create a background for the camera. A hangman's noose was secured by a hook in the ceiling and was tied off to the side. Directly below the hanging noose was a small platform upon which the subject could stand to place the noose over his head and around his neck. The subject was observed walking into the camera's view wearing a pair of women's panties over his head. He looked into the direction of the camera and placed the noose over his head and around his neck. He then stood with his hands behind his back. The hypoxia began to take effect. He suddenly lost his balance and the noose became tightened around his neck. At this point he could have saved himself. However, he was not aware of the impending danger and again placed his hands behind his back and continued with the fantasy. In less than 20 seconds he lost consciousness and went into fatal cerebral anoxia. He attempted to escape, however, it was too late. He had lost muscle coordination and began to convulse. His video production had gone from fantasy to reality in less than 4 minutes. It was an extremely dramatic portrayal of the reality of sexual asphyxia.

Sexual Asphyxia—The Psychosexual Aspects of Autoerotic Activity

The purpose of this section is to acquaint the investigator with some of the clinical terminology used to define bizarre and deviant human sexuality. The psychopathology of this pheomenon is better left to the clinicians and other professionals trained in the fields of medicine and psychiatry. I refer the reader to the *Diagnostic and Statistical Manual of Mental Disorders* (DSM-III) (American Psychiatric Association, 1980), *Abnormal Psychology and Modern Life* (7th edition by Coleman et al.), and Chapter 5 of *Autoerotic Fatalities* (Hazelwood et al., 1983).

The investigative interpretation of the psychosexual aspects of auto-erotic activities can be found in a group of persistent sexual arousal patterns defined in DSM-III as *paraphilias*.

The essential feature of disorders in this subclass is that unusual or bizarre imagery or acts are necessary for sexual excitement. Such imagery or acts tend to be insistently and involuntarily repetitive and generally involve either: 1) preference for use of a nonhuman object for sexual arousal, 2) repetitive sexual activity with humans involving real or simulated suffering or humiliation, or 3) repetitive sexual activity with nonconsenting partners. In other classifications these disorders are referred to as sexual deviations. The term paraphilia is preferable because it correctly emphasizes that the deviation (para) is in that to which the individual is attracted (philia) . . .

Since paraphiliac imagery is necessary for erotic arousal, it must be included in masturbatory or coital fantasies, if not actually acted out alone or with a partner and supporting cast or paraphernalia. In the absence or paraphiliac imagery there is no relief from nonerotic tension, and sexual excitement or orgasm is not attained.

The imagery in a paraphiliac fantasy or the object of sexual excitement in a paraphilia is frequently the stimulus for sexual excitement in individuals without a Psychosexual Disorder. For example, women's undergarments and imagery of sexual coercion are sexually exciting for many men; they are paraphiliac only when they become necessary for sexual excitement.[7]

DSM-III recognizes nine paraphilias, which I have listed with a brief description of the paraphilia for investigative recognition.

Fetishism:	Use of nonliving objects for sexual arousal. (Female undergarments, panties, shoes, etc.)
Transvestism:	Cross-dressing by heterosexual male for sexual excitement. (Ranges from solitary wearing of female clothes to extensive involvement in a transvestite subculture.)

According to Hazelwood et al., "Individuals found cross-dressed at death are more likely to have worn female clothes for their masochistic value than as a reflection of transvestism.[8]

Zoophilia:	Use of animals for sexual arousal. (Includes intercourse with animals as well as training the animal to lick or rub the human partner.)
Pedophilia:	Engaging in sexual activity with prepubertal children.
Exhibitionism:	Exposing the genitals to an unsuspecting stranger for the purposes of obtaining sexual excitement.
Voyeurism:	Repetitive looking at unsuspecting people, who are either naked, in the act of disrobing, or engaging in sexual activity ("The Peeping Tom").

Fantasy Drawings. [A] The victim has drawn a woman, which is actually himself, dressed in "LaFemme" undergarments. His fantasy involved cross dressing. [B] Here we see a female victim who has supposedly hung herself with her own bra. In both drawings the victim has created a fantasy which involves

Sexual Masochism: Getting pleasure from being humiliated, bound, beaten, or otherwise made to suffer for sexual arousal. (Considered a chronic disorder.)

Sexual Sadism: The infliction of physical or psychological pain on another person in order to achieve sexual excitement. (Considered a chronic and progressive disorder.)

Atypical Paraphilia: This is a residual category of DSM-III for individuals with Paraphilias which cannot be classified in any of the other categories.

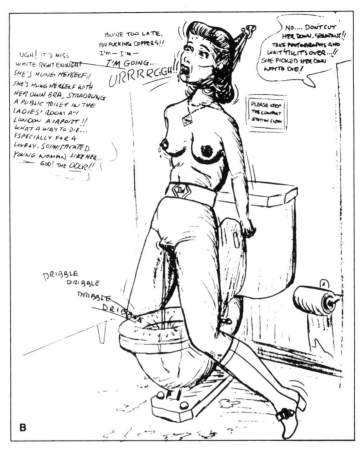

urophilia. There were approximately twenty of these drawings found at the death scene. Additionally, the victim had taken Polaroid photos of himself dressed in female attire acting out similar fantasies.

These include the following: coprophilia (feces), frotteurism (rubbing), klismaphilia (enemas), mysophilia (filth), necrophilia (corpse), telephone scatologia (lewdness), urophilia (urine).[9]

Case Histories

Hanging. A 40-year-old married salesman was discovered in the basement of his residence totally suspended from a floor joist with a large piece of rope ending in a hangman's noose encircling his head. The body was dressed in a white shirt, a white panty-girdle with nylons, and a pair of women's open-toed shoes. A woman's girdle was over the victims' head and his hands were bound by a belt.[10]

Hanging. A white, male in his late forties, never married, living at home with his mother and sister was found hanging in his basement workshop. He was wearing street clothing, which covered woman's undergarments. A bra stuffed with padding, woman's panties, woman's boots, and leather gloves. A mask, which he had apparently been wearing, was found on the floor beneath him. He was hanging by a rope affixed to a hook in the ceiling. There was a Polaroid camera positioned on the workbench and a number of photographs of the deceased participating in this conduct. There were a number of pornographic magazines, depicting female bondage, lesbian conduct, and sadomasochistic behavior found in his room. In addition to these commercial products, police discovered sadomasochistic drawings depicting the deceased dressed as a woman. In these drawings, this "woman" is observed with an erect penis threatening and abusing other women. There were also a number of these sexually explicit drawings of nude and seminude women urinating. These "fantasy drawings" were further illustrated with words indicating that the deceased was actually verbalizing his sadomasochistic fantasies. Also discovered were two legal-size sheets of paper listing approximately 200 pieces of woman's apparel and undergarments that the deceased had purchased. The victim had listed these items by number, description, price, and the name of the store from which the item was purchased. He then had a separate column which indicated whether or not he had photographed himself in the item. This individual's total sex life was involved with solo sexual activities. His drawings further suggested paraphilias of transvestism, sadism, and masochism with fantasies of necrophilia and urophilia.

Chest Compression. The victim was a 49-year-old commercial airline pilot who was married and the father of two small children. On his day off he left his residence, advising his wife that he was going to target practice. A fisherman discovered him a short time later crushed against the left rear fender of his 1968 Volkswagen. The scene was a large turnaround area at the end of a secluded road. The left door was open and the motor was running. The steering wheel was fixed in an extreme left turn position and the automatic transmission was in low gear. Tire tracks indicated that the automobile had been moving in concentric circles. The body was held against the car by a heavy linked chain and was totally nude except for a chain harness. The harness had a moderately tight loop around the neck and was bolted in front. The chain passed down the sternum and abdomen and around the waist to form a second loop. From the waist loop, strands of chain passed on each side of the testicles and into the gluteal fold and was secured to the waist loop in the small of the back. A ten-foot length of chain was attached from the waist loop to the rear bumper and had become wound around the rear axle five times. It is not known whether he jogged behind the car or was dragged; however, when he tired of the exercise he approached the car intending to turn off the motor. In so doing, the chain became slack and the back tire rolled over it causing the chain to become wound onto the rear axle. The trunk of the car contained his clothing, a zippered bag holding locks, bolts, chains, and wrenches. A lock and key were on the ground beside the body and another lock was found twenty feet from the body.[11]

Suffocation. A white male, 66 years of age, was discovered lying upon his bed by police, who had been called to the man's apartment. The deceased was wearing women's clothing, which consisted of a grey turtle neck sweater with crotch snaps and red panty hose. The upper torso was bound with straps and chains which were interconnected by a series of locks. A rubber mask covered his face and the mask was connected to the bedboard by rope. There was an electrical apparatus attached to a hook in the ceiling, which consisted of a timer and two wires. This equipment was plugged into a wall socket. One of the wires extended down to the crotch area of the victim. A copper wire loop had been fitted beneath the snaps of the turtle neck sweater and this could be connected to the electrical device. In the man's room, police investigators discovered three suitcases full of woman's undergarments, wigs, and "falsies," as well as other sexual paraphernalia consisting of dildos, discipline masks, and pornographic materials. When the body was examined, the victim was found to be wearing women's undergarments. Under the head mask, duct tape covered his eyes, foam rubber was stuffed in his mouth, and a headband held a small rubber ball in each ear. He was totally in the dark and couldn't hear a thing, but all of the bindings and chains were within his grasp.

His escape mechanism was a single lock, which secured all of the chains wrapped around his body. The deceased had held the keys for this lock in his right hand. He had apparently dropped his keys on the floor, where the police discovered them. The duct tape and rubber balls in his ears certainly shut out any possibility of seeing the keys or hearing them drop to the floor. He had been bound to the bed in such a manner that he would not have been able to reach down to the floor even if he had heard the keys drop. The cause of death was suffocation. The police supervisor as well as the detective investigating this case had both been to one of my Practical Homicide Investigation lectures. They immediately recognized the death to be an autoerotic fatality based on the

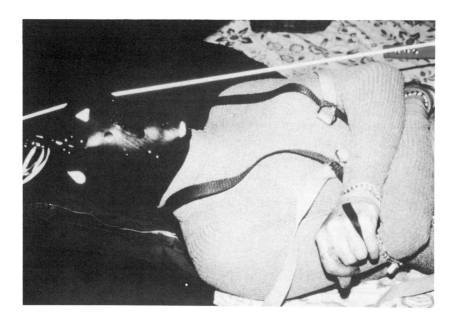

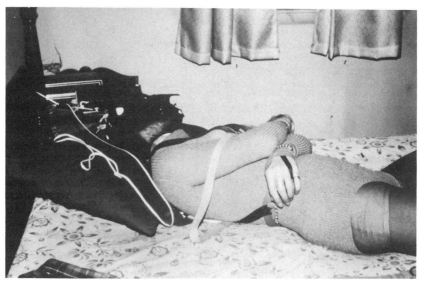

Autoerotic Death Sequence. A male has dressed in female attire with a discipline mask over his head. His eyes were covered with duct tape, his mouth stuffed with foam rubber, a small rubber ball was in each ear, and he had a headband around the ears. The victim was wearing pantyhose and female undergarments beneath this outfit. All of the chains and binds were intercon-

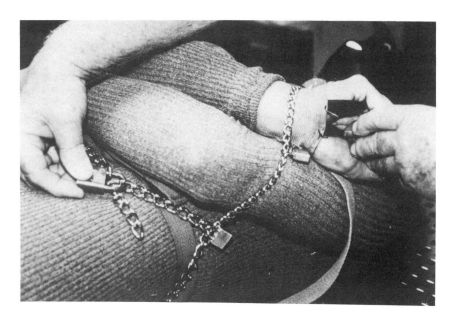

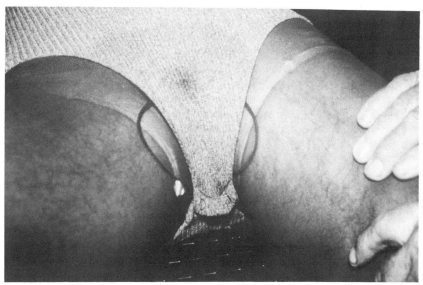

nected. A copper loop of wire in the crotch area had been connected to an electrical apparatus with a timer, which sent intermittent shocks to the victim. The victim was a 66-year-old man. (Courtesy of Det. Lt. Raymond Krolak, Commanding Officer, Investigations Division, Colonie, New York Police Department.)

above information. However, when the medical examiner of the jurisdiction arrived at the scene, he told the detectives it appeared to be a homicide related to "biker-gang" activity. He obviously was not familiar with such cases and based his conclusion of homicide on the bizarre binding of the body.

Oxygen Exclusion. A deceased male was discovered lying on a bed in a rental cabin with a plastic bag over his head. This male had rented the summer cabin during the off-season. The proprietor, who was checking on the rental, made the discovery when he entered the premises and noticed the nude body of the deceased on the bed. Police were called to the location and discovered an array of pornographic magazines opened to the centerfolds on the floor next to the bed. Also next to the bed was a cannister of nitrous oxide. The investigators learned that the man, who had been involved with this activity in the past, had been sniffing the pure nitrous oxide by releasing the gas into the plastic bag from the tank. He would then write down his sexual fantasies on a pad while viewing the pictures of the nude models in the magazines next to the bed. When he placed the plastic bag over his head, the oxygen which had been excluded resulted in asphyxiating the victim.

Female Victims of Autoerotic Fatality

Although most of the cases of autoerotic death involve males, it is important to realize that this type of practice is not limited to males. For example, what may appear to be a sex slaying, involving the bondage and suffocation of a female victim, may in fact be the accidental death of a female practitioner of autoerotic activities. One such case was reported by retired Special Agent Frank Sass of the FBI. A 35-year-old female divorcee was discovered dead by her nine-year-old daughter. The woman was nude and lying on a small shelved space in the rear of a closet in her bedroom. She was on her stomach and an electric vibrator with a hard rubber massaging head was between her thighs and in contact with her vulva. The vibrator was operating when the victim was discovered. Attached to the nipple of her right breast was a spring-type clothespin, compressing her nipple. Immediately below her left breast another clothespin was found. Around the victim's neck was a handtowel; a nylon stocking went over the towel in loop fashion and was fastened to a shelf bracket above her head. The lower portion of the body was supported by the shelf and the victim's upper body rested on her arms, which were extended downward from her body in a push-up position. The clothespins were used to cause discomfort, the vibrator was used in a masturbatory exercise, and the ligature reduced oxygen flow. She obviously intended to support her upper body

Victim of an Autoerotic Fatality. A metal bolt was inserted into the victim's vagina from the rear. The victim was discovered bent over a tub filled with water. The actual cause of death was drowning. This case, at first, was thought to be a sex-related homicide.

weight with her arms, but she lost consciousness and the weight of her body, hanging from the nylon stocking, caused her to strangle.[12]

It should be noted that the female victim of an autoerotic fatality, who has involved herself in binding and some sort of sadomasochistic scenario, presents authorities with circumstances which actually resemble a sex-related homicide.

Hazelwood et al. cite the following case. A 23-year-old black woman was found dead in her bathroom. The victim's upper torso rested on the edge of the bathtub, her face was in the water, and her knees were on the floor. The faucets were turned on, and the water had filled the tub, spilled on the floor, and ran throughout the house. There was vomitus in the tub water. A piece of rope had been doubled and looped around her on the left side of her neck, with the loose ends coming across and over her right shoulder. Her wrists were wrapped together in front of her body and the end of the rope securing them rested in her right hand. The decedent was nude, and a 9 1/2-inch bolt was on the floor beside the body. There was a bruise on the left side of her forehead and drops of blood were found on the edge and side of the tub. Autopsy revealed the cause of death to be aspiration of vomitus.[13]

This case was investigated initially as a suicide, based upon statements by a relative and friend of the victim. It was also investigated as a possible homicide, with the boyfriend, who had discovered the body, as a primary suspect. Actually, this case had enough factors to support both possibilities. In actuality, the case was eventually classified as an autoerotic fatality. According to the authors, "A theory that accounts for all of the facts in this case is that the victim had been drawing a bath while asphyxiating herself with the rope, intending to use the bolt for manual masturbation, or already having done so. Through asphyxiation, she lost consciousness, struck her head on the bathtub, and aspirated vomitus . . ."[14]

Notification and Advising the Surviving Family of the Mode of Death

Advising surviving family members of the circumstances and nature of this type of death can be quite stressful and difficult. The tragedy is often compounded by survivor reactions, which range from guilt, shame, and humiliation to anger and rage.

As professional investigators, we are entrusted with a profound duty and responsibility—not only to the deceased, but to the surviving family as well. It is imperative that we do all in our power to assist the surviving family by our professionalism. The official explanation of the circumstances of the death is best undertaken with the assistance of clergy or a professional practitioner after considering the family's ability to cope with the facts of the case. However, it is important to note that each case and set of circumstances will dictate the proper course of action. In some instances, I believe investigators, who recognize what has happened, may make a conscious decision to spare the family and allow them to believe the death to be a suicide. Under certain circumstances this action might be an entirely appropriate alternative. I offer this personal advice as a veteran homicide cop. Whatever course of action you decide, "just make sure you do the right thing."

Investigative Considerations

Although each autoerotic death scene may be unique, there are many common factors for the investigator to consider in making his or her determination of the mode of death. I have listed some of these considerations within this section.

Victim Profile. Research has indicated that most victims of this activity are white males ranging from 13 years of age to their late thirties. This group is followed by white females in their early twenties, black males 20 to 40 years of age, and one reported black female in her late twenties. The victims are considered to be basically moral people, successful in their respective occupations. They may be considered shy by friends because they are not sexually or romantically active. However, they may be married or involved with a significant other person. Interviews and investigations do not disclose any indications of depression or suicidal tendencies.

Location. The location selected is usually secluded or isolated and affords the practitioner the opportunity to involve himself or herself in a private fantasy. Some examples are as follows: locked rooms at home, attics, basements, garages or workshops, motel rooms, places of employment during nonbusiness hours, summer houses, or outdoor locations.

Nudity. Most victims of suicide are not found in the nude. Although this is not a conclusive indicator, the discovery of a nude victim should alert the investigator to the possibility of an autoerotic fatality if other indicators, such as those listed below, are present.

Determining the Involvement of Sexual Asphyxia: Autoerotic Checklist

There are certain questions which the investigator should consider in determining whether or not the death is related to autoerotic activity.

1. Is the victim nude, sexually exposed, or—if a male—is he dressed in articles of feminine attire: transvestism, make-up, wigs?
2. Is there evidence of masturbatory activity: tissues, towels, or hanky in hand, or in shorts to catch semen? Seminal fluids?
3. Is there evidence of infibulation: piercing or causing pain to the genitalia, self-torture, masochism, pins in penis, etc.?
4. Are sexually stimulating paraphernalia present: vibrators, dildos, sex aids, pornographic magazines, butt plugs, etc.?
5. Is bondage present: ropes, chains, blindfolds, gags, etc.? Are any constrictive devices present: corset, plastic wrap, belts, ropes, or vacuum cleaner hoses around the body or chest constraints?
6. Is there protective padding between the ligature and the neck: towels, rags, or cloth to prevent rope burns or discomfort?
7. Are the restraints interconnected? (Do the ropes and ties come together or are they connected? Are the chains interconnected

through one another? Is the victim tied to himself, so that by putting pressure on one of the limbs the restraints are tightened?

8. Are mirrors or other reflective devices present? Are they positioned so that the victim can view his or her activities?

9. Is there evidence of fantasy (diaries, erotic literature, etc.) or fetishism (woman's panties, bras, girdles, leather, rubber, latex, high-heel shoes, etc.)?

10. Is the suspension point within reach of the victim or is there an escape mechanism (keys, lock, slip knot, etc.)?

11. Is there evidence of prior such activities (abrasions or rope burns on suspension point)? Unexplained secretive behavior, or long stays in isolated areas, rope burns on neck, etc.?

12. Does the victim possess literature dealing with bondage, escapology, or knots?

13. Is there a positioned camera? (Check film and/or videotapes. Look for photos and view any videotapes in camera.)

While not all such deaths will involve the above characteristics, their presence will certainly alert the investigator to the possibility of death occurring as the result of sexual misadventure.

Summary

The investigation of sexual asphyxia and the appropriate determination of mode of death require that the investigator conduct a knowledgeable scene examination. This obviously means that the investigator should have an understanding of clues that may be present both at the scene and in the background of the deceased.

The psychological autopsy (see "Suicides") can be helpful in resolving those cases in which it is not clear whether the motivational intent was suicidal or autoerotic in nature.[15] As further information on this mode of death becomes available through research, the investigator will be afforded additional assistance in making this determination and properly classifying these cases.

References

1. H. L. P. Resnick. "Eroticized Repetitive Hangings—A Form of Self-Destruction." *American Journal of Psychotherapy*, January 1972, p. 10.

2. Robert R. Hazelwood, Ann Wolbert Burgess, and Nicholas Groth. "Death During Dangerous Autoerotic Practice." *Social Science and Medicine.* Elmsford, New York: Pergamon Press, Vol. 15E, pp. 129–133.

3. Robert R. Hazelwood, Park Elliot Dietz, Ann Wolbert Burgess. *Autoerotic Fatalities.* Lexington, Massachusetts: Lexington Books, D. C. Heath & Company, 1983.

4. Paul Raeburn, "Autoerotic Deaths—Shocking Practice Often Mistaken for Teen Suicide." *Sunday Journal News.* December 2, 1984.
5. Hazelwood et al. "Death During Dangerous Autoerotic Practice," p.2.
6. Dominick J. DiMaio and Vincent J. DiMaio. *Practical Aspects of Forensic Pathology.* New York: Elsevier Science Publishing Co., 1989.
7. American Psychiatric Association. *Diagnostic and Statistical Manual of Mental Disorders,* 3rd ed. Washington D.C.: American Psychiatric Association, 1980, pp. 266–267.
8. Hazelwood et al. *Autoerotic Fatalities,* p. 100.
9. American Psychiatric Association, p. 275.
10. Hazelwood et al. "Death During Dangerous Autoerotic Practice," p. 3.
11. J. Rupp. "The Love Bug." *Journal of Forensic Science* 18: 259–262(1973).
12. Frank Sass. "Sexual Asphyxia in the Female." *Journal of Forensic Science* 20:181–185(1975); also in *Psychiatric Nursing in the Hospital and the Community, 3rd ed.* Ann Wolbert Burgess (Ed.), Englewood Cliffs, New Jersey: Prentice-Hall, Inc., 1981, pp. 316–319.
13. Hazelwood et al. *Autoerotic Fatalities,* pp. 136–137.
14. *Ibid.,* p. 138.
15. N. Hibbler. "The Psychological Autopsy." *Forensic Science Digest* 5:42(1978).

Selected Reading

Adelson, Lester. *The Pathology of Homicide.* Springfield, Illinois: Charles C. Thomas, 1974.

American Psychiatric Association. *Diagnostic and Statistical Manual of Mental Disorders,* 3rd ed. (DSM-III). Washington, D.C.: American Psychiatric Association, 1980.

Burgess, Ann W. *Psychiatric Nursing in the Hospital and the Community,* 3rd ed. Englewood Cliffs, New Jersey: Prentice-Hall, Inc., 1981.

DiMaio, Dominick J., and DiMaio, Vincent J. M. *Forensic Pathology.* New York: Elsevier Science Publishing Company, Inc., 1990.

Geberth Vernon J. "Sexual asphyxia—the phenomenon of autoerotic fatalities." *Law and Order* vol. 37 (1989).

Harris, Raymond I. *Outline of Death Investigation.* Springfield, Illinois: Charles C. Thomas, 1962.

Hazelwood, Robert R., Burgess, Ann W., and Groth, Nicholas. "Death During Dangerous Autoerotic Practice," in *Social Science and Medicine.* Elmsford, New York: Pergamon Press, Ltd.

Hazelwood, Robert R., Dietz, Park Elliot, and Burgess, Ann W. *Autoerotic Fatalities.* Lexington, Massachusetts: D. C. Heath & Company, 1983.

Hughes, D. J. *Homicide Investigative Techniques.* Springfield, Illinois: Charles C. Thomas, 1974.

O'Hara, Charles E. *Fundamentals of Criminal Investigation.* 5th ed. Springfield, Illinois: Charles C. Thomas, 1980.

Raeburn, Paul. "Autoerotic Deaths—Shocking Practice Often Mistaken for Teen Suicide." *New York Sunday Journal News,* December 2, 1984.

Resnick, H. L. P. "Eroticized Repetitive Hangings—A Form of Self-Destruction." *American Journal of Psychotherapy,* January 1972.

Sass, Frank. "Sexual Asphyxia in the Female." *Journal of Forensic Science* 20:181–185(1973).

Snyder, LeMoyne. *Homicide Investigation.* 3rd ed. Springfield, Illinois: Charles C. Thomas, 1977.

Spitz, Werner U., and Fisher, Russell S. *Medicolegal Investigation of Death: Guidelines for the Application of Pathology to Crime Investigation.* Springfield, Illinois: Charles C. Thomas, 1973.

Svensson, Arne, Wendel, Otto, and Fisher, Barry A. J. *Techniques of Crime Scene Investigation,* 3rd ed. New York: Elsevier North Holland, Inc., 1981.

The Investigation of Sex-Related Homicides

12

Sex-related homicides include rape-murders, serial murders, killings that involve both anal and oral sodomy and other acts of sexual perversion, as well as other sexually oriented interpersonal violence cases.

A homicide is classified as "sex-related" when there is evidence of sexual activity observed at the crime scene or upon the body of the victim. This evidence includes:

1. type or lack of attire on the victim;
2. evidence of seminal fluid on, near, or in the body;
3. evidence of sexual injury and/or sexual mutilation;
4. sexualized positioning of the body;
5. evidence of substitute sexual activity, i.e., fantasy, ritualism, symbolism, and/or masturbation;
6. multiple stabbings or cuttings to the body, including slicing wounds across the abdomen of the victim, throat slashing, and overkill-type injuries, which are considered highly suggestive of sexual motivation.[1]

The victims of these crimes are usually females and young children; however, sex-related homicides can involve homosexual relationships (see "Homosexual Homicide"). The killers are usually male.

The homicide might have sexual implications even without an overt sex act or observable sexual activity at the crime scene. It is important to note that, unlike other murders, the motive or reason for the killing may not always be readily discernable or as "clear-cut" as in a robbery-homicide or organized crime "hit."

Practically speaking, if the body is that of a female, and it is found nude or partially clothed, the investigator should think "sex crime."

Crime Scene Investigation

The search of the homicide crime scene is the most important phase of the scene investigation, and has a twofold purpose:

1. The complete documentation of events should be accomplished prior to any other police procedures at the scene and should include photographs (both black and white and color) and/or videotape, as well as crime scene sketches.
2. A careful and complete search should be conducted for any forensic materials and other evidence, which might provide a clue to the identity of the killer.

Sex-Related Crime Scene Checklist

☐ Seminal fluid must be collected as soon as possible before it is lost or destroyed. *Consider DNA testing technique requirements.*

☐ Bloodstains, spittle, and hair (including pubic combings) should be obtained at the scene, properly packaged, and forwarded to lab. *Consider DNA testing techniques.*

☐ Trace evidence found on the victim and/or upon victim's clothing should be collected.

☐ Bruises and marks on the victim, including the presence of sadistic injuries, should be noted and documented in the investigative notes.

☐ Urine or feces left at the scene by the assailant should be recorded and collected. *DNA Testing can be performed on urine.*

☐ Fingernail scrapings should be obtained for an analysis of any blood, skin, or hair from the suspect. *Consider DNA testing technique.*

☐ Confer with the medical examiner and ensure that specimens are taken from the body (e.g., hair from various areas of the body). In addition, vaginal washings, as well as anal, nasal, and oral swabs, should be requested for serological evaluation and examination. *Consider DNA testing technique.*

☐ Examine the scene for evidence of a struggle: the presence of torn clothing, missing buttons, ripped textiles, marks on the ground or floor and blood splatters must all be photographed, documented, and collected as evidence.

☐ Homicides involving mutilation may yield clues, such as style of attack, type of weapon used, amount and location of mutilation, position of the body, etc. These items should be recorded (see Chapter 17).

☐ If a suspect has been taken into custody, his or her clothing should be taken and an examination conducted for any physical evidence.

☐ Each piece of evidence should be packaged in a separate container.

☐ The suspect's body should be examined for any fingernail scratches, bite marks, or other indications of a violent struggle.

☐ Hair and blood samples should be obtained. (Assure that any such samples are obtained legally.)

☐ The body should be examined for the presence of bite-mark evidence. Collect and record:

    ☐ Saliva washing of the bite-mark area for blood grouping. Use 100% cotton dampened in distilled water. *Important:* Obtain a control sample from another area of the body.

    ☐ Photograph the bite mark. Obtain B&W and color photos. Use a rule of measure and obtain an anatomical landmark.

    ☐ Casting (if possible); use dental materials.

In sex-related homicide cases, basic evidence-collection procedures acquire an increased importance. Human behavior patterns and psychosexual activities, not generally amenable to ordinary collection techniques, become additional factors to consider in determining the reason and motive for the killing.

Human Sexuality and Sexual Deviance

The three components of the human sex drive are biological (instinctive), physiological (functional), and emotional (mental). According to experts, the emotional component is the strongest of the three, accounting for approximately 70% of the human sex drive. As emotions are controlled by the mind, it follows that *the mind controls the act.* The mind determines what is and what is not sexually arousing to an individual, which can be an important consideration when analyzing *what took place* in a sex-related crime scene.

Essentially, our human sexuality is established in our psychosexual development through conditioning. Sexual behaviors are learned behaviors in which the individual develops a perception of what is sexually satisfying and what is socially appropriate within the context of his or her environment. Sex is also a sensory act that involves the five senses (touch, sight, sound, smell, and taste) to varying degrees. For example, the sight of a scantily clothed woman might be an arousal factor for a man. Or, the sense of touch as it relates to a tender caress might be the stimulus that serves as an arousal factor for a woman. These are perfectly appropriate responses because they are generally viewed as acceptable behaviors. However, persons who are sexually inhibited may develop unconventional forms of sexual expression. The person who becomes aroused looking at a scantily clad woman could possibly become obsessed with this type of behavior. A deviance might then emerge in the form of compulsive voyeurism. The determination of acceptable versus unacceptable behavior is based upon statistical, cultural, religious, and subjective considerations. The subjective determination of what is sexually pleasing to the individual could be, and many times is, in conflict with the *acceptable* standards.

Unacceptability of a behavior does not prevent the individual from expressing his or her sexual needs. According to Coleman et al. (1984) "The sex drive is normally sufficiently powerful enough to override all but the most severe social sanctions. Thus we see variant sexual needs frequently erupting into variant sexual behaviors."[2]

These variations are divided into two groupings. The distinction between the categories is based on social effect. Does the activity infringe on the public welfare? Or is the activity a victimless sexual variant. We in law enforcement become involved in what are described as sexual deviations. According to Coleman et al., *sexual deviations* are described as "acts which involve nonconsent or assault and those acts which can be described as problematic from the standpoint of the welfare of society." The sexual deviations are:[3]

Voyeurism,	Incest and rape,
Sexual sadism,	Pedophilia,
Exhibitionism,	Masochism.

The term paraphilia (*para*—deviance; *philia*—attraction) is an attraction to deviance.[4] "The paraphilias are a group of persistent sexual arousal patterns in which unusual objects, rituals, or situations are required for full sexual satisfaction to occur."[5]

According to DSM-III there are nine paraphilias as listed below. For further information consult the *Diagnostic Manual of Mental Disorders III* and *Abnormal Psychology* (7th ed.) by Coleman et al.

Fetishism: Using nonliving objects for sexual arousal (female undergarments, shoes, etc.).

Transvestism: Cross-dressing by heterosexual males for sexual excitement. It ranges from solitary wearing of female clothes to extensive involvement in a transvestite subculture.

Zoophilia: Using animals for sexual arousal, including intercourse with animals as well as training the animal to lick or rub the human partner.

Pedophilia: Engaging in sexual activity with prepubertal children.

Exhibitionism: Exposing genitals to an unsuspecting stranger for the purpose of obtaining sexual excitement.

Bondage as Fantasy—Cordophilia. This bondage scenario shows a person as a willing participant in a sex game.

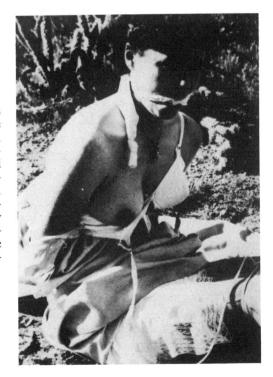

Bondage as Reality—Sadistic Murder. In this photo we see the bound victim of a serial killer. While acting out a sadistic fantasy, he would bind and sexually abuse his victims prior to killing them. The killer took this photograph of the victim shortly before her death. Police recovered a number of these type photos at the killer's residence.

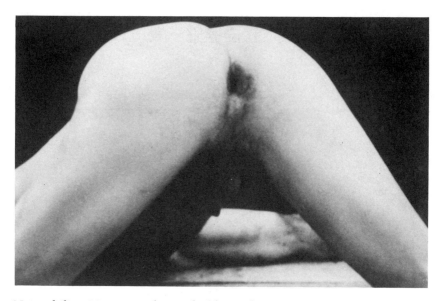

Necrophilia—Homosexual Assault. This male victim was stabbed to death and *then* sexually assaulted anally in an act of necrophilia.

Sadomasochistic Paraphernalia. S&M paraphernalia that was removed from the scene of a sex-related death.

Voyeurism:	Repetitive looking at unsuspecting people, who are either naked, in the act of disrobing, or engaging in sexual activity—the "Peeping Tom."
Sexual Masochism:	Getting pleasure from being humiliated, bound, beaten, or otherwise made to suffer for sexual arousal (considered a chronic disorder).
Sexual Sadism:	Inflicting physical or psychological pain on another person in order to achieve sexual excitement (considered a chronic and progressive disorder).
Atypical Paraphilias:	A residual category of DSM-III for individuals with paraphilias that cannot be classified in any of the other categories. These include the following:[6]

Coprophilia:	A sexual arousal by feces.
Frotteurism:	A sexual arousal by rubbing against the genitalia or body of another.
Klismaphilia:	A sexual arousal by the giving or receiving of enemas.
Mysophilia:	A sexual arousal by filth.
Necrophilia:	A sexual attraction to dead bodies; having intercourse with a dead body.
Telephone Scatolgia:	A sexual arousal by making obscene telephone calls. Lewdness.
Urophilia:	A sexual arousal by urine.

Determining Motivation

An extremely important aspect of the homicide investigation is the determination of the *motive* for the killing. In the sex-related homicide, there are a number of possibilities to consider. Remember, sex-related homicides include rape-murders, serial murders, killings that involve anal and oral sodomy and other acts of sexual perversion, as well as interpersonal violence scenarios.

No one acts without motivation. According to the late James A. Brussel, M.D., a criminal psychiatrist:

> . . . the motivations behind the acts of a madman possess their own logic. The psychotic murderer does not act wholly irrationally. There is a method to his madness: there is a logic, a rationale, hidden behind what he does and how he does it, however wildly bizarre and completely without reason it appears to be . . .[7]

The investigative challenge is to discover this seemingly irrational logic and apply this information to the case.

A careful search for evidence of sexual activity should always be conducted at the crime scene and surrounding area. The investigator should search for the presence of sexual assault activity as well as substitute and paraphiliac behaviors. This evidence may be seminal fluid in the vagina, mouth, or rectum, or semen and other evidence discovered on the surface of the body or upon the clothing. Pornographic books, videos, magazines, and/or photographs may be found at the crime scene. The photographs may depict the victim involved in sexual activity. Writings or messages may have been left by the offender at the crime scene and/or upon the body of the deceased. In any event, these are important factors in determining the type of sexual activity that may have taken place.

Human behavior, although unpredictable, is often repetitive. Research indicates that certain actions engaged in at the homicide crime scene by certain types of personalities will repeat themselves in other homicide investigations. The homicide detective who has enhanced his experience with a comprehension of the psychodynamics of human behavior will be able to develop a base of knowledge that can be applied to the review of similar cases.

There are certain preliminary questions an investigator should ask when examining a crime scene. *What took place? Why did it occur? Who could have done it?*

The reason or motivation for the crime is an extremely important consideration in establishing the investigative direction. Was the mur-

Crime Scene—Sex-Related Homicide. This is a crime scene photograph of a sex-related homicide. The first question is, "What took place?"

der the result of a lover's quarrel? Can the case be attributed to interpersonal violence? Does it appear the victim was killed during a rape or sodomy attempt? Is the killing sexually oriented? Is there a psychotic motive, which sometimes appears to be motiveless or bizarre? Or, is the homicide the work of a sexual psychopath, with sadistic or impulsive implications? Each of these scenarios suggests a specific course of action.

However, in sex-related homicide investigations the motivation behind the killing may not be immediately ascertained. And, even when you do believe you have determined the motive, my personal experience suggests caution.

I remember reviewing an investigation in which the partially clad body of a 28-year-old college coed had been found on campus of a large university. Her pants and panties had been removed, her legs had been spread apart, and her blouse had been pushed up to reveal her breasts. The cause of death was not readily apparent at the scene; however, there was evidence of sexual activity at the crime scene, which the medical examiner confirmed by the presence of semen in the girl's vagina. The motive was determined to be a rape-homicide. Upon further investigation it was discovered that the young woman, who was a pharmaceutical student at the university, had actually committed suicide the evening before. A suicide note was found in her dorm that

Rape-Murder? or Sexual Perversion? This victim of a suicide was sexually assaulted 12 hours after death. At first viewing, one can see how this scenario might be mistaken for a rape-murder. (Courtesy of Detective Earl McKee, University of Utah Police Department.)

explained that she was extremely depressed and had taken an overdose of prescription drugs. The medicolegal autopsy confirmed that her death was related to an overdose of drugs. Eventually, the homicide inquiry revealed that the grounds-keeper, who had initially reported finding the body, was responsible for the sexual act. He confessed to police that he had come across the body and experienced a "sexual urge." The girl's body, which had been lying there for some 12 hours, was in rigor. He broke the rigor to loosen her legs, removed her clothing, and engaged in an act of necrophilia. What had appeared to be a rape-homicide was actually a suicide with an act of sexual deviance committed upon the body after death.

Remember, things are not always what they appear to be.

The identification of the victim is a crucial consideration in determining motivation. An intensive investigation into the victim's background, life-style, and associations many times will reveal a possible motive. An examination of any relationships, acquaintances, and risk factors may provide a clue to the "Who could have done it?" scenario. For example, who does the victim live with? Who was with the victim last? Does it appear that the victim knew his or her assailant? What is the victim's current social status? Why was this particular victim selected? Does the crime appear to be a "stranger-homicide"? Was the deceased in a high-risk occupation (call girl or prostitute)? Was the victim a runaway or hitchhiker? Or, was the victim a late-hours worker, e.g., waitress or service worker, who had to travel alone at night? What method of transportation did she use? What route did she travel?

There are any number of questions which can be asked and answered depending upon the circumstances of the crime scene. Consequently, an important factor in the proper formulation of a hypothesis will be the experience and knowledge of the investigator assigned to the case.

Examining a crime scene with the purpose of identifying and interpreting certain items, which may serve as clues to the type of personality, is an excellent technique. (See "Investigative Assessment—Criminal Personality Profiling," Chapter 17.) There are common denominators between the psychological make-up of the criminal and the psychological clues the crime scene reveals.

Research by the FBI's Behavioral Science Unit into sex-related homicides has disclosed a remarkable consistency in the type of person who commits certain acts. Although there is a wide range of differences among offenders who commit similar offenses, these offenders also share similarities and common traits.

Organized and Disorganized Offenders

The organized and disorganized dichotomy devised by the FBI's Behavioral Science Unit is a description of criminal-offender typologies. The information herein presented as it relates to the phenomena of organized and disorganized offenders is based upon the studies and research of the Behavioral Science Unit, personal interviews with Supervisory Special Agent Robert K. Ressler, and others involved in the project, as well as the personal experience of the author as a homicide investigator.

What is the Motive?

PSYCHOPATHIC	PSYCHOTIC
Sadistic	Motiveless
Impulsive	Bizarre
Organized	*Disorganized*

The Organized Offender

The organized offender is usually above-average in intelligence. He is methodical and cunning. His crime is well thought out and carefully planned. The crime is usually committed out of his area of residence or work. He is likely to own a car that is in good condition. He is mobile and travels many more miles than the average person. Fantasy and ritual are important to the organized-type personality. He selects a victim who he considers to be the "right" type, someone he can control (either through manipulation or strength), usually a stranger. Most of his victims will share some common traits.

He is considered socially adept. He uses his verbal skills to manipulate his victims and gain control over them until he has them within his "comfort zone." He is fully cognizant of the criminality of his act and takes pride in his ability to thwart the police investigation. He is likely to follow news reports of the event and will often take a "souvenir" from his victim as a reminder, which is sometimes used to relive the event or continue with the fantasy. (The souvenir is referred to as a "trophy" when describing this particular action by the organized offender.)

He is excited by the cruelty of the act and may engage in torturing the victim. Sexual control of the victim plays an important part in this scenario. He avoids leaving evidence behind and usually brings his own weapon. He is aware of police procedures. The body is often removed from the crime scene. He may do this to "taunt" the police or to prevent its discovery by transporting it to a location where it will be well hidden. (See Chapter 17 for a more in-depth profile of the Organized Offender.)

The Disorganized Offender

The disorganized offender is usually below-average in intelligence. He is generally a loner type, who usually is not married, lives either alone or with a relative in close proximity to the crime scene. He experiences difficulty in negotiating interpersonal relationships and is described as socially inadequate.

He acts impulsively under stress and will usually select a victim from his own geographic area. In most instances, this type of offender will not own a vehicle. Generally, he will avoid people and can be described as sexually incompetent, i.e., without any meaningful sexual relationships. He uses a "blitz" style of attack, which catches the victim off guard. This spontaneous action, in which the offender suddenly "acts out" his fantasy, does not allow for a conscious plan or even the thought of being detected, which is why the crime scene will be disorganized.

The disorganized offender usually depersonalizes his victim by facial

Defeminization. A disorganized offender mutilated this female victim and removed her breasts.

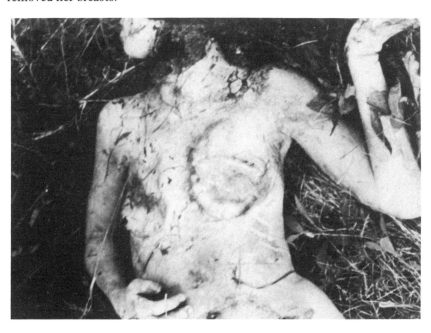

destruction or overkill-type wounds. Any sexually sadistic acts are performed postmortem. Mutilation to the genitalia, rectum, breasts of females, neck, throat, and buttocks are performed because these parts of the body contain a strong sexual significance to him. (See Chapter 17 for an in-depth profile of the Disorganized Offender.)

According to Ressler et al. (1986) ". . . there are significant differences between the organized and disorganized offender. However, there are no situations where the organized and disorganized offenders are mutually exclusive. That is, both types of murderers are capable of all types of behavior."[8]

Homosexual Homicides

Homosexual homicides are quite common and may involve male victims killed by other males, or female victims involved in some sort of lesbian relationship and killed by another female.

Homosexual homicides include serial murders, killings that involve forced anal and/or oral sodomy, other acts of sexual perversion, as well as sexually oriented interpersonal violence cases and robbery.

It has been my experience that male homosexual homicides involving interpersonal violence often present overkill patterns of injuries.

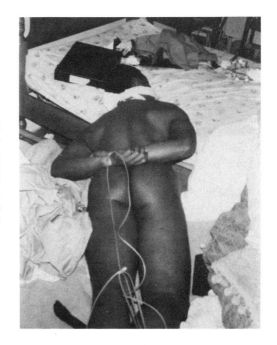

Homosexual Robbery-Homocide. This victim met his assailant, who pretended to be gay, at a homosexual bar. He brought the man back to his apartment for a sexual liaison. During the sexual activity the offender killed the victim and robbed the apartment.

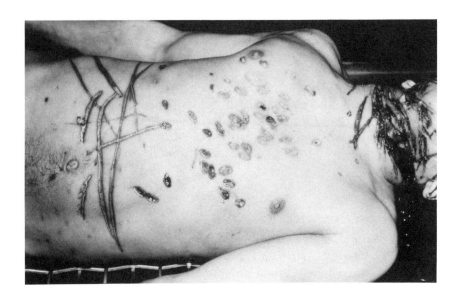

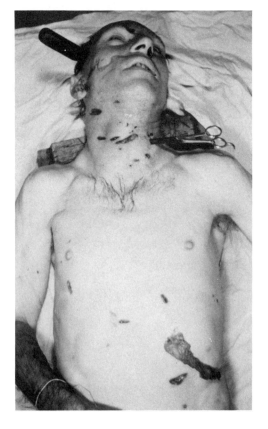

Homosexual Homicides Involving "Lover's Quarrels". Slashing and Cutting to Throats of Victims. Note the increased level of violence and "overkill" injuries that are common in homosexual homicides. (Courtesy of Dr. Dominick J. DiMaio, M.D., Former Chief Medical Examiner, City of New York.)

These injuries are usually directed to the throat, chest, and abdomen of the victims. It has been suggested, but not empirically proven, that the assault to the throat takes place because of the sexual significance of the mouth and throat in male homosexual "love-making." In any event, if presented with the death of a male in a crime scene that suggests sexual activity, and there is cutting or slashing of the throat, consider a homosexually oriented interpersonal violence motivation. I would suggest that these "lover's quarrels" between male homosexuals manifest an increased level of violence due to the fact that the parties involved in the emotional conflict are both sexual aggressors.

There are homosexual homicides in which the victim is killed by a person described as homophobic. I remember a case that took place in Greenwich Village in New York City. The homophobic son of a minister was apparently distressed over his own homosexual tendencies and went on a shooting rampage with an automatic rifle and "sprayed" street corners where homosexual men would congregate. More recently, in New York City, a Corrections Officer was arrested and charged with a series of killings. He reportedly would cruise a certain area in his vehicle looking for gay men whom he would proposition. He then would bring them to a secluded location and kill them with his newly issued off-duty revolver. Three murders were linked to this individual.

The murders by six serial homosexual killers (attributed to John Wayne Gacy from the Chicago area of Illinois; Wayne Williams "the Atlanta Child Killer" from Georgia; William Bonan from Los Angeles, California; Bruce A. Davis from Illinois; Dean Coril from Texas; and Randy Steven Kraft from California) accounted for the deaths of 142 young men and boys.

Homosexual homicides involving forced anal and/or oral sex are to some extent analogous to the rape-homicide among the heterosexual population. These can be extremely brutal homicides, where death occurs from the amount of force used to overcome the victim's resistance, or the victim is killed to prevent identification.

I remember supervising the investigation of a homicide on a South Bronx rooftop landing. The deceased, who lived in the building, was discovered at the location by a male resident of the building. The reporting witness told police that he had gone to the roof to urinate when he came upon the body. He told the officers that he had lit a match and recognized the dead man as a fellow resident. He then reportedly summoned his wife to the roof and she called the police. The victim was fully clothed but there was a belt around his neck. Once again, I caution the reader. I do not have any independent empirical data to support this theory. However, it has been my experience that when you observe a belt, or strap, or ligature around the neck of a male victim

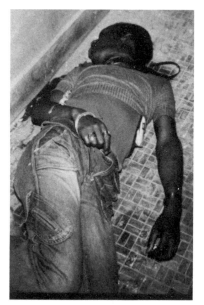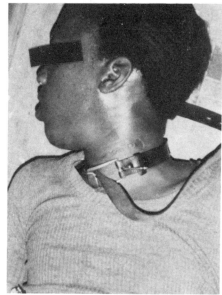

Homosexual Homicide—Victim Anally Assaulted. Belt Used to Overcome Victim's Resistance. These photographs show a homosexual homicide crime scene. Note the belt around the neck of the victim may be a clue, which suggests that the offender may have spent time in a prison or institution.

Standard Color Codex for Homosexual Handkerchief Codes

		Where worn	
Handkerchief color	Sexual activity	Left	Right
Red	Fisting	Top	Bottom
Dark blue	Anal intercourse	Giver	Receiver
Light blue	Fellatio	Desires	Provides
Robin egg blue	Sixty-nine	Both	Both
Mustard	Penis more than 8''	Has	Desires
Orange	Anything	Top	Bottom
Yellow	Golden shower	Giver	Receiver
Green	Hustler	Seller	Buyer
Olive drab	Into uniforms	Both	Both
White	Masturbation	Desires	Dual
Grey	Bondage	Giver	Desires
Brown	Scat (Fecal matter)	Spreads	Receives
Black	Heavy S & M	Top	Bottom
Purple	Genital torture	Piercer	Receiver

311

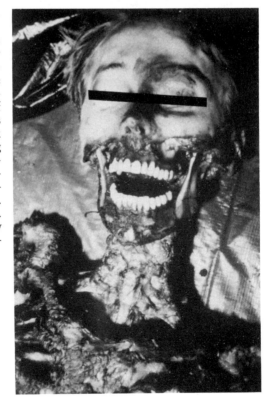

Homosexual "Snuff-Killings." The "Death-Mask" Case. These two photos show the decomposed body of a male victim of a homosexual "snuff-killing." Note the leather mask on the skeleton. Ironically, the face of the victim, which was tightly covered by the mask in an outdoor location during the winter months, was preserved well enough for physical identification of the deceased by family members. (Courtesy of Stephen G. Scurti, Chief of Police, Stony Point, New York Police Department.)

you can expect that there has been forced anal sodomy. This method of controlling the victim by choking off the air is a "prison trick" employed by the more aggressive male inmates to intimidate and sexually dominate other weaker males. I immediately recognized the significance of the belt and directed that the male who found the body be brought in for questioning as a "witness." Investigation at the scene indicated this to be a sex-related death. A canvass of the building yielded evidence that the victim and the reporting witness were observed going to the roof together. The "witness" had just been released from prison. Originally, he told his wife that some "faggot" in the building had "hit-on-him" sexually. He then explained to her how he got mad and beat the guy to death. He conveniently forgot to tell his wife that he had anal intercourse with the deceased before strangling him. When the wife was advised of what had actually transpired on the roof landing, she became the state's best witness.

Often male-oriented homosexual homicides involve bizarre and sadistic methodologies, such as "S&M" (sadomasochism) or "B&D" (bondage and discipline) scenarios. Homosexual activities involving "fisting" (the "top-man" inserts his lubricated fist and forearm up to the elbow into the anal cavity of the "bottom-man") and other dangerous and life-threatening sexual perversions can result in death, including homosexual "snuff" killings.

The Rockland County, New York, "Death-Mask" case, which made national headlines, is an example of depraved sexual violence involving bondage, beatings, and torture. The victim, who was a male Norwegian fashion student, was brought to the home of one of the perpetrators. He was stripped, sexually abused, tightly laced into a leather bondage mask, and then shot in the head at point blank range during an evening of sadistic homosexual depravity.

Classifications

In my opinion as an expert in the sphere of homicide investigation, sex-related homicides can be classified into *four distinct categories* based upon frequency of occurrence.

1. Interpersonal violence-oriented disputes and assaults.
2. Rape- and/or sodomy-oriented assault.
3. Deviant-oriented assault, commonly referred to as a lust murder or psychotic killing. (*In these situations the motive for the murder is not readily discernible.*)
4. The serial murder.

Interpersonal Violence-Oriented Disputes and Assaults

The most common type of sex-related homicide originates from interpersonal violence. "Sexual domestic disputes" involve husbands and wives, men and women, boyfriends and girlfriends, boyfriends and boyfriends, girlfriends and girlfriends, and on occasion even siblings. They may also involve third-party relationships, such as "love triangles," former husbands and/or wives, and jilted lovers.

In some instances the death may not appear to be sexually motivated. However, upon examination into the background and relationships of the victim, a new possibility soon presents itself to the authorities.

I remember a case in which a 36-year-old female executive was found shot to death "execution style." She had been shot three times in the head at close range, and her body was left in her automobile, which was found parked under the George Washington Bridge. The police investigation revealed that the victim had an ongoing lesbian relationship with a 31-year-old female bartender. Detectives ascertained that the deceased had become embroiled in an argument with her lesbian girlfriend over another woman. The victim had met this woman at an East Side "singles" bar. When the "other woman" arrived, the argument began and the three women ended up leaving the bar together. The deceased drove the auto with her "new friend" sitting in the front seat and her lover sitting in the rear seat. The argument continued as they drove. During the argument, the jealous lover shot her friend in the head from the back seat. The woman passenger fled from the scene as the "shooter" exited the vehicle and got behind the wheel of the auto. She then drove the victim's car and body to the location of discovery. The "witness-passenger" eventually came forward, and police arrested the jealous lover, who was hiding out at another woman's Manhattan apartment. Initially, this case did not appear to be a sex-related homicide.

The motive in this category of slayings is most often based upon elements of rage, hate, anger, jealousy, or revenge. Scenarios that involve violent behaviors and statements such as, "If I can't have you then nobody will have you," are often revealed during the inquiry.

The following is a common scenario in sexual domestic-dispute cases. The woman petitions the court for an "Order of Protection." The court order directs the man to stay away from the petitioner and refrain from any further harassment. The man becomes enraged with this attempt by the woman to "break the relationship." A violent homicidal episode in which sexual aggression is evident in the crime scene often culminates the drama.

I remember another case in which the nude body of an apparent rape

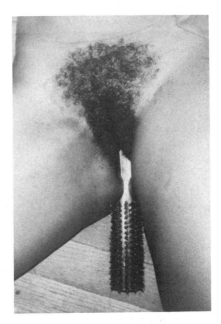

Sex-Related Homicide—Interpersonal Violence. At first impression, the hair brush might be considered an item used to sexually abuse the victim or a form of penis substitution. In fact, the hair brush had been jammed into the vagina after the victim was strangled to death. The case was actually an interpersonal dispute between the victim and her former husband who jammed the hairbrush into his ex-wife's vagina in a fit of anger.

victim was found in a city park. Initially, it was believed that the victim had been raped at an undisclosed location, shot to death, and transported to the park where the body was "dumped." However, upon identification of the victim, it was ascertained that she had been reported missing the previous day. Investigation revealed that she had been abducted by her estranged husband, who kept her captive in his auto where he repeatedly raped her and subsequently killed her for refusing to reconcile with him.

In some domestic-dispute cases, especially those involving "crack" (a concentrated form of cocaine), the crime may appear to be based upon some sort of psychotic episode. The nude body of a murdered woman was found in her neatly furnished apartment. She had been stabbed seven times in the back, chest, and neck. There was evidence that she had been sexually assaulted following her death. Her boyfriend was a 24-year-old ex-marine who had smoked six vials of crack earlier that day. He worked for a Long Island electronics firm and was reportedly a good employee. He did not have any criminal history, and according to family members had apparently been happy in his relationship with the woman. Yet, while under the influence of "crack," he had sexually assaulted her and stabbed her to death with a 9-inch carving knife.

An enraged lover or spouse, who is acting under extreme emotional circumstances, is capable of anything. I recall a number of cases in which offenders attempted to dispose of their wives and girlfriends through dismemberment. Initially, the police are confronted with a complete mystery and some unidentified body parts. However, once the identity is ascertained, the investigation usually leads to a relative or friend and an interpersonal violence scenario.

There may be an attempt to destroy the victim by depersonalizing the body: facial destruction, multiple cuttings and stabbings, sexual assault, overkill, and even postmortem attack.

I remember supervising the investigation of a case which appeared to have been committed by a lust murderer or a psychotic killer. The partially clad body of a 22-year-old black female was discovered in her apartment. She had been savagely beaten on the head with a baseball bat, and her throat had been slashed. Next to the body was a blood-stained drinking glass. I observed a lip print in blood upon the rim of the glass, suggesting that the glass had been used to drink blood. On the coffee table in the living room were a number of kitchen knives, which had been used to slice the victim's body. The utensils were lined up on a coffee table operating-room style. The victim had been eviscerated, and a large soda bottle had been thrust into her abdominal cavity. Her intestines could be observed inside of the clear plastic bottle. There were a number of postmortem slicings to her breasts and chest. In addition, the killer had also carved diagonal wounds into both of the victim's legs. This murder was actually committed in a fit of rage by the victim's live-in boyfriend.

It is important to note that the *motivation* in an interpersonal violence-oriented dispute may be obscured by what was done to the body of the victim, or how the crime scene was staged or changed. Originally, what appears to be a rape-murder, the work of a sexual psychopath, or a lust murder is often based on interpersonal violence.

Rape- and/or Sodomy-Oriented Assault

In this category of sex-related homicide, the offender's primary intent is to rape and/or sodomize the victim. These cases are extremely brutal, and death usually results from the assailant overcoming the resistance of the victim to the rape, sodomy, or homosexual assault. The victim may be choked or strangled into submission, or the mouth and nose may be held tightly in order to stifle the victim's screams, thereby causing asphyxia. Blunt-force injuries may be present when the killer

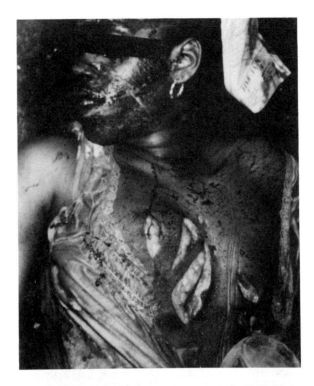

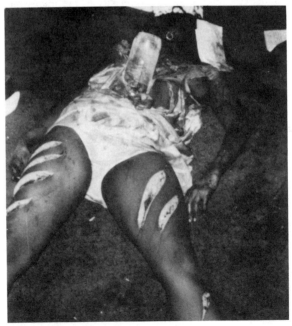

Sex-Related Homicide Involving Bizarre Activities. Anthropophagy and Postmortem Mutilation of Body. These photographs show the partially clad body of an eviscerated female. The victim was hit in the head with a baseball bat. Her throat was cut, and there are multiple cuttings to the breasts and legs of the victim. A soda bottle was placed in the abdominal cavity and there was evidence that the offender had drunk the victim's blood.

---

has attempted to beat the victim into submission. In addition to the brutality of the attack, a victim may also die of shock or other trauma, especially young children and older persons.

The "Murder at the Met" case in New York City is a classic rape-homicide. In this case a young violinist, who was performing at the Metropolitan Opera House, was attacked and killed by a stagehand. The young woman was walking through one of the many hallways back stage when she was spotted by the stagehand, who had been drinking. He followed her to an elevator, forced her to accompany him into a stairwell, and attempted to rape her. He then brought her up to the roof, where he bound and gagged her. He returned a short time later when he heard her making noise as she struggled to break free. He then pushed her from the roof into a ventilating shaft, where she was battered to death in the fall. The offender killed the victim to prevent her from identifying him.

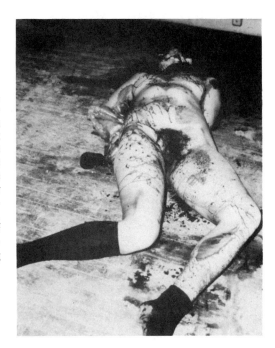

Rape-Homicide Crime Scene. This is the victim of a rape-homicide that occurred in an unoccupied apartment within a building in the South Bronx. The victim was raped and sodomized by the killer, who had forced her into this location after confronting her in the building. She was a classic "victim of opportunity" who just happened to be at the wrong place at the wrong time.

In some cases, the offender may actually attempt to mislead the authorities by staging the crime scene to make it appear to be something other than a sex crime. For instance, I remember a case in which the police were requested to respond to a "possible suicide." When they arrived, Emergency Medical Services (EMS) personnel were attempting to revive a partially clothed female. The EMS personnel advised the officers that when they arrived they observed the unconscious female with a ligature around her neck. Her body was partially suspended by this ligature, which was affixed to some molding. However, upon closer examination of the death scene, the officers noticed signs of a struggle. The officers noticed that the victim's blouse had been ripped open. They also observed some buttons on the floor along with a broken wrist watch that belonged to the deceased. In addition, closer examination of the victim's neck revealed concentric fingernail marks, which would be consistent with manual strangulation. The officers immediately initiated basic crime scene procedures and notified detectives. As a result, additional evidence was located and a proper crime scene investigation was conducted.

Investigative Strategy. The usual intent of the offender in sexual assault is to rape and/or sodomize. The offender in this category generally does not receive any sexual satisfaction from the murder. As a practical matter, the police are dealing with a rapist who has killed and not a murderer who has raped.

Investigatively speaking, it has been my experience that a rape-murder is usually preceded by other sexual offenses, including rapes and/or sodomies in which the victim has not been killed. The investigative approach should be to first ascertain whether or not other cases involving a similar MO have taken place in the jurisdiction. This check can then be expanded to include other jurisdictions within the immediate area. This avenue of inquiry can then be expanded to research records for similar offenses committed in the past by persons who have since been released from confinement.

In the investigation of rape/sodomy-oriented homicides, remember that you are dealing with a sexual offender. Large, progressive police departments usually maintain specialized operations, such as Homicide, Robbery, and Sex Crimes units. The investigators in these specialized units have a unique advantage. They become experts within their respective fields and are able to gain an insight into certain criminal behaviors beyond the experience of the average, generalist detective. I personally think it is good procedure to assign a member of the Sex Crimes Unit to work with the homicide detectives on sex-related homicide investigations. In fact, on *major case investigations*, involving a series of rapes or homicides, I recommend that teams of Sex

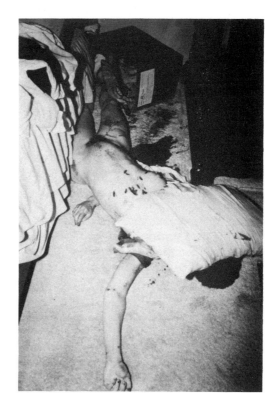

Rape-Homicide Crime Scene—Depersonalization. This young woman was raped and murdered by an *organized offender.* The woman, who had been bound for the purposes of sexual assault, was "under the control" of this killer for a number of hours. The covering of the face and/or turning over of the body is referred to as *depersonalization.* (Courtesy of Det. Sgt. (Ret.) Robert L. Bittle, Cumberland County Sheriff's Department, North Carolina.)

Crimes and Homicide detectives work together in a *Task Force* type operation.

I remember a particularly brutal rape-homicide in which the semi-nude body of a 21-year-old victim was found "dumped" in a Bronx lot. The victim was an art therapist, who was last seen at a college campus in New Rochelle, New York. Her body was discovered at approximately noontime on Saturday. At the time of the body's discovery, the victim's car was missing, as was her wallet and keys. She had been at The New Rochelle Public Library the previous day and had checked out a few books. An autopsy confirmed that the young woman had been raped and that the cause of death was due to manual strangulation. The day after her body was discovered someone found her wallet in Pelham, New York, which is a town between the Bronx and New Rochelle. Three days after the murder, her car was found in a parking lot in New Rochelle. In the victim's auto were four library books she had checked out of The New Rochelle Public Library. There was also a slip of paper from the library upon which she had written the "key numbers" for the books she had borrowed.

It was quite apparent to the New York City Police investigators that

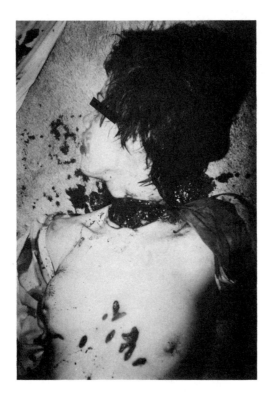

Rape-Homicide Crime Scene—Prevent Identification. The offender engaged in multiple breast assault by knife and assured the victim's death by cutting her throat. The police investigation indicated that the victim could have identified her assailant. She was killed by the offender to prevent identification. (Courtesy of Det. Sgt. (Ret.) Robert L. Bittle, Cumberland County Sheriff's Department, North Carolina.)

the abduction of the deceased had taken place in the Westchester County City of New Rochelle, and that in reality this investigation should be focused in New Rochelle and Pelham.

The detectives got their first break from a fingerprint on the slip of library paper, which had been found in the victim's car. Although there weren't any suspects with which to compare this print, detectives from the Bronx decided to look into all rapes and sex crimes within Westchester County during the period of the murder. They came up with a rape-pattern involving a black male, 27 years of age, who had been arrested and convicted for a rape-abduction. In fact, he had been apprehended with the rape victim less than one-half mile from where the Bronx victim's body had been found. Detectives requested a latent print check of the suspect's fingerprints with the slip of paper from the victim's car. The first fingerprint technician missed the match. However, detectives were certain that this rape suspect was the killer. They resubmitted the latents of the print to another fingerprint technician who determined that the latent print from the murder case matched the suspect, who was incarcerated in the Westchester County Jail. Unfortunately, when the information was presented to the Bronx

District Attorney's Office in 1984, the late Mario Merola, District Attorney for the Bronx declined to prosecute, citing police error.

I ordered this investigation to be reopened in 1985. The detective who had originally discovered the rape pattern was assigned to the investigation. However, once again, our efforts were thwarted by the failure of the Bronx District Attorney's Office to prosecute. In 1989, approximately nine years after the murder, a detective and detective sergeant decided to try a different tactic. Using DNA information supplied by the author as well as current newspaper articles dealing with this state-of-the-art forensic technique, they constructed an interview strategy. The strategy was to allow the suspect to peruse the materials on DNA and then convince the offender through explanation of DNA technology that he would probably be forensically identified as the rapist.

The suspect who had since been released from prison on unrelated rape charges, was invited in for an interview with the New York City detectives. The suspect, who was "jail-smart," thought that he could invoke the statute of limitations on the rape charge. He would have been correct if the only charge was rape. The statute of limitations on felonies in the state of New York is seven years. However, the authorities in this case were pursuing a *rape-homicide* investigation. *There isn't any statute of limitations on homicide.*

During the interview, the suspect made statements implicating himself in the rape and indicated that he had an accomplice, who actually did the killing. The original police investigation had never revealed an accomplice in the rape-pattern for which the suspect had been convicted. Often, an offender, who is providing police with an inculpatory statement, will attempt to minimize his participation. The detectives presumed that this suspect was likewise trying to minimize his involvement and allowed the suspect to continue with his statement. Surprisingly, when the detectives conducted a record check for the alleged accomplice, they were able to document the existence of this person as described by their suspect.

This individual was located and invited in for questioning. This suspect came up the exact same story as the first suspect. The only difference was in *who* did the killing. The second suspect predictably blamed the first suspect. However, both suspects were charged with the rape-murder of the 21-year-old victim.

I personally feel that this case is an excellent example of the principles of practical homicide investigation. Murders are solved because of the tenacity of homicide detectives who care. I was personally involved in the above case, as were a number of other detectives. You can imagine our frustration when the district attorney's office refused to prosecute. However, that did not prevent the detectives from utilizing

Table 12.

Type of Rapist	Motivation	Profile
Power Reassurance	This type assaults to assure himself of his masculinity. Lacks the confidence to interact socially and sexually with women.	Indoor type Victim alone with small children Local victims Attacks victims as they sleep Uses ski mask or pillow or makes victim turn over Loner type; dominant mother May keep a diary or scrapbook Nonathletic Victim can negotiate Takes a souvenir Probably is married Weapon only for show Maintains guilt; may call victim: wants to please her Underachiever
Power Assertive	This type has no doubts as to his masculinity. Uses rape to express his dominance over women. Uses force.	Same age as victim Cruises for victims Resides in area near crime Selects victims of opportunity Short time-span between attacks Prior institutionalization Selfish actions Poor record if in armed service Sports-minded Flashy vehicle Tears clothing Oral assault Direct approach Commits crime outdoors Alcohol user
Anger Retaliatory	This type is getting even with women. Uses sex as a weapon to punish and degrade (anger oriented).	Strikes out at women; may select prostitutes or elderly Does not spend much time Blitz-style of attack Selects symbolic victims Tears clothing Uses alcohol Random times (no pattern)
Anger Excitation	This type is sexually turned-on by the victim's response to the infliction of physical and/or emotional pain. The sexual acts will be varied and experimental and intended to cause pain.	Might work with an accomplice No mental or health problems Uses auto Uses degrading language Into S&M activities No remorse Brings weapon Good IQ

[a] Author recommends the textbook, *Practical Aspects of Rape Investigation: A Multidisciplinary Approach*, to the investigator for further information and case studies of these types of offenders.[11]

tactics, procedures, and forensic techniques to continue to pursue this case. Allow me to quote from the Oath of Practical Homicide Investigation.

. . . Death investigation constitutes a heavy responsibility, and as such, let no person deter you from the truth and your own personal commitment to see that justice is done, not only for the deceased, but for the surviving family as well.[9]

Categories of Rapists. According to Groth et al., there are four categories of rapists: power reassurance, power assertive, anger retaliatory, and anger excitation.[10]

Deviant-Oriented Assault—The Lust Murder

This type of sex-related homicide is usually committed by someone who is defined as a lust murderer. The lust murderer is oriented toward deviant and sexually sadistic assault and is distinguished from other sex-related homicide offenders by his involvement in mutilation of the victim. According to studies conducted by the FBI, most of these offenders do not engage in penis penetration of the victim. Instead, they may masturbate upon their victims and engage in postmortem mutilation. There may be displacement of the breasts of females (defeminization), postmortem attack of the genitalia of males and females, evisceration, the insertion of objects into the body cavities of victims, and sometimes anthropophagy (the consumption of human flesh and blood).

I remember participating in an investigation in which a nude body of a 26-year-old woman had been discovered on the roof landing of her Bronx building. She had been the victim of a classic lust murderer. The young woman's jaw and nose had been broken, suggesting a "blitz-style" of attack. She had been manually strangled with a strap from her purse, and her panties had been placed over her face (depersonalization). Her body had been placed in a grotesque position (a position that was probably sexually significant to the offender). Her nylon stockings had been loosely tied around her wrists, suggesting evidence of symbolic postmortem binding (fantasy and symbolism). The items used to create this postmortem binding came from the victim and included a belt, which was draped across her abdomen, representing bondage.

The killer had cut off her nipples and placed them upon the victim's chest. An umbrella and a pen had been inserted into the dead girl's vagina (penis substitution), and a comb was placed in her pubic hair. The words "fuck you" were written upon her abdomen; and on the inside of her left thigh the killer had etched in pen, "You can't stop me." In addition, there were postmortem bite marks on the victim's thighs. This offender was classified as disorganized, based on the analysis of the

Classic Lust Murder—Sex Related Homicide, Disorganized Personality. After, postmortem mutilation and sexual abuse, the body was positioned in a sexually provocative manner significant to the offender. There is postmortem binding as well as penis substitution into the vaginal canal with foreign objects. (*See* Case History.)

crime scene information. The profile, which was prepared by the FBI, matched one of the suspects developed during the police investigation. This suspect was a patient at a local psychiatric hospital, who claimed to have been in the hospital on the day of the murder. Although the authorities knew that the suspect had been absent from the institution on the day of the murder, the hospital records did not indicate his absence. The poor record-keeping created an additional problem for the police, who were attempting to obtain a court order for teeth impressions of the suspect. When the court order was finally approved, the suspect's teeth impressions were compared to the bite mark evidence. Three forensic dentists agreed that the suspect had inflicted the bite mark wounds on the victim's body. The suspect was arrested after an exhaustive 13-month police investigation. The bite-mark evidence was crucial in the outcome of the case. The suspect was found guilty and is presently serving 25 years to life in a New York State facility.

Lust murders are primarily heterosexual and intraracial, yet there are recorded instances of homosexual lust murder. I performed a case analysis for a jurisdiction that experienced a vicious lust murder of a young boy. He had been multiply stabbed, sticks and dirt had been forced into his throat, and the body had been sexually mutilated.

Lust murderers usually live or work in close proximity to the crime scene. They act on the spur of the moment and are obsessed by some sort of perverse fantasy. In their own minds they have planned the event; however, when the opportunity presents itself, they do not have a plan for avoiding detection. They either panic or become so involved in the fantasy that they are totally oblivious to the fact that they are leaving evidence behind.

I had the opportunity to assess a sex-related homicide for the United States Postal Inspections Service. The case involved the lust murder of a female letter carrier. The crime had originally been classified as an attempted rape. Upon analysis of the case reports, the crime scene information, the victimology, and the facts of the case, it was soon apparent that the offender in this investigation was a classic disorganized personality. In my opinion this offender would not have been able to perform sexually with a live victim. Any sexual activity that would have taken place would have occurred after death.

The victim was a 30-year-old letter carrier. Her partially nude body had been discovered in the rear seat of her postal vehicle in a church parking lot. This location was approximately one mile from the deceased's assigned route. There was evidence of blunt force trauma to the head and multiple stabbings to the torso. The victim's uniform shirt and bra had been pulled up over her arms exposing the woman's breasts. The obvious lack of blood for such devastating injuries suggested that the victim had been killed elsewhere and transported to this location.

There was an extensive amount of evidence in and upon the postal vehicle. In fact, police used a flat-bed truck to transport the vehicle directly to the lab. The large amount of bloodstained mail suggested that the victim had not gotten too far along her route. The murder weapon was found in the trunk of the car, along with the victim's shoes and additional bloodstained mail. The mail bore bloody footprints, which did not match the victim's shoes, as well as bloody fingerprints. On the rear of the trunk was a patent print in blood. Crime scene technicians also located vegetative matter consistent with plant debris, long strands of blond hair (the victim was a brunette), a large leaf from a philodendron plant, small flecks of green and blue paint, and a portion of panty hose that did not belong to the victim. An inspection of the odometer of the postal auto did not show any significant deviation from the carrier's assigned route except for the distance between the delivery area and the church parking lot. The autopsy revealed the cause of death to be cerebral hemorrhage and stabbing wounds. The victim had 18 stab wounds from a hunting knife, which was matched to the knife recovered at the scene, and had suffered extreme blunt-force trauma to the head. The time of death was placed between 12:00 noon and 2:00 PM that day. The victim had last been seen at approximately 11:30 AM, and only a small portion of her mail had actually been delivered.

It was obvious to seasoned detectives that the actual assault and murder had taken place somewhere along the victim's mail route. However, they couldn't use the undelivered mail to ascertain deliveries as the mail that was recovered from the victim's auto contained evidence. Investigators targeted her postal route and conducted a door-to-door canvass in an attempt to locate the crime scene. Tracking dogs were brought in and scented with the leather steering wheel cover of her auto. The dogs led investigators back to the victim's route. Detectives located the crime scene and discovered blood on the driveway of the murderer's home. In addition, there was a large philodendron plant on the front porch. The vegetative matter found on the victim's body came from a juniper bush in front of the house. The blue and green flecks of paint came from the weathered Christmas bulbs that were left on the house year round. The paint had flecked and fallen into the cracks in the driveway. When the suspect had dragged the body from the house, the trace evidence had adhered to the woman's body.

Police obtained a search warrant for the premises. Although the interior of the house had been cleaned and scrubbed, additional evidence of the crime was recovered, which included the matching piece of panty hose found in the auto.

The offender was an 18-year-old who had dropped out of high school. A loner type with a drug habit, he was enrolled in a community college but was doing poorly. He was described as weird and argumentative by persons who knew him. For a six-month period he had lived in a tent behind his house. The long strands of blond hair found at the crime scene came from the family dog. The suspect had been having sex with his dog and was reportedly into solo sex-related activities, which involved sadistic fantasies. The pieces of panty hose in this particular case were fetish items for the offender. He was found guilty and is presently incarcerated.[12]

The Serial Murder

Serial murder is the killing of three or more separate victims with emotional time breaks between the killings. These breaks or "cooling-off" periods range from days to weeks or months between victims.

In recent years, based upon the revelations of the FBI's Behavioral

Science Unit, there has been a lot of public interest generated in the phenomenon of serial murder. Several books and articles have been published on the subject. There has even been an NBC mini-series based upon the deviant exploits of Ted Bundy, a convicted serial killer, who was finally executed by the State of Florida in 1989.

In my professional opinion, the most complete study and research into the serial killer can be found in *Sexual Homicide: Patterns and Motives*.[13]

In psychiatric terminology, a serial killer may be defined as either psychotic or psychopathic, depending on the information supplied during the examination and the facts as presented to the clinician. In the experience of the author, serial killers are rarely psychotic. They are more properly defined as *sexual psychopaths* or *psychopathic sexual sadists*, depending on the circumstances of the homicide and what was done to the victim. They obviously have a profound personality disorder, but are keenly aware of their own criminality and certainly not out of touch with reality. If serial killers were psychotic, they probably wouldn't be as successful in eluding the police.

In the case of the psychotic killer, one could propose that he kills because his psychosis drives him to kill. An example of this type of serial killer was Joseph Kallinger, the shoemaker, who reportedly was acting under orders from God to kill his victims.

In any event, it is not the purpose of this section to present psychiatric information or engage in an in-depth psychological analysis of the serial murderer. Instead, I present this information from an investigative perspective for the purpose of analyzing the sex-related murder investigation.

In the case of the psychopathic killer who is a serial murderer, I suggest that this type of offender kills because he likes to kill. According to Ressler et al., "These men have conscious, detailed plans for murder. Often these plans are improved upon with each successive killing; each new experience gives the offender insight into his next murder."[14]

Serial killers have been described as intelligent, charismatic, streetwise, charming, and generally good looking. They are mobile individuals capable of traveling any number of miles in search of the "right" victim. I analyzed one case in which the killer cruised a local strip for three hours and put over 120 miles on his van while searching for a victim. They target a certain type of victim: someone who is vulnerable and easy to control. Their victims are males and females. They may select children, vagrants, prostitutes, or homosexuals. If the victim is a female, she may resemble other female victims in some aspect: long hair, hair color, coed, nurse, waitress, etc.

Serial killers are extremely manipulative. Often they are able to talk their victim into what has been described as their "comfort zone." This is a location where they feel comfortable and safe and can control the victim. Many times they use a ruse to gain access to a potential victim. Ted Bundy used a cast on his arm. John Wayne Gacy offered young men jobs in his construction business. Others have offered hitchhikers a lift, or posed as talent scouts, offered modeling assignments, posed as police officers, etc. They continually perfect their ruse and seem to have an uncanny knack at recognizing potential victims. They are quickly able to gain the victim's confidence with their verbal skills.

Many serial killers have a fascination for police procedure. Some have even worked as police officers, reserve officers, or security guards. They use this experience to avoid detection. They have been known to frequent police hangouts and eavesdrop on police conversations during a case. They may even interject themselves into the investigation.

In some instances, these type of killers have gone back to the crime scene or location where the body was discovered, either to assess the police investigation or to taunt police with additional clues. I remember one case in which the killer complained that the police had discovered the body sooner than he had anticipated. He was upset because he hadn't had time to make sure he hadn't left any evidence behind.

The serial killer, despite his outward facade, is a very insecure individual. He is without power unless he is in control. This is reflected in his personal life and in his behaviors. He is at his "peak" when he has a victim under his control.

They enjoy the publicity of their crimes for the same reason. They are likely to follow news events of their crimes very closely and gain satisfaction in the knowledge that they have defeated the police. Some serial killers communicate with the press. David Berkowitz, "The Son of Sam" serial killer in New York City, communicated with authorities by sending cryptic messages to a major metropolitan newspaper.

Another serial killer sent messages to the press, demanding that they acknowledge his killings by affording him a title like other serial murderers.

This type of offender engages in purposeful mutilation of the corpse, as opposed to the disorganized offender who engages in sexual or exploratory mutilation. The organized offender will employ mutilation to hinder identification or for shock value. In one of the New York City serial murders the offender removed the heads and hands of two prostitutes in order to prevent the identification of the victims. In another case this same offender removed the breasts of one of his victims and left them on the bed board for police to find.

Serial killings are considered by several experts in the field of psychology and psychiatry to represent the ultimate extension of violence. From a rational standpoint, serial killings are completely senseless acts. However, in the mind of the serial killer, he experiences great pleasure in exerting power and control over his victim, including the power of life and death. The sex act is secondary. He is excited by the cruelty of the act and will engage in physical and psychological torture of the victim. His pleasure is derived by watching the victim writhe in pain as he or she is humiliated and tortured to death. Offenders have used a variety of torture techniques, such as biting, whipping, burning, electricity, and forcing the victim to ingest a caustic cleaning fluid.

The serial killer operates in an emotionally detached manner. It is almost as if he is following a script. The script is usually based upon a sadistic fantasy.

Police investigations of serial murderers have revealed intricate and precise planning on the part of the serial killer. Detectives have seized recorded evidence of the offense, such as audio tape recordings of the victim's screams of pain, writings, photos, and even videotape segments of their sadistic activities. In one case, an offender, who had kidnapped, raped, and murdered a young woman, forced the victim to describe his sexual assault on tape. He then recorded the victim's hysterical screams for help as he savagely tortured her by pinching and ripping her nipples with a pair of pliers.

Many of these serial killers seemingly maintain respectable lifestyles and engage in sexual relations with a primary female in their lives. However, they really don't have any type of satisfactory relationship with anyone. They are obsessed with self-gratification, to the point where nothing else matters.

Most of the serial killers interviewed by the FBI's Behavioral Science Unit, or by psychiatrists conducting independent examinations, reported that they had been victims of child abuse, usually at the hands of a female parent or parent figure. Many of the offenders were reportedly under the influence of alcohol or marijuana while committing the crime, which tended to exacerbate their sadistic fantasies.

The serial killer tends to increase his killings. It appears that they have to kill more often to maintain an equilibrium. The fantasy and psychic high that they obtain through their conduct induces bold and more frequent attacks, sometimes with a complete disregard of risk. Consequently, many of the country's most notorious serial killers were caught either by accident or during some independent police action that was not related to the murder investigation.

Current estimates from the United States Department of Justice are that 35 to 40 serial murderers are roaming throughout the country. This type of killer never stops killing. In my opinion, there is no cure for the sadistic sexual psychopath except life in prison or death.

Conclusion

The criminal investigator confronted with a sex-related homicide investigation should first address the basic crime scene techniques as outlined in this text. He or she should concentrate on the total documentation and preservation of the scene, including those factors that suggest the possible psychodynamics of the event.

Remember, there are four classifications of sex-related homicide: (1) interpersonal violence-oriented disputes and assaults; (2) rape-and/or sodomy-oriented assault; (3) deviant-oriented assault—the lust murder; and (4) the serial murder.

I have presented them in the order of frequency of occurrence. Start your investigation with an eye toward an interpersonal violence scenario and then work your way through the other options. Specific law enforcement strategies can be applied to the investigation upon identification of the motive. An example would be: computer analysis of similar offenses, a request for a criminal personality profile through VI-CAP, or simply a recanvass of the neighborhood wherein the crime took place.

Remember, within each of the categories there exist elements of human behavior, human sexuality, and possible sexual deviance.

In any event, there aren't any simple clues, solutions, or explanations that account for the logic of a person who commits a sex-related homicide. *Just remember that "things are not always what they appear to be."*

References

1. Vernon J. Geberth. "The Investigation of Sex Related Homicides." *Law and Order Magazine* July 1986, p. 40.
2. James C. Coleman, James N. Butcher, and Robert C. Carson. *Abnormal Psychology and Modern Life*, 7th ed. Texas: Scott, Foresman and Company, 1984, p. 457.
3. *Ibid.*, p. 457.
4. American Psychiatric Association. *Diagnostic and Statistical Manual of Mental Disorders*, 3rd ed. Washington, D.C.: American Psychiatric Association, 1980, p. 267.
5. Coleman et al., *op. cit.*, p. 460.
6. American Psychiatric Association, *op. cit.*, p. 267.
7. James A. Brussel. *Casebook of a Crime Psychiatrist.* New York: Geis Publishing Company, 1968, p. xii.
8. Robert K. Ressler, Ann W. Burgess, John E. Douglas, Carol R. Hartman, and Ralph B. D'Agostino. "Sexual Killers and Their Victims." *Journal of Interpersonal Violence* 1:293(1986).
9. Vernon J. Geberth. "The Oath of Practical Homicide Investigation." 1988.

10. Nicholas A. Groth, Ann W. Burgess, and L. L. Holmstrom. "Rape: Power, Anger and Sexuality." *American Journal of Psychiatry* 134:1239–1243(1977).
11. Robert R. Hazelwood and Ann W. Burgess. *Practical Aspects of Rape Investigation: A Multidisciplinary Approach.* New York: Elsevier Science Publishing Company, 1987, pp. 175–180.
12. Inspector T. M. Fail, U.S. Postal Inspections Service. Personal interview, January, 1987.
13. Robert K. Ressler, Ann W. Burgess, and John E. Douglas. *Sexual Homicide: Patterns and Motives.* Lexington, Massachusetts: D.C. Heath & Company, 1988.
14. *Ibid.*, p. 49.

Selected Reading

American Psychiatric Association. *Diagnostic and Statistical Manual of Mental Disorders,* (DSM-III), 3rd ed. Washington, D.C.: American Psychiatric Association, 1980.

Brussel, James A. *Casebook of a Crime Psychiatrist.* New York: Bernard Geis Publishing Company, 1968.

Coleman, James C., Butcher, James N., and Carson, Robert C. *Abnormal Psychology and Modern Life.* 7th ed. Texas: Scott, Foresman and Company, 1984.

DiMaio, Dominick J., and DiMaio, Vincent J. M. *Forensic Pathology.* New York: Elsevier Science Publishing Company, 1990.

Geberth, Vernon J. "Mass, Serial and Sensational Homicides: The Investigative Perspective." *Bulletin of the New York Academy of Medicine* 62:492–496(1986).

Geberth, Vernon J. "The Investigation of Sex Related Homicides." *Law and Order Magazine* 34:40–47(1986).

Geberth, Vernon J. "Homicide Investigation." In *The Encyclopedia of Police Science,* edited by W. G. Bailey. New York: Garland Publishing, 1989, pp. 255–261.

Hazelwood, Robert R., and Burgess, Ann W. *Practical Aspects of Rape Investigation: A Multidisciplinary Approach.* New York: Elsevier Science Publishing Company, 1987.

Ressler, Robert K., Burgess, Ann W., Douglas, John E., et al. "Crime Scene and Profile Characteristics of Organized and Disorganized Murderers." *FBI Law Enforcement Bulletin* 54(1985).

Ressler, Robert K., Burgess, Ann W., Douglas, John E., Hartman, Carol R., and D'Agostino, Ralph B. "Sexual Killers and Their Victims: Identifying Patterns Through Crime Scene Analysis." *Journal of Interpersonal Violence* 1:288–308(1986).

Ressler, Robert K., Burgess, Ann W., and Douglas, John E. *Sexual Homicide: Patterns and Motives.* Lexington, Massachusetts: D.C. Heath & Company, 1988.

Svensson, Arne, Wendel, Otto, and Fisher, Barry A. J. *Techniques of Crime Scene Investigation,* 4th ed. New York: Elsevier Science Publishing Company, 1987.

Collection of Evidence 13

Physical evidence is any tangible article, small or large, which tends to prove or disprove a point in question. It may be used to:

1. Reconstruct the crime.
2. Identify the participants.
3. Confirm or discredit an alibi.

The proper collection and disposition of physical or trace evidence from the crime scene and the body of the deceased is of utmost importance to the investigation and eventual court presentation. The evidence must have been obtained legally in order for it to be admissible. Therefore, it is imperative that both the legal authority to collect the evidence and the proper collection techniques be considered prior to the actual collection of the evidence.[1]

Procedures for Collection of Evidence

In order to be introduced as physical evidence in a trial, an article must:

Be properly identified,

Show a proper chain of custody,

Be material and relevant,

Meet all legal requirements.

---

[1] The techniques of collection presented in this chapter are based on the recommendations and procedures of Dr. Robert C. Shaler, Ph.D. In addition, I have provided the recommendations and procedures for submitting evidence to the FBI Laboratory as specified in the Federal Bureau of

(continued)

The crime scene technician or crime scene investigator who is summoned to the scene should have operational supervision over gathering, collection, and marking of evidence for identification. However, the investigator assigned to the case is still in charge of the investigation and should be consulted prior to any evidence gathering or crime scene processing.

The proper collection and disposition of evidence will be accomplished if the following guidelines are adhered to:

1. Each piece of evidence should be marked (on the container or item as applicable) to show its original position and location. This information should also be recorded in the investigator's notebook.
2. Each article should be marked distinctively by the searching officer to identify the person who found the particular piece of evidence. In cases of small or fluid specimens this marking is done on the container.
3. Each item should be described exactly and completely with the corresponding case numbers affixed and the date and time of collection indicated.
4. Each item should be packaged in a separate, clean, and proper-sized container to prevent cross-contamination or damage.
5. Each package should be sealed to retain evidence and prevent any unauthorized handling.
6. Each piece of evidence should show proper disposition:
   a. Police department laboratory
   b. Property clerk's office
   c. F.B.I. Laboratory
7. Proper records should be kept regarding each piece of evidence showing chain of custody. These records should reflect any movement of the evidence from the point of origin to its final disposition.

Remember, each item should be photographed before it is collected as evidence. These photographs should include a long-range view to show the relationship of the object to its surroundings and a close-range view to show the actual item being collected. (See Chapter 6.)

Footnote 1 (continued)
Investigation's *Handbook of Forensic Science.* This material is reprinted with permission of the Director, Federal Bureau of Investigation.

Doctor Shaler, who holds a M.S. and Ph.D. in Biochemistry from Pennsylvania State University, is the Director of Serology for the New York City Medical Examiners Office. Doctor Shaler has lectured at various universities and forensic symposia and has published several articles related to the forensic sciences.

Collection of Specific Types of Evidence

The homicide investigator is usually confronted with the same general type of evidence in most murder investigations, such as blood, bullets, and fingerprints. The evidence ordinarily falls within three distinct categories, *body materials, objects,* and *impressions.*

This text will focus on the practical methods for collection of those types of evidence commonly found at the scene of a homicide. The more advanced and detailed methodologies have been purposefully omitted from this section because they are usually beyond the capability of the average investigator and are best performed by crime scene technicians and other experts who have been specially trained in forensic science techniques.[2]

Body Materials

BLOOD (WET)

1. Large amounts or pools:
   a. Use an eyedropper or hypodermic syringe to collect the fluid and transfer to a sterile container (5cc is sufficient for testing purposes).
   b. Transfer immediately to laboratory or refrigerate specimen. However, *do not freeze blood.*
   c. In some instances, depending on the jurisdiction regulations, a chemical preservative such as Sodium Azide can be used to prevent blood spoilage.
2. Small amounts of wet blood:
   a. Use a 100 percent cotton swab, #8 cotton thread, or gauze pad to collect specimen.
   b. Allow swab or gauze pad to air dry.
   c. Place in sterile test tube or other clean container.

BLOOD STAINS (DRY)

1. Nonporous surface:
   a. If there is a sufficient amount of dry blood it can be scraped from the surface with a clean razor blade or sterile scalpel. These scrapings should be shaved into a sterile container.
2. Porous surface (fabric, unfinished wood, etc.):
   a. Collect and submit the article containing the stain to the laboratory as found.

---

[2]These advanced methodologies are covered in several comprehensive works on the subject. If the reader wishes a more in-depth knowledge of evidence collection, he or she is advised to consult the more technical textbooks on forensic science. See for example, Paul Kirk. *Crime Investigation,* 2nd ed., New York: John Wiley and Sons, Inc., 1974.

Blood Evidence—Victim Removed to Hospital. (**A**) An assault has taken place in this hallway of a South Bronx Housing Project. There is a large amount of blood on the floor. The victim has been removed to the hospital and police officers have secured the hallway as a crime scene. Blood should be collected from this site. (**B**) The knife, which was used in the assault, is lying next to one of the pools of blood. This knife should be carefully collected as evidence. (*See* Weapons.)

b. Wrap in separate and sterile container. If the article is too large or inappropriate to transport, remove a portion of the material containing an adequate amount of the stain for transport to the laboratory for analysis.

3. Traces or smears which cannot be scraped into container:
   a. Moisten a 100 percent cotton swab or gauze pad with distilled water. Also obtain a control sample which should be forwarded to the lab for analysis with the specimen.
   b. Stain will soften and soak into swab or gauze pad.
   c. Allow to air dry.
   d. Place into a sterile test tube or container for laboratory.

Remember, do not use a swab or other instrument to collect blood from more than one stain. Use separate swabs, razors, scalpels, or other instruments for each separate stain to be sampled. This is to prevent contamination of samples.

It is possible that the assailant's blood may also be present. If the same instrument is used to collect all samples, the evidence will be tainted. Furthermore, you should be careful not to touch the surface which has contacted the blood sample because your own secretions may contaminate the collected sample.

SEMEN. Next to blood, semen is the physiological fluid most commonly discovered at homicide crime scenes. If a sexual assault is suspected, the investigator should carefully examine the body and clothing of the deceased prior to moving the body. If any stains are observed, procedures to collect this evidence should be performed at the scene. Later at autopsy, the medical examiner or coroner will take a vaginal swab or vaginal aspirant to obtain any semen traces from within the vaginal canal. In addition, oral and anal swabs may be taken, if sodomy is also suspected, and air dried immediately.

The following techniques should be employed at the scene.

1. Wet stain:
   a. Swab or wash (by medical examiner if possible).
   b. Draw the fluid into an eyedropper or hypodermic syringe.
   c. Place in sterile test tube.
   d. Use swab or cotton gauze pad for samples of smaller quantities which are still moist.
   e. Allow to air dry immediately and place in sterile container.
2. Dry stain:
   a. Dry stain will have a stiff "starchy" texture.
   b. If it is on clothing, submit the entire article, being careful not to break or contaminate the stained area.

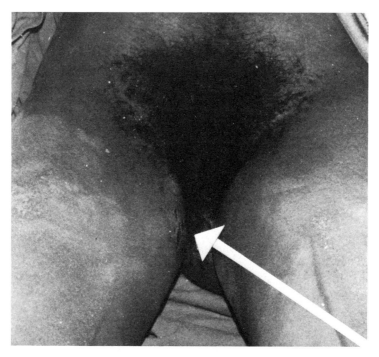

Dried Semen Evidence. This close-up shot of the vaginal area of a rape-homicide victim discloses the traces of dried semen. (See arrow.) Notice the "starchy" appearance. This trace should be gathered using 100% cotton moistened with distilled water, allowed to air-dry, and then placed in a sterile container for delivery to the laboratory.

    c. On body, using 100 percent cotton gauze pad moistened with distilled water, gently remove stain and place in sterile test tube or container after allowing to air dry.

Sometimes an ultraviolet light can be utilized to locate seminal stains. However, in many instances a false reading will be obtained due to the "brighteners" used in certain laundry detergents.

URINE
1. Remove by eyedropper or gauze pad.
2. Place in sterile test tube or other container.
3. If on clothing, the entire article should be submitted.

SPITTLE OR SALIVA
1. Remove with eyedropper or 100 percent cotton gauze pad.
2. Place in sterile test tube or other clean container after drying.

FECES

1. Large amount:
   a. Remove with a small clean shovel. Allow to air dry.
   b. Place in sterile container.
2. Small amount:
   a. Remove with 100 percent cotton swab or gauze pad moistened with distilled water, then air dry or scrape into container.
   b. Place in sterile test tube.

VOMIT

1. Remove with eyedropper or small shovel depending on amount.
2. Place into sterile container.

It should be noted that any physiological fluid found at the scene, such as urine, saliva, feces, perspiration, ear wax, nasal mucus, etc., can be typed into the same grouping as blood providing the material comes from an individual who is a secretor. Secretors make up approximately 80 percent of the general population. Physiological fluids of these secretors can be blood-typed by the serologist. Other genetic factors sometimes can also be identified regardless of secretor status.

TISSUE

1. Remove with tweezers.
2. Place in glass container or sterile test tube.
3. Forward to the medical examiner.

HAIR. During crimes of violence, specifically against persons, certain trace materials such as hair or fibers will be transferred between the victim and the perpetrator. These traces may also be left at the scene. Hairs are considered a *class characteristic*—although they cannot be identified as being absolutely identical to a given suspect's hair, they can be classified as similar to a known sample. In addition, they can be used to exclude a suspect. However, from an investigative point of view, hairs and/or fibers can:

1. Help determine the extent of the crime scene.
2. Place the perpetrator at the scene of the crime.
3. Connect the suspect to the weapon.
4. Corroborate statements of witnesses.
5. Determine the route to and from the crime scene.
6. Be located in any number of areas involved in the homicide:
   a. The victim,
   b. The crime scene,
   c. The weapon,
   d. A tool,
   e. A vehicle,
   f. An article of clothing,
   g. The suspect.

Trace Evidence—Documentation. With the use of macro photography, we see the various pieces of trace evidence that have been transferred from the victim to the site of recovery. This forensic evidence consists of the victim's blood, a long strand of hair, as well as vegetative matter from the primary crime scene which was approximately one mile from this location.

Hair Evidence. Detectives recovering hair from a woolen cap; evidence in a homicide case. (*Courtesy of* Lt. Daniel Guiney, Commanding Officer, Crime Scene Unit, New York City Police Department.)

DETERMINATIONS FROM HAIR

1. Species—human or animal.
2. Race—Caucasoid, Negroid, or Mongoloid. (In certain instances, the determination of a combination of racial characteristics can be ascertained.)
3. Location of growth—body area from where the particular hair originated (head, thorax, chest, pubis, etc.)
4. Treatment—dyed, bleached, straightened, etc.
5. How it was removed—pulled, fell out, cut, etc.
6. Disease and/or damage.
7. Genetic information:
   a. Blood type, from shaft of hair,
   b. Other genetic markers, from roots of pulled hair,
   c. Sex, from roots of pulled hair.

It is recommended that a sample of hair from various parts of the body be obtained in all homicide cases. Even though hair evidence may not be crucial or known to exist in the early stages of the investigation, it may be discovered later even after the body has been buried or destroyed through cremation. Samples should always be taken from various parts by pulling or plucking so as to obtain a piece of the root. If pulling or plucking absolutely cannot be undertaken for some reason, cutting the hair close to the scalp will suffice. An ordinary sampling will comprise approximately twenty-four to forty-eight pieces of hair. Hair removed from the head should be taken as follows: front, back, left side, right side, and top. The sample roots should then be air dried.

COLLECTION OF HAIRS FROM THE SCENE. Using oblique lighting, scan the surfaces of the crime scene.

a. If hairs or fibers are located, gather by tweezers, being careful not to bend or break.
b. Masking or Scotching tape can be used to gather small fibers or hairs.
c. Place in sterile container and seal. (Folded paper or envelopes may also be used.)

CONCLUSIONS FROM HAIR SAMPLES

1. Hair did not come from unknown hair source.
2. Hair could have come from known hair source.
3. Hair sampling too limited for meaningful comparison.
4. No conclusion.

Objects

BULLETS. When a bullet is fired from a weapon, certain distinctive characteristics are imparted to the bullet by the gun. These markings can be examined through internal ballistics and provide the investigator with certain general information regarding the type of weapon used. In addition, ballistics evidence is highly individualistic, and a fired bullet recovered from the scene can be positively matched with the suspect weapon.

1. Bullets should be collected without damaging or marking the *rifling,* the series of grooves or lines on the interior surface of the barrel which cause the bullet to spin and travel forward through the barrel with accuracy. These grooves and lines are transferred to the bullet as it is fired and are used by the ballistics expert to make comparisons.
2. Bullets embedded in doors, trees, walls, etc. should be removed by taking out a portion of the object in which the bullet has become lodged rather than by probing or digging. Digging for the bullet may cause additional marks which may destroy the ballistics value of the evidence.
3. Recovered bullets should be examined for blood or other materials before packaging.
4. Bullets should be marked on the base or nose.
5. Each bullet should be packaged separately in an appropriate con-

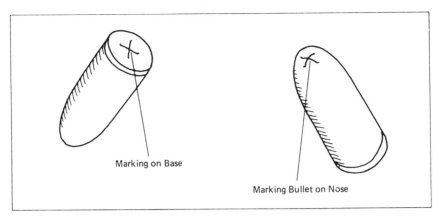

Marking of Ballistics Evidence on the Base and Nose of the projectile. Recommended procedure.

tainer, preferably one which will prevent any cross-contamination or accidental abrasion of the rifling marks.
6. Package should be marked to show identification and location of discovery.

DISCHARGED CASINGS OR CARTRIDGES. The recovery of discharged shells may indicate the direction and location of the attack as well as how many shots were fired. In addition, certain class characteristics such as make and caliber can be ascertained. Furthermore, if an automatic weapon was used, certain ejector or clip markings may be present.

1. Recovered casings should be marked on the inside wall of the shell by the mouth end, or, if this is not possible, as near to the opening as possible.
2. Never mark the recovered casing on or near the end which contains the primer cap, because examination of weapon markings may be destroyed.
3. Always consider the possibility of fingerprints on the sides of these casings and take appropriate methods to preserve them.
4. Package in separate containers with proper documentation.

SHOTGUN SHELLS
1. Plastic or paper shotgun shells should be handled in the same manner as other discharged casings.
2. These items can be marked on the metal side part of the casing.
3. *Never mark on base of shell casing.*

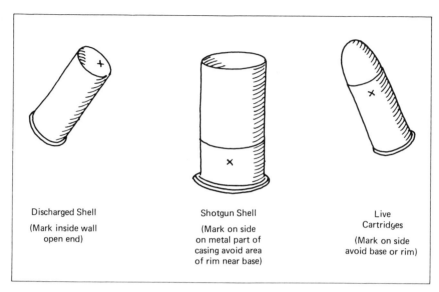

Discharged Shell	Shotgun Shell	Live Cartridges
(Mark inside wall open end)	(Mark on side on metal part of casing avoid area of rim near base)	(Mark on side avoid base or rim)

Marking Discharged Casings, Shotgun Shells, and Live Cartridges. Recommended procedure.

LIVE CARTRIDGES OR ROUNDS OF AMMUNITION
1. Examine for fingerprint evidence prior to marking.
2. Mark on side of casing.
3. Package, indicating the location of recovered rounds.

SHOTGUN WADDING
1. Recover and submit for laboratory examination.
2. Place in a separate container.

WEAPONS
1. Photograph and examine for fingerprints.
2. Examine for any serology or other trace evidence.
3. Place in special container according to size to protect evidence and prevent handling.
4. Forward to serology or crime lab for further analysis.

FIREARMS
1. Photograph in original position.
2. Examine for fingerprints.
3. Examine for any serology (e.g., blow-back of close-range firing may result in blood, hair, or tissue being transferred to weapon or in barrel of weapon).
4. Upon completion of preliminary examination for above, unload weapon and render safe before transporting.

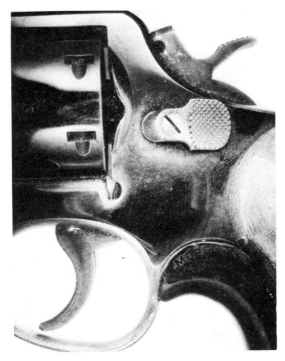

Latent Print. The print on this revolver is photographed in order to preserve the evidence. The camera used for this particular latent impression is the Polaroid CU-5. (*Courtesy of* the Polaroid Corporation, Cambridge, Massachusetts.)

5. Package individually in an appropriate container. (In circumstances in which the firearm must be transported for further examination at a proper facility, use a cardboard box. Draw a string through the trigger guard and attach this string at either end of the box, leaving the gun in a suspended position. For larger firearms like rifles or shotguns, cut a notch in each end of the box and lay weapon across container.)
6. Indicate the brand name, model designation, serial numbers, caliber, and number of shots the weapon is capable of firing, e.g., 5- or 6-shot revolver, etc. in reports and on evidence containers. Also indicate the type of finish—nickel plate, etc.
7. All weapons recovered should be marked for identification as soon as possible in the following manner:
   a. Revolvers—mark on frame, barrel, and cylinder.
   b. Rifles and shotguns—mark on receiver, bolt and barrel.
   c. Semiautomatic weapons—receiver (frame), the slide, barrel, and any clips.

FIBERS. Fibers, like hairs, may be transferred between the victim and perpetrator, and provide the investigator with an additional piece of class evidence which can be subjected to microscopic and microchemical testing. Items such as fibers, rope, string, or twine should be collected for examination.

1. Examination of fibers will indicate origin as follows:
   a. Vegetable—cotton and hemp,
   b. Animal—wool and mink,
   c. Mineral—glass wool and asbestos,
   d. Synthetic—nylon and orlon.
2. Examination of fiber evidence will determine if the fiber is similar to the control sample.
3. Collect fibers as follows:
   a. Forceps,
   b. Tape,
   c. Vacuum sweeping. (It should be noted that this is the least desirable method because too many contaminants are also collected.)
4. Collecting samples by using sticky side of tape is considered the most practical method.
5. Place samples in individual containers from each area gathered, mark appropriately, and forward to laboratory for examination.

FABRIC
1. Pieces of fabric found at the scene can be examined in a manner similar to fibers to determine:
   a. Color,
   b. Type of cloth and fiber,
   c. Thread count,
   d. Direction of fiber twist,
   e. Dye.
2. Class as well as individual characteristics can be obtained from fragments of fabric when matched by physically fitting the evidence pieces into its source.

CIGARETTE/CIGAR BUTTS. Cigarette or cigar butts found at the crime scene, especially those with filter tips, can be examined by serologists for the determination of blood type and sometimes other genetic factors (e.g., sex) of individuals who are secretors.

1. Collect with forceps or tweezers and insure dryness.
2. Place into separate containers to prevent contamination.
3. Containers should be appropriately marked.
4. Forward to serology.

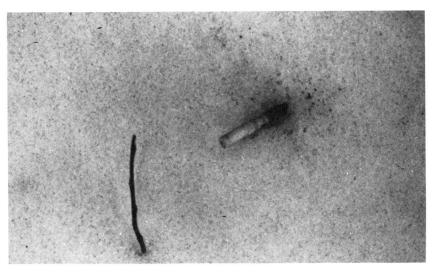

Outdoor Crime Scene Search. Here you can see a partially smoked cigarette butt lying in the snow. The cigarette butt contains lipstick and has apparently burned out in the snow. This piece of evidence was discovered by investigators who were searching the area where a body was found. In fact, the cigarette's condition was consistent with the time element of how long the body had been lying at the location. It is important to note that saliva will be transferred to the cigarette and can be typed in certain instances to reveal the blood type of the person who smoked it.

DISPLACED FURNITURE
1. Examine for any fingerprints or serology.
2. Useful in crime reconstruction.

SOIL
1. Soil on shoes, clothing, tools, weapons, and other objects may be useful in placing a suspect at the scene and providing the investigator with additional evidence. Also microbiological comparisons in addition to mineral comparisons can be made.
   a. Color of soil may be distinctive.
   b. Minerals can be distinctive.
   c. Bacterial profiles can be distinctive.
   d. Vegetation (fungal spores, etc.) can be distinctive.
2. Collection of soil samples:
   a. Collect several samples at the scene from various locations since mineral and organic contents vary within short distances.
   b. Gather at least a cupful or handful from each location.

c. Insure dryness.
d. Package in separate containers.
e. Mark properly for identification and location.

TOOLS. Tools which are suspected of being used in the crime should be examined as follows:

1. Examine for serology or fingerprints.
2. If the tool contains any serological evidence, it must be carefully packaged to preserve this evidence.
3. If tool contains traces of certain materials that are to be matched up with known samples, care must be taken so that this material is not rubbed off.
4. Portion of tool to be matched must be protected.
5. Broken tools and/or knives can be fracture-matched to provide positive identification.
6. *Never try to fit tool into tool mark or match broken pieces together.*

VEHICLES
1. Photograph and examine for serology.
2. Process for fingerprints.
3. Examine for other items of evidence.
4. Search for weapons.

CLOTHING. Each item of clothing collected as evidence should be individually wrapped in order to prevent cross contamination. If the clothing to be collected is wet, it should be air dried before it is packaged. Clothing may provide the investigator with additional evidence:

1. Stains on clothing may match stains from the scene, the victim, or the suspect.
2. A suspect's clothing may contain blood similar to the victim's.
3. The victim's clothing may contain saliva and/or seminal fluid from the perpetrator.
4. Hairs or fibers may be present on clothing that match similar hairs or fibers from a particular scene or location or from the victim.
5. Tears or cuts in clothing made by the weapon can be matched to show the position of the victim at the time of the assault.
6. The deposit of gunshot residues on clothing can be analyzed to determine the approximate distance from which the gun was fired.

DOCUMENTS (LETTERS, NOTES, PAPERS). These items may be examined to ascertain authenticity, locate fingerprints, or determine authorship in suicide cases, or for more advanced techniques such as psycholinguistic examination. (See Chapter 15, "Psycholinguistics.")

1. The primary consideration in handling this type of evidence is the preservation of any fingerprints which may be on the item.
2. Evidence should be collected by using tweezers or forceps to gently pick up the paper.
3. Each item should be placed in a separate package. A package which is clear or see-through it best since it will allow the investigator to examine contents without contaminating the document with additional fingerprints.
4. If see-through packages are not available, the object can be photocopied using forceps to place the object on the machine and later to transfer it to the evidence envelope. (This will allow for reading and other examination of content without disturbing evidence value of the original document.)
5. Marking this type of evidence depends on the type of examination to be conducted. In some instances, a mark can be placed on a back corner of the paper. In other instances just the package in which the document is placed will be marked.
6. Documents should not be folded.
7. Examine for latent prints.
8. Saliva on envelopes can be blood-typed and sometimes analyzed for sex origin.

EXAMINATION OF DOCUMENTS. The examination for latent prints on papers, documents, and other porous materials such as wood proceeds in a series of steps.

First step. Iodine fuming—reacts with oil or fatty fluids in latent print.

Second step: Ninhydrin—penetrates material and reacts with amino acids in perspiration. Heat should be applied and print will emerge.

Third step: Silver nitrate—reacts to salt in the perspiration. The document is then exposed to strong light.

GLASS. Examinations can be conducted on glass and glass fragments using a *refractive index,* which proves that the known sample and the evidence glass may have come from a similar source. In addition, in certain cases the fragments can by physically matched. Furthermore, the direction and sequence of bullet holes through glass can be determined by examination of radial and concentric fractures and may prove important in reconstructing the crime. Glass should be collected as follows:

a. Small pieces should be placed in a vial or pillbox.
b. Large pieces should be placed in a sturdy cardboard box with proper padding or protection to prevent further breakage during transport.

Impressions

FINGERPRINT EXAMINATION. The most valuable evidence that an investigator can obtain from the homicide crime scene are the fingerprints of the suspect. From an investigative point of view, any crime scene search should include a detailed examination for visible, plastic, and latent prints. It is important to note that the officer(s) performing this function should preserve all developed prints. Even partial prints which may seem insignificant may become valuable later when compared to prints taken from a suspect. It should be noted that fingerprint powders *do not* interfere with serological analyses. However, ninhydrin sprays and other chemical means to make prints visible may interfere with serology tests.

TYPES OF FINGERPRINTS. Fingerprints are divided into three separate categories: plastic prints, visible prints, and latent prints.

1. *Plastic prints.* These impressions occur when the finger touches or presses against a soft pliable surface such as putty, gum, a newly painted area, the glue on a stamp or envelope, wax, flour, thick dust, soap, grease, tar, resin, clay, etc. A negative impression of the friction ridge pattern is produced, resulting in a *plastic print.*
2. *Visible prints.* These prints occur when the fingers, palms, or feet which have been contaminated with a foreign substance come into contact with a clean surface and are pressed onto the surface, leaving a print. The most common type is the dust print. However, substances such as ink, blood, soot, paint, grease, face powders, oils, etc. contaminate the friction ridges of the fingers, when they are pressed against another surface, an image is transferred.
3. *Latent prints.* These prints occur from the natural skin secretions such as perspiration. When grease or dirt is mixed with the natural secretions a stable print may be deposited on the surface. Latent prints, which are not visible, are usually found on objects with smooth or polished surfaces or on paper. The latent print is developed by dusting or chemical process. In some instances these latent prints can be developed on rougher surfaces by using certain chemical processes.

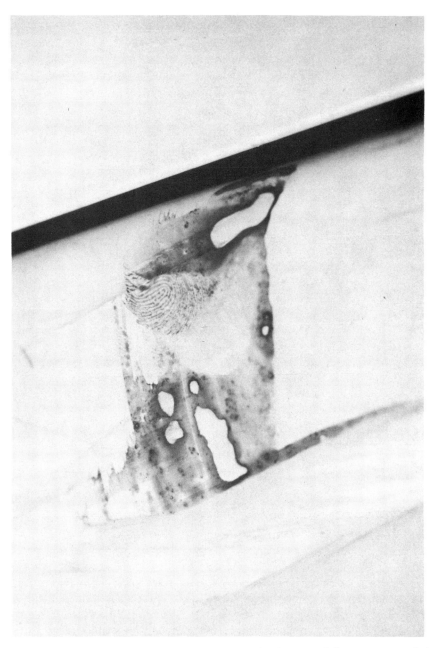

Visible Print (also referred to as a Patent Print). This actual fingerprint was left in blood at the crime scene. This is a Visible or Patent Print. The offenders blood-drenched hands and fingers transferred this fingerprint to the glossy surface of an automobile.

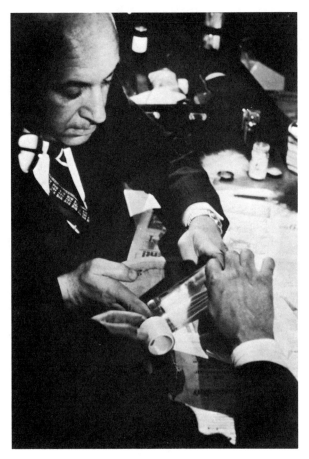

Detective Lifting a
Latent Print.

DEVELOPMENT OF FINGERPRINTS. The most common and practical method of developing prints at crime scenes is through the "dusting" technique. This is done by dusting or spreading fingerprint powder with a brush over the surface of the object suspected of bearing prints. The choice of the color of the powder to be used depends on the background of the object to be dusted. If the object is dark or black, a light powder is used, and conversely, if the object is light or white, a dark or black powder is used. The most common color powders are black, silver, grey, and white. However, fingerprint powders come in many other colors which can be used to contrast with any background. The brushes available are composed of camel's hair, feather dusters, fiberglass, or nylon.

1. A small amount of powder is poured onto a clean piece of paper.

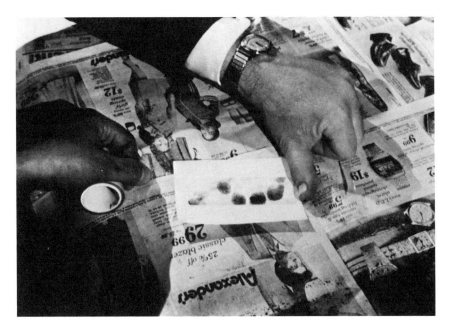

Placing the Lift on a Card. (*Courtesy of* Lt. Daniel Guiney, Commanding Officer, Crime Scene Unit, New York City Police Department.)

2. The brush is drawn across the powder and then tapped with the finger to remove excess material.
3. The surface of object to be searched is then lightly brushed by the investigator who uses curved strokes to locate prints.

The fingerprint powder adheres to the material and forms the latent print. This latent print will first appear as a smudge and will require further treatment before it becomes a distinct print. This is done by brushing the powder parallel to the ridge structure of the print, being careful not to rub the print too hard. After the print is developed it should be photographed first and then lifted.

Another method of dusting is done with magnetic powders. The Magna-Brush is dipped into the magnetic powder which then adheres to the magnet in the brush. When the powder, which is actually fine iron fillings, is evenly distributed on the end of the brush, the investigator uses the applicator like any other fingerprint brush. The advantage of this method is that there is no mess or excess powder left on the object. The disadvantage is that the Magna-Brush method cannot be used on ferrous metals and is very expensive. The prints that are located are lifted in the same manner as those obtained with the regular fingerprint powder.

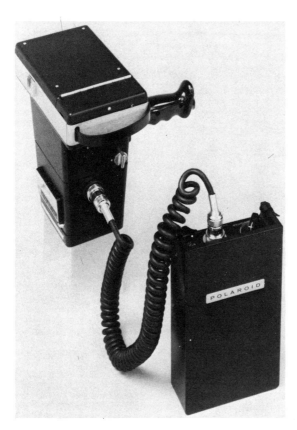

Polaroid's CU-5 Camera.

PRESERVATION OF FINGERPRINTS. Prints found at the scene of a homicide should be immediately recorded by photography before any attempt is made to "lift" the print. This procedure is recommended in the event lifting is not successful or the print is damaged during attempts to remove it from the item on which it is found.

In addition, photography also makes it easier to introduce the fingerprint evidence into court, since parts of the object that contained the print can be seen in the picture. The method of photography used will vary with the expertise of the technician. I recommend that the investigator use the 1 × 1 or "fingerprint" camera. Polaroid produces a fixed-focus camera called the CU-5 which is ideal for this type of work. (See Figure 12.8.)

It should be noted that in addition to latent fingerprints, *palmar* (palm, wrist) or *plantar* (foot, toe) skin designs may also be found at the scene.

Firearms. Latent print developed after the gun has been processed for prints, using dusting powders. The developed print is then photographed with the CU-5 camera. It is recommended procedure to photograph any latent prints before attempting the lift. In the event that the lift fails, the photograph can still be used to evaluate and compare the latent print. (*Courtesy of* the Polaroid Corporation, Cambridge, Massachusetts.)

Remember, these impressions or prints can also be used to positively identify suspects and should be preserved accordingly.

CHEMICAL PROCESSES. In addition to the powders, there are a series of chemical procedures which can be employed to develop latent prints. These are: iodine fuming, ninhydrin, and silver nitrate. Furthermore, there have been some remarkable results in developing latent prints by use of the lasar. Practically speaking, the average investigator will not be employing these procedures. However, one should be aware of the availability of these methods in the event that further examination of evidence is necessary in order to discover and develop latent print evidence.

TIRE TRACKS AND FOOTPRINTS. These impressions may be left in various types of material. The footprint is the most common impression left at or near the scene of a crime. A *footprint* is formed when the foot or sole and heel of a shoe becomes contaminated with some for-

Bloodstained Sneakers. These are the bloodstained sneakers of an offender who was apprehended while standing in a crowd of on-lookers at a homicide scene. The offender had gotten the blood on his sneakers during an assault. He had stabbed the victim multiple times during a dispute in a hallway. He then fled from the scene, but had to walk through the blood thereby leaving sneaker prints in blood at the crime scene. The sneaker prints matched the impressions and the blood on the sneakers matched the blood type of the deceased.

eign substance, such as blood, paint, or dust. A *foot impression* is formed like a tire track, when the foot or tire treads are pressed into some type of moldable material such as dirt, clay, or snow. Any such impression should be preserved and used for comparison with suspects or vehicles. Impressions may be identifiable by wear, damage, characteristic properties, or repair marks. Impressions should be collected in the following manner.

1. Photograph: Prior to photography, the impression should be cleaned of all foreign matter. Lighting should be employed so as to enhance the details. A scale of measure should be included in the photo. Then a long-range view and a close-up should be taken.
2. Casting: A casting kit should be available for use at the crime scene which contains the following materials:
   a. Plaster of paris (five pounds).

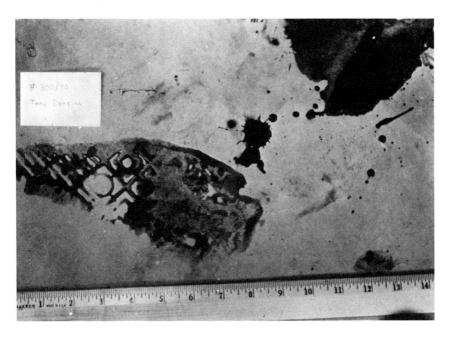

Evidence Photograph Depicting a Bloody Sneaker Print. Note the rule of measure. (*Courtesy of* Dr. Robert C. Shaler, Chief of Serology, New York City Medical Examiner's Office.)

    b. Mixing container (flexible for reuse).
    c. Stirring stick.
    d. Reinforcement material (sticks, wire, etc. to hold form).
    e. Shellac or plastic spray (to form soft earth or dust).
    f. Oil spray (to serve as release agent).
3. Preparation for casting:
    a. Clean out the loose material without disturbing impression.
    b. Plastic spray to fix soil prior to plaster.
    c. Build a form around impression to avoid run-off.
    d. Gently pour plaster of paris over impression.
    e. Add reinforcement sticks as form builds.
4. Preservation of dust prints:
    a. Photograph first.
    b. Use a special lifter (black rubber with a sticky surface) placed sticky-side down over impression. Press on the impression and then remove lifter.

Remember, do not overlook soil evidence which may later be found on suspect's shoes.

In addition to obtaining castings, the investigator should collect soil samples from the location.

TOOL MARKS. Tool marks, like footprints and tire tracks, may contain minute imperfections which are unique and can sometimes be microscopically compared to the tool or object in question. It is better if the investigator can remove the object which bears the tool mark. This can be done by removing the surface for submission to the laboratory. In instances where this would be impractical, the tool mark can be cast with a silicone rubber material. To collect tool marks:

1. Photograph (long-shot and close-up with 1 × 1 camera).
2. Cast with a silicone rubber casting after spraying surface with silicone release agent.

BITE MARKS. Practically speaking, bite marks may be considered as tool marks and are valuable physical evidence. (See Chapter 15, "Bite Mark Identification.")

BULLET HOLES
1. In walls or furniture, first photograph and then examine trajectory.
2. In garments:
   a. Photograph.
   b. Safeguard for examination for powder residue.
   c. Wrap (do not fold) and place in proper container. Direction of fire can be ascertained by using a color test to determine presence of lead (the Harrison Test).

NEWLY DAMAGED AREAS. The presence of damaged furniture, objects, and any other newly damaged areas are indicative of some sort of violence or struggle.

1. Photograph.
2. Examine for any serology.
3. Process for fingerprints.

Application of DNA Technology

Biological evidence retrieved from a victim or crime scene can now be examined at its most fundamental level—the deoxyribonucleic acid (DNA) molecule.

The purpose of this section is to acquaint the reader with the application of DNA and genetic identification techniques in criminal investigation. In addition to the FBI, there are three private corporations that perform forensic DNA analysis: Lifecodes Corporation in New York,

Forensic Science & Associates in California, and Cellmark Corporation in Maryland.

The author serves as an investigative consultant for The Lifecodes Corporation. The information within this section is based on the research and experience of the Lifecodes Corporation and personal interviews with Robert C. Shaler, Ph.D. (former Forensic Director of Lifecodes Corporation, and presently Chief of Serology for the New York Medical Examiner's Office) who is a nationally recognized authority on forensic DNA applications.

The Lifecodes Corporation is a DNA-based genetic diagnostic research laboratory in Valhalla, New York, which developed a testing system known as the DNA-PRINT^{TM} Identification Test. This system was the first of its kind in the United States and has enabled forensic scientists to examine the specific genetic code of a biological specimen for individual characteristics. The specimens may be blood, tissue, semen, hair with root, bone, urine, or any evidence containing or exhibiting traces of the genetic code (DNA).

Deoxyribonucleic Acid

Deoxyribonucleic acid is housed in every nucleated cell in the body. These DNA molecules are often described as the body's blueprints because they carry the genetic codes that govern the structure and function of every component of the body. DNA has been described as the fundamental natural material that determines the genetic characteristics of all life-forms. Although there are portions of our DNA that are relatively conserved through the evolutionary process, as humans we share a human form that is basically human-specific, while other classes of organisms share a DNA composition unique to that particular species—an elephant is an elephant, a fish is a fish.

In fact, the DNA molecule carries the genetic information that establishes each person as separate and distinct. We as humans create human offspring through the transfer of this DNA to our children.

According to the genetic experts, the DNA molecule's configuration does not vary from cell to cell. Therefore, the billions of cells which comprise each person contain the same molecules of DNA carrying the same codes in precisely the same sequence.

The Cell

The cell is the basic unit of all living organisms, including humans, animals, insects, and plants. The human body has more than 10 trillion cells. It is composed of two parts: the nucleus, which contains the chromosomes and the nucleli, and the cytoplasm, which is all of the material inside the cell membrane outside of the nucleus. The nucleus contains the cells genetic program—a sort of master plan that controls everything the cell does. The chromosomes within the nucleus are composed mainly of DNA and associated proteins. The chromosome stores and transmits genetic information.

The DNA molecule is tightly coiled within the nucleus of a cell, similar to a ball of yarn. When unraveled, a molecule of DNA is approximately six feet in length. This molecule is recognized by the scientists as a double-stranded helix.

According to the 1953 studies of Watson and Crick, each chromosome consists of a double spiral of deoxyribonucleic acid in the shape of a twisted ladder—hence, the term double-stranded helix. The sides or backbone of the ladder are composed of alternating sugar (deoxyribose) and phosphoric acid (phosphate) molecules. The "rungs" of the ladder are composed of "pairs" of purine and pyrimidine bases.

DNA is built up of units called nucleotides, composed of the sugar, a phosphate group, and a base. Millions of these nucleotides form a single strand. However, there are only four bases:

Two (2) purines: (A) adenine and (G) guanine
Two (2) pyrimidines: (T) thymine and (C) cytosine

The purine and pyrimidine bases interact with each other through hydrogen bonding and form predictable associations. Adenine (A) always binds to (T) thymine, and (G) guanine always binds to (C) cytosine. These are the only possible combinations which form the "rungs" of the ladder and are referred to as complimentary base pairs. Thus, we have a T–A, A–T, C–G, and G–C formulation within the helix.

It is important to note that these genetic base sequences are fairly fixed, and that they determine the protein and enzyme make-up of the our human cells.

Research and Development

Since the early 1970s a number of remarkable discoveries have been made in DNA by a new breed of molecular biologists known as genetic engineers. These scientists have learned to "edit" the language of the DNA molecule using a technique called recombinant DNA, referred to as rDNA technology. Through this research, scientists have learned to synthesize or clone these molecules, and have generally engineered certain structural changes within organisms.

A modern-day application of this research is found in genetic diagnostics. Scientists have been able to isolate and produce individual fragments of DNA that carry the code for specific inherited disorders. These DNA fragments, known as gene probes, are applied to a test specimen of DNA, where they act as genetic sleuths seeking out and binding to areas of DNA carrying defective gene codes.

In their long-time study of specific diseases, molecular biologists came across small areas of the DNA molecule that showed marked variations in base sequence from one individual to the next. They called these naturally occurring variations *polymorphisms.*

As human beings we all share a common species of DNA. Long stretches of DNA remain the same from person to person. For instance, we all have a head, a heart, lungs, legs, arms, etc. However, within the *polymorphic areas,* the DNA can vary quite dramatically from one individual to another.

The scientists referred to some of these highly polymorphic regions as anonymous sequence or "junk DNA" because their function was not clearly understood. These *polymorphic* DNA regions are known to repeat themselves over and over again like a stutter and are called *variable number of tandem repeats* or *VNTRs,* which are uniqe to the individual.

Research soon revealed that the chance of any two individuals, except identical twins, having the same polymorphisms in these segments of the DNA molecule was quite remote. These highly variable polymorphic regions, or sequences of DNA, provided the basis for DNA fingerprinting.

Forensic investigators reasoned that a technique which enabled them to identify the polymorphisms in the DNA of one individual and compare them with the polymorphisms in the DNA of another individual could serve as a means of genetic indentification.

To find these polymorphisms, they needed a gene probe similar to the one used in diagnostic medicine. However, instead of seeking out the codes of disease, they utilized DNA technology to create a probe that would seek out and label the genetic polymorphisms peculiar to the DNA of each individual.

Two types of probes are used in forensic DNA identification: the multilocus probe, which was first developed by Jeffreys (1985) to identify specific fingerprints of human DNA by focusing on multiple points on multiple chromosomes; and the single-locus probe, which focuses on one region within one chromosome. The law enforcement community has chosen the single-locus probe, used by Lifecodes Corporation and the FBI, for analysis of forensic evidence in criminal investigations.

Scientific Techniques Employed in DNA-Print Tests

DNA purified. The DNA must first be extracted from the nucleus of the cells of the biological specimen. The goal is to remove protein bound to the DNA so that restriction enzyme digestion and other manipulation of DNA is not inhibited. Another goal is to isolate the DNA in as close to a native form as possible. Native DNA, called high molecular weight or intact DNA, is easily isolated from fresh biological specimens (i.e., whole blood). However, DNA present in forensic specimens (i.e., vaginal swabs, bloodstains) may not be intact. Therefore, the extraction procedure should be gentle permitting DNA with as high a molecular weight as possible to be isolated.

DNA cleaved into fragments. Restriction endonucleases are enzymes that work like a pair of molecular scissors, actually cutting the DNA at specific base sequences. For example, Lifecodes Corporation uses a cutting enzyme designated Pst 1. It is obtained from bacteria and is designed to cleave the DNA molecule whenever it recognizes the base sequence CTGCAG. It cuts the DNA molecule at this specific "A–G" point along the entire helix where the CTGCAG occurs. In other words, in the sequence of (C) cytosine, (T) thymine, (G) guanine, (C) cytosine, (A) adenine, and (G) guanine, CTGCAG, whenever Pst-1 sees this *CTGCAG* sequence it cuts the DNA fragment. The FBI uses HAE III as a cutting enzyme that recognizes the sequence GGCC. Whenever the enzyme recognizes this particular base sequence, it cuts the DNA at this point.

The enzyme action results in millions of DNA fragments. In the areas of the helix, which are highly variable or polymorphic, there are differences in the length due to the VNTRs or the varying number of base pairs that lie between the cutting points that the enzyme selects. These varying number of base pairs are referred to as variable number of tandem repeats or VNTRs. As the fragments can be created by the actions of the restriction enzymes, and as these fragments are polymorphisms, they are termed *restriction fragment length polymorphisms*, or RFLPs. It is important to understand that a VNTR does not have to be an RFLP, and that an RFLP does not have to contain a VNTR.

RFLP technology. The above process is referred to as *RFLP technology*. The fragments of DNA are cut with a restriction enzyme, and the lengths of the polymorphisms differ for each individual. Under RFLP technology, DNA can be extracted and analyzed at the molecular level and then compared with DNA from a known biological specimen for identification purposes.

Fragments are size-separated. The DNA fragments, which have been digested into RFLPs, are separated in a gel medium using an electrical charge in a process known as *electrophoresis*. This technique is used to arrange the biological particles on an agarose gel through exposure to electricity. The distance each fragment travels depends on its length. The longer the fragment, the slower its rate of migration. Positively charged particles will migrate toward the negative pole, whereas negatively charged particles will migrate toward the positive electrode of the electrophoretic field. All DNA carries a negative charge and will migrate toward the positive pole. The fragments separate by size into bands and create a pattern on the gel.

Southern blotting. This is a process by which the DNA fragments separated during electrophoresis are transferred from the wobbly surface of the agarose gel onto a sheet of nylon membrane. Once blotted, the pattern is ready for the gene probe.

Hybridization. Probes are then applied to the nylon membrane. These probes, usually tagged with a radioactive marker, are designed to "seek-out" a predetermined chromosomal locus containing a polymorphic region of DNA.

A probe is a segment of recombinant DNA (rDNA) that is engineered to go to a particular predetermined locus on a particular chromosome. Lifecodes Corporation uses four probes D2S44, D14S1, D17S79, and DXYS14 in this test. The "D" stands for DNA; the numbers "2," "14," "17," and "XY" indicate the numbered chromosome; "S" is the submission or application number which focuses on the polymorphic area.

Upon finding a DNA fragment that carries all or part of its complimentary base sequence, the probe "binds" to or *hybridizes* to that fragment.

The autoradiograph. The *autoradiograph* or *autorad* is the final product. The excess probe is washed away from the nylon membrane. The nylon membrane is then placed against a piece of x-ray film and exposed for several days. When the film is processed, black bands appear where the radioactive probes stuck to the fragments. Single-locus probes normally will each produce one or two dark bands on a white column in each individual.

Interpretation of the results. The pattern of bands can be unique for each individual, except for identical twins. When comparing the two DNA fragment patterns, the forensic investigator simply looks to see where the probe landed on the two patterns. If the specimens are from the same person, the investigator can expect to find the probe on fragments of identical length and, consequently, in identical positions on the two patterns.

However, the statistical rarity of each pattern is based on population genetics, which takes into account specific allele frequencies and other

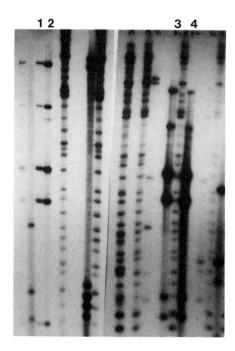

In this autoradiograph (autorad), we know the match between a serial murder suspect and the autorad of two of his victims. Lanes 1 and 2 show suspect evidence and whole blood of the suspect, and lanes 3 and 4 show the victim.

considerations that may require additional experiments, techniques, and controls in arriving at a justifiable scientific conclusion.

It has been reported in some forensic journals that the probability of positive identification has been calculated to be some 30 billion to one that two unrelated individuals will have the same genetic make-up.

DNA Identification Tests.

Human cells. In each human cell there are 46 chromosomes arranged in pairs of 22 plus two sex chromosomes. Twenty-three are contributed by the fathers' sperm and 23 by the mother's egg. *Practically speaking, we are part of our mother and part of our father in that we each inherit part of our parent's DNA.*

DNA technology can be utilized in paternity testing in order to establish a child's rightful parentage. Lifecodes has performed approximately 3,000 such testings. DNA-PRINT™ Identification Test allows investigators to compare DNA patterns and establish positive identification. DNA identifications can also be used in forensic paternity, immigration disputes, missing persons cases, and unidentified body cases, etc.

Application in Forensic Medicine

Victim identification. The DNA-PRINT™ test has been successfully used in a number of criminal investigations to positively identify the deceased. In one particular case, Lifecodes scientists were able to confirm that the brain matter found in a missing woman's vehicle belonged to the victim, who was identified through her DNA and that of her parents. Skeletonized remains (bone marrow), body parts, and other materials which contain nucleated cells can be analyzed for DNA and can provide authorities with identification.

Case History[3]

In December of 1987, Wichita homicide detectives encountered a bizarre crime. The suspect in this case had allegedly killed his wife by putting her into a crematorium. Police were alerted to this possible crime by a civilian complainant, who was suspicious of a bucket that had been left in her garage. The police recovered the burnt remains consisting of a number of small fragments of bone and burned flesh, which the medical examiner, Dr. William Eckert, had determined to be human. A forensic anthropologist was also brought in to assist the police and medical examiner's office in establishing an identity.

The homicide investigation revealed that the offender thought that he had planned the perfect murder. His reasoning, according to witnesses, was "no body—no crime." Police learned that he had lured his former wife to a shopping mall on the pretense of shopping together for Christmas presents for their child. At the time, he had been involved in a bitter custody battle over this child with his ex-wife.

Somehow, he managed to get his wife to the funeral home, where he was employed as an usher. And somehow, no one knows for sure whether she was dead or alive, he managed to place her body into the crematorium and activated the furnace.

The crematorium could reach temperatures of 1500°F, and it would take approximately two and one-half hours to reduce the body to ashes. However, the suspect didn't know that one of the burners wasn't working properly. He realized that he was running out of time. He wasn't even authorized to operate the crematorium. The suspect then decided to get the evidence of the burning out of the crematorium and out of the building before his employer found out. He tried to clean-up but was left with a bucket full of cremains. This bucket of cremains was subse-

---

[3] Based upon a personal interview with Major John Dotson, Wichita, Kansas Police Department.

Note this interior view of the crematorium. (A) The crematorium is operating in normal fashion. (B) Malfunctioning of the crematorium is evident with only one jet operating. The killer was unaware of the second burner malfunction. (*Courtesy of* Major John Dotson, Wichita, Kansas Police Department.)

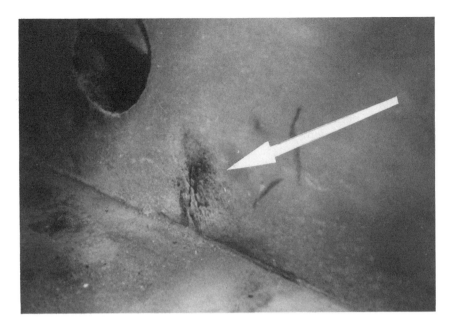

An arrow points to the dried blood of the victim on the inside wall of the crematorium. This blood was collected by authorities and submitted to The Lifecodes Corporation, which provided positive identification of the deceased after comparing evidence to the whole blood samples of the victim's parents. (*Courtesy of* Major John Dotson, Wichita, Kansas Police Department.)

quently seized by Wichita police and resulted in the suspect's arrest. The cremains provided circumstantial evidence of this brutal slaying. In addition, a unique piece of jewelry, which the deceased wore, was found in the catch basket of the crematorium. However, prosecutors wanted more.

The District Attorney's office decided on establishing the victim's identity, beyond the jewelry and anthropological evidence.

In February 1988, the following evidence was sent to Lifecodes Corporation. A partial femur bone as well as tissue from the pelvis and blood scrapings from the crematorium were forwarded along with whole blood samples of the victim's parents. Lifecodes extracted DNA from the blood scrapings from the crematorium, which they were able to compare with the DNA from the whole blood samples of the victim's parents. Identification of the remains was positively established through the DNA-PRINT™ identification test, which was in actuality a paternity-type testing.

Assailant idenfication (forcible rape). DNA offers the criminal justice system an unprecedented opportunity to obtain the strongest possible evidence from semen specimens. Prior to DNA technology, the best that forensic scientists could provide was an exclusion or suggestion of inclusion based on specimens that were analyzed for blood type and protein enzymes. Semen would be mixed with the vaginal fluids, which also contain protiens. This would make determining identity by protein analysis difficult. In other cases, in which there were multiple assailants, several semen samples would become intermingled making any determination of identity by protein analysis almost impossible.

The DNA-PRINT™ identification test, however, provides positive individual identification. This test can separate vaginal and sperm cells; it can identify mixtures; and interference by bacteria is eliminated. It is also applicable to old stains. It amounts to the criminal leaving his name, address, and social security number at the scene of the crime.

Investigation of a Series of Crimes

The DNA-PRINT™ test is useful in investigations of a series of similar crimes. If several rapes have been committed in the same general area, forensic experts can test the semen specimens from the victims and know whether they should be looking for one suspect or multiple suspects. Lifecodes Corporation has provided forensic evidence in a number of serial rape cases, and has provided prosecutors with crucial evidence in a significant serial-murder case.

Case History

On September 19, 1987, the dead body of a 35-year-old woman was found in the bedroom of her first-floor apartment in Richmond, Virginia. Her body was discovered by a police officer who went to her apartment after her car, which had been abandoned and running, was found a few blocks away. She had been strangled and there was evidence of sexual activity at the scene.

On October 3, 1987, two weeks later, a 32-year-old female physician was found dead in a second-floor bedroom closet in her home in Richmond, Virginia. Her body was discovered by her husband, who had returned home from school in Washington. She also had been strangled, and there was also evidence of sexual activity at the scene.

Police investigation indicated that in both cases the murderer had entered the homes of the women by cutting a screen and climbing through an open window. In the first murder scene police recovered semen samples from the bedding of the victim. In the second murder scene, the killer left semen on the victim's slip. Medicolegal examination revealed that the first victim had been raped and strangled to death with a sock, which had been tightened around her neck with a pipe from a vacuum cleaner. According to the medical examiner, the second

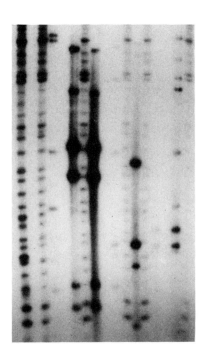

DNA-Print Autorad. This autoradiograph (autorad) shows the DNA of two Richmond victims indicating a positive match. This autorad establishes that the semen at each of the crime scenes was from the same source. Later in the investigation, the blood sample taken from the suspect was also submitted for DNA analysis and indicated him to be the donor.

victim had been raped, sodomized, and then strangled to death with a belt. Both women had been bound with their hands tied behind their backs and both women had been strangled with ligatures. The police investigation immediately focused on the similar *modus operandi* of the two murders. However, the only evidence that the police had recovered in these two cases was biological. At the time this forensic evidence seemed insignificant in comparison to any solid "leads" in the case.

A special task force operation, which involved uniform as well as plainclothes officers, was initiated within the two neighborhoods where the killings had taken place. Community apprehension over these two murders was at a peak as police attempted to identify a possible serial killer, whom the media called Richmond's "South Side Strangler."

As the police intensified their presence within the areas of the murders, the community began to regain composure. However, 51 days later in an adjoining county another vicious sex-related homicide had occurred. This time, the victim was a teenager.

On November 22, 1987 a 15-year-old woman was found dead in her parent's apartment in Chesterfield County, which is just south of Richmond city limits. The killer had entered her bedroom through a window as the family was asleep. The victim had been strangled, her

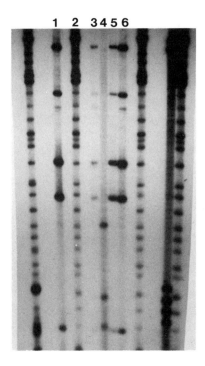

Autorad Indicating Match of Suspect to
Arlington Victim. In lane 1 we see the
DNA of suspect Spencer. Lane 2 is a
marker. Lane 3 is the sleeping bag of the
victim upon which the sperm was retrieved. Lane 4 is the DNA of the victim's blood. Lane 5 is the nightgown of
the victim, which also contained semen
evidence. Lane 6 is the DNA of the suspect spencer. NOTE the DNA match between Spencer and the semen evidence
from the crime scenes. (*Courtesy of* The
Lifecodes Corporation, Valhalla, New
York.)

hands were tied behind her back, and once again there was evidence of
sexual activity at the crime scene.

Police authorities from Richmond and Chesterfield Counties met to
compare notes on what was apparently the work of the Richmond's
"South Side Strangler."

Nine days later and over 100 miles away in Northern Virginia, another rape-homicide was being investigated by the Arlington County
Police. On December 1, 1987, a 44-year-old woman was found dead on
her bed on the second floor of her two-story home in Arlington County
in Northern Virginia. She had been strangled and there was evidence
that she had been raped. Police recovered semen from the victim's
nightgown and a sleeping bag at the crime scene.

Detective Joseph Horgas was in charge of this seemingly unrelated
homicide in Arlington. The first thing Horgas looked for was if any
similar cases had occurred within the jurisdiction. A 1984 rape-
homicide seemed to fit the MO but there had been an arrest and the
suspect was still in jail. As Det. Horgas began the tedious job of searching through old files, he came upon a series of rapes in 1983 in which the
victims had not been killed. The detective would later forward this
evidence from the 1983 rape case to Lifecodes for a DNA analysis. This
1983 evidence matched the DNA of the evidence from the 1987 rape-
murder in Arlington. Meanwhile, Det. Horgas began to develop infor-

mation on a black male named Timothy Spencer who had lived in the Arlington area before going to jail on an unrelated charge. He discovered that Spencer had recently been released and was living in the Richmond area in a half-way house. A check of parole records indicated that this very same suspect had been given a two-week furlough to visit his family in the Arlington area for Thanksgiving. This put Spencer in the immediate area at the time of the rape-murder in Arlington. After conferring with authorities in Richmond, Horgas was sure that his suspect Timothy Spencer was the "South Side Strangler."

In fact, Detective Horgas believed that Timothy Spencer had perpetrated the rape-homicide in 1984, and that the suspect who had been jailed was innocent. *Ultimately, the evidence developed by Det. Horgas proved this man to be innocent and he was released after being pardoned by the Governor of the State of Virginia.*

On January 20, 1988, Horgas traveled to Richmond where he arrested Timothy Wilson Spencer for the homicide in Arlington. Spencer, who had been released from prison to a half-way house in Richmond, was finally exposed as "The South Side Strangler." In fact, all four murders had occurred within three months of Spencer's release.

The most important evidence in this series of rapes and murders was the biological fluids recovered from the crime scenes. In fact, three of the rape-murders had been connected forensically through the DNA analysis of the semen.

Lifecodes Corporation, which did the analysis of the evidence from the two Richmond cases as well as the Arlington murder, was provided with blood samples from the suspect. The evidence from the Chesterfield murder was forwarded to Forensic Science & Associates by Lifecodes for *DNA amplification* due to the limited amount of genetic material.

The DNA-PRINT™ identification test indicated that the DNA patterns in Spencer's blood were identical to the DNA patterns from the semen left at the murder scenes.

Spencer went to trial as his attorneys tried to exclude genetic fingerprint evidence from being introduced. However, prosecutors were able to convince the court that DNA evidence should be presented in each of the murder trials.

Lifecodes Corporation was allowed to testify to their DNA-PRINT™ analysis, which showed a match between Spencer's blood and semen found at each of the murder scenes.

The DNA analysis also enabled prosecutors to pass the legal test for "signature crimes," meaning enough similarities exist to believe that the crimes were committed by the same person. This "signature-crime" tactic was used in the Chesterfield County case as well as the subsequent penalty phase hearings on each of the convictions.

Timothy Wilson Spencer was ultimately convicted of all four rape-

372

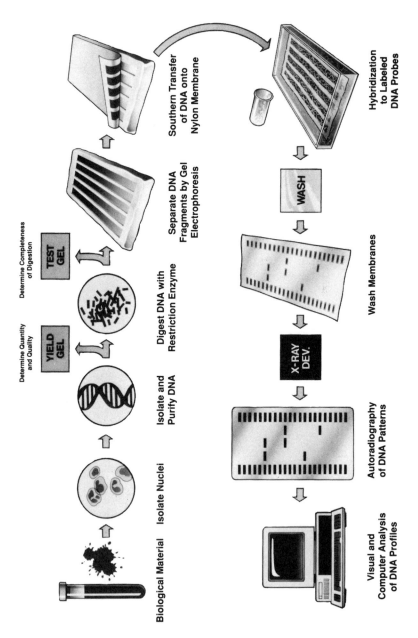

Determine Quantity and Quality

Determine Completeness of Digestion

YIELD GEL

TEST GEL

Biological Material

Isolate Nuclei

Isolate and Purify DNA

Digest DNA with Restriction Enzyme

Separate DNA Fragments by Gel Electrophoresis

Southern Transfer of DNA onto Nylon Membrane

Hybridization to Labeled DNA Probes

WASH

Wash Membranes

X-RAY DEV.

Autoradiography of DNA Patterns

Visual and Computer Analysis of DNA Profiles

The DNA-Print™ Process (*Courtesy of* Lifecodes Corporation, Valhalla, New York.)

murders. DNA evidence was also utilized in the penalty phase of the trials, and Spencer has been sentenced to death on each one of the murders. In September 1989 the convictions and sentences on two of the rape-murders were upheld on appeal before the Virginia Supreme Court. This case was significant because it is the nation's first murder conviction based on the use of DNA fingerprinting.

Reopening Unsolved Cases

Since DNA maintains its integrity in dried specimens for prolonged periods, the DNA-PRINT™ identification test can be utilized on old evidence. In my capacity as an investigative consultant I have reopened a number of cases for DNA-PRINT™ analysis. I conferred with the detectives in a case which was approximately 12 years old to consider this forensic technique. The authorities in that jurisdiction now have forensic evidence linking a serial killer to crimes a dozen years old.

DNA patterns from old evidence can also be compared with DNA patterns of recently apprehended suspects. Or, cases from the past, in which evidence was inconclusive, can now be tested using DNA technology.

Admissibility Criterion

In determining the admissibility of any evidence into trial, there must be method validation and laboratory validation. The scientific acceptance of this technology is the basis for the legal acceptance in a court of law. The medical research, Nobel Prize awards, peer level publications, as well as general acceptance by the scientific community comprise the bases for legal argument.

In the early 1900s a Nobel Prize was awarded for the discovery of DNA as the genetic basis for life. In 1953, Drs. James Watson and Francis Crick were awarded a Nobel Prize in connection with defining the structure of DNA. Their elucidation of the *double helix structure* of DNA revolutionized the field of molecular biology and genetics.

In the 1970s further genetic research produced the *restriction enzymes.* Genetic engineering through gene splicing and cloning were soon accepted procedures within the scientific community. In the early 1980s scientists discovered *RFLP technology,* which was the basis for determining individual identity.

The American Society of Crime Laboratory Director's Guidelines for Forensic Laboratory Management has established procedures for the validation and implementation of methods for DNA analysis.

Dr. Richard J. Roberts, Assistant Director for Research at the Cold Spring Harbor Laboratory on Long Island, New York, serves as Deputy

Table 13.1 DNA-PRINT™ Test: Preservation of Sample and Minimum Amounts[a]

Blood (White Cells)	
Liquid	1–100 μl (size of a quarter, one drop)
Preservation	EDTA (Purple Cap) refrigeration
Dried	Approximately, size of a dime
Preservation	Dried; keep dry; refrigerate/freeze

Semen	
Liquid	1–20 μl (approximately dime size)
Preservation	Add EDTA and refrigerate
Dried	Requires an appropriate amount of sperm
Preservation	Keep dry; refrigerate or freeze; laboratory/separate sperm

Urine	
Cellular Material	10,000 cells (approximately 60 ml)
	60–100 cc (approximately 2 ounces)
Liquid	Isolate cellular material; freeze (−70°C)
Dried	keep dry; freeze

Saliva	
Buccal Cells	10,000 cells (one drop)
Liquid	Separate buccal cells; dry/freeze
Dried	Keep dry; refrigerate or freeze

Tissues (Bones)	
Minimum Amount	100–500 Mg (one inch)
Fresh	Freeze (−70°C)
Dried	keep dry; freeze

[a] The DNA-PRINT identification test can be utilized to: (1) establish the link between evidential DNA with that of the possible suspect's DNA; and (2) identify whether the DNA in quesiton is human or nonhuman and establish sex.

to the Director of the laboratory. The Director is Dr. James Watson—the very same James Watson who in 1953, together with Francis Crick, received a Nobel Prize for the elucidation of the double helix structure. Dr. Roberts, in his testimony during a Frye hearing in New York, *People v. Wesley*, County of Albany, 1988, stated that the protocols used by Lifecodes Corporation," . . . were not only acceptable by the scientific community, and deemed reliable therein, but were among the most detailed and specific laboratory protocols for the procedures involved . . ."

The availability of appropriate controls and procedures to assure reliability of DNA laboratory results promises favorable judicial reviews for the admissibility of DNA evidence in trial courts.

The Legal Standard of Admissibility

A majority of jurisdictions follow the Frye rule for determining admissibility of evidence. This is based on the Supreme Court ruling in *Frye v. United States*, F. 1013 at 1014 (D.C. Cir. 1923). The court in this case held:

> Just when a scientific principle or discovery crosses the line between the experimental and demonstrable stages is difficult to define. Somewhere in this twilight zone the evidential force of the principle must be recognized, and while courts will go a long way in admitting expert testimony deduced from a well-recognized scientific principle or discovery, the thing from which the deduction is made must be sufficiently established to have gained general acceptance in the particular field in which it belongs.

Practically speaking, the Frye rule requires that the evidence to be introduced has gained general acceptance in the scientific community. It has been established in a number of courts that DNA identification is capable of producing reliable results and that there is general scientific acceptance of the theories underlying DNA identification.

The courts have also concluded that DNA forensic identification tests to determine inclusions are reliable and meet the Frye standard of admissibility.

Conclusion

DNA and genetic fingerprinting represent the most important breakthrough in crime detection since the discovery of the fingerprint. DNA technology represents the future of forensic medicine; the experts have only begun to scratch the surface with this technology. It is a powerful tool that protects the innocent just as surely as it pinpoints the guilty. Genetic identification takes the "gamesmanship" out of the trial—it either is the defendant, who committed the crime, or it is not.

The Lifecodes Corporation has been a pioneer of DNA technology in this country. They are considered the most experienced DNA testing laboratory in the world. Lifecodes trains personnel in DNA technology and supplies the probes, reagents, and enzymes to a number of forensic laboratories in the United States, including the FBI.

Selected Reading

Balazs, I., Wexler, K., Nicholas, L., Guisti, A., Baird, M., Rubinstein, P., Allen, F. H., Sussman, L. "The use of Restriction Length polymorphisms for the Determination of Paternity." Toronto, Canada. Presented to the American Society of Human Genetics. November 1984.

Blake, E. T., and Sensabaugh, G. F. "Genetic Markers in Human Semen: A Review." *Journal of Forensic Sciences* 21:784–796 (1976).

FBI *Handbook of Forensic Science.* Washington, D.C.: U.S. Department of Justice, Federal Bureau of Investigation, 1979.

Geberth, Vernon J. "DNA-PRINT Identification Test Provides Crucial Evidence in Lust Murder Case." *Law and Order Magazine* 36 (1988).

Geberth, Vernon J. "The Application of DNA in Criminal Investigations." *Law and Order Magazine* (1990). Vol. 38. No 3 March, 1990.

Gill, P., Jeffreys, A. J., and Werret, D. J. "Forensic Application of DNA Fingerprints". *Nature* 318:577–579 (1985).

Guisti, A., Baird, M., Pasquale, S., Balazs, I., and Glassberg, J., "Application of DNA Polymorphisms to the Analysis of DNA Recovered from Sperm." *Journal of Forensic Sciences* 31:409–417 (1986).

Harris, Joseph. Frye Ruling. *People v. Wesley,* 140 Misc. 2nd 306 Supreme Court County of Albany, July 15, 1988.

Jeffreys, A. J., Wilson, V., and Thein, S. L. "Individual Specific Fingerprints of Human DNA. *Nature* 316:76–79 (1985).

Kanter, E., Baird, M., Shaler, R., and Balazs, I. "Analysis of Restriction Fragment Length Polymorphisms in DNA Recovered from Dried Bloodstains." *Journal of Forensic Sciences.* 31:403–408 (1986).

Kirk, Paul L. *Crime Investigation,* 2nd. ed. New York: John Wiley and Sons Inc., 1974.

McNally, Lorah, Shaler, Robert, Giusti, Alan, Baird, Michael, Balazs, Ivan, DeForest, Peter, and Kobilinski, Lawrence. "The Effects of Environment and Substrata on DNA: The Use of Case Work Samples from New York City. *Journal of Forensic Sciences* 34 (1989).

McNally, Lorah, Shaler, Robert, Giusti, Alan, Baird, Michael, Balzas, Ivan, DeForrest, Peter, and Koblinski, Lawrence. "Evaluation of Deoxyribonucleic Acid (DNA) Isolated from Human Bloodstains Exposed to Ultraviolet Light, Heat, Humidity, and Soil Contamination." *Journal of Forensic Sciences* 34 (1989).

Rabson, A. B., and Rabson, A. S. "Recombinant DNA Technology and Laboratory Medicine." *Archives of Pathology and Laboratory Medicine* 107:505–509 (1983).

Scott, James D. *Investigative Methods.* Reston, Virginia: Reston Publishing Company, Inc., 1978.

Shaler, Robert C. "Forensic Serology—An Increasingly Important Tool for the Criminal Justice System." *Brooklyn Barrister,* 1980, pp. 51–57.

Sheindlin, Gerald. "Decision on the Admissibility of DNA Identification Tests." *People v. Castro,* Supreme Court County of the Bronx, August 14, 1989.

Svensson, Arne, Wendel, Otto, and Fisher, Barry A. J. *Techniques of Crime Scene Investigation,* 3rd ed. New York: Elsevier North Holland, Inc., 1981.

Stuver, W. C., Shaler, R. C., Marone, P. M., and Plankenhorn, R. "Forensic Bloodstain and Physiological Fluid Analysis." *ACS Symposium Series* 13.Washington, D.C.: American Chemical Society, 1975, pp. 142–150.

The Bureau of National Affairs. "Virginia Upholds Admission of Results of 'DNA Fingerprint' Analysis." *The Criminal Law Reporter* 46:1026–1027.

Requesting Laboratory Assistance

The information under this caption as well as that contained elsewhere in this section under the particular type of examination or assistance desired should be consulted to facilitate the submission of requests to the Laboratory Division.

Requests for Examination(s) of Evidence

All requests should be made in a written communication, in triplicate, addressed to the Director, Federal Bureau of Investigation, with an attention line in accordance with instructions below and contain the following information:

A. Reference to any previous correspondence submitted to the Laboratory in the case.

B. The nature of and the basic facts concerning the violation insofar as they pertain to the Laboratory examination.

C. The name(s) and sufficient descriptive data of any subject(s), suspect(s), or victim(s).

D. The list of the evidence being submitted either "herewith" or "under separate cover." (Note: Due to evidential "chain of custody" requirements, all evidence sent through the U.S. Postal Service (USPS) system must be sent by registered mail and not by parcel post or regular mail. If United Parcel Service, Federal Express, or air freight is used, utilize their "acknowledgement of delivery," "protective signature," "security signature," or any other such service which provides the same protection as USPS registered mail.)

1. "Herewith": This method is limited to certain small items of evidence which are not endangered by transmission in an envelope marked clearly as contained evidence sealed, and attached securely to the written communication which should state "Submitted herewith are the following items of evidence . . . ."

2. "Under separate cover": This method is generally used for shipment of numerous and/or bulky items of evidence. The written communication should state "Submitted under separate cover by (list the method of shipment be it USPS Registered, United Parcel Service, Federal Express, or air freight) are the following items of evidence." For further information concerning the preparation of packages send under separate cover see Packaging Chart elsewhere in this section.

E. A request. State what types of examinations are desired, to include, if applicable, comparisons with other cases.
   1. Evidence will not be forwarded by the Laboratory Division to the Latent Fingerprint Section, Identification Division, for latent fingerprint examinations unless specifically requested to do so in the written communication.

F. Information as to where the original evidence is to be returned as well as where the original Laboratory report is to be sent.

G. A statement, if applicable, as to whether
   1. The evidence has been examined previously by another expert in the same technical field.
   2. Any local controversy is involved in the case.

H. Notification of the need and the reason(s) for an expeditious examination; bearing in mind this treatment should not be routinely requested.

Attention Lines for Communications and Packages

The following guidelines should be adhered to as closely as possible to avoid any unnecessary delay in the routing of mail at FBI Headquarters.

A. Requests for Laboratory examination *only*, should be marked "Attention: FBI Laboratory."

B. Requests for a fingerprint examination *only*, should be marked "Attention: Identification Division, Latent Fingerprint Section."

C. Requests for *both* a fingerprint examination and Laboratory examination of any type should be marked "Attention: FBI Laboratory."

Shipment of Evidence

The following steps should be followed to properly prepare a package for shipment of numerous and/or bulky items of evidence. (Note: Comply with steps A through I if a cardboard box is used and step J if a wooden box is used):

FEDERAL BUREAU OF INVESTIGATION

Washington, D. C. 20537

REPORT

SAMPLE LETTER

of the

SAMPLE LETTER

LATENT FINGERPRINT SECTION

IDENTIFICATION DIVISION

YOUR FILE NO. 12-741
FBI FILE NO.   95-67994
LATENT CASE NO.
              A-73821

March 22, 19_ _

REGISTERED

TO: Mr. James T. Wixling
    Chief of Police
    Right City, State (Zip Code)

RE: GUY PIDGIN:
    EMPALL MERCHANDISE MART
    RIGHT CITY, STATE
    MARCH 16, 19_ _
    BURGLARY

REFERENCE: Letter March 17, 19_ _
EXAMINATION REQUESTED BY: Addressee
SPECIMENS: Piece of bent metal, Q5
             Ten transparent lifts
             Fingerprints of Guy Pidgin, FBI #213762J9

Four latent fingerprints of value were developed on the piece of metal,

Q5. Seven latent fingerprints of value appear on three lifts marked "safe door"

and five latent fingerprints of value appear on two lifts marked "side window."

No latent prints of value appear on the remaining lifts.

A. Take every precaution to preserve the items of evidence as outlined in the applicable sections of the Evidence Chart as well as
afford appropriate physical protection of the latent fingerprints
thereon to include identification with the word "latent."

B. Choose a cardboard box suitable in size.

C. Wrap each item of evidence separately to avoid contamination.

D. Do not place evidence from more than one investigation case in
the same box.

E. Pack the evidence securely within the box to avoid damage in
transit.

The four latent fingerprints developed on the piece of metal, designated
Q5, have been identified as finger impressions of Guy Pidgin, FBI #213762J9.

The remaining twelve latent fingerprints are not identical with the
fingerprints of Pidgin.

Photographs of the unidentified latent fingerprints have been prepared
for our files and will be available for any additional comparisons you may desire.

Should you desire the assistance of one of the FBI's fingerprint experts
in the trial of this case, we should be notified in ample time to permit the
necessary arrangements. This report should be used, however, if legal considerations permit, in lieu of the appearance of our expert in any pretrial action such
as a preliminary hearing or grand jury presentation. Our representative cannot
be made available to testify if any other fingerprint expert is to present testimony on the same point, namely, that the impressions in question are identical.

The lifts and the fingerprints of Pidgin, which should be retained for
possible future court action in this case, are enclosed.

The results of the laboratory examinations, as well as the disposition
of the piece of metal, Q5, are the subjects of a separate report.

Enclosures (11)

Page 2
LC #A-73821

F. Seal the box with gummed tape and clearly mark the outer portions of the box with the word(s) "evidence." (Note: If any of the
evidence in the box is to be subjected to a latent fingerprint examination, also clearly mark the outer portions of the box with
the word "latent.")
G. Place a copy of the original written request for the examination(s)
in an envelope marked "invoice" and securely affix this envelope
to the outside of the sealed box.
H. Enclose the sealed box in wrapping paper, seal the wrapping paper
with gummed tape, and address the package to the Director, Fed-

eral Bureau of Investigation, Washington, D.C. 20535, with the proper attention line as outlined above.
I. Ship the package via U. S. Postal Service, Registered Mail, United Parcel Service, Federal Express, or air freight.
J. Choose a durable wooden box suitable in size and
  1. Comply with the above steps A, C, D, and E.
  2. Securely fasten the lid on the box and address it to the Director, Federal Bureau of Investigation, Washington, D.C. 20535, with the proper attention line.
  3. Place a copy of the original written request for the examination(s) in an envelope marked "invoice," place the invoice envelope in a clear plastic cover, and tack it to the box.
  4. Comply with step I above.

Evidence Chart

The following chart is provided to give assistance in the collection, identification, preservation, packaging, and sending of evidence to the laboratory. This chart should be used in conjunction with similar evidence information contained elsewhere in this section under each type of examination desired. This evidence information and chart are not intended to be all-inclusive.

Hazardous Materials

Over 3,000 items, including flash paper, live ammunition, explosives, radioactive materials, flammable liquids and solids, flammable and nonflammable gases, spontaneously combustible substances, and oxidizing and corrosive materials are currently considered as hazardous materials. All require special packaging, and the amount of each item which can be shipped is regulated. Therefore, the applicable action listed at the top of the opposite page is to be taken:

A. Flash paper: Contact the FBI Technical Evaluation Unit for shipping instructions *each and every time* this item is to be submitted to the Laboratory.
B. Live ammunition: For shipping instructions see paragraph regarding Live Ammunition.
C. Other hazardous materials: Contact the FBI Explosives Unit for shipping instructions *each and every time* any hazardous material, except flash paper or live ammunition, is to be submitted to the Laboratory.

Nonhazardous Materials

If evidence of this type is not found in this chart or elsewhere in this section, locate a specimen which is most similar in nature and take the appropriate actions or call the Laboratory at 202-FBI-4410 for general instructions.

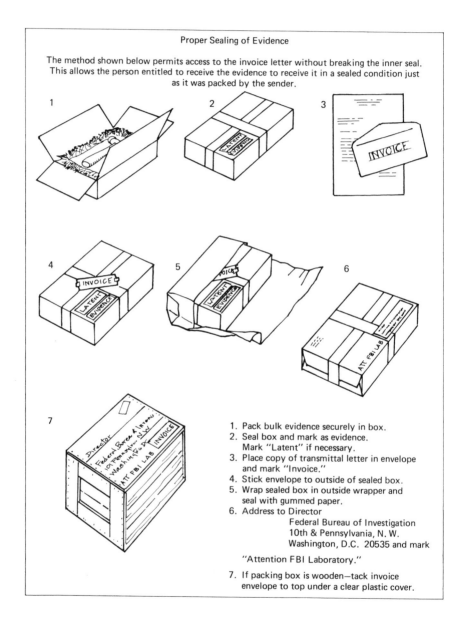

Proper Sealing of Evidence

The method shown below permits access to the invoice letter without breaking the inner seal. This allows the person entitled to receive the evidence to receive it in a sealed condition just as it was packed by the sender.

1. Pack bulk evidence securely in box.
2. Seal box and mark as evidence. Mark "Latent" if necessary.
3. Place copy of transmittal letter in envelope and mark "Invoice."
4. Stick envelope to outside of sealed box.
5. Wrap sealed box in outside wrapper and seal with gummed paper.
6. Address to Director
   Federal Bureau of Investigation
   10th & Pennsylvania, N. W.
   Washington, D.C. 20535 and mark

   "Attention FBI Laboratory."

7. If packing box is wooden—tack invoice envelope to top under a clear plastic cover.

Table A.1

Specimen	Amount Desired		Send by
	Standard	Evidence	
Abrasives, including carborundum, emery, sand, etc.	Not less than one ounce	All	Registered mail or Federal Express
Acids	250 milliters (ml.)	All to 250 ml.	Contact FBI Explosives Unit for instructions.
Adhesive tape	Recovered roll	All	Registered mail
Alkalies—caustic soda, potash, ammonia, etc.	250 ml. 100 gms.	All to 250 ml. All to 100 gms.	Contact FBI Explosives Unit for instructions.
Ammunition (cartridges)			
Anonymous letters, extortion letters, bank robbery notes		All	Registered mail
Blasting caps	(Contact FBI Explosives Unit for instructions.)		

Identification	Wrapping and Packing	Remarks
On outside of container: Type of material. Date obtained. Name or initials	Use containers, such as ice-cream box, pillbox, or plastic vial. Seal to prevent any loss.	Avoid use of envelopes.
Same as above	Plastic or all-glass bottle. Tape stopper. Pack in sawdust, glass, or rock wool. Use bakelite or paraffin-lined bottle for hydrofluoric acid.	Label acids, glass, corrosive.
Same as above	Place on waxed paper or cellophane.	Do not cut, wad, or distort.
Same as above	Plastic or glass bottle with rubber stopper held with adhesive tape	Label alkali, glass, corrosive.
Same as above		Unless specific examination of cartridge is essential, do not submit.
Initial and date each unless legal aspects or good judgment dictates otherwise.	Place in proper enclosure envelope and seal with "evidence" tape or transparent cellophane tape. Flap side of envelope should show 1) wording "Enclosures(s) to FBIHQ from (name of submitting office)," 2) title of case, 3) brief description of contents, and 4) file number, if known. Staple to original letter of transmittal.	Do not handle with bare hands. Advise if evidence should be treated for latent fingerprints.

(continued)

Table A.1 *(continued)*

Specimen	Amount Desired		Send by
	Standard	Evidence	
Blood:			
1. Liquid known samples	Two tubes each (sterile) 5cc, 1 tube—blood only. 1 tube—EDTA and blood or heparin and blood.	All	Registered airmail special delivery
2. Small quantities: a. Liquid questioned samples		All	Registered airmail special delivery
b. Dry stains, not on fabrics		As much as possible	Registered mail
c. For toxicological use		20 cc. (Blood and preservative mixture)	Registered airmail special delivery
3. Stained clothing, fabric, etc.		As found	Registered mail, Federal Express, United Parcel Service (UPS)
Bullets (not cartridges)		All found	Registered mail

Identification	Wrapping and Packing	Remarks
Use adhesive tape on outside of test tube, with name of donor, date taken, doctor's name, name or initials of investigator.	Wrap in cotton, soft paper. Place in mailing tube or suitably strong mailing carton.	Submit immediately. Don't hold awaiting additional items for comparison. Keep under refrigeration, *not* freezing, until mailing. *No* refrigerants and/or dry ice should be added to sample during transit. Fragile label.
Same as above	Same as above	If unable to expeditiously furnish sample, allow to dry thoroughly on the nonporous surface, and scrape off; or collect by using eyedropper or clean spoon, transfer to nonporous surface and let dry; or absorb in sterile gauze and let dry.
On outside of pillbox or plastic vial: type of specimen, date secured, name or initials.	Seal to prevent leakage.	Keep dry. Avoid use of envelopes.
Same as liquid samples	Medical examiner should use a standard blood collection kit.	Preservative desired (identify preservation used). Refrigerate. *Can freeze.*
Use tag or mark directly on clothes: type of specimens, date secured, name or initials.	Each article wrapped separately and identified on outside of package. Place in strong box placed to prevent shifting of contents.	If wet when found, dry by hanging. *Use no heat to dry.* Avoid direct sunlight while drying. Use no preservatives.
Initials on base, nose, or mutilated area	Pack tightly in cotton or soft paper in pill, match or powder box. Label outside of box as to contents.	Unnecessary handling obliterates marks.

(continued)

Table A.1 *(continued)*

Specimen	Amount Desired		Send by
	Standard	Evidence	
Cartridges (live ammunition)		All found	
Cartridge cases (shells)		All	Registered mail
Charred or burned documents		All	Registered mail
Checks (fraudulent)		All	Registered mail
Check protector, rubber-stamp, and/or date-stamp known standards. (Note: send actual device when possible.)	Obtain several copies in full word-for-word order of each questioned check-writer impression. If unable to forward rubber stamps, prepare numerous samples with different degrees of pressure.		Registered mail
Clothing		All	Registered mail, Federal Express, or United Parcel Service (UPS)
Codes, ciphers, and foreign language material		All	Registered mail
Drugs: 1. Liquids		All	Registered mail, UPS, or air express

Identification	Wrapping and Packing	Remarks
Initials on outside of case near bullet end	Same as above	
Initials preferably on inside near open end and/or on outside near open end	Same as above	
On outside of container indicate fragile nature of evidence, date obtained, name or initials.	Pack in rigid container between layers of cotton.	Added moisture, with atomizer or otherwise, not recommended.
See anonymous letters.	See anonymous letters.	Advise what parts questioned or known. Furnish physical description of subject.
Place name or initials, date, name of make and model, etc., on sample impressions.	See anonymous letters and/or above.	Do not disturb inking mechanisms on printing devices.
Mark directly on garment or use string tag: type of evidence, name or initials, date.	Each article individually wrapped with identification written on outside of package. Place in strong container.	Leave clothing whole. Do not cut out stains. If wet, hang in room to dry before packing.
Same as anonymous letters	Same as anonymous letters	Furnish pertinent background and technical information.
Affix label to bottle in which found, including name or initials and date.	If bottle has no stopper, transfer to glass-stoppered bottle and seal with adhesive tape.	Mark "Fragile." Determine alleged normal use of drug and if prescription, check with druggist for supposed ingredients.

(continued)

Table A.1 *(continued)*

Specimen	Amount Desired		Send by
	Standard	Evidence	
2. Powders, pills, and solids		All to 30 gms.	Registered mail, UPS, or air express
Dynamite and other explosives	(Contact FBI Explosives Unit for instructions.)		
Fibers	Entire garment or other cloth item	All	Registered mail
Firearms		All	Registered mail, UPS, or Federal Express
Flash paper	One sheet	All to 5 sheets	Contact FBI Technical Evaluation Unit for instructions.
Fuse (safety)	(Contact FBI Explosives Unit for complete instructions.)		
Gasoline	500 ml.	All to 500 ml.	Contact FBI Explosives Unit for instructions.
Gems		All	Registered mail, insured
General unknown 1. Solids (nonhazardous)	500 gms.	All to 500 gms.	Registered mail

Identification	Wrapping and Packing	Remarks
On outside of pillbox, name or initials and date.	Seal with tape to prevent any loss.	
On outside of sealed container or on object to which fibers are adhering	Folder paper on pillbox. Seal edges and openings with tape.	Do not place loose in envelope.
Mark inconspicuously as if it were your own. String tag gun, noting complete description on tag. Investigative notes should reflect how and where gun marked.	Wrap in paper and identify contents of packages. Place in cardboard box or wooden box.	Unload all weapons before shipping. Keep from rusting. See Ammunition, if applicable.
Initials and date	Individual polyethylene envelopes double-wrapped in manila envelopes. Inner wrapper sealed with paper tape.	Fireproof, place in vented location away from any other combustible materials, and if feasible, place in watertight container immersed in water. Mark inner wrapper "Flash Paper Flammable."
On outside of all-metal container, label with type of material, name or initials, and date.	Metal container packed in wooden box.	Fireproof container
On outside of container	Use jeweler's box or place in cotton in pillbox.	
Name or initials, date on outside of sealed container	Same as drugs	If item is suspected of being a hazardous material, treat as such and contact FBI Explosives Unit for shipping instructions.

(continued)

Table A.1 *(continued)*

| Specimen | Amount Desired | | Send by |
	Standard	Evidence	
2. Liquids (nonhazardous)	500 ml.	All to 500 ml.	Registered mail
Glass fragments		All	Registered mail, UPS, or air express
Glass particles	All of bottle or headlight. Small piece of each broken pane.	All	Registered mail
Glass wool insulation	1″ mass from each suspect area	All	Registered mail
Gunshot residues 1. Cotton applicator swabs with plastic shafts *(do not use wood shafts).*		All	Registered mail
2. On cloth		All	Registered mail
Hair	Dozen or more full-length hairs from different parts of head and/or body	All	Registered mail
Insulation (See glass wool insulation.)			
Handwriting and hand printing, known standards			Registered mail

Identification	Wrapping and Packing	Remarks
Same as for liquid drugs	Same as drugs	Same as above
Adhesive tape on each piece. Name or initials and date on tape. Separate questioned and known.	Wrap each piece separately in cotton. Pack in strong box to prevent shifting and breakage. Identify contents.	Avoid chipping and mark "Fragile."
Name or initials, date on outside of sealed container	Place in pillbox, plastic or glass vial; seal and protect against breakage.	Do not use envelopes.
Same as above	Sealed container	
On outside of container, date and name or initials. Label as to name of person and which hand.	Place swabs in plastic containers.	Do not use glass containers.
Attach string tag or mark directly: type of material, date, and name or initials.	Place fabric flat between layers of paper and then wrap so that no residue will be transferred or lost.	Avoid shaking.
On outside of container:type of material, date, and name or initials	Folded paper or pillbox. Seal edges and openings with tape.	Do not place loose in envelope.
Name or initials, date, from whom obtained, and voluntary statement should be included in appropriate place.	Same as anonymous letters	

(continued)

Table A.1 *(continued)*

| Specimen | Amount Desired | | Send by |
	Standard	Evidence	
Matches	One to two books of paper. One full box of wood.	All	UPS or Federal Express
Medicines	(See Drugs.)		
Metal	One pound	All to one pound	Registered mail, UPS, or air express
Oil	250 ml. together with specifications	All to 250 ml.	UPS
Obliterated, eradicated, or indented writing		All	Registered mail
Organs of the body		200 gms. of each organ	UPS, air express, or registered airmail special delivery
Paint:			
1. Liquid	Original unopened container up to 1 gallon if possible	All to 1/4 pint	Registered mail, UPS, or air express
2. Solid (paint chips or scrapings)	At least 1/2 sq. in. of solid, with all layers represented	All. If on small object, send object.	Registered mail, UPS, or air express

Identification	Wrapping and Packing	Remarks
On outside of container: type of material, date, and name or initials.	Metal container and packed in larger package to prevent shifting. Matches in box or metal container packed to prevent friction between matches.	Keep away from fire. Use "Keep away from fire" label.
Same as above	Use paper boxes or containers. Seal and use strong paper or wooden box.	Melt number, heat treatment, and other specifications of foundry if available. Keep from rusting.
Same as above	Metal container with tight screw top. Pack in strong box using excelsior or similar material.	*Do not use dirt or sand for packing material.* Keep away from fire.
Same as anonymous letters	Same as anonymous letters	Advise whether bleaching or staining methods may be used. Avoid folding.
On outside of container: victim's name, date of death, date of autopsy, name of doctor, name or initials	Plastic or glass containers. Metal lids must have liners.	"Fragile" label. Keep cool. Send autopsy report. Add no preservatives to the organs. Use dry ice in the package.
On outside of container: type of material, origin if known, date, name or initials.	Friction-top paint can or large-mouth, screw-top jars. If glass, pack to prevent breakage. Use heavy corrugated paper or wooden box.	
Same as above	If small amount, round pillbox or small glass vial with screw top. Seal to prevent leakage. Envelopes not satisfactory. Do not pack in cotton.	Avoid contact with adhesive materials. Wrap so as to protect smear.

(continued)

Table A.1 *(continued)*

Specimen	Amount Desired		Send by
	Standard	Evidence	
Plastic casts of tire treads and shoe prints	Send in shoes and tires of suspects. Photographs and sample impressions are usually not suitable for comparison.	All shoe prints; entire circumference of tires	Registered mail, UPS, or air express
Powder patterns (See gunshot residues)			
Rope, twine, and cordage	One yard or amount available	All	Registered mail
Saliva samples	1 1/2″ diameter stain in center of filter paper	All	Registered mail
Safe insulation	Sample all damaged areas	All	Registered mail, UPS, or air express
Shoe print lifts (impressions on hard surfaces)	Photograph before making of dust impression.	All	Registered mail
Soils and minerals	Samples from areas near pertinent spot	All	Registered mail
Tools		All	Registered mail, UPS, or air express

Identification	Wrapping and Packing	Remarks
On back before plaster hardens: location, date, and name or initials	Wrap in paper and cover with suitable packing material to prevent breakage. Do not wrap bags.	Use "Fragile" label. Mix approximately four pounds of plaster to one quart of water. Allow casts to cure (dry) before wrapping.
On tag or container: type of material, date, name or initials.	Wrap securely.	
On outside envelope and on filter paper put type of sample, name of donor, date of collection, and collector's initials or name.	Seal in envelope.	Stain should be circled in pencil for identification. Filter paper available from hospitals and drug stores. Allow to dry.
On outside of container: type of material, date, name or initials.	Use containers, such as pillbox or plastic vial. Seal to prevent any loss.	Avoid use of glass containers and envelopes.
On lifting tape or paper attached to tape: name or initials and date.	Prints in dust are easily damaged. Fasten print or lift to bottom of a box so that nothing will rub against it.	Always secure crime scene area until shoe prints or tire treads are located and preserved.
On outside of container: type of material, date, name or initials	Pillbox or plastic vial	Avoid glass containers and envelopes.
On tools use string tag: type of tool, identifying number, date, name or initials	Wrap each tool in paper. Use strong cardboard or wooden box with tools packed to prevent shifting.	

(continued)

Table A.1 *(continued)*

| Specimen | Amount Desired | | Send by |
	Standard	Evidence	
Toolmarks	Send in the tool. If impractical, make several impressions on similar materials as evidence, using entire marking area of tool.	All	Registered mail, UPS, or air express
Typewriting, known standards			Registered mail
Urine	Preferably all urine voided over a period of 24 hours	All	Registered mail
Vaginal samples 1. Slides (microscope)		Minimum of two slides	Registered mail
2. Swabs	Two unstained swabs from same package as stained	Minimum of two swabs	Registered mail
Water	2 liters	2 liters	Registered mail
Wire (See also toolmarks.)	Three feet (Do not kink.)	All (Do not kink.)	Registered mail
Wood	One foot or amount available	All	Registered mail

Identification	Wrapping and Packing	Remarks
On object or on tag attached to or on opposite end from where toolmarks appear: name or initials and date.	After marks have been protected with soft paper, wrap in strong wrapping paper, place in strong box, and pack to prevent shifting.	
Place name or initials, date, serial number, name of make and model etc., on specimens.	Same as anonymous letters	Examine ribbon for evidence of questioned message thereon.
On outside of container: type of material, name of subject, date taken, name or initials.	Bottle surrounded with absorbent material to prevent breakage. Strong cardboard or wooden box.	Use any clean bottle with leakproof stopper.
Same as for saliva samples	Use commercial slide box.	Slide box available at hospitals. Doctor should not fix slides. No cover slips. Air dry.
Same as above	Seal in envelope.	Allow swabs to dry before packaging.
Same as for urine	Same as for urine	Same as for urine
On label or tab: type ot material, date, name or initials	Wrap securely.	Do not kink wire.
Same as above	Wrap securely.	

The News Media in Homicide Investigations 14

A free press serves the public by supplying needed information, stimulating thought, and providing a medium for expression. An informed public is essential to the maintenance of a free society, and the public is entitled to be informed on topics of public interest. Crime, especially homicide, is always a subject for public concern and interest. Therefore, law enforcement officials can and should expect news media people to be present, make inquiries, and actively pursue the event.

The purpose of this chapter is to act as a guide in fostering better relations between the police investigative team and the news media in homicide investigations. To make better relations possible, I advocate mutual cooperation and understanding of each other's goals. The news media can be a tremendous asset in a homicide investigation or an equally staggering liability. Realistically, their impact usually falls between these two extremes.

Throughout the United States, law enforcement agencies and the news media are in daily contact. The days of "No comment" by the police to the media have been replaced by a more open and candid dialogue between the two. Therefore, there needs to be a thoughtful policy of police-media relationships which provides for the integrity of the investigation and the proper dissemination of information to the public.

Establishing a News Media Policy

Today, most large police departments and law enforcement agencies maintain a public information office staffed by designated public information officers or news media representatives to handle requests for information. These public information officers act as spokesmen for the department and maintain regular liaison with the media. In addition, most departments have established guidelines for the release of information by the members in the field to representatives of the media.

In homicide investigations, however, there must be a tighter control over the news release, justified by the legal considerations and the strategic aspects of the case. The public information officer should be kept advised of any such incidents and is responsible for notifying the media that police are investigating a homicide. However, all subsequent information and news releases from the department during the investigative stage should come from the detective supervisor or his equivalent in other agencies, who is in charge of the investigation at the scene.

Generally, local media will be more responsive than national to a request for cooperation because they are more sympathetic to local needs and sentiments. Likewise, representatives of major media organizations whom you have dealt with before will usually cooperate with you as long as they know they will be provided with information and given a statement from the investigator in charge. The trick is to engage in as much give-and-take as you can without compromising the case. However, as the newsworthiness of an event increases, out-of-town reporters or representatives of the wire services, radio, and television may become involved in gathering news, and this usually creates a strain.

The competitive nature of multimedia coverage usually presents law enforcement officers with problems they are ill-equipped to deal with. Too often there has been no previous thought given to how to handle a media-worthy situation. Suddenly, you're surrounded with an army of reporters seeking details of interest, ferreting out "new" information, interviewing witnesses, family, and anyone they feel might give them an edge over another news team. Photographers will be attempting to obtain photos of the body, the suspect, the scene of the crime, the investigators, and so on. Obviously, these media people will be "doing their own thing" without any consideration of the investigative needs of the case and the legal impact involved, not to mention consideration for the family. This is where planning comes into the picture. An intelligent news media policy will take into consideration the legal, strategic, and humanitarian aspects of the case and at the same time provide for the comprehensive release of news to the media.

Any policy instituted by a police department should provide guidelines for preserving the delicate balance between a free press and a fair trial when disseminating information. Most states and the federal government have provisions that are intended to promote accuracy and fairness in the release of information. The following "Fair Trial Free Press Principles and Guidelines for the State of New York" (reproduced in full here) are provided to the reader as a model.

"Fair Trial Free Press Principles"

Freedom of the press is guaranteed by the First Amendment of the Constitution of the United States. The right to a speedy and public trial by an impartial jury is guaranteed in criminal cases by the Sixth Amendment. The New York State bar, bench, law enforcement agencies, and news media, as represented by the organizations that have signed this document, recognize and uphold these guarantees and grant them equal validity.

They also recognize the right of the public in a democratic society to be informed about crime, law enforcement, and the administration of justice, and the right, in general, to have trials openly conducted.

While the news media recognize the responsibility of the judge to preserve order in the court and seek the ends of justice by all those means available to him, decisions about handling the news rest with the editors, who, in the exercise of news judgments should remember that:

a. An accused person is presumed innocent until proven guilty.
b. Accused persons and civil litigants are entitled to be judged in an atmosphere free from passion, prejudice, and sensationalism.
c. Readers, listeners, and viewers are potential jurors.
d. No one's reputation should be injured needlessly.

The proper administration of justice is the concern of the judiciary, bar, the prosecution, law enforcement personnel, news media, and the public. None should relinquish its share in that concern. None should condone injustices on the ground that they are infrequent.

1. When and after an arrest is made, the following information should be made available for publication:
   a. The accused's name, age, residence, employment, marital status, and similar background information.
   b. The substance or text of the charge such as a complaint indictment, information and, where appropriate, the identity of the complainant.
   c. The identity of the investigating and arresting agency and length of the investigation.
   d. The circumstances immediately surrounding the arrest, including the time and place of arrest, resistance, pursuit, possession and use of weapons, and description of items seized at the time of arrest.

2. The release of certain types of information by law enforcement personnel, the bench, and bar and the publication of this information by news media may tend to create dangers of prejudice without serving a significant law enforcement or public interest function. Therefore, all concerned should be aware of the dangers of prejudice in making pretrial disclosure of the following:
   a. Statements as to the character or reputation of an accused person or prospective witness.
   b. Admissions, confessions, or the contents of a statement or alibi attributable to an accused person.
   c. The performance or results of tests or the refusal of the accused to take a test.
   d. Statements concerning the credibility or anticipated testimony of prospective witnesses.
   e. The possibility of a plea of guilty to the offense charged or to a lesser offense, or other disposition.
   f. Opinions concerning evidence or argument in the case, whether or not it is anticipated that such evidence or argument will be used at trial.
3. Prior criminal charges and convictions are matters of public record and are available to the news media. Police, corrections, and other law enforcement agencies should make such information available to the news media on request. The public disclosure of this information by the news may be highly prejudicial without any significant addition to the public's need to be informed. The publication of such information should be carefully considered by the news media.
4. Law enforcement and court personnel should NOT prevent the photographing of defendants when they are in public places outside the courtroom. They should neither encourage nor discourage pictures or televising, but *they should not pose the accused.*
5. Photographs of a suspect may be released by law enforcement personnel provided a valid law enforcement function is served thereby. It is proper to disclose such information as may be necessary to enlist public assistance in apprehending fugitives from justice. Such disclosure may include photographs as well as records or prior arrests and convictions.

The preceding guidelines are those which address themselves to the law enforcement function. A separate set of guidelines is recommended for cases involving juveniles. Generally speaking, the following information should *not* be given to the press:

1. The names of children under sixteen years of age who are charged with a crime *or* are complainants in a criminal proceeding; and
2. The identity of a victim of a sex crime.

In homicide cases, witnesses and others involved in the investigation should be cautioned not to speak to the press. However, it should be noted that the only persons whom police can effectively isolate from the media are suspects. It is utterly impossible to prevent others from speaking to reporters. If their disclosures present legal or other problems, you must be prepared to request cooperation from the media to withhold certain information in the interests of justice.

Remember, the best way to promote good media relations is through preparation and communication.

Know what you need to say to the media, and how to say it, in order to cooperate while still maintaining the integrity of the case.

Building a Relationship with the News Media

The relationship between the news media representative and the homicide spokesman usually starts off in a somewhat adversarial setting. The news reporter will be attempting to uncover facts of the investigation to obtain a better story, and the homicide spokespersons will be trying their best to keep certain strategic information out of the hands of the press.

How the police and the media deal with any given contact generally determines the ultimate associations, since a good relationship is usually the product of many individual contacts over a span of time. It is during these contacts that these persons get to know one another and learn to respect each other's professional position—for instance, I wouldn't expect a news representative to "kill" a story which was detrimental to the police, and likewise a news person shouldn't be insulted because an officer doesn't go along with an "off-the-record" request for information which might jeopardize the police investigation.

Professional homicide-news media relationships are usually built upon past experiences which have been mutually successful to both parties.

It also helps for each party to understand the other's pressures, particularly those relating to *time.* A murder investigation may take anywhere from a few hours to several days, weeks, or months. The news media representative, on the other hand, must complete his or her initial coverage of the event prior to a deadline which may amount to only hours or minutes. This is where a strain may set in between the two groups. A story which might rate front-page coverage prior to today's deadline, might tomorrow rate only a paragraph inside. A potential lead item on the "Eleven O'Clock News" that evening may not even be considered the following day. Time is of the essence to newspeople because other newsworthy events are taking place, deadlines must be met, and the space for newsprint and the time for broadcasts are tightly constrained. By the same token, time is of the essence to the homicide supervisor and detectives who are conducting the investigation. There is a tremendous amount of information generated in a very short period of time at the homicide crime scene. Furthermore, there are many investigative duties to perform and steps to be taken before valuable evidence is lost and suspects can be identified. The homicide spokesman cannot be expected to drop everything and engage in a news conference, nor should the reporter expect the police to prematurely disclose information in the early stages of the case so he or she can get a better story. In addition, news media people should resist the temptation to become part of the event. They should realize that their selection of news sources and the questions they ask may not only affect the story, but strain police-media relations by creating issues that jeopardize the homicide case. Practically speaking, a little flexibility and common sense in most cases will ultimately benefit both the news media and the police. Frictions can be minimized, issues put in proper perspective, and goals attained through mutual cooperation.

The homicide supervisor at the scene should be aware of media needs, and without neglecting investigative duties direct that a notification of the homicide be given to the public information officer along with some basic facts. In the event that there is no public information officer, the homicide supervisor can still encourage cooperation by providing for notifications to local media so that they may cover the story. This notification and subsequent release of information to the media will encourage cooperation and set the tone for future good relations.

Contacts between the homicide spokesman and the news media representatives are not limited to the formal news conference during a homicide investigation. Informal meetings reinforce relationships and encourage cooperation. It is usually during these informal exchanges that certain barriers to communication and misunderstandings can be discussed and eliminated. I have found from personal experience that the more frequent the meetings, the more candid the dialogue.

When reporters and police have been in daily contact over a period of time, they can come to a mutual understanding whereby both groups can benefit. This relationship, however, should never be abused, since any breach of trust on the part of either party may destroy in an instant a relationship which took years to develop.

News media people who handle crime stories pride themselves on their ability to develop sources of information within any given police agency. Similarly, homicide officials should also strive to develop sources and relationships within the media which are mutually beneficial and serve an intelligent investigative end. If the homicide spokesman has developed a good rapport with certain news media representatives, he or she may be able to obtain news coverage, which can benefit an investigation, for a case which ordinarily wouldn't be considered newsworthy enough.

Sometimes, a case which must be kept "under wraps" comes to the attention of the news media through other sources. If there has been an effective and cooperative relationship between the media and the agency, a request to withhold the story pending some investigative consideration will usually be granted. However, the agency cannot expect the news media to cover up an otherwise newsworthy event. Practically speaking, when you take the media into your confidence on a particularly sensitive case, you will have to rely on their good intentions and judgment not to compromise the investigation or prematurely release information to the public. However, by taking them into your confidence you have effectively made them part of the "team" and psychologically have set the tone for a cooperative venture.

I can recall many cases over the years which the media had access to and, upon conferring with the chief investigator, delayed release to give police the opportunity to perform a specific investigative step.

The key word in building relationships is *credibility*—the law enforcement representative and the news media person must be honest with each other if this relationship is to survive. If each can come to rely on the other's credibility, tested by time, there can evolve a compatible arrangement between the police and the press.

I remember reading about a particularly sensational murder case in which a news reporter purposely ignored a request by the police to withhold certain information. This official request was made when it had become apparent that the reporter had become aware of certain confidential information through a series of "leaks." In fact, the chief investigator had personally asked this reporter not to print this information. Instead, this reporter published a blow-by-blow description of every piece of physical evidence and detail of the murder investigation. This caused irreparable damage to the investigation, created additional legal problems, and embarrassed the police officials involved. Needless to say, such an obvious violation of trust destroyed not only this reporter's credibility with the agency concerned, but all future contacts between the news media and police officials in this jurisdiction. The agency subsequently changed its policy for dealing with the news media and has drastically curtailed the release of information to the press.

Hopefully, such situations as described above are the exception, not the rule. However, law enforcement personnel must be aware of such possibilities and take appropriate measures to prevent disclosures which may adversely effect the outcome of a case.

Homicide News Release Policy

The indiscriminate release of information in a homicide investigation is an invitation to disaster. An erroneous or improper statement can damage the confidentiality of the investigation, the future prosecution, the reputation of the department, the rights of the accused, or the sensibilities of the family of the victim. Therefore, I have provided the following guidelines for officers to follow in the dissemination of information to the news media:

1. During the investigative stage, all information from the police department should come from one person and one person only. Generally, this person should be the detective supervisor, the chief investigator, or some other ranking officer, so designated in advance. The reason for this restriction should be obvious. The person in charge of the investigation is familiar with all phases and will be aware of those items which can or cannot be released because of legal or investigative reasons.

2. Designating one person to handle news releases allows reporters an opportunity to obtain information about the case without interfering with operations at the scene. More importantly, however, it precludes the possibility of having conflicting information emanating from members of the same department. This tight control is necessary and all members of the department must abide by this rule if its purposes are not to be defeated.

3. Officers at the scene can and should expect news reporters to be present. It is a mistake to treat the news media rudely or shut them off entirely. Frequently, they can be exceedingly helpful in uncovering information which is valuable to the case. Officers on the scene or wherever any investigative activity is taking place may be approached and asked to comment on the investigation. All they need do is explain that the department will make information available to them through the person designated for this function "to assure equal treatment and accurate information." The homicide investigator is expected to act as a professional and should handle each media contact in a manner which encourages cooperation.

4. The detective supervisor or designated police spokesman should confer with the medical examiner and the prosecutor in these

early stages, so as to avoid any confusion or embarrassment from conflicting or inappropriate releases being issued by the various officers. During the preliminary activities only the police agency charged with the responsibility of conducting the homicide investigation should be making any official news-release statements. Later on, after the autopsy, the medical examiner and/or coroner may elect to make an appropriate statement as to cause of death. However, all initial statements as to investigative inquiry, discovery of a body, or arrest of suspected persons lies within the jurisdiction of the police. During the prosecutorial stage, beginning with the suspect's arraignment, all information about the case should come from the office of the prosecutor. Practically speaking, this thin line of jurisdictial prerogative can oftentimes result in conflict or embarrassment, particularly in sensational murder cases—the appropriate source to make the news release is determined by the expertise and authority of the agency concerned, whether investigatory, medical, or prosecutorial.

5. When releasing details of the homicide investigation, do not furnish the name of the deceased until there has been an acceptable identification and the next of kin have been notified. In some instances, the media will have been able to ascertain the identity from police radio transmissions, teletype alarms, bystanders, witnesses, etc. In these cases, a request should be made that they withhold this information pending official notification to the family. Generally such a request will be complied with. However, in keeping with the theme of mutual cooperation, the media should be advised when the police have notified next of kin so they may properly file their story.

6. In cases where the perpetrator has not been arrested and the investigation for suspects is continuing, it is imperative that certain information be withheld. During the course of a murder investigation, news items appearing in the press may be helpful or harmful depending on what *preparation* has been given to what is said. One of the classic means of establishing the veracity of a confession is to have the suspect give information which only the actual perpetrator could know. The more sensational the case, the more the likelihood of persons coming forward with false information or even confessions. Obviously, it is always wise to withhold certain information from the media. This will preserve the integrity of the investigation.

7. When talking to the media, do not permit yourself to be maneuvered into a situation where you theorize or speculate, where you make predictions, or where you give personal opinions about the case. Statements such as "We expect to have the suspect in cus-

tody within the next 24 hours" have come back to haunt many
an officer foolish enough to make that prediction. Such a personal
observation can do nothing to assist the investigation and may,
in fact, become a liability later on. The investigator is a fact
finder, open to all possibilities. When asked, "Is it possible . . . Could he have . . . Have you ruled out . . . ," the
most practical approach is to merely state, "At this time, we are
keeping all of our options open, and we would rather not speculate on any specific possibility."

8. Never pose for photographs, either at the scene or when transporting the suspect. Posed photographs can create the wrong
impression with the public and can create legal problems during
the prosecution. If the press is able to take photos outside the
crime scene area of the investigators as they carry out their duties
at the scene, there shouldn't be any problems. However, officers
should be cognizant of their presence and maintain a professional
demeanor.

9. If the news release is a taped interview, which will be aired on
television or radio, the police spokesman should be aware that
whatever he or she says will be recorded. It is best to prepare
oneself by writing out, prior to the interview, a brief narrative
account of the event, being careful to withhold information
which might adversely affect the case. Prior to the actual taping,
the news media people will usually go over your release and ask
certain questions. This is done for their own benefit so that they
can get a "feel" for the case. Practically speaking, this preliminary
question-and-answer session can benefit both parties. The questions which are asked during this preliminary conference are basically the same questions which the reporter will be asking you
on tape, so you will have an idea of the type of questions you
will be responding to.

If there is a particular question which you cannot answer, either for legal or strategic reasons, explain this to the news media
people and set the ground rules. It is important to note that the
entire interview will usually not be broadcast but will be edited
to fit into an allotted amount of time. Therefore, to be sure that
the interview gives the complete coverage you desire, stick to
short and concise sentences.

Sometimes a reporter will try to force an issue by waiting for
the television lights to go on and the camera to start rolling and
then purposely ask a question which you had previously indicated you couldn't answer. At this point, without hesitation, look
directly into the camera and state, "Excuse me, Mr. or Ms. So-
and-So, I told you before we went on camera that it would be

improper for me to respond to that question." I am pretty sure you will not be bothered by that kind of question again. However, more importantly, you will have maintained control over the interview and not compromised the investigation.

10. The news media provide an excellent vehicle for making appeals to the public for information. I have found that media personnel will usually make a special effort to assist law enforcement officials in requesting public assistance in a homicide investigation. For example, an unidentified body may be found whose physical qualities or possessions and clothing can be described. An appeal can be made through the media to ascertain if anyone recognizes the description with a request to call police with any information. A general appeal can also be made to anyone with information on a specifically heinous crime to obtain citizen involvement, thereby reaching persons not readily available through ordinary investigative means. It is usually a good idea to stress the fact that callers can remain anonymous, if they desire, and that the information will remain confidential.

The offering of rewards. A question often arises regarding rewards and what role the police should play. The offering of rewards usually results in additional unproductive investigative time as police check out vague tips which offer no help with the investigation. However, there is always the possibility that someone will come forward with useful information. It is usually better not to discourage the offer of a reward, even though it means more wasted effort. If the police reject the offer, they risk criticism for not doing everything possible to find the murderer. However, there should be two stipulations in connection with any reward offer: 1) No law enforcement officer is eligible to receive it; and 2) Any information must be given directly to the police.

Handling the News Media at the Scene

News media people at the scene should be advised that any information will come from the homicide supervisor and not the officers who are actually working on the case. News media people usually learn about the homicide through police radio transmissions. All police press rooms monitor the police communications system, and most media organizations maintain mobile units which are similarly equipped that will respond to the scene. In some instances, these reporters will arrive before the investigators. First officers who are maintaining lines at the scene should tactfully explain to these media representatives that information will be made available to them as soon as possible by the homicide commander. Point out that it would be unfair to make information available to some members of the press which would not be equally available to all others. I have seen some police officers handle this situation quite tactfully, while others have embarrassed me by their ignorance or rudeness. In any event, most news media people who have dealt with the police before can appreciate the emergency nature of this preliminary phase of the homicide investigation, and they realize that any information must come from a ranking official. If there is a good, consistent homicide news-release policy, the media will usually cooperate.

It should be noted that members of the news media have a right to be present at the scene and perform their task of gathering information. However, this right to be present at the scene and gather news information does not include interfering with the police investigation, nor entering restricted areas such as the crime scene where valuable evidence may be lost or destroyed.

In homicide cases there are usually police lines established to prevent unauthorized persons from entering the scene. In most instances, news media people who are authorized to cross police lines to cover stories will be allowed entry. This entry is permissible as long as it does not interfere with police operations, jeopardize the integrity of the scene, or create a hazard. Witnesses or suspects who are being detained must be kept away from the media. However, the press should generally be permitted to report or photograph anything they observe while legally present at an emergency scene. Where publication of specific items would interfere with the investigation or place witnesses, suspects, or others in jeopardy, the homicide official in charge should advise the reporters and their editors of the consequences of publication and request their cooperation. If some member of the media is pushy or overzealous and threatens the security of the scene or interferes with the police operation, merely exercise intelligent police procedure and physically remove him or her from the crime scene just as you would any other unauthorized person.

In homicide cases, especially in the preliminary stages of the investigation at the scene, uniformed officers and detectives assigned to the case are usually in possession of information which must be withheld from the general public; for example, the identity of the deceased prior to notification of next of kin. News media people who have responded to the murder scene are anxious to obtain as much information as possible to "cover the story." Usually they will question bystanders and others at the scene in order to get a feel for the story, and probably will ask any officers present for information about the case. These officers must keep in mind that certain disclosures may harm the investigation, subvert justice, or infringe on individual rights to privacy. The professional response to such inquiry is simply to refer these reporters to the detective supervisor.

The more sensational murder cases and those involving well-known persons or celebrities result in a more aggressive style of reporting, as the various representatives from different news organizations strive to meet deadlines or outscoop each other. In situations like these, various pressures will escalate and strain relationships. The highest degree of cooperation between the police and the media will be necessary in order to reduce this pressure and neutralize these strains before they get out of hand.

There must be a policy as to what kind of information is given and who is to release it. Only one person should make the press release. If the release represents the formal position of the department, the public information officer should perform the duty. If the release is a news briefing of an active investigation, the homicide supervisor, who has been kept up to date on the investigation, is in the best position to determine what information can and cannot be released. This eliminates the possibility of two or more detectives independently releasing conflicting details or facts. News items given by others working on the case are usually a source of trouble, because jealousies can be created and information which embarrasses other phases of the investigation may result.

Generally, the chances for a successful outcome of the investigation are improved by being completely candid with the press. If the press is aware of what information should not be prematurely released and is kept informed of developments, they will be more receptive to investigative requests. If every minute detail of the crime appears in the local paper, it will be impossible to determine the truthfulness of some statement by the suspect later on.

Remember, always withhold certain details of the crime which only the murderer and the police can know about.

In connection with photographs, the police should neither discourage nor encourage reporters from taking pictures of a suspect.

Remember, prisoners should never be posed or allowed to make statements to the press.

However, if suspects or prisoners are in a public place, news media people are allowed to take pictures, just as they are allowed to take pictures of officers at the scene performing their duties. The identity of the suspect prior to arrest should not ordinarily be made public unless in the opinion of the homicide supervisor such information is necessary to assist in the apprehension of a suspect or warn the public of a possible danger. Photographs should likewise be released only if they serve a valid purpose such as identifying a victim or enlisting public assistance in finding a fugitive suspect.

From an investigative point of view, I would advise you to be very careful in making any predictions about solution or arrest, regardless of what your prospects appear to be at the moment. I remember one case which involved a shoot-out in a local social club. Although we had a double homicide on our hands, we had been able to determine within hours the identity of the shooter. I must admit it was very tempting to tell the press that we knew who did it and that we would be making an arrest imminently. The two victims had been innocent of any involvement in the shooting and were merely patrons in the club who had been caught in a cross-fire. The resultant community concern and subsequent media attention added to the pressure for immediate action. However, my gut feeling was based on knowledge of the "players," and so I merely indicated the basic facts—there were two dead, apparently the innocent victims of a shooting between two groups, and police were investigating to determine what person or persons were responsible. Later on, I was glad to have taken this route. The suspect wasn't apprehended for three months and then only after a tremendous amount of time and effort.

At-the-scene news releases can be just as effective as the formal news release if you maintain your composure and control.

Remember, know what you are going to say and how you are going to say it.

Before you speak, consider the following:

1. Will the release cause the suspect to flee?
2. What information should be held for future interrogation?
3. Does the information you are releasing hinder the investigation?
4. Is the information released consistent with department policy?

Preparing the News Release

The news release in homicide investigations should either be personally prepared by the homicide supervisor or by the public information officer after consulting the homicide official. As mentioned earlier, the homicide commander is in the best position to know what can and cannot be released in any given case.

A basic principle to keep in mind is that the news release is an investigative tool which represents the official police position in the investigation. Therefore, any news release and subsequent news media coverage should be included in the official case folder because it is a public record and may ultimately affect the outcome of the investigation. The news release should be written in a clear and comprehensible manner and its organization and style should be simple and direct.

The acronymn NEOTWY—whe*n*, wher*e*, wh*o*, wha*t*, ho*w*, and wh*y* should be considered when preparing the news release, and the following items should be included in the release.

1. The date and time of the homicide. (Avoid reference to military time and express the time in civilian hours; for example, 9:30 P.M. instead of 2130 hours.)
2. The exact location of the homicide.
3. The name of the deceased, if proper notification has been made to next of kin, and residence.
4. The type of homicide (gunshot, stabbing, etc.).
5. The facts of the preliminary investigation, including a summary of how the homicide occurred and the present status of the case.
6. The motive, if known.
7. If there are any arrests, the name, address, and age of the suspect(s) including nicknames and background information.
8. The exact charge or charges. (This refers to the charge under which the suspect was arrested. If there is a possibility of other charges, simply state, "additional charges pending.")
9. Place of the arrest and facts and circumstances surrounding it.
10. Officers involved in the investigation.

There are different methods for constructing the news release. One method which is recommended by journalists and students of communication is the "inverted pyramid." According to Charles W. Steinmetz, Instructor at the FBI Academy and an expert in the area of mass media and effective communication, the inverted pyramid is effective because it meets police requirements and can help avoid a distorted or rewritten story. Place the facts in a diminishing order of importance, with the most important facts at the top, or beginning, of the release, and the lesser facts placed in order of descending importance. This allows for shortening the article by a newspaper without changing the official facts of the release.

The length of the release depends on how much information the agency wishes to make available in any given homicide. I recommend that the spokesman first write out a narrative description of the event

INVERTED PYRAMID

```
    Who, What, Where, When, (Why, How)?

         Additional Information

           Embellishments


             Placed in
             Descending
             Importance
```

Guide for Media Release

The Inverted Pyramid.

before making any official release. Then he or she can review the statement and eliminate information which might hinder the investigation. An example of a completed release is as follows:

> I am (name of official) of (name of agency). On (date and time) the body of a (male or female) identified as (name) was found at (location). (He or She) had been (shot, stabbed, etc.). Investigation revealed that the deceased had been killed during (robbery, etc.). At this time the investigation (is continuing, indicates, etc.).

or

> An arrest has been effected in connection with this investigation. The suspect is identified as (name, age, address, nickname, etc.). (He or She) was arrested at (location) and has been charged with (charges). (Relationship of victim to suspect optional.) The officers assigned to this investigation are (names).

Of course each department should design a format which suits its particular needs.

Handling Questions During News Conferences

If the murder case is a sensational type of homicide, or there is a considerable amount of public interest in the investigation, the agency will usually hold a news conference when they release the information. During these news conferences certain "loaded" questions may be asked by the media representative. The best course for the homicide spokesman to follow is to give straightforward and honest answers to such questions within the framework of his or her investigative priorities. The following suggestions are provided as a guide.

1. Repeat each question to the group. This will allow you to clear the question in your own mind, bide time, and allow the group to hear the question.
2. Avoid the original questioner, instead directing your response to the group.
3. Avoid a one-to-one exchange.
4. Keep your answers short and concise.
5. Rephrase unclear questions.
6. Have the question repeated if unclear.
7. Defuse and depersonalize antagonistic questions.
8. If you do not know the answer or cannot answer the question because of some legal or strategic reason, say so.
9. Do not allow yourself to theorize, speculate, or make predictions.

Conclusion

The homicide official who recognizes and understands the role of the news media and follows the principles and guidelines discussed in this chapter will better be able to deal with press inquiries and news releases as they relate to homicide investigations.

Sooner or later, every community will experience a murder case which arouses widespread attention. The results can be catastrophic if no thought has been given on how to deal with this situation. The subsequent pressure of the media blitz as reporters try to get the best story for their particular news agency mandates that there be a sensible news release policy. Although the police will not be able to manipulate the media, they can use the news release as a tool in performing certain functions. For instance, the release of certain information may stimulate the investigation, while withholding certain facts guarantees that only the police and the killer are aware of them. Good relations between the media and the police will keep pressures at a minimum.

Police agencies must strive to protect the rights of the victim's family, the rights of the accused, and the right to knowledge of society in general. Sometimes under the pressure of major media organizations this is not always possible. However, somewhere between the right of freedom of the press—as guaranteed in the First Amendment—and the rights of the accused—as specified in the Sixth Amendment—there exists a delicate balance. It can be maintained if there is cooperation and good faith between the news media and the law enforcement agency.

Selected Reading

Shaw, David. *Journalism Today—A Changing Press for a Changing America.* New York: Harper College Press, 1977.

Steinmetz, Charles W. "The News Release as a Tool." *Law and Order Magazine,* July 1980.

Steinmetz, Charles W. "No Comment . . . Law Enforcement and the Media." *F.B.I. Law Enforcement Bulletin*, July 1979.

The Autopsy

A *medicolegal autopsy,* an examination of a body after death, is always required in homicide cases. In this chapter we will look at the purpose of the autopsy and describe the examination. I have also included a brief section on human anatomy to acquaint the investigator with some basic terminology used by the medical profession.

The Medical Examiner/Coroner

The medical examiner's or coroner's office is primarily concerned with the investigation of violent, sudden, unexpected, and suspicious deaths. The procedures used in the official medicolegal investigation of death fall under the supervision of the chief medical examiner or coroner, who is responsible for the evaluation and interpretation of the results of this inquiry. It should be noted that the terms pathologist, coroner, and medical examiner may be but are not always synonymous. In some jurisdictions the coroner is not a physician, but an elected or appointed official responsible for taking legal charge of the body. In other jurisdictions, medical examiners are not pathologists, and pathologists are not necessarily medical examiners. The recommended standards for a medical examiner system are that the chief medicolegal officer—whether referred to as medical examiner or coroner—be a qualified doctor of medicine who is also a certified pathologist skilled in forensic pathology. In those jurisdictions lacking a forensic pathologist, the author recommends that the investigator seek out the services of a pathologist, preferably one with some experience in forensic medicine, and refer this pathologist to the

Modern Medicolegal Facilities: Storage. (*Courtesy of* Dr. Leslie I. Lukash, Chief Medical Examiner, Nassau County, New York.)

Modern Medicolegal Facilities: Autopsy Room. (*Courtesy of* Dr. Leslie I. Lukash, Chief Medical Examiner, Nassau County, New York.)

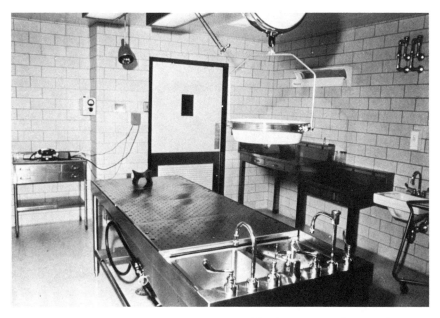

Modern Medicolegal Facilities: Autopsy Table. (*Courtesy of* Dr. Leslie I. Lukash, Chief Medical Examiner, Nassau County, New York.)

procedures recommended by the National Association of Medical
Examiners.[1]

For the purposes of this chapter the term medical examiner or coroner will be synonymous with forensic pathologist and will refer to
the medicolegal authority responsible for conducting the investigation.

The certified pathologist has received advanced training in recognizing and interpreting diseases and injuries in the human body. It is
this knowledge that enables the medical examiner/coroner to make
significant contributions to the homicide investigation. Practically
speaking, forensic experts play an active part in the homicide investigation and should be considered an important part of the investigative team. If the investigation is to be successful, the homicide detective and the forensic pathologist must work together.

[1]Leslie I. Lukash (Chairman) et al. *Standards for Inspection and Accreditation of a Modern Medicolegal Investigative System.* National Association of Medical Examiners, Wilmington, Delaware,
1974.

420

OFFICE OF CHIEF MEDICAL EXAMINER
OF THE CITY OF NEW YORK

IDENTIFICATION OF BODY

STATE OF NEW YORK
CITY AND COUNTY OF NEW YORK, ss.:
BOROUGH OF

....age................, residing at

....in the ....

being duly sworn, deposes and says: That   he is a...

of the person whose body was found at..., 19 .....,

and subsequently sent to the Office of Chief Medical Examiner; that deponent has seen the................................

of said deceased, and has every reason to believe that the body now recorded at the Office of Chief Medical

Examiner as...

is..who was last seen or heard from by deponent on

...., 19 ......

Deponent therefore prays that   identification of said deceased person be accepted by the Chief

Medical Examiner of The City of New York.

Age:..................... Sex:..................... Color:.....................

Marital Status: ....

Occupation: ....

Residence: ....

Sworn to before me this

day of...........................19 .....   X...

Identified to:...........................Death Ctf. issued by:...........................Date:...................

ME-21 (1/79)

Family Identification Form.

2010A-20M-315055(76) 346

Compartment No. ....

OFFICE OF CHIEF MEDICAL EXAMINER
CITY OF NEW YORK

Police Identification of Body

STATE OF NEW YORK
CITY AND COUNTY OF NEW YORK, ss
BOROUGH OF ....

PATROLMAN .... SHIELD .... PCT. ....

1. That he was the Patrolman who first saw the body of deceased:

....
Name of Deceased   M. E. Case No.

at ....
Place of Death   Date of Death

2. PLACE of OCCURRENCE (State exact location, streets, apt. etc.):

....

....
Time   Date

THAT HE OBTAINED THE FOLLOWING INFORMATION AS TO THE CIRCUMSTANCES
OF THE OCCURRENCE:

....

....

....

THAT HE IDENTIFIED THE BODY OF THE DECEASED AT THE OFFICE OF THE
CHIEF MEDICAL EXAMINER, IN THE PRESENCE OF OR TO:

DRS. ....

....

....

Sworn to before me this ....

day of .... 19 ......

Time ....

....
Signature of Patrolman

Police Identification Form.

Investigation of Death

An autopsy is always required in homicide cases. However, the chief medical examiner or coroner has the authority to investigate and certify any death which falls in the following categories.

Criminal violence

Suicide

Accident

Suddenly when in apparent good health

Deaths under unusual or suspicious circumstances

Abortion, (legal and criminal)

Prisoner and inmate deaths or any death while in legal custody

Deaths where the deceased was unattended by a physician

Poisoning

Unclaimed bodies

Diseases constituting a threat to public health

Disease, injury, or toxic agent resulting from employment

Death associated with diagnostic or therapeutic procedures

When a body is to be cremated, dissected, or buried at sea

When a dead body is brought into a new medicolegal jurisdiction without proper medical certification.

The medical examiner takes charge of the body upon notification of death. The medical examiner/coroner or a duly authorized representative should respond to the scene of the homicide to conduct an investigation into the circumstances of death. In order to conduct the investigation properly, he or she must obtain as much information as possible from the homicide investigator at the scene. An investigator fully apprised of all developments of the case should be present later at the autopsy.

In some jurisdictions, only the first officer is required to attend the autopsy, and only then to identify the body for the chain of custody. From an investigative point of view, I recommend that the investigator who is familiar with the facts of the case be present to brief the pathologist. Many times, during the autopsy, questions will arise that only someone who was present at the scene can answer. The investigator who was present at the crime scene can provide the pathologist with a detailed account of all that transpired from the discovery of the body to the preliminary investigation at the scene and thereby assure that both parties will have the benefit of all available information. In addition, sometimes certain changes take place in the body during transportation and storage. These changes may be misinterpreted if someone who was present at the scene and observed the body in its original condition is not present at the autopsy to point out these changes. I recall one case in which the deceased's face was flattened, giving the impression that the body had been face down, when in fact the body was on its back when discovered. A heavy piece of furniture placed on the deceased's face by the killer had created this postmortem artifact. The pathologist who performed the autopsy was at first confused by this apparent contradiction. However, since I had been at the scene and observed the body in its original position with the piece of furniture on the face, I was able to explain.

Purpose of the Autopsy

The purpose of the medicolegal autopsy is to establish the cause of death and make a medical determination of all the other factors which may be involved in the death. The autopsy provides the forensic pathologist with an opportunity to examine the body externally and internally to determine what wounds and injuries were sustained and to determine the cause of death.

Body Being Weighed and Measured prior to Autopsy. (*Courtesy of* Dr. Leslie I. Lukash, Chief Medical Examiner, Nassau County, New York.)

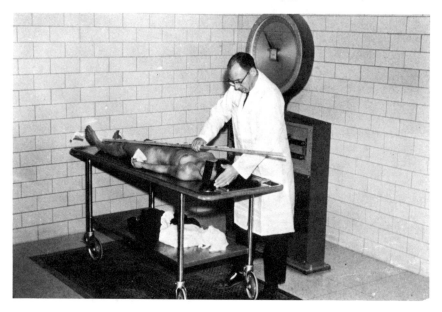

Body Being X-Rayed prior to Autopsy. (*Courtesy of* Dr. Leslie I. Lukash, Chief Medical Examiner, Nassau County, New York.)

Cause, Manner, and Mode of Death

From an investigative point of view, we can consider the *cause of death* as the pathological condition which produced the death; the *manner of death* as the instrument or physical agent which was used; and the *mode of death* as the intent (or lack of intent) when the instrumentality was employed, and by whom. Four modes are possible: natural, accidental, suicidal, or homicidal. For example, the cause of death may be a subdural hemorrhage; the manner of death may be an injury to the skull by blunt force; and the mode of death may be homicidal. In other types of cases the death may be natural as in a myocardial infarct (cardiac arrest), which may be caused by arteriosclerosis (hardening of the arteries).

There may be instances where the cause of death cannot be determined, but because of the condition of the body and the circumstances surrounding its discovery, the medical examiner will determine that the death should be considered a homicide.

The findings of the autopsy will usually determine whether or not death is the result of a homicide. This is important since some conditions which are in fact natural may sometimes suggest homicidal violence. Such cases can present serious problems for the homicide detective. For example, a person suffering a cerebral hemorrhage may become convulsive, compelling the police to subdue him or her. Actually, the victim may have suffered a subarachnoid hemorrhage due to a spontaneous rupture of a small aneurysm (dilatation of the wall of an artery) in the brain. The spontaneous nature of this condition is unaffected by the fact that the deceased may have been slapped, punched, or otherwise subjected to physical abuse during any minor argument or restraining activity. The hemorrhage may be either rapid or slow. If it is slow, the victim usually remains conscious, but may become disturbed or assaultive and may cause a commotion. In certain instances, these persons may expire while police are attempting to subdue them, prompting the erroneous assumption that the use of force by the police caused the death. The pathologist's findings during the autopsy will determine that the death was caused by the ruptured aneurysm and not by any physical restraint. Likewise, death from lobar pneumonia is sometimes preceded by delirium or excitement which may require that police be summoned. This situation may also produce minor injuries which are totally unrelated to the death.

The death of an alcoholic may at times cause investigators to believe that the death is suspicious or possibly homicidal, based on the general condition of the body. It should be noted that alcoholics may physically deteriorate to a point where they continually fall or cut themselves, resulting in numerous cuts, abrasions, and contusions which may be fresh or in various stages of healing. Furthermore, such persons are generally untidy and during their delirium may upset furniture, drop things, throw things around, and generally create an appearance of some sort of violent assault which did not in fact occur.

Investigators should also be aware of the various postmortem changes, as well as the possibility of the presence of postmortem artifacts which can appear to be wounds or additional injuries on the body. Examples of postmortem artifacts are insect and animal activity and decomposition. Discolorations in the skin may resemble bruises or injuries and may mislead the investigator. All observations at the scene should be recorded in the investigative notes and brought to the attention of the pathologist to assure that he or she can separate antemortem from postmortem conditions.

Conversely, investigators should realize that fatal violence may be inflicted without any external signs of trauma. Poisoning is probably the most obvious type of homicide in which no external wound is present. However, in any number of circumstances an injury may not be readily observed, such as a torn spleen from a kick or other trauma to the abdomen, or an asphyxiation where the victim has had a pillow held over the nose and mouth. I remember reading about a series of senior citizen deaths, all of which were thought to have been natural. There wasn't any evidence of a crime, and preliminary medical examination did not reveal any trauma. However, later on a suspect was developed after evidence of asphyxia was discovered in a similar case. A review of the other cases both by the medical examiner, who ordered the exhumation of certain bodies, and the police, who reopened their investigation, indicated that these "natural" deaths were in fact homicidal. It was later learned that the suspect would enter the bedrooms of the victims and hold a pillow over their faces as they lay in bed, causing suffocation. The suspect would then steal the TV and other small items of value without disturbing the general condition of the scene. In most instances, the bodies had begun to decompose before discovery. Police later located a witness who had observed the suspect leaving the apartment of one of the victims with a TV. Although evidence of this type of trauma could have been identified earlier, the procedures involved in cases of apparent natural death where no suspicion was involved were not sufficient to address this possibility. The jurisdiction involved subsequently changed its policy.

Determining mode of death obviously requires the expertise of the forensic pathologist. The detective should be constantly aware that things are not always as they appear to be. He or she should keep an open mind, conduct a thorough investigation, and remember that teamwork is essential. Then the two will be able to pool their knowledge to reach a successful conclusion.

Investigative Information Provided by the Autopsy

In addition to supplying the homicide investigator with an official cause of death, the forensic pathologist conducting the autopsy can assist the investigation by answering such questions as:

1. What type of weapon was involved in the death? (A hammer or screwdriver might leave impression-type wounds, for example.)
2. Are the wounds consistent with investigative evidence?
3. Which wound was the fatal wound? (Where there are numerous gunshot or stab wounds this determination frequently cannot be made.)

4. Approximately how long could the deceased have lived after the assault? (Survival time.)
5. How far could the deceased have walked or run?
6. Was the body dragged or dumped?
7. From what direction was the force applied?
8. What was the position of the deceased at the time of injury (sitting, standing, lying down, etc.)?
9. Are the injuries antemortem or postmortem?
10. Is there any evidence of sexual assault (rape or sodomy)?
11. Was the deceased under the influence of drugs?
12. Was the deceased under the influence of alcohol?
13. Are there any foreign objects in the cadaver (bullets, broken blades, fibers, etc.)?
14. Is there any evidence of a struggle (defense wounds, etc.)?
15. What is the estimated time of death?

It is important to note that most initial injuries do not cause immediate death. There is often a "survival interval" during which the person may engage in considerable activity before collapsing and dying. In fact, instances have been documented in which persons who have been severely injured, or who have suffered multiple gunshot wounds, have performed unusual physical accomplishments. This type of activity before death will be readily observable to the trained pathologist, who will be able to reasonably determine the survival time by noting the condition of internal organs and the forms of hemorrhage in the body cavities or stomach of the deceased. For example, hemorrhage into the chest and heart cavities following a penetrating wound usually indicates that the individual survived for only a short time, while bleeding into the stomach or lower abdominal tract indicates a longer survival time.

The presence of a wound on a body does not necessarily mean that someone else inflicted the wound. Suicide must always be considered. It is a common error to believe that certain wounds would have been too painful to be self-inflicted.

Remember, there is no such thing as a wound which is too painful if the person is determined to take his or her own life.

The pathologist considers the location, size, shape, character, and type of wound before the death is determined a homicide. For wounds to be self-inflicted, the locations must be accessible to the deceased. In most suicides, the instrument of death will be nearby. (However, the absence of a weapon is not conclusive evidence that the death is a homicide.)

The number, type, and location of wounds may also provide information to the investigator. Unusual types of wounds—such as mutilation of the body, removal of private parts, or eyes put out—may offer clues. Secondary wounds or "overkill" injuries may indicate extreme emotion.

The pathologist can ascertain how recent a wound is and which wound caused the death. The pathologist can also distinguish between wounds produced before and after death. Furthermore, in cases where the body has been out of doors or in water, there will be evidence of feeding by wild animals or postmortem injuries due to marine life or boat propellers, which the investigator might mistakenly interpret as being related to the cause of death. The pathologist also looks for defense wounds; these are usually found on the arms and legs of the victim, particularly between and on the inside of the fingers.

In some instances, the autopsy examination will reveal a specific type of weapon. When the barrel of a gun is pressed close to skin of a victim, it will leave a mark of the barrel.

The investigator can assist the medical examiner by keeping the crime scene under police control until after the autopsy has been completed. This procedure allows for further search in case additional information is discovered during the autopsy, and assures admissibility of any additional evidence.

The Medicolegal Autopsy

The complete *medicolegal autopsy* or *postmortem examination* involves the following steps:

Examination of the crime scene,

Identification of the body,

External examination of the body,

Internal examination of the body,

Toxicological examination of body fluids and organs.

The medicolegal autopsy is ordered by the medical examiner or coroner for the purposes of:

1. Determining the cause, manner, mode, and time of death.
2. Recovering, identifying, and preserving evidentiary material.
3. Providing interpretation and correlation of facts and circumstances related to death.
4. Providing a factual, objective medical report for prosecution and defense.

5. Separating natural death from unnatural death for protection of the innocent in suspicious deaths.

It is important to note that an autopsy must be complete if it is to be accurate. The basic principle of homicide investigation is "do it right the first time, you only get one chance." Theoretically a body can be exhumed for further examination. However, exhumation is costly and usually unnecessary if the examination was complete the first time. There is no excuse for haphazard or short-cut methods to be taken in this crucial investigative step. Once a body has been embalmed and buried, many forms of evidence—especially toxicological and pathological—will be lost forever. Therefore, a systematic routine must be followed in postmortem examinations.

The medicolegal autopsy is much more involved than a general autopsy, which is performed in a hospital. It involves special training, skill, and cooperation between independent organizations including the police, the prosecutor's office, and specialized personnel such as serologists, toxicologists, anthropologists, and odontologists. Usually when the autopsy is performed by the pathologist it is impossible to foresee the questions which may arise hours, weeks, or years later. Therefore, if an autopsy is to be done professionally, it must be done completely and all possible information obtained.

Remember, the purpose of the medicolegal autopsy is more than just to establish cause of death. It involves the determination of all other factors which may or may not be involved.

In order to acquaint the investigator with the requirements of the medicolegal autopsy, I have provided the following guidelines based on the National Association of Medical Examiners' *Standards for Inspection and Accreditation of a Modern Medicolegal Investigative System.*

Examination of the Crime Scene

In many jurisdictions a medical investigator, medical examiner, or coroner will respond to the crime scene to ascertain the essential facts concerning the circumstances of death and make a preliminary examination of the body. Once the body has been identified, the examiner looks for and evaluates any external evidence of trauma. Then a more complete examination of such factors as body heat, lividity, rigor mortis, decomposition, etc. is made to determine the approximate time of death. Often a determination of cause of death will hinge on facts or circumstances derived from an examination of the scene. However, although cause of death can frequently be determined during the scene investigation, particularly in gunshot or stab wound cases, the exact number of bullet or stab wounds cannot usually be ascertained until the autopsy. This is particularly true in cases where the body is clothed or has been covered with blood or dirt. The medical examiner or coroner takes charge of the body, any clothing on the body, and any article on or near the body that may assist the pathologist in determining cause and manner of death.

The crime scene examination does not end at the location of death. If the medical examiner who was present at the scene will not be performing the autopsy, the information from the crime scene investigation must be conveyed to the pathologist who will conduct the autopsy. The homicide detective who conducted the preliminary police investigation and was present at the crime scene should attend the autopsy and provide the medical examiner or coroner with the following.

1. Description of the circumstances of death.
2. Description of the scene of death. (Complete notes taken at the scene include a description of the deceased, color of any blood, injuries and wounds observed, etc.)
3. Condition of the body when first discovered (rigor mortis, lividity, temperature, putrefaction, decomposition, maggots or other insect activity, etc.).
4. Statements taken from witnesses and/or suspects.
5. Police photographs taken at scene. (Polaroid photos can be taken in addition to the usual police photos since they are ready for viewing immediately and can be available at autopsy.)
6. Diagrams and sketches of the crime scene.
7. Any weapons or articles found at the scene which relate to the death (knives, guns, other weapons, notes, papers, drugs, etc.).
8. Any questions formulated during the initial phase of the investigation. These may be evaluated in light of the medical evidence found by the pathologist.

Identification of the Body

The body must be properly identified to the medical examiner. The legal identification of the body is one of the requirements in the chain of custody and is vital to the homicide investigation. In criminal cases both a personal and a police identification must be made directly to the medical examiner. These identifications are made on official affidavits, sworn to in the presence of witnesses, with the time and date affixed, and signed by the person or official making the identification.

The police identification is made by an officer who observed the body at the scene, saw where it was found, or saw where the crime was committed. A personal identification is made by a relative or someone who knew the deceased.

The medical examiner assumes responsibility for the proper identification of the dead body. In homicide cases, all available means of identification should be employed to ascertain the identity of the deceased. The various methods of identification are as follows.

Personal identification (next of kin, relatives, friends, etc.)

Fingerprints

Teeth

Scars and/or surgical procedures (medical records)

Tattoos

Body build

Congenital malformations

Comparison x-rays

Identification of clothing on the body and its contents

Photographs

If the body is badly decomposed or skeletonized an additional function of the autopsy will be to identify the remains. The pathologist is in the best position to know what additional experts—odontologists, anthropologists, etc.—may be needed.

External Examination of the Body

The date, time, and place of autopsy should be recorded, where and by whom it was performed, and the identity of any witnesses and/or participants. This recording can either be done by a stenographer or by use of mechanical recording equipment.

PRELIMINARY PROCEDURE

1. The body is examined before the clothing is removed to determine the condition of the clothing and to correlate any tears or other defects with obvious injuries to the body. These observations are then recorded.

2. The clothing, body, and hands of the deceased should be protected from possible contamination prior to the examination. (Hands

should have been covered with paper bags at scene before body was transported.)

3. Clothing should then be carefully removed by unbuttoning, unzippering, or unhooking without tearing or cutting. This should be done systematically, and the condition of the clothing as well as any torn buttons, unsnapped garments, etc., should be recorded so the cutting is not confused with any tearing or cutting from the weapon or incident which caused death.

4. Clothing should then be laid out on a table so that a relationship can be established between the wounds on the body and the damages to the clothing. This procedure enables the pathologist to determine the position of the body at the time the wounds were inflicted, and to know where to look for external and internal damage.

5. Each item of clothing should be properly marked for identification. (If clothing is wet or bloody, it should be hung to air dry in order to prevent any putrefaction.)

THE EXTERNAL EXAMINATION

1. The body is identified for the record and a complete physical description is taken as follows.
   a. Age
   b. Height
   c. Weight
   d. Sex
   e. Color of hair and eyes
   f. State of nutrition
   g. Muscular development
   h. Scars
   i. Tattoos
   j. Detailed description of teeth (number and general condition)
   k. Any abnormalities or deformities
   l. Evidence of any fractures

2. The body should then be carefully washed to remove any dried blood and/or dirt from the surface. (In gunshot cases, the pathologist should record the presence of any smoke or powder residue prior to this washing.)

3. A detailed description of the injuries should then be recorded, noting the number and characteristics such as size, shape, pattern, and location in relation to anatomic landmarks.

4. Photographs should then be taken of the body for identification and to record specific injuries.
   a. Photographs of injuries should include a scale and an identification number.

b. If police have recovered a weapon, this weapon can be photographed alongside the wound. However, the weapon should be held away from the body in order to prevent any contamination of evidence, such as blood or hair being transferred between the body and the weapon.

5. The presence of any bite marks should be noted and these wounds or marks photographed with a 1 × 1 (fingerprint) camera, using a scale and measure along with an identifier label. (If these bite marks were observed prior to the body washing, a saliva swabbing should have been obtained for a possible blood grouping.)

6. X-ray and fluoroscope examination should then be undertaken to:
   a. Locate bullets, broken blades, or other radio-opaque objects.
   b. Document any old or new fractures, anatomic deformities, postsurgical materials such as metal plates, screws, nails, etc.
   c. Identify remains where there is no personal identification. (These x-rays can then be held pending the comparison of any antemortem records when and if located.)
   (*Note:* In all decomposition and child-abuse cases, the remains are x-rayed to document past trauma.)

7. During this external examination a record is made of any postmortem artifacts, such as:
   a. Artifacts of decomposition.
   b. Third-party artifacts, e.g., animal or insect activity, emergency medical treatment, deliberate mutilation, or any dismemberment.
   c. Artifacts of storage and/or transportation prior to autopsy.

8. Examination of the hands, wrists, and arms for evidence of defense wounds. In addition in certain types of homicides, the pathologist will clip the fingernails to obtain trace evidence from the deceased's fingers, which may include tissue and blood specimens from suspects. Hands may also be examined for powder residue by neutron activation analysis.

9. In sex homicides, samples of scalp and pubic hair should be obtained from the body of the deceased. All hair should be plucked to secure the entire hair including the root. The pubic area should first be combed to secure any foreign or loose hairs which may be compared with suspect's hair. Other samples should be obtained which represent different parts of the body. In addition, oral, vaginal, and anal swabs should be taken for further examination.

Internal Examination of the Body

An internal examination of the head, neck, cervical spine, thorax, abdomen, and genitalia is then performed by the pathologist. The examination records the course of wounds through the various structures and any evidentiary items such as bullets, pieces of weapons, pellets, and foreign material are preserved. Their particular point of recovery is noted for the record, and each item is labeled for proper identification. The internal examination generally proceeds as follows.

THE HEAD

a. The exterior of the scalp is first examined for any injuries which may be hidden by the hair.

b. The eyes and eyelids are then examined for any petechiae in the conjunctivae. (This is a pathological condition caused by asphyxia. Tiny hemorrhages in the form of specks are seen on the mucous membrane lining the inner surface of the eyelids.)

c. The ear canals are then examined for evidence of hemorrhage.

d. The interior of the mouth, lips, and cheeks are examined for evidence of trauma.

e. The teeth are then examined for any injury or breakage. The pathologist can use a dental chart to identify each tooth, its condition, location of fillings, evidence of injury, etc.

f. A *coronal mastoid incision* is then made across the head. The scalp is pulled back exposing the cranium. The interior of the scalp is examined for any evidence of trauma, and the cranium is examined for fractures. The calvarium is then removed, exposing the dura and the brain.

g. The brain is removed and examined for any injury or disease.

h. The brain is weighed.

i. A slice of brain tissue is taken for later examination.

j. The dura is then stripped from the cranial cavity and the interior of the skull is examined for any fractures or injury.

THE CHEST

a. An incision is then made across the chest of the subject. This incision is called the *thoracoabdominal incision,* more commonly referred to as the "Y" or primary incision.

b. The chest is then examined for any fractures of ribs, noting their specific anatomic location. In cases where an ambulance crew has attempted resuscitation, there may be additional injuries to the body which will not be properly evaluated if the medical examiner is not given this information. I cannot overemphasize that an investigator assigned to the case should be present during the autopsy so the pathologist can be briefed about what transpired at the scene.

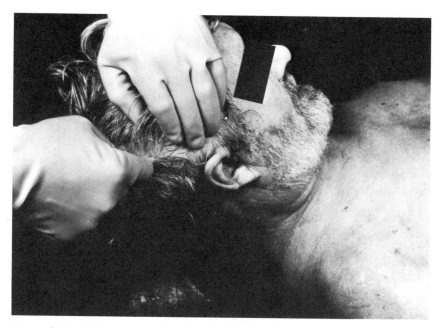

Coronal Mastoid Incision—Head Incision. (*Courtesy of* Dr. Leslie I. Lukash, Chief Medical Examiner, Nassau County, New York.)

Head Incision. (*Courtesy of* Dr. Leslie I. Lukash, Chief Medical Examiner, Nassau County, New York.)

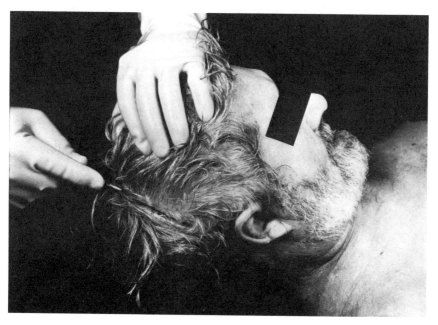

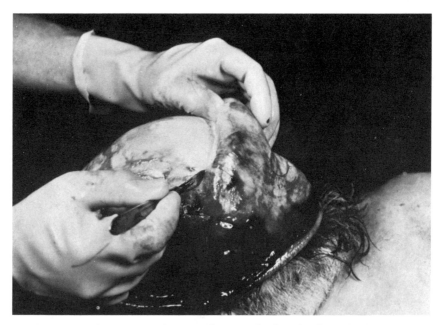

Head Incision. (*Courtesy of* Dr. Leslie I. Lukash, Chief Medical Examiner, Nassau County, New York.)

Head Incision. (*Courtesy of* Dr. Leslie I. Lukash, Chief Medical Examiner, Nassau County, New York.)

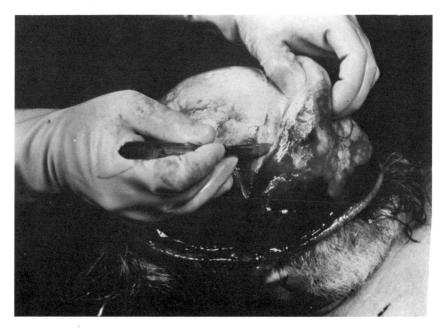

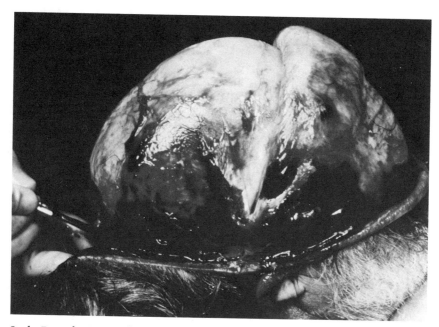

Scalp Brought Forward to Expose the Cranium. (*Courtesy of* Dr. Leslie I. Lukash, Chief Medical Examiner, Nassau County, New York.)

Opening of the Skull Cavity. (*Courtesy of* Dr. Leslie I. Lukash, Chief Medical Examiner, Nassau County, New York.)

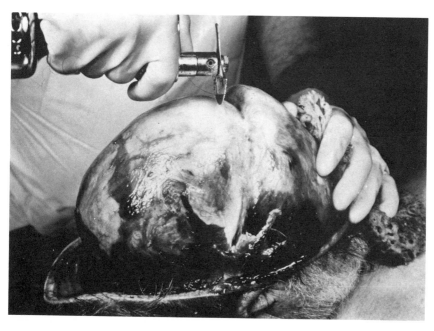

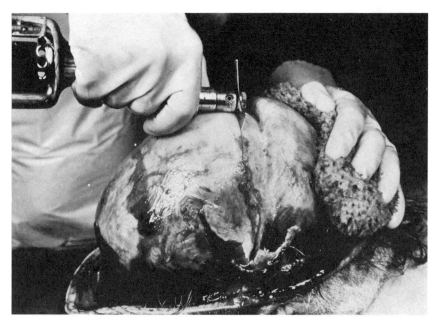

Opening of the Skull Cavity. (*Courtesy of* Dr. Leslie I. Lukash, Chief Medical Examiner, Nassau County, New York.)

Opening of the Skull Cavity. (*Courtesy of* Dr. Leslie I. Lukash, Chief Medical Examiner, Nassau County, New York.)

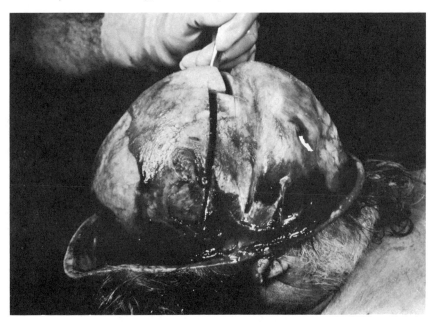

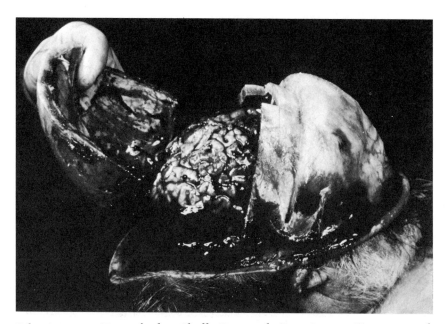

Calvarium or Top of the Skull Removed Exposing a Hemmorraged Brain. (*Courtesy of* Dr. Leslie I. Lukash, Chief Medical Examiner, Nassau County, New York.)

Brain Being Removed from Skull. (*Courtesy of* Dr. Leslie I. Lukash, Chief Medical Examiner, Nassau County, New York.)

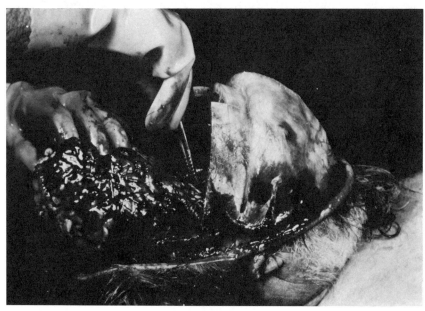

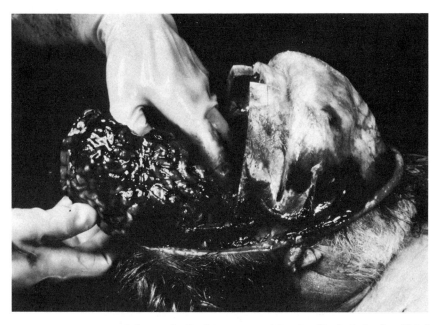

Brain Being Removed from Skull. (*Courtesy of* Dr. Leslie I. Lukash, Chief Medical Examiner, Nassau County, New York.)

Skull Cavity after Brain Removed. (*Courtesy of* Dr. Leslie I. Lukash, Chief Medical Examiner, Nassau County, New York.)

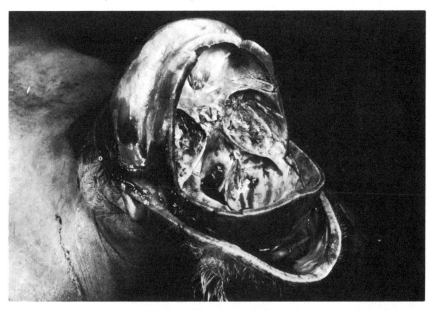

c. The breast plate is then removed by cutting through the ribs, exposing the heart and lungs for examination.
d. A sample of blood is then taken directly from the heart, after opening the pericardial sac, for determining blood type and later toxicological examination.
e. The heart and lungs are then removed, weighed, and examined and a slice of tissue taken for later examination.
f. The quantity of fluids in the pericardial and pleural cavities is measured and recorded.
g. The chest flap is then pulled upward to chin level to examine structures of the neck muscles and organs. Any hemorrhage is noted, and the organs of the neck and throat are removed including the tongue for further examination.
h. Signs of asphyxia are noted within these structures, the upper chest, and in the pericardium and pleurae.
i. The tongue is then examined by lateral dissection for any evidence of trauma. (In many instances the deceased will bite his or her tongue during strangulation.)
j. The interior of the chest is then examined for any trauma or other injuries along the cervical and thoracic spine.

THE ABDOMEN
a. The abdomen is examined, noting the positions and condition of the organs.
b. The course of injuries is traced and recorded before any organs are removed.
c. All fluids in this cavity are measured and recorded.
d. Each separate organ is weighed and dissected for later toxicological examination after it has been examined for any projectiles. In addition a section of the intestines is kept for testing.
e. Stomach contents are measured and recorded and a sample kept for toxicology.
f. The fluid in the gall bladder is kept intact for testing.

THE PELVIC CAVITY
a. The external and internal genitalia are examined for evidence of foreign matter and injury.
b. In sex homicides, vaginal and anal swabs are taken (oral swabs should also be obtained).
c. The urinary bladder is removed and the fluid measured and kept for toxicological examination.

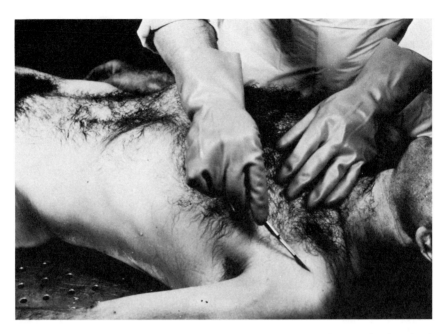

Preparing to Open the Chest Cavity. *(Courtesy of* Dr. Leslie I. Lukash, Chief Medical Examiner, Nassau County, New York.)

The Thoracoabdominal or "Y" Incision. (*Courtesy of* Dr. Leslie I. Lukash, Chief Medical Examiner, Nassau County, New York.)

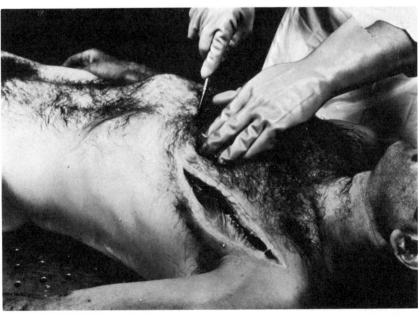

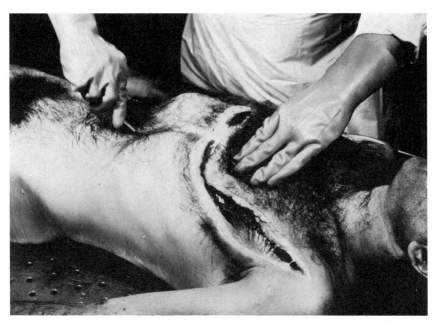

The Thoracoabdominal or "Y" Incision. (*Courtesy of* Dr. Leslie I. Lukash, Chief Medical Examiner, Nassau County, New York.)

The Thoracoabdominal or "Y" Incision. (*Courtesy of* Dr. Leslie I. Lukash, Chief Medical Examiner, Nassau County, New York.)

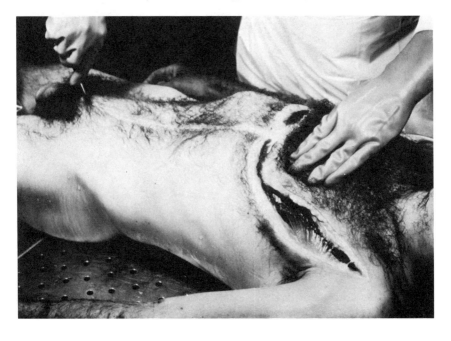

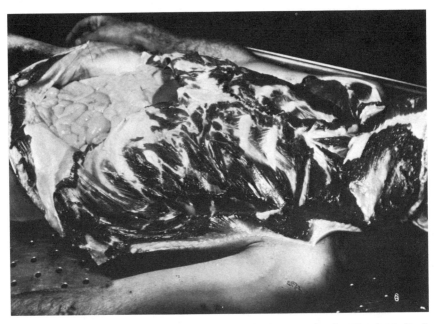

Chest and Ribs Exposed. (*Courtesy of* Dr. Leslie I. Lukash, Chief Medical Examiner, Nassau County, New York.)

Removal of the Chest Plate. (*Courtesy of* Dr. Leslie I. Lukash, Chief Medical Examiner, Nassau County, New York.)

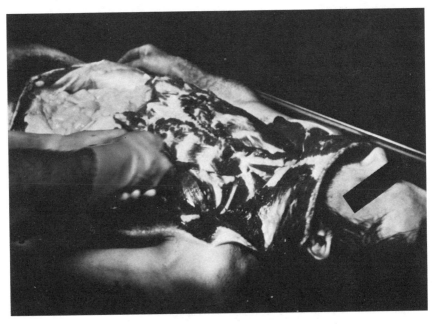

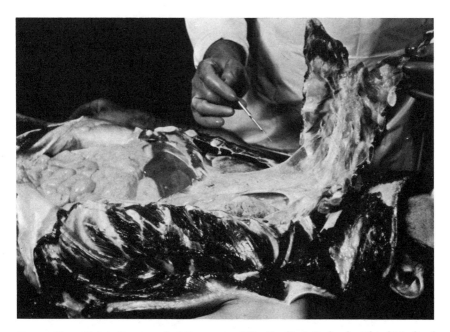

Breast Plate Being Removed. (*Courtesy of* Dr. Leslie I. Lukash, Chief Medical Examiner, Nassau County, New York.)

The Protocol

The *protocol* is the official report of the autopsy by the medical examiner or coroner. It may be dictated to a stenographer or recorded into a mechanical recorder for later transcription. The preparation of this report is the responsibility of the chief medical examiner or coroner. The protocol or autopsy report reflects the entire examination, both negative and positive, and gives the official cause of death expressed in acceptable terminology. It contains the following information:

1. External examination:
   a. Description of the clothing,
   b. Description of the body.
2. Evidence of injury:
   a. External,
   b. Internal.
3. Central nervous system (head and brain).
4. Internal examination—cardiovascular system, pulmonary system, GI (gastrointestinal) system, stomach, small and large intestines, etc.

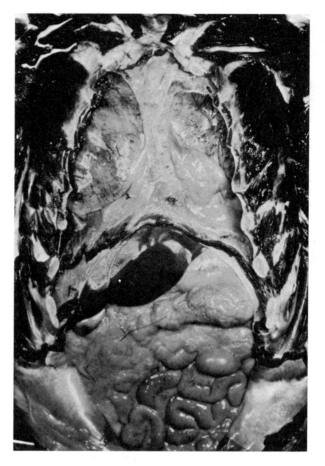

Internal Organs of the Chest Exposed for Autopsy. (*Courtesy of* Dr. Leslie I. Lukash, Chief Medical Examiner, Nassau County, New York.)

5. Anatomical findings.
6. Toxicological findings.
7. Opinion.

The medical examiner at the end of this protocol then reports the official diagnosis of the cause of death. Today, many pathologists use a prepared autopsy form that not only guides the procedure but assures the completion of the autopsy. If death is determined to be the result of a homicide, the pathologist will indicate this by placing the word "homicidal" on the protocol. The opinion will then be expressed in simple, understandable English, avoiding medical terminology, indicating the nature of the injury which caused death and any major complicating factors. For example: "It is my opinion that John Smith,

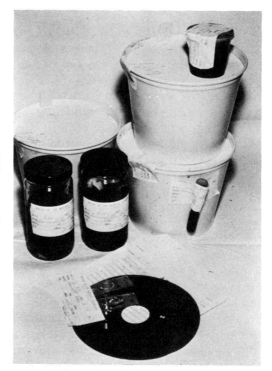

Containers of Physiologic Fluids and Organs to be sent for Further Toxicologic Examination. (*Courtesy of* Dr. Leslie I. Lukash, Chief Medical Examiner, Nassau County, New York.)

a 30-year-old male, died as a result of a gunshot wound to the chest. The bullet, a 38-caliber which was recovered from the body, passed through the right lung and heart causing massive internal hemorrhage. No other injuries or significant natural disease process was found at the time of autopsy."

The value of the diagnosis and protocol from an investigative point of view is that it provides a factual and medical opinion of the death. This can then be used to determine if the facts and evidence gathered during the homicide investigation are consistent with the cause of death as determined by the medical examiner.

Summary

The success of the medical examination and the homicide investigation is assured when there exists a mutual cooperation between the pathologist and the homicide investigator. Teamwork is essential in this phase of the investigation, just as it is in other phases. It requires an appreciation and understanding of each other's duties and responsibilities so that all parties can benefit from one another's contributions and expertise in the professional investigation of homicide.

Human Anatomy

In order to provide the reader with some basic reference material and understanding of the terminology used in medicolegal investigations, I have included this section on human anatomy.[2] Investigators are not expected to have the medical knowledge of a forensic pathologist. However, they should have a working knowledge of anatomical terminology in order to communicate intelligently with the pathologist and comprehend the final autopsy report. Furthermore, an understanding of the fundamental structures of the human body and the location of vital organs and bones can enable the investigator to make intelligent observations at the scene.

The word *anatomy* is derived from two Greek words which mean, literally, "to cut apart." Through usage, it has come to mean the study of the structure of the body, describing the size, shape, composition, and relative positions of the organs and various parts of the body. In order to describe the structures within the body, medical terminology employs a number of "points of reference," which assist in visualizing each organ's position within the human body. For example, to describe the heart's position it is necessary to detail what is above, below, to the right and left, and in front and back of it, and where all these positions are located in reference to easily identified points on the outside of the body. In order for these points of reference to be meaningful, there must be a set position of the body known as *anatomical position.*

All terminology used in describing the body and its parts is based on this anatomical position, which is that of the body standing erect, arms at the sides, with the palms facing forward and the thumbs to the outside.

Therefore, when studying anatomical plates, like the figures presented in this section, the right side of the body will be on the left side of the drawing, and the left side of the body will be on the right side of the drawing, as when looking at a person facing you.

Directional Terms

These are the terms used in anatomy to describe the position of a particular organ in relation to other organs.

1. *Superior:* Indicates direction toward the head end or upper part of the body. Hence, the lungs are *superior* to the liver.
2. *Inferior:* Indicates direction further away from the head end of

---

[2]The material in this section is based on *Gray's Anatomy* and *Life Sciences for Nursing and Health Technologies* by Virginia E. Thomas.

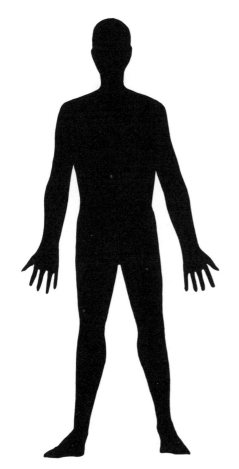

Anatomical Position. (*Courtesy of* Virginia E. Thomas, Technicourse, Long Beach, California.)

the body or toward the lower part of the body. Hence, the intestines are *inferior* to the stomach.

3. *Anterior (ventral):* Indicates the front or belly side of the body. Hence, the toes are *anterior* or *ventral.*

4. *Posterior (dorsal):* Indicates the backside of the body. Hence, the heels are *posterior* or *dorsal.*

5. *Proximal:* Indicates nearer to a point of reference, usually the center of the body. Hence, the shoulder is *proximal* to the elbow.

6. *Distal:* Indicates farther away from the center of the body. Hence, the elbow is *distal* to the shoulder.

7. *Medial:* Indicates closer to the midline of the body. Hence, the little finger is *medial* in anatomical position.

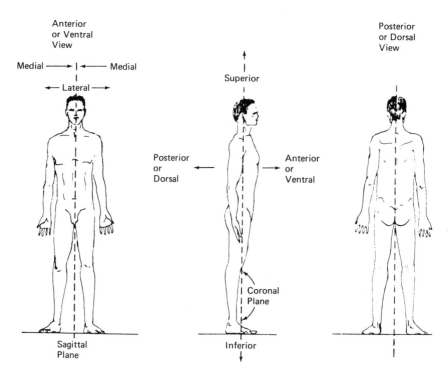

Directional Terms. (*Courtesy of* Virginia E. Thomas, Technicourse, Long Beach, California.)

8. *Lateral:* Indicates toward the side of the body or away from the midline. Hence, the thumb is *lateral* in anatomical position.
9. *Saggital plane:* Is an imaginary line dividing the body into a right and left portion.
10. *Coronal plane:* Is an imaginary line dividing the body into a front and back portion.

Body Cavities

The body is divided into two large cavities called the *dorsal* (back) and *ventral* (front) cavities, which are then subdivided into smaller sections.

DORSAL CAVITY. This cavity is subdivided into the *cranial* and *vertebral* cavities.

1. *Cranial cavity:* Is formed by the skull and contains the brain and the pituitary gland.
2. *Vertebral cavity:* Is contained within the vertebral column and houses the spinal cord.

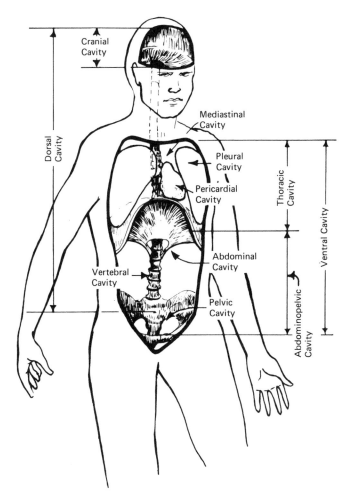

Body Cavities. (*Courtesy of* Virginia E. Thomas, Technicourse, Long Beach, California.)

VENTRAL CAVITY. This cavity is subdivided into two major sections, the *thoracic cavity* and the *abdominopelvic cavity*. These two sections are divided by the diaphragm. These two major sections are then subdivided into additional cavities as follows.

1. Thoracic cavity: This is the portion above the diaphragm and contains the following cavities.
   a. Two *pleural cavities:* These contain the two lungs.
   b. *Pericardial cavity:* This contains the heart.
   c. *Mediastinal or interpleural cavity:* This contains everything, located in the thoracic cavity other than the heart and lungs. Includes the trachea, bronchi, esophagus, etc.

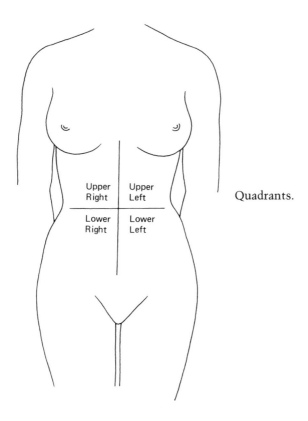

Quadrants.

2. Abdominopelvic cavity: This is the portion below the diaphragm and contains two sections:
   a. *Abdominal cavity:* The upper portion of the abdominopelvic cavity. It contains the stomach, liver, gallbladder, spleen, pancreas, and most of the large and small intestines. The kidneys, ureters, and adrenal glands lie deep in the cavity.
   b. *Pelvic cavity:* The lower portion of the abdominopelvic cavity, which begins roughly on a line with the iliac crests and ends at the inferior end of the abdominopelvic cavity. It contains the urinary bladder, the sex organs, and part of the small and large intestines.

Quadrants

There are additional points of reference to locate precisely the organs in the abdominopelvic cavity, because the cavity is both large and contains several organs. The medical description divides the cavity into four *quadrants*.

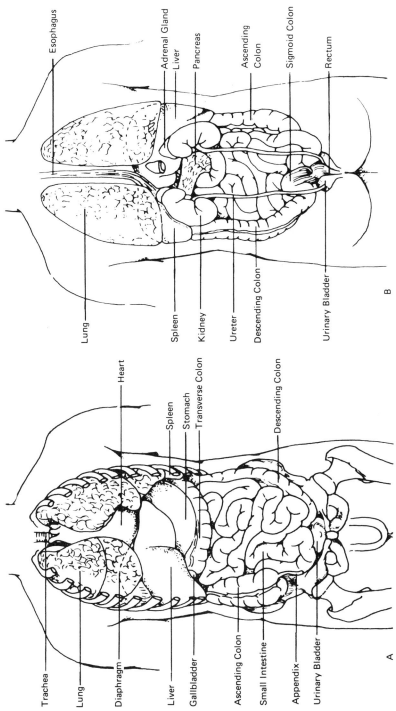

Anterior and Posterior Views of the Thoracic and Abdominal Pelvic Cavities. (*Courtesy of Virginia E. Thomas, Technicourse, Long Beach, California.*)

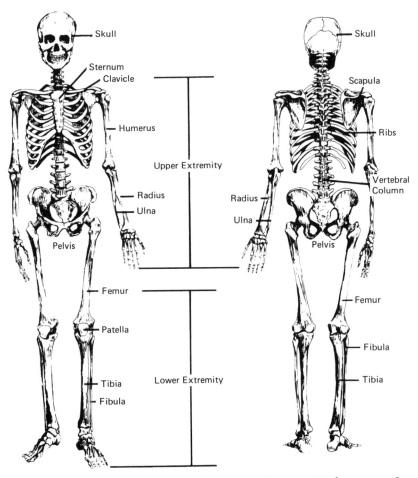

Bones of the Skeleton. (*Courtesy of* Virginia E. Thomas, Technicourse, Long Beach, California.)

1. *Upper right quadrant:* Contains part of the small intestine, the descending duodenum, the upper ascending colon, most of the liver, gallbladder, and bile ducts, head of pancreas, right adrenal gland, right kidney, and upper part of right ureter.
2. *Lower right quadrant:* Contains the lower ascending colon, cecum, appendix, lower right ureter, terminal ileum, part of urinary bladder, and sex organs.
3. *Upper left quadrant:* Contains ascending part of duodenum, upper

descending colon, left half of transverse colon, spleen, small part of liver, left adrenal gland, left kidney, and upper part of left ureter.
4. *Lower left quadrant:* Contains descending colon, small intestine (part of ileum), lower part of left ureter, part of urinary bladder, and sex organs.

The Skeletal System

The *skeletal system* consists of all of the bones in the body. The skeleton provides support, protects certain body organs beneath the bones, and serves as a system of connection for the muscles and ligaments. Practically speaking, it is not necessary for the homicide detective to understand the make-up, development, or detailed structure of the bones. However, the investigator should have some basic knowledge of the anatomical location of certain major bones in the human body, such as the *long bones* of the arms and legs, the *humerus, ulna, radius, femur, tibia,* and *fibula.* In addition, the location of the *clavicle, scapula, sternum, vertebral column, ribs, pelvis,* and *patella* may be useful in visualizing a specific portion of the body.

The Heart

The heart is basically a pump that maintains the circulation of blood throughout the human body. It is about the size of a man's fist and is located in the pericardial cavity between the lungs, posterior to the sternum, lying about two-thirds to the left of midline. The heart is divided into four chambers. The upper two chambers are called *atria* and the lower two chambers are called *ventricles.*

The heart is the major organ of the cardiovascular system. The pumping action maintains the circulation of blood to and from the heart through a series of blood vessels. These blood vessels are:

1. *Arteries:* carry blood away from the heart.
2. *Veins:* carry blood to the heart.
3. *Capillaries:* connect arteries and veins.

The purpose of circulation is to bring the deoxygenated blood from various parts of the body through the veins to the lungs for purification. The oxygenated blood is then returned to the heart from the lungs for circulation to the body through the arteries.

It is not necessary for the investigator to have an in-depth knowledge of the workings of the heart and cardiovascular system. How-

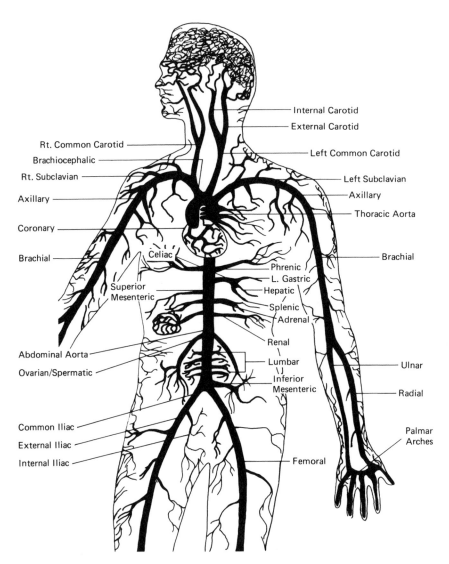

The Arteries. (*Courtesy of* Virginia E. Thomas, Technicourse, Long Beach, California.)

ever, he or she may want to be familiar with the general location of the heart and the major veins and arteries in order to appreciate the trauma or damage which can be done to the body if one of these major blood vessels is injured. The following table lists the major arteries and veins for reference purposes.

457

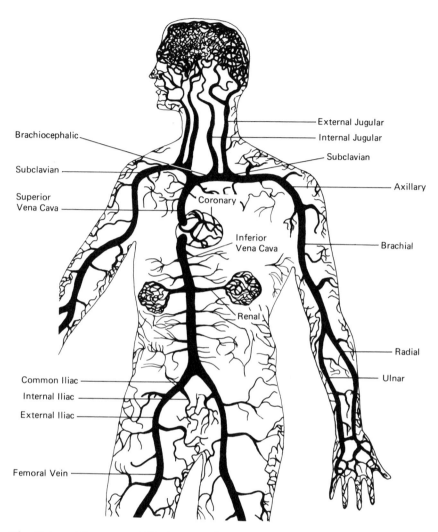

The Veins. (*Courtesy of* Virginia E. Thomas, Technicourse, Long Beach, California.)

ARTERIES		VEINS	
Carotid	Femoral	Jugular	Femoral
Subclavian	Brachial	Subclavian	Brachial
Aorta	Ulnar	Superior vena cava	Ulnar
Abdominal aorta	Radial	Inferior vena cava	Radial
Iliac		Iliac	

The author wishes to acknowledge the assistance and contributions of the following forensic pathologists who were instrumental in providing the technical data and information relative to the medicolegal autopsy. Dr. Dominick J. DiMaio, Former Chief Medical Examiner, City of New York. Doctor DiMaio has lectured at various forensic symposia and instructed various law enforcement agencies in the role of the medical examiner in homicide investigations. He is a professorial lecturer in pathology at Downstate Medical Center, State University of New York, and an Associate Professor of Forensic Medicine at New York University's Medical Center. Dr. Leslie I. Lukash, Chief Medical Examiner of Nassau County, East Meadow, New York. Doctor Lukash is Professor of Forensic Pathology at Stony Brook University, Long Island, New York, and served as chairman of the committee on Standards for Inspection and Accreditation of Modern Medicolegal Systems of the National Association of Medical Examiners. Dr. Elliot M. Gross, Chief Medical Examiner for the City of New York, Associate Professor of Forensic Medicine, New York University, and Adjunct Professor of Pathology at Cornell University Medical College.

The author also wishes to acknowledge Dr. John L. E. Wolff, Clinical Associate Professor of Medicine at New York Medical College and Police Surgeon, New York City Police Department, who reviewed the section on anatomy for technical content.

Finally, the author wishes to acknowledge the assistance of Virginia E. Thomas who also contributed to the illustrations herein.

Selected Reading

Adelson, Lester. *The Pathology of Homicide.* Springfield, Illinois: Charles C. Thomas, 1974.

Fisher, Russell S. and Petty, Charles S. (Eds.). *Forensic Pathology: A Handbook for Pathologists.* Washington, D.C.: National Institute of Law Enforcement and Criminal Justice Law Enforcement Assistance Administration, U.S. Department of Justice, 1977.

Gray, Henry F. R. S. *Gray's Anatomy.* edited by T. Pickering. Philadelphia, Pennsylvania: Pick Running Press, 1974.

New York City Charter and Administrative Code Chapter 39 Chief Medical Examiner.

Snyder, LeMoyne. *Homicide Investigation,* 3rd ed. Springfield, Illinois: Charles C. Thomas, 1977.

Spitz, Werner U. and Fisher, Russell S. *Medicolegal Investigation of Death.* Springfield, Illinois: Charles C. Thomas, 1973.

Thomas, Virginia, *Life Sciences for Nursing and Health Technologies.* Long Beach, California: Technicourse, Inc., 1977.

Identification of Suspects 16

The purpose of this chapter is to familiarize homicide detectives with the availability of certain technical and psychological tools, which can be utilized in professional investigations. Practically speaking, these techniques may be limited to specific cases. However, they are viable adjuncts to the investigation and may provide additional facts, information, and identification of suspects. In order to acquaint detectives with these investigative methodologies, I have provided information, case histories, and recommendations for the following techniques:

Bite mark identification,

Hypnosis,

Latent prints on human skin,

Polygraph,

Psychological profiling,

Psycholinguistics,

Psychics.

Bite-Mark Identification

The purpose of this section is to acquaint investigators with practical information and procedures which can be employed in the investigation of homicides involving bite-mark evidence.

Bite marks are usually found in cases involving extremely emotional and violent episodes such as child abuse, felonious assault, sex-

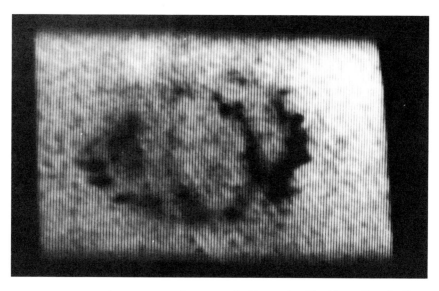

High-Contrast Enhancement of Bite Mark. From the *Florida v. Bundy* Case. (*Courtesy of* Dr. Lowell J. Levine, Forensic Odontologist.)

Bite Mark. Subtle bite mark on the cheek of a child assaulted and murdered by another child. (*Courtesy of* Dr. Levine, Forensic Odontologist.)

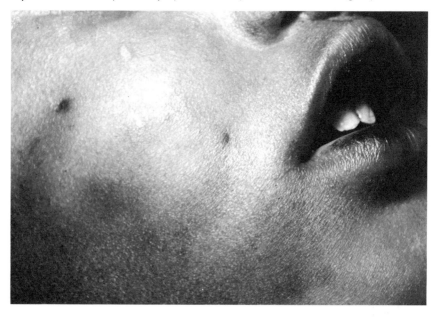

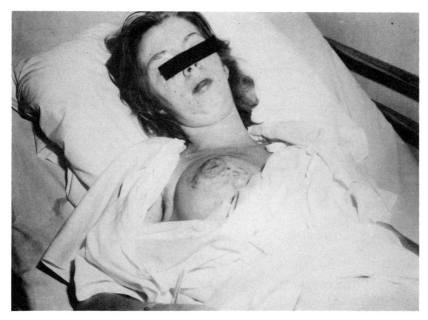

Bite Marks from a Sadistic Breast Assault. Multiple bite marks were inflicted upon the breast of a victim, who survived an attack by a serial killer. (*Courtesy of* Lt. Frank P. Del Prete, Bergen County Prosecutor's Office, Bergen County, New Jersey.)

ual assault, and sex-related homicides. However, in order for investigators to utilize this evidence, they must first be able to recognize and discover the existence of this type of wound. I have included various photos of bite-marks herein to assist investigators in making this observation.

The homicide detective will obviously need the expertise of a forensic odontologist to interpret this type of evidence. Here we will look at certain basic steps which investigators must employ at the scene in order to assist the odontologist in his evaluations.

Forensic odontology has become a highly important and technically complex area, as a medicolegal investigation of bite-mark evidence has proved to be successful in many noteworthy cases which have occurred in recent years. The "Theodore Bundy" case in Florida is an example of the value of bite-mark evidence in homicide investigations. Bundy, who was convicted for murder, had inflicted bite marks on his victims during sexual assaults. These were examined by forensic odontologists who later testified with reasonable medical and dental certainty at the trial that the defendant had inflicted the bite marks.

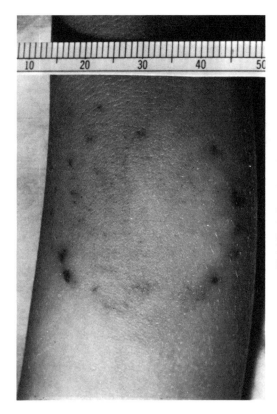

Bite Mark on the Arm of a Child Victim of a Single Homicidal Assault. Photo is taken with a camera perpendicular to the center of pattern with a stiff ruler in position. (*Courtesy of* Dr. Levine, Forensic Odontologist.)

The Bite Mark

Practically speaking, the bite mark should be viewed as an additional piece of evidence which may be utilized to identify a suspect. The teeth are actually used by people as "tools," and, in the simplest terms, tooth marks are tool marks. It has been well documented that owing to such factors as size, shape, wear, rotations, restorations, fillings, loss of certain teeth, and accidental characteristics such as breakage and injury, no two sets of teeth are exactly alike. The relative positions of the teeth, their width, and the distance between them together with ridges on the edges of the teeth and grooves on the back or front, vary for different individuals. These factors provide the forensic odontologist with specific and characteristic information about the person who has inflicted the bite mark and can be used to positively identify a suspect.

Generally, tooth marks come from the front teeth in the upper and lower jaws. The type of impression varies with the age of the individual. For example, children and young people have ridges on the lower edges of their front teeth, while persons over twenty years of age generally have front teeth which are smoother.

Bite mark identification is not limited to skin. Teeth leave impressions or scraping marks in the form of bite marks in chewing gum, cheese, fruit, chocolate, and similar materials. The discovery of a piece of discarded chewing gum at the scene of a homicide should certainly be considered a significant find. Its value is not only in its distinctive bite-mark impressions, but also in its ability to yield additional information through a serological test to determine the blood grouping of the suspect who chewed the gum.

According to Dr. Lowell Levine,[1] the markings found on the skin of a victim are more than just marks. The musculature of the lips, tongue, and cheeks, and the mental state of the biter, all seem to play a role in the infliction of the tooth-mark pattern on the skin. The skin itself contributes to the bite mark in that it is elastic, yielding, and variable from body area to body area and from body to body. Most

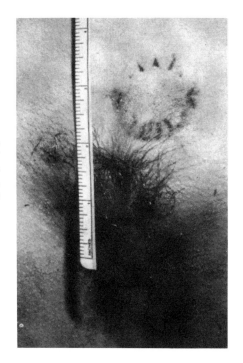

Sexually Oriented Bite Mark. This is a typical example of a sexually oriented bite mark. In this case the victim was sadistically bitten above vagina in the area of the pubis. (*Courtesy of* Dr. Levine, Forensic Odontologist.)

---

[1]Dr. Lowell J. Levine is President of the American Academy of Forensic Sciences and Consultant in Forensic Dentistry, Office of the Chief Medical Examiner, Nassau County. He is also a teacher, writer, and lecturer of Forensic Odontology.

464   Identification of Suspects

bite marks are found in the following types of homicides: 1) The homicide victim involved in sexual activity around the time of death; and 2) the battered-child homicide victim.

Sexually oriented homicides can be either homosexual or heterosexual and may involve voluntary sexual activity or forcible attack. Child victims may be either battered children or children murdered by other children in a single homicide assault. According to Dr. Levine, there are two types of bite-mark patterns:

1. Those which are inflicted slowly, almost sadistically, exhibiting a central *ecchymotic area* or "suck mark," and a radiating linear abrasion pattern surrounding the central area resembling a sunburst. This type is most often found in the sexually oriented homicide.
2. The second type more closely resembles a tooth-mark pattern. This is an attack or defense bite-mark and is seen most often in the battered-child type of homicide.

Collection of Bite-Mark Evidence at the Scene

The proper handling of bite-mark evidence begins at the scene of the crime, where the homicide investigator must initiate procedures to insure that it is not destroyed or lost. The best course of action is to secure photographs of the bite-mark wounds. If the material is other than skin, consideration must be given to casting the object. Bite marks are usually found in materials which cannot be kept for long periods of time; once the materials have dried up or decomposed, the bite mark's appearance will change drastically and be of no value to the odontologist. It is therefore imperative to obtain photographs or casts of the bite mark before the material begins to change. Even if an object is to be cast, the bite mark should first be photographed in case the casting goes wrong. These first photographs are usually taken by the police photographer at the scene, followed by medical examiner photographs taken at autopsy. I recommend that the investigator take photos of any pattern of injury he or she observes on the body while at the scene, giving special attention to any ovoid-shaped wounds or marks which are less than two inches in diameter.

The following procedures at the crime scene are recommended.

PHOTOGRAPHS OF THE BITE-MARK WOUND
1. The best type of camera to utilize is the Fingerprint type, which gives a 1 × 1 exposure or life-size photo of the wound.
2. Use a rule of measure in the photo to document size. (The rule

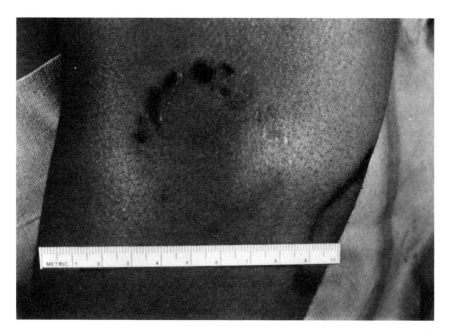

Photograph of Bite-Mark Wound with Ruler in Place to Show Actual Size. (*Courtesy of* Dr. Arthur D. Goldman, Forensic Odontologist.)

which is used should not be white in color because white is not conducive to enhancement.)

3. Use oblique lighting to enhance bite mark.
4. Provide for an anatomical landmark in photo.
5. Take photos in black-and-white and color.
6. Take an overall photo and a close-up of each wound.
7. Do *not* throw away any "bad" shots but save all negatives and photos. They are evidence.

SALIVA WASHINGS

1. Take a saliva washing of the bite-mark area for a blood grouping and serological examination.
2. Washing should be done with distilled water and 100 percent cotton. Start at the periphery and work inward, use a separate swab for each bite mark. (If there is no distilled water available, use tap water, but take a control sample for examination.)
3. Air dry each swab.
4. Place each swab in a separate container, preferably a sterile test tube.

5. Take a saliva swab from victim for control.
6. Take a controlled swab from an area of the body other than bite mark.
7. Label each sample; keep items separate.

Remember, always keep track of the chain of custody.

Interpretation of the Bite-Mark Evidence

The interpretation of the bite mark requires the forensic odontologist to consider at least four factors:

1. The teeth of the biter.
2. Distortion.
3. The mental state of the biter at the time the bite was inflicted.
4. The portion of the body upon which the bite was inflicted.

Bite marks have been found almost everywhere on the body. However, certain patterns are most prominent in particular kinds of cases. For example, homosexual cases often involve bite marks of the back, arms, shoulders, axillae (armpits), face, and scrotum of the victim. Heterosexual cases usually involve the breasts and thighs. Battered children most often have randomly placed bite marks on the cheeks, back, and sides. However, bite marks on battered children have also been found on the abdomen, scrotum, and buttocks. In child cases, the biting seems to be done in a rapid, random, and enraged manner leaving tissue laceration, diffuse areas, and poor detail, as opposed to sexually associated bite marks, usually inflicted in a slow and sadistic manner and resulting in excellent detail.

Factors such as size and shape are helpful in establishing whether the bite mark was inflicted by a human being or an animal. If the bite mark is human, the time it was inflicted (antemortem or postmortem), tissue reaction of the surrounding area, and position of the body when found are all taken into consideration by the odontologist.

Examination of the Bite Mark

The examination of the bite mark by a forensic odontologist can generally provide the investigator with sufficient information to rapidly include or exclude a suspect in a particular investigation. For instance, in a case involving a battered child, only a limited number of persons would have the opportunity to bite and murder the child. The suspect in such cases might include one or two adults (the mother and father) and siblings. On the basis of the size of the arch, the forensic odontologist can usually determine whether the attacker was an adult or a child. In addition, there may be enough individual characteristics (wear, missing teeth, dental restorations, rotations, arch form, etc.) to exclude all but the perpetrator of the bite.

The forensic examination includes the following procedures:

1. Saliva washings of the area for blood grouping (using 100 percent cotton dampened in distilled water).
2. Photographs of the bite mark:
   a. 1 × 1 camera fingerprint type model,
   b. Black and white and color photographs,
   c. Rule of measure,
   d. Anatomical landmark.
3. Examination of dental casts of possible suspects. Models of the teeth of all suspects which will subsequently be used for comparisons are taken only by informed consent or by court order. The models are made either by the forensic odontologist or another licensed dentist. This varies from case to case and from court order to court order. All models, however, are made according to accepted dental standards and labeled for evidentiary purposes.
4. Comparisons are made of the life-size photographs of the bite marks with bite marks made in wax either by the suspect or by models of the suspect's teeth.
5. A report is prepared indicating whether the bite marks are or are not consistent with the teeth of the suspect.

Summary

The application of forensic odontology to bite-mark identification, and matching a serological group with a saliva washing of the suspected bite mark, are two viable investigative techniques which can provide the investigator with the necessary evidence to present a case for prosecution.

Bite-mark identification has been recognized by the superior courts of several jurisdictions in noteworthy homicide trials. It is the opinion of the author that this excellent investigative technique should be utilized in every case of homicide involving bite marks. Even in cases where there has been a confession or other evidence linking the suspect to the crime, bite-mark evidence should still be obtained and submitted to the forensic odontologist. There is no such thing as "enough evidence" in homicide prosecution.

Remember, bite-mark identification represents individual characteristic evidence which can positively identify a suspect.

Hypnosis

The purpose of this section is to acquaint the homicide detective with the utilization of hypnosis in murder investigations.[2] In addition, there is a discussion of *psychodynamics*, the science pertaining to motives and other causative factors in mental life, and how these factors can affect the outcome of an investigation.

What Is Hypnosis?

The word *hypnosis* is derived from the Greek word *hypnos* which means "sleep." However, the person under hypnosis is not really asleep but is aware of his or her surroundings. Hypnosis may be defined as "an altered state of consciousness involving focused attention, heightened awareness, and concentration."[3] The person in a hypnotic state can increase his or her capacity to restructure events by reorganizing his or her usual perceptions of things.

Psychodynamics. In order to comprehend how hypnosis works, it is useful to understand the systems of the mind referred to as the *conscious, preconscious,* and *unconscious.* The *conscious* consists of the thoughts, feelings, and actions we are aware of. The *preconscious* includes mental activity that we can be aware of if we attend to it. It will receive and remember those impressions that are classified as "safe," i.e., that have passed the screening of the ego's defenses. According to Sgt. Byrnes, these defenses ward off that which is dangerous and harmful to the ego. The *unconscious* contains all the rest of our memories, including the "unsafe" ones, which are not available, for recall. This is why witnesses to very traumatic crime situations, such as homicides are often unable to recall what they have seen. The investigator should be aware that this is not a deliberate effort on the part of these individuals to frustrate the investigation. They may very well not recall "seeing" the details of the incident in the trauma situation.

The unconscious consists of approximately seven-eighths of the brain. It not only receives repressed material that has been blocked by the defenses and classified as "harmful," but also stores impulses which were conscious and preconscious at one time. Furthermore, it

---

[2]The technical data on hypnosis are based on materials and information provided by Sergeant Timothy P. Byrnes, Commanding Officer of the New York City Police Department's Hypnosis Unit.

[3]Martin Reiser. *Handbook of Investigative Hypnosis.* Los Angeles, California: Lehi Publishing, Co., 1980, p. 30.

is alert to responses on a twenty-four-hour-a-day basis. It never sleeps. It records every stimulus regardless of the condition of the conscious of the individual. Thus, in spite of intoxication or trauma, accurate records are being received and recorded by the senses and stored in the subconscious.

Value to the Investigator

Hypnosis offers the homicide investigator a means of obtaining additional information, and its application in certain murder investigations has been very effective. Hypnosis has been used to enable people to recall names, places, or details including the actual verbalizations which took place during the crime. In addition, there are many cases in which persons under hypnosis have described vehicles including make, model, color, and complete license number.

When a person is hypnotized, the conscious mind is somewhat subdued. This allows the subconscious to become a little more active. When the hypnotist talks to the person under hypnosis, the subconscious mind is more acceptable to what it is told and governs the body accordingly. In other words, a person in a hypnotic state is prone to the suggestions of the hypnotist who acts as a guide. Thus, hypnosis and other related techniques designed to remove trauma may enable the subject to recall that which was stored in the subconscious and relate this information to the hypnotist in a clear and concise fashion.

Shortcomings of Hypnosis

There are some shortcomings of hypnosis which should be understood by the investigator prior to using this technique.

1. People can lie while under hypnosis. Although it is not policy to routinely explain this to the subject to be hypnotized, it should be noted that if the investigator seeks to know whether or not the subject is telling the truth, the polygraph should be employed. Hypnosis is not truth serum.
2. People see and remember things in various manners. Recollection may be colored by previous experience. Therefore, memory of numbers, letters, or phrases can be jumbled or mistakenly affiliated with previous associations.
3. The investigator must be vigilant about *confabulation*, whereby the mind fills in memory gaps with imagined or distorted information.

Case History

The following case history is typical of those handled by the New York City Police Department's Hypnosis Unit.

An investigator called the unit and stated that he had reached a dead end in his investigation. He remarked that he only had one witness, who had looked out a window after the shooting. This witness was very quiet in nature but told police that the auto which the suspect had fled in was brown, and he was able to supply one number of the license plate.

At a prehypnosis introduction, Sgt. Byrnes noticed that the subject wore heavy, dark glasses that covered his eyes and part of his face. He spoke very little and nodded his yes-and-no answers, rather than saying them.

In conforming with legal parameters, the hypnotist was given limited information—only the subject's name, that he was a college graduate who lived alone, and that he had looked out the window after the shooting.

During the prehypnosis interview, the subject again only nodded when asked questions. Finally, when asked to relate the incident that he had witnessed, he replied slowly and with some difficulty. He suffered from a nervous condition of stammering, which was in fact totally out of character for this young educated individual. Apparently he was conscious of this condition and chose not to speak at length in order to avoid making the condition known to others.

Under hypnosis, Sgt. Byrnes asked him to remove his glasses, (and thereby shed a defense mechanism). The subject did so and the session proceeded without incident until the discussion finally returned to the date and time in question. At that point, to the amazement of both Sgt. Byrnes and the investigator, the subject began to rapidly relate the details of the incident without even a trace of stammering. In addition, he provided the entire license plate number (explaining how he remembered the numbers in his own method of association), the type of vehicle, the conversation that he had heard immediately after the shooting, the description of the suspect, his route of travel, the fact that he had stopped and had a conversation with another person on a distant corner, and the fact that another person was present and had voiced his horror about the shooting (thereby supplying an additional witness to the crime).

As a direct result, the investigator was able to continue his investigation and eventually independently verify the veracity of the statements made by the subject under hypnosis. The result was an indictment for murder.

Sgt. Byrnes adds as a postscript that the subject of the hypnosis, immediately after the session, returned to his previous stammering condition.

Summary

Practically speaking, most law enforcement agencies using hypnosis have found this technique to be quite successful. It should be noted, however, that hypnosis is not the final answer. Any information obtained through this method must be independently corroborated by further investigation. From an investigative point of view, hypnosis may provide the police with additional facts and information and should be viewed as an additional investigative tool.

Latent Prints on Human Skin

There have been some recent advances in forensic science in the area of latent print development from human skin. The development of latent prints on human skin can be extremely valuable in homicide investigations and other crimes in which the perpetrator has touched the victim. Some of the methods used are simple and inexpensive, while other more advanced techniques require the use of a laser and other sophisticated equipment. The techniques presented in this section will be limited to those simple and practical methods which the average investigator can employ at the scene.

These methods are still in an experimental stage and may not be effective in all instances. However, their application should be encouraged, since fingerprints represent the ultimate piece of physical evidence in any criminal investigation. In homicide cases their presence takes on an added value because the victim, who is deceased, will never be able to "point the finger" at the suspect.

General Considerations

Experiments conducted in developing latent prints on human skin indicate that fingerprints on living skin seem to last for approximately 1 to 1½ hours. In dead-body cases it is recommended that these procedures be employed as soon as possible. The state of the skin and atmospheric conditions will affect results. The ideal temperature is between 60 and 75 degrees Fahrenheit.

Procedures

1. Kromekote lift technique or unexposed Polaroid film. This method involves the use of the following equipment:

a. Fiberglass filament brush
b. Black fingerprint powder
c. Kromekote cards (5 × 7)[4]
d. Unexposed Polaroid film can be substituted for Kromekote.

The Kromekote card or unexposed polaroid film is placed over the area of the skin where the suspected latent print is located, and pressure is applied to the card or film piece for approximately three seconds. The card or film is then carefully removed and dusted with the black fingerprint powder to develop the print which was transferred onto the card or film. The latent print obtained will be a mirror image of a normal print and can be reversed through photography.

2. Magna-Brush and powder direct to the skin: This method may be employed in the absence of Kromekote or unexposed Polaroid film, or in addition to the above procedure. The following equipment is necessary:
   a. Magna-Brush with magnetic powders
   b. Fiberglass filament brush with volcanic powders. The powder is applied directly to the skin. The use of volcanic or magnetic powders depends on the condition of the skin. When the skin is dry, you may obtain better results with the magnetic powder. If a print is developed, it should first be photographed using a 1 × 1 fingerprint camera. It is then lifted in conventional fashion, using cellophane "lifting" tape.

Certain areas of the body will usually yield latent prints, because these areas are usually touched by the perpetrator, for example,

Upper arms of the victim

Areas directly behind the ear and ear lobe

Inner thighs directly below the crotch area (sex cases)

Heels and skin around the ankles (body dragged)

The neck area

Wrists

3. The Iodine-Silver Transfer Method.[5] The equipment needed for this procedure is as follows:
   a. Conventional iodine fuming gun
   b. A number of silver sheets approximately 2" square. These silver

---

[4]The cards are similar to photographic paper, with a very high gloss. They are manufactured by various companies; however, unexposed Polaroid film can be used.

[5]The following description is based on information in the FBI *Police Instructor's Bulletin*, Quantico, Va.: Law Enforcement Training Division, 1976. The information compiled in this document was based on research by Robert J. Hazen and Clarence E. Phillips, both Supervising Fingerprint Specialists assigned to the FBI Training Division in Quantico, Virginia.

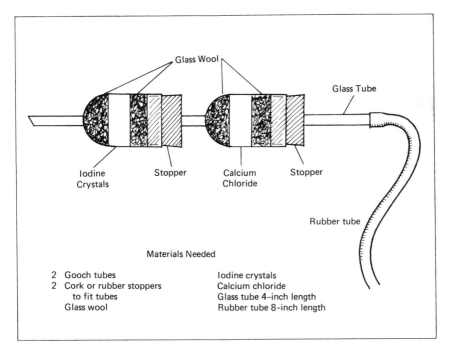

Materials Needed

2 Gooch tubes	Iodine crystals
2 Cork or rubber stoppers	Calcium chloride
to fit tubes	Glass tube 4-inch length
Glass wool	Rubber tube 8-inch length

The Iodine Gun.

sheets should be between .005 and .010 inches thick in order to conform to the skin surface. These sheets can be cleaned with whiting or silver polish and may be reused.

c. A strong light (photoflood light is ideal).

There are four basic steps in this process, as follows.

1. Fume the skin tissue with vapor from the iodine gun.
2. Press the silver plate directly onto the skin, covering the area where the latent prints are believed to be.
3. Remove the silver plate.
4. Expose the silver plate to the strong light.

It should be noted that the prints on the silver sheets are laterally inverted; i.e., the left side of the print on the silver sheet corresponds to the right side of the original print. In order to reproduce the position correctly, it will be necessary when preparing prints on the negative to place the glossy side of the negative next to the emulsion side of the printing paper.[6]

---

[6]Further information on this technique can be obtained by writing to the Law Enforcement Arts Research Unit, FBI Training Division, Quantico, Virginia 22135.

Polygraph Examinations

The purpose of this section is to familiarize the homicide investigator with the utilization of the *polygraph*—or, as it is more commonly referred to, the lie detector—in homicide investigations.[7]

Basically, the polygraph examination uses mechanical and electronic instrumentation to graphically record the physiological changes that take place in persons questioned under controlled conditions. Changes in cardiovascular activity, respiratory activity, and galvanic skin reflex are recorded on a moving chart as the examiner asks the subject specific questions. These charts are then evaluated to determine whether or not the person's answers were truthful, untruthful, or inconclusive.

Although polygraph results are generally inadmissible in a court of law unless an agreement and stipulation by counsel is obtained, the test can be very useful to the investigators during a homicide investigation. For example, during the early stages of the investigation when the number of suspects is large, the polygraph can be utilized to eliminate certain suspects so that investigative resources can be employed more productively.

The proper and intelligent utilization of the polygraph coupled with the ability and expertise of the polygraph examiner may be able to do what the deceased cannot; "point the investigation in the right direction."

The Examination

The polygraph is always a supplement to a good field investigation and never a substitute for it. Often the results of a polygraph examination will be only as good as the information developed by field investigation. The polygraphist should be consulted at the early stages of the investigation as to the feasibility of using the polygraph in the investigation; it should never be used as a last resort.

Polygraphs are conducted on a strictly voluntary basis. The subject cannot be forced into taking an examination, and the examination cannot be rushed. A properly conducted polygraph test lasts approximately two hours or more depending on the circumstances of the case.

There are four phases of a polygraph examination.

1. *First phase—pretest interview.* The polygraphist learns about the

---

[7]The information and technical data presented herein was provided by Detective Donald F. Sullivan of the New York City Police Department.

subject's medical history, physical condition, and psychological background. The pretest interview determines whether the subject is capable of taking the examination.

2. *Second phase—explanation of how the polygraph works.* During this phase the polygraphist discusses the crime with the subject, and he has the subject explain what he knows, if anything, about the crime. The polygraphist is looking for any changes in the subject's original statement given to the investigator.
3. *Third phase—preparation of test questions.* The subject is aware of the questions to be asked and there are no surprise questions. If the subject objects to one of the questions, the question is either changed or eliminated.
4. *Fourth phase—the actual testing.* After the examination, the polygraphist analyzes the charts and then renders one of three opinions: truthful, lying, or inconclusive. It must be noted that re-examinations are necessary in some cases.

Possible Subjects for Polygraph Examinations

The majority of examinations are conducted with suspects. If suspects are to be questioned, they should be advised of their rights prior to testing. If the suspect has an attorney, the polygraphist should have the attorney witness the waiver.

Informants may also be tested to ascertain that the information being supplied to the investigator is correct. Witnesses may be tested for the same reason, as well as to see if they are withholding any other details pertinent to the crime.

Subjects that Cannot Be Tested

Persons with physical disabilities, such as a serious heart condition (verified by a doctor), should not be tested, nor should pregnant women.

Investigator's Duties Prior to the Examination

The investigator should provide the polygraphist with correct and adequate case facts and not withhold anything from him or her.

Remember, homicide investigation requires a teamwork approach. The polygraphist and the investigator must work together in order to be successful.

The polygraphist must know the subject's history. The investigator should provide the polygraphist with the following information:

1. Prior record, especially any arrests or investigations for a similar crime.
2. Possible motive for committing the crime.
3. Religion and how faithful.
4. Financial status.
5. Anything else the investigator can think of that might be of value to the polygraphist to get an insight into the subject.

The subject should be properly prepared for the examination. Like other physical evidence, he or she should be handled with care so that the examination can be done properly.

The investigator should find out why this person initially decided to take the test and the person's attitude toward it. The investigator should never assume the subject's truthfulness based solely on the fact that the subject agrees to take an examination. Any police polygraphist will show you cases of confirmed liars who are willing to take a polygraph examination.

Needless to say, certain information about the crime should always be withheld from all parties, including the news media, prior to the examination. The investigator should take the polygraphist into his or her confidence and inform the examiner of facts about the crime, which only the one who committed the crime or who was present when the crime was committed would know, for example, how the person was killed; where the entry was made; what weapon was used; what items were stolen or removed from scene; or unusual facts about the crime, such as sex mutilation, tying up of victim, etc.

Polygraph Procedures

The polygraphist usually has the final decision on who can be tested, when the examination will begin, and whether or not the examination will continue.

Never use the polygraph as a bluff. The subject should only be asked if he is willing to take an examination when the investigator fully intends to have the subject examined.

The polygraphist is responsible for the issues to be covered in the examination. The exact wording of all test questions on the examination should be decided by the investigator and the polygraphist after conferral with each other regarding the facts of the case. Only one crime will be covered during the examination. If the subject is suspected of committing other crimes, then separate examinations should be conducted at later dates.

The polygraph examination should be conducted, if possible, first thing in the morning after the subject has had a night's sleep. On the day of the examination, the investigator should not interrogate the subject. When a person agrees to the polygraph, the investigators should cease all interrogation until after the completion of the examination.

Summary

The polygraph is an investigative aid and a supplement to a good field investigation. The homocide detective should be encouraged to use this tool and to discuss its capabilities with the polygraphist who will conduct the examination. The polygraph examination is not admissible in a court of law; however, statements made to a polygraphist are admissible. The polygraph represents an extremely valuable technique in homicide investigation when employed by a competent technician working as a member of the investigative team.

Psycholinguistics

The purpose of this section is to acquaint the investigator with psycholinguistic analysis and explain how this technique can be utilized to obtain information on the origin, background, and psychology of a homicide suspect who communicates with the authorities. The communication can either be verbal or written.[8]

What Is Psycholinguistic Analysis?

Psycholinguistic analysis is a sophisticated method of examining the spoken or written communication for clues as to origins, background, and psychology of the speaker or writer. Every sentence, phrase, syllable, word, pause, and comma is automatically scanned by computer for what it can reveal about the person who has communicated the message. These messages can also establish the author's identity by comparison with other messages whose authors are known. Psycholinguistic analysis combines the two disciplines of psychology and linguistics to provide an understanding of the type of personality who has originated the communication as well as a strategy for dealing with such persons. Although the primary purpose of the program, initiated by

---

[8] The material presented herein is based on documents and information supplied by the FBI and on personal interviews with Dr. Murray S. Miron, a professor at Syracuse University, who has performed extensive research in the area of psycholinguistic analysis.

Professor Miron, was to analyze threats in connection with terrorist activities, psycholinguistics can provide the homicide detective with an effective investigative tool to identify certain suspects who taunt police with verbal or written communications.

Methodology

Upon receipt of the message or communication, the psycholinguistic expert enters the information into a computer by means of a terminal keyboard. The computer then scans the message and assigns each word to a set of categories which research has identified as important in the characterization of a threat. In addition, the computer tabulates occurrences of such things as punctuation, speech hesitancies, misspellings, and sentence structure.

The computer used to analyze a wide range of threats over the years has established what is referred to as a "threat dictionary." This threat dictionary has continued to grow in size and comprehensiveness, composing more than 350 categories representing more than 250,000 words. These threats range from suicide notes to terrorist communications, including both hoaxes and threats which have actually been carried out. Furthermore, the computer stores over 15 million words gathered from analyses of ordinary spoken and written English. Any unusual usages or word occurrences which differ from this stored data are flagged by the computer for closer analysis. By weighing the vocabulary usages of an author or speaker against the usage employed by the average speaker, the psycholinguistic expert can derive a set of "signature" words which are unique to an individual and which can be expected to match across differing communications.

Case History

The following case history represents the sort of information that psycholinguistic techniques can provide to law enforcement.[9]

Prepared from communications received from an unidentified subject (UNSUB) who threatened a flight from New York to Geneva, Switzerland, Dr. Miron drew several conclusions. On the basis of psycholinguistic analyses, he judged that the UNSUB was a German-born male of at least fifty years of age who had immigrated to the United States as an adult and had resided in this country for at least twenty years. Further, the analyses indicated that the UNSUB had

---

[9] Reprinted from Murray S. Miron and John E. Douglas, "Threat Analysis—The Psycholinguistic Approach," *FBI Law Enforcement Bulletin*, September, 1979.

probably written previous messages to prominent officials in both the United States and Germany. Perhaps most revealing was the conclusion that the perpetrator's personality compelled him to leave clues as to his identity in the message itself. At the conclusion of the extortion message, there was a series of three-digit code numbers which seemed to correspond to the fictitious name of the group UNSUB claimed he directed. The following code appeared at the end of the message:

> Sig: 604 247 945 305 734 430
> 915 837 907 Reciprocal Relief
> Alliance for Peace, Justice and
> Freedom Everywhere

Each of the nine code groups appears to correspond to the nine words of the group name. No words are duplicated in the group name or in the three-digit code groups.

However, if the code groups are rearranged so that each group is written as a column of numbers, the code would look as follows:

$$6 \ 2 \ 9 \ 3 \ 7 \ 4 \ 9 \ 8 \ 9$$
$$0 \ 4 \ 4 \ 0 \ 3 \ 3 \ 1 \ 3 \ 0$$
$$4 \ 7 \ 5 \ 5 \ 4 \ 0 \ 5 \ 7 \ 7$$

When arranged in this way, the first three code numbers, 6 2 9, correspond to the alphabet letters of FBI. Using a standard coding device which employs a displacement key for the remaining text, the next code groups translate as "IM" followed by two initials repeated twice. Together the translation would read "FBI, I'm JK JK." A search of the names of the passengers on the flight revealed that one of the travelers matched the profile description and part of the initials of the deciphered code. Search of the records revealed that this passenger had written and signed his name to a series of similar messages written in 1969. Subsequent psycholinguistic comparisons established that these earlier messages were written by the same suspect. After this identification, the psycholinguistic tools were then used to suggest methods for conducting the interview with the suspect. Using the clues gleaned from the messages as to the personality of the suspect, specific stratagems for approaching him were devised. These involved predictions as to how the subject would react, and whether or not he might contemplate suicide or escape.

Psycholinguistics As an Investigative Tool

One of the more dramatic applications of psycholinguistic methods by Dr. Miron took place during the Patricia Hearst case. Soon after the first of the tape recordings sent by the Symbionese Liberation Army (SLA) had been received by the authorities, Dr. Miron prepared a series of reports for the FBI. He described the individual calling himself "Cinque" as one who fit the known background of Donald DeFreeze. Perhaps more important, these reports predicted that Patricia Hearst would join the SLA and commit some criminal acts with them. The analyses further indicated that DeFreeze and his followers were suicidal and that they would undoubtedly die in a final shootout with the authorities rather than surrender.

Practically speaking, the use of this technique in the investigation of homicide is limited to those occasions when the murderer chooses to communicate with or taunt the police with his messages. However, when such communications are received during a murder investigation, psycholinguistic analysis can be invaluable in providing authorities with an insight into the personality type of the suspect. The "Son of Sam" case in New York City is a good example of the type of homicide case in which psycholinguistics has been used.

In this particular investigation, the killer David Berkowitz, who called himself the "Son of Sam," roamed through the streets seeking out young couples and then gunning them down with a .44-caliber revolver. In a series of cryptic messages which he sent to a local newspaper, he claimed that he was acting under instructions communicated to him by a neighbor's dog.

The psycholinguistic method drew a profile of this killer early in the investigation which later turned out to closely fit the subject. Despite the fact that several eye-witness reports had indicated that the killer was in his mid-thirties (Berkowitz had a receding hairline), the psycholinguistic profile based on the written communications correctly placed the killer's age between 20 and 25. As an indication of just how detailed such a profile can be, even though based only upon what the perpetrator may choose to write or say, Dr. Miron's profile of Berkowitz included the information that the killer was of average height and overweight (he was both), that his mother was either dead or separated from the family (Berkowitz had been adopted and his adoptive mother had died when he was fourteen), that his father was ill or aged (he was retired), and that Berkowitz would continue to attack young attractive women until caught and when finally caught would surrender meekly to the authorities, as he eventually did.

According to Dr. Miron, a typical psycholinguistic profile consists of three sections. First, and most important from the standpoint of the homicide investigator, is a demographic profile of the author of the communication which attempts to identify the author's age, sex, birthplace, and other details that can be gleaned from the communication. Second, the profile presents such aspects of the psychology of the author as his or her motivations, personality, and pathology, if any. Finally, the profile provides an assessment of the determination and capabilities of the writer to carry out the threatened or claimed actions.

Utilizing Psycholinguistic Analysis

Requests for psycholinguistic analysis should be made through the Technical Evaluation Unit (TEU) of the FBI. The request can be made through the local FBI field office covering the jurisdiction requesting this service, or can be sent direct to the following address:

Federal Bureau of Investigation Hdq.
Technical Evaluation Unit
F.B.I. Laboratory Division
J. Edgar Hoover Building
10th and Pennsylvania Ave
Washington, D.C. 20535

A request for psycholinguistic analysis should include reference to any previous communications or correspondence submitted to the laboratory in the case, and the facts concerning the violation insofar as they pertain to the specific laboratory examination. For further information refer to Chapter 12.

Summary

This method of investigation is still considered to be in a developmental stage, and its adaptability to homicide investigation is limited to those cases in which there is some form of communication. The investigator should be aware of its limitations and not assume that psycholinguistics can replace traditional homicide investigation procedures. However, psycholinguistic analysis has proven to be a valuable investigative tool in those cases where it has been used. In homicide cases psycholinguistics has been used in just about every major investigation, from the Alphabet Bomber to the Zodiac and Zebra Kebra Killing.

Psychics

The professional homicide detective utilizes many tools in the investigation to assist in the retrieval of information, some of which may be inaccessible through ordinary methods. A somewhat sensational and often controversial practice is the use of psychics. The purpose of this section is to provide the investigator with information on the use of a psychic in homicide investigations.[10]

Practically speaking, police officers are naturally skeptical of psychics and psychic phenomena. However, from an investigative point of view, anything which has proven to be successful in one investigation should certainly be considered in other cases. It should be noted that information provided by the psychic may not always be accurate and in some instances may have no value to the investigation. However, this should not discourage authorities from using a psychic, especially in homicide cases where there is limited information. The use of a psychic can be considered as an additional investigative aid.

What Is a Psychic?

A *psychic* is a person who is especially sensitive to nonphysical forces of life energy. According to Ms. Renier, being a psychic "involves getting rid of logic and rationale." A psychic is not someone with magical or mystical powers. Instead, the psychic is a person who learns to control a portion of the brain which is not generally used in order to see and feel things which the average person cannot experience.

How Can the Police and Psychics Work Together?

The police and the psychic must understand each other's roles and respect each other's expertise before a proper working relationship can be developed. The credibility of the psychic will ultimately be tested by performance and results. However, the police have a responsibility to assure that the psychic is properly handled.

Before an agency decides to seek the assistance of a psychic, certain facts must be considered. The first consideration is that there is very limited information and knowledge on how psychics perform. Each psychic has his or her own distinctive method of operation. The second consideration is how to know whether or not the psychic is "legitimate." This is very difficult to ascertain, because even those scientists involved in the study of these phenomena cannot provide definitive guides for law enforcement. There is an abundance of exaggeration and

---

[10] The information presented in this section is based on research of specific cases, personal interviews, and correspondence with several psychics including Ms. Noreen Renier, a psychic and recognized authority on the phenomena of extrasensory perception. Ms. Renier has worked with various police agencies including the FBI on homicide cases and other criminal investigations.

sensationalism attached to psychic phenomena, yet there have been a number of instances where information provided by a psychic has been beneficial to authorities.

It should be noted that the police and not the psychic solve crime. Ideally, the psychic will be able to provide clues and information for the police to act on. The psychic should therefore be considered as an aid in developing clues that are not recognizable to the police. The police should then provide the necessary follow-up investigation in order to corroborate the information provided by the psychic.

In order to present the reader with an insight into how the police and psychic can work together, I have provided Ms. Renier's personal comments on her method of procedure and technique.

Ms. Renier states, "Because a psychic is usually called into an investigation as a last resort, when little or no clues to the identity of the criminal have been uncovered, there is often a lot of skepticism on the part of the police. First, because they do not understand psychic phenomena. The police deal in logic and hard facts and usually have never worked with a psychic. They have strong doubts. Secondly, a psychic is not a police officer and therefore is considered an outsider. I, as a psychic, have to contend with these areas of negativism before I even start to work on the crime. If the people I am working with are filled with doubts and animosity, I will pick-up on these feelings and it will definitely hamper my work.

"I prefer murder cases, but will work on other crimes as well. I prefer *not* to know any details of the crime or personal backgroud of the victim. I need only to know the first name of the victim and the type of case I am working on in order to use my talents. For example, Alice/ Murder.

"I also like to hold an object that was on the victim at the time of the murder. I prefer metal objects, such as a ring or watch." This technique is called *psychometry*. Ms. Renier states that she is able to tune into impressions or vibrations left by the owner in or around metal objects. For example, the earring of a murder victim was sent to Ms. Renier by Michigan police. She was able, through psychometry, to reconstruct what the victim looked like, where she lived, what the house looked like, and how the victim was killed. In addition, she states that she "saw" the murderer washing his hands and combing his hair. She even "saw" the tattoos on his arms. She was able to describe this person to the police, who later arrested their suspect based on physical evidence developed during the investigation.

"I try to see physically what the victim looked like. I then try to recreate the scene of the murder. I do these things for two reasons.

"First, to make sure that I am tuning into the correct case, and secondly, to give the police confidence in me as a psychic.

"Once the police start believing I'm real, and can do the things I say I can, we can continue.

"As I describe the victim and the scene of the crime, I insist on feedback. A simple 'Yes' or 'I understand' is sufficient. I do not need additional clues or information.

"After describing the victim and the scene of the crime, if it is a murder, I try to feel the way the person was murdered. I switch from psychic 'seeing' to psychic 'feeling.' During the session I will use all of my five senses to a degree which is beyond the average person. I have been 'shot,' 'stabbed,' and 'strangled' numerous times during this psychic 'feeling.' This usually is painful, since I can actually feel where the bullet or knife entered 'my' body. I often moan and groan. However, I can shake this feeling off instantly. The people who I am working with should understand this and not become upset for me. At this point, I have satisfied myself, and hopefully the police, who are present, that I am 'tuned' into the case.

"I then like to describe the murderer. I explain to the police before we start the session how to question me. If they have not asked questions before, it is important that they do so now. I can see the murderer but the way I am questioned will help me see him or her more clearly. The police can then obtain the necessary information to help them apprehend this person. It is helpful to have a police or quick sketch artist on hand to sketch the face I describe.

"Besides the murderer's appearance, I am able to go into his or her personality, mode of travel from the scene, etc. I can even switch back and become the victim again, whatever the police investigators request me to do.

"One thing which is vitally important, is how the police phrase the questions. They have to question me in a casual, gentle manner. I cannot be interrogated like a criminal, even when I am playing the part of the criminal. There should be no leading type questions, such as 'Is his hair black?' Instead, the question should be, 'What is the color of his hair?' Preferably, there should be no series of 'Yes' and 'No' questions, as sometimes I lose my train of thought. If it looks like I'm dying down, the question must be rephrased or I must be redirected. If an answer is unclear, it should be rephrased. If an answer doesn't sound right, instead of a negative, 'No, no you're all wrong,' I prefer, 'Let's go back to that later.' I may be slightly off in my interpretation of what I see, or maybe what I see is true, but totally unbelievable at that point. Sometimes, when we go back later, it will be clearer or 'fit in.' "

It should be noted that Ms. Renier does not claim to be 100 percent accurate in her interpretations, nor does she claim to be able to work on all cases equally well.

As far as the police working with the psychic, it has been determined that psychics respond better and are more accurate when the individuals working with them have a positive attitude.

Practically speaking, if an officer feels that he or she cannot accept or work with the psychic, then this officer should not get involved in this segment of the investigation. Instead, someone who may be skeptical, but is able to put aside this personal prejudice, should be assigned to work with the psychic.

Charlatans and Frauds

The agency which decides to utilize the psychic in a particular investigation should first establish the authenticity of the psychic by routine inquiry. Generally speaking, the decision to use a psychic is based on a report of a successful investigation attributed to psychic phenomena. This report may appear in a local newspaper or come about by word of mouth. Official contact and interagency communication will usually indicate whether or not the psychic was of any investigative value.

It is important to note that charlatans and frauds exist in all professions. However, they fluorish in the area of extrasensory perception. From an investigative point of view, the best way to avoid being taken in by a phony psychic is in the proper handling and control of this person. For example, many frauds merely "feed back" information to the police which is already a matter of public record, having read a newspaper account of the crime. Or a fraud may have access to information on the case through family members or "official leaks" which give the impression that he or she has some psychic knowledge of events.

It should be noted that the police should not be telling the psychic, the psychic should be telling the police. Once the agency decides to employ the services of the psychic, all information supplied about the case to the psychic, and all information provided by the psychic, should flow through one contact officer, in order to maintain proper control. In addition, certain facts should be purposely withheld from the psychic in order to maintain the integrity of the investigation and assure that the information provided by the psychic is genuine and not the result of the police investigation. All conversations relative to the psychic investigation should be taped. This is extremely important, since psychics can generate a tremendous amount of information in a short span of time. Also this information is often in the form of disjointed impressions. An investigator cannot be expected to accurately take notes and intelligently formulate questions in the face of such voluminous information. Later on the tape can be analyzed by other investigators for acuracy and follow-up, and additional questions can be formulated. Furthermore, the tape serves as a control and documentation of the information exchanged.

According to Ms. Renier, the reason for an abundance of phonies in the area of extrasensory perception is that the average person is ignorant about psychic phenomena. Wherever there is lack of knowledge, it is easy to trick and deceive people. The phonies like conditions they can control. They do a lot of key bending and blindfold tricks which are impressive. Their clarity and accuracy are usually overwhelming. Even individuals who have been involved in psychic phenomena for years are sometimes deceived by these frauds. Real psychics are human, and therefore are subject to error.

Conscious of the poor image the public has of psychics, Ms. Renier advocates strict licensing procedures by a recognized board. She states that if there were proper testing and licensing procedures, psychic ability could be proven and properly evaluated before official recognition. This would not only legitimize psychics in the eyes of the public, but could also serve as a referral system.

At present there are no plans for such a system, but there are groups involved in researching this phenomenon. If a law enforcement agency is interested in utilizing a psychic, a representative of the agency should contact one of these groups. Dr. Karlis Osis of the American Society for Psychical Research, which is a respected and conservative organization involved in the study of this phenomenon, can be contacted at 5 West 73rd Street, New York, N.Y. 10023. The telephone number is (212) 799-5050.

Summary

Empirical research into psychic phenomena has been limited, and there just isn't any "hard" research data available to indicate an accurate percentage of cases materially aided by the use of psychic phenomena. However, investigatively speaking, there has been sufficient documentation of successes to merit the consideration of this technique on a case-by-case basis.

The police have much to learn about the relative value of psychic phenomena in criminal investigations. Furthermore, there is a definite need for an evaluation of the successes and failures of psychic phenomena as they relate to law enforcement before they can be recognized as a "legitimate" investigative tool. Perhaps in time, the psychic and the homicide investigator may form the perfect partnership against crime. In any event, I neither encourage nor discourage the use of psychics in homicide investigations.

The author wishes to acknowledge the assistance of Dr. Lowell J. Levine for the technical information and for contributing the case histories in the section on bite marks.

The author also wishes to acknowledge the contribution of Sgt. Timothy Byrnes. He holds a B.S. Degree from St. John's University and an M.A. from John Jay College of

Selected Reading

Bite Mark Identification
Levine, Lowell J. "Forensic Odontology Today—A New Forensic Science." FBI Law Enforcement Bulletin, August 1972.
Levine, Lowell J. "Bite Mark Evidence." *Dental Clinics of North America* 21 (1977).
Sperber, Norman D. "Bite Mark Evidence in Crimes Against Persons." FBI Law Enforcement Bulletin, July 1981.

Hypnosis
Reiser, Martin (Ed.). *Handbook of Investigative Hypnosis.* Los Angeles, California: Lehi Publishing Co., 1980.

Latent Prints on Human Skin
Federal Bureau of Investigation. *Police Instructor's Bulletin.* Quantico, Virginia: Law Enforcement Training Division, 1976.
Svensson, Arne, Wendel, Otto, and Fisher, Barry A. J. *Techniques of Crime Scene Investigation,* 3rd ed. New York: Elsevier North Holland, Inc., 1981.

Psycholinguistics
Foss, Donald J. and Hakes, David T. *Psycholinguistics.* Englewood Cliffs, New Jersey: Prentice-Hall, Inc., 1978.
Jakobovits, L. and Miron, Murray S. (Eds.), *Readings in the Psychology of Language.* Englewood Cliffs, New Jersey: Prentice-Hall, Inc., 1967.
Miron, Murray S. and Douglas, John E. "Threat Analysis—The Psycholinguistic Approach." *FBI Law Enforcement Bulletin,* September 1979.
Miron, Murray S. and Goldstein, A. P. *Hostage.* New York: Pergamon Press, 1979.
Miron, Murray S. and Pasquale, A. "Psycholinguistic Analyses of Coercion." *Journal of Psycholinguistic Research* 2 (1978).

Criminal Justice. He received his initial training in hypnosis at the Ethical Hypnosis Training Center in South Orange, New Jersey. In addition, Lt. Byrnes studied under Dr. Martin Reiser who is Director of Behavioral Science Services, Los Angeles Police Department and is Director of the Law Enforcement Hypnosis Institute, Inc. He is considered to be an expert in the field of hypnosis as used by law enforcement agencies.

Finally, the author wishes to acknowledge the contribution of Det. Donald Sullivan (retired), who has conducted over 500 forensic polygraph examinations and participated in many homicide investigations. He is a graduat of the National Training Center of Polygraph Science, Vice President of the New York State Polygraph Association, Research Editor for the *Journal of Polygraph Science,* and lecturer and instructor in the field of polygrafh examinations.

Investigative Assessment: Criminal Personality Profiling

History of Profiling

Profiling is not an entirely new concept. During World War II, the Office of Strategic Services (OSS) employed psychiatrist William Langer to profile Adolf Hitler.[1] Such cases as the "Boston Strangler" and the "Mad Bomber" were similarly profiled by a psychiatrist. Traditionally psychiatrists and psychologists entered into an analysis of a crime only after the suspect was in custody. Their evaluations were usually aimed at determining whether or not the suspect was "sane" at the time of the offense.

An exception to this traditional role took place during the late 1950s and early 1960s when Dr. James A. Brussel, a New York City psychiatrist, provided law enforcement authorities with valuable information on such sensational cases as the Mad Bomber of New York City and the Boston Strangler of Massachusetts. There were other important investigations in which he "profiled" the suspect based on the psychodynamics of an event and the psychiatric "clues" he deduced from the crimes he examined.

In the Mad Bomber case, police authorities asked Dr. Brussel to provide them with his professional opinion. Dr. Brussel reviewed the huge case file, the photographs, and a number of letters that the suspect had mailed over a 16-year period. Without engaging in what best can be described as a lot of psychoanalytic doubletalk, he simply rendered the following opinion: "Look for a heavy man. Middle-aged. Foreign born. Roman Catholic. Single. Lives with a brother or sister." He also added, ". . . when you find him, chances are he'll be wearing a double-breasted suit. Buttoned."[2]

On January 20, 1957 police arrested George Metesky and charged him with being the infamous Mad Bomber. He was exactly as described by Dr. Brussel. When he was taken into custody he was even wearing a double-breasted suit.

In April, 1964, Dr. Brussel was again invited into a major police investigation. A group of physicians and psychiatrists were brought together in Boston, Massachusetts in connection with the Boston Strangler cases, which had occurred between June 14, 1962 and January 4, 1964. The official name of the group was the Medical-Psychiatric Committee. There had been 11 sex-related murders in the Boston area (later this total would be amended to 13), and all investigative efforts to identify the person or persons responsible had failed. The circumstances of the deaths seemed to indicate that there were two stranglers involved. The Committee members based this opinion on the fact that the first group of stranglings involved older women, whereas the second group involved the stranglings of younger women. Also, the psychosexual activity in both sets of killings differed. Dr. Brussel, however, did not agree with the Committee. He maintained that one man was responsible. The killings mysteriously stopped and the Committee was eventually disbanded. In November, 1964, a man identified as Albert DeSalvo came to the attention of authorities. He was ultimately identified as the Boston Strangler. He fit the profile that Dr. Brussel had provided to the police.[3]

Dr. Brussel's ability to interpret bizarre behaviors and then translate this psychiatric knowledge into investigative realities proved to be an extrememely effective tactic. He had his own unique method of applying psychiatric principles in reverse, with a blend of science and intuition. Dr. Brussel also applied the results of studies by the late Ernst Kretschmer, a German psychiatrist who demonstrated that a person's physical build is often associated with a certain type of personality, and in the event of psychiatric illness, with a particular disorder, e.g., 85% of persons suffering from paranoia have an "athletic" body type.[4] A schizophrenic, according to Kretschmer would most likely be asthenic in build, thin, small-framed, and angular[5]; whereas a paranoid schizophrenic individual, with strong paranoid features, would most likely have the well-proportioned build of a paranoiac-type person.[6]

Psychiatry and psycholgy were also enlisted into the investigation of the "Son of Sam" case that occurred in New York City over a period of 13 months during 1976–1977. The police were attempting to identify a mad man who shot young couples as they sat in parked autos at various locations within the city. The New York City Police Department sought the assistance of these forensic experts in an attempt to assess the personality of this serial killer. In addition, Dr. Murray S. Miron, a professor at Syracuse University, performed a *psycholinguistic* analysis of the communications sent by Son of Sam to local newspapers. This profile turned out to fit the suspect closely (see "Psycholinguistics," Chapter 16).

Professional investigators soon realized that involving psychiatrists and psychologists with the proper experience and background to assist the police was a practical and logical procedure in certain criminal investigations. Use of profiles remained sporadic until 1978 when the FBI established a *Psychological Profiling Program* within its Behavioral Science Unit in Quantico, Virginia.

Research by the Behavioral Science Unit had revealed a serious deficiency in the number of credible and experienced forensic professionals available to assist law enforcement with psychological profiles. The Profiling Program attempted to fill this void by reviewing and researching specific types of cases, such as those previously described in this section and sexual homicides, which yield much information about the mind and motivation of the killer.

The profilers worked closely with qualified psychiatrists and psychologists to assist authorities in the interpretation of crimes that demonstrated some sort of psychotic or psychopathic motivation on the part of the offender. These professionals were soon providing law enforcement agencies with strategic information in the form of psychological profiles. This program has proven to be a viable investigative tool that has been successful in pinpointing potential suspects in certain types of murder cases.

In 1981, a system designed to identify serial murderers was introduced by Pierce Brooks, a retired Chief of Police and former Homicide Commander of the Los Angeles Police Department. This system was called VI-CAP, an acronym for Violent Criminal Apprehension Program. It was designed to collect, collate, and analyze all aspects of an investigation using the latest computer and communications technology.

The combined success of both the Psychological Profiling Program and the VI-CAP concept consequently produced congressional legislation establishing a National Center for the Analysis of Violent Crime in July 1984.[7] The Center is based at the FBI Academy in Quantico, Virginia and operates as a subdivision of the Behavioral Science Unit. It is composed of four sections: Research and Development, VI-CAP, Training, and Criminal Personality Profiling and Consultation.

Law enforcement professionals can now submit investigations of mass, serial, and sensational homicides, as well as sex crimes and other specified investigations, to a central location for analysis and identification of similar crime patterns that may exist in other jurisdictions and may possibly be related.

In order to present the reader with a practical understanding of criminal personality profiling, the author, with the cooperation of the FBI, researched this particular investigative technique by examining certain cases profiled by the Behavioral Science Unit. In addition, I have included interviews of Supervisory Special Agent Robert K. Ressler, commander of the original project, and Supervisory Special Agent John E. Douglas, coordinator of the original program. They provided the author with a case history, which appears in this section, along with the technical information, which has been enhanced with current publications (cited herein) and information supplied in the FBI *Law Enforcement Bulletin* (August, 1985).[8] It should be noted that the term "psychological profile" has since been changed to "*criminal investigative analysis.*"

Criminal Personality Profile

A criminal personality profile is an educated attempt to provide investigative agencies with specific information as to the type of individual who would have committed a certain crime. It can be a valuable tool in identifying and pinpointing suspects; however, it has its limitations. It should be used in conjunction with sound investigative techniques ordinarily employed at the scene of a homicide.

The Purpose of the Profile

The objective of criminal profiling is to provide the investigator with a personality composite of the unknown suspect(s) that will aid apprehension. By studying the crime scene from a psychological standpoint, the criminal psychologist is able to identify and interpret certain items of evidence at the scene, which provide clues to the personality type of the individual or individuals who have committed the crime. Certain clues at a crime scene, by their very nature, do not lend themselves to ordinary collection techniques, such as the emotions of rage, hate, love, fear, and irrationality. According to Ressler and Douglas, there is nothing mystical about their work; the procedures they use are well-founded in sociological and psychological roots.

When Profiling Can Be Productive

Criminal personality profiling is usually productive in crimes in which an unknown subject has demonstrated some form of psychopathology in his crime. For example:

Sadistic torture in sexual assault,
Evisceration,
Postmortem slashing and cutting,

Motiveless fire-setting,
Lust and mutilation murders,
Ritualistic crimes,
Rapes.

Practically speaking, in any crime in which available evidence indicates a mental, emotional, or personality aberration by an unknown perpetrator, the criminal personality profile can be instrumental in providing the investigator with information that narrows down the leads. It is the behavioral characteristics of the perpetrator as evidenced in the crime scene and not the offense per se that determines the degree of suitability of the case for profiling.

According to Douglas and Ressler of the FBI, all people have personality traits that can be more or less identified. However, an abnormal person becomes more ritualized, displaying a distinct pattern to his behavior. Many times, the behavior and personality are reflected in the crime scene in the same manner that furnishings in a home reflect the character of the owner.

In certain instances agents of the Criminal Personality Profiling and Consultation section have been able to supply police with such details as height, weight, body type, age, general occupation, and family environment of an unknown suspect. Such a description is based on their initial examination of the scene, using crime scene photos, and preliminary information concerning the crime provided by the requesting agency. However, as an expert in homicide, I must caution the reader that viewing crime scene photographs without making a personal visit to the crime scene to get a "feel" for the area may prove to be very embarrassing. In addition, there may be other considerations not readily discernible to persons unfamiliar with the geographical areas, local customs, or unique patterns of behavior endemic to an area. Whenever I perform an investigative assessment of a case I make it a point to visit the crime scene and conduct personal interviews with the assigned investigators, who many times have already "profiled" possible suspects, based on their expertise and knowledge of their jurisdiction.

Case History: Disorganized Offender

The following case history of a particularly bizarre series of homicides shows how criminal profiling can be of value in an investigation. This case, known as "the vampire killer" case, concerns an individual identified as Richard Trenton Chase. Chase, who may have also committed additional homicides, was conclusively linked to the murders of six individuals; five of whom were killed in one week. This case history information was provided by Lieutenant Ray Biondi, Commanding

Officer of the Homicide Bureau of the Sacramento County, California Sheriff's Department.[9]   The first known murder occurred on December 29, 1977. A 51-year-old man exited his house to retrieve groceries from his car in the driveway and was shot once in the chest with a .22-caliber automatic. The man's wife, who was about to follow him out the door, heard two shots. Neighbors also reported hearing shots as well as a car drive off. The authorities had no suspects nor motive for the murder. They did, however, have a comparable bullet from the victim's body as well as a shell casing found in the street.

On Monday, January 23, 1978, a man entered his home and discovered the body of his 22-year-old wife sprawled dead on the bedroom floor. She had been shot in the head as she walked out her front door, carrying some garbage bags. Her body was then dragged into the rear

Mutilated Body of the Vampire Killer. This eviscerated body is the female victim of Richard Trenton Chase, the "Vampire Killer", who was positively linked to six murders. He fit the category of a disorganized serial killer. (*Courtesy of* Lt. Ray Biondi, Commanding Officer Homicide Bureau, Sacramento, California Sheriff's Department.)

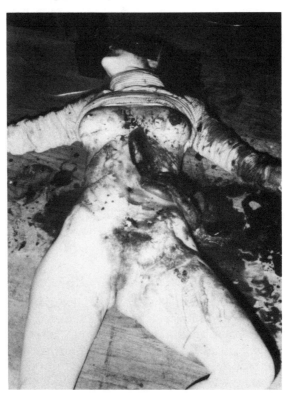

Evidence of Anthropophagy—Ringlets of Blood. In this crime-scene photograph, you can see the ringlet of blood from the cup that the killer used to drink the victims blood. [*Courtesy of* Lt. Ray Biondi, Commanding Officer Homicide Bureau, Sacramento, California Sheriff's Department.]

bedroom and was savagely mutilated. The victim's blouse had been pulled up over her chest, her pants forced down to her ankles, and fecal matter (later determined to be canine) had been placed into her mouth. The killer, using steak knives taken from the kitchen, had opened the victim's midsection and removed her intestines. In addition, the victim's blood had apparently been scooped out of her body cavity with a paper cup, which had been discarded at the scene. Investigators found various ringlets corresponding to the diameter of this cup on the floor next to the body. Later it was determined that the killer had drunk the woman's blood. Certain body parts were taken from the scene along with several steak knives.

    The Sacramento Sheriff's detectives were completely baffled by this strange and vicious homicide and readily admitted to never having encountered such a bizarre crime. According to Ray Biondi, investigators recognized that this murder could be related to the homicide that had occurred a month earlier. There were some compelling reasons to believe that these two murders were linked: primarily, the attacks had occurred in the same residential area; both victims were attacked in blitz-style confrontations; both victims had been shot with a .22-caliber automatic; and similar shell casings had been recovered at both scenes.

On the other hand, the activity in the most recent case was totally bizarre, compared to the "execution" type attack on the male victim. To add to this mystery, the next day within the same neighborhood a young store clerk was executed while on his knees in a cold storage box. Ballistics later indicated that the weapon used in this case was .38 caliber. This case was eventually determined to be an unrelated event. However, one can imagine how this case complicated an already confusing series of events.

Sheriff's detectives relied heavily upon standard investigative techniques. The neighborhood was thoroughly canvassed for information. The investigators learned that a few days earlier there had been a burglary on the same block at which the burglar had defecated on the bed in the master bedroom. According to Ray Biondi, "We were sure the burglary was related to the murder, we just could not establish the 'why'." Biondi and his fellow detectives began to look into some possible psychological motivations in an effort to establish the "why."

Later that same week, sheriff's investigators learned that a Labrador puppy had been shot to death in the owner's back yard within this same neighborhood. Biondi arranged for an autopsy on the dog in order to recover the projectile.

Meanwhile, homicide investigators were performing the traditional routine "spade" work of interviewing the husband, who had discovered his wife's body, checking old boyfriends of the deceased, looking into friends and associates of the victim. It was during this victimology phase that investigators were served another curve ball. A former girlfriend of the deceased's husband was extremely jealous of their marriage. When she had originally learned that the deceased had become pregnant, she had reportedly remarked to friends that she would like to kill the deceased and cut out the baby. Needless to say, this information certainly added to an already bizarre chain of events.

The investigation into Monday's murder had hardly begun, when later that same week, five blocks away, another even more grisly discovery was made. On Friday, January 27, 1978, Sacramento Sheriff's deputies were called to a residence within the same general area on a report of a multiple murder. A woman, who had gone to visit her next-door neighbor, opened the door to her friend's house and discovered the whole family murdered. The dead woman, who was 36 years of age, had been shot three times and had been eviscerated. Her 52-year-old godfather (who had been visiting) had died of gunshot wounds of the head; the woman's 6-year-old boy had been shot dead; and her 22-month-old baby was missing from a bloodstained crib. Once again, the victim of the evisceration was female.

In this case there was an attempt at anal sodomy with the corpse. A kitchen knife taken from the first crime scene had been left behind. It had been used to mutilate this victim as in the first case, there was evidence of *anthropophagy* (consumption of the victim's flesh or blood). An examination of the woman's body revealed that certain body organs had been removed. In addition, a piece of rubber glove was found in the body cavity. (Later, sheriff's detectives would learn that the killer wore these gloves because he believed he was performing surgery.) When the detectives searched the house, they discovered that the bathtub was filled with bloody water as well as brain matter and pieces of human entrails. The female victim's hair was soaking wet. Evidence at the scene indicated that she had probably been taking a bath when the offender came into the house and began killing people. The killer took the male victim's car, which was found abandoned late Friday evening about a mile from the scene.

At this point in the investigation it was quite evident to investigators that this series of murders was being committed by a single individual, who was obviously quite disturbed. Ray Biondi was given full resources of the Sacramento County Sheriff's Detective Division.

Sheriff's detectives "profiled" their suspect to be a white male (the area was primarily white). The canvass had not indicated any suspicious black males. The suspect would be in his twenties (males of this age commit most of the crimes). The suspect was probably schizophrenic (based upon the cutting and probing of the bodies in what detectives perceived to be curiosity). The suspect might have recently been released from a mental institution (this was based on the fact that these bizarre crimes had suddenly occurred within a short span of time within one area). The suspect seemed unconcerned about being apprehended, based upon the daylight attacks, as well as the apparent lack of effort to hide the crimes or evidence—a loner type of individual, unmarried (based on who could live with a "wacko" like this). If the suspect did work, it would be a menial job at best. The suspect probably lived within the one-mile circle, due to the fact that the crimes were committed within the area as well as the fact that the stolen car was recovered in a parking lot of a building complex within the area.

According to Ray Biondi, "This profile generally suggested that investigators were looking for a psychotic individual who lived and/or worked in the neighborhood and was committing the crimes and murders on impulse or opportunity."

Ray Biondi and Sergeant Don Habecker established an investigative plan, which would focus the probe. As all of the murders, as well as the bizarre incidents, had occurred within a one-mile radius, a large circle encompassing this one-mile radius was drawn on a map of the area. An extensive canvass operation was initiated. The entire investigative effort was effectively concentrated on these locations within the circle. In addition, detectives continued their inquiries at the present crime scene as well as the location where the stolen auto was later recovered. The stolen vehicle was put under 24-hour police surveillance Friday evening.

A supervisor was put in charge of the canvass, with explicit instruction to assure that each and every person within this circle be interviewed and asked whether or not they had observed any strangers or suspicious persons in the area.

The following day, Saturday, Biondi received information about a witness who had talked to an individual identified as Richard Chase. This civilian witness had seen Richard in a supermarket parking lot behind the residence of the first female victim on the day of the murder. Richard had asked this witness, whom he knew from high school, for a ride. The witness declined due to the fact that Richard was unkempt and acting really weird. Biondi assigned the Chase lead to three general assignment detectives for follow-up investigation. The three detectives, Ken Baker, Wayne Irey, and Bill Roberts, contacted the building manager of the apartment complex where Chase lived. The manager told the detectives about dogs and cats missing from the buildings within the complex. The manager and the detectives went to Chase's apartment and knocked on the door. Unbeknownst to them, other detectives had already attempted to interview the occupant of this apartment with negative results. The manager opened the door to an unoccupied apartment next door. Through an interior wall Detective Baker could hear movement inside Chase's apartment. As Detective Roberts returned with the manager to his office and called Ray Biondi, detectives Baker and Irey staked out the suspect's apartment. The suspect suddenly came running out of the apartment carrying a box that contained bloody rags, fast-food containers with blood and other body parts enclosed, and other evidence of the crimes. When the detectives searched him they found a gun in a shoulder holster. This gun was the same .22-caliber automatic he had used to kill his victims. The apartment revealed extensive evidence of the murders, including three blenders containing blood and human entrails. A diaper from the missing baby was also found in the apartment. (The baby's body was found three months later in mummified condition. The body had been drained of blood and was beheaded.) There was dried blood caked on the suspect's mouth and hands, and additional evidence indicated that he had cooked, eaten, and drunk his victim's blood and body parts. In the refrigerator there was a can containing brain matter. The remaining steak knives, which he had taken from the residence of the first victim, were found in the suspect's apartment.

According to the suspect, the reason for his vampire-like activity and grisly behavior was that flying saucers were drying up his blood through some sort of radiation, and that in order to survive he had to replenish his supply. The suspect was eventually convicted. However, while awaiting appeal, he committed suicide or accidently overdosed trying to cure his imaginary illness on medication he had secreted in his cell.

According to Lt. Ray Biondi, this series of bizarre murders enabled the investigators to use some of the information they had received during an FBI Homicide School he had attended in 1976. The principle instructor was Special Agent Russell Vorpagle, who had presented a segment on the "Psychology of Murder." Ray Biondi stated,

> The training that I and the other detectives in our Homicide Detail received from this school greatly influenced the tactics we took when the Chase murders were occurring. In fact, on the day we arrested Chase, we had a meeting with Agent Vorpagle, who lived in the area. Vorpagle agreed with our evaluation of the suspect and refined our profile to include additional psychological factors. When we arrested Chase later that day, many of the psychological factors we had discussed were applicable to the offender.

Ray Biondi, as a homicide expert, believes that criminal profiling is an excellent investigative tool when combined with the street expertise of the homicide detective.

Factors that can be determined by a criminal personality profile:

1. Age
2. Sex
3. Race
4. Marital status/ adjustment
5. Intelligence
6. Scholastic achievement/ adjustment
7. Life-style
8. Rearing environment
9. Social adjustment
10. Personality style/ characteristics
11. Demeanor
12. Appearance and grooming
13. Emotional adjustment
14. Evidence of mental decompensation
15. Pathological behavioral characteristics
16. Employment/occupational history and adjustment
17. Work habits
18. Residency in relation to crime scene
19. Socioeconomic status
20. Sexual adjustment
21. Type of sexual perversion or disturbance (if applicable)
22. Motive

The Investigative Approach to Profiling

The criminal personality profile is based upon a good crime scene examination and adequate information supplied to the profiler. In order to facilitate this process there are certain investigative steps that must be taken at the scene by the detective.

1. The complete documentation of events. Photographs (both B&W and color) and/or videotape as well as crime scene sketches should be accomplished prior to any other police procedures at the scene.
2. A careful and complete search conducted for any forensic materials and other evidence that might provide a clue to the identity of the killer.

Furthermore, an extensive and thorough investigation of the victim's background must be undertaken in order for the profiler to appraise the type of suspect for which police should be looking. *Assessing the victimology of the deceased is standard operating procedure for any good homicide investigator. Many times the detective ends up learning more about the deceased than the victim knew about him- or herself.* From the perspective of the profiler, however, the victim's background information takes on an added value as the profiler seeks a behavioral pattern or scenario upon which to build his or her hypothesis.

The following items are necessary to create a profile:

I. Photographs (the larger the photo the better) should focus on the depth and extent of the wounds.
   A. Complete photographs of the crime scene.
   B. Color photos of the victim.
   C. Body positioning from different angles.
   D. If residence is involved, photos of other rooms, including a crime scene sketch that depicts the entire scene, and floor plan of the residence.
   E. Photo of the area to include aerial shot to show relationship of body placement to area (so the profiler can get a feel for the area).
II. Neighborhood and complex.
   A. Racial, ethnic, and social data.
III. Medical examiner's report (autopsy protocol).
   A. Photos to show full extent of damage to body.
      1. Stabs, cuts (number of).
      2. Gunshots.
      3. Bruises.
      4. Lividity.
   B. Toxicology reports.
      1. Drugs, alcohol.
      2. Sperm present; sperm in anus; hair cut off; bits and pieces of hair; and oral swabs of mouth for semen.
   C. Are wounds postmortem?
   D. Feelings of the medical examiner, which are not committed to the report.
IV. Map of the victim's travels prior to death.
   A. Place employed.
   B. Residence.

C. Where last seen.
D. Crime scene location.
V. Complete investigation report of the incident.
  A. Standard report of date, time, location, etc.
  B. Weapon used if known.
  C. Investigative officer's reconstruction of the sequence of events.
  D. Detailed interviews of witnesses.
VI. Background of the victim.
  A. Age.
  B. Sex.
  C. Race.
  D. Physical description (including dress at time of incident.)
  E. Marital status/adjustment.
  F. Intelligence, scholastic achievement/adjustment.
  G. Life-style (recent changes).
  H. Personality style/characteristics.
  I. Demeanor.
  J. Residency (former and present) in relation to the crime scene.
  K. Sexual adjustment.
  L. Occupation (former and present).
  M. Reputation at home and work.
  N. Medical history (physical and mental).
  O. Fears.
  P. Personal habits.
  Q. Use of alcohol or drugs/social habits.
  R. Hobbies.
  S. Friends and enemies.
  T. Recent court action.

In addition to providing a criminal personality profile of an unknown suspect based upon an analysis of the crime scene, the Behavioral Science Unit profilers of the National Center for the Analysis of Violent Crime (NCAVC) can also make an assessment of possible suspects based on an evaluation of certain background information on a specific suspect supplied by local police.

The following information should be obtained on the individual to be profiled:

1. Name.
2. Age.
3. Sex.
4. Race.
5. Height and weight.
6. Marital status; ages and sex of children; recent births; children on the way.
7. Education level.

8. Socioeconomic status.
9. History (criminal record or psychiatric problems).
10. Physical abnormalities and/or defects (e.g., acne, speech impediment, obese, walks with limp).
11. Residence (condition of, etc.).
12. Automobile (color; how maintained).
13. Behavior (describe any recent change.)
14. Mannerisms and personality traits.
15. Employment (recently laid off? skills associated with job).
16. Day or night person.
17. User of drugs or alcohol (recent increase?).
18. Dress (sloppy or neat, type of clothing).
19. Known to carry, collect, or display weapons? (what type?).
20. Rigid vs. flexible personality.
21. Prior military experience (branch of service).

Investigative Assessment: The Profiling Process

According to Ressler et al., "The process used by the profiler is quite similar to that used by clinicians to make a diagnosis and treatment plan: data is collected, the situation reconstructed, hypotheses are formulated, a profile developed and tested, and the results reported back. The profilers combine brainstorming, intuition, and educated guesswork with prior experience in similar case scenarios to arrive at hypothetical formulations."[10]

Basically, a homicide detective follows these steps at the crime scene. The detective gathers information, attempts to reconstruct the incident, develops a theory about the incident, and then assesses these data to see whether or not the theory is consistent with the facts of the case. The investigators brainstorm the case during the investigative critique. They use their intuition, follow hunches, and make educated guesses based upon their extensive personal experience in homicide investigation.

In fact, an effective homicide detective is usually someone who has taken his experience and has enhanced it with knowledge, flexibility, and common sense.

Crime Scene and Profile: Characteristics of Organized and Disorganized Murderers

The organized and disorganized dichotomy devised by the FBI's Behavioral Science Unit is a description of criminal offender typologies. The information herein presented as it relates to the phenomena of organized and disorganized offenders is based upon the studies and research of the FBI's Behavioral Science Unit, personal interviews with members of the Behavioral Science Unit, research in the field, and the author's personal experience with these type of cases.

The terms *organized* and *disorganized* are excellent descriptions of human behaviors as they relate to the characteristics of sex-related murderers. *It is important to note, however, that there may be a combination of both organized and disorganized behaviors evidenced in a crime scene, which in effect presents a "mixed" personality profile.*

These are not clinical classifications, but they are based upon recognized clinical diagnoses. The organized offender can be compared to the psychopath, whereas the disorganized offender may evince indications of a psychosis (schizophrenic disorders and/or paranoid diagnoses).

Psychopathic Personality

A psychopathic person's behavior is largely amoral and asocial and is characterized by irresponsibility, lack of remorse or shame, perverse or impulsive (often criminal) beahvior, and other serious personality defects.[11]

Psychopathic characteristics include:[12]

Complete disregard for community standards of behavior;
Apparent absence of guilt feelings;
Failure to learn by punishment;
Desire for immediate satisfaction;
Continuous sexual experimentation;
Usually an extrovert;
Can "go in" and "out" of feelings;
Undue dependence on others.

Psychotic Personality (Psychosis)

Psychosis is a major mental disorder in which the personality is very seriously disorganized and contact with reality is usually impaired.[13]

Psychotic characteristics include[14]:

Loner-type personality;
Generally remains isolated or secluded;
Uncomfortable around people;
Lacks interpersonal skills.

The following organized and disorganized profiles are an example of investigative assessment. These profiles, however, do not provide for local geography, sociology, ethnic make-up, forensics, victimology, or special considerations that are unique to the local area. The investiga-

Table 17.1 Profile Characteristics of Organized and Disorganized Murders

Organized	Disorganized
Average to above-average intelligence	Below average intelligence
Socially competent	Socially inadequate
Skilled work preferred	Unskilled work
Sexually competent	Sexually incompetent
High birth order status	Low birth order status
Father's work-stable	Father's work-unstable
Inconsistent childhood discipline	Harsh discipline as child
Controlled mood during crime	Anxious mood during crime
Use of alcohol with crime	Minimal use of alcohol
Precipitating situational stress	Minimal situational stress
Living with partner	Living alone
Mobility with car in good condition	Lives/works near crime scene
Follows crime in news media	Minimal interest in news media
May change jobs or leave town	Significant behavior change (drug/alcohol abuse, religiosity, etc.)

Reprinted from the *FBI Law Enforcement Bulletin*, August, 1985.

tor is advised that these profiles are provided as a basic investigative tool for the purposes of focusing investigative resources on specific classifications of personality early-on in the investigation. (A more comprehensive criminal personality profile can be obtained through VI-CAP at the National Center of the Analysis of Violent Crime Behavioral Science Unit, FBI Academy Quantico, Virginia 22135.)

Note how Tables 1 and 2 compare with these clinical descriptions.[15] However, it should be noted also that the *organized/disorganized* classifications go into much more investigative detail. The expertise of the criminal profiler rests in his or her ability to identify the clusters of

Table 17.2 Crime Scene Differences Between Organized and Disorganized Murderers

Organized	Disorganized
Planned offense	Spontaneous offense
Victim a targeted stranger	Victim/location known
Personalizes victim	Depersonalizes victim
Controlled conversation	Minimal conversation
Crime scene reflects overall control	Crime scene random and sloppy
Demands submissive victim	Sudden violence to victim
Restraints used	Minimal use of restraints
Aggressive acts prior to death	Sexual acts after death
Body hidden	Body left in view
Weapon/evidence absent	Evidence/weapon often present
Transports victim or body	Body left at death scene

Reprinted from the *FBI Law Enforcement Bulletin*, August, 1985.

information that demonstrate the psychopathology of the event and provide an insight into the behavioral make-up of the offender.

The Organized Offender

Age. This offender is approximately the same age as his victim. The mean or average age of this type of offender is usually under 35 years old; however, they range in age from 18 to 45 years of age.

Sex. Male

Race. Usually the same race as the victim. However, the investigator should consider local ethnic make-up, victimology, geography, customs, culture, and other considerations unique to the area of the offense.

Marital status. Married or living with a partner. This type of offender is sexually competent and usually has a significant female in his relationship.

Education/intelligence level. This offender is of normal to superior intelligence. He is also street-wise. He has completed high school and may have some college experience; however, he was a school disciplinary problem. He was known as a troublemaker due to his senseless and aggressive acts against others. Academically, he would be considered an underachiever.

Socioeconomic level. Middle-class.

Mental health history. None.

Physical characteristics. Usually well-built. Tends to take good care of himself.

Residence. Lives some distance from the crime scene. (The exception to this is in the first offense, which often is close to home.) Lives in a middle-class rental. Takes good care of his residence. Married or may be living with a significant female in his life.

Automobile. Middle-class vehicle. May be a sedan or possibly a station wagon. The auto may be dark in color and may resemble local police cars. This vehicle will be clean and well-maintained. In the event that you believe your offender to be young (early twenties), expect him to drive a red or black "muscle" or macho-type vehicle. If a pick-up truck is a masculine status symbol in the area of investigation, expect the offender to have a similarly colored vehicle.

Employment. This offender has the ability to handle almost any type of employment. However, he tends to seek jobs that project a "macho" image. Some examples are as follows: truck driver, bartender, construction worker, cowboy, security guard, police officer, paramedic, gunsmith, demolition worker, or possibly a job that brings the offender into contact with bloodshed and death. His work record will be sporadic. He may have a reputation for walking off the job or being fired for unsatisfactory performance. His job is usually some distance from the crime scene. However, the crime scene may be along the route he takes to and from his place of employment.

Military history. Army or marines. Volunteered. May have been discharged under other than honorable conditions. While in the service, he was a disciplinary problem, AWOL, fights, etc.

Arrest record. Arrests for interpersonal violence, sex offenses. May have a poor driving record, DWI arrests as well as unpaid traffic violations, including parking tickets. The interpersonal violence arrests, if any, will involve sadistic acts, and/or beatings beyond the normal "fist-fight," which indicates an extreme cruelty and violence. He likes to "hurt" those with which he is angry, and probably planned his assaults with this objective in mind.

GENERAL BEHAVIOR CHARACTERISTICS

1. This type of person fits well in society—contemporary in style.
2. A gregarious, outgoing person. Seemingly the type of person with whom you might want to be friends. However, you soon realize that this outgoing person is actually a self-centered individual, who cares only about himself. His social nature is actually a facade.
3. A good talker who is socially competent with good interpersonal skills. He uses these skills in a manipulative manner and usually "gets his way" with people.
4. An irresponsible person who is indifferent to the welfare of society.
5. A ladies man, known to frequent bars and lounges noted for large numbers of female patrons.
6. Someone who dresses well, wears designer clothes, and is style-conscious.
7. A person who dates frequently with many different women, has multiple sex partners, and is known to brag about his sexual conquests.

8. He is methodical and cunning. He plans his crimes and selects his victims. He selects the site and is known to research his craft.

9. Travels frequently. Cruises, seeking the right victim. Known for his mobility. Drives a car in good condition. Lives some distance from the actual crime scene. (Note exception to this is usually in the first incident, which often is close to offender's home or place of work.)

10. Acquaintances know him to have a violent temper and usually try to avoid becoming involved in any arguments with him out of fear or a desire to "keep the peace."

11. When insulted or threatened he will respond with violence—if not immediately, within a very short time. He externalizes his anger and is known to hold a grudge. *This person cannot accept criticism.*

12. He is a *"pathological liar,"* makes promises he has no intention of keeping, and cannot be relied upon to "keep his word."

13. Does not meet his financial obligations.

14. He feels no guilt or remorse for his actions. *He is an amoral person,* who usually blames his troubles on others.

15. *"Chameleon"* personality, who leads a *compartmentalized life-style.*

16. He does not alter his behavior as a result of punishment. He fails to learn from his mistakes and will often repeat the same offense. When caught, he will say he is sorry; however, he is really sorry he got caught.

17. He is a consummate actor. He can play any role he desires. He has the ability to go in and out of feelings, cry real tears, evoke sympathy, and manipulate people's feelings.

18. Has a history of physical and/or sexual abuse by a female parent or parent figure. Important information for the structuring of any interviews of this type personality.

19. The *triad* are three significant components that form a pattern of behaviors among offenders involved in lust murders. These activities include childhood cruelty to animals (severe cruelty that might involve sadistic acts, such as disemboweling the family cat), childhood fire-setting (arson that causes damage), and childhood bedwetting. These three factors can be used to predict violent behavior.

20. High birth order status, may be first born son.

21. Inconsistent childhood discipline.

22. Father's work known to be stable.

23. This offender may select a victim who resembles a significant female in his life. Or, chooses victims of similar appearance, occupation, or life-style.

24. He selects victims he can *control* and *dominate*. This type of offender demands a submissive victim.
25. The crime scene will reflect controlled rage. Restraints will have been used. Items such as ropes, chains, tape, belts, pieces of the victim's clothing, gags, handcuffs, and/or blindfolds may be evident.
26. This type of offender will possess a "murder-kit," which will consist of weapons and/or restraints brought to and taken from the scene.
27. There will be evidence of torture, rape, and aggressive acts prior to death, including sexual experimentation with the live victims.
28. This offender collects "trophies" of his victims as opposed to souvenirs, which are items taken by the disorganized type of offender. The trophies may be in the form of *costume* jewelry or other personal items of the deceased. The organized offender had been known to present such items to significant females in his life as gifts which actually serve a psychological remembrance of the event and provides the offender with a continuance of the fantasy.
29. Follows the news media and may keep newclippings of the event. Reads the daily newspapers, listens to the radio, and watches TV in order to judge the extent of the police investigation. This type of offender concentrates and focuses on police statements.
30. May communicate with authorities. Sometimes this type of offender likes to "bait" the police with information or he may communicate through the media. This type of activity on the part of the offender has as its objective the continuation of the fantasy. It also serves to reinforce the offender's feeling of superiority over the police. This type of offender is encouraged by the apparent inability of the police to solve the crime and takes great pleasure in designing his communications to frustrate and confuse the authorities.

It should be noted that this type of offender can be stressed through the effective utilization of "proactive techniques." Any subsequent news releases by the agency should be designed with this purpose in mind.

---

31. This type of offender may hang around establishments frequented by the police for the purposes of "overhearing" some shop talk about the crime. He is usually thought of as a police buff or friendly nuisance.
32. He is angry or depressed before the crime.
33. Precipitating situational stressors include problems with money, work, or women prior to the crime.
34. This type of offender may exhibit a fascination with firearms, guns, explosives, etc.

35. This type of offender will transport the victim or body.
36. This type of offender will usually conceal the body to hide it from authorities. The exception is the organized offender, who wishes to make a statement by blatantly displaying the body for shock value.
37. This offender many times has a collection of S&M pornography, and shows an avid interest in torture, sadistic fantasies, and bondage materials. There is also research that indicates a propensity for "detective" type magazines, which describe particularly brutal sex crimes and the police investigation techniques. In some instances the crime scene and the activities engaged in by the offender will be similar to specific sadistic acts as portrayed in the pornographic materials collected by the offender. This is important investigative information, especially when considering the search warrant application.
38. This type of offender, who is focusing on the media as well as assessing the police investigation, may change jobs or leave town after a homicide if he feels threatened.
39. This type of offender has also been known to involve himself in the police investigation by providing information to authorities or participating in searches for the body.
40. Remember, The organized offender plans the crime, selects the site, hunts the victim, and researches his craft. *He needs to be in control even after the crime.* Use this against him.[16]

Serial Killing—Organized Offender. This female victim was sadistically tortured and killed. Note that the body is partially clothed, but has been arranged so as to expose the breasts and vagina. This homicide was the first in a series of killings by a sadistic sexual psychopath. The body has been purposefully displayed by the offender. (*Courtesy of* Delaware State Police.)

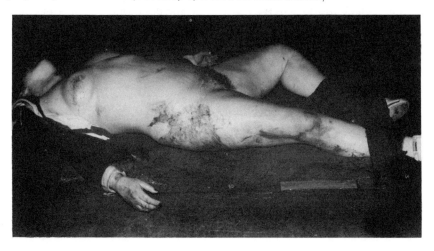

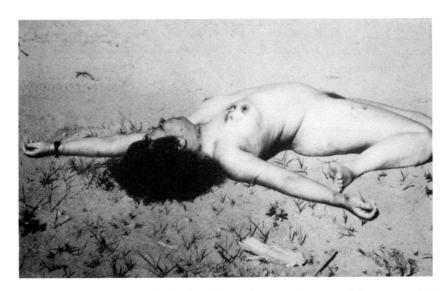

Serial Killing—Organized Offender. This is the second victim of the same serial killer. This offense took place approximately 6 months later. She also has been sadistically tortured and killed. However, note the progression of the offense. Sexual sadism is recognized as a progressive disorder. The injuries to this victim were even more severe than those of the first victim. She is totally nude and there is evidence of severe breast assault as well as additional injuries of torture, including paddling. The body has been provocatively displayed in a public area by the killer for the purposes of "shock value." There were, in total, five victims. (*Courtesy of* Captain George O. Haggerty, New Castle County, Delaware, Department of Public Safety.) *Authors note:* These offenses, which occurred 6 months apart, took place under the jurisdiction of two separate law enforcement jurisdictions: New Castle County and the Delaware State Police. Early in the case I was invited to review the investigation with the respective lead detectives, who had immediately recognized the murders as the work of a possible serial killer. Due to the cooperation and intelligent exchange of information among investigators and between the agencies involved, this case was effectively and successfully cleared.

The Disorganized Offender

Age. These offenders range in age from 16 to their late thirties. The age of the victim does not matter to the offender. The victim is selected randomly and may be unknown or simply a victim of opportunity. Research indicates that many of these offenders experience their acting-out phase between the ages of 17 and 25.

Sex. Male.

Race. Usually the same race as the victim. However, the investigator should consider the local ethnic make-up of the area, victimology, geography, customs, culture, and other considerations unique to the area of offense.

Marital status. Single.

Education/intelligence level. High school drop-out. Possibly community college. Below-average intelligence. Considered a marginal student.

Socioeconomic level. Lower to middle class.

Mental health history. This type of offender may have some history of mental disorders or may have been treated for depression as an out-patient. If he did receive any professional help, he may have been classified as exhibiting schizoid behavior.

Physical characteristics. Thin, possibly with acne or some physical malady that contributes to an appearance that is different from the general population.

Residence. Close to the area of the crime scene. Usually lives alone in a rental property or with his parents.

Automobile. Generally does not own a vehicle. However, if he does own a vehicle it will be an older model that looks junky both inside and out. The investigator should consider his area of jurisdiction. If the area is rural, expect the offender to have an older-type vehicle, messy interior and not well-maintained. If the area is within an urban setting, the offender will probably not own a car.

Employment. This type of offender may not be employed. If he is employed, he will most likely seek out unskilled work. His job will be a simple or menial one, requiring little contact with the public, e.g., dishwasher, bus boy, janitor, maintenance man, stock boy.

Military history. Probably none. If in the military, he was probably in the army and he may have been discharged as unsuitable.

Arrest record. Arrests for voyeurism, fetish thefts, burglary, exhibitionism, and other nuisance offenses.

GENERAL BEHAVIOR CHARACTERISTICS

1. Someone who has a societal aversion. He rejects society, which he feels has rejected him, and is considered socially inadequate.

2. A loner, he becomes secluded and isolated. He is quiet and withdrawn, and might be considered a recluse.
3. An underachiever, he has a poor self-image, and his clothes are dirty and messy.
4. He has poor personal hygiene habits.
5. His acquaintances consider him weird or odd. He may have delusional ideas, and seems strange in appearance and behavior.
6. He internalizes hurt, anger, and fear.
7. He is sexually incompetent, and may never have had a sexual experience with someone of the opposite sex. He does not date; interpersonal relationships are difficult for this subject.
8. This offender is heavily into solo-sex-related activities (substitute sex). Voyeurism, exhibitionism, panty thefts, autoerotic activities, sadistic fantasies, pornography, and masturbation are used to compensate for his lack of interpersonal relationships.
9. He is nocturnal, a night person.
10. He has no close personal friends.
11. This offender usually lives alone or with a significantly older female relative.
12. Low birth order status.
13. Father's work known to be unstable.
14. Harsh discipline as a child.
15. Anxious mood during crime.
16. Minimal use of alcohol.
17. Minimal interest in the news media.
18. This type of offender lacks the cunning of the organized offender.
19. He commits the crime in a frenzy, "blitz-style" of attack, and attempts to quickly silence the victim, usually with blunt-force trauma. Sudden violence to the victim and death follows quickly.
20. His is a spontaneous offense. The crime scene is tightly clustered. The weapon is usually one of opportunity. There usually will be evidence found. The weapon may be present, and the body may be left at the location of assault.
21. The crime scene will be random and sloppy. There may be evidence of blood smearing on self, the victim, or upon surface areas at the scene, as well as uncontrolled stabbing or slashing.
22. There may be depersonalization of the victim, with extreme assault to the face.
23. Postmortem bite marks to breasts, buttocks, neck, thighs, and abdomen may be present.
24. Postmortem dissection of the body may be inflicted, which is exploratory in nature. Investigators may find mutilation of the body, and evidence of anthropophagy, the consumption of the victim's flesh and blood.

25. Sexual acts may be performed with the body: insertion of foreign objects into the anal or vaginal cavities; masturbation upon the victim or her clothing; ejaculation into stab wounds; and sexual experimentation. *Usually there is no penis penetration of the body by this type of offender.*
26. The crime scene may be isolated, but there is no real effort to hid or conceal the body. *The crime scene will be in proximity to the offender's residence or place of employment.*
27. The body may be positioned by the offender for some symbolic purpose.
28. There may be evidence of ritualism. This type of offender may be expressing some sort of psychosexual need in the symbolic positioning of the body or in some ritualistic aspect of the crime scene. Since this type of offender is known to be extensively involved in pornography and solo-sex-related activities, it would be good investigative technique to record this psychological aspect of the crime scene. Later on this information may serve as the basis for a search warrant of the suspect's home.
29. The triad are three significant components which form a pattern of behavior among offenders involved in lust murders. These activities include childhood cruelty to animals (the family pet), childhood fire-setting (arson as a nuisance offense), and childhood bedwetting.
30. This type of offender may take a *souvenir*. The souvenir can be an object or article of clothing taken as a remembrance. Or, in some instances, the souvenir may even be a body part. *This type of offender has been known to return souvenirs to either the gravesite or the crime scene.*
31. This type of offender has been known to undergo a significant behavior change after the crime—drug and/or alcohol abuse, religiosity, etc.[17]

What is the Motive?	
PSYCHOPATHIC	PSYCHOTIC
Sadistic	Motiveless
Impulsive	Bizarre
Organized	*Disorganized*

The above chart can be utilized by the investigator in making an assessment relative to the type of personality that may be involved in a particular investigation.

Case History: Disorganized/Organized

The following case history is presented to explain how the FBI Behavioral Science Unit evaluates information and requests for a criminal personality profile based upon crime scene analysis. This case involves a mix of both organized and disorganized behaviors. Supervisory Special Agent John E. Douglas prepared this profile based on information supplied by the requesting jurisdiction.[18]

According to police reports, the victim was apparently abducted at about 10:15 PM on the evening of her disappearance after she left a babysitting job in the area of her residence. Her nude mutilated body was discovered three days later in a local garbage dump. According to the autopsy report, the victim was probably murdered shortly after her abduction. Based on an analysis of the stomach contents, it was theorized she died about midnight that same evening. The cause of death was a massive head injury; the mutilation, according to the medical examiner, was postmortem.

The first questions, according to Douglas, are, Why was the victim killed? Why was the victim mutilated? and Why was the victim's body placed at the garbage dump?

The scene where the body was discovered was merely a disposal site. The body had been placed there after being bled elsewhere. Douglas stated that the body was probably placed at the garbage dump so it could be discovered. The deceased was discovered in a face-down position. She had been spread-eagled in a sexually provocative position, and there was evidence of mutilation to the buttocks and the left thigh. Furthermore, none of her clothing was found at the site, supporting the theory that she had been killed at another location. The victim's hair, which was in a long pony-tail style, had been cut from her head and hung on a nearby branch. When her body was rolled over, additional injuries were discovered. There was extensive trauma to the face, and both the jaw and nose bones had been broken. The deceased's throat had been cut, and her breasts had been removed. Only one breast was found at the crime scene, and the other one was missing. In addition to this mutilation, there was a deep stab wound in the center of the stomach, and the offender had made an incision across the pelvic area of the deceased.

Douglas states that based on his experience with these types of lust murders, the mutilation is usually performed after death. Also, the fact that one breast was missing provides additional information about the personality of the offender. In fact, based on just the circumstances described above, a definite type of offender can be profiled and focused upon. However, there was a circumstance in this case that didn't fit the profile. The autopsy report had indicated that there was seminal fluid in the deceased's vagina. Douglas said, "Generally the type of offender who removes breasts and mutilates his victim cannot complete a sex-

Lust Murder—Disorganized Offender. The deceased had been killed elsewhere and was placed in this position by the killer.

ual act and usually engages in some sort of masturbatory activity at the scene. He may ejaculate on the victim's face or on the victim or her clothing, or he may masturbate with the victim's clothing. This case really threw us a curve."

In order to formulate a profile, it is important to get as much information as possible about the victim and the suspects to make an accurate appraisal. In this case, Douglas first examined the victimology of the deceased.

The victim was a white female, 22 years of age, 5'5" tall, 120 lbs., with brown hair, and blue eyes. A check into the victim's character and morals revealed that she was sexually promiscuous. She had both a lesbian relationship with a black female, and a heterosexual relationship with a white male. In addition, she was presently living with a white male 26 years of age.

The local police submitted the names of six suspects to the FBI, which included a suspect who had discovered the body and the live-in boyfriend of the deceased. The first suspect, although initially thought to be a good prospect, didn't fit the profile of a person who would engage in the activity described. He was in his late twenties, married with

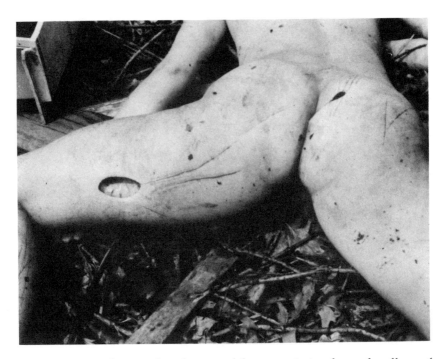

Postmortem Mutilation. This close-up of the same victim shows the effects of postmortem mutilation. The incised wound is open due to the cutting across the lines of cleavage. Note the lack of bleeding around the wounds.

children, an outdoors type, who had had a few minor skirmishes with the law. He had been observed urinating at the location of the crime scene and, after being questioned by police, secured an attorney. However, this suspect was quickly eliminated based on the FBI's profile, as were four others.

One suspect evaluated by Douglas was the live-in boyfriend of the deceased. He is described as a white male, 26 years of age, close to the victim, a loner, who according to his own admissions, had limited social and/or sexual relations—in other words, a socially retarded person.

The profile prepared by Douglas indicated that this suspect would probably be a high school drop-out, who sat in the back of the room, was a slow learner with a reading disability, and by junior year had social problems. If he had gotten into the military service, primarily the army or marines, he wouldn't have lasted and probably would have been kicked out in a few months.

This profile along with additional information fit the suspect and also fit the pattern of the case with one exception, the sperm in the vagina.

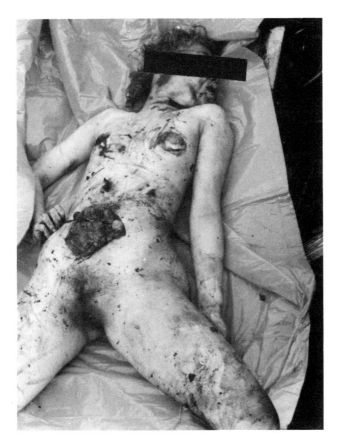

Gross Postmortem Mutilation. This turned-over body shows gross postmortem mutilation. The breasts have been removed (*defeminization*), and we observe evisceration and severe trauma to the head and facial area (*depersonalization*). These types of cases indicate certain traits in the murderers make-up, which may provide police with additional investigative clues. An investigative assessment of this crime would indicate that the killer is a *disorganized personality.*

The Behavioral Science experts decided that there must be two suspects. According to John Douglas, the key ingredient in any profile is intelligent gathering of information. The type of personality who mutilates his victims usually does not have normal social relationships and relies heavily upon fantasy. Douglas stated that the suspect would probably keep a scrapbook or diary, and he advised local police to try to locate these items in order to discover the suspect's innermost thoughts and secrets and maybe even recover additional evidence.

The information about the suspect's background and the FBI analysis indicated that the suspect was extremely influenced by his mother, who exercised an inordinate amount of control over his personal life. In fact, just before the incident, the suspect's mother had come to the house and asked the deceased when she was going to "put out sexually" for her son. The facts indicated that although the deceased was living with the suspect for two months, she had not engaged in any sexual relations with him. She had broken off a relationship with another male and would often boast to the suspect how great her other lovers were, including her lesbian girlfriend. When the deceased finally agreed to have sex with the suspect, she told him that he couldn't satisfy her. According to police reports, the deceased kept comparing the suspect with her other lovers and constantly reminded him how poorly he performed sexually. According to Douglas, this obviously distressed the subject and is an important factor to note, especially in the extreme facial damage and overkill of the victim. According to psychological studies, these types of injuries to the face of the victim usually indicate that the killer knew his victim and felt extreme rage. The sperm in the vagina, however, just didn't fit the suspect's profile. The police were requested to obtain additional information on the suspect's associates. It was the determination of the experts at the Behavioral Science Unit that although the primary suspect had probably done the mutilation, someone else had to have completed the sex act. This other person, it was reasoned, would be close to both the primary suspect and the deceased. This person would be the one who teamed up with the primary suspect, had the sexual relations, and supplied the vehicle. An individual like the primary suspect, according to Douglas, may possess a driver's license but generally does not own a vehicle and relies on public transportation.

Information about the brother of the primary suspect made the two-perpetrator theory more plausible. The primary suspect's brother had a history of assaultive behavior, was more explosive than the primary suspect, and had recently been hospitalized for this condition. The FBI began to look at the second suspect's background for certain "stressors," such as a recent marriage, a recent divorce, separation, a pregnant wife, etc. The fact was that this subject was married and had a wife, who was delivering a baby on the evening of the murder. The profiles had been instrumental in identifying and pinpointing both suspects in the investigation.

The next question, according to Douglas, is, "How do you get the information from the suspects?" From extensive research with disorganized types of personalities, certain actions on the part of these individuals can be forecasted. Douglas felt that the primary suspect would be a nocturnal type and would probably go to the cemetery. It was suggested that the local police "wire up" the headstone when they staked out the cemetery.

The profile and information was correct. The primary suspect showed up at the grave site and openly conversed with the deceased. It had not been possible to wire up the headstone; however, the observation of the suspect at the site and his activities gave the police additional evidence. Later, when police went back to the crime scene, they found jewelry that belonged to the deceased. This scene had been thoroughly searched by police, and the only explanation was that the suspect had planted the items at the site. According to Douglas, this could possibly be an attempt to "enshrine" the victim.

The removal of the body from the place of death to the disposal site is also a factor to consider in these types of murders. In the "Yorkshire Ripper" case in England, the killer would often move his victims' bodies either to taunt the police or assist them in locating the victim. Douglas contended that the suspect in this case moved the body so it would be discovered and have a proper burial.

Apparently, the body had been preserved in some manner, which would be consistent with the suspect not wanting the body to decompose. In this case the suspect would probably attend the funeral; however, his actions and behavior would be inappropriate. For example, he would be smiling when he should be sad.

According to Douglas, the suspect might turn toward religion, alcohol, or drugs in order to repress unwanted memories or thoughts of the crime. Often this type of offender would move from the area in order to get away from the crime scene. This activity on the part of the subject is an attempt to cope. Douglas points out that this is where the investigator may be able to take advantage of a weakness. If this activity is identified in a suspect, he should be reminded of his act either through the media, or by being exposed to a high police profile. For example, allow him to observe police presence around him, but make no attempt to interview him.

The next question in this case was, Who would be the best subject to interrogate? One of the benefits of the profile is that it gives you an insight into how the suspect will react to any given circumstance. In this case, the brother of the primary suspect, who had raped the victim, would be the best one to approach. He had only raped the victim as opposed to killing and mutilating her. The interrogation suggested by the FBI was to approach the suspect directly. He would be picked up and questioned on not whether or not he did it, but why. The assumption was correct, just as the profile had indicated. This suspect admitted his participation and made statements regarding the primary suspect's cutting and mutilation activities.

In the meantime, police had obtained a search warrant and found the suspect's diaries and scrapbooks, which according to the profile linked the suspect to the crime. Douglas suggested that the interview take place in the evening, as the primary suspect was nocturnal. In this case, it was suggested that the interrogation be indirect. Provide the suspect with a pencil and pad and allow him to write out his own statement. The suspect was allowed to continue at his own pace, and before long was describing things only the killer would know. He placed himself at the scene and then began talking in the third person, discussing someone else committing the crime. It was interesting to note that the brother of the primary suspect had stated that the primary suspect had taken the breast, which was never found, and had kept it in a container. This possibility was part of the initial criminal personality profile. In addition, it was learned that the primary suspect had kept the body wrapped in sheets in a cool area to preserve it. This also was significant to the original profile. This case was successfully concluded through the intelligent use of a criminal personality profile. The facts indicated that there were two different personalities, disorganized and organized, involved in this crime.

Offender Profiles

The success of the Psychological Profiling Program resulted in the expansion of the project to include the formulation of criminal offender profiles through interviews of the some of the nation's most notorious murderers. Ressler and Douglas have interviewed such killers as Edmund Kemper, David "Son of Sam" Berkowitz, Charles Manson, Sirhan Sirhan, Richard Speck, Lynette "Squeaky" Fromme, Kenneth Bianchi, "The Hillside Strangler," and many others.

FBI agents are involved in a joint project with an internationally recognized authority in the field of sexual assault and psychiatry, Dr. Ann Wolbert Burgess, R.N., D.N.Sc., van Ameringen Professor of Psychiatric Mental Health Nursing at the University of Pennsylvania School of Nursing. The objective of the program is to eventually recognize certain profiles as typical of certain types of crime. The project represents a multidisciplinary approach to violent crime, which combines the efforts of law enforcement with the behavioral sciences.

To understand the minds of the killers involved in such crimes, Ressler and Douglas as well as other specially trained FBI agents have interviewed them after prosecution. These experts delve into the killer's early childhood, filling out a 57-page questionnaire that addresses such matters as overeating, bedwetting, nail biting, nightmares, rebelliousness, destructiveness, religion, family, school, military, sexual deviation, marital and criminal histories, victim selection, and crime scene.

Ressler and Douglas discovered common denominators between the psychological make-up of the criminal and the psychological "clues" that the crime scene reveales. In fact, the patterns have been so consistent and revealing that the experts involved in this project have developed a system of recording and coding this data to permit computer analysis and retrieval. The program, which initially focused on sexual homicides, serial murders (murders spaced over a period of time), and mass murders in the United States, has been expanded to include cases from Canada, Australia, West Germany, and England. In fact, Ressler and Douglas provided British police with some psychological help on the "Yorkshire Ripper," Britain's knife-wielding killer who was arrested in January, 1981 after he killed 13 women.

Although no two offenders are exactly alike, and there is a wide range of individual differences found among offenders who commit similar offenses, they also share some similarities or common traits. It is both these important differences and the important similarities that serve to differentiate and identify specific types of offenders within the same offense category.

The backgrounds of certain types of killers make it possible to profile suspects in subsequent homicides. The organized personality is methodical and cunning. His actions indicate a controlled and structured plan. He knows police procedure and is fully aware of his criminal actions. The disorganized personality is severely mentally disturbed. The symptoms of this aberration are revealed in the way an individual acts out the crime, especially a bizarre crime. The criminal psychologist, who has been exposed to these types through the interview program and is knowledgeable of the psychopathology of the crime scene, begins to recognize certain patterns.

According to Ressler, these characteristics and others, such as the way they kill and what was done to the bodies, provide "clues" to the personality of the killer. In other words, these killers leave their "signature."

The results of this in-depth study were published in the text, *Sexual Homicide: Patterns and Motives* by Robert K. Ressler, Ann W. Burgess, and John E. Douglas.[20]

Ted Bundy: Serial Killer

Offender Profile

On January 24, 1989, convicted murderer and serial killer Theodore Robert Bundy was finally executed in Florida's electric chair for the 1978 abduction and murder of 12-year-old Kimberly Diane Leach, the last of his many victims.

Ted Bundy, who has been described as charming, charismatic, intelligent, and articulate, was in fact a *classic organized offender* who killed

Ted Bundy Shortly Before Execution. Ted Bundy (right) is giving a statement to Supervisory Special Agent William Hagmaier of the F.B.I. (left). This photo, taken on January 23, 1989, is one of the last photos taken of this infamous serial killer who was responsible for the deaths of over thirty young woman. (*See* interview). (*Courtesy of* Supervisory Special Agent William Hagmaier FBI.)

over 30 young women in various jurisdictions of the Northwest United States and Florida between 1973 and 1978. He was finally apprehended after a crude, murderous, and animal-like rampage in Florida, where he killed two college coeds at the Chi Omega sorority house, left three others for dead, and two weeks later ravaged and killed young Kimberly Leach.

Investigatively speaking, Ted Bundy was a sexual psychopath, who enjoyed killing women in the context of expressing his sadistic sexual fantasies. Obsessed with the idea of total possession of his victims, Ted Bundy killed with impunity until the end, when he regressed into the classic disorganized offender.

Ted Bundy became the subject of interest to many writers and clinicians as they attempted to recreate and present the motivations and machinations of such a sophisticated serial killer. In death, the activities and revelations of Ted Bundy will continue to be analyzed as psychiatrists, psychologists, and other behavioral scientists theorize about and attempt to explain the rationale behind this modern-day horror.

A number of books and articles have been written about Ted Bundy, which provide interesting information about his life and his murderous activities. *The Only Living Witness* (1989 updated version) by Stephen Michaud and Hugh Aynesworth provides an excellent insight into the mind of Ted Bundy, the serial killer, as Bundy relates to the authors in the third person how such an offender might think.

However, the most dramatic disclosures, which finally revealed the "entity" of Ted Bundy, took place on death row in Florida State Prison during the final hours of Ted Bundy's life in January 1989.

The following information relative to Ted Bundy was provided to me during a personal interview with Supervisory Special Agent Bill Hagmaier on November 20, 1989.[21]

Offender Profile Program

William Hagmaier, a Supervisory Special Agent assigned to the FBI's Behavioral Science Unit at Quantico, Virginia, first met Theodore Bundy as part of the FBI's efforts to gain a better understanding of serial killers and their crimes. Supervisory Special Agent Hagmaier became Bundy's official contact with the FBI and maintained intermittent correspondence with the serial killer, who refused to admit any guilt but never denied his involvement in the crimes.

Background. At 41 years of age, Hagmaier was just a year younger than Ted Bundy. Over a period of some four years, Hagmaier visited Bundy at Florida State Prison on a number of occasions. They began to exchange letters and greeting cards regularly. As they got to know each other, they established a relationship based on mutual understanding and trust.

Bundy, according to Hagmaier, perceived himself as highly intellectual. He liked to challenge the system and to play mind games. According to Hagmaier, "Bundy even told me that he had tested my motives. However, I was totally honest with him. I even told him I thought he deserved the full penalty of the law for what he had done. I think it became clear to him after a while that I wasn't trying to judge him. I wasn't trying to get any new evidence on him, I wasn't writing a book or trying to profit from him. What I wanted from him was information on the thinking of serial killers."

Eventually, Bundy began to communicate more freely with Hagmaier. Ted Bundy, a former law school student, apparently enjoyed sharing his insights into criminal investigations. In fact, Bundy would provide his personal insights into other murders across the country. Hagmaier stated, "those he chose to discuss were somewhat similar to his crimes and his insights were very good."

Bundy indicated to the FBI agent that he trusted him. He even told Hagmaier that if he ever decided to be totally candid about his activities he would ask for him to be there.

In the last few days before his execution, Bundy, who had maintained his innocence throughout the appeals process, made a last ditch effort to prolong his life by offering to provide authorities with additional information and confessions on open homicide cases. At Bundy's request, agent Hagmaier was contacted and requested to participate in the negotiations.

In fact, Bill Hagmaier was the only law enforcement person that Ted Bundy would see alone, and he insisted that Hagmaier be present when he was interviewed by other investigators. It was during these last four days before his execution that Bundy confessed to the murder of over 30 young women and girls.

Hagmaier sat through each of the confessions, which consisted of 11 murders in Washington, three in Colorado, eight in Utah, three in Florida, two in Idaho, two in Oregon, and one in California.

Supervisory Special Agent Bill Hagmaier was directly responsible for obtaining the confessions and facilitating the opportunity for law enforcement officials to meet with Ted Bundy during the week prior to his execution.

Investigative analysis. According to Hagmaier, Bundy's attacks on women centered around control and total domination. Bundy wanted his victims to be totally submissive to the extent that in some instances he performed necrophilia shortly after killing them. Most of the murders that Bundy told him about were planned, with the exception of five or six that were committed impulsively. In fact, Bundy's first killing was an impulsive act of displaced aggression. Bundy's plans involved sadistic fantasies with a combination of sex and violence, featuring a dominant male and a submissive and terrified female. All of his victims were raped, traumatized, and then killed.

The victim would be directed to act or dress in a certain way, thereby affording Bundy a firsthand "experience" of his fantasy.

In fact, some of Bundy's victims were discovered in clothes they had never worn, and the bodies indicated that their hair had been washed and fresh fingernail polish had been applied to their fingernails. Bundy admitted that he used his victims to recreate for him the covers of detective magazines or scenes from "slasher" movies.

According to Hagmaier, Bundy would first select a disposal site. He would then plan on targeting a specific type of victim, by age, physical appearance, dress, etc.

Hagmaier states, "Bundy thought of himself as a predator. He liked the hunt as much as the kill and he selected what he called "worthy prey," which he described as "attractive, intelligent young women with good backgrounds." Hagmaier added, "It was the thrill of the hunt and the challenge. It was competitive for him in a heinous way."

Bundy would approach his victims and make verbal contact while faking an injury. He would have his arm in a sling or would be using crutches while he asked for help. Ironically, Bundy had picked up this technique while participating in a psychology course that was designed to examine whether people would be more trusting if a person asking for help appeared disabled, wearing a cast, or using crutches. During his "official" mode, Bundy would pretend to be a police officer when approaching potential victims.

Bundy told Hagmaier that he usually was drinking before his homicidal hunts. He would kill his victim by ligature strangulation as he was having sex, and later would dispose of the body at a preselected burial site.

Hagmaier said, "Bundy could never understand why people couldn't accept the fact that he killed because he wanted to kill. He did it of his own volition. Although he chose the time, the place, and method, people were always looking for some mysterious reason for his motivation."

Instead, Bundy had a conscious detailed plan to kill. He selected the burial site beforehand, he selected a location where he could act upon his fantasy, he stalked a specific type of victim, and then acted upon his sadistic fantasies dehumanizing the victim. This organized offender consciously was able to keep his heinous criminal behavior separate from his day-to-day "normal" life. According to Hagmaier, "Bundy had an uncanny ability to compartmentalize. He could actually disassociate himself from these brutal and sadistic crimes."

Postcrime behavior. According to Hagmaier, Bundy concentrated and focused upon police statements about the crimes and adjusted his activities accordingly. In fact, Bundy revealed that his success at avoiding apprehension was directly attributable to the inappropriate and revealing press releases made by certain police authorities during the investigation, as well as the obvious failure of police agencies to cooperate with one another and share information relative to their cases.

Bundy returned to certain burial sites, which were available to him, and was able to assess the police investigation as well as change the crime scene. This often was based upon the news media information, which had been provided by the authorities. He engaged in dismemberment and decapitation to preclude identification of the bodies.

According to Hagmaier, Bundy also engaged in necrophilia with the corpses of some of his victims. The dissection of the bodies was for the purposes of transportation and/or the making of the crime to appear to have a different *modus operandi*. He buried some of his victims, placed others in the water, and spread the remains of his victims between burial sites.

Bundy was extremely conscious of the value of forensic evidence and took pains to assure that he had left no traces behind. He told Hagmaier that on one occasion he had steam-cleaned his car three times to assure that there wouldn't be any evidence available for authorities. This included cleaning the car inside and out and even changing the upholstery in his car.

Ironically, one of the most crucial pieces of evidence introduced at Bundy's trial was forensic evidence in the form of bite marks upon one of the Chi Omega coeds. Ted Bundy, despite his clever attempts to avoid detection, apparently was not aware of the then relatively new technique of forensic odontology. In fact, the Bundy case firmly established the use of forensic dentistry in future murder trials across the United States.

Conclusion

I have provided this section on Bundy because he represented the epitome of the serial killer. He was an organized offender with a psychopathic personality that enabled him to manipulate people and systems right to the very end. In my opinion as an expert in homicide investigation, the information relative to the inappropriate news releases, as well as law enforcement's inability to cooperate with one another, should be considered by law enforcement professionals as an investigative precaution.

Case History: Organized Offender

The following case history concerns a serial killer, who operated within New York City and Bergen County, New Jersey. He is a classic organized offender, who could be clinically classified as a psychopathic sexual sadist. This case history includes information from a personal interview of Lt. Frank Del Prete, Bergen County Prosecutor's Office.[22]

New York City homicide detectives first became involved in this serial murder investigation when the bodies of two women were discovered in the Travel Lodge Motor Inn on West 42nd Street. The Fire Department had responded to this location to extinguish a fire in one of the motel rooms. In the room were the nude and mutilated bodies of the two young women. Their heads and hands had been removed almost surgically, according to the pathologist, who confirmed that both women had been sexually abused and physically tortured. This investigation became known as the "Mid-Town Torso Case." It was believed that both women were prostitutes, who had somehow been lured to the room. A check of the hotel register indicated that this room had been occupied for three days by an unknown white male who gave a fictitious address in New Jersey. Radiological tests on the bones of the victims revealed one woman to be in her early twenties and the other was estimated to be approximately 16 years of age. The newspapers printed everything they could lay their hands on, including how the police were attempting to identify the young women by dressing man-

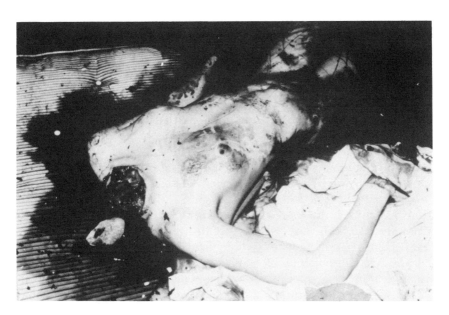

Mid-town Torso Case.

Serial Killings. In these figures you see the mutilated bodies of two women found in a midtown hotel. Both women had been sadistically tortured over a period of days. Note that the heads as well as the hands have been severed from the bodies. The mutilation in this particular circumstance was purposeful and performed by the killer so as to prevent authorities from identifying the victims. The killer then set the room on fire before leaving the hotel. Note the linear torture marks on the body in the bottom figure.

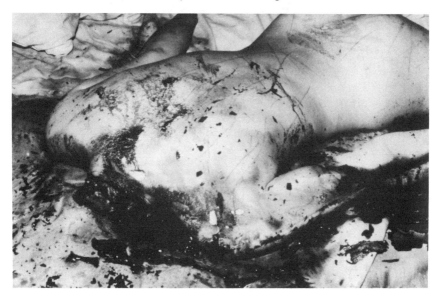

nequins with the clothing recovered at the murder scene. There were stories on the progress of the investigation, including stories on "Johns" who had been arrested for abusing prostitutes. The newspapers also reported on the efforts by the police in the area to come up with information. Approximately one month later the body of one of the victims was identified as a high-priced prostitute who worked the Atlantic City–New York City set. Despite this break, the investigation was still going nowhere.

Four months later, in Hasbrouck Heights, in Bergen County, New Jersey, the nude body of a 19-year-old woman would be found in the Quality Inn Motel by a maid who was cleaning the room. This victim was identified through fingerprints as a prostitute who was originally from Miami, Florida but was now working the streets of New York City. She had been tortured and sexually abused. In fact, the killer had left behind a pair of handcuffs, which had been used to bind the victim. Her body bore evidence of bondage-type injuries, nipple and breast assault, as well as superficial torture-type cuttings to the skin. The Bergen County Prosecutor's Office took over this investigation. They

Victim of Serial Murderer. Another female victim from the same serial killer was found beneath a bed in a New Jersey motel. This victim had also been tortured and sexually abused. There is breast assault as well as bondage activity (handcuffs) in the crime scene. Note the linear lines of torture on the body that are similar to the victim in the previous figure. (Courtesy of Lt. Francis P. Del Prete, Bergen County Prosecutor's Office.)

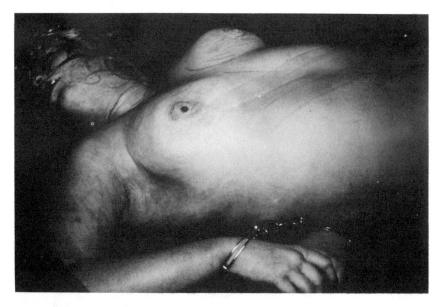

got their first break when a partial latent fingerprint was discovered on the handcuffs that the killer had left on the body. Although the New Jersey authorities conducted interviews in New York City and conferred with New York City Police, this case was not considered related to the Mid-Town Torso case because of the different MO and crime scene information.

Eleven days after the Bergen County homicide, New York City Police were once again summoned to a hotel room fire by the Fire Department, which discovered a nude and mutilated body. New York City homicide detectives immediately linked this death to the Mid-Town Torso case. However, this time the killer did not remove the victim's head and hands. Instead, the killer removed both of the woman's breasts, which he left on the headboard of the bed. Once again there was evidence of bondage and torture. This victim, like the one who had been identified in the Mid-Town Torso case, was a high-class prostitute who ordinarily

Serial Killer Victim. In this photo we see the victim of the same serial killer found in a New York City hotel. This victim had also been tortured and sexually abused. The offender had removed the breasts of the victim and placed them on the bed board to shock the police. He did attempt to change his modus operandi, however, and set the room on fire. New York City authorities immediately linked this killing to the midtown case. He was finally caught on his next attempt in New Jersey.

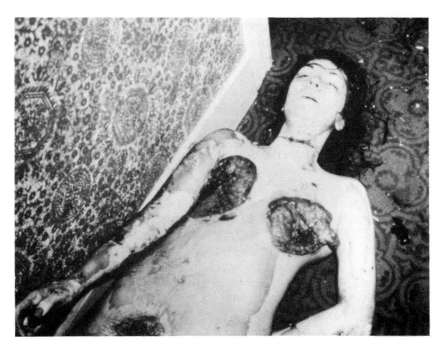

wouldn't be operating out of this type of premises. This time there wasn't any clothing left behind for police to analyze. Had the killer been focusing on the news reports? The New York City Police still had no viable leads.

One week after the New York City case, and approximately three weeks since the discovery of the body at the Quality Inn Motel in Hasbrouck Heights, police once again were called to the motel. This time, Hasbrouck Heights Police were responding to cries for help coming from one of the rooms. A 33-year-old white male, identified as Richard Cottingham, was arrested by police as he attempted to flee from the motel. An 18-year-old prostitute from New York City was found in the room. She had been bound with handcuffs and sadistically tortured by Cottingham. Her screams for help had been heard by the motel staff, who immediately called police. Cottingham tried to talk his way out of the assault by stating he had "paid for this service from a prostitute" and that he wasn't trying to kill her. He feigned cooperation, readily admitting to sadomasochistic activities with the prostitute, but steadfastly denied any involvement with the three-week old murder investigation. However, Bergen County detectives were convinced that they had just apprehended a killer. The New Jersey officials secured a search warrant for Cottingham's house in Lodi, New Jersey. Police were shocked to discover that Cottingham maintained his own private room, that even his wife was not allowed to enter. It became known as the "Trophy Room." Cottingham would take souvenirs from his victims, which are referred to as *trophies*. In this room would be the crucial evidence linking Cottingham to both the New Jersey and New York City homicides. In addition to the murders, Cottingham also became the primary suspect in a series of abductions and rapes of New York City prostitutes, who had been drugged and then brought to New Jersey motels, where he would torture and sexually abuse them.

The latent print on the handcuffs was matched to Richard Cottingham. The evidence recovered in the Trophy Room became the basis of the New York City investigation; and the victims of the abductions and sex-torture were able to identify Cottingham in the subsequent line-ups conducted by Bergen County Prosecutor's detectives.

Bergen County detectives were convinced that Cottingham had killed before in New Jersey. In fact, three years earlier, the body of a beautiful 27-year-old nurse had been found in the parking lot of the Quality Inn Motel in Hasbrouck Heights. She had died of asphyxiation from a gag, as she was being abducted. Ironically, this victim had been a neighbor of Cottingham when he lived in Little Ferry, New Jersey.

Her body bore some similar wounds to those of other victims. There were enough similarities to convince the prosecutor, Dennis Calo, to seek an additional murder charge against Richard Cottingham. This case subsequently became known as the "Signature Case," when Dennis Calo was able to convince the court that the *modus operandi* in respect to the cases was so unique and so novel as to be personal to Richard Cottingham. Cottingham was eventually convicted of the New Jersey murders and rapes, and is currently serving several lifetime prison sentences in Trenton State Prison.

Cottingham displayed the following classic organized-offender traits:

His activities with the victims are consistent with the clinical diagnosis of psychopathic sexual sadist in that he became sexually excited by the suffering of his victims.

He selected each of his victims for the purpose of sexual and psychosexual gratification.

He was methodical and cunning and planned his offense. He had his "murder-kit" and props, which he used on his victims.

He maintained control over his victims (handcuffs, restraints, tape across mouths, etc.).

He was excited by the cruelty of the acts.

He had an extensive collection of S&M pornography, which displayed his avid interest in sadistic fantasies, torture, and bondage paraphernalia.

He demanded submission from his victims, engaged in sexual experimentation, and degraded his victims.

He engaged in mutilation for the purposes of hindering identification in the Mid-Town Torso case. He removed the breasts of the other victim for "shock value."

Most of his crime scenes were sparse of evidence. He used fire to destroy evidence in two of the cases.

He followed the news media accounts; changed his MO accordingly, and changed his location.

He took souvenirs from his victims. In the case of organized offenders these become "trophies" of his conquests.

He lived some distance from his crime scenes, and his victims were targeted strangers, except in the nurse killing, which may have been his first murder.

He led a compartmentalized life-style. He was married with three children and had a home in New Jersey. He worked in Manhattan and maintained a separate life-style in New York City. He had two girlfriends in the city, each of whom was unaware of the other. He was involved with prostitutes, whom he would date, or abduct and rape. And, he was also torturing and killing certain prostitutes in between his other activities.

National Center for the Analysis of Violent Crime

The National Center for the Analysis of Violent Crime (NCAVC), based at the FBI Academy in Quantico, Virginia, functions as a subdivision of the Behavioral Science Unit. It is a law-enforcement-oriented Behavioral Science and Data Processing Center designed to consolidate research, training, and operational support functions for the purpose of providing expertise to law enforcement agencies confronted with unusual, vicious, or repetitive violent crimes. The NCAVC is composed of four sections: Research and Development, VI-CAP, Training, and Criminal Personality Profiling and Consultation Program.

Research and Development Program

This was originally the Offender Profile Program, which was designed to contribute to advances in the study of sexual homicide. It has now been expanded to include other crimes. The Research and Development program studies violent criminals, their victims, and crime scenes from the law enforcement perspective in order to gain insight into their personalities, to understand the motivations for their behavior, and to examine how they have been able to evade law enforcement efforts to identify, locate, apprehend, prosecute, and incarcerate them. The program personnel interview serial and exceptionally violent criminals, such as murderers, rapists, child molesters, and arsonists. The goal has been to explore how murderers commit their crimes. An in-depth analysis of the interviews with the convicted killers has resulted in procurement of first-hand information about their patterns of values and beliefs, patterns of information storage, levels of recall on the crimes, as well as admissions of responsibility. In addition, this program has served to improve interrogation techniques and interviewing skills and identify those techniques of questioning, which are most productive with each type of offender. The data derived from the interviews of offenders and analysis of specific crimes, and the research of the experts involved in the program, has now been data-banked on a national basis within the NCAVC.

The Violent Criminal Apprehension Program

This system to identify serial murders was introduced to the FBI by Pierce Brooks, a retired Chief of Police and former Homicide Commander of the Los Angeles Police Department.

This VI-CAP system, an acronym for Violent Criminal Apprehension Program, was designed to collect, collate, and analyze all aspects of an investigation using the latest computer and communications technology. It provides a national clearinghouse for unsolved violent crimes. A staff of VI-CAP analysts and investigative case specialists review unsolved violent crimes, such as homicides, rapes, child molestations, and arsons, which are submitted by law enforcement agencies on a VI-CAP form. The VI-CAP goal has been to centralize all active and unsolved homicide investigations wherein mutilation, dismemberment, torture, or violent sexual trauma was involved.

Proponents of this program suggested that if VI-CAP had been in effect during the time when Theodore Bundy was traveling across the Northwest United States, he would have been apprehended in Utah, well before his murderous rampage in Florida, where he was finally apprehended.[23] Currently, cases that meet the following criterion are accepted by VI-CAP:

1. Solved or unsolved homicides or attempts, especially those that: involve an abduction; are apparently random, motiveless, or sexually oriented; or are known or suspected to be part of a series.
2. Missing persons, where the circumstances indicate a strong possibility of foul play and the victim is still missing.
3. Unidentified dead bodies, where the manner of death is known or suspected to be homicide.[24]

Profiling and Consultation Program

The NCAVC's Profiling and Consultation Program provides law enforcement agencies with consultation and opinion of experienced criminal personality profilers. It conducts careful and detailed analysis of violent crimes on a case-by-case basis in order to construct *Criminal Personality Profiles* of the unknown offenders. Consultation is furnished on serial and exceptional cases; this also includes case-planning strategies, developing probable cause for search warrants, personality assessments, interviewing techniques, coaching of prosecutors of violent criminals, and on-site major case analysis, consultation, and training, which falls under the Training division of NCAVC.

The overall goal of the National Center for the Analysis of Violent Crime is to develop a sophisticated and comprehensive knowledge-based computer system to assist law enforcement. Eventually, detectives who are working on a murder, rape, arson, or sexual mutilation case, will be able to obtain assistance through a nationwide computer network. The expert-based computer system under development will allow the NCAVC to:

1. Eliminate useless investigative paths, which historically have proven fruitless in profiling and identifying the offender.
2. Preserve and recall knowledge of similar cases, criminal personality profiles, and research studies.

3. Display the hierarchy of complex criminal network problems from the general to specific level.
4. Develop and use decision rules that accelerate computation time, as well as allow the investigator to understand the problem better.
5. Receive advice and consultation from the expert system on new and existing cases based upon prior knowledge captured by the system.
6. Preserve information in an active form as a knowledge base, rather than a mere passive listing of facts and figures.
7. Train novices to think as an experienced crime profiler would.
8. Create and preserve in an active environment a system that is not subject to human failings, will respond to constant streams of data, and can generalize large bodies of knowledge.[25]

Regional Organized Crime Information Center

The Regional Organized Crime Information Center (ROCIC) is one of six projects called Regional Information Sharing Systems (RISS), which were formed to help local, state, and federal law enforcement agencies track and apprehend traveling criminals. ROCIC developed the *HUMP* system to serve as a foundation of a national clearinghouse on unsolved *homicide/unidentified body* and *missing person* cases, in which the suspect, known or unknown, may travel and operate multijurisdictionally.

The information is submitted to ROCIC on a HUMP card and is entered into a database. The ROCIC computer then analyzes and collates the information to identify any possible matches and trends on a national basis. Any cases with key similarities in the database are further analyzed, and each submitting agency is notified of the possible match so that their investigators can *compare notes and exchange information* about their respective cases.

Since its inception, the HUMP system has proven successful in identifying related and potentially related cases across the country, and in providing new leads and a direct line of communication between investigators.

The advantage of the HUMP system over the VI-CAP system is that it allows for immediate access by telephone and only requires a one-page report as opposed to a 15-page report for a VI-CAP analysis. In addition, ROCIC puts the inquiring investigator directly in touch with his counterpart on the related case (see "HUMP Card.")

Submission of Cases

The investigator simply fills out a HUMP card. In addition to the information on the card, ROCIC requests a short narrative on the back

Table 17.3 Regional Information Sharing Systems (RISS)

N E S P I N (800)343-5682	New England State Police Information Network Maine, Vermont, New Hampshire, Rhode Island, Massachusetts, Connecticut
W S I N (800)824-7868	Western States Information Network Alaska, Hawaii, Washington, Oregon, California
M A G L O C L E N (800)345-1322	Mid Atlantic-Great Lakes Organized Crime Law Enforcement Network Michigan, Indiana, Ohio, Delaware, Pennsylvania, New York, New Jersey, Maryland
R M I N (800)821-0640	Rocky Mountain Information Network Montana, Idaho, Wyoming, Nevada, Utah, Colorado, Arizona, New Mexico
M O C I C (800)798-0110	Mid States Organized Crime Information Center North Dakota, South Dakota, Nebraska, Kansas, Minnesota, Iowa, Missouri, Wisconsin, Illinois
R O C I C (800)238-7985	Regional Organized Crime Information Center Virginia, West Virginia, Kentucky, Oklahoma, Arkansas, Tennessee, Georgia, North Carolina, South Carolina, Alabama, Mississippi, Louisiana, Texas, Florida

of the card or on a separate sheet of paper. ROCIC will accept telephone inquiries at 1-800-238-7985, or through FAX at (615)871-0013. A card may be mailed to:

> Regional Organized Crime Information Center
> 545 Marriott Drive, Suite 740,
> Nashville, Tennessee 37210

Conclusion

Criminal profiling can be a valuable investigative tool in identifying and pinpointing potential suspects in certain types of murder cases. The VI-CAP program as well as the additional knowledge-based systems being developed offer law enforcement exciting new capabilities. However, criminal personality profiling cannot replace sound investigative techniques, nor eliminate the need for experienced homicide investigators. It should be noted that knowledge-based systems, as well as criminal profiles, are *only* investigative tools.

Practically speaking, these tools are meaningless unless the primary and basic investigative functions of information-gathering—through crime scene process, interviews, and interrogation—and medicolegal autopsy are effectively accomplished.

I would like to close this section with an investigative precaution that I came across in my research:

Investigators . . . should gain enough insight into scientific psychology to see how unreliable and unsuitable psychological evidence from character is in criminal detection, and how rarely and cautiously it should be used.[26]

My years of personal homicide investigation experience in the field have taught me a valuable lesson. The theories and strategies involved in the application of criminal profiling techniques to a homicide investigation are subject to the realities of human behavior, which is at best an unpredictable commodity. Although, I am an advocate of profiling, I also personally advise against putting all your investigative eggs into a psychological basket.

References

1. Richard L. Ault and James T. Reese. "A Psychological Assessment of Crime Profiling." *Law Enforcement Bulletin*, March 1980, p. 23.
2. James A. Brussel. *Casebook of a Crime Psychiatrist.* New York: Bernard Geis Publishing Company, 1968, p. 47.
3. *Ibid.*, pp. 136–162.
4. *Ibid.*, p. 33.
5. *Ibid.*, p. 101.
6. *Ibid.*, p. 117.
7. Vernon J. Geberth. "Mass, Serial and Sensational Homicides: The Investigative Perspective." *Bulletin of the New York Academy of Medicine* 62:495 (1986).
8. Robert K. Ressler, Ann W. Burgess, Roger L. Depue, John E. Douglas, Robert R. Hazelwood, Kenneth V. Lanning, et al. "Crime Scene and Profile Characteristics of Organized and Disorganized Murderers." *FBI Law Enforcement Bulletin*, August, 1985.
9. Lt. Ray Biondi, Commanding Officer Homicide Bureau Sacramento County, California Sheriff's Department. Personal interview with Ray Biondi, December 19, 1989.
10. Robert K. Ressler, Ann W. Burgess, and John E. Douglas, *Sexual Homicide: Patterns and Motives.* Lexington, Massachusetts: D.C. Heath & Company, 1988, p. 135.
11. *Webster's New World Dictionary.* New York: Simon & Schuster, 1982, p. 1147.
12. James C. Coleman, James N. Butcher, and Robert C. Carson. *Abnormal Psychology and Modern Life*, 7th ed. Texas: Scott, Foresman & Co., 1984, pp. 247–50.
13. *Webster's, op. cit.*, p. 1147.
14. Coleman et al., *op. cit.*, pp. 237–239.
15. R. K. Ressler et al, *FBI LEB*, 1985, p. 19.
16. Vernon J. Geberth. Profile "A" Prepared for IPAC CAP Program. Computer Assisted Profiling, 1989.
17. Vernon J. Geberth. Profile "B" Prepared for IPAC CAP Program. Computer Assisted Profiling, 1989.

18. John E. Douglas. This case history was described in a personal interview with Douglas, March 1981.

19. Ann W. Burgess, Robert K. Ressler, and John E. Douglas. "Offender Profiles: A Multidisciplinary Approach." *FBI Law Enforcement Bulletin*, September 1980.

20. Robert K. Ressler, Ann W. Burgess, and John E. Douglas. *Sexual Homicide: Patterns and Motives.* Lexington, Massachusetts: D.C. Heath & Company, 1988.

21. William Hagmaier. This information was provided in a personal interview with Hagmaier, November 20, 1989.

22. Frank Del Prete. Personal interview with Lieutenant Del Prete, Bergen County Prosecutor's Office, January 1984.

23. Vernon J. Geberth. "Mass, Serial and Sensational Homicides: The Investigative Perspective." *Bulletin of the New York Academy of Medicine* 62:495 (1986).

24. R. K. Ressler et al., *op. cit.* (1988), p. 117.

25. *Ibid.,* p. 115.

26. Theodore Reik. *The Compulsion to Confess.* Toronto Canada: Ambassador Books, Ltd. 1959, pp. 34–35.

Selected Reading

American Psychiatric Association. *Diagnostic and Statistical Manual of Mental Disorders,* (DSM-III), 3rd ed. Washington, D.C.: American Psychiatric Association, 1980.

Ault, Richard L., and Reese, James T. "A Psychological Assessment of Crime Profiling." *FBI Law Enforcement Bulletin* (1980).

Brussel, James A. *Casebook of a Crime Psychiatrist.* New York: Bernard Geis Publishing Company, 1968.

Burgess, Ann Wolbert, Ressler, Robert K., and Douglas, John E. "Offender Profiles: A Multidisciplinary Approach." *FBI Law Enforcement Bulletin* (1980).

Coleman, James C., Butcher, James N., and Carson, Robert C. *Abnormal Psychology and Modern Life,* 7th ed. Texas: Scott, Foresman and Company, 1984.

Geberth, Vernon J. "Mass, Serial and Sensational Homicides: The Investigative perspective." *Bulletin of the New York Academy of Medicine* 62:492–496 (1986).

Geberth, Vernon J. "The Investigation of Sex Related Homicides." *Law and Order Magazine* 34:40–47 (1986).

Geberth, Vernon J. "The Serial Killer—The Revelation of Ted Bundy." *Law and Order Magazine* 38;5 (1990)

Keppell, Robert D. Serial Murder: *Future Implications for Police Investigations.* Cincinnati, Ohio: Anderson Publishing Company, 1989.

Michaud, Stephen G., and Aynesworth, Hugh. *The Only Living Witness.* New York: Simon & Schuster, 1983 and 1989.

Michaud, Stephen G., and Aynesworth, Hugh. *Ted Bundy: Conversations with a Killer.* New York: Signet Books, 1989.

Reik, Theodore. *The Compulsion to Confess.* Toronto, Canada: Ambassador Books, Ltd., 1959.

Ressler, Robert K., Burgess, Ann W., Douglas, John E., et al. "Crime Scene and Profile Characteristics of Organized and Disorganized Murderers." *FBI Law Enforcement Bulletin* 54 (1985).

Ressler, Robert K. Burgess, Ann W., Douglas, John E., Hartman, Carol R., and D'Agostino, Ralph B. "Sexual Killers and Their Victims: Identifying Patterns Through Crime Scene Analysis." *Journal of Interpersonal Violence* 1:288–308 (1986).

Ressler, Robert K., Burgess, Ann W., and Douglas, John E. *Sexual Homicide: Patterns and Motives.* Lexington, Massachusetts: D.C. Heath and Company, 1988.

Teton, Howard D. "Offender Profiling." In The Encyclopedia of Police Science, edited by William G. Bailey. New York: Garland Publishing, 1989, pp. 365–367.

Practical Homicide Investigation: Supervision and Management of the Homicide Investigation

18

The purpose of this chapter is to provide the homicide supervisor with practical and specific considerations for formulating management objectives in the investigation of homicide. Practically speaking, the administrative policies and procedures employed by police agencies are usually determined on a jurisdiction-to-jurisdiction basis. Therefore, the author cannot and will not attempt to present an all-inclusive management technique applicable to all law enforcement agencies. However, it should be noted that certain basic principles of homicide investigation, along with interagency responsibility, can be proceduralized into police department guidelines that contribute to the proper and intelligent handling of murder cases.

Management Policy

Two basic principles of homicide investigation are documentation and preservation. In order to ensure that these principles are accomplished, there must be an established management policy that gives direction to the investigative unit. Management is necessary to assure that the preliminary investigation and initial actions taken at the scene, as well as the total investigative effort, have been properly documented, and that any evidence recovered has been properly handled and preserved.

The effective and professional investigation of homicide is the responsibility of the entire police organization and not just the individual investigator assigned to the case. Hence, there is a need for an efficient coordination of activities and procedures critical to the processing of the case. Some of these activities are the collection of evidence, procedural tactics, duties of patrol officers at the scene, preparation of official forms and required reports, overtime allowance, case-officer responsibility, confidential informant funds, allocation of police department equipment, supervisor's duties, and notifications. These activities must be properly managed in order to bring the entire organization into play to effect the successful conclusion of the case.

However, the intelligent management of homicide investigations must provide for flexibility and common sense. Therefore, any system that is implemented to direct and manage murder cases should be realistic and allow for policy variations at the point of execution.

Teamwork

All members of the police department can contribute to the process of crime-solving. Whether it be the operator in the communications division who initially takes the call and elicits additional information from the person reporting the crime, or the officer in the patrol car who responds to the scene and detains a key witness or suspect, the fact remains that patrol officers and investigators must be willing to work together toward a common goal—solving the homicide.

Therefore, the duties of detectives and the activities of patrol officers must be integrated to complement one another, and the management policy should stress the principle of teamwork.

Police Department Policy

Each police department must establish guidelines and procedures that will allow their organization to function efficiently within their jurisdictional purview. Homicide investigations, however, present additional management considerations because two distinctively unique operational divisions are involved. For example, the investigation of homicide is usually initiated by the patrol division, which operates under patrol guidelines. The patrol division, in turn, notifies the investigative division, which operates under investigative guidelines. Investigators, upon their arrival, assume responsibility of the case and take over the investigation from patrol officers, possibly directing uniformed officers and additional police units at the scene as required by the investigation.

Police department policy must provide for the efficient coordination of these various units by either the investigator assigned to the case or the detective supervisor, if present, in order to maintain control over the homicide investigation.

In addition, any policy established by the police department must meet the legal requirements of, and be compatible with, the responsibilities of other agencies. For example, the offices of the district attorney, state's attorney, or solicitor have a specific responsibility for the ultimate prosecution of the case, and the medical examiner or coroner's office has the legal responsibility for determination of the cause of death. As each of these organizations is required by law to conduct independent investigations into the facts and circumstances of death, police department policy will have to make provision for mutual cooperation and exchange of information.

Criminal Investigation Management

1. The structure of the department and how it is organized to perform investigative functions; this includes selection and training of personnel for investigative assignment, management of investigative personnel, and the designated units which are responsible for conducting criminal investigations.

How are members selected for assignment to investigations?

Is the selection based upon legitimate qualifications, i.e., department exam, aptitude testing, seniority in rank, supervisor's recommendation, board qualification? Or, is someone within the police department's hierarchy trying to create some sort of "Rainbow Coalition" that fails to recognize the need for qualified personnel without regard to sex, race, creed, or color?

What type and quality of training is afforded the members?

Is the training level provided to members sufficient for the assignment or does the department allow the new investigator to "just feel his or her way" around the assignment? Are outside sources utilized for more advanced in-service training? Are members encouraged to attend training sessions both within and without the agency?

Is specialization, generalization, or rotation assignment utilized?

Specialization for Homicide assignment is the ideal situation if the agency can justify specialists for the workload. Even in agencies where the workload is not sufficient for full-time homicide specialists, a select few are generally chosen to investigate the homicide cases. Generalization is acceptable for smaller departments that do not have a substantial case load. Rotation has proven to be an abortion. It was designed and created by officials with absolutely no understanding nor appreciation of the investigative mission. It is demoralizing for officers, who are transferred out of a preferred assignment; it does not allow for career growth and actually frustrates professional ambition. Practically speaking, it takes at least two years for an officer to become somewhat familiar with investigations work. What moron would want to transfer periodically these experienced investigators back to patrol for the purposes of rotation?

How are supervisors selected for investigative assignment?

Are qualified members from within the department's investigative units selected for assignment as supervisors or commanding officers within detective commands? Or, does the policy of your department erroneously dictate that when an investigator is promoted he or she must first go back to a uniform assignment for some sort of "cleansing." This policy has also proven to be a failure that has adversely effected the overall success of the investigations sections. The inexperienced supervisor fails to delegate properly routine matters and involves him or herself in operations rather than the supervision of operations.

2. Case management, which relates directly to the processes involved in monitoring the progress of an investigation. This begins with the initial report or officer-initiated police action, and continues through all phases of the investigation until the case is closed.

What administrative procedures have been implemented to provide for the proper documentation of the case and preservation of evidence?

The official police report as well as the major case folder are extremely important instruments. The documentation of events as well as the official police response to the investigation form the basis for the prosecution. The path from arrest to conviction is fraught with technical and legal "booby traps." Hence, there is a need for intelligent case management, which takes into account the reality of *discovery vs. documentation.* Investigatively speaking, proper case management should require pertinent official documentation of the facts of the case and not police administrative matters, i.e., supervisory reviews, case recommendations, meal times, travel to and from, roll call assignments, and DARs (daily activity reports). This type of information does not belong in the major case folder. However, rest assured, some individual who has never been involved in a major case criminal trial or investigation will attempt to "enhance" the operation with some administrative obstacle. My personal advice is to assure him that he will be receiving a subpoena later on requiring him to testify in court if his procedure is implemented. That should be sufficient.

Major Pitfalls to Practical Homicide Case Management

1. Inappropriate departmental policy and/or procedures regarding investigative strategies.

   Usually based upon bureaucratic, political, and/or personal considerations not related to the primary objective which should be solving the case.

2. Inappropriate interference by high-ranking officials.

   Police commissioners, chiefs of police, sheriffs, majors, and/or colonels are supposed to be police administrators, not detectives or squad commanders. The immediate mission of the detective supervisor is to provide coordination to investigative personnel. High-ranking officials are supposed to communicate their orders and directions through the squad commander. This is referred to as the "chain of command." The chain of command is necessary to maintain order and responsibility. Therefore, high-ranking officials should not be communicating orders directly to officers, and definitely should not be involved in operational processes such as interrogating suspects and other tactical procedures best left to the detectives.

   Too many times, I have seen chiefs of police and others in command positions interfere in an investigation by interjecting themselves or their personal opinions into an investigation.

3. Interagency rivalry.

   Practically speaking, a working relationship must be established among police, prosecutors, and medical examiner/coroners based upon cooperation, trust, and respect. The police and the prosecution should complement one another, and both should feel at ease in giving and receiving advice from each other during the investigation.

There is no room for interagency rivalry in professional homicide investigation. Law enforcement agencies with dual responsibility for the investigation of sudden and unexplained deaths must reach an accord as to ultimate case responsibility among the state, county, and local jurisdictions involved.

The best way to accomplish this cooperative venture is through continued personal contact and understanding of each other's roles and duties. Each of these three official agencies of inquiry has specific responsibilities and duties that may at times overlap. This overlap is where a misunderstanding can sometimes take place, especially in the more sensational murder cases where there is an inordinate amount of pressure, with requests for day-to-day progress reports, coupled with requests by the news media for a story.

Professionally speaking, the duties of each agency involved in the investigation of homicide will be determined by both tradition and law. However, policies should be instituted within each organization that transcend individual positions and address the common goal or objective. Courtesy and tact are always helpful in interagency dealings. Basically, the duties of each agency are as follows:

1. The ultimate responsibility for the investigation of crime rests with the law enforcement agency. The chief law enforcement official within any community is the chief of police, the sheriff, or the police commissioner and his or her designated representatives.
2. The district attorney, states attorney, or solicitor, in turn, is responsible for the ultimate prosecution of the crime, and as such should be kept aware of all developments of the police investigation. He is responsible for all legal investigative operations such as search warrants, arrest warrants, and grand jury presentations.
3. The medical examiner/coroner is responsible for the determination of cause, manner, and mode of death, and as such should be apprised of all developments of the police investigation.

Practically speaking, a little flexibility and common sense by the representatives of each of these agencies will ultimately benefit all concerned and eliminate any misunderstanding.

Procedures for Effective Management and Supervision of Homicide Investigation

Practically speaking, the management and supervision of the homicide investigation can be separated into five specific segments listed below. The case preparation for court and prosecution as well as any subsequent case analysis are separate prosecutorial and administrative functions, which do not apply to the following practical homicide investigation supervision techniques. The first three segments are presented as a checklist, whereas the remaining segment follows the list in an expanded form.

1. Supervising the preliminary investigation at the scene,
2. Directing specific investigative duties,
3. Supervising the homicide crime scene search,
4. Providing for the effective documentation of events,
5. Conducting the investigative critique.

Supervisor's Homicide Checklist

SUPERVISING THE PRELIMINARY INVESTIGATION AT THE SCENE

☐ Initial receipt of information. It is imperative that the Supervisor, upon being notified that detectives are requested to respond to a possible homicide, record the following information:

   ☐ Date and time received.

   ☐ How initial report was received.

   ☐ Name of person making report (this includes police officers).

   ☐ Complete details.

At this point the homicide supervisor either responds directly with investigators in their unit, or responds in his or her own unit. I recommend that the supervisor take his or her own unit to the scene.

☐ Assign a member to maintain communications within the command. This member's responsibility will be to make follow-up notifications, record checks, requests for special services, as well as take requests from the command post at the crime scene. This assignment becomes critical in major case investigations when overhead commands attempt to assess the investigation.

☐ Duties upon arrival at the scene.

   ☐ Record the exact time of arrival.

   ☐ Record the exact address.

   ☐ Record police units present.

   ☐ Confer with detectives at the scene. Ascertain that there is an investigator assigned to the case. If an investigator has not been officially assigned as *case officer* do so immediately.

   ☐ Confer with uniform supervisor and establish cooperation.

   ☐ Confer with first officer—obtain a quick briefing.

   ☐ Make a visual inspection of the crime scene and victim. Have the first officer or detective escort you in order to get a feel for the case and establish perimeters.

   ☐ Solicit any opinions and/or theories from police personnel at the scene. Evaluate these with you own observations.

   ☐ Determine any investigative needs—make assignments as necessary. Establish your authority by providing any manpower and equipment.

   ☐ Implement an assignment sheet. Record assignments, know who is performing what assignment to assist in the coordination effort.

The author takes notes while he is briefed by one of his detectives at the scene of a multiple drug-related homicide in the South Bronx. Detective First Grade Andrew Lugo from Bronx Homicide is pointing out the rear of the location from which shots were heard by a possible witness. This briefing will determine the focus of the subsequent neighborhood canvass. Throughout the early stages of a homicide investigation the supervisor engages in a number of these on-scene briefings from the detectives "working" the case in order to properly assess and manage the investigation.

The supervisor's notebook becomes a log detailing exactly who has what assignment. This enables the supervisor to properly assign members and record exactly what has transpired at the crime scene. As members report back, the supervisor jots down a brief paragraph detailing their activities. Later, this notebook can be utilized to conduct the investigative critique and designate responsibility for the subsequent written reports.

☐ Initiate an investigative canvass. The investigative canvass is simply a door-to-door inquiry or road-block operation in order to obtain information and/or locate witnesses.

The supervisor should assign a sufficient number of officers to effectively cover the area to be canvassed. I recommend assigning a supervisor to coordinate the canvass and instruct members to use canvass questionnaires and canvass control sheets for effective follow-up surveys.

☐ Victim removed to hospital. If the victim has been removed to a hospital, assign either a patrol unit or detective to respond to the hospital to assure proper evidence-collection procedures (re: clothing, ID papers, etc.) are undertaken. In addition, there may be an opportunity to obtain a dying declaration.

☐ Transmittal of alarms. Ascertain what alarms have been transmitted. Review alarms for appropriate information and consider updating them based upon information developed at the scene.

☐ Dissemination of information. Provide for the dissemination of information to all units and personnel involved in the investigation. Keep the command post and investigators informed of all relative and current information as it becomes available.

☐ Handling curious onlookers. Utilize patrol officers to maintain lines and instruct detectives to use courtesy and tact in dealing with people at the scene.

    ☐ Assign members in street clothes to "work-the-crowd" to obtain any overhears and direct bilingual officers to mingle with bystanders, etc. (depending upon circumstances).

    ☐ Direct that photos be taken of crowd.

☐ Interview of ambulance personnel. Direct that ambulance or EMS personnel be interviewed if they arrived before police relative to their activities at the scene as well as any persons they may have seen or things they may have overheard.

DIRECTING SPECIFIC INVESTIGATIVE DUTIES

☐ The suspect in custody.

    ☐ Establish the probable cause for arrest.

    ☐ Determine the scope of the preliminary investigation.

    ☐ Ascertain the location of any evidence.

    ☐ Advise detectives to instruct patrol officers to document their observations (re: any overhears, statements, and any information provided by informants and/or witnesses).

☐ Interview and interrogation of suspect in custody.

    ☐ Direct investigators to document their Miranda warnings.

    ☐ If the suspect is cooperative, have detectives take a preliminary statement at the scene, which can be used to assist in the recovery of any evidence, etc.

☐ Formal interrogation. This is best undertaken at the station house.

    ☐ Direct that no one interfere with an investigator who is in the process of taking a statement from a suspect.

The cardinal rule of interrogation—Never intrude on an interview of a suspect. This includes supervisors as well.

☐ Examination of a suspect for evidence.

    ☐ Advise investigators to document by both photography and sketch any scratches, bruises, injuries, etc., observed on suspect.

    ☐ Advise transporting officers to be aware of evidential considerations. (Do *not* allow suspect to wash.)

☐ Dying declarations. Anytime you have a seriously injured victim, a consideration should be made to obtain a dying declaration.

    ☐ Direct investigators to respond to the hospital, obtain a witness if possible, and attempt to obtain a statement from the injured victim.

Actually, there are no set guidelines for the exact sequence of questions. Basically, you want to establish that the victim is competent, lucid, and does believe that he or she is about to die.

☐ Evaluation of a suspect's demeanor and/or mental capacity.

    ☐ Direct detectives to document the suspect's demeanor and/or mental capacity from the time of arrest to arraignment. This procedure is necessary to prepare against a possible *diminished capacity defense.*

SUPERVISING HOMICIDE CRIME SCENE SEARCH

Supervision of the investigation conducted at the scene is a *separate* and *distinct* function. Ideally, there should be a Crime Scene Investigator or Evidence Technician assigned to conduct the search. I recommend that departments select and train a sufficient number of investigators for this extremely important function.

People have come to expect that evidence of a crime will be found and retrieved by police investigators at the scenes of crimes. This may not be true in all instances. *Often agencies do not put enough emphasis on this phase of the investigation, opting, instead, for something less time-consuming, e.g., a confession. Make sure you do a proper search.*

The purpose of the crime scene search is to obtain evidence. The function of the supervisor is to document and preserve the event. Practically speaking, if there is any possibility that any evidence you are about to seize for use in a homicide prosecution requires a search warrant, it's your job as the *supervisor* to assure that this warrant is obtained. Supervisors should also be aware of the warrant exceptions: emergency, plain view, consent, and search of persons after arrest.

Practically any method of search can be used, depending on the size, location, and complexity of the scene, as long as the search is *systematic* and *complete.*

The scope of the search is usually determined by a theory or hypothesis arrived at by the detective supervisor and investigators based upon their initial observations of the scene. This *theory,* which is provisional, is based upon simple assumptions of how and why the homicide occurred.

Remember, anything and everything can be evidence.

The primary responsibility is the isolation and protection of the crime scene. The objective is to establish the *corpus delicti* and the identity of the criminal.

- [ ] Preliminary steps.
  - [ ] Upon arrival ascertain boundaries. Do not move blindly into an area (confer before moving).
  - [ ] Decide how to approach the crime scene. Paths of entry and exit (Confer with first officer, etc.).
  - [ ] The initial survey (escort by first officer). Use this opportunity to develop a mental image.
  - [ ] Ascertain whether or not any fragile evidence is present (assure collection).
  - [ ] Prior to any crime scene search direct that photographs and crime scene sketches be made.

- [ ] The supervisory hypothesis. The supervisory hypothesis is as follows. You ask yourself what happened. You keep an open mind; don't be influenced by the original report, the police call, or initial statements. Note all the information. Make your own determination based upon the total information available. Was the death caused by homicide, suicide, accident, or natural causes? The answer to this question is based upon the facts, crime scene, statements, and physical evidence supporting this explanation.

Remember, things are not always as they appear to be. Don't be afraid to change your mind. Any hypothesis is only provisional at best.

- [ ] Examination of the body at the scene.

☐ Direct that all photographs and sketches be completed before examining the body.

☐ Direct that a complete description of the body as well as clothing be obtained.

☐ Portions of the body which were not accessible prior to the photos can now be examined and photographed.

☐ Direct a complete examination of the body, note wounds, and direct that this information be recorded.

☐ Release of the body. This decision is critical. Once the body is released from the scene *no additional* procedures can be undertaken, i.e., photos, etc.

☐ Direct that the body be wrapped in a clean white sheet before being placed in a body bag.

☐ Examining an outdoor crime scene.

☐ Direct the following:

☐ Rope off the largest area.

☐ Establish a path of entry and exit.

☐ Conduct examination as soon as possible (before losing daylight or experiencing weather changes).

☐ Direct that surrounding area be searched.

☐ If weather changes suddenly—order that evidence be collected immediately.

☐ Examining an outdoor scene at night. Under ordinary circumstances an outdoor scene should not be searched during nighttime hours—this is common sense.

☐ Direct the following:

☐ Safeguard and secure the area.

☐ Direct that photographs be taken before body is moved.

☐ Safeguard body against additional damage in transport.

The search should be postponed until daylight because it is utterly impossible to discover or detect minute traces of evidence under nighttime conditions. Weather changes the rule. Under no circumstances should the crime scene and/or body be left unguarded and unprotected until daylight hours. *Assign sufficient coverage for the purposes of "chain of custody."*

☐ Release of the crime scene. This decision is also critical. Practically speaking, the authorities should hold onto the scene as long as possible. There may be a need for additional photos, or information may reveal the need to collect additional materials, an additional search may be necessary, etc.

Before releasing the crime scene, consider: A good defense attorney will visit the crime scene to judge the extent of the police investigation. He or she will be alert to areas that were or were not processed.

☐ Recommended procedure.

    ☐ Direct that all materials used to process scene be placed in a receptacle that can be taken from the scene when the police leave.

    ☐ Direct members to make sure that all police equipment has been secured and removed from premises before release.

Providing for the Effective Documentation of Events

Case Management

Practically speaking, case management is the official documentation of events and should be an extension of good investigative techniques. Investigatively speaking, the most perturbing problem in relation to management is that all too often the "designers" of case management have no conception of what constitutes the proper and intelligent documentation of a criminal investigation. It is quite apparent to the experienced detective and supervisor that these "designers" have never investigated a case in their careers and/or certainly never had to testify in court. Otherwise, they wouldn't perpetrate some of the nonsense I have seen mandated in various investigative units. Some tips on the intelligent documentation process in a criminal investigation follow.

Documentation

Notekeeping. Practically speaking, no one, no matter how many homicides he or she has investigated, can know for sure at the beginning just what witness, suspect, feature, or piece of physical or trace evidence will be important. Therefore, notetaking is of the utmost importance in homicide investigations. The investigator's notebook will eventually accumulate vast amounts of information, which may later be instrumental in proving or disproving a specific point or fact in question.

Because notekeeping is essential to any good homicide investigation, it is imperative that investigative notes be comprehensive, accurate, and reflective of a proper chronological time frame. In fact, on each separate notation, the investigator should record the time and date of the event. These notes must be preserved for later review and/or admission into evidence.

Official reports. The official police report is the tool used by the criminal investigator to document the findings of his investigative actions. It is the principal source used by the courts, the defense, the district attorney's office, and the police department to evaluate the thoroughness of an investigation, and the ability of the reporting detective. A thorough field investigation, accompanied by an accurate and readable report, reflects professionalism and underlies success. A good report starts with an organized approach to the investigation. A new steno pad should be used for each homicide case, and the information available at the start of the homicide investigation should be immediately recorded. There are three basic steps involved: (1) collecting the information; (2) collating the information and organizing the notes; and (3) writing the report.

1. *Collecting the information.* A good report requires a good field investigation. No amount of rhetoric or literary expertise can disguise the fact that an investigator has failed to conduct a thorough investigation. In fact, even a good investigation may look haphazard if the report is not properly prepared or written. The investigator should:
   a. Gather and record as much information as possible while conducting the investigation, e.g., time of initial report, who notified you, condition of the body when you arrived, who was present, etc.
   b. Record the facts in a clear and logical order. Remember that your notes are subject to subpoena during trial, so you had better be able to read and interpret them at a later date.
   c. When collecting the information, make a clear distinction between hearsay, opinions, and facts.
   d. Keep you notes on file with the case folder. If you are transferred or otherwise unavailable, the detective who is assigned to your case will be aware of your investigative efforts.
2. *Collating the information and organizing the notes:*
   a. Review completely the information obtained during the investigation, including any information that was obtained by other investigators at the scene, such as interviews, names, and canvass results. The value of this procedure is twofold:
      1. It enables the investigator to prepare a better report.
      2. It highlights what future steps may be required in the investigation.
   b. As all the information gathered during the investigation cannot possibly be put in the report, the detective must decide what is

appropriate and needs to be included. The official report must be a complete and true account of what has transpired, whether favorable or not to the suspect, victim, or witness. Hence, the investigator should attempt to include all the facts necessary to present a candid account to the reader.

    c. Organize the material in a logical order so that it can be understood by anyone who reads it.

    d. Include all the investigative steps that were taken, with their results, both positive and negative.

    e. Occasionally, it helps to compose a rough draft on scrap paper first, in order to get an idea how the finished report will look and read.

3. *Writing the report.* If you have collected and organized your material as discussed, the actual writing of the report is relatively simple.

    a. The information must be accurate and complete.

    b. The language should be clear and concise.

    c. The entire report should be as brief as possible, yet still contain the necessary information.

Below is an example of an official report referred to as a "response report." This report is required by the New York City Police Department's Detective Bureau to show receipt of the homicide investigation:

COMPLAINT: Homicide   METHOD: gun   DATE: 5/4/89
VICTIM: Mary Smith F/B/18   HOMICIDE: 122/89
SUBJECT: Response to the scene

1. On the above date at 2205 hours, the undersigned Officer was informed by Police Officer Moffett 48th Pct. that there was a homicide at 637 Jefferson Place. 4th floor landing.
2. Lieutenant Commander Geberth and Detective Lugo 7th Homicide Zone responded and arrived at 2215 hours.
3. The deceased identified as Mary Smith F/B/18 yrs. old, address 1392 Crotona Park No. Apt. 6D Tel#998-0000 was lying face up on the 4th floor landing, dressed in brown coat,· blue sweater, blue shirt, gray pants, rust-colored boots, and a type of blue kerchief on her head. It appeared that she was shot in the right chest area.
4. Attendant O'Grady #1721 Jacobi Hospital Ambulance #237 pronounced the victim DOA at 2230 hours.
5. The deceased's cousin Sarah Brown 1679 Franklin Avenue Apt. 3B Tel#783-000 present and identified the body.

The structure and process of homicide report writing is flexible and usually varies with the length of the investigation and the number of investigators who are involved. If, for example, the perpetrator has been arrested on the scene, or shortly after the commission of the crime or

COMPLAINT: Homicide   METHOD: Shotgun   DATE: 2/21/78

VICTIM: Mary Smith F/B 18   HOMICIDE: 32/78

SUBJECT: Response to the scene

1. On the above date at 2205 hours, the undersigned officer was informed by Police Officer Moffett 48th Pct. that there was a homicide at 637 Jefferson Place, 4th Fl. landing.

2. Detective Sergeant Geberth and Detective Scroope 7th Homicide Zone responded and arrived at 2215 hours.

3. The deceased identified as MARY SMITH F/B 18 yrs. address 1392 Crotona Park No. apt. 6D Tele. # 998-   was lying face-up on the 4th. floor landing, dressed in a brown coat, blue sweater, blue shirt, gray pants, rust colored boots, and a type of blue kerchief on her head. It appeared that she was shot in the right chest area.

4. Attendant O'Grady #1721 Jacobi Hospital Ambulance #237 pronounced the victim DOA at 2230 hours.

5. The deceased's cousin Sarah Brown 1679 Franklin Avenue apt. 3B Tele. # 783-present and identified the body.

The Response Report.

discovery of the body, the assigned detective will be able to assemble all the facts from his notes and type them into a unified, complete, and well-structured report. Usually this can be accomplished shortly after the initial chaos that is characteristic at homicide crime scenes. In these cases, the report itself serves primarily as a record of details of the crime, the subsequent investigation, and the apprehension. Normally, such rapidly cleared cases present no major problems; however, the investigator must be careful that he does not leave out any significant facts, or treat the report too lightly.

On the other hand, in a large-scale continuing investigation, involving a relatively large number of investigators, reports must be filed on a daily basis to expedite the indexing of the vast amount of information being gathered, thereby making the information available to the various investigators when needed. Some of the investigators may be from different units. This varied mass of reports can create a problem in terms of format, structure, and readability of the whole report when finally collated. The prosecutor, and possibly some other investigator who may be assigned to the investigation at some future time, will have to decipher these reports (which are, in effect, reports of numerous separate investigations into distinct phases of the case) and be able to relate them to the entire case.

In order to clarify these voluminous reports and provide for uniformity, the report filed for each new facet of an investigation should begin with an assignment paragraph which sets forth:

1. The date and time of the assignment.
2. The rank, name, shield number, if any, and the command of the person who made the assignment.
3. Full details as to the source and nature of the lead, if there is such.
4. The objective of the investigation, if it arises in the normal course of investigative routine, or because of the particular needs of the investigation.

Without these explanatory "pegs," a long report can possibly degenerate into a meaningless mass of disjointed interviews. An example of a proper format would be as follows:

ASSIGNMENT: At 2115 hours, Thursday, May 4, 1989, the undersigned and Detective Andrew Lugo were assigned by Lieutenant Commander Geberth Bronx Homicide Squad, to investigate a lead that was received by P. O. Coyne, shield #2107 Communications Division. P. O. Coyne, on duty at Communications Division on Thursday, May 4, 1989, at 2040 hours received a call as follows: "The man you are looking for in the cop killing works as a bag packer at the Triple A Supermarket on Jerome Avenue." The voice appeared to be that of a male, Hispanic. There was no further conversation and no other identifying information. Triple A Supermarket: The undersigned and Det. Lugo present at. . . .

The report will now continue with the results of the investigation in chronological order, until that particular avenue of inquiry is exhausted or abandoned due to more pressing priorities. Where the investigation of one lead produces another, the report of the investigation should continue in a chronological fashion. If for some reason in the future abandoned lines of inquiry are resumed, the assignment paragraph should clearly reflect that fact and refer to the earlier reports. Each new line of inquiry or new phase of an investigation should begin on a new page. This will ease the grouping of similar leads and investigative processes so that the final report will have a logical arrangement.

When the final report is correlated, it should be arranged with the main portion of the investigation appearing first, followed by a grouping of reports on the results of neighborhood canvassing, grouping of leads

An Example of Report Writing which Involves Explanatory "Pegs."

ASSIGNMENT: At 1815 hours, Thursday, August 18, 1978, the undersigned and Detective

Scroope were assigned by Det. Sgt. Geberth, Shield #16, 7th Homicide Squad, to investigate a

lead that was received by Police Officer Regino, shield #2801 Communications Division. P. O.

Regino, on duty at Communications Division on Thursday August 18, 1978, at 1740 hours

received a call as follows: "The man you are looking for in the Mendex homicide case worked at

the E/Z Car Wash on Washington Avenue." The voice appeared to be that of a male, Hispanic.

There was no further conversation and no other identifying information. E/Z CAR WASH: The

undersigned and Det. Scroope present at etc.

---

checked under appropriate subtitles, and so on. The final report, whether short or long, should begin with a resume or summary of the case. This summary will enable the reader to relate to the overall picture as he or she goes through the case.

In a large-scale investigation, investigators are generally too busy the first day to type any formal reports, with the exception of brief official reports, such as "the response report." At this stage, investigators should take copious notes, while orally keeping the chief investigator informed of developments. This should be a two-way communication, so the investigators can better evaluate any information they receive. The chief investigator at this phase of the investigation should appoint someone to act as recorder, who will list any assignments that are given out with the names and commands of the investigators assigned, to fix responsibility for each report and prevent duplication of effort. I recommend a logbook as a running chronological record. The first entries in this log can be taken from the assignment sheets used at the scene of the crime. At this stage of the investigation, the command post should be moved to the station house and all activities in connection with the case should originate and be directed from this central location. The command post at the crime scene or place of occurrence is temporary and used only initially during emergency operations. Once the emergency or crime scene work is complete, the operations center should be at a police facility where the necessary equipment and resources are available within a secure building. If by the second day an arrest has not been made or perpetrators identified, and the department has involved numerous investigators, formal typed records should be filed at the conclusion of each investigator's tour. Needless to say, this will require typewriters, supplies, and space to accommodate the number of personnel involved. It helps to avoid confusion if the newly assigned and regular investigators are thoroughly briefed on what is required from them.

FIRST DAY OF INVESTIGATION

SUPERVISOR CHECKLIST

☐ Implement assignment sheet assign recorder to command post.

    ☐ List all assignments of personnel at the scene.

    ☐ Indicate individual assignments by name, rank, and command.

☐ Chief investigator keeps track of various assignments in his notebook. Usually a brief paragraph relating to results obtained, facts of interviews, results of canvass, evidence recovered, etc.

☐ Implement major case forms (delegate recorder to issue as members arrive at crime scene): Checklists, assignment sheets, canvass questionnaires, interview reports, investigative plans, witness forms, canvass control sheets, and lead sheets.

Indexing the Homicide Investigation

As the volume of daily reports grows, the amount of information becomes unmanageable without an effective indexing procedure.

Index cards should be prepared for names of all persons that arise in an investigation, locations or premises mentioned, vehicles, license plate numbers, or other such categories as may be required in a particular investigation. An investigator should be assigned to type and file the index cards that will be required, according to the following procedure.

Daily reports should be reviewed and signed by the supervising officer or chief investigator. They should be prepared in duplicate. The original is handled per department requirements; the duplicate is given to the index officer for processing. The officer who prepares the report will underline in red, on the case folder copies of the report, all names, addresses, vehicles, plate numbers, phone numbers, and any other information that the chief investigator decides is necessary. The case folder copies of the reports are filed chronologically and numbered consecutively with the response report as number 1.

The index officer then prepares an index card for each name, address, etc. The name cards will be filed alphabetically by last name. If only a first name or nickname appears, it will be filed according to that single name. Name cards will be cross-referenced with location cards, vehicle cards, etc., when applicable.

Each card will list the case number, a brief summary of the information, and a reference to the original report by listing the consecutive

```
Homicide #192

VICTIM   John W. Doe    M/W/38Yrs. old
TIME   2230 Hrs.        DATE   December 14, 1981
PLACE OF OCCURRENCE   3335 Webster Avenue
METHOD   Gunshot
COMPLAINT NO.   7881              PCT.   52
DET. ASSIGNED   Det. George Scroope
DET. ASSISTING   Det. Andrew Lugo
FIRST OFFICER   Police Officer Michael Regino
PHOTO   Det. Charles Carway
FORENSIC   Det. Arne Roussine
LAB.   Dr. Shaler
BALLISTICS   Det. Sgt. Scaringe
M.E.   Di Maio
A.D.A.   Kelly
```

CASE NO. 192 COMPLAINT NO. 7881 PCT. 52 DATE OF OCC. 12/14/81 DATE OPENED Same

The Case Folder.

number from the case folder copy. Below is an example of such a index card:

JONES, HOWARD A.   HOMICIDE #78/89
1368 Bathgate Avenue
Apt. 3D Bronx   Report# 37
Name found in wallet of deceased

A quick glance at the index card indicates that the name Howard Jones was in the deceased's wallet. As other information relative to Jones surfaces, it can be added to the card with a reference to the original report. If further information is required, the investigator can refer back to the report by number.

The location cards can be filed according to any plan, i.e., alphabetically by name of the street, then in numerical house number order. When necessary, a category can be prepared for different towns or communities, or by borough or county.

The vehicle cards can be filed alphabetically by make, year, etc., and license plates can be filed alphabetically or numerically.

Before the index officer prepares an index card for any red-lined name, location, etc., he will first consult the existing file to determine if any such information has previously appeared. Where a card already exists, that information should be brought to the attention of the chief investigator and other investigators concerned. The index officer then adds the new information to the existing card, with the number of the corresponding report from the case folder. This system of calling "hits" to the attention of the investigators minimizes the possibility of important information being lost or delayed in a mass of uncatalogued information. Although a computerized system is much more effective, this system is still recommended as a back-up.

The index officer becomes a valuable aid in the investigation, especially when he becomes meticulously aware of each phase of the case. He or she should attend all conferences and freely contribute to all discussion of the case. Even when there is insufficient typing and filing to keep the index officer busy, he or she should remain with the investigation until it is cleared, if possible. The index officer can be used to fill in on teams where a partner may be sick or in court, can be assigned to investigations that can be handled by one man on a part-time basis, and can use his remaining time to attend to typing and filing.

News Clipping File

Investigators should maintain a file of news clippings relating to the crime. These clippings may prove important later if a suspect admits to an intimate knowledge of the crime which he or she claims to have perpetrated. A news file on the case will assist the police in determining the veracity of any statements. In addition, investigators should be aware of what information has been released by the press so that they can make proper investigative decisions. The index officer can also be assigned to clip and file all newspaper clippings about the case. This file can also be expanded to include recordings of any television newscasts on videotape using a VCR. In larger departments, with a more sophisti-

INVESTIGATIVE PLAN   PART 1

Assigned Supervisor _____   Date Received _____

Supervisor _____   Complaint # _____ Precinct _____

                                                 Case # _____ Command _____

ACTIVITY CHECKLIST   REMARKS

Activity		Remarks
Weapon Used	☐	_____
Vehicle Used	☐	_____
Injury Involved	☐	_____
Canvass Conducted	☐	_____
Crime Scene Searched	☐	_____
Evidence Obtained	☐	_____
Print Kit Used	☐	_____
Polaroid Camera Used	☐	_____
Forensic Notified	☐	_____
Reporting P. O. Interviewed	☐	_____
Alarm Transmitted	☐	Date _____
Wanted Card Forwarded	☐	Date _____
Visit to B.C.I.	☐	Date _____
View Photos at Command	☐	Date _____

Additional Activity and/or comments:

The Investigative Plan.

INDEX SHEET

ITEM NO.	DATE	ITEM

ALL COMPLAINT FOLLOW-UPS will be consecutively numbered on this sheet.
All other items submitted (Photographs, Laboratory Reports, Property Vouchers,
etc.) will also be included on the sheet, but will not be numbered.

The Index Sheet. All reports are chronologically numbered on this sheet and
placed into the case folder.

		7th HOMICIDE ZONE		

COMPLAINT # _____

CASE # _____

NAME OF DECEASED   DATE & TIME OF OCCURRENCE PLACE OF OCCURRENCE

DATE	DET. ASSIGNED	ASSIGNMENT	REPORTS	FOLLOW UP

Assignment Sheet. All assignments are recorded on this running sheet in order to "fix" responsibility for certain "jobs."

INTERVIEW REPORT

Case # _____

Date: _____ Day: _____ Time Start: _____ Time Finished _____

Location and Room # of Interview:_____

Name of Person Interviewed: _____

Address: _____ Date of Birth:_____

B # _____ Marital Status: _____ Wife/Husband Name: _____

Address of Wife/Husband: _____

Where Employed: _____ Employer: _____ Position: _____

Telephone: _____ Ext.: _____

Children's Names _____ Age _____ School _____

Previous Arrests: Date   Jurisdiction   Charge   Disposition

Present at Interview: _____

A.D.A.: _____ Bureau: _____

Investigator: _____ Command: _____ Shield # _____

Name of Attorney: _____ Address: _____

Others Present at Interview: _____

_____

Advised of Rights: Yes/No   N/A   By: _____

Interview:

Interview Report. This form is used as a preliminary interview form at the scene. A more extensive report appears in Chapter 4.

cated taping system, a number of news stations can be monitored at the same time and the newscasts videotaped for the investigative unit's library. I have been involved in a number of major cases during the past few years that received an inordinate amount of news coverage. It was to our advantage to have copies of the TV coverage, both during the investigation as well as later for court purposes.

Good press-relations policy can come in handy. If the agency and the news media are cooperating, the news media people will make available to the law enforcement agency any publications relating to the case. This will eliminate the possibility of missing any printed item in the local papers. (See Chapter 13 "The News Media in Homicide Investigations.")

I remember one case in which we had requested the local newspapers to print a story on a gang-style execution in an attempt to identify the deceased. As the story was carried in a number of different newspapers, we had missed one of the articles for the file. Later, we developed two suspects who had claimed to have read of the death in a certain paper. This was approximately three weeks after the original story. Because the paper involved and the news person were generally cooperative with the police, and the police cooperative with them, the reporter had someone research the files and find the particular article involved. We were then able to properly evaluate the alibi.

Conducting the Investigative Conference

The investigative conference is one of the most important phases of any well-run homicide investigation. The conference need not be a formal gathering back at the station house. In fact, the investigative conference takes place during and after each of the other four phases. The conference is directed by the chief investigator at each critical point of the investigation. The object is to assess the investigation by gaining an overall synopsis. Each member and/or team relate their progress and ideas; everyone is kept abreast of all developments, and there is a general discussion. The daily investigative conference, which is somewhat different and usually takes place at the station house, attempts to assess the entire investigation on a daily basis.

In my professional opinion, the investigative critique should be used as a guide by the experienced members to conduct the homicide investigation.

The Investigation of Police-Related Shootings

Law enforcement officers, in their capacity as the guardians of law, are authorized to be armed with a firearm to protect themselves and others against the immediate threat of death or serious bodily injury. This authority is also extended to apprehend a fleeing felon who has committed a violent crime, i.e., an armed robbery, murder, or serious felonious assault, and whose escape presents a substantial risk of death or serious bodily injury to others.

The necessary and appropriate use of this authority is an awesome responsibility. The decision to use deadly force is based on the circumstances as presented at the time of incident. The final determination of justification, however, is based on law.

Police administrators must establish fair and appropriate guidelines within their respective departments for the use of deadly physical force, which instill public confidence by assuring official accountability. Commensurate with this formulation of policy relative to the justifiable use of force, however, should be a mandate not to unduly place the law enforcement officer in an unnecessary position of any danger or harm. The justification for the use of deadly physical force is usually decided on a case-by-case basis within the context of the law and interests of society. Therefore, it is not the intent of the author to argue the necessity for the use of deadly physical force by police officials, for the protection of others and the general public, or the legal basis of any justification defense. Instead, the purpose of this section is to provide practical guidelines to the investigator who is charged with the responsibility of conducting an official investigation in connection with a police-related shooting that results in death.

Police-related shooting incidents involve the discharge of a firearm by a sworn officer in the performance of duty, which results in injury or death. The investigation of these matters can have far-reaching consequences for all parties involved. The outcome may involve criminal as well as civil litigation, not to mention the psychological trauma inherent on the part of the officer. I know because I have been there.

The official police investigation usually concentrates on the issue of whether or not the officer acted within the agency guidelines. The determination is based upon the law as it relates to the "Justifiable Use of Force," ethics, good judgment, and departmental policies established within the agency. The author acknowledges that there may be variances in the law, and that case management and/or investigative techniques are usually determined on a jurisdiction-to-jurisdiction basis.

However, in situations where a death has occurred in connection with a police-related shooting incident, I personally recommend that a homicide investigation take precedent over any type of internal investigations inquiry. An internal investigation can always be conducted after the homicide probe.

Pierce R. Brooks recommends that an Incident Case Book be prepared for each fatal shooting incident. The initial Officer Involved Shooting report and the information added as addendum become the *Incident Case Book*. The addendum includes:

all scene diagrams,

other related reports,

supplemental reports,

transcribed or lengthy statements,

medical examiner's protocol,

EMT/hospital treatment reports,

lab reports,

evidence reports,

suspect's criminal record,

photos,

news clips,

Review Board decision,

other pertinent information.

I have provided the following checklist format, which has been designed to assure that a complete, factual, and unbiased report can be generated.

POLICE-RELATED SHOOTING REPORT

OPENING PARAGRAPH

☐ Summarize the basic incident in concise terms.

☐ Time and date.

☐ Location (exact address, intersection, etc.).

☐ Name of officer(s).

☐ ID numbers: badge number and/or shield number.

☐ Agency/command and/or assignment.

☐ Number of shots fired.

☐ At whom (identify suspects, etc.).

☐ State the reason for the shooting (i.e., attempted robbery, assault, effecting an arrest, narcotics buy operation, etc.).

PARAGRAPH TWO

☐ Identity of department and/or other agency investigators preparing the report.

PARAGRAPH THREE

☐ Explanation of the event: when, where, who, what, how, and why.

    ☐ Explain the events leading up to, during, and following the incident.

- ☐ Use descriptive matter as necessary to clarify the *facts* and/or *support conclusion.*
- ☐ Document officer's duty status.
  - ☐ On or off duty.
  - ☐ Last tour of duty performed.
  - ☐ Next tour of duty.
  - ☐ Where was officer going to or coming from?
- ☐ Detail the following information in appropriate format, covering the areas listed below.
  - ☐ Detail the extent of the investigation conducted.
  - ☐ Identify all persons involved.
  - ☐ Provide a complete list of all notifications made during the investigation.
- ☐ Crime scene search.
  - ☐ Identity of searchers.
  - ☐ Description of area searched.
  - ☐ Time of search.
  - ☐ Results of search.
  - ☐ Property damage (if any).
  - ☐ Spent bullets recovered.
  - ☐ Weapons found, etc.
  - ☐ Complete crime scene sketch.
    - ☐ Accurate measurements.
    - ☐ Positions of law enforcement officers as well as others involved in the event.
    - ☐ Identity of sketcher.
- ☐ Injuries and/or wounds.
  - ☐ List injuries and/or wounds; identify victim with injury and/or wounds.
  - ☐ Name of hospital.
  - ☐ Admitting or attending physician.
  - ☐ Medical examiner's report and appropriate photographs.
    - ☐ ME photographs.
    - ☐ Investigation photographs taken at crime scene.
- ☐ Statements.
  - ☐ Insure that all statements from law enforcement persons are complete and exact.

☐ What did civilian witnesses see and/or hear relative to the discharge?

☐ Document attempts to locate witnesses.

  ☐ By whom.

  ☐ Submit list of witnesses; document names and addresses.

☐ Perpetrator's pedigree.

  ☐ Description of suspect (pedigree, age, DOB, address, etc.).

  ☐ Clothing.

  ☐ Criminal record.

☐ Officer's pedigree.

  ☐ Describe officer's pedigree (age, DOB, assignment, etc.; personal information omitted from pedigree).

  ☐ Uniform or plainclothes.

☐ Examination of firearm.

  ☐ Who examined firearm.

  ☐ Is the firearm authorized? listed with agency?

  ☐ Was the ammunition authorized?

  ☐ Statement of the above inspection.

☐ Ballistics.

  ☐ Notify the ballistics section.

  ☐ Have the firearm examined by ballistics.

  ☐ Obtain ballistics report.

FINAL PARAGRAPH

☐ Make appropriate recommendation. The recommendation is based upon the results of the investigation as well as interviews of all parties concerned. The report should indicate within this final paragraph whether or not the shooting incident was within agency guidelines.

Conclusion

The management and supervision of the homicide investigation is unique in its comparison to other police management operations. The management of day-to-day patrol operations and administrative functions can be proceduralized because of their routine and repetitive nature. In fact, management and supervision of many police operations are interchangeable and allow for supervisory reassignment and career growth within the organization. The supervisor's experience with the function is not considered a prerequisite for assignment.

This rationale is based on the theories of police administrators, whom I refer to as "the police intelligentsia." They believe that "police managers" should not participate operationally in the function. Instead, these managers should be taught to rely strictly upon the written rules and procedures of the organization. This, the "police intelligentsia" believe, will assure operational uniformity.

Generally speaking, this strict and rigid bureaucratic control does not allow for on-site common sense, and the flexibility necessary in a practical homicide investigation. These administratively oriented rules eventually become insulative and effectively relieve the "manager" of the on-line supervisory responsibility commensurate with the direction of operations.

Investigatively speaking, the intelligent management and supervision of homicide investigations requires a different approach that takes into account the unpredictable aspects of a murder investigation. There are rules and procedures, established policies that give direction and coordination to the function, as well as guidelines implemented for specific investigative actions.

In homicide investigation, the on-scene supervisor directs and coordinates a team effort based upon established policies. However, as a manager, he or she is given the authority to allow for variations of the guidelines to occur when needed at the point of execution. This flexibility is based upon necessity and common sense.

The supervision and management function requires the supervisor to actively participate in the investigation. This does not mean "playing detective" and/or jumping into the operational aspects, such as interrogation of suspects, searching the crime scene, collecting and/or handling evidence, interviewing prospective witnesses, etc.

Active participation means sharing an interest in the investigation intelligently directing activities and utilizing the investigative critiques to establish priorities properly. In addition, active participation enables the supervisor to assess the case and provide the necessary resources to his people so that they may effectively investigate the case.

The supervisor of homicide should ideally have a homicide or an investigative background as experience is a prime asset. This does not mean that a supervisor who lacks a homicide or investigative background cannot effectively supervise investigations. However, it does suggest that there is a need for learning the investigative processes involved. Even for the experienced supervisor, managing investigations is an on-going educational process. And remember, you're never too smart to learn.

Epilogue

As far as homicide detectives are concerned, there are two types of homicide: one in which the suspect is caught quickly, and the unsolved homicide. In New York City, the former are referred to as "ground-balls," and the latter are appropriately called "Mysteries." Mystery or ground-ball, the fact remains that you are dealing with the ultimate crime—murder. Whether you have the killer-in-cuffs or it's a who-done-it-and-ran, the investigation should remain the same. Each case must be properly managed and the investigation must be thorough and complete. This is what professional homicide investigation is all about.

Homicide investigation is a profound duty. As an officer entrusted with such a duty, it is incumbent upon you to develop an understanding of the dynamics and principles of professional homicide investigation.

Practical Homicide Investigation suggests that "things be done right the first time," and "knowledge is power"—knowledge that has been enhanced with experience, flexibility, and common sense.

Practitioners must be prepared to use tactics, procedures, and forensic techniques in their pursuit of the truth, and then to follow the course of events and the facts as they are developed to their ultimate conclusion.

Death investigation constitutes a heavy responsibility and as such let no person deter you from the truth and your own personal commitment to see that justice is done—not only for the deceased, but for the surviving family as well.

And remember, "You're working for God."

Glossary

Abdomen Portion of the body between the thorax (chest area) and pelvic area.

Abdominal cavity Contains the stomach, liver, gallbladder, spleen, pancreas, and most of the large and small intestines. The kidneys, ureters, and adrenal glands lie deep in the cavity.

Abdomino-pelvic cavity This is the portion of the ventral cavity below the diaphragm, consisting of the *abdominal cavity* and the *pelvic cavity.*

Abortion Uterus empties itself prematurely. Criminal abortion is a willful production of a miscarriage of a woman who is pregnant, by drugs, instruments, or any other means not authorized by law.

Abrasion An injury to the skin in which there is a removal of the superficial epithelial layer of the skin (the epidermis) due to friction against a rough surface with resultant scraping away of the superficial portions of the epidermis. (Wearing away of the skin in small shreds by friction.)

Abrasion collar The circular perforation and blackening effect on the edges of the skin as a bullet passes through the skin.

Accident An unforeseen occurrence, especially one of an injurious character.

Acid phosphatase An enzyme found in the kidneys, serum, semen, and prostate gland. Acid phosphatase is found in high concentrations in semen. It is most useful as an indicator of recent sexual intercourse.

Acute Sharp or severe.

Adhesions Places where the tissues adhere to the skin, normally found at previous operation scars.

Adipocere Waxy soap-like substance formed during the decomposition of animal bodies buried in moist places. It consists principally of insoluble salts of fatty acids. Also called "grave wax." Composed of oleic, palmitic, and stearic acids.

Adrenals Either of two secretory organs perched atop the kidneys. Each consists of two parts, the cortex and the medulla, which secrete hormones.

AIDS Acquired Immune Deficiency Syndrome (HTLV-3). A disease involving a defect in cell-mediated immunity. Usually transmitted through sexual contact or exposure to contaminated blood.

Allele Alternative forms of a gene (as, e.g., an allele for blue eyes).

Amnesia Lack of, or loss of, memory, especially for past experiences.

Anatomy Study of the structure of the human body.

Anemia Insufficient oxygen-carrying capacity of the blood.

Anesthetics A group of drugs capable of producing either localized or general loss of sensation. Examples: (1) chloroform—a heavy, colorless liquid with a characteristic odor and taste; and (2) ether—a colorless volatile liquid with penetrating odor.

Aneurysm A sac formed by the dilation of the walls of an artery or a vein and filled with blood.

Angina Spasmodic pain.

Angina pectoris Spasmodic pain in chest caused by sudden decrease of blood supply to the heart muscle.

Anoxia Total oxygen deprivation.

Antemortem Before death.

Anterior (Ventral) The Front. Indicates the front or belly side of the body. Hence, the toes are anterior or ventral.

Antitoxin A substance found in the blood serum and in other body fluids, which is specifically antagonistic to some particular toxin.

Anus The distal end, and outlet of, the alimentary canal.

Aorta The great trunk artery, which carries blood from the heart to be distributed by branch arteries throughout the body.

Arachnoid membrane Thin covering of the brain and spinal cord.

Areola The pigmented ring around the nipple of the breast.

Arrhythmia Any deviation from the normal pattern of the heartbeat.

Arsenic A medicinal and poisonous element; a brittle, lustrous, graying solid, with garlic odor.

Artery Any one of the vessels through which the blood passes from the heart to the various parts of the body.

ASHD hardening of the arteries, (arteriosclerotic heart disease) frequent in old age and resulting from the accumulation of fat in the arteries.

Asphyxia The end stage of significant interference with the exchange of oxygen and carbon dioxide, as in suffocation.

Aspiration of vomitus Breathing or drawing vomitus into the respiratory tract, blocking same.

Asthma Wheezing and coughing, usually caused by allergies affecting the bronchi or air passages to the lungs.

Auto A combining form meaning self.

Autoeroticism Arousal and satisfaction of sexual emotion within or by oneself through fantasy and/or genital stimulation.

Autolysis The breakdown of cells and organs from the aseptic chemical process caused by intracellular enzymes.

Autopsy The internal examination of the body after death.

Autoradiograph The autoradiograph or AUTORAD is the final product in a DNA probe. The nylon membrane, which has been probed by the radioactive marker, is placed against a piece of x-ray film and exposed for several days. Black bands appear where the radioactive probes stuck to the fragments.

Autosadism Sexual gratification through self-inflicted pain.

Avulsion The separation, by tearing, of any part of the body from the whole.

Barbiturates Depressant medicines prescribed by doctors; common in suicide by overdose.

Bases The chemical units adenine, thymine, guanine, and cytosine, whose order in DNA molecules governs the genetic code.

Biliary tract Of or pertaining to bile or gallbladder and its ducts, which transport bile.

Bondage A masochistic involvement with ligatures, restraints, blindfolds, gags, hoods, or restrictive containers. In autoerotic episodes, these restraints may vary from the very simple to very complex and bizarre.

Bottom man The homosexual male, who receives the fist of the "top man" during a "fisting."

Bradycardia Abnormally slow heartbeat. Cardiac output is decreased causing faintness, dizziness, and chest pains.

Bullet track The path of the bullet or projectile as it passes through the body.

Burking Mechanical asphyxia plus smothering that is homicidal in nature. Murder by suffocating so as to leave the body unmarked. (William Burke, executed in Edinburgh 1829, and an accomplice would supply bodies for anatomical dissection. They would get an individual intoxicated and Burke would sit on the victim's chest while the mouth and nose were covered.)

Cadaveric spasm Stiffening and rigidity of a single group of muscles occurring immediately after death.

Carbon dioxide A heavy, colorless gas. Forms in tissues during respiration and is eliminated by the lungs.

Carbon monoxide (CO) A colorless, odorless, very toxic gas, formed by burning carbon or organic fuels.

Carcinoma Cancer. This will usually be defined by the organ or body affected.

Cardio A combining form denoting relationship to the heart.

Cardiovascular system The network of structures, including the heart and the blood vessels, that pump and convey the blood throughout the body.

Carotid Arteries of the neck.

Cartilage The gristle or white elastic substance attached to articular bone surfaces and forming certain parts of the skeleton.

Castration Removal of the gonads (primary sex organs).

Cause of death Any injury or disease that produces a physiological derangement in the body that results in the individual dying.

Cavity A hollow place or space.

Cell The cell is the basic unit of all living organisms, including humans, animals, insects, and plants. The cell consists of a nucleus and cytoplasm. The human body has more than 10 trillion cells.

Cerebral Pertaining to the cerebrum, which is the main portion of the brain occupying the upper part of the cranium.

Cervical Pertaining to the neck.

Choking Asphyxia caused by obstruction within the air passages.

Chop wounds These wounds are caused by a heavy object that has an edge, e.g., an axe, machete, or meat cleaver.

Chromosome A structure in the cell nucleus composed mainly of DNA and other proteins, which stores and transmits genetic information.

Chronic Of long duration (said of sickness).

Circulation Movement in a regular course, as the circulation of the blood.

Cirrhosis A disease of the liver marked by progressive destruction of liver cells.

Coagulate To become clotted.

Colon The part of the large intestine that extends from the cecum to the rectum.

Comatose Unconscious and unresponsive to stimuli. Note that a comatose person is not dead.

Congenital Existing at or dating from birth.

Contact wound Occurs when the firearm is pressed against the head or body. Consequently, gases from the explosion expand between the skin and the bone, producing a bursting effect and ragged wound.

Contrecoup contusions These occur in the brain directly opposite to the point of impact. They are seen most commonly in the frontal and temporal lobes. Contrecoup contusions are classically associated with falls.

Contusion An area of hemorrhage into soft tissue due to the rupture of blood vessels caused by blunt trauma.

Convulsion A violent, involuntary contraction or series of contractions of the voluntary muscles.

Coprolangia A sexual desire to consume feces.

Coprophilia A sexual attraction to feces.

Coronary Of or pertaining to the heart.

Corpse The dead body of a human being.

Crack Concentrated form of cocaine, which is used in vapor form. It is smoked or inhaled through "crack pipes." It is a highly addictive drug that causes psychotic behavior, which is often violent.

Craniotomy The opening of the skull, as for brain surgery.

Cranium The skull or brain pan.

Cremains Human remains which have been cremated.

Cricoid A ring-shaped cartilage connected to the thyroid cartilage.

Criminal investigative analysis The current term used by the FBI Behavioral Sciences Unit at Quantico to define their Psychological Profile and Criminal Personality Profiles of Offenders.

Culpable Meriting condemnation or blame.

Cutaneous Pertaining to the skin.

Cyanosis Blueness of the skin, often due to cardiac malformation resulting in insufficient oxygenation of the blood.

Decomposition The separation of compound bodies into their constituent principles; postmortem degeneration of the body. It involves two principles: autolysis and putrefaction.

Defecation Elimination of solid waste matter from the intestines.

Defeminize To remove a woman's breast as in defeminization.

Defense wounds Cuts, abrasions, and contusions on the hands, wrists, forearms, and arms, which occur during a violent struggle as the victim attempts to ward-off his or her attacker.

Degeneration Deterioration.

Delirium A mental disorder marked by illusions, hallucinations, physical restlessness, and incoherence.

Depersonalization The actions taken by a murderer to obscure the personal identity of the victim. Face may be beaten beyond recognition, or the face of the victim may be covered.

Depraved Corrupt or perverted.

Deteriorate To become worse.

Diagnosis The art of distinguishing one disease from another.

Diaphragm The musculomembranous partition that separates the abdomen from the thorax.

Disarticulation Amputation or separation at a joint.

Disease Any departure from a state of health; illness or sickness.

Disembowel To take out the bowels or entrails; eviscerate.

Disinterment Digging up a body after burial.

Distal Indicates farther away from the center of the body. Hence, the elbow is distal to the shoulder.

DNA Deoxyribonucleic acid; this molecule is housed in every nucleated cell of the body. Often described as the body's blueprint, since it carries the genetic codes that govern the structure and function of every component of the body.

Dorsal Pertaining to the back.

Dorsal cavity Subdivided into the *cranial* and *vertebral* cavities.

Double homicide Two victims killed during one event and at one location.

Drowning Asphyxiation because of submersion in a liquid. Sequence of events are breath holding, involuntary inspiration and gasping for air at the breaking point, loss of consciousness, and death.

Duodenum The first portion of the small intestine.

Dura mater Outermost and toughest membrane covering the brain.

Dysentery Term given to a number of disorders marked by inflammation of the intestines, attended pain in the abdomen, and frequent stools containing blood and mucus.

Dyspnea Difficult or labored breathing.

Ecchymosis Swelling from a bruise caused by bleeding beneath the skin.

Eczema An inflammatory skin disease.

Ejaculate To discharge.

Electrophoresis A technique for separating by size biological molecules by exposing them to an electrical charge.

Entomology Branch of science that deals with the study of insects. For example, in making a determination of "time-of-death," a forensic entomologist evaluates the structure's and habits of certain necrophagous insects collected from the carrion, which provide cycle time frames for the species.

Entrails The inner organs of humans and animals. Specifically, the intestines.

Enzyme Proteins that initiate specific biochemical reactions.

Erotic Arousing sexual desire.

Eroticism Sexual or erotic quality or character of something.

Evisceration Removal of the viscera from the abdominal cavity; disembowelment.

Exhibitionism Exposing the genitals to an unsuspecting stranger for the purposes of obtaining sexual excitement.

Exsanguination Loss of blood.

Fantasy An imaginative sequence in which one's desires are fulfilled.

Feces Excrement discharged from the intestines.

Fetish Any object or nongenital part of the body that causes a habitual erotic response or fixation.

Fetishism Compulsive use of nonliving objects for sexual arousal (usually female undergarments, i.e., panties, shoes, etc.).

Fibrillation Fluttering of the heart not controlled by motor nerves.

Fisting A sexual deviant act that is practiced among homosexual males. The human hand is inserted into the anal cavity of the other participant during sadomasochistic sex.

Fistula An abnormal passage leading from an abscess to the body surface.

Flaccid Soft, limp.

Floater A dead body in the water, which comes to the surface due to decompositional gases.

Fratricide The act of killing one's brother or sister.

Frotteurism A sexual attraction to rubbing against the genitalia or body of another.

Frye rule A legal standard of admissibility used by a number of jurisdictions, which requires that scientific evidence to be introduced into court must have gained general acceptance by the scientific community. Based on Supreme Court decision *Frye v. U.S.,* F 1013 at 1014 (D.C. Cir. 1923). A number of these Frye rulings have occurred as a result of DNA technology. Most courts have upheld DNA.

Gangrene Death of tissue, characterized by anoxia and marked inflammation.

Gastrointestinal tract Of or pertaining to the organs of the GI tract, from mouth to anus. Specifically, of the stomach and intestines.

Gene A segment of DNA that codes for the production of a specific protein.

Genitalia The sexual organs (genitals). In males, the testes and penis; in females, the vulva and vagina.

Glycoprotein (P30) A semen-specific glycoprotein (P30) of prostatic origin discovered in 1978. This substance is only present in semen and has essentially replaced analysis for acid phosphatase in rape investigations, except for rapid screening tests.

Helix A double-spiral of deoxyribonucleic acid in the shape of a twisted ladder, i.e., DNA as a double-stranded helix.

Hematoma A large focal collection of blood in an area of contusion. Or, local swelling filled with effused blood.

Hemolysis Breakdown of red blood cells and the release of hemoglobin.

Hemophilia Condition in which blood is slow to clot or does not clot, allowing a person to bleed to death.

Hemorrhage Heavy bleeding. A loss of a large amount of blood in a short period of time, either externally or internally. May be arterial, venous, or capillary.

Hemothorax An accumulation of blood and fluid in the pleural cavity, between the parietal and visceral pleural, usually the result of trauma.

Histology The science dealing with the microscopic identification of cells and tissues; the structure of organ tissues, including the composition of cells and their organization into various body tissues.

Histotoxin Any substance that is poisonous to the body tissues. It is usually generated within the body rather than introduced externally.

HLA Human leukocyte antigen. A polymorphic protein system commonly identified for paternity testing.

Homeostasis A relative constancy in the internal environment of the body, naturally maintained by adaptive responses that promote healthy survival. An example of some functions controlled by homeostatic mechanisms are: heartbeat, blood pressure, and respiration.

Homicidomania Impulsive desire to commit murder.

Homosexual A person who is attracted to and obtains sexual gratification from acts performed with a person of the same sex.

Homosexual handkerchief codes The color-coded handkerchief signals employed by certain homosexual subcultures to indicate their sexual proclivities and/or preferences.

Hybridization Probes, usually tagged with a radioactive marker, are applied to the nylon membrane (see Southern blotting). These probes are designed to "seek-out" a predetermined chromosomal locus containing a polymorphic region of DNA.

Hyoid bone Small U-shaped bone at base of tongue.

Hypertension High blood pressure.

Hyperthermia A much higher than normal body temperature.

Hypothermia An abnormal and dangerous condition in which the body is below 95°F. Usually caused by prolonged exposure to cold.

Hypoxia Partial deprivation of oxygen.

Incised wound Caused by a sharp instrument or weapon. A wound which is longer than deep, with minimum bruising, no bridging of skin, and bleeds freely.

Incision A wound inflicted by an instrument with a sharp cutting edge.

Infanticide The act of killing an infant soon after birth.

Infarct An area of necrosis (death of a cell or group of cells) in a tissue, produced by sudden arrest or circulation in vessel.

Inferior Indicates direction further away from the head end of the body or toward the lower part of the body.

Infibulation Self-infliction of pain on the genitals.

Inguinal Of the groin.

Inhalation The drawing of air or other vapor into the lungs.

Intestine The membranous tube that extends from the stomach to the anus.

Intra Prefix meaning within.

Klismaphilia A sexual attraction to the giving or receiving of enemas.

Laceration A split or tear of the skin, usually produced by blunt force (shearing or crushing-type injuries from blunt objects, falls, or impact from vehicles). These injuries tend to be irregular with abraded contused margins. Internal organs can also have lacerations.

Laryngeal prominence The bulge at the front of the neck produced by the thyroid cartilage of the larynx (Adam's apple).

Lateral Pertaining to a side.

Ligament Any fibrous, tough band that connects bones or supports viscera.

Ligature Anything that binds or ties.

Liver The largest glandular organ situated in the upper part of the abdomen on the right side, usually of a dark red color.

Lividity or livor mortis Postmortem discoloration due to the gravitation of blood into the dependent capillaries and veins.

Locus The specific position occupied by a particular gene or allele on a chromosome.

Lumbar Pertaining to or near the lower region of the back.

Mandible The large bone constituting the lower jaw.

Manic depressive A psychosis characterized by alternating periods of mania and mental depression.

Manner of death Explains how the cause of death came about. Medicolegal manners of death are: homicide, suicide, accident, natural, and undetermined.

Marbling Produced by hemolysis of blood vessels with reaction of hemoglobin and hydrogen sulfide and development of greenish-black coloration along the vessels.

Masochism Sexual perversion in which an individual takes delight in being subject to degrading, humiliating, or cruel treatment, such as flogging or choking.

Mass murder A homicide involving the killing of four or more victims during a single event at one location. *Classic:* Involves a single individual, who kills more than four persons at one location during a period of time (minutes, hours, or days). *Family-member murder:* More than three family members are killed and the perpetrator takes his own life (a mass murder/suicide). *Family killing:* Four or more family members killed by a family member who does not commit suicide.

Masturbation Manual manipulation of the genitals resulting in sexual excitement.

Maxilla One of a pair of large bones that form the upper jaw.

Mechanical asphyxia Asphyxia created by pressure on the outside of the body, which prevents respiration. Examples are: traumatic asphyxia, positional asphyxia, and riot crush or "human pile" deaths.

Mechanism of death The physiological derangement produced by the resulting cause of death, i.e., hemorrhage, septicemia, cardiac arrhythmia.

Medial Pertaining to the middle. Indicates closer to the midline of the body.

Membrane A thin layer of tissue which covers a surface or divides a space or organ.

Meningitis Inflammation of the meninges (thin membranous covering of the brain).

Miscarriage The premature emptying of a uterus prior to 28 weeks of gestation.

Misdemeanor murders A "Geberthism" suggesting that when two "shitbirds" (less-than-productive citizens) kill each other in some sort of drug-related homicide that the crime might actually be considered a less-than-felony offense. (The author obviously uses the term in a facetious manner.)

Monomania Insanity on a single subject or class of subjects.

Mummification The complete drying-up of the body as the result of burial in a dry place, or by exposure to dry atmosphere.

Musculoskeletal system All of the muscles, bones, joints, and related structures, as the tendons, and connective tissue, that function in the movement of the parts and organs of the body.

Myocardial infarction (MI) An occlusion of a coronary artery, caused by atherosclerosis or an embolus resulting from a necrotic area in the vasculature myocardium.

Myocardium The heart muscle.

Mysophilia A sexual attraction to filth.

Narcomania An insane desire for narcotics or alcohol.

Natal Pertaining to birth.

NCAVC National Center for the Analysis of Violent Crime: A subdivision of the FBI's Behavioral Science Unit located in Quantico, Virgina. Composed of four sections: Research and Development; VICAP; Criminal Personality Profiling Program; and Consultation Program.

Necrophagia The eating of dead bodies or feeding-off of carrion, e.g., necrophagous insects such as flies and beetles can provide entomological evidence in death investigations.

Necrophilia A sexual attraction to dead bodies; having sexual intercourse with a dead body.

Necrosis Localized tissue death that occurs in groups of cells in response to disease or injury.

Neonaticide The killing of a child within 24 hours of its birth.

Nitroglycerine Medicine to treat heart patients; a pill taken under the tongue.

Non compos mentis Not sound of mind; insane.

Nucleus The part of the cell which contains the chromosomes, which are composed of DNA and associated proteins—the genetic program.

Occlusion In anatomy, a blockage in a canal, vessel, or passage of the body.

Organized crime "hit" A murder of a known or recognized member of an organized criminal enterprise.

Ossification Formation of bone or a bony substance.

Osteitis Inflammation of bone caused by pyogenic organism.

Overlay Mechanical asphyxia combined with smothering. An example would be an infant in bed with one of the parents, who inadvertently rolls on top of the child, thus compressing the chest and occluding the nose and mouth with the bedding or the body.

Padding Material placed between a body portion and the ligature or device used to alter the physiological state of the victim.

Pancreas A large elongated gland located behind the stomach.

Papillary Pertaining to or resembling a nipple, ridges, or grooves.

Paralysis The loss of power of voluntary motion.

Paranoia A mental disorder characterized by systematized delusions, as of grandeur, or especially those of persecution, often—except in a schizophrenic state—with an otherwise intact personality.

Parenticide The act of killing one's own parents.

Parietal Of or pertaining to the outer wall of a cavity or organ.

Pathognomonic Of a sign or symptom; specific to a disease or condition.

Pedophilia Engaging in sexual activity with prepubertal children.

Pelvic cavity Contains the urinary bladder, the sex organs, and part of the small and large intestines.

Peritoneum An extensive serous membrane that covers the entire abdominal wall of the body and is reflected over the contained viscera.

Peritonitis An inflammation of the peritoneum produced by bacteria or irritating substances introduced into the abdominal cavity by a penetrating wound or perforation of an organ.

Permeation The spreading through a tissue or organ of a disease process.

Petechial hemorrhage Minute (pin-like) hemorrhages that occur at points beneath the skin; usually observed in conjunctiva; the mucous membrane lining the inner surface of the eyelids and anterior part of the sclera.

Phalanx Any bone of a finger or toe.

Phonomania Insanity marked by a tendency to commit murder.

Physiological mechanism The ligature or device used to alter the physiological state of the victim.

Piquerism Sexual inclinations to stab, pierce, or cut. Obtaining a sexual gratification from the shedding of blood, tearing of flesh, and/or observing such pain and suffering of a victim who is being subjected to this activity.

Pneumatic Pertaining to air or respiration.

Pneumothorax Air in the chest cavity.

Polymorphism A naturally occurring or induced variation in the sequence of bases on a segment of DNA.

Positional asphyxia Asphyxia that occurs as a result of body position, which restricts respiration.

Posterior Dorsal, indicates the backside of the body; hence, the heels are posterior or dorsal.

Postmortem After death.

Postpartum Pertaining to the period following childbirth.

Probe In genetic engineering, a fragment of DNA carrying the complementary code for a specific base sequence. Probes can be used to detect variations in base sequence that establish individual identity.

Protein A molecule consisting of linked amino acids. Proteins serve as the "building blocks" of body structures or as the enzymes that initiate specific biochemical reactions.

Proximal Indicates nearer to a point of reference, usually the center of the body. Hence, the shoulder is proximal to the elbow.

Psychiatry Branch of medicine concerned with the study, treatment, and prevention of disorders of the mind, including psychoses, neuroses, etc.

Psychodynamics The study of the mental and emotional processes underlying human behavior and its motivation.

Psycholinguistic analysis A sophisticated method of examining the spoken or written communication as to origins, background, and psychology of the speaker or writer.

Psychological autopsy A collaborative procedure involving law enforcement and mental health experts, who attempt to determine the state of a person's mind prior to a sudden death.

Psychology The science dealing with the mind and with the mental and emotional processes; the science of human and animal behavior.

Psychopathic killer A person who kills for pleasure.

Psychopathic personality A person whose behavior is largely amoral and asocial and who is characterized by irresponsibility, lack of remorse or shame, perverse or impulsive (often criminal) behavior, and other serious personality defects, generally without psychotic attacks or symptoms.

Psychopathic sexual sadist A person who inflicts pain, either physical or psychological on another for the purposes of causing suffering, submission, humiliation, fear, and terror in another. The suffering of the victim is sexually arousing for the offender.

Psychopathology The science dealing with the causes and development of mental disorders. Psychological malfunctioning, as in mental disorder.

Psychosis A major mental disorder in which the personality is very seriously disorganized and contact with reality is impaired.

Psychosomatic Pertaining to the mind–body relationship.

Psychotic Of, or having the nature of, a psychosis; having a psychosis—a person who has a psychosis.

Psychotic killer A person whose psychosis drives him to kill.

Pubic Pertaining to the pubes (anterior pelvic bones).

Pugilistic attitude Position the body assumes in fire deaths. Coagulation of the muscle due to heat causes contraction of muscle fibers with resultant flexion of the limbs.

Pulmonary Pertaining to the lungs.

Pulmonary embolism The closure of the pulmonary artery or one of its branches by an embolus.

Pulmonary infarction An area of necrosis in lung tissue, produced by sudden arrest of circulation in a vessel.

Purge fluid Decomposition fluid which drains from the mouth or nose. Sometimes mistaken as blood and head trauma.

Purines Basic chemicals of life, as in DNA molecule, adenine (A) and guanine (G).

Putrefaction Decomposition of soft tissues by bacteria and fermentation and enzymes. After death, the bacterial flora of the gastrointestinal tract invades the vascular system, spreading throughout the body, producing putrefaction.

Pyrimidines Basic chemicals of life, as in DNA molecule; thymine (T) and cytosine (C).

Rancid Having a musty, rank taste or smell.

rDNA Recombinant DNA—rDNA technology in which a molecule of DNA is cloned or synthesized.

Reproductive system The male and female gonads, associated ducts and glands, and the external genitalia which function in the procreation of offspring. In women these include the ovaries, fallopian tubes, uterus, vagina, clitoris, and vulva. In men these include the testes, epididymis, vas deferens, seminal vesicles, ejaculatory duct, prostate, and penis.

Respiration The act or function of breathing.

Respiratory tract The complex of organs and structures that performs the pulmonary ventilation of the body and the exchange of oxygen and carbon dioxide between the ambient air and the blood circulating through the lungs.

Restriction endonuclease Enzyme that "cuts" the DNA molecules at specific locations.

Resuscitation To revive, as in drownings or electrical shock.

Retardation Delay or hindrance.

RFLP Restriction fragment length polymorphisms.

Rigor mortis A rigidity or stiffening of the muscular tissue and joints of the body after death due to the disappearance of adenosine triphosphate (ATP) from muscle.

Ritual Any practice or pattern of behavior repeated in a precise manner.

Ritualism Adherence to or insistence on ritual.

Sacro Combining form, denoting relationship to the sacrum (the large, triangular bone at the dorsal part of the pelvis).

Schizophrenia A major mental disorder of unknown cause typically characterized by separation between thought processes and the emotions; a distortion of reality accompanied by delusions and hallucinations; a fragmentation of the personality, motor disturbances, bizarre behavior, etc., often with no loss of basic intellectual functions.

Schizophrenic Of or having schizophrenia; a person who is schizophrenic.

Sclerosis Induration or hardening of tissue.

Self-rescue mechanism The object (knife, key) or method (pressure point change) utilized by the victim to alleviate the effects of the physiological mechanism.

Semen Thick, whitish secretion of the reproductive organs in the male.

Senile Pertaining to or characteristic of old age, i.e., physical or mental deterioration.

Septicemia Systematic infection in which pathogens (microorganisms capable of producing disease) are present in the bloodstream, having spread from an infection in any part of the body.

Serial murder Three or more separate murders with an emotional cooling-off period, which may consist of days, weeks, or months, between the homicides.

Serology The science dealing with the properties and actions of serums, e.g., blood analysis.

Sexual masochism Getting pleasure from being humiliated, bound, beaten, or otherwise made to suffer for sexual arousal (considered chronic).

Sexual sadism The infliction of physical or psychological pain on another person in order to achieve sexual excitement (considered chronic).

SIDS Sudden Infant Death Syndrome, or crib death, is characterized by the sudden, unexpected death of an apparently healthy infant.

Smothering Asphyxia due to mechanical obstruction or occlusion of the external airways, e.g., mouth and nose.

Sororicide The act of murdering one's own sister.

Southern blotting Process by which the DNA fragments separated during electrophoresis are transferred from the wobbly surface of the agarose gel onto a sheet of nylon membrane.

Spasm Sudden, violent, involuntary contraction of a muscle or group of muscles.

Sperm A combining form meaning seed. The male germ cell (spermatozoon) found in semen, which penetrates the ovum or egg of the female.

Spree murder The murder of more than one person at two or more locations during a single event without any cooling-off period.

Sputum Matter ejected from the mouth; saliva and mucus. This substance contains DNA.

Stab wounds Caused by relatively sharp, pointed instruments such as knives, screwdrivers, ice picks, daggers, scissors, or pieces of glass. These wounds are deeper than they are wide, with possible damage to vital organs beneath the skin and bone, and internal bleeding with little or no external blood.

Sternum The breastbone.

Stillbirth A fetus at least 28 weeks old, born dead.

Stippling Also referred to as *tattooing;* pinpoint hemorrhages due to the discharge of burning powder against the skin.

Strangulation Any abnormal constriction of the throat, causing a suspension of breathing.

Stroke Cerebrovascular accident; a sudden or severe attack, with rupture of the blood vessels of the brain.

Subdural Under the dura matter, or between the dura and arachnoid membranes covering the brain, as in subdural hematoma.

Subdural hematoma The most common lethal injury associated with head trauma.

Suffocation The failure of oxygen to reach the blood. This can occur through entrapment, smothering, choking, mechanical asphyxia combined with smothering, or through suffocating gases.

Superior Indicates direction toward the head end or upper part of the body. Hence the lungs are superior to the liver.

Survival interval The period of time between the infliction of injury and the actual death.

Suspension point That location from which the victim has suspended himself.

Tache noire An artifact of the drying eye after death, consisting of a brown to black band of discolored sclera where the eyes are partly open and exposed to the air.

Tachycardia An abnormally fast heartbeat.

Tarsus The instep proper of the foot with its seven bones.

Telephone scatologia A sexual attraction to making obscene telephone calls (lewdness).

Tetanus An acute, potentially fatal infection of the central nervous system caused by bacteria which release a powerful toxin.

Thermo Combining form, denoting relationship to heat.

Thoracic cavity This is the portion of the ventral cavity above the diaphragm which contains two *pleural cavities* that contain the two lungs; the *pericardial cavity*, which contains the heart; and the *mediastinal* or *interpleural cavity*, which contains everything located in the thoracic cavity other than the heart and lungs, e.g., trachea, bronchi, esophagus, etc.

Thorax Chest; a bony-cartilaginous cage containing and protecting the heart, the lungs, and their major blood vessels.

Thrombo Combining form, denoting relationship to clot.

Tibia The inner and large bone of the leg below the knee.

Tissue An aggregation of cells united in the performance of a particular function.

Top man The "fister" who inserts his hand into the anal cavity of the "bottom" man.

Torso The trunk of the body without the head or extremities.

Toxic Poisonous.

Toxicologist An expert in the knowledge and detection of poisons.

Toxicology The scientific study of poisons, their detection, their effects, and methods of treatment for conditions they produce.

Trachea Commonly referred to as the windpipe. It is a nearly cylindric tube of cartilage and membrane that extends from the larynx to the bronchi. It conveys air to the lungs.

Tracheotomy An incision into the trachea, below the larynx to gain access to the airway below the point of blockage.

Transvestism Cross dressing by heterosexual males for the purpose of sexual excitement. Ranges from solitary wearing of female clothes to extensive involvement in a transvestite subculture.

Trauma A physical injury caused by violent or disruptive action, or by the introduction into the body of a toxic substance.

Traumatic asphyxia Occurs when a large weight falls onto or presses down on an individual's chest or upper abdomen, making respiration impossible.

Tremor An involuntary trembling or quivering.

Triage Military medicine; a classification of casualties of war and other disasters according to the gravity of injuries, urgency of treatment, and place for treatment. A process in which a group of patients is sorted according to their need for care, the kind of illness or injury, the severity of the problem, and the facilities available. Disaster medicine; a process in which a large number of patients is sorted so that care can be concentrated on those who are likely to survive.

Triple homicide The murder of three victims during one event at one location.

Umbilical Pertaining to the umbilicus (navel).

Unconscious Being unaware of the surrounding environment; unresponsive to any stimuli; comatose.

Uremia Presence of urinary materials in the blood. Could indicate renal failure.

Urinary tract All organs and ducts involved in the secretion and elimination of urine from the body. These include the kidneys, ureters, and bladder.

Urolangia A sexual desire to consume urine.

Urophilia A sexual attraction to urine.

Vagina The part of the female genitalia that forms a canal from the orifice through the vestibule to the uterine cervix.

Vascular Pertaining to a blood vessel.

Vein A vessel that conveys the blood to or toward the heart.

Ventricle One of the two lower cavities of the heart.

VI-CAP Violent Criminal Apprehension Program; a system designed to collect, collate, and analyze all aspects of an investigation.

Victimology Pedigree, such as, sex, age, height, weight, etc., the essential information about the victim, such as family, friends, and acquaintances, education, employment, residence, neighborhood, etc. This also includes the background information on the life-style of the victim. Was this person a low risk, moderate, or high risk victim?

Viscera The internal organs enclosed within a body cavity, primarily the abdominal organs.

Visceral peritoneum One of two portions of the largest serous membrane in the body. The free surface of the visceral peritoneum is a smooth layer of mesothelium exuding a serous fluid that lubricates the viscera and allows them to glide freely against the wall of the abdominal cavity or over each other. The attached surface of the membrane is connected to the viscera and the abdominal wall by subserous fascia.

VNTRs Variable number of tandem repeats; polymorphic DNA regions known to repeat themselves over and over, which are unique to an individual.

Voyeurism Repetitive looking at unsuspecting people, who are either naked, in the act of disrobing, or engaging in sexual activity ("The Peeping Tom").

Vulva The external genitalia of the woman. It includes the mons pubis, the labia majora, the labia minora, the vestibule of the vagina, and the vestibular glands.

Zoophilia Use of animals for sexual arousal; includes intercourse with animals as well as training the animal to lick or rub the human partner. This sexual disorder is also commonly referred to as beastiality.

Index

Vernon J. Geberth is a retired Lieutenant Commander of the New York City Police Department with over twenty-five years of law enforcement experience. He retired as the Commanding Officer of the Bronx Homicide Task Force, which handled over 400 murder investigations a year. During his career he was a detective, a Precinct Detective Squad Commander, and Temporary Commander of the 7th Homicide Zone in the South Bronx. He has personally investigated, supervised, assessed, and consulted on approximately five thousand death investigations.

Lieutenant Commander Geberth, who has a BBA degree from Iona College in New Rochelle, New York and a graduate degree (MPS) from C. W. Post College, Long Island University, has served as Adjunct Professor of Criminal Justice at both Mercy College, Dobbs Ferry, New York, and John Jay College of Criminal Justice in New York City. He is also a graduate of the FBI National Academy in Quantico, Virginia. He was affiliated with the University of Deleware's Continuing Education Program as an Associate Professor and served as a Police Instructor for the New York City Police Department, The New York City Housing Police, and the Police Training Division of the New York Office of the FBI. At present he is on the Faculty of Northwestern University Traffic Institute as a Homicide Instructor.

Vernon J. Geberth is the Series Editor of *Practical Aspects of Criminal and Forensic Investigations* for Elsevier Science Publishing Company, Inc. He is a nationally renowned lecturer, author, educator, consultant, and expert witness on the subject of death investigations.

Lieutenant Commander Geberth is President of P.H.I. Investigative Consultants, Inc., a New-York-based corporation which provides state-of-the-art instruction and consultation in homicide and forensic case investigations for a number of law enforcement agencies throughout the United States and Canada.

In addition, Commander Geberth has been the recipient of more than 60 awards for bravery and exceptional police work and is a member of the Honor Legion of the City of New York Police Department.